SCHAUM'S OUTLINE OF

THEORY AND PROBLEMS

of

MANAGERIAL FINANCE

•

JAE K. SHIM, Ph.D.
Professor of Business Administration
California State University at Long Beach

and

JOEL G. SIEGEL, Ph.D., CPA
Professor of Finance and Accounting
Queens College
City University of New York

•

SCHAUM'S OUTLINE SERIES

McGRAW-HILL BOOK COMPANY

New York   St. Louis   San Francisco   Auckland   Bogotá   Guatemala   Hamburg
Lisbon   London   Madrid   Mexico   Montreal   New Delhi   Panama   Paris
San Juan   São Paulo   Singapore   Sydney   Tokyo   Toronto

JAE K. SHIM is currently Professor of Business Administration at California State University at Long Beach. He received his M.B.A. and Ph.D. from the University of California at Berkeley. Professor Shim has published numerous articles in such journals as *Financial Management, Decision Sciences, Econometrica, Journal of Urban Economics, Long Range Planning,* and *Business Economics.* He is a coauthor of Schaum's Outlines of *Financial Accounting* and *Managerial Accounting.* Dr. Shim has seven other books to his credit and is a recipient of the 1982 Credit Research Foundation Award for his article on financial management.

JOEL G. SIEGEL is Professor of Finance and Accounting at Queens College of the City University of New York. He received his Ph.D. in accounting from Bernard M. Baruch College and is a certified public accountant. In 1972, Dr. Siegel received the Outstanding Educator of America Award. He has written on numerous finance topics in professional journals, including *The Financial Executive* and *The Financial Analyst Journal.* Dr. Siegel is the author of *How to Analyze Businesses, Financial Statements and Quality of Earnings* and is coauthor of Schaum's Outlines of *Financial Accounting* and *Managerial Accounting.*

SCHAUM'S OUTLINE OF THEORY AND PROBLEMS OF MANAGERIAL FINANCE
INTERNATIONAL EDITION

Copyright © 1987
Exclusive rights by McGraw-Hill Book Co., Singapore for manufacture and export. This book cannot be re-exported from the country to which it is consigned by McGraw-Hill.

1st Printing 1987

Sponsoring Editor, Elizabeth Zayatz
Editing Supervisor, Marthe Grice
Production Manager, Nick Monti

Library of Congress Cataloging in Publication Data

Shim, Jae K.
    Schaum's outline of theory and problems of managerial finance.
    Includes index.
    1. Business enterprises—Finance.   2. Corporations—Finance.
I. Siegel, Joel G.   II.Title.
III. Title: Theory and problems of managerial finance.
IV. Title: Managerial finance.
HG4026.S455   1986   658.1′5   85-14910
ISBN 0-07-057306-9

When ordering this title use ISBN 0-07-099172-3

Printed and Bound in Singapore by Fong & Sons Printers Pte Ltd

Preface

Managerial Finance, designed for finance and business students, presents the theory and application of corporate finance. As in the preceding volumes in the Schaum's Outline Series in Accounting, Business, and Economics, the solved-problems approach is used, with emphasis on the practical application of principles, concepts, and tools of financial management. Although an elementary knowledge of accounting, economics, and statistics is helpful, it is not required for using this book since the student is provided with the following:

1. Definitions and explanations that are clear and concise.
2. Examples that illustrate the concepts and techniques discussed in each chapter.
3. Review questions and answers.
4. Detailed solutions to representative problems covering the subject matter.
5. Comprehensive examinations, with solutions, to test the student's knowledge of each chapter; the exams are representative of those used by 2- and 4-year colleges and M.B.A. programs.

In line with the development of the subject, two professional designations are noted. One is the Certificate in Management Accounting (CMA), which is a recognized certificate for both management accountants and financial managers. The other is the Chartered Financial Analyst (CFA), established by the Institute of Chartered Financial Analysts. Students who hope to be certified by either of these organizations may find this outline particularly useful.

This book was written with the following objectives in mind:

1. To supplement formal training in financial management courses at the undergraduate and graduate levels. It therefore serves as an excellent study guide.
2. To enable students to prepare for the business finance portion of such professional examinations as the CMA and CFA examinations. Hence it is a valuable reference source for review and self-testing.

Managerial Finance was written to cover the common denominator of managerial finance topics after a thorough review was made of the numerous managerial finance, financial management, corporate finance, and business finance texts currently available. It is, therefore, comprehensive in coverage and presentation. In an effort to give readers a feel for the types of questions asked on the CMA and CFA examinations, problems from those exams have been incorporated within this book.

Our appreciation is extended to the National Association of Accountants and the Institute of Chartered Financial Analysts for their permission to incorporate their examination questions in this book. Selected materials from the CMA examinations, copyrighted by the National Association of Accountants, bear the notation (CMA, adapted). Problems from the CFA examinations bear the notation (CFA, adapted).

PREFACE

Finally, we would like to thank our assistants, Su-chin Tsai and Jackie Steinke, for their assistance and our wives, Chung and Roberta, who helped with the typing. We also would like to extend our gratitude to John Aliano, Schaum's Outline Series senior editor, for his generous assistance and Elizabeth Zayatz, editor, for her outstanding editorial contribution to the manuscript.

JAE K. SHIM
JOEL G. SIEGEL

Contents

CONTENTS

CONTENTS

CONTENTS

Chapter 1

Introduction

1.1 THE GOALS OF MANAGERIAL FINANCE

Typical goals of the firm include (1) stockholder wealth maximization, (2) profit maximization, (3) managerial reward maximization, (4) behavioral goals, and (5) social responsibility. Modern managerial finance theory operates on the assumption that the primary goal of the firm is to *maximize the wealth of its stockholders*, which translates into *maximizing the price of the firm's common stock*. The other goals mentioned above also influence a firm's policy but are less important than stock price maximization. Note that the traditional goal frequently stressed by economists—*profit maximization*—is not sufficient for most firms today.

Profit Maximization versus Stockholder Wealth Maximization

Profit maximization is basically a single-period or, at the most, a short-term goal. It is usually interpreted to mean the maximization of profits within a given period of time. A firm may maximize its short-term profits at the expense of its long-term profitability and still realize this goal. In contrast, stockholder wealth maximization is a long-term goal, since stockholders are interested in future as well as present profits. Wealth maximization is generally preferred because it considers (1) wealth for the long term, (2) risk or uncertainty, (3) the timing of returns, and (4) the stockholders' return. Table 1-1 provides a summary of the advantages and disadvantages of these two often conflicting goals.

Table 1-1. Profit Maximization versus Stockholder Wealth Maximization

Goal	Objective	Advantages	Disadvantages
Profit maximization	Large amount of profits	1. Easy to calculate profits 2. Easy to determine the link between financial decisions and profits	1. Emphasizes the short term 2. Ignores risk or uncertainty 3. Ignores the timing of returns 4. Requires immediate resources
Stockholder wealth maximization	Highest market value of common stock	1. Emphasizes the long term 2. Recognizes risk or uncertainty 3. Recognizes the timing of returns 4. Considers stockholders' return	1. Offers no clear relationship between financial decisions and stock price 2. Can lead to management anxiety and frustration

1

EXAMPLE 1.1 Profit maximization can be achieved in the short term at the expense of the long-term goal, that is, wealth maximization. For example, a costly investment may experience losses in the short term but yield substantial profits in the long term. Also, a firm that wants to show a short-term profit may, for example, postpone major repairs or replacement, although such postponement is likely to hurt its long-term profitability.

EXAMPLE 1.2 Profit maximization does not consider risk or uncertainty, whereas wealth maximization does. Consider two products, A and B, and their projected earnings over the next 5 years, as shown below.

Year	Product A	Product B
1	$10,000	$11,000
2	10,000	11,000
3	10,000	11,000
4	10,000	11,000
5	10,000	11,000
	$50,000	$55,000

A profit maximization approach would favor product B over product A. However, if product B is more risky than product A, then the decision is not as straightforward as the figures seem to indicate. It is important to realize that a trade-off exists between risk and return. Stockholders expect greater returns from investments of higher risk and vice versa. To choose product B, stockholders would demand a sufficiently large return to compensate for the comparatively greater level of risk.

1.2 THE ROLE OF FINANCIAL MANAGERS

The financial manager of a firm plays an important role in the company's goals, policies, and financial success. The financial manager's responsibilities include:

1. *Financial analysis and planning:* Determining the proper amount of funds to employ in the firm, i.e., designating the size of the firm and its rate of growth
2. *Investment decisions:* The efficient allocation of funds to specific assets
3. *Financing and capital structure decisions:* Raising funds on as favorable terms as possible, i.e., determining the composition of liabilities
4. *Management of financial resources* (such as working capital)

In a large firm, these financial responsibilities are carried out by the treasurer, controller, and financial vice president (chief financial officer). The treasurer is responsible for managing corporate assets and liabilities, planning the finances, budgeting capital, financing the business, formulating credit policy, and managing the investment portfolio. He or she basically handles *external* financing matters. The controller is basically concerned with *internal* matters, namely, financial and cost accounting, taxes, budgeting, and control functions. The financial vice president supervises all phases of financial activity and serves as the financial adviser to the board of directors.

The Financial Executives Institute, an association of corporate treasurers and controllers, distinguishes their functions as shown in Table 1-2. (For a typical organization chart highlighting the structure of financial activity within a firm, see Problem 1.4.)

The financial manager can affect stockholder wealth maximization by influencing

1. Present and future earnings per share (EPS)
2. The timing, duration, and risk of these earnings
3. Dividend policy
4. The manner of financing the firm

Table 1-2.   **Functions of Controller and Treasurer**

Controller	Treasurer
Planning for control	Provision of capital
Reporting and interpreting	Investor relations
Evaluating and consulting	Short-term financing
Tax administration	Banking and custody
Government reporting	Credits and collections
Protection of assets	Investments
Economic appraisal	Insurance

1.3 FINANCIAL DECISIONS AND RISK-RETURN TRADE-OFF

Integral to the theory of finance is the concept of a risk-return trade-off. All financial decisions involve some sort of risk-return trade-off. The greater the risk associated with any financial decision, the greater the return expected from it. Proper assessment and balance of the various risk-return trade-offs available is part of creating a sound stockholder wealth maximization plan.

EXAMPLE 1.3 In the case of investment in stock, the investor would demand higher return from a speculative stock to compensate for the higher level of risk.

In the case of working capital management, the less inventory a firm keeps, the higher the expected return (since less of the firm's current assets is tied up), but also the greater the risk of running out of stock and thus losing potential revenue.

A financial manager's role is delineated in part by the financial environment in which he or she operates. Three major aspects of this environment are (1) the organization form of the business, (2) the financial institutions and markets, and (3) the tax structure. In this book, we limit the discussion of tax structure to that of the corporation.

1.4 BASIC FORMS OF BUSINESS ORGANIZATION

The three *basic* forms of business organization are (1) the sole proprietorship, (2) the partnership, and (3) the corporation.

A *sole proprietorship* is a business owned by one individual. Of the three forms of business organization, sole proprietorships are the greatest in number. The advantages of a sole proprietorship are:

1.   No formal charter is required.
2.   Organizational costs are minimal.
3.   Profits and control are not shared with others.

The disadvantages are:

1.   Its ability to raise large sums of capital is limited.
2.   It carries unlimited liability for the owner.
3.   It is limited to the life of the owner.

A *partnership* is similar to the sole proprietorship except that the business has more than one owner. Its advantages are:

1.   It is easily established with minimal organizational effort and costs.
2.   It is free from special governmental regulation.

Its disadvantages are:

1. It carries unlimited liability for the individual partners.
2. It is dissolved upon the withdrawal or death of any of the partners.
3. Its ability to raise large amounts of capital is limited.

A *corporation* is a legal entity that exists apart from its owners (better known as stockholders). Ownership is evidenced by possession of shares of stock. In terms of types of businesses, the corporate form is not the greatest in number, but it is the most important in terms of total sales, assets, profits, and contribution to national income. The corporate form is implicitly assumed throughout this book. The advantages of a corporation are:

1. It has an unlimited life.
2. It carries only a limited liability for its owners.
3. Ownership is easily transferred through transfer of stock.
4. It has the ability to raise large amounts of capital.

Its disadvantages are:

1. It is difficult and expensive to establish, as a formal charter is required.
2. It is subject to double taxation on its earnings and dividends paid to stockholders.

1.5 THE FINANCIAL INSTITUTIONS AND MARKETS

A healthy economy depends heavily on efficient transfer of funds from savers to individuals, businesses, and governments who need capital. Most transfers occur through specialized *financial institutions* (see Fig. 1-1) which serve as *intermediaries* between suppliers and users of funds.

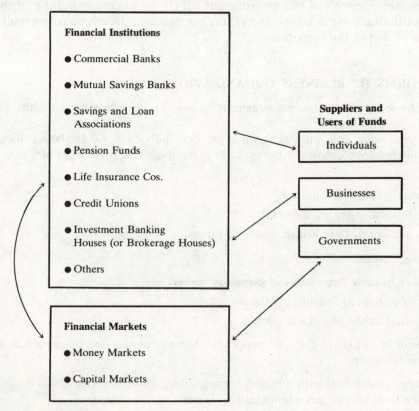

Fig. 1-1 General flow of funds among financial institutions and financial markets

It is in the *financial markets* that entities demanding funds are brought together with those having surplus funds. Financial markets provide a mechanism through which the financial manager may obtain funds from a wide range of sources, including financial institutions. The financial markets are composed of money markets and capital markets. Figure 1-1 depicts the general flow of funds among financial institutions and markets.

Money markets are the markets for short-term (less than 1 year) debt securities. Examples of money market securities include U.S. Treasury bills, federal agency securities, bankers' acceptances, commercial paper, and negotiable certificates of deposit issued by government, business, and financial institutions.

Capital markets are the markets for long-term debt and corporate stocks. The New York Stock Exchange, which handles the stocks of many of the larger corporations, is a prime example of a capital market. The Americal Stock Exchange and the regional stock exchanges are still another example. In addition, securities are traded through the thousands of brokers and dealers on the *over-the-counter market*, a term used to denote all buying and selling activities in securities that do not take place on an organized stock exchange.

1.6 CORPORATE TAX STRUCTURE

In order to make sound financial and investment decisions, a corporation's financial manager must have a general understanding of the corporate tax structure, which includes the following:

1. Corporate tax rate schedule
2. Interest and dividend income
3. Interest and dividends paid by a corporation
4. Capital gain
5. Operating loss carryback and carryforward
6. Depreciation and accelerated cost recovery system (ACRS)
7. Investment tax credit

Corporate Tax Rate

At present, the corporate tax on the first $100,000 of taxable income is taxed at graduated rates:

15 percent on first $25,000
18 percent on next $25,000
30 percent on next $25,000
40 percent on next $25,000
46 percent on an amount greater than $100,000

EXAMPLE 1.4 If a firm has $20,000 in taxable income, the tax liability is $3,000 ($20,000 × 15%).

EXAMPLE 1.5 If XYZ Corporation has $150,000 in taxable income, the tax is calculated as follows:

Income ($)	×	Marginal Tax Rate (%)	=	Taxes ($)
25,000		15		3,750
25,000		18		4,500
25,000		30		7,500
25,000		40		10,000
50,000		46		23,000
150,000				48,750

The company's total tax liability is $48,750. Note that the rates used in computing a corporation's total tax liability are called the *marginal tax rates*, which indicate the rate applicable for the next dollar of income.

In addition to the marginal tax rate, the *average tax rate* may be calculated as follows: Average tax rate = total tax liability ÷ taxable income.

In the present tax rate schedule, the average tax rate ranges from 15 percent to a maximum of 46 percent.

EXAMPLE 1.6   Using the data in Example 1.5, the average tax rate is 32.5 percent, calculated as follows:

$$\text{Average tax rate} = \text{total tax liability} \div \text{taxable income}$$
$$= \$48,750 \div \$150,000 = 32.5\%$$

Interest and Dividend Income

Interest income is taxed as ordinary income at the regular corporate tax rate.

Dividends represent the distribution of earnings to the stockholders of a corporation. A corporation may exclude from its taxable income 85 percent of any dividends received from *another* corporation.

EXAMPLE 1.7   ABC Corporation owns stock in XYZ Corporation and receives dividends of $10,000 in a given year. Only $1,500 will be subject to tax, with the remaining $8,500 (85% × $10,000) being tax-exempt. If the company is in the 46 percent tax bracket, the company's tax liability on this dividend is $690 (46% × $1,500).

Interest and Dividends Paid

Interest paid is a tax-deductible business expense. Thus, interest is paid with *before-tax* dollars. Dividends on stock (common and preferred), however, are not deductible and are therefore paid with *after-tax* dollars. This means that our tax system favors debt financing over equity financing.

EXAMPLE 1.8   Yukon Corporation has an operating income of $200,000, pays interest charges of $50,000, and pays dividends of $40,000. The company's taxable income is:

$200,000   (operating income)
−50,000   (interest charge, which is tax-deductible)
$150,000   (taxable income)

The tax liability, as calculated in Example 1.5, is $48,750. Note that dividends are paid with after-tax dollars.

Capital Gain

Capital gains are one major form of corporate income (see also Chapter 8). They result when old assets are sold at prices above the original purchase prices.

$$\text{Capital gain} = \text{sales price} - \text{purchase price}$$

Capital gains may be short-term or long-term, with *short-term gains* resulting from the sale of assets held for 1 year or less. Short-term capital gains are treated as ordinary income and therefore taxed at the ordinary rate. *Long-term gains*, resulting from the sale of assets held longer than 1 year, are taxed at a rate of 28 percent or the ordinary rate, whichever is lower.

If a firm sells an old asset for a price above the original purchase price and also above the book value, the amount by which the purchase price exceeds the book value is considered to be *recaptured depreciation* and taxed as ordinary income. To summarize,

$$\text{Total gain} = \text{sales price} - \text{book value}$$

For determining the tax, total gain is split as follows:

$$\text{Total gain} = \text{capital gain (taxes at 28\% maximum if long-term)} + \text{recaptured depreciation}$$
$$\text{(taxed at ordinary rate)}$$
$$= \text{(sales price} - \text{purchase price)} + \text{(purchase price} - \text{book value)}$$

EXAMPLE 1.9 Assume that the United Corporation has an operating income of \$100,000 and has just sold for \$28,000 a machine purchased 2 years ago for \$25,000. Assume further that the machine is to be depreciated over 5 years using the straight-line method. What is the company's total tax liability?

$$\text{Annual depreciation charge} = \text{cost} \div \text{number of years}$$
$$= \$25,000 \div 5 \text{ years} = \$5,000/\text{year}$$
$$\text{Book value} = \text{cost} - \text{depreciation}$$
$$= \$25,000 - (\$5,000/\text{year} \times 2 \text{ years}) = \$15,000$$

The total gain is therefore

$$\text{Total gain} = \text{sales price} - \text{book value}$$
$$= \$28,000 - \$15,000 = \$13,000$$

The gain is split as follows:

$$\text{Total gain} = \text{capital gain} \qquad\qquad + \text{recaptured depreciation}$$
$$= \text{(sales price} - \text{purchase price)} + \text{(purchase price} - \text{book value)}$$
$$= (\$28,000 \quad - \$25,000) \quad + (\$25,000 \quad - \$15,000)$$
$$= \$3,000 \qquad\qquad\qquad + \$10,000$$

The company's total tax liability from its operating income and the sale of the machine is calculated as follows:

Ordinary income:

Operating income	\$100,000
Recaptured depreciation	10,000
	\$110,000

$$\text{Tax on ordinary income} = 15\% \ (\$25,000) + 18\% \ (\$25,000) + 30\% \ (\$25,000) + 40\% \ (\$25,000)$$
$$+ 46\% \ (\$110,000 - \$100,000)$$
$$= \$3,750 + \$4,500 + \$7,500 + \$10,000 + \$4,600 = \$30,350$$

Tax:

Ordinary income	\$30,350
Capital gain (28% × \$3,000)	840
Total tax	\$31,190

Operating Loss Carryback and Carryforward

If a company has an operating loss, the loss may be applied against income in other years. The loss can be carried back 3 years and then forward for 15 years (capital losses can be carried forward for 5 years). Note that the taxpayer must first apply the loss against the taxable income in the 3 prior years. If the loss is not completely absorbed by the profits in these 3 years, it may be carried forward to each of the 15 following years. At that time, any loss remaining may no longer be used as a tax deduction. To illustrate, a 1985 operating loss may be used to recover, in whole or in part, the taxes paid during 1982, 1983, and 1984. If any part of the loss remains, this amount may be used to reduce taxable income, if any, during the 15-year period of 1986 through 2000.

EXAMPLE 1.10 The Loyla Company's taxable income and associated tax payments for the years 1982 through 1989 are presented below:

Year	Taxable Income ($)	Tax Payments ($)
1982	120,000	35,950 [a]
1983	80,000	18,250 [a]
1984	40,000	6,850 [a]
1985	(400,000)	
1986	80,000	17,250
1987	100,000	25,750
1988	150,000	48,750
1989	150,000	48,750

[a] Old tax rates were used.

In 1985, the company had an operating loss of $400,000. By carrying the loss back 3 years and then forward, the firm was able to reduce its before-tax income as follows:

$$\begin{array}{r}
\$120,000 \text{ in } 1982 \\
80,000 \text{ in } 1983 \\
40,000 \text{ in } 1984 \\
80,000 \text{ in } 1986 \\
\underline{80,000} \text{ in } 1987 \\
\$400,000
\end{array}$$

The total tax savings was $101,050 as shown below:

$$\begin{array}{r}
\$\ 35,950 \text{ in } 1982 \\
18,250 \text{ in } 1983 \\
6,850 \text{ in } 1984 \\
17,250 \text{ in } 1986 \\
\underline{22,750} \text{ in } 1987\ [\$25,750 - (15\% \times \$20,000)] \\
\$101,050
\end{array}$$

As soon as the company recognized the loss of $400,000 in 1985, it was able to file for a tax refund of $61,050 ($35,950 + $18,250 + $6,850) for the years 1982 through 1984. It then carried forward the portion of the loss not used to offset past income and applied it against income for the next 2 years, 1986 and 1987.

Depreciation and Accelerated Cost Recovery System (ACRS)

The method used to calculate depreciation for tax purposes depends on the acquisition date of the asset. For assets acquired before January 1, 1981, any one of the following three depreciation methods may be used:

1.   Straight-line method
2.   Sum-of-the years'-digits (SYD) method
3.   Double-declining-balance (DDB) method

The SYD method and the DDB method are referred to as *accelerated depreciation methods* since they provide for a more rapid rate of expensing the cost of the asset and thereby offer the advantage of deferring the payment of taxes. For assets acquired in 1981 or later, the accelerated cost recovery system (ACRS) is to be used. The three traditional depreciation methods noted above are explained below. The ACRS is discussed in depth in Chapter 8.

Straight-Line Method

This is the easiest and most popular method of calculating depreciation. It results in equal periodic depreciation charges. The method is most appropriate when an asset's usage is uniform from period to period, as is the case with furniture. The annual depreciation expense is calculated by using the following formula:

$$\text{Depreciation expense} = \frac{\text{cost} - \text{salvage value}}{\text{number of years of useful life}}$$

EXAMPLE 1.11 An auto is purchased for $20,000 and has an expected salvage value of $2,000. The auto's estimated life is 8 years. What is its yearly depreciation?

$$\text{Depreciation expense} = \frac{\text{cost} - \text{salvage value}}{\text{number of years of useful life}} = \frac{\$20,000 - \$2,000}{8 \text{ years}} = \$2,250/\text{year}$$

An alternative means of computation is to multiply the *depreciable* cost ($18,000) by the annual depreciation *rate*, which is 12.5 percent in this example. The annual rate is calculated by dividing the number of years of useful life into one ($\frac{1}{8}$ = 12.5%). The result is the same: $18,000 × 12.5% = $2,250.

Sum-of-the Years'-Digits Method

In this method the number of years of life expectancy is enumerated in reverse order in the numerator, and the denominator is the sum of the digits. For example, if the life expectancy of a machine is 8 years, write the numbers in reverse order: 8, 7, 6, 5, 4, 3, 2, 1. The sum of these digits is 36, or $(8 + 7 + 6 + 5 + 4 + 3 + 2 + 1)$. Thus, the fraction for the first year is 8/36, while the fraction for the last year is 1/36. The sum of the eight fractions equals 36/36, or 1. Therefore, at the end of 8 years, the machine is completely written down to its salvage value.

The following formula may be used to find the sum-of-the-years' digits (S):

$$S = \frac{(N)(N+1)}{2}$$

where N represents the number of years of expected life.

EXAMPLE 1.12 In Example 1.11, the cost of an auto having an estimated life of 8 years is $20,000, and its salvage value is $2,000. The amount subject to depreciation is $18,000 ($20,000 − $2,000). Using the sum-of-the-years'-digits method, the computation for each year's depreciation expense is

$$S = \frac{(N)(N+1)}{2} = \frac{8(9)}{2} = \frac{72}{2} = 36$$

Year	Fraction	×	Depreciable Amount ($)	=	Depreciation Expense ($)
1	8/36		18,000		4,000
2	7/36		18,000		3,500
3	6/36		18,000		3,000
4	5/36		18,000		2,500
5	4/36		18,000		2,000
6	3/36		18,000		1,500
7	2/36		18,000		1,000
8	1/36		18,000		500
Total					18,000

Double-Declining-Balance Method

Under this method, depreciation expense is highest in the earlier years. First, a depreciation rate is determined by doubling the straight-line rate. For example, if an asset has a life of 10 years, the straight-line rate is 1/10 or 10 percent, and the double-declining rate is 20 percent. Second, depreciation expense is computed by multiplying the rate by the book value of the asset at the beginning of each year. Since book value declines over time, the depreciation expense decreases each successive period. This method *ignores* salvage value in the computation. However, the book value of the fixed asset at the end of its useful life cannot be below its salvage value.

The double-declining-balance method is advantageous for tax purposes since higher depreciation charges in the earlier years result in less income and thus less tax to be paid. The tax savings may then be invested for a return. Of course, over the life of the fixed asset, the total depreciation charge will be the same no matter what depreciation method is used; only the timing of the tax savings will differ.

EXAMPLE 1.13 Assume the data in Example 1.11. Since the straight-line rate is 12.5 percent (1/8), the double-declining-balance rate is 25 percent (2 × 12.5%). The depreciation expense for each year is shown below.

Year	Book Value at Beginning of Year ($)	× Rate (%) =	Depreciation Expense ($)	Year-end Book Value ($)
1	20,000	25	5,000	15,000
2	15,000	25	3,750	11,250
3	11,250	25	2,813	8,437
4	8,437	25	2,109	6,328
5	6,328	25	1,582	4,746
6	4,746	25	1,187	3,559
7	3,559	25	890	2,669
8	2,669	25	667	2,002

Note that if the original estimated salvage value had been $2,100, the depreciation expense for the eighth year would have been $569 ($2,669 − $2,100) rather than $667, since an asset cannot be depreciated below its salvage value.

Investment Tax Credit

The investment tax credit (ITC) was designed to stimulate business investment. The ITC is a direct reduction of taxes. Under the 1981 Economic Recovery Act, the ITC is set at 6 percent on property with a 3-year ACRS life and at 10 percent on longer-lived property. For used property, a maximum cost basis subject to ITC of $125,000 is allowed. The law maintains the current limit until 1987, when it will increase to $150,000. ITC is taken up in depth in Chapter 8, "Capital Budgeting."

EXAMPLE 1.14 During 1982, the Rachel Mirror Company purchased two machines. One was a new machine (X) having a 5-year ACRS life and costing $80,000; the other was a used machine (Y) having a 3-year ACRS life and costing $150,000. The total ITC available may be computed as follows:

Machine	Calculations	ITC
X	10% × $80,000	$ 8,000
Y	6% × $125,000	7,500
		$15,500

The $15,500 credit can be applied to the current year's tax liability. Note that machine Y, which is a used machine, is entitled to a maximum value of only $125,000 for ITC purposes.

Review Questions

1. Modern financial theory assumes that the primary goal of the firm is the maximization of stockholder _____ , which translates into maximizing the _____ of the firm's common stock.

2. _____ is a short-term goal. It can be achieved at the expense of the firm and its stockholders.

3. A firm's stock price depends on such factors as present and future earnings per share, the timing, duration, and _____ of these earnings, and _____ .

4. A major disadvantage of the corporation is the _____ on its earnings and the _____ paid to its owners (stockholders).

5. A _____ is the largest form of business organization with respect to the number of such businesses in existence. However, the corporate form is the most important with respect to the total amount of _____, assets, _____, and contribution to _____ .

6. A corporation is a(n) _____ that exists separately from its owners, better known as _____ .

7. A partnership is dissolved upon the _____ or _____ of any one of the _____ .

8. The sole proprietorship is easily established with no _____ and does not have to share _____ or _____ with others.

9. Corporate financial functions are carried out by the _____ , _____ , and _____ .

10. The financial markets are composed of money markets and _____ .

11. Money markets are the markets for short-term (less than 1 year) _____ .

12. The _____ is the term used for all trading activities in securities that do not take place on an organized stock exchange.

13. Commercial banks and credit unions are two examples of _____ .

14. _____ represent the distribution of earnings to the stockholders of a corporation.

15. _____ are the rates applicable for the next dollar of taxable income.

16. A capital gain is _____ minus initial purchase price.

17. A total gain is the sum of a capital gain and _____ . The capital gain receives _____ .

18. If a corporation has a net loss, the loss may be _____ and then _____ .

19. The traditional depreciation methods include _____ , _____ , and _____ methods.

20. The _____ is designed to stimulate business investment.

Answers: (1) wealth, market price; (2) Profit maximization; (3) risk, dividend policy; (4) double taxation, dividends; (5) sole proprietorship, sales, profits, national income; (6) legal entity, stockholders; (7) withdrawal, death, partners; (8) formal charter, profits, control; (9) treasurer, controller, financial vice president; (10) capital markets; (11) debt securities; (12) over-the-counter market; (13) financial institutions (or intermediaries); (14) Dividends; (15) Marginal tax rates; (16) sale price; (17) recaptured depreciation, special tax treatment; (18) carried back, carried forward; (19) straight-line, double-declining-balance, sum-of-the-year's-digits; (20) investment tax credit (ITC).

Solved Problems

1.1   Profit Maximization versus Stockholder Wealth Maximization. What are the disadvantages of profit maximization and stockholder wealth maximization as the goals of the firm?

SOLUTION

The disadvantages are:

Profit Maximization	**Stockholder Wealth Maximization**
Emphasizes the short run	Offers no clear link between financial decisions and stock price
Ignores risk	
Ignores the timing of returns	Can lead to management anxiety and frustration
Ignores the stockholders' return	

1.2   The Role of Financial Managers. What are the major functions of the financial manager?

SOLUTION

The financial manager performs the following functions:

1. Financial analysis, forecasting, and planning
    (*a*) Monitors the firm's financial position
    (*b*) Determines the proper amount of funds to employ in the firm
2. Investment decisions
    (*a*) Makes efficient allocations of funds to specific assets
    (*b*) Makes long-term capital budget and expenditure decisions
3. Financing and capital structure decisions
    (*a*) Determines both the mix of short-term and long-term financing and equity/debt financing
    (*b*) Raises funds on the most favorable terms possible
4. Management of financial resources
    (*a*) Manages working capital
    (*b*) Maintains optimal level of investments in each of the current assets

1.3   Stock Price Maximization. What are the factors that affect the market value of a firm's common stock?

SOLUTION

The factors that influence a firm's stock price are:

1. Present and future earnings
2. The timing and risk of earnings
3. The stability and risk of earnings
4. The manner in which the firm is financed
5. Dividend policy

1.4   Organizational Chart of the Finance Function. Depict a typical organizational chart highlighting the finance function of the firm.

SOLUTION

See Fig. 1-2.

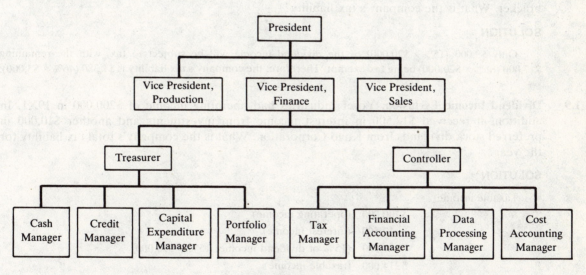

Fig. 1-2

1.5   Tax Liability and Average Tax Rate. A corporation has a taxable income of $15,000. What is its tax liability and average tax rate?

SOLUTION

The company's tax liability is $2,250 ($15,000 × 15%). The company's average tax rate is 15 percent.

1.6   Tax Liability. A corporation has $120,000 in taxable income. What is its tax liability?

SOLUTION

Income ($)	×	Marginal Tax Rate (%)	=	Taxes ($)
25,000		15		3,750
25,000		18		4,500
25,000		30		7,500
25,000		40		10,000
20,000		46		9,200
120,000				34,950

The company's total tax liability is $34,950.

1.7   Average Tax Rate. In Problem 1.6, what is the average tax rate of the corporation?

SOLUTION

Average tax rate = total tax liability ÷ taxable income = $34,950 ÷ $120,000 = 0.291 = 29.1%

1.8   Dividend Income Exclusion. Rha Company owns stock in Aju Corporation and receives dividends of $20,000 in a given year. Assume that the company is in the 46 percent tax bracket. What is the company's tax liability?

SOLUTION

Only $3,000 (15% × $20,000) of the dividend income will be subject to tax, with the remaining $17,000 (85% × $20,000) being tax-exempt. Therefore, the company's tax liability is $1,380 (46% × $3,000).

1.9   Dividend Income Exclusion. Yosef Industries had operating income of $200,000 in 19X1. In addition, it received $12,500 in interest income from investments and another $10,000 in preferred stock dividends from Koyo Corporation. What is the company's total tax liability for the year?

SOLUTION

Taxable income:

$200,000	(operating income)
12,500	(interest income)
1,500	(15% of dividend income: 15% × $10,000)
$214,000	(taxable income)

The company's total tax liability is computed as follows:

Taxable Income ($)	×	Marginal Tax Rate (%)	=	Taxes ($)
25,000		15		3,750
25,000		18		4,500
25,000		30		7,500
25,000		40		10,000
114,000		46		52,440
214,000				78,190

1.10 Interest and Dividends Paid. Johnson Corporation has operating income of $120,000, pays interest charges of $60,000, and pays dividends of $20,000. What is the company's tax liability?

SOLUTION

The company's taxable income is:

$120,000   (operating income)

−60,000   (interest charge)

$ 60,000   (taxable income)

The tax liability is then calculated as follows:

Income ($)	×	Marginal Tax Rate (%)	=	Taxes ($)
25,000		15		3,750
25,000		18		4,500
10,000		30		3,000
60,000				11,250

Note that since dividends of $20,000 are paid out of after-tax income, the dividend amount is not included in the computation.

1.11 Capital Gain and Recaptured Depreciation. The Theisman Company purchased a machine 4 years ago for $50,000 that had a depreciable life of 10 years with no salvage value. The company sold the machine this year for $70,000. The machine has a book value of $30,000 based on the use of straight-line depreciation [$50,000 − ($5,000 × 4)]. The firm has a marginal tax rate of 46 percent and a long-term capital gain rate of 28 percent. Calculate the company's tax liability resulting from the sale.

SOLUTION

$$\text{Total gain} = \$70,000 \text{ sale price} - \$30,000 \text{ book value} = \$40,000$$

The total gain is split as follows:

$40,000 Total Gain

Long-Term Capital Gain	Recaptured Depreciation
$70,000 sale price	$50,000 purchase price
−50,000 purchase price	−30,000 book value
$20,000 (taxed at 28%)	$20,000 (taxed at 46%)

$$\text{Tax liability} = (28\% \times \$20,000) + (46\% \times \$20,000) = \$5,600 + \$9,200 = \$14,800$$

1.12 Capital Gain and Recaptured Depreciation. Two years ago the JKS Company purchased machinery for $50,000 that has a depreciable life of 10 years and a zero salvage value. The company just sold the equipment for $65,000. The firm has a marginal tax rate of 46 percent and a long-term capital gain rate of 28 percent and uses straight-line depreciation. What is the total tax liability resulting from the sale?

SOLUTION

$$\text{Annual depreciation} = \$50,000 \div 10 \text{ years} = \$5,000/\text{year}$$

$$\text{Current book value} = \$50,000 - (\$5,000 \times 2) = \$40,000$$

$$\text{Total gain} = \$65,000 \text{ sale price} - \$40,000 \text{ book value} = \$25,000$$

This is split into a long-term capital gain of $15,000 and recaptured depreciation of $10,000 as follows:

$25,000 Total Gain

Long-Term Capital Gain		Recaptured Depreciation	
$65,000	sale price	$50,000	purchase price
−50,000	purchase price	−40,000	book value
$15,000	(taxed at 28%)	$10,000	(taxed at 46%)

Tax liability = 28% ($15,000) + 46% ($10,000) = $4,200 + $4,600 = $8,800

1.13   Operating Loss Carryback and Carryforward. The Kenneth Parks Company's taxable income and tax payments/liability for the years 1982 through 1988 are given below.

Year	Taxable Income ($)	Tax Payments/Liability ($)
1982	60,000	12,250[a]
1983	20,000	3,400[a]
1984	40,000	6,850[a]
1985	(150,000)	0
1986	50,000	8,250
1987	60,000	11,250
1988	100,000	35,750

[a] Old tax rates were used.

Compute the company's tax refund.

SOLUTION

By carrying the loss in 1985 back 3 years and then forward, the company is able to reduce its taxable income by $60,000 in 1982, $20,000 in 1983, $40,000 in 1984, and $30,000 in 1986. As soon as the company recognizes the $150,000 loss in 1985, it may file for a tax refund of $22,500 ($12,250 + $3,400 + $6,850) for the years 1982 through 1984.

1.14   Operating Loss Carryback and Carryforward. The Bruce Gross Company's taxable income and associated tax payments for the years 1982 through 1988 are presented below.

Year	Taxable Income ($)	Tax Payments ($)
1982	20,000	3,400[a]
1983	15,000	2,550[a]
1984	50,000	8,750[a]
1985	(90,000)	
1986	10,000	1,500
1987	15,000	2,250
1988	75,000	15,750

[a] Old tax rates were used.

Calculate the company's tax benefit in each year.

SOLUTION

By carrying the loss back 3 years and then forward, the firm was able to reduce its before-tax income as follows:

1982	$20,000
1983	15,000
1984	50,000
1986	5,000
	$90,000

Therefore, the yearly and total tax savings are as follows:

1982	$3,400 [a]
1983	2,550 [a]
1984	8,750 [a]
1986	750 [b]
	$15,450

---

[a] To be refunded.

[b] $1,500 - (15\% \times \$5,000)$

1.15   Straight-Line Depreciation. On January 1, 19X5, a machine was purchased for $30,000. The estimated life is 6 years and the salvage value is $1,500. Determine the annual depreciation using the straight-line method.

SOLUTION

$$\text{Depreciation expense} = \frac{\text{cost} - \text{salvage value}}{\text{number of years of useful life}}$$

$$= \frac{\$30,000 - \$1,500}{6 \text{ years}} = \$4,750/\text{year}$$

1.16   Sum-of-the-Years'-Digits Method. Using the information supplied in Problem 1.15, compute the depreciation expense for the first 3 years by the sum-of-the-years'-digits method.

SOLUTION

$$S = \frac{(N)(N+1)}{2} = \frac{6(6+1)}{2} = 21$$

Year.	Fraction	×	Depreciable Amount ($)	=	Depreciation ($)
1	6/21		28,500		8,143
2	5/21		28,500		6,786
3	4/21		28,500		5,429

1.17   Double-Declining-Balance Method. Solve Problem 1.15 using the double-declining-balance method.

SOLUTION

The double-declining rate is 1/3 ($2 \times 1/6$). Salvage value is ignored in the computation.

Year	Book Value at Beginning of Year ($)	× Rate =	Depreciation Expense ($)	Year-End Book Value ($)
1	30,000	1/3	10,000	20,000
2	20,000	1/3	6,667	13,333
3	13,333	1/3	4,444	8,889

1.18 **Depreciation Methods.** Fonda corporation has purchased a mixing machine for $20,000. The machine has an estimated life of 4 years with an estimated salvage value of $6,000. Compute the annual depreciation expense for each year using (*a*) the straight-line method, (*b*) the sum-of-the-years'-digits method, and (*c*) the double-declining-balance method. Which method gives the greatest tax advantage in the first year?

SOLUTION

(*a*) Straight-line depreciation:

$$\frac{\$20,000 - \$6,000}{4 \text{ years}} = \$3,500/\text{year}$$

(*b*) Sum-of-the-years'-digits depreciation:

$$S = \frac{(N)(N+1)}{2} = \frac{(4)(5)}{2} = 10$$

Year	Fraction ×	Depreciable Amount ($) =	Depreciation Expense ($)
1	4/10	14,000	5,600
2	3/10	14,000	4,200
3	2/10	14,000	2,800
4	1/10	14,000	1,400
			14,000

(*c*) The straight-line rate is 1/4 = 25 percent. Therefore, the double-declining rate is 50 percent.

Year	Book Value at Beginning of Year ($)	× Rate =	Depreciation Expense ($)
1	20,000	0.5	10,000
2	10,000	0.5	4,000 [a]
3	6,000		
4	6,000		14,000

[a] Note that the depreciation expense is not $5,000 ($10,000 × 0.5) since the asset cannot be depreciated below its salvage value of $6,000.

The double-declining method gives the greatest tax advantage in the first year since its depreciation expense is highest ($10,000). The higher the depreciation deduction, the less the taxable income and, therefore, the less the tax.

1.19 **Investment Tax Credit (ITC).** During 1985, Wanda Ballanger Corporation purchased two machines. One was a new machine (A) having a 3-year ACRS life and costing $100,000; the other was a used machine (B) having a 5-year ACRS life and costing $200,000. What is the company's total investment tax credit?

SOLUTION

Machine	Calculations	Investment Tax Credit
A	6% × $100,000	$ 6,000
B	10% × $125,000 [a]	12,500
		$18,500

---

[a] Note that machine B, which is a used machine, is entitled to a maximum value of only $125,000 for ITC purposes.

Chapter 2

Financial Analysis

2.1 THE SCOPE AND PURPOSE OF FINANCIAL ANALYSIS

Financial analysis is an evaluation of both a firm's past financial performance and its prospects for the future. Typically, it involves an analysis of the firm's financial statements and its flow of funds. *Financial statement analysis* involves the calculation of various ratios. It is used by such interested parties as creditors, investors, and managers to determine the firm's financial position relative to that of others. The way in which an entity's financial position and operating results are viewed by investors and creditors will have an impact on the firm's reputation, price/earnings ratio, and effective interest rate.

Funds flow analysis is an evaluation of the firm's statement of changes in financial position in order to determine the impact that its sources and uses of funds have on the firm's operations and financial condition. It is used in decisions that involve corporate investments, operations, and financing.

2.2 FINANCIAL STATEMENT ANALYSIS

The financial statements of an enterprise present the summarized data of its assets, liabilities, and equities in the balance sheet and its revenue and expenses in the income statement. If not analyzed, such data may lead one to draw erroneous conclusions about the firm's financial condition. Various measuring instruments may be used to evaluate the financial health of a business, including *horizontal*, *vertical*, and *ratio analyses*. A financial analyst uses the ratios to make two types of comparisons:

1. *Industry comparison.* The ratios of a firm are compared with those of similar firms or with industry averages or norms to determine how the company is faring relative to its competitors. Industry average ratios are available from a number of sources, including:
    (*a*)   *Dun & Bradstreet.* Dun & Bradstreet computes 14 ratios for each of 125 lines of business. They are published annually in *Dun's Review* and *Key Business Ratios.*
    (*b*)   *Robert Morris Associates.* This association of bank loan officers publishes *Annual Statement Studies.* Sixteen ratios are computed for more than 300 lines of business, as well as a percentage distribution of items on the balance sheet and income statement (common size financial statements).

2. *Trend analysis.* A firm's present ratio is compared with its past and expected future ratios to determine whether the company's financial condition is improving or deteriorating over time.

After completing the financial statement analysis, the firm's financial analyst will consult with management to discuss their plans and prospects, any problem areas identified in the analysis, and possible solutions.

2.3 HORIZONTAL ANALYSIS

Horizontal analysis is used to evaluate the trend in the accounts over the years. A $3 million profit year looks very good following a $1 million profit year, but not after a $4 million profit year. Horizontal analysis is usually shown in comparative financial statements (see Examples 2.1 and 2.2). Companies often show comparative financial data for 5 years in annual reports.

EXAMPLE 2.1

The Ratio Company
Comparative Balance Sheet
(In Thousands of Dollars)
December 31, 19X3, 19X2, and 19X1

	19X3	19X2	19X1	Increase or (Decrease) 19X3–19X2	Increase or (Decrease) 19X2–19X1	Percentage of Increase or (Decrease) 19X3–19X2	Percentage of Increase or (Decrease) 19X2–19X1
ASSETS							
Current assets							
Cash	$ 30.0	$ 35	$ 35	$(5.0)	—	(14.3)	—
Accounts receivable	20.0	15	10	5.0	$ 5	33.3	50.0
Marketable securities	20.0	15	5	5.0	10	33.3	200.0
Inventory	50.0	45	50	5.0	(5)	11.1	(10.0)
Total current assets	$120.0	$110	$100	$10.0	$10	9.1	10.0
Plant assets	100.0	90	85	10.0	5	11.1	5.9
Total assets	$220.0	$200	$185	$20.0	$15	10.0	8.1
LIABILITIES							
Current liabilities	$ 55.4	$ 50	$ 52	$ 5.4	$(2)	10.8	(3.8)
Long-term liabilities	80.0	75	70	5.0	5	6.7	7.1
Total liabilities	$135.4	$125	$122	$10.4	$ 3	8.3	2.5
STOCKHOLDERS' EQUITY							
Common stock, $10 par value, 4,500 shares	$ 45.0	$ 45	$ 45	—	—	—	—
Retained earnings	39.6	30	18	$ 9.6	$12	32.0	66.7
Total stockholders' equity	$ 84.6	$ 75	$ 63	$ 9.6	$12	12.8	19.0
Total liabilities and stockholders' equity	$220.0	$200	$185	$20.0	$15	10.0	8.1

EXAMPLE 2.2

The Ratio Company
Comparative Income Statement
(In Thousands of Dollars)
For the Years Ended December 31, 19X3, 19X2, and 19X1

	19X3	19X2	19X1	Increase or (Decrease) 19X3–19X2	Increase or (Decrease) 19X2–19X1	Percentage of Increase or (Decrease) 19X3–19X2	Percentage of Increase or (Decrease) 19X2–19X1
Sales	$100.0	$110	$50	$(10.0)	$60	(9.1)	120.0
Sales returns and allowances	20.0	8	3	12.0	5	150.0	166.7
Net sales	$ 80.0	$102	$47	$(22.0)	$55	(21.6)	117.0
Cost of goods sold	50.0	60	25	(10.0)	35	(16.7)	140.0
Gross profit	$ 30.0	$ 42	$22	$(12.0)	$20	(28.6)	90.9
Operating expenses							
Selling expenses	$ 11.0	$ 13	$ 8	$ (2.0)	$ 5	(15.4)	62.5
General expenses	4.0	7	4	(3.0)	3	(42.9)	75.0
Total operating expenses	$ 15.0	$ 20	$12	$ (5.0)	$ 8	(25.0)	66.7
Income from operations	$ 15.0	$ 22	$10	$ (7.0)	$12	(31.8)	120.0
Nonoperating income	3.0	0	1	3.0	(1)	—	(100.0)
Income before interest expense and taxes	$ 18.0	$ 22	$11	$ (4.0)	$11	(18.2)	100.0
Interest expense	2.0	2	1	—	1	—	100.0
Income before taxes	$ 16.0	$ 20	$10	$ (4.0)	$10	(20.0)	100.0
Income taxes (40% rate)	6.4	8	4	(1.6)	4	(20.0)	100.0
Net income	9.6	12	6	(2.4)	6	(20.0)	100.0

Because horizontal analysis stresses the trends of the various accounts, it is relatively easy to identify areas of wide divergence that require further attention. In the income statement shown in Example 2.2, the large increase in sales returns and allowances coupled with the decrease in sales for the period 19X2 to 19X3 should cause concern. One might compare these results with those of competitors to determine whether the problem is industrywide or just within the company.

Note that it is important to show both the dollar amount of change and the percentage of change, because either one alone might be misleading. For example, although the interest expense from 19X1 to 19X2 increased 100 percent (Example 2.2), it probably does not require further investigation since the dollar amount of increase is only $1,000. Similarly, a large change in dollar amount might result in only a small percentage change and therefore not be a cause for concern.

When an analysis covers a span of many years comparative financial statements may become cumbersome. To avoid this, the results of horizontal analysis may be presented by showing trends relative to a base year. In this method, a year representative of the firm's activity is chosen as the base. Each account of the base year is assigned an index of 100. The index for each respective account in succeeding years is found by dividing the account's amount by the base year amount and multiplying by 100. For example, if we let 19X1 be the base year in the balance sheet of Example 2.1, Accounts Receivable would be given an index of 100. In 19X2, the index would be 150 [(15/10) × 100], and in 19X3 it would be 200 [(20/10) × 100]. A condensed form of the balance sheet using *trend analysis* is shown in Example 2.3.

EXAMPLE 2.3

The Ratio Company
Trend Analysis of the Balance Sheet
(Expressed as Percent)
Dec. 31, 19X3, 19X2, and 19X1

	19X3	19X2	19X1
ASSETS			
Current assets	120	110	100
Plant assets	117.6	105.9	100
Total assets	118.9	108.1	100
LIABILITIES AND STOCKHOLDERS' EQUITY			
Liabilities			
Current liabilities	106.5	96.2	100
Long-term liabilities	114.3	107.1	100
Total liabilities	111.0	102.5	100
Stockholders' equity			
Common stock	100	100	100
Retained earnings	220	166.7	100
Total stockholders' equity	134.3	119	100
Total liabilities and stockholders' equity	118.9	108.1	100

2.4 VERTICAL ANALYSIS

In *vertical analysis*, a significant item on a financial statement is used as a base value, and all other items on the financial statement are compared to it. In performing vertical analysis for the balance sheet, total assets is assigned 100 percent. Each asset account is expressed as a percentage of total assets. Total liabilities and stockholders' equity is also assigned 100 percent. Each liability and equity account is then expressed as a percentage of total liabilities and stockholders' equity. In the income statement, net sales is given the value of 100 percent and all other accounts are evaluated in comparison to net sales. The resulting figures are then given in a *common size statement*. The common size analysis of Ratio Company's income statement is shown in Example 2.4.

EXAMPLE 2.4

The Ratio Company
Income Statement and
Common Size Analysis
(In Thousands of Dollars)
For the Years Ended Dec. 31, 19X3 and 19X2

	19X3		19X2	
	Amount	**%**	**Amount**	**%**
Sales	$100.0	125.0%	$110	107.8%
Sales returns and allowances	20.0	25.0	8	7.8
Net sales	$ 80.0	100.0	$102	100.0
Cost of goods sold	50.0	62.5	60	58.8
Gross profit	$ 30.0	37.5	$ 42	41.2
Operating expenses				
Selling expenses	$ 11.0	13.8	$ 13	12.7
General expenses	4.0	5.0	7	6.9
Total operating expenses	$ 15.0	18.8	$ 20	19.6
Income from operations	$ 15.0	18.7	$ 22	21.6
Nonoperating income	3.0	3.8		
Income before interest				
expense and taxes	$ 18.0	22.5	$ 22	21.6
Interest expense	2.0	2.5	2	2.0
Income before taxes	$ 16.0	20.0	$ 20	19.6
Income taxes	6.4	8.0	8	7.8
Net income	$ 9.6	12.0%	$ 12	11.8%

Vertical analysis is used to disclose the internal structure of an enterprise. It indicates the existing relationship between each income statement account and revenue. It shows the mix of assets that produces the income and the mix of the sources of capital, whether by current or long-term liabilities or by equity funding. In addition to making such internal evaluation possible, the results of vertical analysis are also used to further assess the firm's relative position in the industry.

As with horizontal analysis, vertical analysis is not the end of the process. The financial analyst must be prepared to probe deeper into those areas that either horizontal or vertical analysis, or both, indicate to be possible problem areas.

2.5 RATIO ANALYSIS

Horizontal and vertical analyses compare one figure to another within the same category. It is also essential to compare figures from different categories. This is accomplished through *ratio analysis*. There are many ratios that an analyst can use, depending upon what he or she considers to be important relationships.

Financial ratios can be classified into five groups:

1. Liquidity ratios
2. Activity ratios

3. Leverage ratios
4. Profitability ratios
5. Market value ratios

Some of the most useful ones in each category are discussed next.

Liquidity Ratios

Liquidity is a company's ability to meet its maturing short-term obligations. Liquidity is essential to conducting business activity, particularly in times of adversity, such as when a business is shut down by a strike or when operating losses ensue due to an economic recession or a steep rise in the price of a raw material or part. If liquidity is insufficient to cushion such losses, serious financial difficulty may result. Poor liquidity is analogous to a person having a fever—it is a symptom of a fundamental problem.

Analyzing corporate liquidity is especially important to creditors. If a company has a poor liquidity position, it may be a poor credit risk, perhaps unable to make timely interest and principal payments.

Liquidity ratios are static in nature as of year-end. Therefore, it is also important for management to look at expected *future* cash flows. If future cash outflows are expected to be high relative to inflows, the liquidity position of the company will deteriorate.

A description of various liquidity measures follows.

Net Working Capital. Net working capital[1] is equal to current assets less current liabilities. *Current assets* are those assets that are expected to be converted into cash or used up within 1 year. *Current liabilities* are those liabilities that must be paid within 1 year; they are paid out of current assets. Net working capital is a safety cushion to creditors. A large balance is required when the entity has difficulty borrowing on short notice.

$$\text{Net working capital} = \text{current assets} - \text{current liabilities}$$

The net working capital for the Ratio Company for 19X3 is:

$$\$120,000 - \$55,400 = \$64,600$$

In 19X2, net working capital was $60,000. The increase in net working capital is a favorable sign.

Current Ratio. The current ratio is equal to current assets divided by current liabilities. This ratio, which is subject to seasonal fluctuations, is used to measure the ability of an enterprise to meet its current liabilities out of current assets. A high ratio is needed when the firm has difficulty borrowing on short notice. A limitation of this ratio is that it may rise just prior to financial distress because of a company's desire to improve its cash position by, for example, selling fixed assets. Such dispositions have a detrimental effect upon productive capacity. Another limitation of the current ratio is that it will be excessively high when inventory is carried on the last-in, first-out (LIFO) basis.

$$\text{Current ratio} = \frac{\text{current assets}}{\text{current liabilities}}$$

The Ratio Company's current ratio for 19X3 is:

$$\frac{\$120,000}{\$55,400} = 2.17$$

In 19X2, the current ratio was 2.2. The ratio showed a slight decline over the year.

---

[1] Some textbooks define *working capital* as current assets less current liabilities. Therefore, the terms *net working capital* and *working capital* are often used interchangeably throughout those books.

Quick (Acid-Test) Ratio. The quick ratio, also known as the acid-test ratio, is a stringent test of liquidity. It is found by dividing the most liquid current assets (cash, marketable securities, and accounts receivable) by current liabilities. Inventory is not included because of the length of time needed to convert inventory into cash. Prepaid expenses are also not included because they are not convertible into cash and so are not capable of covering current liabilities.

$$\text{Quick ratio} = \frac{\text{cash} + \text{marketable securities} + \text{accounts receivable}}{\text{current liabilities}}$$

The quick ratio for the Ratio Company in 19X3 is:

$$\frac{\$30,000 + \$20,000 + \$20,000}{\$55,400} = 1.26$$

The ratio was 1.3 in 19X3. The ratio went down slightly over the year.

Activity (Asset Utilization) Ratios

Activity ratios are used to determine how quickly various accounts are converted into sales or cash. Overall liquidity ratios generally do not give an adequate picture of a company's *real* liquidity, due to differences in the kinds of current assets and liabilities the company holds. Thus, it is necessary to evaluate the activity or liquidity of specific current accounts. Various ratios exist to measure the activity of receivables, inventory, and total assets.

Accounts Receivable Ratios. Accounts receivable ratios consist of the accounts receivable turnover ratio and the average collection period. The *accounts receivable turnover ratio* gives the number of times accounts receivable is collected during the year. It is found by dividing net credit sales (if not available, then total sales) by the average accounts receivable. *Average accounts receivable* is typically found by adding the beginning and ending accounts receivable and dividing by 2. Although average accounts receivable may be computed annually, quarterly, or monthly, the ratio is most accurate when the shortest period available is used. In general, the higher the accounts receivable turnover, the better since the company is collecting quickly from customers and these funds can then be invested. However, an excessively high ratio may indicate that the company's credit policy is too stringent, with the company not tapping the potential for profit through sales to customers in higher risk classes. Note that here, too, before changing its credit policy, a company has to weigh the profit potential against the risk inherent in selling to more marginal customers.

$$\text{Accounts receivable turnover} = \frac{\text{net credit sales}}{\text{average accounts receivable}}$$

Ratio Company's average accounts receivable for 19X3 is:

$$\frac{\$15,000 + \$20,000}{2} = \$17,500$$

The accounts receivable turnover ratio for 19X3 is:

$$\frac{\$80,000}{\$17,500} = 4.57 \text{ times}$$

In 19X2, the accounts receivable turnover ratio was 8.16. The drop in this ratio in 19X3 is significant and indicates a serious problem in collecting from customers. The company needs to reevaluate its credit policy, which may be too lax, or its billing and collection practices, or both.

The *collection period* (days sales in receivables) is the number of days it takes to collect on receivables.

$$\text{Average collection period} = \frac{365}{\text{accounts receivable turnover}}$$

The Ratio Company's average collection period for 19X3 is:

$$\frac{365}{4.57} = 79.9 \text{ days}$$

This means that it takes almost 80 days for a sale to be converted into cash. In 19X2, the average collection period was 44.7 days. With the substantial increase in collection days in 19X3, there exists a danger that customer balances may become uncollectible. One possible cause for the increase may be that the company is now selling to highly marginal customers. The analyst should compare the company's credit terms with the extent to which customer balances are delinquent. An *aging schedule*, which list the accounts receivable according to the length of time they are outstanding, would be helpful for this comparison.

Inventory Ratios.   If a company is holding excess inventory, it means that funds which could be invested elsewhere are being tied up in inventory. In addition, there will be high carrying cost for storing the goods, as well as the risk of obsolescence. On the other hand, if inventory is too low, the company may lose customers because it has run out of merchandise. Two major ratios for evaluating inventory are inventory turnover and average age of inventory.

Inventory turnover is computed as:

$$\text{Inventory turnover} = \frac{\text{cost of goods sold}}{\text{average inventory}}$$

Average inventory is determined by adding the beginning and ending inventories and dividing by 2. For the Ratio Company, the inventory turnover in 19X3 is:

$$\frac{\$50,000}{\$47,500} = 1.05 \text{ times}$$

In 19X2, the inventory turnover was 1.26 times.

The decline in the inventory turnover indicates the stocking of goods. An attempt should be made to determine whether specific inventory categories are not selling well and if this is so, the reasons therefore. Perhaps there are obsolete goods on hand not actually worth their stated value. However, a decline in the turnover rate would not cause concern if it were primarily due to the introduction of a new product line for which the advertising effects have not been felt yet.

Average age of inventory is computed as follows:

$$\text{Average age of inventory} = \frac{365}{\text{inventory turnover}}$$

The average age of inventory in 19X3 is:

$$\frac{365}{1.05} = 347.6 \text{ days}$$

In 19X2, the average age was 289.7 days. The lengthening of the holding period shows a potentially greater risk of obsolescence.

Operating Cycle

The *operating cycle* of a business is the number of days it takes to convert inventory and receivables to cash. Hence, a short operating cycle is desirable.

$$\text{Operating cycle} = \text{average collection period} + \text{average age of inventory}$$

The operating cycle for the Ratio Company in 19X3 is:

$$79.9 \text{ days} + 347.6 \text{ days} = 427.5 \text{ days}$$

In 19X2, the operating cycle was 334.4 days. This is an unfavorable trend since an increased amount of money is being tied up in noncash assets.

Total Asset Turnover.   The total asset turnover ratio is helpful in evaluating a company's ability to use its asset base efficiently to generate revenue. A low ratio may be due to many factors, and it is important to identify the underlying reasons. For example, is investment in assets excessive when compared to the value of the output being produced? If so, the company might want to consolidate its present operation, perhaps by selling some of its assets and investing the proceeds for a higher return or using them to expand into a more profitable area.

$$\text{Total asset turnover} = \frac{\text{net sales}}{\text{average total assets}}$$

In 19X3 the total asset turnover ratio for the Ratio Company is:

$$\frac{\$80,000}{\$210,000} = 0.381$$

In 19X2, the ratio was 0.530 ($102,000/$192,500). The company's use of assets declined significantly, and the reasons need to be pinpointed. For example, are adequate repairs being made? Or are the assets getting old and do they need replacing?

Interrelationship of Liquidity and Activity to Earnings.   A trade-off exists between liquidity risk and return. *Liquidity risk* is minimized by holding greater current assets than noncurrent assets. However, the rate of return will decline because the return on current assets (i.e., marketable securities) is typically less than the rate earned on productive fixed assets. Also, excessively high liquidity may mean that management has not aggressively searched for desirable capital investment opportunities. Maintaining a proper balance between liquidity and return is important to the overall financial health of a business.

It must be pointed out that high profitability does not necessarily infer a strong cash flow position. Income may be high but cash problems may exist because of maturing debt and the need to replace assets, among other reasons. For example, it is possible that a growth company may experience a decline in liquidity since the net working capital needed to support the expanding sales is tied up in assets that cannot be realized in time to meet the current obligations. The impact of earning activities on liquidity is highlighted by comparing *cash flow from operations* to net income.

If accounts receivable and inventory turn over quickly, the cash flow received from customers can be invested for a return, thus increasing net income.

Leverage (Solvency, Long-Term Debt) Ratios

Solvency is a company's ability to meet its long-term obligations as they become due. An analysis of solvency concentrates on the long-term financial and operating structure of the business. The degree of long-term debt in the capital structure is also considered. Further, solvency is dependent upon profitability since in the long run a firm will not be able to meet its debts unless it is profitable.

When debt is excessive, additional financing should be obtained primarily from equity sources. Management might also consider lengthening the maturity of the debt and staggering the debt repayment dates.

Some leverage ratios follow.

Debt Ratio.   The debt ratio compares total liabilities (total debt) to total assets. It shows the percentage of total funds obtained from creditors. Creditors would rather see a low debt ratio because there is a greater cushion for creditor losses if the firm goes bankrupt.

$$\text{Debt ratio} = \frac{\text{total liabilities}}{\text{total assets}}$$

For the Ratio Company, in 19X3 the debt ratio is:

$$\frac{\$135,400}{\$220,000} = 0.62$$

In 19X2, the ratio was 0.63. There was a slight improvement in the ratio over the year as indicated by the lower degree of debt to total assets.

Debt/Equity Ratio.   The *debt/equity ratio* is a significant measure of solvency since a high degree of debt in the capital structure may make it difficult for the company to meet interest charges and principal payments at maturity. Further, with a high debt position comes the risk of running out of cash under conditions of adversity. Also, excessive debt will result in less financial flexibility since the company will have greater difficulty obtaining funds during a tight money market. The debt/equity ratio is computed as:

$$\text{Debt/equity ratio} = \frac{\text{total liabilities}}{\text{stockholders' equity}}$$

For Ratio Company, the debt/equity ratio was 1.60 in 19X3 ($135,400/$84,600) and 1.67 in 19X2. The ratio remained fairly constant. A desirable debt/equity ratio depends on many variables, including the rates of other companies in the industry, the access for further debt financing, and the stability of earnings.

Times Interest Earned (Interest Coverage) Ratio.   The times interest earned ratio reflects the number of times before-tax earnings cover interest expense.[2] It is a safety margin indicator in the sense that it shows how much of a decline in earnings a company can absorb. The ratio is computed as follows:

$$\text{Times interest earned ratio} = \frac{\text{earnings before interest and taxes (EBIT)}}{\text{interest expense}}$$

In 19X3, interest of Ratio Company was covered 9 times ($18,000/$2,000), while in 19X2 it was covered 11 times. The decline in the coverage is a negative indicator since less earnings are available to meet interest charges.

Profitability Ratios

An indication of good financial health and how effectively the firm is being managed is the company's ability to earn a satisfactory profit and return on investment. Investors will be reluctant to associate themselves with an entity that has poor earning potential since the market price of stock and dividend potential will be adversely affected. Creditors will shy away from companies with deficient profitability since the amounts owed to them may not be paid. Absolute dollar profit by itself has little significance unless it is related to its source.

Some major ratios that measure operating results are summarized below.

Gross Profit Margin.   The gross profit margin reveals the percentage of each dollar left over after the business has paid for its goods. The higher the gross profit earned, the better. Gross profit equals net sales less cost of goods sold.

$$\text{Gross profit margin} = \frac{\text{gross profit}}{\text{net sales}}$$

The gross profit margin for the Ratio Company in 19X3 is:

$$\frac{\$30,000}{\$80,000} = 0.38$$

In 19X2 the gross profit margin was 0.41. The decline in this ratio indicates the business is earning less gross profit on each sales dollar. The reasons for the decline may be many, including a higher relative production cost of merchandise sold.

---

[2] Note that some textbooks use *after*-tax earnings to calculate this ratio.

Profit Margin. The ratio of net income to net sales is called the profit margin. It indicates the profitability generated from revenue and hence is an important measure of operating performance. It also provides clues to a company's pricing, cost structure, and production efficiency.

$$\text{Profit margin} = \frac{\text{net income}}{\text{net sales}}$$

In 19X3, the Ratio Company's profit margin is:

$$\frac{\$9,600}{\$80,000} = 0.120$$

In 19X2, the ratio was also 0.120. The constant profit margin indicates that the earning power of the business remained static.

Return on Investment. Return on investment (ROI) is a key, but rough, measure of performance. Although ROI shows the extent to which earnings are achieved on the investment made in the business, the actual value is generally somewhat distorted.

There are basically two ratios that evaluate the return on investment. One is the return on total assets, and the other is the return on owners' equity.

The *return on total assets* (ROA) indicates the efficiency with which management has used its available resources to generate income.

$$\text{Return on total assets} = \frac{\text{net income}}{\text{average total assets}}$$

For the Ratio Company in 19X3, the return on total assets is:

$$\frac{\$9,600}{(\$220,000 + \$200,000)/2} = 0.0457$$

In 19X2, the return was 0.0623. The productivity of assets in deriving income deteriorated in 19X3.

The Du Pont formula shows an important tie-in between the profit margin and the return on total assets. The relationship is:

$$\text{Return on total assets} = \text{profit margin} \times \text{total asset turnover}$$

Therefore,

$$\frac{\text{Net income}}{\text{Average total assets}} = \frac{\text{net income}}{\text{net sales}} \times \frac{\text{net sales}}{\text{average total assets}}$$

As can be seen from this formula, the ROA can be raised by increasing either the profit margin or the asset turnover. The latter is to some extent industry dependent, with retailers and the like having a greater potential for raising the asset turnover ratio than do service and utility companies. However, the profit margin may vary greatly within an industry since it is subject to sales, cost controls, and pricing. The interrelationship shown in the Du Pont formula can therefore be useful to a company trying to raise its ROA since the area most sensitive to change can be targeted.

For 19X3, the figures for the Ratio Company are:

$$\text{Return on total assets} = \text{profit margin} \times \text{total asset turnover}$$
$$0.0457 = 0.120 \times 0.381$$

We know from our previous analysis that the profit margin has remained stable while asset turnover has deteriorated, bringing down the ROI. Since asset turnover can be considerably higher, Ratio Company might first focus on improving this ratio while at the same time reevaluating its pricing policy, cost controls, and sales practices.

The *return on common equity* (ROE) measures the rate of return earned on the common stockholders' investment.

$$\text{Return on common equity} = \frac{\text{earnings available to common stockholders}}{\text{average stockholders' equity}}$$

In 19X3, Ratio Company's return on equity is:

$$\frac{\$9,600}{(\$84,600 + \$75,000)/2} = 0.1203$$

In 19X2, the ROE was 0.17. There has been a significant drop in the return earned by the owners of the business.

ROE and ROA are closely related through what is known as the *equity multiplier* (leverage, or debt ratio) as follows:

$$\text{ROE} = \text{ROA} \times \text{equity multiplier}$$
$$= \text{ROA} \times \frac{\text{total assets}}{\text{common equity}}$$

or

$$= \frac{\text{ROA}}{1 - \text{debt ratio}}$$

In 19X3, the Ratio Company's debt ratio was 0.62. Thus,

$$\text{ROE} = \frac{0.0457}{1 - 0.62} = 0.1203$$

Note that ROA = 0.0457 and ROE = 0.1203. This means that through the favorable use of leverage (debt), the Ratio Company was able to increase the stockholders' return *significantly*.

Market Value Ratios

A final group of ratios relates the firm's stock price to its earnings (or book value) per share. It also includes dividend-related ratios.

Earnings per Share. Earnings per share indicates the amount of earnings for each common share held. When preferred stock is included in the capital structure, net income must be reduced by the preferred dividends to determine the amount applicable to common stock. When preferred stock does not exist, as is the case with the Ratio Company, earnings per share is equal to net income divided by common shares outstanding. Earnings per share is a useful indicator of the operating performance of the company as well as of the dividends that may be expected.

$$\text{Earnings per share} = \frac{\text{net income} - \text{preferred dividends}}{\text{common stock outstanding}}$$

In 19X3, earnings per share is:

$$\frac{\$9,600}{4,500 \text{ shares}} = \$2.13$$

In 19X2, earnings per share was $2.67. The decline in earnings per share should be of concern to investors.

Almost all of the Ratio Company's profitability ratios have declined in 19X3 relative to 19X2. This is a very negative sign.

Price/Earnings Ratio (Multiple). Some ratios evaluate the enterprise's relationship with its stockholders. The often quoted price/earnings (P/E) ratio is equal to the market price per share of stock divided by the earnings per share. A high P/E multiple is good because it indicates that the investing public considers the company in a favorable light.

$$P/E \text{ ratio} = \frac{\text{market price per share}}{\text{earnings per share}}$$

Let us assume that the market price per share of Ratio Company stock was $20 on December 31, 19X3, and $22 on December 31, 19X2. Therefore, the P/E ratio in 19X3 is:

$$\frac{\$20}{\$2.13} = 9.39$$

The ratio in 19X2 was 8.24 ($22/$2.67). The rise in the P/E multiple indicates that the stock market has a favorable opinion of the company.

Book Value per Share.   Book value per share is net assets available to common stockholders divided by shares outstanding, where net assets is stockholders' equity minus preferred stock. Comparing book value per share with market price per share gives another indication of how investors regard the firm.

The Ratio Company book value per share in 19X3 equals:

$$\text{Book value per share} = \frac{\text{total stockholders' equity} - \text{preferred stock}}{\text{shares outstanding}}$$
$$= \frac{\$84,600 - 0}{4,500} = \$18.80$$

The book value per share in 19X2 was $16.67.

If we assume the stock has a market price of $20 per share, then Ratio Company's stock is favorably regarded by investors since its market price exceeds book value.

Dividend Ratios.   Many stockholders are primarily interested in receiving dividends. The two pertinent ratios are *dividend yield* and *dividend payout*:

$$\text{Dividend yield} = \frac{\text{dividends per share}}{\text{market price per share}}$$

$$\text{Dividend payout} = \frac{\text{dividends per share}}{\text{earnings per share}}$$

Obviously, a decline in these ratios signals a decline in the value of dividends and would cause concern on the part of stockholders. (See Problem 2.12 for a computation of the dividend ratios.)

EXAMPLE 2.5

Summary of Financial Ratios

Ratio	Formula	19X2	19X3	Evaluation of Trend
Liquidity Net working capital	Current assets − current liabilities	$60,000	$64,600	Improved
Current ratio	$\dfrac{\text{Current assets}}{\text{Current liabilities}}$	2.2	2.17	Deteriorated
Quick ratio	$\dfrac{\text{Cash + marketable securities + receivables}}{\text{Current liabilities}}$	1.3	1.26	Deteriorated

(continued)

Summary of Financial Ratios (*cont.*)

Ratio	Formula	19X2	19X3	Evaluation of Trend
Activity				
Accounts receivable turnover	$\dfrac{\text{Net credit sales}}{\text{Average accounts receivable}}$	8.16	4.57	Deteriorated
Average collection period	$\dfrac{365}{\text{Accounts receivable turnover}}$	44.7 days	79.9 days	Deteriorated
Inventory turnover	$\dfrac{\text{Cost of goods sold}}{\text{Average inventory}}$	1.26	1.05	Deteriorated
Average age of inventory	$\dfrac{365}{\text{Inventory turnover}}$	289.7 days	347.6 days	Deteriorated
Operating cycle	Average collection period + average age of inventory	334.4 days	427.5 days	Deteriorated
Total asset turnover	$\dfrac{\text{Net sales}}{\text{Average total assets}}$	0.530	0.381	Deteriorated
Leverage				
Debt ratio	$\dfrac{\text{Total debt}}{\text{Total assets}}$	0.63	0.62	Improved
Debt/equity ratio	$\dfrac{\text{Total liabilities}}{\text{Stockholders' equity}}$	1.67	1.60	Improved
Times interest earned	$\dfrac{\text{Earnings before interest \& taxes}}{\text{Interest expense}}$	11 times	9 times	Deteriorated
Profitability				
Gross profit margin	$\dfrac{\text{Gross profit}}{\text{Net sales}}$	0.41	0.38	Deteriorated
Profit margin	$\dfrac{\text{Net income}}{\text{Net sales}}$	0.12	0.12	Constant
Return on total assets	$\dfrac{\text{Net income}}{\text{Average total assets}}$	0.0623	0.0457	Deteriorated
Return on common	$\dfrac{\text{Net income}}{\text{Common equity}}$	0.17	0.1203	Deteriorated
Market value				
Earnings per share	$\dfrac{\text{Net income} - \text{preferred dividends}}{\text{Common stock outstanding}}$	$2.67	$2.13	Deteriorated
Price/earnings ratio	$\dfrac{\text{Market price per share}}{\text{Earnings per share}}$	8.24	9.39	Improved
Book value per share	$\dfrac{\text{Stockholders' equity} - \text{preferred stock}}{\text{Common stock outstanding}}$	$16.67	$18.80	Improved
Dividend yield	$\dfrac{\text{Dividends per share}}{\text{Market price per share}}$			
Dividend payout	$\dfrac{\text{Dividends per share}}{\text{Earnings per share}}$			

Collective Inference of All the Ratios

By examining the trend in the company's ratios from 19X2 to 19X3, shown in Example 2.5, we find from the decline in the current and quick ratios that there has been a slight deterioration in liquidity. However, net working capital has improved. A significant deterioration in the activity ratios has taken place, indicating that better credit and inventory policies are needed. Ratio Company should improve its collection efforts. The increased age in inventory may point to obsolescence problems. On a positive note, the company's leverage has improved, so it is generally better able to meet long-term debt. However, less earnings are available to meet interest charges. Ratio Company's profitability has worsened over the year. As a result, the return on the owner's investment and the return on assets have gone down. Part of the reason for the earnings decrease may be the company's higher cost of short-term financing. The higher costs may have come about because of the problems with receivables and inventory that forced a decline in the liquidity and activity ratios. Also, as receivables and inventory turn over fewer times per year, earnings will drop from a lack of sales and the costs associated with holding higher current asset balances.

2.6   SUMMARY AND LIMITATIONS OF RATIO ANALYSIS

Financial statement analysis is an attempt to work with the reported financial figures in order to assess the entity's financial strengths and weaknesses.

Most analysts tend to favor certain ratios. They may leave out some of those mentioned in this chapter and include some not mentioned. Although other ratios may be of interest, depending on one's perspective (i.e., manager, stockholder, investor, creditor), there is no use in computing ratios of unrelated items such as sales returns to income taxes.

A banker, for example, is concerned with the firm's liquidity position in deciding whether to extend a short-term loan. On the other hand, a long-term creditor has more interest in the entity's earning power and operating efficiency as a basis to pay off the debt at maturity. Stockholders are interested in the long-run profitability of the firm since that will be the basis for dividends and appreciation in the market price of stock. Management, naturally, is interested in all aspects of financial analysis since they are concerned with how the firm looks to both the investment and credit communities.

Once a ratio is computed, it is compared with related ratios of the company, the same ratios from previous years, and the ratios of competitors. The comparisons show trends over a period of time and hence the ability of an enterprise to compete with others in the industry. Ratio comparisons do not mark the end of the analysis of the company, but rather indicate areas needing further attention.

Although ratio analysis is useful, it does have its limitations, some of which are listed below.

1. Many large firms are engaged in multiple lines of business, so that it is difficult to identify the industry group to which the firm belongs. Comparing their ratios with those of other corporations may be meaningless.

2. Operating and accounting practices differ from firm to firm, which can distort the ratios and make comparisons meaningless. For example, the use of different inventory valuation methods (LIFO versus FIFO) and different depreciation methods would affect inventory and asset turnover ratios.

3. Published industry average ratios are only approximations. Therefore, the company may have to look at the ratios of its major competitors, if such ratios are available.

4. Financial statements are based on historical costs and do not take inflation into account.

5. Management may hedge or exaggerate their financial figures; thus, certain ratios will not be accurate indicators.

6. A ratio does not describe the quality of its components. For example, the current ratio may be high but inventory may consist of obsolete goods.

7. Ratios are static and do not consider future trends.

2.7 FUNDS FLOW ANALYSIS THROUGH THE STATEMENT OF CHANGES IN FINANCIAL POSITION

Along with financial ratio analysis, *funds flow analysis* is a valuable tool to financial managers. *The statement of changes in financial position* (often referred to as the *sources and uses of funds statement*) is used by financial managers to evaluate the uses of funds by a firm and to determine how those uses are financed.

The statement of changes in financial position provides concise information as to how a company generated and used its net working capital[3] during the period; that is, it shows why net working capital increased or decreased. An analysis of the statement is useful in appraising past performance, forecasting net working capital trends, and evaluating the firm's ability to satisfy its debts at maturity. Because the statement lists the specific sources and applications of net working capital during the period and the changes which occurred during the year in the noncurrent accounts, it can be used to answer the following questions:

1. How was the expansion in plant and equipment financed?
2. What use was made of net income?
3. Where did the firm obtain its funds?
4. How much of its required capital has the firm been able to generate internally?
5. Is the business expanding faster than it can generate funds?
6. Is the firm's dividend policy in balance with its operating policy?

We will discuss both the *net working capital* basis and the *cash* basis of preparing this statement.

2.8 NET WORKING CAPITAL BASIS OF PREPARING THE STATEMENT OF CHANGES IN FINANCIAL POSITION

Sources of Funds

Funds Provided from Operations. Funds derived from sales, including cash and accounts receivable, generate net income. The funds are used for expenses and the purchase of goods. Hence, the excess of sales over costs and expenses represents the increase in net working capital.

The computation of funds provided from operations is complex. Net income must be adjusted for income statement components from other than net working capital sources (i.e., nonworking capital). Those nonworking capital expenses that have been deducted in determining profits but did not result in a decrease in net working capital must be added back to net income. For example, depreciation expense reduces earnings but does not reduce net working capital. Other expenses added back to net income are depletion expense, amortization expense, and loss on the sale of fixed assets. Revenue that has been added to determine profit but did not result in an increase in net working capital must be subtracted from

---

[3] Note that *working capital* and *net working capital* are not synonymous here. Working capital is current assets and is called *gross working capital* in some textbooks, whereas net working capital is current assets minus current liabilities.

net income. Common examples include the amortization of deferred income and the gain on the sale of fixed assets.

Net working capital provided from operations is the first source of funds listed in the statement of changes in financial position.

EXAMPLE 2.6 A business reports net income of $80,000. Depreciation expense is $12,000, amortization expense is $6,000, and the amortization of deferred income is $4,000. Funds provided from operations is calculated as follows:

Net income		$80,000
Add: Nonworking capital expenses[a]		
Depreciation expense	$12,000	
Amortization expense	6,000	18,000
Less: Nonworking capital revenue[a]		
Amortization of deferred income		(4,000)
Funds provided from operations		$94,000

[a] Nonworking capital means other than from net working capital.

Decrease in Noncurrent Assets. When noncurrent assets (e.g., fixed assets, long-term investments) are sold, net working capital is increased.

Increase in Noncurrent Liabilities. The issuance of long-term obligations (e.g., bonds payable, mortgage payable, long-term notes payable) results in an increase in net working capital.

Increase in Stockholders' Equity. The issuance of equity securities (common stock and preferred stock) results in an increase in net working capital. However, transactions involving only stockholder equity accounts (intrastockholder equity transactions) are not shown since they do not affect net working capital. Examples are stock dividends and appropriations of retained earnings.

Net working capital is *not* affected by a transaction that affects only individual accounts in current assets or current liabilities but not current assets or current liabilities themselves. Therefore, this type of transaction is not reported in the statement of changes in financial position. Examples are the *collection* of an account receivable or the *payment* of an account payable.

Applications of Funds

Increase in Noncurrent Assets. The acquisition of property, plant, equipment, and long-term investments reduces net working capital. The purchase usually requires the payment of cash or the incurrence of a current liability.

Decrease in Noncurrent Liabilities. The payment of long-term debt (e.g., bonds payable, long-term notes payable) also reduces net working capital.

Decrease in Stockholders' Equity. The reduction in stockholders' equity represents a use of net working capital funds. An example is the declaration of a cash dividend that results in the current liability Cash Dividends Payable. Other applications are the purchase of treasury stock[4] and the redemption of preferred stock, both of which require the payment of cash.

---

[4] Treasury stock is the company's own stock that it has bought back from its stockholders.

2.9 SCHEDULE OF CHANGES IN NET WORKING CAPITAL ACCOUNTS

The initial step in preparing a statement of changes in financial position is to determine the net increase or decrease in net working capital for the period. The net change is shown in a *schedule of changes in net working capital accounts* (see Example 2.7).

EXAMPLE 2.7   The balance sheet for APB Corporation is shown below.

APB Corporation
Comparative Balance Sheet
(In Thousands of Dollars)
Dec. 31, 19X3 and 19X2

ASSETS	19X3		19X2	
Current assets				
Cash	$ 35		$ 40	
Marketable securities	18		15	
Accounts receivable	20		22	
Inventory	75		70	
Prepaid expenses	4		7	
Total current assets		$152		$154
Noncurrent assets				
Land	$125		$100	
Plant and equipment (net of accumulated depreciation)	220		238	
Total noncurrent assets		345		338
Total assets		$497		$492

LIABILITIES AND STOCKHOLDERS' EQUITY				
Current liabilities				
Notes payable	$ 14		$ 15	
Accounts payable	50		53	
Current portion of long-term debt	10		12	
Total current liabilities		$ 74		$ 80
Noncurrent liabilities				
Long-term debt		90		108
Total liabilities		$164		$188
Stockholders' equity				
Common stock	$258		$240	
Retained earnings	75		64	
Total stockholders' equity		333		304
Total liabilities and stockholders' equity		$497		$492

Using the above information, prepare a schedule showing the change in net working capital accounts for the period.

APB Corporation
Schedule of Changes in Net Working Capital Accounts
(In Thousands of Dollars)
Dec. 31, 19X3 and 19X2

	19X3	19X2	Increase or (Decrease) in Working Capital
Current assets			
Cash	$ 35	$ 40	$(5)
Marketable securities	18	15	3
Accounts receivable	20	22	(2)
Inventory	75	70	5
Prepaid expenses	4	7	(3)
Total current assets	$152	$154	
Current liabilities			
Notes payable	$ 14	$ 15	1
Accounts payable	50	53	3
Current portion of long-term debt	10	12	2
Total current liabilities	$ 74	$ 80	
Net working capital	$ 78	$ 74	
Increase in net working capital			$ 4

According to the above schedule, the increase in net working capital for the period is $4,000. This increase will be reflected in the statement of changes in financial position. Example 2.8 illustrates the preparation of the statement of changes in financial position using the net working capital basis.

EXAMPLE 2.8   The following additional information is available for APB Corporation:

APB Corporation
Income Statement
(In Thousands of Dollars)
For the Year Ended Dec. 31, 19X3

Sales	$105	
Cost of goods sold	62	
Gross profit		$43
Expenses		
Selling and administrative	$ 15	
Depreciation	2	
Interest	4	
Total expenses		21
Income from operations		$22
Gain on sale of equipment		3
Income before taxes		$25
Income taxes		10
Net income		$15

Also, (1) the company sold equipment with a book value of $22,000 for $25,000, (2) long-term debt of $8,000 was converted into common stock, and (3) dividends of $4,000 were declared and paid.

Prepare a statement of changes in financial position using the above information and the schedule of changes prepared in Example 2.7.

APB Corporation
Statement of Changes in Financial Position
(In Thousands of Dollars)
For the Year Ended Dec. 31, 19X3

Sources of Funds

Funds provided from operations

Net income	$15	
Add: Nonworking capital expenses[a]		
Depreciation	2	
Less: Nonworking capital revenue[a]		
Gain on sale of equipment	(3)	
Funds provided from operations		$14
Sale of equipment		25
Issuance of common stock		10
Conversion of long-term debt to common stock		8
Total sources of funds		$57

Applications of Funds

Purchase of plant and equipment	$ 6
Declaration of dividends	4
Purchase of land	25
Reclassification of long-term debt to current debt	10
Conversion of long-term debt to common stock	8
Total applications of funds	$53
Increase in net working capital	$ 4

---

[a] *Nonworking capital* means other than from net working capital.

An explanation of the components of the statement of changes in financial position in the order in which they appear follows.

Funds provided from operations is the first item under the heading Sources of Funds. The net income amount ($15,000) is taken from the income statement. Depreciation expense ($2,000) must be added back to net income since this expense does not require the application of net working capital; it affects only the plant and equipment account in the form of accumulated depreciation. The gain on the sale of equipment ($3,000) is subtracted from net income because it represents revenue that does not increase net working capital. However, the proceeds from the sale of equipment are listed as a separate source later in the statement. The net working capital provided from operations in this example is $14,000 ($15,000 + $2,000 − $3,000).

The proceeds received from the sale of equipment ($25,000) is listed next. Part of the $25,000 amount is the $3,000 gain that was deducted earlier from net income.

As indicated in the balance sheet (Example 2.7), common stock increased by $18,000. However,

$8,000 of the increase was due to the conversion of long-term debt to common stock. (See item 2 after the income statement in Example 2.8. Therefore, APB Corporation sold only $10,000 of additional shares, which is listed next.

The conversion of $8,000 of long-term debt to equity does not affect net working capital but is a material, noncurrent transaction that must be disclosed in the statement of changes in financial position. Therefore, the $8,000 conversion is listed under sources of funds. This $8,000 conversion will be recognized again as an application of net working capital in order to produce a net effect of zero upon net working capital.

The total of the sources of net working capital is $57,000.

The application of funds begins with the purchase of plant and equipment in the amount of $6,000. This amount is determined by finding in the balance sheet that the plant and equipment account has a net decrease of $18,000. Of that decrease, $2,000 is due to accumulated depreciation. The sale of equipment having a book value of $22,000 further decreased the plant and equipment account, making the total decrease thus far $24,000. Since the net decrease in the account was $18,000, there must have been an additional purchase of plant and equipment in the amount of $6,000. The net change in the plant and equipment account is shown below.

<table>
<tr><td colspan="2"></td><td>Plant and Equipment (net)</td><td>18,000</td><td></td></tr>
<tr><td>Purchase</td><td>6,000</td><td>Accumulated depreciation</td><td></td><td>2,000</td></tr>
<tr><td></td><td></td><td>Sale of equipment</td><td></td><td>22,000</td></tr>
<tr><td></td><td></td><td></td><td></td><td>24,000</td></tr>
</table>

The declaration of cash dividends ($4,000) is a use of funds since it involves an increase in the current liability account Cash Dividends Payable. It is the *declaration* of the cash dividend that is the application, not the payment. When the cash dividend is actually paid, there is no effect on net working capital since only current accounts (Cash Dividends Payable and Cash) are involved.

As indicated in the balance sheet, land increased by $25,000, which represents a purchase of additional property.

The balance sheet also shows that long-term debt decreased by $18,000. Since only $8,000 was converted to equity, the remaining $10,000 of long-term debt was reclassified as current. This reclassification represents a decrease in net working capital since current liabilities are increased. The $8,000 conversion of long-term debt to equity also must be recognized as an application in order to balance the $8,000 source mentioned earlier.

The total for applications of net working capital is $53,000. The difference between the sources and the applications gives an increase in net working capital of $4,000 ($57,000 − $53,000).

2.10 CASH BASIS OF PREPARING THE STATEMENT OF CHANGES IN FINANCIAL POSITION

The statement of changes in financial position prepared on the *cash basis* typically provides more information for financial analysis. Its preparation is shown in the following example.

EXAMPLE 2.9 In addition to the information presented in the following balance sheet for the beginning and end of 19X1, Long Beach Corporation had a net income after taxes of $182 million and paid out $40 million in cash dividends.

Long Beach Corporation
Balance Sheet
(In Millions of Dollars)

	Jan. 1, 19X1	Dec. 31, 19X1	Source	Use
ASSETS				
Cash	$ 51	$ 27	$ 24	
Marketable securities	30	2	28	
Receivables	62	97		$ 35
Inventories	125	211		86
Total current assets	$268	$337		
Gross fixed assets	$225	$450		225
Less: Accumulated depreciation	(62)	(85)	23	
Net fixed assets	$163	$365		
Total assets	$431	$702		
LIABILITIES AND EQUITY				
Accounts payable	$ 65	$ 74	9	
Notes payable	45	9		36
Other current liabilities	21	45	24	
Long-term debt	24	78	54	
Common stock	114	192	78	
Retained earnings	162	304	142	
Total liabilities and equity	$431	$702	$382	$382

Note the purchase of fixed assets in the amount of $225 million and depreciation expense of $23 million. Prepare the statement of changes in financial position.

Long Beach Corporation
Statement of Changes in Financial Position
(In Millions of Dollars)

	Amount	% of Total
SOURCES		
From operations		
Net income	$182	45.73%
Depreciation	23	5.78
Sale of marketable securities	28	7.04
Increase in accounts payable	9	2.26
Increase in other liabilities	24	6.03
Issuance of long-term debt	54	13.57
Sale of common stock	78	19.60
Total sources	$398	100.00%
USES		
Payment of dividends	$ 40	9.48%
Increase in receivables	35	8.29
Increase in inventories	86	20.38
Decrease in notes payable	36	8.53
Purchase of fixed assets	225	53.32
Total uses	$422	100.00%
Decrease in cash	$ 24	

An analysis of the statement of changes in financial position shows the following information. Large investments were made in fixed assets and inventories (53.32 percent and 20.38 percent, respectively). Funds were also used to reduce outstanding notes payable and to increase accounts receivable. The uses of funds were met from internal sources, which provided 51.51 percent of the funds used (45.73 percent from retained earnings and 5.78 percent from depreciation), while another 33.17 percent of the total funds were raised through new issues of long-term debt and common stock (33.17% = 13.57% + 19.60%.)

Review Questions

1. Comparing an account to the same account in a prior year is known as _____.

2. In a common size income statement, _____ is given the value of 100 percent.

3. _____ is the ability of a company to meet its current liabilities out of current assets.

4. The current ratio is equal to _____ divided by _____.

5. _____ is included in computing the current ratio but not the quick ratio.

6. Accounts receivable turnover is equal to _____ divided by _____.

7. The number of days for converting inventory sold on credit into cash is found by adding the _____ to the _____.

8. The ratio of total liabilities to _____ is used to determine the degree of debt in the capital structure.

9. The number of times interest is earned is equal to _____ divided by _____.

10. Return on owners' equity is found by dividing _____ by _____.

11. The price/earnings ratio is equal to the _____ per share divided by the _____ per share.

12. Two measures that are of interest to stockholders in evaluating the dividend policy of a firm are the dividend _____ and the dividend _____ ratios.

13. When the comparison of ratios indicates a significant change in a company's financial position, the analyst should investigate further: (a) true; (b) false.

14. The most common definition of "funds" when preparing the statement of changes in financial position is _____.

15. An application of funds may represent _____ in noncurrent assets, _____ in noncurrent liabilities, or _____ in stockholders' equity.

16. Depreciation expense is one of the items that must be _____ to net income to determine funds provided from operations.

17. A gain on the sale of a fixed asset must be _____ from net income in order to derive funds provided from operations.

18. The issuance of common stock for cash _____ net working capital.

19. The purchase of treasury stock is a(n) _____ of funds.

20. The sale of a building for $125,000 that has a book value of $150,000 would result in $_____ being added back to net income to obtain the funds provided from operations and $_____ as a source of funds from the sale.

21. Transactions involving two current accounts (*are/are not*) reported in the statement of changes in financial position.

22. The receipt of $10,000 from an account receivable (*does/does not*) affect net working capital.

23. A stock dividend (*is/is not*) shown in the statement of changes in financial position.

Answers: (1) horizontal analysis; (2) net sales; (3) Liquidity; (4) current assets, current liabilities; (5) Inventory; (6) net credit sales, average accounts receivable; (7) collection period, average age of inventory; (8) stockholders' equity; (9) income before interest and taxes, interest expense; (10) net income, average stockholders' equity; (11) market price, earnings; (12) yield, payout; (13) (*a*); (14) net working capital; (15) an increase, a decrease, a decrease; (16) added back; (17) subtracted; (18) increases; (19) application; (20) 25,000, 125,000; (21) are not; (22) does not; (23) is not.

Solved Problems

2.1   Horizontal Analysis. Smith Corporation provides the following comparative income statement:

Smith Corporation
Comparative Income Statement
For the Years Ended Dec. 31, 19X3 and 19X2

	19X3	19X2
Sales	$570,000	$680,000
Cost of goods sold	200,000	170,000
Gross profit	$370,000	$510,000
Operating expenses	100,000	210,000
EBIT	$270,000	$300,000

(*a*) Calculate the percentage change using horizontal analysis and (*b*) evaluate the results.

SOLUTION

(a)

Smith Corporation
Comparative Income Statement
For the Years Ended Dec. 31, 19X3 and 19X2

	19X3	19X2	% Increase or (Decrease)
Sales	$570,000	$680,000	(16.2)
Cost of goods sold	200,000	170,000	17.6
Gross profit	$370,000	$510,000	(27.5)
Operating expenses	100,000	210,000	(52.4)
EBIT	$270,000	$300,000	(10.0)

(b) Gross profit declined 27.5 percent due to the combined effects of lower sales and higher cost of sales. However, operating expenses were sharply cut. This kept the decline in net income to only 10 percent.

2.2   Index Numbers. Jones Corporation reports the following for the period 19X1 to 19X3:

	19X3	19X2	19X1
Current liabilities	$34,000	$25,000	$20,000
Long-term liabilities	$60,000	$45,000	$50,000

The base year is 19X1. Using trend analysis, determine the appropriate index numbers.

SOLUTION

	19X3	19X2	19X1
Current liabilities	170	125	100
Long-term liabilities	120	90	100

2.3   Vertical Analysis. The Lyons Corporation reported the following income statement data:

	19X2	19X1
Net sales	$400,000	$250,000
Cost of goods sold	$280,000	$160,000
Operating expenses	$75,000	$56,000

(a) Prepare a comparative income statement for 19X2 and 19X1 using vertical analysis, and (b) evaluate the results.

SOLUTION

(a)

The Lyons Corporation
Income Statement and
Common Size Analysis
For the Years Ended Dec. 31, 19X2 and 19X1

	19X2		19X1	
	Amount	%	Amount	%
Net sales	$400,000	100	$250,000	100
Cost of goods sold	280,000	70	160,000	64
Gross profit	$120,000	30	$ 90,000	36
Operating expenses	75,000	18.8	56,000	22.4
EBIT	$ 45,000	11.2%	$ 34,000	13.6%

(*b*) Cost of goods sold may have increased because of higher costs in buying merchandise. Expenses may have dropped due to better cost control. However, the drop in expenses has not offset the rise in the cost of goods sold and so the company's profits have declined from 19X1 to 19X2.

2.4   Net Working Capital, Current Ratio, and Quick Ratio. Charles Corporation's balance sheet at December 31, 19X7, shows the following:

Current assets	
Cash	$ 4,000
Marketable securities	8,000
Accounts receivable	100,000
Inventories	120,000
Prepaid expenses	1,000
Total current assets	$233,000
Current liabilities	
Notes payable	$ 5,000
Accounts payable	150,000
Accrued expenses	20,000
Income taxes payable	1,000
Total current liabilities	$176,000
Long-term liabilities	$340,000

Determine the following: (*a*) net working capital, (*b*) current ratio, and (*c*) quick ratio.

SOLUTION

(*a*)
$$\text{Net working capital} = \text{current assets} - \text{current liabilities}$$
$$= \$233,000 - \$176,000 = \$57,000$$

(*b*)
$$\text{Current ratio} = \frac{\text{current assets}}{\text{current liabilities}} = \frac{\$233,000}{\$176,000} = 1.32$$

(*c*)
$$\text{Quick ratio} = \frac{\text{cash} + \text{marketable securities} + \text{accounts receivable}}{\text{current liabilities}}$$

$$\frac{\$4,000 + \$8,000 + \$100,000}{\$176,000} = \frac{\$112,000}{\$176,000} = .64$$

2.5   Liquidity Position. Based upon the answer to Problem 2.4, does Charles Corporation have good or poor liquidity if industry average for current ratio is 1.29 and quick ratio is 1.07?

SOLUTION

While the company's current ratio is slightly better than the industry norm, its quick ratio is significantly below the norm. Charles Corporation has more current liabilities than highly liquid assets and so has a poor liquidity position.

2.6   Accounts Receivable. The Rivers Company reports the following data relative to accounts receivable:

	19X2	19X1
Average accounts receivable	$ 400,000	$ 416,000
Net credit sales	$2,600,000	$3,100,000

The terms of sale are net 30 days. (*a*) Compute the accounts receivable turnover and the collection period, and (*b*) evaluate the results.

SOLUTION

(*a*)
$$\text{Accounts receivable turnover} = \frac{\text{net credit sales}}{\text{average accounts receivable}}$$

For 19X2:
$$\frac{\$2,600,000}{\$400,000} = 6.5 \text{ times}$$

For 19X1:
$$\frac{\$3,100,000}{\$416,000} = 7.45 \text{ times}$$

$$\text{Collection period} = \frac{365}{\text{accounts receivable turnover}}$$

For 19X2:
$$\frac{365}{6.5} = 56.2 \text{ days}$$

For 19X1:
$$\frac{365}{7.45} = 49 \text{ days}$$

(*b*) The company's management of accounts receivable is poor. In both years, the collection period exceeded the terms of net 30 days. The situation is getting worse, as is indicated by the significant increase in the collection period in 19X2 relative to 19X1. The company has significant funds tied up in accounts receivable that otherwise could be invested for a return. A careful evaluation of the credit policy is needed; perhaps too many sales are being made to marginal customers.

2.7 **Net Sales.** Utica Company's net accounts receivable were $250,000 as of December 31, 19X8, and $300,000 as of December 31, 19X9. Net cash sales for 19X9 were $100,000. The accounts receivable turnover for 19X9 was 5.0. What were Utica's total net sales for 19X9?

SOLUTION

$$\text{Average accounts receivable} = \frac{\text{beginning accounts receivable} + \text{ending accounts receivable}}{2}$$

$$\frac{\$250,000 + \$300,000}{2} = \$275,000$$

$$\text{Accounts receivable turnover} = \frac{\text{net credit sales}}{\text{average accounts receivable}}$$

$$5 = \frac{\text{net credit sales}}{\$275,000}$$

$$\text{Net credit sales} = 5 \times \$275,000 = \$1,375,000$$

Since the cash sales were $100,000, the total net sales must be $1,475,000.

2.8 **Inventory.** On January 1, 19X6, the River Company's beginning inventory was $400,000. During 19X6, River purchased $1,900,000 of additional inventory. On December 31, 19X6, River's ending inventory was $500,000. (*a*) What is the inventory turnover and the age of inventory for 19X6? (*b*) If the inventory turnover in 19X5 was 3.3 and the average age of the inventory was 110.6 days, evaluate the results for 19X6.

SOLUTION

(*a*) First determine the cost of goods sold:

Beginning inventory	$ 400,000
Purchases	1,900,000
Cost of goods available	$2,300,000
Ending inventory	500,000
Cost of goods sold	$1,800,000

$$\text{Average inventory} = \frac{\text{beginning inventory} + \text{ending inventory}}{2} = \frac{\$400,000 + \$500,000}{2} = \$450,000$$

$$\text{Inventory turnover} = \frac{\text{cost of goods sold}}{\text{average inventory}} = \frac{\$1,800,000}{\$450,000} = 4$$

$$\text{Average age of inventory} = \frac{365}{\text{inventory turnover}} = \frac{365}{4} = 91.3 \text{ days}$$

(*b*) River Company's inventory management improved in 19X6, as evidenced by the higher turnover rate and the decrease in the number of days that inventory was held. As a result, there is less liquidity risk and the company's profitability will benefit from the increased turnover of merchandise. Note that this is only a conjecture, based on an evaluation of two ratios in isolation; keep in mind that if the rapid turnover was accomplished by offering excessive discounts, for example, profitability ratios may not show an improvement.

2.9 **Operating Cycle.** Based on your answer to Problem 2.8, what is the River Company's operating cycle in 19X6 if it is assumed that the average collection period is 42 days?

SOLUTION

Average age of inventory	91.3
Average collection period	42.0
Operating cycle	133.3 days

2.10 **Financial Ratios.** A condensed balance sheet and other financial data for the Alpha Company appear below.

Alpha Company
Balance Sheet
Dec. 31, 19X1

ASSETS

Current assets	$100,000
Plant assets	150,000
Total assets	$250,000

LIABILITIES AND STOCKHOLDERS' EQUITY

Current liabilities	$100,000
Long-term liabilities	75,000
Total liabilities	$175,000
Stockholders' equity	75,000
Total liabilities and stockholders' equity	$250,000

Income statement data appear below.

Net sales	$375,000
Interest expense	4,000
Net income	22,500

The following account balances existed at December 31, 19X0:

Total assets	$200,000
Stockholders' equity	$65,000

The tax rate is 35 percent. Industry norms as of December 31, 19X1, are:

Debt/equity ratio	1.75
Profit margin	0.12
Return on total assets	0.15
Return on stockholders' equity	0.30
Total asset turnover	1.71

Calculate and evaluate the following ratios for Alpha Company as of December 31, 19X1: (a) debt/equity ratio, (b) profit margin, (c) return on total assets, (d) return on stockholders' equity, and (e) total asset turnover.

SOLUTION

(a)
$$\text{Debt/equity ratio} = \frac{\text{total liabilities}}{\text{stockholders' equity}} = \frac{\$175,000}{\$75,000} = 2.33$$

Alpha's debt/equity ratio is considerably above the industry norm, indicating a solvency problem. Excessive debt may make it difficult for the firm to meet its obligations during a downturn in business. A high debt position will also make it difficult for Alpha Company to obtain financing during a period of tight money supply.

(b)
$$\text{Profit margin} = \frac{\text{net income}}{\text{net sales}} = \frac{\$22,500}{\$375,000} = 0.06$$

Alpha's profit margin is far below the industry norm. This indicates that the operating performance of the company is poor because the profitability generated from revenue sources is low.

(c)
$$\text{Return on total assets} = \frac{\text{net income}}{\text{average total assets}} = \frac{\$22,500}{(\$200,000 + \$250,000)/2} = \frac{\$22,500}{\$225,000} = 0.10$$

Alpha's return on total assets is below the industry norm; therefore, the company's efficiency in generating profit from assets is low. Profit generation is, of course, different from revenue (sales) generation because for the former, corporate expenses are deducted from sales.

(d)
$$\text{Return on stockholders' equity} = \frac{\text{net income}}{\text{average stockholders' equity}}$$
$$= \frac{\$22,500}{(\$65,000 + \$75,000)/2} = \frac{\$22,500}{\$70,000} = 0.32$$

Since the return earned by Alpha's stockholders is slightly more than the industry norm, investment in the firm relative to competition was advantageous to existing stockholders. This may be due to a currently low stockholders' equity investment in the firm. Note also that although stockholders earned a good return, some ratios show that their investment is riskier than most. Whether the return is good enough to warrant the risk of continued investment in Alpha is a decision each stockholder must make individually.

(e)
$$\text{Total asset turnover} = \frac{\text{net sales}}{\text{average total assets}} = \frac{\$375,000}{\$225,000} = 1.67$$

Alpha's ratio is about the same as the industry norm. Therefore, the company's ability to utilize its assets in obtaining revenue is similar to that of competition. The utilization of assets has a bearing upon the ultimate profitability to stockholders.

2.11   Financial Ratios. The Format Company reports the following balance sheet data:

Current liabilities	$280,000
Bonds payable, 16%	$120,000
Preferred stock, 14%, $100 par value	$200,000
Common stock, $25 par value, 16,800 shares	$420,000
Paid-in capital on common stock	$240,000
Retained earnings	$180,000

Income before taxes is $160,000. The tax rate is 40 percent. Common stockholders' equity in the previous year was $800,000. The market price per share of common stock is $35. Calculate (a) net income, (b) preferred dividends, (c) return on common stock, (d) times interest earned, (e) earnings per share, (f) price/earnings ratio, and (g) book value per share.

SOLUTION

(a)

Income before taxes	$160,000
Taxes (40% rate)	64,000
Net income	$ 96,000

(b)   Preferred dividends = 14% × $200,000 = $28,000

(c)   Common stockholders' equity is computed as follows:

Common stock	$420,000
Paid-in capital on common stock	240,000
Retained earnings	180,000
Common stockholders' equity	$840,000

$$\text{Return on common stock} = \frac{\text{net income} - \text{preferred dividends}}{\text{average common stockholders' equity}}$$

$$= \frac{\$96,000 - \$28,000}{(\$800,000 + \$840,000)/2} = \frac{\$68,000}{\$820,000} = 0.08$$

(d)   Income before interest and taxes equals:

Income before taxes	$160,000
Interest expense (16% × $120,000)	19,200
Income before interest and taxes	$179,200

$$\text{Times interest earned} = \frac{\text{income before interest and taxes}}{\text{interest expense}}$$

$$= \frac{\$179,200}{\$19,200} = 9.33 \text{ times}$$

(e) $$\text{Earnings per share} = \frac{\text{net income} - \text{preferred dividends}}{\text{common stock outstanding}} = \frac{\$96,000 - \$28,000}{16,800 \text{ shares}} = \$4.05$$

(f)   Price/earnings ratio $= \dfrac{\text{market price per share}}{\text{earnings per share}} = \dfrac{\$35.00}{\$4.05} = 8.64$ times

(g)   Book value per share $= \dfrac{\text{stockholders' equity} - \text{preferred stock}}{\text{common stock outstanding}}$

$$= \dfrac{\$840,000}{16,800 \text{ shares}} = \$50 \text{ per share}$$

2.12   Dividends. Wilder Corporation's common stock account for 19X3 and 19X2 showed:

Common stock, \$10 par value   \$45,000

The following data are provided relative to 19X3 and 19X2:

	19X3	19X2
Dividends	\$2,250	\$3,600
Market price per share	\$20	\$22
Earnings per share	\$2.13	\$2.67

(a) Calculate the dividends per share, dividend yield, and dividend payout, and (b) evaluate the results.

SOLUTION

(a)   Dividends per share $= \dfrac{\text{dividends}}{\text{outstanding shares}}$

For 19X3: $\dfrac{\$2,250}{4,500 \text{ shares}} = \$0.50$

For 19X2: $\dfrac{\$3,600}{4,500 \text{ shares}} = \$0.80$

Dividend yield $= \dfrac{\text{dividends per share}}{\text{market price per share}}$

For 19X3: $\dfrac{\$0.50}{\$20.00} = 0.025$

For 19X2: $\dfrac{\$0.80}{\$22.00} = 0.036$

Dividend payout $= \dfrac{\text{dividends per share}}{\text{earnings per share}}$

For 19X3: $\dfrac{\$0.50}{\$2.13} = 0.23$

For 19X2: $\dfrac{\$0.80}{\$2.67} = 0.30$

(b) The decline in dividends per share, dividend yield, and dividend payout from 19X2 to 19X3 will cause concern to both stockholders and management.

   Stockholders will want to determine the reason for the decline. For example, do they know that the company is investing heavily to reposition itself for greater competitiveness in the future? Has the entire industry suffered a decline or only Wilder? Is the company on solid financial footing or is it borderline? What is the company's—and the industry's—potential for the future?

Management will want to deal with similar questions and find solutions to other problems, such as how to manage their finances so as not to lose investors in the short term while ensuring financial health in the long term. Whatever the reasons for the decline in the ratios, this is a situation where management cannot safely ignore the short term and may therefore choose to sacrifice some long-term goals in order to turn the ratios around. The extent to which a company may choose to do this depends on many factors, including its relative financial health, its reputation in the financial world, how much risk managers are willing (or able) to take, what the actual problems are, and what options are available as solutions.

2.13 Financial Ratios. Jones Corporation's financial statements appear below.

Jones Corporation
Balance Sheet
Dec. 31, 19X1

ASSETS

Current assets

Cash	$100,000	
Marketable securities	200,000	
Inventory	300,000	
Total current assets		$ 600,000
Plant assets		500,000
Total assets		$1,100,000

LIABILITIES AND STOCKHOLDERS' EQUITY

Liabilities

Current liabilities	$200,000	
Long-term liabilities	100,000	
Total liabilities		$ 300,000
Stockholders' equity		
Common stock, $1 par value, 100,000 shares	$100,000	
Premium on common stock	500,000	
Retained earnings	200,000	
Total stockholders' equity		800,000
Total liabilities and stockholders' equity		$1,100,000

Jones Corporation
Income Statement
For the Year Ended Dec. 31, 19X1

Net sales	$10,000,000
Cost of goods sold	6,000,000
Gross profit	$ 4,000,000
Operating expenses	1,000,000
Income before taxes	$ 3,000,000
Income taxes (50% rate)	1,500,000
Net income	$ 1,500,000

Additional information includes a market price of $150 per share of stock, total dividends of $600,000 for 19X1, and $250,000 of inventory as of December 31, 19X0.

Compute the following ratios: (*a*) current ratio, (*b*) quick ratio, (*c*) inventory turnover, (*d*) average age of inventory, (*e*) debt/equity ratio, (*f*) book value per share, (*g*) earnings per share, (*h*) price/earnings ratio, (*i*) dividends per share, and (*j*) dividend payout.

SOLUTION

(*a*)
$$\text{Current ratio} = \frac{\text{current assets}}{\text{current liabilities}} = \frac{\$600,000}{\$200,000} = 3.0$$

(*b*)
$$\text{Quick ratio} = \frac{\text{cash} + \text{marketable securities}}{\text{current liabilities}} = \frac{\$300,000}{\$200,000} = 1.5$$

(*c*)
$$\text{Inventory turnover} = \frac{\text{cost of goods sold}}{\text{average inventory}} = \frac{\$6,000,000}{(\$250,000 + \$300,000)/2} = 21.82$$

(*d*)
$$\text{Average age of inventory} = \frac{365}{\text{inventory turnover}} = \frac{365}{21.82} = 16.7 \text{ days}$$

(*e*)
$$\text{Debt/equity ratio} = \frac{\text{total liabilities}}{\text{stockholders' equity}} = \frac{\$300,000}{\$800,000} = 0.375$$

(*f*)
$$\text{Book value per share} = \frac{\text{stockholders' equity} - \text{preferred stock}}{\text{common shares outstanding}} = \frac{\$800,000}{100,000 \text{ shares}} = \$8$$

(*g*)
$$\text{Earnings per share} = \frac{\text{net income}}{\text{outstanding common shares}} = \frac{\$1,500,000}{100,000 \text{ shares}} = \$15$$

(*h*)
$$\text{Price/earnings ratio} = \frac{\text{market price per share}}{\text{earnings per share}} = \frac{\$150}{\$15} = 10$$

(*i*)
$$\text{Dividends per share} = \frac{\text{dividends}}{\text{outstanding shares}} = \frac{\$600,000}{100,000 \text{ shares}} = \$6$$

(*j*)
$$\text{Dividend payout} = \frac{\text{dividends per share}}{\text{earnings per share}} = \frac{\$6}{\$15} = 0.4$$

2.14   Financial Ratios. The 19X9 financial statements for Johanson Co. are reproduced below.

Johanson Co.
Statement of Financial Position
(In Thousands of Dollars)
Dec. 31, 19X8 and 19X9

	19X8	19X9
ASSETS		
Current assets		
Cash and temporary investments	$ 380	$ 400
Accounts receivable (net)	1,500	1,700
Inventories	2,120	2,200
Total current assets	$4,000	$4,300
Long-term assets		
Land	$ 500	$ 500
Building and equipment (net)	4,000	4,700
Total long-term assets	$4,500	$5,200
Total assets	$8,500	$9,500

LIABILITIES AND STOCKHOLDERS' EQUITY

Liabilities		
Current liabilities		
Accounts payable	$ 700	$1,400
Current portion of long-term debt	500	1,000
Total current liabilities	$1,200	$2,400
Long-term debt	4,000	3,000
Total liabilities	$5,200	$5,400
Stockholder's equity		
Common stock	$3,000	$3,000
Retained earnings	300	1,100
Total stockholders' equity	$3,300	$4,100
Total liabilities and stockholders' equity	$8,500	$9,500

Johanson Company
Statement of Income and Retained Earnings
(In Thousands of Dollars)
For the Year Ended Dec. 31, 19X9

Net sales		$28,800
Less: Cost of goods sold	$15,120	
Selling expenses	7,180	
Administrative expenses	4,100	
Interest	400	
Income taxes	800	27,600
Net income		$ 1,200
Retained earnings January 1		300
Subtotal		$ 1,500
Cash dividends declared and paid		400
Retained earnings December 31		$ 1,100

For 19X9, find (a) the acid-test ratio, (b) the average number of days sales were outstanding, (c) the times interest earned ratio, (d) the asset turnover, (e) the inventory turnover, (f) the operating income margin, and (g) the dividend payout ratio. (CMA, adapted.)

SOLUTION

(a)   Acid-test ratio $= \dfrac{\text{cash} + \text{net receivables} + \text{marketable securities}}{\text{current liabilities}} = \dfrac{\$400 + \$1,700}{\$2,400} = 0.875 \cong 0.9$

(b)   Accounts receivable turnover ratio $= \dfrac{\text{net credit sales}}{\text{average accounts receivable}} = \dfrac{\$28,000}{(\$1,500 + \$1,700)/2} = 18$

Number of days sales outstanding $= \dfrac{365}{\text{accounts receivable turnover ratio}} = \dfrac{365}{18} = 20.3$

(*c*) $$\text{Times interest earned ratio} = \frac{\text{net income} + \text{taxes} + \text{interest expense}}{\text{interest expense}}$$

$$= \frac{\$1,200 + \$800 + \$400}{\$400} = 6.0$$

(*d*) $$\text{Asset turnover ratio} = \frac{\text{sales}}{\text{average assets during year}}$$

$$= \frac{\$28,800}{(\$8,500 + \$9,500)/2} = 3.2$$

(*e*) $$\text{Inventory turnover ratio} = \frac{\text{cost of sales}}{\text{average inventory}} = \frac{\$15,120}{(\$2,120 + \$2,200)/2} = 7.0$$

(*f*) $$\text{Operating income margin} = \frac{\text{net income from operations before taxes}}{\text{net sales}}$$

$$= \frac{\$1,200 + \$800 + \$400}{\$28,800} = 8.3\%$$

(*g*) $$\text{Dividend payout ratio} = \frac{\text{dividends}}{\text{net income}} = \frac{\$400}{\$1,200} = 33.3\%$$

2.15 **Financial Ratios.** Warford Corporation was formed 5 years ago through a public subscription of common stock. Lucinda Street, who owns 15 percent of the common stock, was one of the organizers of Warford and is its current president. The company has been successful, but it is currently experiencing a shortage of funds. On June 10, Street approached the Bell National Bank, asking for a 24-month extension on two $30,000 notes, which are due on June 30, 19X2 and September 30, 19X2. Another note of $7,000 is due on December 31, 19X2, but Street expects to have no difficulty in paying this note on its due date. Street explained that Warford's cash flow problems are primarily due to the company's desire to finance a $300,000 plant expansion over the next 2 fiscal years through internally generated funds.

The commerical loan officer of Bell National Bank requested financial reports for the last 2 fiscal years. These reports are reproduced below.

Warford Corporation
Income Statement
For the Fiscal Years Ended Mar. 31, 19X1 and 19X2

	19X1	**19X2**
Sales	$2,700,000	$3,000,000
Cost of goods sold[a]	1,720,000	1,902,500
Gross margin	$ 980,000	$1,097,500
Operating expenses	780,000	845,000
Net income before taxes	$ 200,000	$ 252,500
Income taxes (40%)	80,000	101,000
Income after taxes	$ 120,000	$ 151,500

[a] Depreciation charges of $100,000 on the plant and equipment and $102,500 for fiscal years ended March 31, 19X1 and 19X2, respectively, are included in cost of goods sold.

Warford Corporation
Statement of Financial Position
Mar. 31, 19X1 and 19X2

	19X1	19X2
ASSETS		
Cash	$ 12,500	$ 16,400
Notes receivable	104,000	112,000
Accounts receivable (net)	68,500	81,600
Inventories (at cost)	50,000	80,000
Plant and equipment (net of depreciation)	646,000	680,000
Total assets	$881,000	$970,000
LIABILITIES AND OWNERS' EQUITY		
Accounts payable	$ 72,000	$ 69,000
Notes payable	54,500	67,000
Accrued liabilities	6,000	9,000
Common stock (60,000 shares, $10 par)	600,000	600,000
Retained earnings[a]	148,500	225,000
Total liabilities and owners' equity	$881,000	$970,000

[a] Cash dividends were paid at the rate of $1 per share in fiscal year 19X1 and
$1.25 per share in fiscal year 19X2.

Calculate the following items for Warford Corporation: (*a*) current ratio for fiscal years 19X1 and 19X2; (*b*) quick (acid-test) ratio for fiscal years 19X1 and 19X2; (*c*) inventory turnover for fiscal year 19X2; (*d*) return on assets for fiscal years 19X1 and 19X2; and (*e*) percentage change in sales, cost of goods sold, gross margin, and net income after taxes from fiscal year 19X1 to 19X2. (CMA, adapted.)

SOLUTION

(*a*)
$$\text{Current ratio} = \frac{\text{current assets}}{\text{current liabilities}}$$

For 19X1:
$$\frac{\$235,000}{\$132,500} = 1.77$$

For 19X2:
$$\frac{\$290,000}{\$145,000} = 2.00$$

(*b*)
$$\text{Quick ratio} = \frac{\text{current assets} - \text{inventories}}{\text{current liabilities}}$$

For 19X1:
$$\frac{\$185,000}{\$132,500} = 1.40$$

For 19X2:
$$\frac{\$210,000}{\$145,000} = 1.45$$

(*c*)
$$\text{Inventory turnover} = \frac{\text{cost of goods sold}}{\text{average inventory}}$$

For 19X2:
$$\frac{\$1,902,500}{(\$50,000 + \$80,000)/2} = 29 \text{ times}$$

(d)   Return on assets $= \dfrac{\text{net income}}{\text{total assets}}$

For 19X1: $\dfrac{\$120,000}{\$881,000} = 13.6\%$

For 19X2: $\dfrac{\$151,500}{\$970,000} = 15.6\%$

(e) Percent changes are as follows (in thousands of dollars):

	Amounts		% increase
	19X2	19X1	
Sales	$3,000.0	$2,700.0	$\dfrac{\$300.0}{\$2,700.0} = 11.11\%$
Cost of goods sold	$1,902.5	$1,720.0	$\dfrac{\$182.5}{\$1,720.0} = 10.61\%$
Gross margin	$1,097.5	$980.0	$\dfrac{\$117.5}{\$980.0} = 11.99\%$
Net income after taxes	$151.5	$120.0	$\dfrac{\$31.5}{\$120.0} = 26.25\%$

2.16 **Financial Ratios.** Ratio analysis is employed to gain insight into the financial character of a firm. The calculation of ratios can often lead to a better understanding of a firm's financial position and performance. A specific ratio or a number of selected ratios can be calculated and used to measure or evaluate a specific financial or operating characteristic of a firm. (a) Identify and explain what financial characteristic of a firm would be measured by an analysis in which the following four ratios were calculated: (1) current ratio, (2) acid-test ratio, (3) accounts receivable turnover ratio, and (4) inventory turnover ratio. (b) Do the ratios in part (a) provide adequate information to measure this characteristic or are additional data needed? If so, provide two examples of other data that would be required. (c) Identify and explain what specific characteristic regarding a firm's operations would be measured by an analysis in which the following three ratios were calculated: (1) gross profit margin, (2) operating income margin, and (3) net income to sales (profit margin). (d) Do these ratios provide adequate information to measure this characteristic or are additional data needed? If so, provide two examples of other data that would be required.

SOLUTION

(a) These four ratios are used to measure short-term liquidity and to evaluate the management of net working capital of a firm, i.e., the ability to meet financial obligations in the near future.

(b) For a thorough analysis of the firm's ability to meet its financial obligations in the near future, we would also need to know the normal and/or industry standards for these ratios in order to have a basis of comparison. In addition, we would need to know if any current assets are pledged or restricted for any reason, if open lines of credit are available to the firm, the firm's credit rating, and any capital investment plans that might require an inordinate amount of cash.

(c) These three ratios are used to measure the profitability of a firm; respectively, each ratio relates sales revenue with (1) the cost of goods or services sold; (2) the costs of operating the business, which would include the cost of goods sold, the marketing expenses, the administrative expenses, and other general operating expenses; and (3) the final net result of all the corporate financial activity for the accounting period.

(d) These ratios do provide an indication of the firm's profitability. However, to complete a thorough analysis, it would be necessary to determine the return on investment, earnings per share, inventory valuation methods, depreciation methods, and any nonrecurring items included in the statement. In addition, data about the cost/volume/profit relationships would be useful. All this information should be evaluated while considering industry averages, results of prior periods, and future projections.

2.17   The Du Pont Formula and Return on Total Assets. Industry A has three companies whose income statements and balance sheets are summarized below.

	Company X	Company Y	Company Z
Sales	$500,000	(d)	(g)
Net income	$25,000	$30,000	(h)
Total assets	$100,000	(e)	$250,000
Total asset turnover	(a)	(f)	0.4
Profit margin	(b)	0.4%	5%
Return on total assets (ROA)	(c)	2%	(i)

First supply the missing data in the table above. Then comment on the relative performance of each division.

SOLUTION

(a)
$$\text{Total asset turnover} = \frac{\text{sales}}{\text{average total assets}} = \frac{\$500,000}{\$100,000} = 5 \text{ times}$$

(b)
$$\text{Profit margin} = \frac{\text{net income}}{\text{sales}} = \frac{\$25,000}{\$500,000} = 5\%$$

(c)
$$\text{ROA} = \frac{\text{net income}}{\text{average total assets}}$$

If we multiply both the numerator and denominator by sales, we get

$$\text{ROA} = \frac{\text{net income}}{\text{sales}} \times \frac{\text{sales}}{\text{average total assets}}$$
$$= \text{profit margin} \times \text{total asset turnover}$$
$$= 5\% \text{ [from } (b)\text{]} \times 5 \text{ [from } (a)\text{]} = 25\%$$

(d)
$$\text{Profit margin} = \frac{\text{net income}}{\text{sales}}$$
$$\text{Sales} = \frac{\text{net income}}{\text{profit margin}} = \frac{\$30,000}{0.004} = \$7,500,000$$

(e)
$$\text{ROA} = \frac{\text{net income}}{\text{average total assets}}$$
$$\text{Average total assets} = \frac{\text{net income}}{\text{ROA}} = \frac{\$30,000}{0.02} = \$1,500,000$$

(f)
$$\text{Total asset turnover} = \frac{\text{sales}}{\text{average total assets}}$$

$$= \frac{\$7,500,000 \text{ [from } (d)]}{\$1,500,000 \text{ [from } (e)]} = 5 \text{ times}$$

(g)
$$\text{Total asset turnover} = \frac{\text{sales}}{\text{average total assets}}$$

$$\text{Sales} = \text{total asset turnover} \times \text{average total assets}$$

$$= 0.4 \times \$250,000 = \$100,000$$

(h)
$$\text{Profit margin} = \frac{\text{net income}}{\text{sales}}$$

$$\text{Net income} = \text{profit margin} \times \text{sales}$$

$$= 5\% \times \$100,000 \text{ [from } (g)] = \$5,000$$

(i)
$$\text{ROA} = \text{total asset turnover} \times \text{profit margin}$$
$$= 0.4 \times 5\% = 2\%$$

or

$$\text{ROA} = \frac{\text{net income}}{\text{average total assets}}$$

$$= \frac{\$5,000 \text{ [from } (h)]}{\$250,000} = 2\%$$

Summarizing the results of (a) through (i) gives:

	Company X	Company Y	Company Z
Total asset turnover	5 times	5 times	0.4 times
Profit margin	5%	0.4%	5%
ROA	25%	2%	2%

Company X performed best. It appears that companies Y and Z are in trouble. Company Y turns over its assets as often as company X, but Y's margin on sales is much lower. Thus, company Y must work on improving its margin. The following questions may be raised about company Y: Is the low margin due to inefficiency? Is it due to excessive material, labor, or overhead, or all three?

Company Z, on the other hand, does just as well as company X in terms of profit margin but has a much lower turnover of capital than X. Therefore, company Z should take a close look at its investments. Is there too much tied up in inventories and receivables? Are there unused fixed assets? Is there idle cash sitting around?

2.18 ROA and ROE. The following ratios have been computed for Los Alamitos Company and are compared with the industry averages:

	Los Alamitos	Industry
Return on total assets (ROA)	6.2%	6.0%
Return on common equity (ROE)	16.5%	8.5%

Comment on the comparison of the company to the industry.

SOLUTION

Los Alamitos Company shows a satisfactory return on total investment (6.20 percent versus 6 percent for the industry). The company's 16.5 percent return on common stockholders' investment compares very favorably with that of the industry (16.5 percent versus 8.5 percent). This higher-than-average return reflects the firm's above-average use of financial leverage. Through the favorable use of debt, the firm was able to increase significantly the return earned on the stockholders' investment which would favorably affect its stock price.

2.19 **Financial Statement Analysis and Loan Decision.** The Konrath Company, a wholesaler in the midwest, is considering extending credit to the Hawk Company, a retail chain operation that has a number of stores in the midwest. The Konrath Company has had a gross margin of approximately 60 percent in recent years and expects to have a similar gross margin on the Hawk Company order, which is estimated at $2 million per year. The Hawk Company's order is approximately 15 percent of the Konrath Company's present sales. Recent statements of the Hawk Company are given below.

Hawk Company
Balance Sheet
(In Millions of Dollars)
As of Dec. 31, 19X1, 19X2, and 19X3

	19X1	19X2	19X3
ASSETS			
Current assets			
Cash	$ 2.6	$ 1.8	$ 1.6
Government securities (cost)	0.4	0.2	
Accounts and notes receivable (net)	8.0	8.5	8.5
Inventories	2.8	3.2	2.8
Prepaid assets	0.7	0.6	0.6
Total current assets	$14.5	$14.3	$13.5
Property, plant, and equipment (net)	4.3	5.4	5.9
Total assets	$18.8	$19.7	$19.4
LIABILITIES AND STOCKHOLDERS' EQUITY			
Liabilities			
Current liabilities			
Notes payable	$ 3.2	$ 3.7	$ 4.2
Accounts payable	2.8	3.7	4.1
Accrued expenses and taxes	0.9	1.1	1.0
Total current liabilities	$ 6.9	$ 8.5	$ 9.3
Long-term debt, 6%	3.0	2.0	1.0
Total liabilities	$ 9.9	$10.5	$10.3
Stockholders' equity	8.9	9.2	9.1
Total liabilities and stockholders' equity	$18.8	$19.7	$19.4

Hawk Company
Income Statement
(In Millions of Dollars)
For the Years Ended Dec. 31, 19X1, 19X2, and 19X3

	19X1	19X2	19X3
Net sales	$24.2	$24.5	$24.9
Cost of goods sold	16.9	17.2	18.0
Gross margin	$ 7.3	$ 7.3	$ 6.9
Selling expenses	$ 4.3	$ 4.4	$ 4.6
Administrative expenses	2.3	2.4	2.7
Total expenses	$ 6.6	$ 6.8	$ 7.3
Earnings (loss) before taxes	$ 0.7	$ 0.5	$(0.4)
Income taxes	0.3	0.2	(0.2)
Net income	$ 0.4	$ 0.3	$(0.2)

Hawk Company
Statement of Changes in Financial Position
(In Millions of Dollars)
For the Years Ended Dec. 31, 19X1, 19X2, and 19X3

	19X1	19X2	19X3
Sources of funds			
Net income (loss)	$ 0.4	$ 0.3	$(0.2)
Depreciation	0.4	0.5	0.5
Funds from operations	$0.8	$0.8	$0.3
Sale of building	0.2		
Sale of treasury stock		0.1	0.1
Total sources	$ 1.0	$ 0.9	$ 0.4
Uses of funds			
Purchase of property, plant, and equipment	$ 1.2	$ 1.6	$ 1.0
Dividends	0.1	0.1	
Retirement of long-term debt		1.0	1.0
Total uses	$ 1.3	$ 2.7	$ 2.0
Net increase (decrease) in net working capital	$(0.3)	$(1.8)	$(1.6)

(a) Calculate for the year 19X3 the following ratios: (1) return on total assets, (2) acid-test ratio, (3) profit margin, (4) current ratio, and (5) inventory turnover.

(b) As part of the analysis to determine whether or not Konrath should extend credit to Hawk, assume the ratios below were calculated from Hawk Co. statements. For each ratio indicate whether it is a favorable, unfavorable, or neutral statistic in the decision to grant Hawk credit. Briefly explain your choice in each case.

	19X1	19X2	19X3
(1) Return on total assets	1.96%	1.12%	(0.87)%
(2) Profit margin	1.69%	0.99%	(0.69)%
(3) Acid-test ratio	1.73	1.36	1.19
(4) Current ratio	2.39	1.92	1.67
(5) Inventory turnover (times)	4.41	4.32	4.52
Equity relationships			
Current liabilities	36.0%	43.0%	48.0%
Long-term liabilities	16.0	10.5	5.0
Shareholders' equity	48.0	46.5	47.0
	100.0%	100.0%	100.0%
Asset relationships			
Current assets	77.0%	72.5%	69.5%
Property, plant, and equipment	23.0	27.5	30.5
	100.0%	100.0%	100.0%

(c) Would you grant credit to Hawk Co.? Support your answer with facts given in the problem.

(d) What additional information, if any, would you want before making a final decision? (CMA, adapted.)

SOLUTION

(a) (1) $$\text{Return on total assets} = \frac{\text{net income} + \text{interest expense}}{\text{average assets}} = \frac{-0.2 + 0.45^a}{(19.7 + 19.4)/2} = 0.01$$

$$^a\ \frac{(2.0 + 1.0)0.06}{2} = \$0.09 \text{ interest}; 0.45 \text{ net of taxes.}$$

(2) $$\text{Acid-test ratio} = \frac{\text{cash} + \text{accounts and notes receivable (net)}}{\text{current liabilities}} = \frac{1.6 + 8.5}{9.3} = 1.086$$

(3) $$\text{Profit margin} = \frac{\text{net income}}{\text{sales}} = \frac{-0.2}{24.9} = -0.8\%$$

(4) $$\text{Current ratio} = \frac{\text{current assets}}{\text{current liabilities}} = \frac{13.5}{9.3} = 1.45$$

(5) $$\text{Inventory turnover} = \frac{\text{cost of goods sold}}{\text{average inventory}} = \frac{18.0}{(3.2 + 2.8)/2} = 6$$

(b) (1) The return on total assets is unfavorable. The rate is low and has been declining.

(2) The profit margin is unfavorable. The rate is low and has been declining.

(3) The acid-test ratio is favorable. The direction of change is unfavorable, but ratio itself is probably more than adequate.

(4) The current ratio is unfavorable. The decline has been sharp and the ratio is probably too low.

(5) The inventory turnover is neutral. Inventory turnover has been fairly constant, and we don't know enough about the business to determine if the turnover is adequate.

(c) The facts available from the problem are inadequate to make a final judgment; additional information would be necessary. However, the facts given do not present a good overall picture of Hawk. The company doesn't appear to be in serious trouble at the moment, but most of the trends reflected in the ratios are unfavorable. The company appears to be developing liquidity problems: cash and securities are declining; inventories and plant and equipment are an increasing portion of the assets; and current liabilities are an increasing portion of capital.

The operations of the company also show unfavorable trends: cost of goods sold is increasing as a percent of sales; administrative expenses are increasing as a percent of sales; and if we recognize that prices have risen, it appears that physical volume at Hawk might have actually decreased.

On the basis of these observations and the fact that Hawk would be a very large customer (thus a potentially large loss if the accounts became uncollectible), credit should be extended to Hawk only under carefully controlled and monitored conditions.

(d) For a final decision on whether to grant credit to Hawk, the additional information needed is: quality of management of the Hawk Company, locations of the Hawk stores, current activities of Hawk that have increased plant and equipment but not inventories, industry position of the Hawk Company, credit rating of the Hawk Company, current economic conditions, capacity of the Konrath Company to handle such a large single account, and normal ratios for the industry.

2.20 Corporate and Economic Factors. What factors (a) within the company and (b) within the economy have affected and are likely to affect the degree of variability in the (1) earnings per share, (2) dividends per share, and (3) market price per share of common stock? (CFA, adapted.)

SOLUTION

(a) Within the company
   (1) Earnings
       a. accounting policies
       b. sales volume
       c. new product introduction
   (2) Dividends
       a. capital expenditures
       b. stability of earnings
       c. replacement of fixed assets
   (3) Market price
       a. management quality
       b. growth in earnings
       c. financial leverage

(b) Economy
   (1) Earnings
       a. trend in economy
       b. governmental regulation
       c. labor relations
   (2) Dividends
       a. tax law
       b. recessionary conditions
   (3) Market price
       a. investor confidence
       b. cyclical changes

2.21 Transactions and the Statement of Changes. Indicate how each of the following transactions would be reported in the statement of changes in financial position by placing an "X" in the appropriate column. (Use the net working capital basis.)

		Listed as a Source	Listed as an Application	Not Reported
(a)	Issued common stock for cash			
(b)	Purchased treasury stock			
(c)	Paid an account payable			
(d)	Declared a cash dividend			
(e)	Issued a bond payable			
(f)	Purchased land			
(g)	Sold a machine at book value			
(h)	Appropriated retained earnings			

SOLUTION

		Listed as a Source	Listed as an Application	Not Reported
(a)	Issued common stock for cash	X		
(b)	Purchased treasury stock		X	
(c)	Paid an account payable			X
(d)	Declared a cash dividend		X	
(e)	Issued a bond payable	X		
(f)	Purchased land		X	
(g)	Sold a machine at book value	X		
(h)	Appropriated retained earnings			X

2.22 Schedule of Changes in Net Working Capital Accounts. Travis Corporation reports the following net working capital information as of December 31, 19X3 and 19X2:

	19X3	19X2
Current assets		
Cash	$20	$17
Marketable securities	18	29
Accounts receivable	30	21
Prepaid expenses	5	4
Current liabilities		
Notes payable	10	7
Accounts payable	11	13
Accrued expenses	5	3

Prepare a schedule of changes in net working capital accounts.

SOLUTION

Travis Corporation
Schedule of Changes in Net Working Capital Accounts
Dec. 31, 19X3 and 19X2

	19X3	19X2	Increase or (Decrease) in Net Working Capital
Current assets			
Cash	$20	$17	$ 3
Marketable securities	18	29	(11)
Accounts receivable	30	21	9
Prepaid expenses	5	4	1
Total current assets	$73	$71	
Current liabilities			
Notes payable	$10	$ 7	$ (3)
Accounts payable	11	13	2
Accrued expenses	5	3	(2)
Total current liabilities	$26	$23	
Net working capital	$47	$48	
Decrease in net working capital			$ (1)

2.23 Statement Analysis of Financial Position. The financial statements for XYZ Company for the years 19X1 and 19X2 are given below.

XYZ Company
Balance Sheet
Dec. 31, 19X1 and 19X2

	19X2	19X1
ASSETS		
Current assets		
Cash	$ 200	$ 150
Accounts receivable	600	300
Inventory	600	700
Total current assets	$1,400	$1,150
Fixed assets		
Plant and equipment	$ 900	$ 700
Less: Accumulated depreciation	(200)	(150)
Net fixed assets	$ 700	$ 550
Long-term investments	$ 300	$ 400
Total assets	$2,400	$2,100

LIABILITIES AND
STOCKHOLDERS' EQUITY

Current liabilities		
Accounts payable	$ 800	$ 400
Taxes payable	50	100
Total current liabilities	$ 850	$ 500
Bonds payable	$ 150	$ 500
Stockholders' equity		
Capital stock	$ 800	$ 700
Retained earnings	600	400
Total stockholders' equity	$1,400	$1,100
Total liabilities and stockholders' equity	$2,400	$2,100

XYZ Company
Income Statement
For the Year Ended Dec. 31, 19X2

Sales		$900
Cost of goods sold		200
Gross margin		$700
Operating expenses		
Selling expense	$100	
Administrative expense	150	
Depreciation expense	50	
Total expenses		300
Net income		$400

XYZ Company
Statement of Retained Earnings
For the Year Ended Dec. 31, 19X2

Retained earnings, Dec. 31, 19X1	$400
Add: Net income	400
	$800
Deduct: Dividends paid	200
Retained earnings, Dec. 31, 19X2	$600

Prepare (*a*) the schedule of changes in net working capital accounts, (*b*) the statement of changes in financial position on a net working capital basis, and (*c*) the statement of changes in financial position on a cash basis with percentages. (*d*) Briefly summarize your findings.

SOLUTION

(a)

XYZ Company
Schedule of Changes in Working Capital Accounts
For the Year Ended Dec. 31, 19X2

	19X2	19X1	Net Working Capital Increase (Decrease)
Current assets			
Cash	$ 200	$ 150	$ 50
Accounts receivable	600	300	300
Inventory	600	700	(100)
Total current assets	$1,400	$1,150	$ 250
Current liabilities			
Accounts payable	$ 800	$ 400	$(400)
Taxes payable	50	100	50
Total current liabilities	$ 850	$ 500	$(350)
Net working capital	$ 550	$ 650	$(100)

(b)

XYZ Company
Statement of Changes in Financial Position
For the Year Ended Dec. 31, 19X2

Sources of net working capital	
From operations	
Net income	$ 400
Add: Depreciation	50
Total funds from operations	$ 450
From sale of long-term investments	100
From sale of capital stock	100
Total sources	$ 650
Uses of net working capital	
To pay dividends	$ 200
To purchase plant and equipment	200
To retire bonds payable	350
Total uses	$ 750
Decrease in net working capital	$(100)

(c)

XYZ Company
Statement of Changes in Financial Position (Cash Basis)
For the Year Ended Dec. 31, 19X2

	Dollars	%
Sources		
From operations		
Net income	$ 400	34.78%
Depreciation	50	4.35
Decrease in inventory	100	8.7
Increase in accounts payable	400	34.78
From sale of long-term investments	100	8.7
From sale of capital stock	100	8.7
Total sources	$1,150	100.00%
Uses		
Increase in accounts receivable	$ 300	27.27%
Decrease in taxes payable	50	4.55
Payment of dividends	200	18.18
Purchase plant and equipment	200	18.18
Retire bonds payable	350	31.82
Total uses	$1,100	100.00%
Increase in cash	$ 50	

(d) Major sources for the XYZ Company during 19X2 were internal (39.13 percent) and an increase in accounts payable (34.78 percent). External sources accounted for 17.4 percent of XYZ's funds through the sale of long-term investments and capital stock. The largest uses of funds were for the retirement of long-term bonds (31.82 percent) and an increase in accounts receivable (27.27 percent). There were also additions to plant and equipment (18.18 percent).

2.24   Statement of Changes in Financial Position. The consolidated balance sheets for CSULB Seasonal Products, Inc., at the beginning and end of 19X1 are presented below (in millions of dollars).

	Jan. 1, 19X1	Dec. 31, 19X1
ASSETS		
Cash	$ 12	$ 9
Accounts receivable	14	24
Inventories	4	12
Total current assets	$ 30	$ 45
Gross fixed assets	$120	$145
Less: Accumulated depreciation	45	55
Net fixed assets	$ 75	$ 90
Total assets	$105	$135

LIABILITIES AND EQUITY

Accounts payable	$ 14	$ 11
Notes payable	10	10
Long-term debt	10	25
Common stock	30	30
Retained earnings	41	59
Total liabilities and equity	$105	$135

CSULB earned $20 million after taxes during the year and paid cash dividends of $2 million. The annual depreciation expense during 19X1 was $10 million. The company purchased $25 million of fixed assets.

(a) Add a source and use column to the balance sheet, (b) prepare a statement of changes in financial position on the cash basis, and include percentage computations, and (c) summarize your findings.

SOLUTION

(a)

**CSULB Seasonal Products
Balance Sheet
(In Millions of Dollars)**

	Jan. 1, 19X1	Dec. 31, 19X1	Source	Use
ASSETS				
Cash	$ 12	$ 9	$ 3	
Accounts receivable	14	24		$10
Inventories	4	12		8
Total current assets	$ 30	$ 45		
Gross fixed assets	$120	$145		25
Less: Accumulated depreciation	45	55	10	
Net fixed assets	$ 75	$ 90		
Total assets	$105	$135		
LIABILITIES AND EQUITY				
Accounts payable	$ 14	$ 11		3
Notes payable	10	10		
Long-term debt	10	25	15	
Common stock	30	30		
Retained earnings	41	59	18	
Total liabilities and equity	$105	$135	$46	$46

(b)

CSULB Seasonal Products
Statement of Changes in Financial Position

	Millions of Dollars	% of Total
Sources		
From operations		
Net income	$20	44.44%
Depreciation	10	22.22
Issuance of long-term debt	15	33.33
Total sources	$45	100.00%
Uses		
Pay cash dividends	$ 2	4.17%
Increase in accounts receivable	10	20.83
Increase in inventories	8	16.67
Decrease in accounts payable	3	6.25
Purchase of fixed assets	25	52.08
Total uses	$48	100.00%
Decrease in cash	$ 3	

(c) Most of CSULB's funds were obtained from operations (over 66 percent) along with a relatively large amount of long-term debt (about 33 percent). CSULB allocated these funds primarily to the purchase of fixed assets (52.08 percent), accounts receivable (20.83 percent), and inventories (16.67 percent). It is important to realize that the company does not have an optimal mix of financing since a relatively large portion of long-term debt went toward the purchase of short-term assets, namely accounts receivable and inventories. Furthermore, since the company's sales are seasonal, it could end up with rather costly excess cash on hand if the additional investment in inventories and accounts receivable is not needed.

2.25   **Statement of Changes in Financial Position.** The Golden Company's comparative balance sheet and income statement are presented below.

The Golden Company
Comparative Balance Sheet
(In Thousands of Dollars)
Dec. 31, 19X2 and 19X1

ASSETS				
Current assets				
Cash	$ 48		$ 30	
Accounts receivable (net)	59		69	
Inventory	84		76	
Prepaid expenses	4		3	
Total current assets		$195		$178
Noncurrent assets				
Land	$ 28		$ 26	
Building (net)	71		63	
Machinery (net)	11		10	
Total noncurrent assets		110		99
Total assets		$305		$277

**LIABILITIES AND
STOCKHOLDERS' EQUITY**

Current liabilities			
Accounts payable	$ 14		$ 35
Accrued expenses payable	3.5		2
Income taxes payable	2.5		2
Total current liabilities		$ 20	$ 39
Noncurrent liabilities			
Bonds payable		35	35
Total liabilities		$ 55	$ 74
Stockholders' equity			
Common stock	$224		$200
Retained earnings	26		3
Total stockholders' equity		250	203
Total liabilities and stockholders' equity		$305	$277

The Golden Company
Income Statement
(In Thousands of Dollars)
For the Year Ended Dec. 31, 19X2

Sales	$100	
Cost of goods sold	22	
Gross profit		$78
Expenses		
Selling and administrative	$ 20	
Depreciation—building	6	
Depreciation—machinery	8	
Interest	4	
Total expenses		38
Income before taxes		$40
Income taxes		15
Net income		$25

Cash dividends were $2,000.

Prepare (*a*) the schedule of changes in net working capital accounts, and (*b*) the statement of changes in financial position.

SOLUTION

(*a*)
The Golden Company
Schedule of Changes in Net Working Capital Accounts
(*In Thousands of Dollars*)
Dec. 31, 19X2 and 19X1

	19X2	19X1	Increase or (Decrease) in Net Working Capital
Current assets			
Cash	$ 48.0	$ 30	$ 18.0
Accounts receivable (net)	59.0	69	(10.0)
Inventory	84.0	76	8.0
Prepaid expenses	4.0	3	1.0
Total current assets	$195.0	$178	
Current liabilities			
Accounts payable	$ 14.0	$ 35	21.0
Accrued expenses payable	3.5	2	(1.5)
Income taxes payable	2.5	2	(0.5)
Total current liabilities	$ 20.0	$ 39	
Net working capital	$175.0	$139	
Increase in net working capital			$ 36.0

(*b*)
The Golden Company
Statement of Changes in Financial Position
(*In Thousands of Dollars*)
For the Year Ended Dec. 31, 19X8

SOURCES OF FUNDS

Funds provided from operations		
Net income	$25	
Add: Nonworking capital expenses		
Depreciation	14	
Funds provided from operations		$39
Issuance of common stock		24
Total sources of funds		$63

APPLICATIONS OF FUNDS

Cash dividends	$ 2
Purchase of land	2
Addition to building	14[a]
Purchase of machinery	9[b]
Total applications of funds	$27
Increase in net working capital	$36

[a] 8,000

Building (net)			
Addition	14,000	Depreciation	6,000

[b] 1,000

Machinery (net)			
Purchase	9,000	Depreciation	8,000

2.26 **Statement of Changes in Financial Position.** The financial statements presented below were provided to the Sparton Corporation. Sparton is considering purchasing ARCHCO, Inc. The statements presented did not include a statement of changes in financial position. Sparton's controller would like to have this statement as well as other relevant financial information, before he makes a financial analysis of ARCHCO, Inc.

ARCHCO, Inc.
Statement of Financial Position
(In Thousands of Dollars)
As of Dec. 31, 19X1 and 19X2

	19X2	19X1
ASSETS		
Current assets		
Cash	$ 16,800	$120,000
Accounts receivable	81,900	73,200
Inventories	119,700	97,500
U.S. Treasury bills	33,450	79,500
Total current assets	$251,850	$370,200
Land	217,500	195,000
Plant and equipment (net of accumulated depreciation)	391,500	387,000
Patents (less accum. amortization)	28,500	31,500
Total assets	$889,350	$983,700
LIABILITIES AND OWNERS' EQUITY		
Liabilities		
Accounts payable	$136,500	$198,500
Taxes payable	3,000	2,500
Interest payable	6,000	4,500
Notes payable	30,000	21,750
Total current liabilities	$175,500	$227,250
Deferred income taxes	11,400	9,750
Long-term bonds	150,000	300,000
Total liabilities	$336,900	$537,000
Owners' equity		
Preferred stock	111,000	45,000
Common stock	360,000	337,500
Retained earnings	81,450	64,200
Total liabilities and owners' equity	$889,350	$983,700

ARCHCO, Inc.,
Income Statement
(In Thousands of Dollars)
For the Year Ended
Dec. 31, 19X2

Sales	$441,600	
Gain on retirement of bonds	9,900	$451,500
Expenses, taxes and losses		
Cost of goods sold	$252,000	
Wages and salaries	51,000	
Depreciation	18,000	
Amortization	3,000	
Other	28,200	
Interest	19,500	
Loss on sale of equipment	3,600	
Income taxes	16,950	392,250
Net income		$ 59,250

The following additional information is available to explain the ARCHCO, Inc., financial results for 19X2.

1. The significant decline in cash and Treasury bills occurred because funds from these two sources were used to retire the bonds at a favorable time.

2. Equipment with a cost of $35,000 and a book value of $18,000 was sold for $14,400.

3. A portion of the preferred stock was issued to provide cash to purchase outstanding bonds in the market. The remaining amount was issued to JIS, Inc., for land and the related plant and equipment on the land.

4. Cash dividends of $4,500 and $15,000 were paid to the preferred and common shareholders, respectively. The common shareholders received a stock dividend which had market value of $22,500.

5. The income tax expense account and the deferred income tax account that appear in the statements properly account for all income tax situations of ARCHCO, Inc.

(*a*) Using the net working capital basis, prepare, in good form, a statement of changes in financial position for the year ended December 31, 19X2. The statement should reflect the changes in total financial resources. (*b*) Identify and explain the probable reasons why the Sparton controller would want the statement of changes in financial position of ARCHCO, Inc. (CMA, adapted.)

SOLUTION

(a)

ARCHCO, Inc.
Statement of Changes in Financial Position
(In Thousands of Dollars)
Year Ended Dec. 31, 19X2

Funds provided			
Funds provided from operations			
Net income	$59,250		
Add (deduct): Charges or credits not			
involving resources capital			
Depreciation	18,000		
Loss on sales of equipment	3,600		
Amortization	3,000		
Increase in deferred taxes	1,650		
Gain on retirement of bonds	(9,900)		
Funds provided from operations		$ 75,600	
Proceeds of sale of equipment	$14,400		
Issuance of preferred stock	66,000	80,400	
Total funds provided			$156,000
Applications of funds			
Retirement of bonds		$140,100	
Acquisition of land		22,500	
Acquisition of plant and			
equipment		40,500	
Declaration of cash dividends		19,500	
Total funds applied			222,600
Decrease in net working capital			$ 66,600

(b) The Sparton controller would want the statement of changes in financial position to obtain information on the financing and investing activities to determine the amount of funds provided from operations, to determine where the financial resources were used, and to disclose the amounts and causes of all other changes in financial position during the period.

2.27 Financial Analysis. Motel Enterprises operates and owns many motels throughout the United States. The company has expanded rapidly over the past few years, and company officers are concerned that they may have overexpanded.

The following financial statements and other financial data have been supplied by the controller of Motel Enterprises.

Motel Enterprises
Income Statement
(In Thousands of Dollars)
For Years Ending Oct. 31, 19X1 and 19X2
(Unaudited)

	19X1	19X2
Revenue	$1,920	$2,230
Cost and expenses		
Direct room and related services	$ 350	$ 400
Direct food and beverage	640	740
General and administrative	250	302
Advertising	44	57
Repairs and maintenance	82	106
Interest expense	220	280
Depreciation	95	120
Lease payment	73	100
Total costs and expenses	$1,754	$2,105
Income before taxes	$ 166	$ 125
Provision for income tax	42	25
Net income	$ 124	$ 100

Motel Enterprises
Statement of Financial Position
(For Thousands of Dollars)
As of Oct. 31, 19X1 and 19X2
(Unaudited)

	19X1	19X2
ASSETS		
Current assets		
Cash	$ 125	$ 100
Accounts receivable (net)	200	250
Inventory	50	60
Other	5	5
Total current assets	$ 380	$ 415
Long-term investments	$ 710	$ 605
Property and equipment		
Buildings and equipment (net)	$2,540	$3,350
Land	410	370
Construction in progress	450	150
Total property and equipment	$3,400	$3,870
Other assets	$ 110	$ 110
Total assets	$4,600	$5,000

LIABILITIES AND STOCKHOLDERS' EQUITY

Liabilities		
Current liabilities		
Accounts payable	$ 30	$ 40
Accrued liabilities	190	190
Notes payable to bank	10	30
Current portion of long-term notes	50	80
Total current liabilities	$ 280	$ 340
Long- term debt		
Long-term notes	$2,325	$2,785
Subordinated debentures (due May 1989)	800	800
Total long-term debt	$3,125	$3,585
Total liabilities	$3,405	$3,925
Stockholders' equity		
Common stock ($1 par)	$ 300	$ 300
Paid-in capital in excess of par	730	730
Net unrealized loss on long-term investments		(105)
Retained earnings	165	150
Total stockholders' equity	$1,195	$1,075
Total liabilities and stockholders' equity	$4,600	$5,000

(*a*) Prepare the statement of changes in financial position (net working capital basis) for Motel Enterprises.

(*b*) Compute the following ratios for 19X1 and 19X2: (1) debt/equity ratio, (2) times interest earned, (3) return on total assets, (4) current ratio, (5) return on common stock equity, and (6) accounts receivable turnover.

(*c*) Evaluate the financial condition based on the trend analysis and the statement of changes in financial position. (CMA, adapted.)

SOLUTION

(*a*)
Motel Enterprises
Statement of Changes in Financial Position
(In Thousands of Dollars)
For the Year Ending Oct. 31, 19X2

Sources of funds		
Net income	$100	
Noncash items		
Gain on land sale	(20)	
Depreciation	120	
Total funds from operations		$200
Sale of land		100
Increases in long-term debt		460
Total resources provided		$760
Applications of funds		
Purchase of building and land	$620	
Construction-in-progress, building	50	
Dividends	115	
Total funds applied		$785
Decrease in net working capital		$ (25)

(b) 1.
$$\text{Debt/equity ratio} = \frac{\text{total liabilities}}{\text{stockholders' equity}}$$

For 19X1:
$$\frac{\$3,405}{\$4,600} = 74.0\%$$

For 19X2:
$$\frac{\$3,925}{\$5,000} = 78.5\%$$

2.
$$\text{Times interest earned} = \frac{\text{EBIT}}{\text{interest expense}}$$

For 19X1:
$$\frac{\$386}{\$220} = 1.75$$

For 19X2:
$$\frac{\$405}{\$280} = 1.45$$

3.
$$\text{Return on total assets} = \frac{\text{net income}}{\text{average total assets}}$$

For 19X1:
$$\frac{\$124}{\$4,600} = 2.7\%$$

For 19X2:
$$\frac{\$100}{(\$4,600 + \$5,000)/2} = 2.1\%$$

4.
$$\text{Current ratio} = \frac{\text{current assets}}{\text{current liabilities}}$$

For 19X1:
$$\frac{\$380}{\$280} = 1.36$$

For 19X2:
$$\frac{\$415}{\$340} = 1.22$$

5.
$$\text{Return on common stock equity} = \frac{\text{earnings available to common stockholders}}{\text{average stockholders' equity}}$$

For 19X1 estimated:
$$\frac{\$124}{\$1,195} = 10.4\%$$

For 19X2:
$$\frac{\$100}{(\$1,195 + \$1,075)/2} = 8.8\%$$

6.
$$\text{Accounts receivable turnover} = \frac{\text{net credit sales}}{\text{average accounts receivable}}$$

For 19X1 estimated:
$$\frac{\$1,920}{\$200} = 9.6 \text{ (every 38 days)}$$

For 19X2:
$$\frac{\$2,230}{(\$200 + \$250)/2} = 9.91 \text{ (every 37 days)}$$

(c) Based on the trend analysis for 19X1 and 19X2, the company's financial condition has deteriorated to some degree in this period, and there is going to be a serious liquidity problem as is evidenced by the decline in the current ratio and the decline of net working capital.

In addition, the company's interest coverage has declined and large amounts of debt are coming due in the near future. The statement of changes in financial position shows that a large portion of capital expenditures were financed through long-term debt.

Chapter 3

Financial Forecasting, Planning, and Budgeting

3.1 FINANCIAL FORECASTING

Financial forecasting, an essential element of planning, is the basis for budgeting activities and estimating future financing needs. Financial forecasts begin with forecasting sales and their related expenses. The basic steps involved in projecting financing needs are:

1. Project the firm's sales. Most other forecasts (budgets) follow the sales forecast. The statistical methods of forecasting sales include:
   - (*a*) Time-series analysis
   - (*b*) Exponential smoothing
   - (*c*) Input-output analysis
   - (*d*) Scatter diagrams
   - (*e*) Regression analysis

   (These methods are discussed in other disciplines such as managerial economics and statistics and are not covered here.)

2. Project variables such as expenses.

3. Estimate the level of investment in current and fixed assets that is required to support the projected sales.

4. Calculate the firm's financing needs.

3.2 PERCENT-OF-SALES METHOD OF FINANCIAL FORECASTING

When constructing a financial forecast, the sales forecast is used traditionally to estimate various expenses, assets, and liabilities. The most widely used method for making these projections is the *percent-of-sales method*, in which the various expenses, assets, and liabilities for a future period are estimated as a percentage of sales. These percentages, together with the projected sales, are then used to construct pro forma (planned or projected) balance sheets.

The calculations for a pro forma balance sheet are as follows:

1. Express balance sheet items that *vary directly with sales* as a percentage of sales. Any item that does not vary directly with sales (such as long-term debt) is designated *not applicable* (n.a.).

2. Multiply the percentages determined in step 1 by the sales projected to obtain the amounts for the future period.

3. Where no percentage applies (such as for long-term debt, common stock, and capital surplus), simply insert the figures from the present balance sheet in the column for the future period.

4. Compute the projected retained earnings as follows:

   Projected retained earnings = present retained earnings
   + projected net income − cash dividends paid

   (You'll need to know the percentage of sales that constitutes net income and the dividend payout ratio.)

5. Sum the asset accounts to obtain a total projected assets figure. Then add the projected liabilities and equity accounts to determine the total financing provided. Since liability plus equity must balance the assets when totaled, any difference is a *shortfall*, which is the amount of external financing needed.

EXAMPLE 3.1   For the following pro forma balance sheet, net income is assumed to be 5 percent of sales and the dividend payout ratio is 4 percent.

Pro Forma Balance Sheet
(In Millions of Dollars)

	Present (19X1)	% of Sales (19X1 Sales = $20)	Projected (19X2 Sales = $24)	
ASSETS				
Current assets	$2.0	10%	$24 × 10% = $2.4	
Fixed assets	4.0	20%	4.8	
Total assets	$6.0		$7.2	
LIABILITIES AND STOCKHOLDERS' EQUITY				
Current liabilities	$2.0	10%	$2.4	
Long-term debt	2.5	n.a.^{a}	2.5	
Total liabilities	$4.5		$4.9	
Common stock	$0.1	n.a.^{a}	$0.1	
Capital surplus	0.2	n.a.^{a}	0.2	
Retained earnings	1.2		1.92^b	
Total equity	$1.5		$2.22	
Total liabilities and stockholders' equity	$6.0		$7.12	Total financing provided
			$0.08^c	External financing needed
			$7.2	Total

---

^{a} Not applicable (n.a.). These figures are assumed not to vary with sales.

^{b}

$$\text{19X2 Retained earnings} = \text{19X1 retained earnings} + \text{projected net income} - \text{cash dividends paid}$$
$$= \$1.2 + 5\%(\$24) - 40\%[5\%(\$24)]$$
$$= \$1.2 + \$1.2 - \$0.48 = \$2.4 - \$0.48 = \$1.92$$

^{c}

$$\text{External financing needed} = \text{projected total assets} - (\text{projected total liabilities} + \text{projected equity})$$
$$= \$7.2 - (\$4.9 + \$2.22) = \$7.2 - \$7.12 = \$0.08$$

Although the forecast of additional funds required can be made by setting up pro forma balance sheets as described in Example 3.1, it is often easier to use the following simple formula:

$$\begin{bmatrix} \text{external} \\ \text{funds} \\ \text{needed} \end{bmatrix} = \begin{bmatrix} \text{required} \\ \text{increase} \\ \text{in assets} \end{bmatrix} - \begin{bmatrix} \text{spontaneous} \\ \text{increase in} \\ \text{liabilities} \end{bmatrix} - \begin{bmatrix} \text{increase in} \\ \text{retained} \\ \text{earnings} \end{bmatrix}$$

$$\text{EFN} = \left(\frac{A}{S}\right)\Delta S - \left(\frac{L}{S}\right)\Delta S - (PM)(PS)(1-d)$$

where EFN = external funds needed
    A/S = assets that increase spontaneously with sales as a percentage of sales
    L/S = liabilities that increase spontaneously with sales as a percentage of sales
    ΔS = change in sales
    PM = profit margin on sales
    PS = projected sales
    d = dividend payout ratio

EXAMPLE 3.2   From Example 3.1:

$$\frac{A}{S} = \frac{\$6}{\$20} = 30\%$$

$$\frac{L}{S} = \frac{\$2}{\$20} = 10\%$$

$$\Delta S = \$24 - \$20 = \$4$$

$$PM = 5\% \text{ on sales}$$

$$PS = \$24$$

$$d = 40\%$$

Inserting these figures into the formula, we get

$$EFN = \left(\frac{A}{S}\right)\Delta S - \left(\frac{L}{S}\right)\Delta S - (PM)(PS)(1 - d)$$

$$= 0.3(\$4) - 0.1(\$4) - (0.05)(\$24)(1 - 0.4)$$

$$= \$1.2 - \$0.4 - \$0.72 = \$0.08$$

The $80,000 in external financing can be raised by issuing notes payable, bonds, or stocks, singly or in combination.

One important limitation of the percent-of-sales method is that the firm is assumed to be operating at full capacity. On the basis of this assumption, the firm does not have sufficient productive capacity to absorb projected increases in sales and thus requires an additional investment in assets.

The major advantage of the percent-of-sales method of financial forecasting is that it is simple and inexpensive to use. To obtain a more precise projection of the firm's future financing needs, however, the preparation of a cash budget is required (see the following sections).

3.3   THE BUDGET, OR FINANCIAL PLAN

A company's annual financial plan is called a *budget*. The budget is a set of formal (written) statements of management's expectations regarding sales, expenses, production volume, and various financial transactions of the firm for the coming period. Simply put, a budget is a set of pro forma statements about the company's finances and operations. A budget is a tool for both planning and control. At the beginning of the period, the budget is a plan or standard; at the end of the period, it serves as a control device to help management measure the firm's performance against the plan so that future performance may be improved.

3.4   THE STRUCTURE OF THE BUDGET

The budget is classified broadly into two categories: the *operational budget*, which reflects the results of operating decisions; and the *financial budget*, which reflects the financial decisions of the firm. The operating budget consists of:

1. Sales budget, including a computation of expected cash receipts

2. Production budget

3. Ending inventory budget

4. Direct materials budget, including a computation of expected cash disbursements for materials

5. Direct labor budget

6. Factory overhead budget
7. Selling and administrative expense budget
8. Pro forma income statement

The financial budget consists of:

1. Cash budget
2. Pro forma balance sheet

The major steps in preparing the budget are:

1. Prepare a sales forecast.
2. Determine production volume.
3. Estimate manufacturing costs and operating expenses.
4. Determine cash flow and other financial effects.
5. Formulate projected financial statements.

Follow the illustration of the Johnson Company (Examples 3.3 to 3.12), a manufacturer of a single product, as its annual budget is created for the year 19X2. The company develops its budget on a quarterly basis. The example will highlight the variable cost–fixed cost breakdown throughout.

The Sales Budget

The sales budget is the starting point in preparing the operating budget, since estimated sales volume influences almost all other items appearing throughout the annual budget. The sales budget gives the quantity of each product expected to be sold. (For the Johnson Company, there is only one product.) Basically, there are three ways of making estimates for the sales budget:

1. Make a statistical forecast (using any one or a combination of the methods mentioned in Section 3.1) on the basis of an analysis of general business conditions, market conditions, product growth curves, etc.

2. Make an internal estimate by collecting the opinions of executives and sales staff.

3. Analyze the various factors that affect sales revenue and then predict the future behavior of each of those factors.

After sales volume has been estimated, the sales budget is constructed by multiplying the estimated number of units by the expected unit price. Generally, the sales budget includes a computation of cash collections anticipated from credit sales, which will be used later for cash budgeting. See Example 3.3.

EXAMPLE 3.3 Assume that of each quarter's sales, 70 percent is collected in the first quarter of the sale; 28 percent is collected in the following quarter; and 2 percent is uncollectible.

The Johnson Company
Sales Budget
For the Year Ended Dec. 31, 19X2

	Quarter				
	1	**2**	**3**	**4**	**Total**
Expected sales in units	800	700	900	800	3,200
Unit sales price ($)	×80	×80	×80	×80	×80
Total sales	$64,000	$56,000	$72,000	$64,000	$256,000

Schedule of Expected Cash Collections

	Quarter				
	1	2	3	4	Total
Accounts receivable, Dec. 31, 19X1	$ 9,500				$ 9,500
1st-qtr. sales ($64,000)	44,800 [a]	$17,920 [b]			62,720
2d-qtr. sales ($56,000)		39,200	$15,680		54,880
3d-qtr. sales ($72,000)			50,400	$20,160	70,560
4th-qtr. sales ($64,000)				44,800	44,800
Total cash collections	$54,300	$57,120	$66,080	$64,960	$242,460

[a] $64,000 × 0.70 = $44,800

[b] $64,000 × 0.28 = $17,920

The Production Budget

After sales are budgeted, the production budget can be determined. The number of units expected to be manufactured to meet budgeted sales and inventory is set forth. The expected volume of production is determined by subtracting the estimated inventory at the beginning of the period from the sum of units to be sold plus desired ending inventory. See Example 3.4.

EXAMPLE 3.4 Assume that ending inventory is 10 percent of the next quarter's sales and that the ending inventory for the fourth quarter is 100 units.

The Johnson Company
Production Budget
For the Year Ended Dec. 31, 19X2

	Quarter				
	1	2	3	4	Total
Planned sales (Example 3.3)	800	700	900	800	3,200
Desired ending inventory	70	90	80	100	100
Total needs	870	790	980	900	3,300
Less beginning inventory [a]	80	70	90	80	80
Units to be produced	790	720	890	820	3,220

[a] The same amount as the previous quarter's ending inventory.

The Direct Materials Budget

When the level of production has been computed, a direct materials budget is constructed to show how much material will be required and how much of it must be purchased to meet production requirements. The purchase will depend on both expected usage of materials and inventory levels. The formula for computing the purchase is

$$
\begin{bmatrix} \text{amount of materials} \\ \text{to be purchased} \\ \text{in units} \end{bmatrix} = \begin{bmatrix} \text{materials needed} \\ \text{for production} \\ \text{in units} \end{bmatrix} + \begin{bmatrix} \text{desired ending} \\ \text{material inventory} \\ \text{in units} \end{bmatrix} - \begin{bmatrix} \text{beginning} \\ \text{material inventory} \\ \text{in units} \end{bmatrix}
$$

The direct materials budget is usually accompanied by a computation of expected cash payments for the purchased materials.

EXAMPLE 3.5 Assume that ending inventory is 10 percent of the next quarter's production needs; the ending materials inventory for the fourth quarter is 250 units; and 50 percent of each quarter's purchases are paid in that quarter, with the remainder being paid in the following quarter. Also, 3 pounds of materials are needed per unit of product at a cost of $2 per pound.

The Johnson Company
Direct Materials Budget
For the Year Ended Dec. 31, 19X2

	Quarter				
	1	**2**	**3**	**4**	**Total**
Units to be produced (Example 3.4)	790	720	890	820	3,220
Material needs per unit (pounds)	×3	×3	×3	×3	×3
Material needs for production	2,370	2,160	2,670	2,460	9,660
Desired ending inventory of materials	216	267	246	250	250
Total needs	2,586	2,427	2,916	2,710	9,910
Less: Beginning inventory of materials[a]	237	216	267	246	237
Materials to be purchased	2,349	2,211	2,649	2,464	9,673
Unit price ($)	×2	×2	×2	×2	×2
Purchase cost	$4,698	$4,422	$5,298	$4,928	$19,346

Schedule of Expected Cash Disbursements

	1	2	3	4	Total
Accounts payable, Dec. 31, 19X1	$2,200				$ 2,200
1st-qtr. purchases ($4,698)	2,349	$2,349			4,698
2d-qtr. purchases ($4,422)		2,211	$2,211		4,422
3d-qtr. purchases ($5,298)			2,649	$2,649	5,298
4th-qtr. purchases ($4,928)				2,464	2,464
Total disbursements	$4,549	$4,560	$4,860	$5,113	$19,082

[a] The same amount as the prior quarter's ending inventory.

The Direct Labor Budget

The production budget also provides the starting point for the preparation of the direct labor cost budget. The direct labor hours necessary to meet production requirements multiplied by the estimated hourly rate yields the total direct labor cost.

EXAMPLE 3.6 Assume that 5 hours of labor are required per unit of product and that the hourly rate is $5.

The Johnson Company
Direct Labor Budget
For the Year Ended Dec. 31, 19X2

	Quarter				
	1	**2**	**3**	**4**	**Total**
Units to be produced (Example 3.4)	790	720	890	820	3,220
Direct labor hours per unit	×5	×5	×5	×5	×5
Total hours	3,950	3,600	4,450	4,100	16,100
Direct labor cost per hour ($)	×5	×5	×5	×5	×5
Total direct labor cost	$19,750	$18,000	$22,250	$20,500	$80,500

The Factory Overhead Budget

The factory overhead budget is a schedule of all manufacturing costs other than direct materials and direct labor. Using the contribution approach to budgeting requires the development of a predetermined overhead rate for the variable portion of the factory overhead. In developing the cash budget, remember that depreciation does not entail a cash outlay and therefore must be deducted from the total factory overhead in computing cash disbursements for factory overhead.

EXAMPLE 3.7 For the following factory overhead budget, assume that:

1. Total factory overhead is budgeted at $6,000 per quarter plus $2 per hour of direct labor.
2. Depreciation expenses are $3,250 per quarter.
3. All overhead costs involving cash outlays are paid in the quarter in which they are incurred.

The Johnson Company
Factory Overhead Budget
For the Year Ended Dec. 31, 19X2

	Quarter				
	1	**2**	**3**	**4**	**Total**
Budgeted direct labor hours (Example 3.6)	3,950	3,600	4,450	4,100	16,100
Variable overhead rate ($)	×2	×2	×2	×2	×2
Variable overhead budgeted	$ 7,900	$ 7,200	$ 8,900	$ 8,200	$32,000
Fixed overhead budgeted	6,000	6,000	6,000	6,000	24,000
Total budgeted overhead	$13,900	$13,200	$14,900	$14,200	$56,200
Less: Depreciation	3,250	3,250	3,250	3,250	13,000
Cash disbursements for overhead	$10,650	$ 9,950	$11,650	$10,950	$43,200

The Ending Inventory Budget

The ending inventory budget provides the information required for constructing budgeted financial statements. First, it is useful for computing the cost of goods sold on the budgeted income statement. Second, it gives the dollar value of the ending *materials* and *finished goods inventory* that will appear on the budgeted balance sheet.

EXAMPLE 3.8 For the ending inventory budget, we first need to compute the unit variable cost for finished goods, as follows:

	Unit Cost	Units	Total
Direct materials	$2	3 pounds	$ 6
Direct labor	$5	5 hours	25
Variable overhead	$2	5 hours	10
Total variable manufacturing cost			$41

The Johnson Company
Ending Inventory Budget
For the Year Ended Dec. 31, 19X2

	Ending Inventory		
	Units	Unit Costs	Total
Direct materials	250 pounds	$2	$500
Finished goods	100 units	$41	$4,100

The Selling and Administrative Expense Budget

The selling and administrative expense budget lists the operating expenses involved in selling the products and in managing the business.

EXAMPLE 3.9 The variable selling and administrative expenses amount to $4 per unit of sale, including commissions, shipping, and supplies; expenses are paid in the same quarter in which they are incurred, with the exception of $1,200 in income tax, which is paid in the third quarter.

The Johnson Company
Selling and Administrative Expense Budget
For the Year Ended Dec. 31, 19X2

	Quarter				
	1	2	3	4	Total
Expected sales in units	800	700	900	800	3,200
Variable selling and administrative expense per unit ($)	×4	×4	×4	×4	×4
Budgeted variable expense	$ 3,200	$ 2,800	$ 3,600	$ 3,200	$12,800
Fixed selling and administrative expenses					
Advertising	1,100	1,100	1,100	1,100	4,400
Insurance	2,800				2,800
Office salaries	8,500	8,500	8,500	8,500	34,000
Rent	350	350	350	350	1,400
Taxes			1,200		1,200
Total budgeted selling and administrative expenses	$15,950	$12,750	$14,750	$13,150	$56,600

The Cash Budget

The cash budget is prepared in order to forecast the firm's future financial needs. It is also a tool for cash planning and control. Because the cash budget details the expected cash receipts and disbursements for a designated time period, it helps avoid the problem of either having idle cash on hand or suffering a cash shortage. However, if a cash shortage is experienced, the cash budget indicates whether the shortage is temporary or permanent, i.e., whether short-term or long-term borrowing is needed.

The cash budget typically consists of four major sections:

1. The receipts section, which gives the beginning cash balance, cash collections from customers, and other receipts

2. The disbursements section, which shows all cash payments made, listed by purpose

3. The cash surplus or deficit section, which simply shows the difference between the cash receipts section and the cash disbursements section

4. The financing section, which provides a detailed account of the borrowings and repayments expected during the budget period

EXAMPLE 3.10   For this example, assume the following:

1. The company desires to maintain a $5,000 minimum cash balance at the end of each quarter.

2. All borrowing and repayment must be in multiples of $500 at an interest rate of 10 percent per annum. Interest is computed and paid as the principal is repaid. Borrowing takes place at the beginning and repayments at the end of each quarter.

3. The cash balance at the beginning of the first quarter is $10,000.

4. A sum of $24,300 is to be paid in the second quarter for machinery purchases.

5. Income tax of $4,000 is paid in the first quarter.

The Johnson Company
Cash Budget
For the Year Ended Dec. 31, 19X2

	From Example	Quarter 1	2	3	4	Total
Cash balance, beginning	Given	$10,000	$ 9,401	$ 5,461	$ 9,106	$ 10,000
Add receipts						
Collection from customers	3.3	54,300	57,120	66,080	64,960	242,460
Total cash available		$64,300	$66,521	$71,541	$74,066	$252,460
Less disbursements						
Direct materials	3.5	$ 4,549	$ 4,560	$ 4,860	$ 5,113	$ 19,082
Direct labor	3.6	19,750	18,000	22,250	20,500	80,500
Factory overhead	3.7	10,650	9,950	11,650	10,950	43,200
Selling and administrative	3.9	15,950	12,750	14,750	13,150	56,600
Machinery purchase	Given		24,300			24,300
Income tax	Given	4,000				4,000
Total disbursements		$54,899	$69,560	$53,510	$49,713	$227,682
Cash surplus (deficit)		$ 9,401	$ (3,039)	$18,031	$24,353	$ 24,778
Financing						
Borrowing			$ 8,500			$ 8,500
Repayment				(8,500)		(8,500)
Interest				(425)		(425)
Total financing			$ 8,500	$(8,925)		$ (425)
Cash balance, ending		$ 9,401	$ 5,461	$ 9,106	$24,353	$ 24,353

The Budgeted Income Statement

The budgeted income statement summarizes the various component projections of revenue and expenses for the budgeting period. For control purposes, the budget can be divided into quarters, for example, depending on the need.

EXAMPLE 3.11

The Johnson Company
Budgeted Income Statement
For the Year Ended Dec. 31, 19X2

	From Example		
Sales (3,200 units @ $80)	3.3		$256,000
Less: Variable expenses			
Variable cost of goods sold (3,200 units @ $41)	3.8	$131,200	
Variable selling and administrative	3.9	12,800	144,000
Contribution margin			$112,000
Less: Fixed expenses			
Factory overhead	3.7	$ 24,000	
Selling and administrative	3.9	43,800	67,800
Net operating income			$ 44,200
Less: Interest expense	3.10		425
Net income before taxes			$ 43,775
Less: Income taxes (20%)			8,755
Net income			$ 35,020

The Budgeted Balance Sheet

The budgeted balance sheet is developed by beginning with the balance sheet for the year just ended and adjusting it, using all the activities that are expected to take place during the budget period. Some of the reasons why the budgeted balance sheet must be prepared are:

1. To disclose any potentially unfavorable financial conditions
2. To serve as a final check on the mathematical accuracy of all the other budgets
3. To help management perform a variety of ratio calculations
4. To highlight future resources and obligations

EXAMPLE 3.12

The Johnson Company
Balance Sheet
For the Year Ended Dec. 31, 19X1

ASSETS		LIABILITIES AND STOCKHOLDERS' EQUITY	
Current assets		Current liabilities	
Cash	$ 10,000	Accounts payable	$ 2,200
Accounts receivable	9,500	Income tax payable	4,000
Materials inventory	474	Stockholders' equity	
Finished goods inventory	3,280	Common stock, no par	70,000
	$ 23,254	Retained earnings	37,054
Fixed assets			
Land	$ 50,000		
Building and equipment	100,000		
Accumulated depreciation	(60,000)		
	$ 90,000		
		Total liabilities and stockholders' equity	$113,254
Total assets	$113,254		

86

The Johnson Company
Budgeted Balance Sheet
For the Year Ended Dec. 31, 19X2

ASSETS		LIABILITIES AND STOCKHOLDERS' EQUITY	
Current assets		Current liabilities	
Cash	$ 24,353[a]	Accounts payable	$ 2,464[g]
Accounts receivable	23,040[b]	Income tax payable	8,755[h]
Materials inventory	500[c]		
Finished goods inventory	4,100[c]	Stockholders' equity	
	$ 51,993	Common stock, no par	70,000[i]
		Retained earnings	72,074[j]
Fixed assets			
Land	$ 50,000[d]		
Buildings and equipment	124,300[e]		
Accumulated depreciation	(73,000)[f]		
	$101,300		
		Total liabilities and	
Total assets	$153,293	stockholders' equity	$153,293

[a] From Example 3.10 (cash budget).

[b] From Example 3.3 (sales budget).

$$\text{Accounts receivable} = \text{Beginning balance} + \text{sales} - \text{receipts}$$
$$= \$9,500 + \$256,000 - 242,460 = \$23,040$$

[c] From Example 3.8 (ending inventory budget).

[d] Unchanged from 19X1 balance sheet.

[e] $100,000 (from 19X1 balance sheet) + $24,300 (from Example 3.10) = $124,300

[f] $60,000 (from 19X1 balance sheet) + $13,000 (from Example 3.7) = $73,000

[g] Accounts payable = beginning balance + purchase cost − disbursements for materials
      = $2,200 + $19,346 (Example 3.5) − $19,082 (Example 3.5) = $2,464

or 50% of 4th-quarter purchase = 50% ($4,928) = $2,464.

[h] From Example 3.11 (budgeted income statement).

[i] Unchanged from 19X1 balance sheet.

[j] $37,054 (from 19X1 balance sheet) + $35,020 (from net income, Example 3.11) = $72,074

3.5 A SHORTCUT APPROACH TO FORMULATING THE BUDGET

Examples 3.3 to 3.12 show a detailed procedure for formulating a budget. However, in practice a shortcut approach to budgeting is quite common and may be summarized as follows:

1. A pro forma income statement is developed using past percentage relationships between relevant expense and cost items and the firm's sales. These percentages are then applied to the firm's forecasted sales. This is a version of the percent-of-sales method discussed in Section 3.2.

2. A pro forma balance sheet is estimated by determining the desired level of certain balance sheet items, then making additional financing conform to those desired figures. The remaining items, thus, are estimated to make the balance sheet balance.

There are two basic assumptions underlying this approach:

1. The firm's past financial condition is an accurate predictor of its future condition.
2. The value of certain variables such as cash, inventory, and accounts receivable can be forced to take on specified *desired* values.

3.6 COMPUTER-BASED MODELS FOR FINANCIAL PLANNING AND BUDGETING

More and more companies are developing computer-based quantitative models for constructing a profit planning budget. The models help managerial decision makers answer a variety of *what-if* questions. The resultant calculations provide a basis for choice among alternatives under conditions of uncertainty. There are primarily two approaches to modeling the corporate budgeting process: *simulation* and *optimization*.

Review Questions

1. _____, an essential element of planning, is the basis for budgeting activities.

2. The most widely used method for forecasting future financing needs is _____.

3. In a forecast of additional funds, external funds needed equal required increase in assets minus the sum of _____ plus _____.

4. Budgeting is a tool for _____ and _____.

5. The cash budget contains four major sections. They are the _____ section, _____ section, _____ section, and the financing section.

6. How much to produce is contingent upon expected sales in units and the _____ and _____ inventories of finished goods.

7. Production budget is prepared after the _____ budget is completed. It is prepared in _____.

8. Cash budgets should include noncash charges such as depreciation: (*a*) true, (*b*) false.

9. Cash budgets are prepared on a short-term basis such as on a monthly, quarterly, or even weekly basis: (*a*) true; (*b*) false.

10. Operating budgets would include cash budgets: (*a*) true; (*b*) false.

11. The pro forma _____ shows the expected operating results for the budgeting year, while the pro forma _____ shows the expected financial condition at the end of budgeting period.

12. Desired ending inventory figures appear on both budgeted _____ and _____.

13. The idea behind preparing cash budgets is to avoid unnecessary cash _____ and _____ .

14. _____ are often used to develop budgets in order to evaluate alternative courses of action.

15. A shortcut approach to formulating a budget uses a version of the _____ .

Answers: (1) Financial forecasting; (2) the percent-of-sales method; (3) spontaneous increase in liabilities, increase in retained earnings; (4) planning, control; (5) cash receipt, cash disbursement, cash surplus (or deficit); (6) beginning, ending; (7) sales, physical units; (8) (*b*); (9) (*a*); (10) (*b*); (11) income statement, balance sheet; (12) income statement (or cost of goods sold), balance sheet; (13) surplus, deficit; (14) Computer-based financial planning models; (15) percent-of-sales method.

Solved Problems

3.1   Behavior of Balance Sheet Items. Which of the following balance sheet items generally vary directly with sales?

(*a*)	Common stock	(*f*)	Marketable securities
(*b*)	Accounts payable	(*g*)	Debentures
(*c*)	Retained earnings	(*h*)	Accrued wages
(*d*)	Inventory	(*i*)	Preferred stock
(*e*)	Taxes payable	(*j*)	Mortgage bonds

SOLUTION

(*b*), (*d*), (*e*), (*f*), (*h*)

3.2   Financial Forecasting and External Funds Needed. The following financial data pertain to Barret Company:

Income Statement
(In Millions of Dollars)

Sales	$16.0
Cost of goods sold	13.0
Gross profit	$ 3.0
Operating expenses	1.0
Net profit before taxes	$ 2.0
Tax	1.0
Profit after taxes	$ 1.0
Dividends	0.7
Retentions	$ 0.3

Balance Sheet
(In Millions of Dollars)

ASSETS

Current assets

Cash	$ 2.0
Receivables	2.0
Inventories	4.0
Total current assets	$ 8.0
Fixed assets	8.0
Total assets	$16.0

LIABILITIES AND NET WORTH

Current liabilities	$ 5.0
Long-term debt	2.0
Total debt	$ 7.0
Common stock	7.0
Retained earnings	$ 2.0
Total liabilities and net worth	$16.0

Barret expects its sales to increase by $2,000,000 next year. In this problem, all the asset accounts (including fixed assets) and current liabilities vary with sales. Barret is operating at full capacity. (*a*) Forecast Barret's need for external funds by (1) constructing a pro forma balance sheet and (2) using the simple formula. (*b*) Discuss the limitation of the percent-of-sales method.

SOLUTION

(*a*) (1)

Pro Forma Balance Sheet
(In Millions of Dollars)

	Present	% of Sales (Sales = $16.0)	Next Year (Projected Sales = $18.0)	
ASSETS				
Current assets	$ 8.0	50	$ 9.0000	
Fixed assets	8.0	50	9.0000	
Total assets	$16.0		$18.0000	
LIABILITIES AND NET WORTH				
Current liabilities	$ 5.0	31.25	$ 5.6250	
Long-term debt	2.0	n.a.	2.0000	
Total liabilities	$ 7.0		$ 7.6250	
Common stock	$ 7.0	n.a.	$ 7.0000	
Retained earnings	2.0		2.3375 [a]	
Total net worth	$ 9.0		$ 9.3375	
Total liabilities and net worth	$16.0		$16.9625	Total financing provided
			$ 1.0375 [b]	External financing needed
			$18.0000	Total

---

[a] Next year's retained earnings = present year's retained earnings + projected net income (after taxes) − cash dividends paid. Note that after-tax net income = $1.0/$16.0 = 6.25% and dividend payout ratio = 0.7/1.0 = 7%. Therefore,

Next year's retained earnings = $2.0 + 6.25%($18.0) − 0.7[6.25%($18)] = $2.0 + $1.125 − $0.7875 = $2.3375.

[b] External funds needed = projected total assets − (projected total liabilities + projected equity) = $18.0 − $16.9625 = $1.0375.

90

(2)

$$EFN = \left(\frac{A}{S}\right)\Delta S - \left(\frac{L}{S}\right)\Delta S - (PM)(PS)(1 - d)$$

where $\dfrac{A}{S} = \dfrac{\$16.0}{\$16.0} = 100\%$

$\dfrac{L}{S} = \dfrac{\$5.0}{\$16.0} = 31.25\%$

$\Delta S = \$18.0 - \$16.0 = \$2.0$

$PM = \$1.0/\$16.0 = 6.25\%$

$PS = \$18.0$

$d = \$0.7/\$1.0 = 70\%$, or $1 - d = 30\%$

Thus,

$$EFN = 100\%\,(\$2) - 31.25\%\,(\$2) - (6.25\%)(\$18)(1 - 0.7)$$
$$= \$2 - \$0.625 - \$0.3375 = \$1.0375$$

(b) The calculations for both the pro forma balance sheet and the simple formula are based on percentage of sales. The limitations of the percent-of-sales method are (1) the relationship between sales and the expense item, asset, or liability being projected is assumed to be pure, i.e., free of any other influences; and (2) the method does not provide accurate forecasts when a firm has extra capacity to absorb all or a portion of the projected increase in sales and the related investment in assets.

3.3 **Determination of External Funds Needed.** Ina Corporation is thinking of purchasing a new machine. With this new machine, the company expects sales to increase from \$8,000,000 to \$10,000,000.

The company knows that its assets, accounts payable, and accrued expenses vary directly with sales. The company's profit margin on sales is 8 percent, and the company plans to pay 40 percent of its after-tax earnings in dividends. The company's current balance sheet is given below.

Balance Sheet

Current assets	\$ 3,000,000
Fixed assets	12,000,000
Total assets	\$15,000,000
Accounts payable	\$ 4,000,000
Accrued expenses	1,000,000
Long-term debt	3,000,000
Common stock	2,000,000
Retained earnings	5,000,000
Total liabilities and net worth	\$15,000,000

(a) Prepare a pro forma balance sheet.

(b) Use the simple formula to determine the external funds needed by the company based on the answer in part (a).

(c) Determine, using the simple formula, the external funds needed under each of the following conditions:

(1) The profit margin rises from 8 percent to 10 percent.

(2) The profit margin is 8 percent, but the dividend payout ratio is reduced from 40 percent to 20 percent.

(*d*) Comment on the results from part (*c*).

SOLUTION

(*a*)

Pro Forma Balance Sheet
(In Millions of Dollars)

	Present Level	% of Sales	Projected (Based on Sales of $10)
Current assets	$ 3	37.5	$ 3.75
Fixed assets	12	150.0	15.00
Total assets	$15		$18.75
Accounts payable	$ 4	50.0	$ 5.00
Accrued expenses	1	12.5	1.25
Long-term debt	3	n.a.	3.00
Common stock	2	n.a.	2.00
Retained earnings	5	n.a.	5.48[a]
Total liabilities and net worth	$15		$16.73 Total funds provided
			$ 2.02 Additional funds needed

[a] Retained earnings = $5 + 8\%\,(\$10) - (0.4)[8\%\,(\$10)]$
$= \$5 + \$0.8 - \$0.32 = 5.48$

(*b*)
$$\text{EFN} = \left(\frac{A}{S}\right)\Delta S - \left(\frac{L}{S}\right)\Delta S - (PM)(PS)(1 - d)$$

where $\dfrac{A}{S} = \dfrac{\$15}{\$8} = 187.5\%$

$\dfrac{L}{S} = \dfrac{\$5}{\$8} = 62.5\%$

$\Delta S = \$10 - \$8 = \$2$

$PM = 8\%$

$PS = \$10$

$d = 40\%$

$$\text{EFN} = 187.5\%\,(\$2) - 62.5\%\,(\$2) - 8\%\,(\$10)(1 - 0.4)$$
$$= \$3.75 - \$1.25 - \$0.48 = \$2.02$$

(*c*) (1)
$$PM = 10\%$$
$$\text{EFN} = 187.5\%\,(\$2) - 62.5\%\,(\$2) - 10\%\,(\$10)(1 - 0.4)$$
$$= \$3.75 - \$1.25 - \$0.6 = \$1.9$$

(2)
$$d = 20\%$$
$$\text{EFN} = 187.5\%\,(\$2) - 62.5\%\,(\$2) - 8\%\,(\$10)(1 - 0.2)$$
$$= \$3.75 - \$1.25 - \$0.64 = \$1.86$$

(*d*) As is evident from part (*c*), an improved profit margin [(*c*)(1)] or a lower dividend payout ratio [(*d*)(2)] will decrease the amount of external funds needed.

3.4   Filling in Blanks and Financial Forecasting. The following data pertain to ABC Company:

Balance Sheet Items
On Dec. 31, 19X1
(In Thousands of Dollars)

	19X1	% of Sales (19X1 Sales = $400)	Pro Forma Balance Sheet on Dec. 31, 19X2 (Projected Sales = $600)
Cash	$ 10	2.5	$ 15
Receivables	90	22.5	135
Inventories	200	50.0	300
Total current assets	$300	75.0	$450
Net fixed assets	300	75.0	450
Total assets	$600	150.0	$900
Accounts payable	$ 40	10.0	$ 60
Notes payable	20	n.a.	(c)
Accrued wages and taxes	40	10.0	60
Total current liabilities	$100		(b)
Mortgage bonds	$140	n.a.	(d)
Common stock	60	n.a.	(f)
Retained earnings	300	n.a.	324
Total	$600		(e) Funds provided
			(a) Additional funds needed

In addition, ABC Company must maintain a total debt/total assets ratio at or below 40 percent and a current ratio at or above 2.5. Within these constraints, ABC would prefer to finance using short-term rather than long-term debt or long-term debt rather than equity.

Fill in the missing terms on the December 31, 19X2, pro forma balance sheet.

SOLUTION

(a)

$$\begin{bmatrix} \text{external} \\ \text{funds} \\ \text{needed} \end{bmatrix} = \begin{bmatrix} \text{required} \\ \text{increase} \\ \text{in assets} \end{bmatrix} - \begin{bmatrix} \text{spontaneous} \\ \text{increase in} \\ \text{liabilities} \end{bmatrix} - \begin{bmatrix} \text{increase in} \\ \text{retained} \\ \text{earnings} \end{bmatrix}$$

$$= (\$900 - \$600) - \begin{bmatrix} \text{increase in} \\ \text{accounts} \\ \text{payable} + \\ \text{accrued wages} \\ \text{and taxes} \end{bmatrix} - (\$324 - \$300)$$

$$= \$300 - [(\$60 - \$40) + (\$60 - \$40)] - \$24$$
$$= \$300 - \$40 - \$24 = \$236$$

(b)

$$\text{Current ratio} = \frac{\text{current assets}}{\text{current liabilities}}$$

$$2.5 \text{ (minimum)} = \frac{\$450}{\text{current liabilities}}$$

Current liabilities = $180, which is the maximum allowed.

(c)

$$\text{Notes payable} = \text{current liabilities} - (\text{accounts payable} + \text{accrued wages and taxes})$$
$$= \$180 - (\$60 + \$60) = \$180 - \$120 = \$60$$

$$\frac{\text{Total debt}}{\text{Total assets}} = 40\% \ (\text{maximum})$$

$$\frac{\text{Current liabilities} + \text{mortgage bonds}}{\text{Total assets}} = \frac{\$180 + \text{mortgage bonds}}{\$900}$$

$$\text{Mortgage bonds} = 40\% \ (\$900) - \$180 = \$180$$

(e)

$$\text{Total funds provided} = \text{total assets} - \text{additional funds needed}$$
$$= \$900 - \$236 \ [\text{from } (a)] = \$664$$

(f)

$$\text{Common stock} = \text{total funds provided} - (\text{montgage bonds} + \text{retained earnings})$$
$$= \$664^a - (\$180^b + \$324) = \$664 - \$504 = \$160$$

_____

[a] From (e).

[b] From (d).

3.5 **Credit Sales and Cash Collections.** The following sales budget is given for Van Dyke Sales Co. for the second quarter of 19X1:

	April	May	June	Total
Sales budget	$45,000	$50,000	$60,000	$155,000

Credit sales are collected as follows: 70 percent in month of sale, 20 percent in month following sale, 8 percent in second month following sale, and 2 percent uncollectible. The accounts receivable balance at the beginning of the second quarter is $18,000, of which $3,600 represents uncollected February sales, and $14,400 represents uncollected March sales.

Compute (a) the total sales for February and March, and (b) the budgeted cash collections from sales for each month February through June. Without prejudice to answer (a), assume February sales equal $40,000 and March sales equal $50,000.

SOLUTION

(a)

$$\text{February sales} \ (1 - 0.7 - 0.2) = \$3,600$$

$$\text{February sales} = \frac{\$3,600}{1 - 0.9} = \$36,000$$

$$\text{March sales} \ (1 - 0.7) = \$14,400$$

$$\text{March sales} = \frac{\$14,400}{0.3} = \$48,000$$

(b)

Cash collections	April	May	June
February			
40,000 (8%)	$ 3,200		
March			
50,000 (20%)	10,000		
50,000 (8%)		$ 4,000	
April			
45,000 (70%)	31,500		
45,000 (20%)		9,000	
45,000 (8%)			$ 3,600
May			
50,000 (70%)		35,000	
50,000 (20%)			10,000
June			
60,000 (70%)			42,000
Total cash collections	$44,700	$48,000	$55,600

94

3.6   Cash Collections. The following data are given for Erich From Stores:

	September, Actual	October, Actual	November, Estimated	December, Estimated
Cash sales	$7,000	$6,000	$8,000	$6,000
Credit sales	$50,000	$48,000	$62,000	$80,000
Total sales	$57,000	$54,000	$70,000	$86,000

Past experience indicates net collections normally occur in the following pattern: No collections are made in the month of sale, 80 percent of the sales of any month are collected in the following month, 19 percent of sales are collected in the second following month, and 1 percent of sales are uncollectible.

Compute (a) total cash receipts for November and December, and (b) accounts receivable balance at November 30 if the October 31 balance is $50,000.

SOLUTION

(a)

	November	December
Cash receipts		
Cash sales	$ 8,000	$ 6,000
Cash collections		
September sales		
50,000 (19%)	9,500	
October sales		
48,000 (80%)	38,400	
48,000 (19%)		9,120
November sales		
62,000 (80%)		49,600
Total cash receipts	$55,900	$64,720

(b)   Accounts receivable (Nov. 30) = $50,000 + $62,000 − $9,500 − $38,400 = $64,100

3.7   Cash Collections and Discount Policy. The treasurer of John Loyde Co. plans for the company to have a cash balance of $91,000 on March 1. Sales during March are estimated at $900,000. February sales amounted to $600,000, and January sales amounted to $500,000. Cash payments for March have been budgeted at $580,000. Cash collections have been estimated as follows: 60 percent of the sales for the month to be collected during the month, 30 percent of the sales for the preceding month to be collected during the month, and 8 percent of the sales for the second preceding month to be collected during the month.

The treasurer plans to accelerate collections by allowing a 2 percent discount for prompt payment. With the discount policy, she expects to collect 70 percent of the current sales and will permit the discount reduction on these collections. Sales of the preceding month will be collected to the extent of 15 percent with no discount allowed, and 10 percent of the sales of the second preceding month will be collected with no discount allowed. This pattern of collection can be expected in subsequent months. During the transitional month of March, collections may run somewhat higher. However, the treasurer prefers to estimate collections on the basis of the new pattern so that the estimates will be somewhat conservative.

Estimate (a) cash collections for March and the cash balance at March 31 under the present policy, and (b) cash collections for March and the cash balance at March 31 according to the new policy of allowing discounts. (c) Is the discount policy desirable?

SOLUTION

(*a*) and (*b*)

	(*a*) Cash Collection under the Present Policy:	(*b*) Cash Collection under the Discount Policy:
Balance, March 1	$ 91,000	$ 91,000
Collections		
From March sales	540,000 ($900,000 × 60%)	617,400 [a]
From February sales	180,000 ($600,000 × 30%)	90,000 ($600,000 × 15%)
From January sales	40,000 ($500,000 × 8%)	50,000 ($500,000 × 10%)
Total cash available	$851,000	$848,400
Less: Disbursements	580,000	580,000
Balance, March 31	$271,000	$268,400

[a] $900,000 × 70% × 98% = $617,400

(*c*)   No, the discount policy is not, since under the discount policy, the March 31 cash balance will be smaller.

3.8   **Cash Disbursements.** Eastmark Stores wants to estimate cash disbursements for cash budgeting purposes for the first 3 months of 19X2 from the data given below.

1.   Cost of merchandise sold, estimated:

19X1: December	$225,000
19X2: January	$250,000
February	$280,000
March	$210,000

The cost of merchandise is to be paid for as follows: 35 percent in the month of sale and 65 percent in the following month.

2.   Wages for each month are estimated as follows:

19X1: December	$23,000
19X2: January	$26,000
February	$31,000
March	$25,000

All are paid as incurred.

3.   Utilities are to be paid every other month at the amount of $320 per month. The first payment is to be made in February.

4.   Six months' rent and insurance amounting to a total of $9,700 is to be paid in January.

5.   An income tax of $12,500 is to be paid in March.

6.   Depreciation on office equipment has been estimated at $7,500 for the year.

7.   New equipment costing $50,000 is to be acquired in February, with a down payment of $4,000 required at date of purchase.

8.   Other operating expenses have been estimated at $2,250 per month, which are to be paid each month.

Prepare a cash disbursement budget for each of the first 3 months of 19X2.

SOLUTION

Cash Disbursements Budget
For 3 Months, 19X2

	January	February	March	Total
Cost of merchandise sold				
35% current	$ 87,500	$ 98,000	$ 73,500	$259,000
65% preceding month	146,250	162,500	182,000	490,750
Total	$233,750	$260,500	$255,500	$749,750
Wages	26,000	31,000	25,000	82,000
Utilities		320		320
Rent and insurance	9,700			9,700
Income tax			12,500	12,500
Equipment, down payment		4,000		4,000
Other operation expenses	2,250	2,250	2,250	6,750
Total disbursements	$271,700	$298,070	$295,250	$865,020

3.9   Cash Budget. Some key figures from the budget of Moore Company for the first quarter of operations for 19X2 are shown below.

	January	February	March
Credit sales	$80,000	$70,000	$86,000
Credit purchases	34,000	32,000	40,000
Cash disbursements			
Wages and salaries	4,000	3,500	4,200
Rent	1,500	1,500	1,500
Equipment purchases	25,000		2,000

The company estimates that 10 percent of its credit sales will never be collected. Of those that will be collected, 50 percent will be collected in the month of sale and the remainder will be collected in the following month. Purchases on account will all be paid for in the month following purchase. 19X2 December sales were $90,000.

Using the preceding information, complete the following cash budget.

	January	February	March
Beginning cash balance	$100,000	_____	_____
Cash receipts			
Cash collections from credit sales	_____	_____	_____
Total cash available	_____	_____	_____
Cash disbursements			
Purchases	_____	_____	_____
Wages and salaries	_____	_____	_____
Rent	_____	_____	_____
Equipment purchases	_____	_____	_____
Total disbursements	_____	_____	_____
Ending cash balance	_____	_____	_____

SOLUTION

	January	February	March
Beginning cash balance	$100,000	$146,000	$174,500
Cash receipts			
Cash collection from credit sales	76,500 [a]	67,500 [b]	70,200 [c]
Total cash available	$176,500	$213,500	$244,700
Cash disbursements			
Purchases		$ 34,000	$ 32,000
Salaries	$ 4,000	3,500	4,200
Rent	1,500	1,500	1,500
Fixed assets	25,000		2,000
Total disbursements	$ 30,500	$ 39,000	$ 39,700
Ending cash balance	$146,000	$174,500	$205,000

[a] From December sales: $\dfrac{\$90,000 - (\$90,000 \times 0.1)}{2} = \$40,500$

January sales: $\dfrac{\$80,000 - (\$80,000 \times 0.1)}{2} = \dfrac{36,000}{\$76,500}$

[b] From January sales: $\$36,000$

February sales: $\dfrac{\$70,000 - (\$70,000 \times 0.1)}{2} = \dfrac{31,500}{\$67,500}$

[c] From February sales: $\$31,500$

March sales: $\dfrac{\$86,000 - (\$86,000 \times 0.1)}{2} = \dfrac{38,700}{\$70,200}$

3.10   Incomplete Data on Sales. The following information pertains to merchandise purchased by Westwood Plumbing Co. for July, August, September, and October. During any month, 60 percent of the merchandise to be sold in the following month is purchased. The balance of the merchandise is purchased during the month of sale. Gross margin averages 20 percent of sales.

	Purchases	
	For the Following Month	For the Current Month
July	$87,000	$92,000
August	$96,000	$100,000
September	$120,000	$89,000
October	$110,000	$92,000

Estimate the sales revenue for August, September, and October.

SOLUTION

Cost of sales:

August:	$87,000 ÷ 0.6 = $145,000
September:	$96,000 ÷ 0.6 = $160,000
October:	$120,000 ÷ 0.6 = $200,000

Since gross margin averages 20 percent of sales, cost of goods sold is equal to 80 percent of sales. Thus, sales:

August:	$145,000 ÷ 0.8 =	$181,250
September:	$160,000 ÷ 0.8 =	$200,000
October:	$200,000 ÷ 0.8 =	$250,000

3.11   Selling and Administrative Expense Budget. Foster Company has gathered the following information for the month of July, 19X1:

Sales: $200,000

Sales commissions: 10% of sales

Advertising expenses: $5,000 + 2% of sales

Miscellaneous selling expense: $1,000 + 1% of sales

Office salaries: $7,000

Office supplies: 0.5% of sales

Travel and entertainment: $4,000

Miscellaneous administrative expense: $1,750

Prepare a selling and administrative budget.

SOLUTION

Foster Company
Selling and Administrative Expense Budget
For the Month of July, 19X1

Selling expenses	
Sales staff commissions	$20,000
Advertising expense	9,000
Miscellaneous selling expense	3,000
Total	$32,000
Administrative expenses	
Office salaries	$ 7,000
Office supplies	1,000
Miscellaneous expense	1,750
Travel and entertainment	4,000
Total	$13,750
Total selling and administrative expenses	$45,750

3.12   Budgeted Income Statement. In the fiscal quarter ended December 31, 19X1, Eric Wills Lumber Company plans to sell 52,000 board feet lumber at a price of $125 per board foot. There are to be 5,500 board feet on hand October 1, with a cost of $65 per board foot. The company plans to manufacture 53,000 board feet of lumber during the quarter, with the following manufacturing costs:

Direct materials:	$971,500
Direct labor:	$2,000,000
Factory overhead: (25% of direct labor costs)	

The company uses the last-in, first-out (LIFO) method of inventory costing. Selling expenses are estimated at 25 percent of sales, and administrative expenses are expected to be 10 percent more than the previous quarter's $950,000.

Prepare a budgeted income statement.

SOLUTION

Eric Wills Lumber Co.
Budgeted Income Statement
For the Quarter Ended Dec. 31, 19X1

Sales (52,000 @ $125)		$6,500,000
Less: Cost of goods sold		
Beginning inventory		
(5,500 @ $65)	$ 357,500	
Direct materials	971,500	
Direct labor	2,000,000	
Factory overhead		
(25% of $2,000,000)	500,000	
Cost of goods available for sale	$3,829,000	
Less: Ending inventory		
(6,500 units)[a]	423,000[b]	3,406,000
Gross profit		$3,094,000
Less operating expenses		
Selling expenses		
(25% of $6,500,000)	$1,625,000	
Administrative expenses		
(110% of $950,000)	1,045,000	2,670,000
Net income		$ 424,000

---

[a]   5,500 units + 53,000 units − x = 52,000 units

$$x = 6,500 \text{ units}$$

[b] The unit cost for the last quarter of 19X1 is calculated as follows:

    Unit cost = cost of goods manufactured/number of units

        = ($971,500 + $2,000,000 + $500,000)/53,000 board feet = $65.50

    Then,

5,500 units @ $65.00		$357,500
1,000 units @ $65.50		65,500
6,500 units		$423,000

3.13   **Budgeted Income Statement.** The Moore Distributor, Inc., has just received a franchise to distribute dishwashers. The company started business on January 1, 19X1, with the following assets:

Cash	$45,000
Inventory	$94,000
Warehouse, office, and delivery facilities and equipment	$800,000

All facilities and equipment have a useful life of 20 years and no residual value. First-quarter sales are expected to be $360,000 and should be doubled in the second quarter. Third-quarter sales are expected to be $1,080,000. One percent of sales are considered to be uncollectible. The gross profit margin should be 30 percent. Variable selling expenses (except uncollectible accounts) are budgeted at 12 percent of sales and fixed selling expenses at $48,000 per quarter, exclusive of depreciation. Variable administrative expenses are expected to be 3 percent of sales, and fixed administrative expenses should total $34,200 per quarter, exclusive of depreciation.

Prepare a budgeted income statement for the second quarter, 19X1.

SOLUTION

The Moore Distributor, Inc.
Budgeted Income Statement
For the Second Quarter, 19X1

Sales		$720,000
Cost of goods sold (70%)		504,000
Gross profit (30%)		$216,000
Operating expenses		
Uncollectible accounts (1%)	$ 7,200	
Depreciation[a]	10,000	
Selling		
Variable (12%)	86,400	
Fixed	48,000	
Administrative		
Variable (3%)	21,600	
Fixed	34,200	207,400
Income before income tax		$ 8,600

[a] $\frac{1}{4}($800,000 \div 20 \text{ years}) = $10,000$

3.14 Pro Forma Balance Sheet. Given the following data on the Dunes Corporation, project its balance sheet for the coming year:

Present sales: $500,000

Next year's sales: $800,000

After-tax profits: 5% of sales

Dividend payout ratio: 40%

Present retained earnings: $200,000

Cash as a percent of sales: 4%

Accounts receivable as a percent of sales: 10%

Inventory as a percent of sales: 30%

Net fixed assets as a percent of sales: 35%

Accounts payable as a percent of sales: 7%

Accruals as a percent of sales: 15%

Next year's common stock: $200,000

Dunes Corporation
Balance Sheet
Dec. 31, 19X1

ASSETS		LIABILITIES AND EQUITIES	
Cash	(a)	Accounts payable	(f)
Accounts receivable	(b)	Notes payable	(g)
Inventory	(c)	Accruals	(h)
Net fixed assets	(d)	Common stock	(i)
		Retained earnings	(j)
Total	(e)	Total	(k)

SOLUTION

The completed balance sheet is as follows:

Dunes Corporation
Balance Sheet
Dec. 31, 19X1

ASSETS		LIABILITIES AND EQUITIES	
Cash	$ 32,000	Accounts payable	$ 56,000
Accounts receivable	80,000	Notes payable	32,000
Inventory	240,000	Accruals	120,000
Net fixed assets	280,000	Common stock	200,000
		Retained earnings	224,000
Total	$632,000	Total	$632,000

The calculations are outlined below.

(a) Cash = 4% of sales = 0.04($800,000) = $32,000

(b) AR = 10% of sales = 0.1($800,000) = $80,000

(c) Inventory = 30% of sales = 0.3($800,000) = $240,000

(d) Net fixed assets = 35% of sales = 0.35($800,000) = $280,000

(e) $632,000

(f) AP = 7% of sales = 0.07($800,000) = $56,000

(g) Notes payable = total assets $- \left(\begin{array}{l} \text{accounts} \\ \text{payable} \end{array} + \text{accruals} + \begin{array}{l} \text{common} \\ \text{stock} \end{array} + \begin{array}{l} \text{retained} \\ \text{earnings} \end{array} \right)$

$\qquad$ = $632,000 - ($56,000 + $120,000 + $200,000 + $224,000)

$\qquad$ = $632,000 - $600,000 = $32,000

(h) Accruals = 15% of sales = 0.15($800,000) = $120,000

(i) Given, $200,000

(j) Retained earnings next year = retained earnings of the present year + after-tax profits − dividends
$\qquad$ = $200,000 + 5% ($800,000) − 0.4[5% ($800,000)] = $224,000

(k) $632,000

3.15 The Tony DeBenedictis Company's 19X2 sales is expected to be $12 million. The following financial statement items vary directly with sales by the percentages given.

Cash:	4%
Accounts receivable:	15%
Inventories:	20%
Net fixed assets:	35%
Accounts payable:	18%
Accruals:	15%
Profit margin on sales:	6%

The dividend payout ratio is 40 percent; the 19X1 retained earnings was $4 million; and notes payable, common stock, and retained earnings are equal to the amounts shown on the balance sheet below:

Complete the following pro forma balance sheet:

Pro Forma Balance Sheet
(In Thousands of Dollars)

Cash	$ (a)	Accounts payable	$ (h)
Accounts receivable	(b)	Notes payable	1,200
Inventories	(c)	Accruals	(i)
Total current assets	$ (d)	Total current liabilities	$ (j)
Net fixed assets	(e)	Debentures	(k)
		Common stock	1,000
		Retained earnings	1,680
Total assets	$ (f)	Total liabilities and equity	$ (g)

SOLUTION

The completed balance sheet is as follows:

Pro Forma Balance Sheet
(In Thousands of Dollars)

Cash	$ 480	Accounts payable	$2,160
Accounts receivable	1,800	Notes payable	1,200
Inventories	2,400	Accruals	1,800
Total current assets	$4,680	Total current liabilities	$5,160
Net fixed assets	4,200	Debentures	1,040
		Common stock	1,000
		Retained earnings	1,680
Total assets	$8,880	Total liabilities and equity	$8,880

The calculations are outlined below.

(a) Cash = 4% of sales = 0.04($12,000) = $480

(b) Accounts receivable = 0.15($12,000) = $1,800

(c) Inventories = 0.20($12,000) = $2,400

(d) Total current assets = $480 + $1,800 + $2,400 = $4,680

(e) Net fixed assets = 0.35($12,000) = $4,200

(f) Total assets = $4,200 + $4,680 = $8,880

(g) Therefore, total liabilities and equity is also $8,880

(h) Accounts payable = 0.18($12,000) = $2,160

(i)   Accruals = 0.15($12,000) = $1,800

(j)   Total current liabilities = $2,160 + $1,200 + $1,800 = $5,160

(k)   Therefore, debentures = $8,880 − $5,160 − $1,000 − $1,680 = $1,040

3.16   Budgeted Income Statement and Balance Sheet. A budget is being prepared for the first and second quarters of 19X2 for Aggarwal Retail Stores, Inc. The balance sheet as of December 31, 19X1, is given below

Aggarwal Retail Stores, Inc.
Balance Sheet
Dec. 31, 19X1

ASSETS		LIABILITIES AND EQUITIES	
Cash	$ 65,000	Accounts payable	$ 83,000
Accounts receivable	52,000	Income tax payable	20,000
Merchandise inventory	75,000	Capital stock	70,000
		Retained earnings	19,000
Total assets	$192,000	Total liabilities and equities	$192,000

Actual and projected sales are:

19X1, 3d quarter (actual):	$250,000
19X1, 4th quarter (actual):	$300,000
19X2, 1st quarter (estimated):	$200,000
19X2, 2d quarter (estimated):	$230,000
19X2, 3d quarter (estimated):	$220,000

Experience has shown that 60 percent of sales will be collected during the first quarter of sales and 35 percent of sales will be collected in the following quarter. Gross profit averages 30 percent of sales. There is a basic inventory of $20,000. The policy is to purchase in each quarter the additional inventory needed for the following quarter's sales; payments are made in the quarter following the quarter of purchase. Selling and administrative expenses for each quarter are estimated at 4 percent of sales plus $15,000 and are paid as incurred. Income tax is equal to 40 percent of taxable income. The income tax liability as of December 31, 19X1, is to be paid during the first quarter of 19X2.

Prepare (a) a budgeted income statement for the first and second quarter of 19X2 and (b) a budgeted balance sheet as of June 30, 19X2.

SOLUTION

(a)

Aggarwal Retail Stores, Inc.
Budgeted Income Statement
For the 6 Months Ended June 30, 19X2

	Quarter		
	1	**2**	**Total**
Sales	$200,000	$230,000	$430,000
Less: Cost of goods sold (70%)	140,000	161,000	301,000
Gross margin	$ 60,000	$ 69,000	$129,000
Less: Selling and administrative expenses ($15,000 + 4% of sales)	23,000	24,200	47,200
Net income before tax	$ 37,000	$ 44,800	$ 81,800
Income tax (40%)	14,800	17,920	32,720
Net income	$ 22,200	$ 26,880	$ 49,080

(b)

Aggarwal Retail Stores, Inc.
Budgeted Balance Sheet as of June 30, 19X2

ASSETS		LIABILITIES AND EQUITIES	
Cash	$ 89,800 [a]	Accounts payable	$ 97,000 [d]
Accounts receivable	49,000 [b]	Income tax payable	32,720 [e]
Merchandise inventory	129,000 [c]	Capital stock	70,000
		Retained earnings	68,080 [f]
Total assets	$267,800	Total liabilities and equity	$267,800

The supporting calculations for the balance sheet are as follows:

	Quarter		
	1	2	Total
CASH RECEIPTS			
60% of current sales	$120,000	$138,000	$258,000
35% of prior quarter's sales	105,000	70,000	175,000
Total receipts	$225,000	$208,000	$433,000
CASH DISBURSEMENTS			
Merchandise purchases [g]	$160,000	$181,000	$341,000
Selling and administrative expenses ($15,000 + 4% of sales per month)	23,000	24,200	47,200
Income tax (for previous quarter)	20,000		20,000
Total disbursements	$203,000	$205,200	$408,200

[a] Cash = beginning balance + cash receipts − disbursements
   = $65,000 + $433,000 − $408,200 = $89,800

[b] Accounts receivable = beginning balance + sales − cash receipts
   = $52,000 + ($200,000 + $230,000) − $433,000 = $49,000

[c] Merchandise inventory = beginning balance + purchases − cost of goods sold
   = $75,000 + ($181,000 + $174,000) − 70% ($430,000) = $129,000

[d] Accounts payable = beginning balance + purchases + selling and administrative expenses
       − disbursements (for purchases and selling and administrative expenses)
   = $83,000 + $355,000 + $47,200 − ($341,000 + $47,200) = $97,000

[e] Income tax payable = beginning balance + net income after tax − income tax payment
   = $20,000 + $32,720 − $20,000 = $32,720

[f] Retained earnings = beginning balance + net income = $19,000 + $49,080 = $68,080

[g] **MERCHANDISE**

Purchases	Quarter			
($20,000 basic + 70% of	4	1	2	Total
the quarter's sales)	$160,000	$181,000	$174,000	$515,000
Cash disbursements for merchandise purchases		$160,000	$181,000	$341,000

Chapter 4

The Management of Working Capital

4.1 MANAGING NET WORKING CAPITAL

Working capital is equal to current assets. *Net* working capital is equal to current assets less current liabilities.

EXAMPLE 4.1 Ace Company has the following selected assets and liabilities:

Cash:	$10,000
Accounts receivable:	$30,000
Inventory:	$42,000
Machinery:	$90,000
Long-term investments:	$36,000
Patent:	$4,000
Accounts payable:	$12,000
Taxes payable:	$3,000
Accrued expenses payable:	$5,000
Bonds payable:	$50,000
Common stock:	$70,000

The net working capital is:

CURRENT ASSETS		
Cash	$10,000	
Accounts receivable	30,000	
Inventory	42,000	$82,000
CURRENT LIABILITIES		
Accounts payable	$12,000	
Taxes payable	3,000	
Accrued expenses payable	5,000	20,000
Net working capital		$62,000

Management of net working capital involves regulating the various types of current assets and current liabilities. Management of net working capital also requires decisions about how current assets should be financed, for example, through short-term debt, long-term debt, or equity. Net working capital is increased when current assets are financed through noncurrent sources.

The liquidity of current assets will affect the terms and availability of short-term credit. The greater the liquidity, the easier it becomes, generally, to obtain a short-term loan at favorable terms. Short-term credit, in turn, affects the amount of cash balance held by a firm.

Working Capital Management and Risk-Return Trade-Off

The management of net working capital requires consideration for the trade-off between return and risk. Holding more current than fixed assets means a reduced liquidity risk. It also means greater flexibility, since current assets may be modified easily as sales volume changes. However, the rate of return will be less with current assets than with fixed assets. Fixed assets typically earn a greater return than current assets. Long-term financing has less liquidity risk associated with it than short-term debt, but it also carries a higher cost.

106

For example, when a company needs funds to purchase seasonal or cyclical inventory, it uses short-term, not long-term financing. The short-term debt gives the firm flexibility to meet its seasonal needs within its ability to repay the loan. On the other hand, the company's permanent assets should be financed with long-term debt. Because the assets last longer, the financing can be spread over a longer time. Financing assets with liabilities of similar maturity is called *hedging*.

4.2 CURRENT ASSETS

By optimally managing cash, receivables, and inventory, a company can maximize its rate of return and minimize its liquidity and business risk. The financial manager should determine the amount to be invested in a given current asset. The amount invested may vary from day to day and require close evaluation of the account balances. Current assets are improperly managed if funds tied up in an asset could be used more productively elsewhere. Financing such assets with debt incurs unnecessary interest expense. Also, large account balances indicate risk since, for example, inventory may not be salable and/or accounts receivable may not be collectible. On the other hand, inadequate current asset levels may be costly as, for example, when business is lost because lack of inventory does not permit the timely fulfillment of customer orders.

4.3 CASH MANAGEMENT

Cash refers to currency and demand deposits. *Cash management* involves having the optimum, neither excessive nor deficient, amount of cash on hand at the right time. Proper cash management requires that the company know how much cash it needs, as well as how much it has and where that cash is at all times. This is especially essential in an inflationary environment.

The objective of cash management is to invest excess cash for a return while retaining sufficient liquidity to satisfy future needs. The financial manager must plan when to have excess funds available for investment and when money needs to be borrowed.

The amount of cash to be held depends upon the following factors:

1. Cash management policies
2. Current liquidity position
3. Management's liquidity risk preferences
4. Schedule of debt maturity
5. The firm's ability to borrow
6. Forecasted short- and long-term cash flow
7. The probabilities of different cash flows under varying circumstances

The company should not have an excessive cash balance since no return is being earned upon it. The least amount of cash a firm should hold is the greater of (1) compensating balances (a deposit held by a bank to compensate it for providing services) or (2) precautionary balances (money held for emergency purposes) plus transaction balances (money needed to cover checks outstanding).

Cash management also requires knowing the amount of funds available for investment and the length of time for which they can be invested. A firm may invest its funds in the following:

1. Time deposits, including savings accounts earning daily interest, long-term savings accounts, and certificates of deposit
2. Money market funds, which are managed portfolios of short-term, high-grade debt instruments such as Treasury bills and commercial paper
3. Demand deposits that pay interest
4. U.S. Treasury securities

When cash receipts and disbursements are highly synchronized and predictable, a firm may keep a small cash balance. The financial manager must accurately forecast the amount of cash needed, its source, and its destination. These data are needed on both a short- and a long-term basis. Forecasting assists the manager in properly timing financing, debt repayment, and the amount to be transferred between accounts.

In deciding whether to adopt a cash management system, the financial manager should consider its associated costs versus the return earned from implementation of the system. Costs related to cash management systems include bank charges, financial manager's time, and office employee salaries. Some cash management systems use the firm's computer to make transactions with the computers of banks and money market funds. Computer systems are also useful for purchasing and selling securities in the money market.

Companies with many bank accounts should guard against accumulating excessive balances. Less cash needs to be kept on hand when a company can borrow quickly from a bank, such as under a *line of credit agreement*, which permits a firm to borrow instantly up to a specified maximum amount. A company may also find some cash unnecessarily tied up in other accounts, such as advances to employees. Excess cash should be invested in marketable securities for a return. Note however that cash in some bank accounts may not be available for investment. For instance, when a bank lends money to a company, the bank often requires the company to keep funds on hand as collateral. This deposit is called a compensating balance, which in effect represents *restricted* cash for the company.

Holding marketable securities serves as protection against cash shortages. Companies with seasonal operations may buy marketable securities when they have excess funds and then sell the securities when cash deficits occur. A firm may also invest in marketable securities when funds are being held temporarily in anticipation of short-term capital expansion. In selecting an investment portfolio, consideration should be given to return, default risk, marketability, and maturity date.

The thrust of cash management is to accelerate cash receipts and delay cash payments. Each bank account should be analyzed as to its type, balance, and cost so that corporate return is maximized.

Acceleration of Cash Inflow

To accelerate cash inflow, the financial manager must (1) know the bank's policy regarding fund availability, (2) know the source and location of company receipts, and (3) devise procedures for quick deposit of checks received and quick transfer of receipts in outlying accounts into the main corporate account.

The various types of check processing delays that must be analyzed are: (1) mail float—the time required for a check to move from a debtor to a creditor; (2) processing float—the time it takes for a creditor to deposit the check after receipt; and (3) deposit collection float—the time required for a check to clear.

Mail float can be minimized by having the collection center located near the customer. Local banks should be selected to speed the receipt of funds for subsequent transfer to the central corporate account. As an alternative, strategic post office lockboxes may be used for customer remissions. The local bank collects from these boxes periodically during the day and deposits the funds in the corporate account. The bank also furnishes the company with a computer listing of payments received by account and a daily total. Because the lockbox system has a significant per-item cost, it is most cost-effective with low-volume, high-dollar remissions. However, the system is becoming increasingly more available to companies with high-volume, low-dollar deposits as technological advances (such as machine-readable documents) lower the per-item cost of lockboxes.

Before a lockbox system is implemented, the company should make a cost-benefit analysis that considers the average dollar amount of checks received, the costs saved by having lockboxes, the reduction in mailing time per check, and the processing cost.

EXAMPLE 4.2 Chaset Corporation obtains average cash receipts of $200,000 per day. It usually takes 5 days from the time a check is mailed to its availability for use. The amount tied up by the delay is:

$$5 \text{ days} \times \$200,000 = \$1,000,000$$

EXAMPLE 4.3 It takes Travis Corporation about 7 days to receive and deposit payments from customers. Therefore, a lockbox system is being considered. It is expected that the system will reduce the float time to 5 days. Average daily collections are $500,000. The rate of return is 12 percent.

The reduction in outstanding cash balances arising from implementing the lockbox system is:

$$2 \text{ days} \times \$500,000 = \$1,000,000$$

The return that could be earned on these funds is:

$$\$1,000,000 \times 0.12 = \$120,000$$

The maximum monthly charge the company should pay for this lockbox arrangement is therefore:

$$\frac{\$120,000}{12} = \$10,000$$

EXAMPLE 4.4 Charles Corporation is exploring the use of a lockbox system that will cost $100,000 per year. Daily collections average $350,000. The lockbox arrangement will reduce the float period by 2 days. The firm's rate of return is 15 percent.

The cost-benefit analysis is shown below.

Return on early collection of cash	
$0.15 \times 2 \times \$350,000$	$105,000
Cost	100,000
Advantage of lockbox	$ 5,000

A corporate financial manager should determine whether it would be financially advantageous to split a geographic collection region into a number of parts.

EXAMPLE 4.5 Travis Company has an agreement with Charter Bank in which the bank handles $3 million in collections a day and requires a $700,000 compensating balance. Travis is thinking of canceling the agreement and dividing its western region so that two other banks will handle its business instead. Bank A will handle $1 million a day of collections, requiring a compensating balance of $300,000, and bank B will handle the other $2 million a day, asking for a compensating balance of $500,000. Travis's financial manager anticipates that collections will be accelerated by $\frac{1}{4}$ day if the western region is divided. The company's rate of return is 14 percent.

The financial manager decided that the new arrangement should be implemented, based on the following analysis:

Acceleration in cash receipts	
$3 million per day $\times \frac{1}{4}$ day	$750,000
Additional compensating balance	
required	100,000
Increased cash flow	$650,000
Rate of return	$\times$ 0.14
Net annual savings	$ 91,000

Concentration banking should also be considered for use. With this method funds are collected by several local banks and transferred to a main *concentration* account in another bank. The transfer of funds between banks should be accomplished through the use of depository transfer checks (DTCs) or wire transfers. In the DTC arrangement, there exists a resolution statement with the bank in which signatureless checks are allowed to be deposited. As the initial banks collect the funds, information is immediately transferred to the concentration bank, which then issues a DTC to collect the outlying funds. The funds may be available the same day.

Once remissions have been accelerated, freed cash should be used for investment in marketable securities or to pay off short-term debt. Thus, the freed cash will generate interest revenue to the business. The revenue derived can be determined for a given month by multiplying the monthly average accounts receivable balance times the associated monthly interest rate (i.e., the interest rate on marketable securities or the interest rate applicable to short-term debt).

EXAMPLE 4.6   A firm's weekly average cash balances are as follows:

Week	Average Cash Balance
1	$12,000
2	17,000
3	10,000
4	15,000
Total	$54,000

The monthly average cash balance is:

$$\frac{\$54,000}{4} = \$13,500$$

If the annual interest rate is approximated at 12 percent, the monthly return earned on the average cash balance is:

$$\$13,500 \times 0.1 = \$135$$

For a cash acceleration system to be feasible, the return earned on the freed cash must exceed the cost of the system.

Delay of Cash Outflow

There are various ways to delay cash disbursement, including:

1.   Using drafts to pay bills since drafts are not due on demand. When a bank receives a draft it must return the draft to the issuer for acceptance prior to payment. When the company accepts the draft, it then deposits the required funds with the bank; hence, a smaller average checking balance is maintained.

2.   Mailing checks from post offices having limited service or from locations where the mail must go through several handling points, lengthening the payment period.

3.   Drawing checks on remote banks or establishing cash disbursement centers in remote locations so that the payment period is lengthened. For example, someone in New York can be paid with a check drawn on a California bank.

4.   Using credit cards and charge accounts in order to lengthen the time between the acquisition of goods and the date of payment for those goods.

The cash disbursements of a firm may be controlled by centralizing its payable operation so that it satisfies its obligations at optimum times. Centralization will also facilitate the prediction of the disbursement float.

Payments to vendors should be delayed to the maximum as long as there is no associated finance charge or impairment of the company's credit rating. Of course, bills should not be paid prior to their due dates because of the time value of money.

A company can minimize its cash balances by using probabilities related to the expected time that checks will clear. Deposits, for example, may be made to a payroll checking account based on the expected time needed for the checks to clear.

Although not a delay of cash outflow, a company may reduce its cash outflow by the early repayment of a loan, thus avoiding some payment of interest. The company should consider the wire transfer of funds if a quick payment method is called for, especially if the payment is to be made to a distant location.

EXAMPLE 4.7 Every 2 weeks, company X disburses checks that average $500,000 and take 3 days to clear. How much money can the company save annually if it delays transfer of funds from an interest-bearing account that pays 0.0384 percent per day (annual rate of 14 percent) for those 3 days?

The interest for 3 days is:

$$\$500{,}000 \times (0.000384 \times 3) = \$576$$

The number of 2-week periods in a year is:

$$\frac{52 \text{ weeks}}{2 \text{ weeks}} = 26$$

The savings per year is:

$$\$576 \times 26 = \$14{,}976$$

Opportunity Cost of Foregoing a Cash Discount

An *opportunity cost* is the net revenue lost by rejecting an alternative action. A firm should typically take advantage of a discount offered by a creditor because of the associated high opportunity cost. For example, if the terms of sale are 2/10, net/30, the customer has 30 days to pay the bill but will get a 2 percent discount if he or she pays in 10 days. Some companies use seasonal datings such as 2/10, net/30, July 1 dating. Here, with an invoice dated July 1, the discount can be taken until July 10.

The following formula may be used to compute the opportunity cost in percentage, on an annual basis, of not taking a discount:

$$\text{Opportunity cost} = \frac{\text{discount percent}}{100 - \text{discount percent}} \times \frac{360}{N}$$

where N = the number of days payment can be delayed by foregoing the cash discount
   = days credit is outstanding − discount period

The numerator of the first term (discount percent) is the cost per dollar of credit, whereas the denominator (100 − discount percent) represents the money made available by foregoing the cash discount. The second term represents the number of times this cost is incurred in a year.

EXAMPLE 4.8 The opportunity cost of not taking a discount when the terms are 3/15, net/60 is computed as follows:

$$\text{Opportunity cost} = \frac{3}{100 - 3} \times \frac{360}{60 - 15} = \frac{3}{97} \times \frac{360}{45} = 24.7\%$$

Determination of Optimal Transaction Size

A model formulated by W. Baumol can be used to compute the optimum amount of transaction cash under conditions of certainty. The objective is to minimize fixed costs applicable to the transactions and the opportunity cost of retaining cash balances. The relevant costs take the following form:

$$\frac{F \cdot T}{Q} + \frac{i \cdot Q}{2}$$

where Q = the amount of marketable securities (such as Treasury bills) sold each time the cash
       balance is replenished
   F = the fixed cost associated with a transaction
   T = the total cash required for the given time period
   i = the interest rate earned on marketable securities

The optimum transaction size is

$$Q = \sqrt{\frac{2FT}{i}}$$

EXAMPLE 4.9   Harris Corp. predicts a cash requirement of $3,000 over a 1-month period in which cash is expected to be paid constantly. The opportunity interest rate is 12 percent per annum. The transaction cost associated with each borrowing or withdrawal is $50. (*a*) What is the optimal transaction size? (*b*) So we know how much cash is usually available to meet operating needs, what is the average cash balance?

(*a*)   Optimal transaction size:

$$Q = \sqrt{\frac{2FT}{i}} = \sqrt{\frac{2(\$50)(\$3,000)}{0.12 \div 12}} = \sqrt{\frac{\$300,000}{0.01}} = \$5,477.23$$

(*b*)   Average cash balance:

$$\frac{Q}{2} = \frac{\$5,477.23}{2} = \$2,738.62$$

4.4   MANAGEMENT OF ACCOUNTS RECEIVABLE

Consideration should be given to the company's investment in accounts receivable since there is an opportunity cost associated with holding receivable balances. The major decision regarding accounts receivable is the determination of the amount and terms of credit to extend to customers. The credit terms offered have a direct bearing on the associated costs and revenue to be generated from receivables. For example, if credit terms are tight, there will be less of an investment in accounts receivable and less bad debt losses, but there will also be lower sales and reduced profits.

In evaluating a potential customer's ability to pay, consideration should be given to the firm's integrity, financial soundness, collateral to be pledged, and current economic conditions. A customer's credit soundness may be evaluated through quantitative techniques such as regression analysis. Such techniques are most useful when a large number of small customers are involved. Bad debt losses can be estimated reliably when a company sells to many customers and when its credit policies have not changed for a long period of time.

The collection period for accounts receivable partly depends on the firm's credit policy and economic conditions, such as a recessionary environment, a period of limited or tight credit, or both.

In managing accounts receivable, the following procedures are recommended. First, establish a *credit policy*:

1.   A detailed review of a potential customer's soundness should be made prior to extending credit. Procedures such as a careful review of the customer's financial statements and credit rating, as well as a review of financial service reports (e.g., Dun & Bradstreet), are common.

2.   As customer financial health changes, credit limits should be revised.

3.   Marketing factors must be noted since an excessively restricted credit policy will lead to lost sales.

4.   If seasonal datings are used, the firm may offer more liberal payments than usual during slow periods in order to stimulate business by selling to customers who are unable to pay until later in the season. This policy is financially appropriate when the return on the additional sales plus the lowering in inventory costs is greater than the incremental cost associated with the additional investment in accounts receivable.

Second, establish policy concerning *billing*:

1.   Customer statements should be sent within 1 day subsequent to the close of the period.

2.   Large sales should be billed immediately.

3. Customers should be invoiced for goods when the order is processed rather than when it is shipped.

4. Billing for services should be done on an interim basis or immediately prior to the actual services. The billing process will be more uniform if cycle billing is employed.

5. The use of seasonal datings should be considered. (See item 4, concerning credit policy.)

Finally, establish policy concerning *collection*:

1. Accounts receivable should be aged[1] in order to identify delinquent and high-risk customers. The aging should be compared to industry norms.

2. Collection efforts should be undertaken at the very first sign of customer financial unsoundness.

EXAMPLE 4.10 Jones Corporation sells on terms of net/60. Its accounts are on the average 30 days past due. Annual credit sales are $500,000. The investment in accounts receivable is:

$$\frac{90}{360} \times \$500,000 = \$125,000$$

EXAMPLE 4.11 The cost of a given product is 40 percent of selling price, and carrying cost is 12 percent of selling price. On average, accounts are paid 90 days subsequent to the sale date. Sales average $40,000 per month. The investment in accounts receivable from this product is:

Accounts receivable:	
3 months × $40,000 sales =	$120,000
Investment in accounts receivable:	
$120,000 × (0.40 + 0.12) =	$ 62,400

EXAMPLE 4.12 A company has accounts receivable of $700,000. The average manufacturing cost is 40 percent of the sales price. The before-tax profit margin is 10 percent. The carrying cost of inventory is 3 percent of selling price. The sales commission is 8 percent of sales. The investment in accounts receivable is:

$$\$700,000(0.40 + 0.03 + 0.08) = \$700,000(0.51) = \$357,000$$

EXAMPLE 4.13 If a company's credit sales are $120,000, the collection period is 60 days, and the cost is 80 percent of sales price, what is (*a*) the average accounts receivable balance and (*b*) the average investment in accounts receivable?

(*a*)   Accounts receivable turnover: $\dfrac{360}{60} = 6$

$$\text{Average accounts receivable} = \frac{\text{credit sales}}{\text{turnover}} = \frac{\$120,000}{6} = \$20,000$$

(*b*)   Average investment in accounts receivable = $20,000 × 0.80 = $16,000

It pays for a firm to give a discount for early payment by customers when the return on the funds received early is greater than the cost of the discount.

---

[1] Aging is simply determining the length of time an account is past due.

EXAMPLE 4.14   Lakeside Corporation provides the following data:

Current annual credit sales	$12,000,000
Collection period	2 months
Terms	net/30
Rate of return	15%

Lakeside proposes to offer a 3/10, net/30 discount. The corporation anticipates 25 percent of its customers will take advantage of the discount. As a result of the discount policy, the collection period will be reduced to 1½ months. Should Lakeside offer the new terms?

The discount policy is disadvantageous, as indicated below.

Current average accounts receivable balance ($12,000,000/6)	$2,000,000

Average accounts receivable
    balance—after policy change
    ($12,000,000/8)
	1,500,000

Reduction in average accounts receivable	$ 500,000
Rate of return	×0.15
Dollar return earned	$ 75,000
Cost of discount (0.25 × $12,000,000 × 0.03)	$ 90,000
Disadvantage of discount policy ($90,000 − $75,000)	$ 15,000

A firm may consider offering credit to customers with a higher-than-normal risk rating. Here, the profitability on additional sales generated must be compared with the amount of additional bad debts expected, higher investing and collection costs, and the opportunity cost of tying up funds in receivables for a longer period of time. When idle capacity exists, the additional profitability represents the incremental contribution margin (sales less variable costs) since fixed costs remain the same. The incremental investment in receivables represents the average accounts receivable multiplied by the ratio of per-unit cost to selling price.

EXAMPLE 4.15   Joseph Corporation, which has idle capacity, provides the following data:

Selling price per unit	$80
Variable cost per unit	$50
Fixed cost per unit	$10
Annual credit sales	300,000 units
Collection period	2 months
Rate of return	16%

The corporation is considering a change in policy that will relax its credit standards. The following information applies to the proposal:

1.   Sales will increase by 20 percent.
2.   Collection period will go to 3 months.
3.   Bad debt losses are expected to be 3 percent of the increased sales.
4.   Collection costs are expected to increase by $20,000.

The analysis of its proposed credit policy change follows:

Concerning incremental profitability:

Increased unit sales (300,000 × 0.20)	60,000
Per-unit contribution margin ($80 − $50)	×$30
Incremental profit	$1,800,000

Concerning additional bad debts:

Incremental dollar sales (60,000 × $80)	$4,800,000
Bad debt percentage	×0.03
Additional bad debts	$ 144,000

New average unit cost is:

	Units	Unit Cost	Total Cost
Current	300,000	$60	$18,000,000
Increment	60,000	$50[a]	3,000,000
Total	360,000		$21,000,000

$$\text{New average unit cost} = \frac{\$21,000,000}{360,000} = \$58.33$$

[a] Since idle capacity exists, the per-unit cost on the incremental sales is solely the variable cost of $50.

Additional cost of higher investment in average accounts receivable is:

Investment in average accounts receivable after the change in policy	$5,249,700[a]
Current investment in average accounts receivable	3,000,000[b]
Incremental investment in average accounts receivable	$2,249,700
Rate of return	×0.16
Additional cost	$ 359,952

$$^{a}\; \frac{\text{Credit sales}}{\text{turnover}} \times \frac{\text{unit cost}}{\text{selling price}} = \frac{\$28,800,000}{4} \times \frac{\$58.33}{\$80.00} = \$5,249,700$$

$$^{b}\; \frac{\$24,000,000}{6} \times \frac{\$60}{\$80} = \$3,000,000$$

The net advantage/disadvantage is:

Incremental profitability		$1,800,000
Less: Additional bad debts	$144,000	
Additional collection costs	20,000	
Opportunity cost	359,952	523,952
Net advantage/disadvantage		$1,276,048

Since the net advantage is considerable, Joseph Corporation should relax its credit policy.

EXAMPLE 4.16 Wise Corporation is considering liberalizing its credit policy to encourage more customers to purchase on credit. Currently, 80 percent of sales are on credit and there is a gross margin of 30 percent. Other relevant data are:

	Currently	Proposal
Sales	$300,000	$450,000
Credit sales	$240,000	$360,000
Collection expenses	4% of credit sales	5% of credit sales
Accounts receivable turnover	4.5	3

An analysis of the proposal yields the following results:

Average accounts receivable balance (credit sales/accounts receivable turnover)	
Expected average accounts receivable ($360,000/3)	$120,000
Current average accounts receivable ($240,000/4.5)	53,333
Increase	$ 66,667
Gross profit	
Expected increase in credit sales ($360,000 − $240,000)	$120,000
Gross profit rate	0.30
Increase	$ 36,000
Collection expenses	
Expected collection expenses (0.05 × $360,000)	$ 18,000
Current collection expenses (0.04 × $240,000)	9,600
Increase	$ 8,400

Wise Corporation would benefit from a more liberal credit policy.

When a company is considering initiating a sales campaign in order to improve income, incremental profitability is compared to the cost of the discount and the opportunity cost associated with the higher investment in accounts receivable.

EXAMPLE 4.17 Drake Company is planning a sales campaign, during which Drake will offer credit terms of 4/20, net/60. Drake anticipates its collection period will rise from 70 days to 90 days. Data for the contemplated campaign are:

	% of Sales Prior to Campaign	% of Sales During Campaign
Cash sales	30	20
Payment from		
1–20	50	45
21–100	20	35

The proposed sales strategy will likely increase sales from $6 million to $7 million. The gross profit rate is 20 percent, and the rate of return is 12 percent. Sales discounts are given on cash sales.

An analysis of the proposed sales campaign is as follows:

	Sales Campaign		
	Without Campaign		With Campaign
Gross profit		$1,200,000		$1,400,000
Sales subject to discount				
0.8 × $6,000,000	$4,800,000			
0.65 × $7,000,000			$4,550,000	
Sales discount	×0.04	− 192,000	×0.04	− 182,000
Investment in average accounts receivable				
70/360 × $6,000,000 × 0.8	$ 933,333			
90/360 × $7,000,000 × 0.8			$1,400,000	
Rate of return	×0.12	− 112,000	×0.12	− 168,000
Net profit		$896,000		$1,050,000

Drake should initiate the sales program since it will generate an additional profit of $154,000.

A business may wish to evaluate a credit policy that would extend credit to currently limited-credit or no-credit customers. Full credit should only be given to a customer category if net earnings ensue.

EXAMPLE 4.18 TGD Corporation has three credit categories (X, Y, Z) and is considering changing its credit policy for categories Y and Z. The pertinent data are:

Category	Bad Debt (%)	Collection Period (Days)	Credit Terms	Additional Annual Sales if Credit Restrictions Are Eased
X	2	30	Full	$100,000
Y	5	50	Restricted	$400,000
Z	13	80	No credit	$900,000

Gross profit approximates 15 percent of sales. The rate of return is 16 percent.
Analysis of the data yields the following results:

	Category Y	Category Z
Gross profit		
$400,000 × 0.15	$60,000	
$900,000 × 0.15		$135,000
Increment in bad debts		
$400,000 × 0.05	− 20,000	
$900,000 × 0.13		− 117,000
Incremental average in accounts receivable		
50/360 × 0.85 × $400,000	$47,222	
80/360 × 0.85 × $900,000		$170,000
Rate of return	×0.16	×0.16
Additional cost	−7,556	−27,200
Net profitability	$32,444	$ −9,200

Credit should be eased only for category Y. Extending credit to category Z is likely to incur a loss for the company.

4.5 INVENTORY MANAGEMENT

The three types of inventory are: (1) raw materials, which are materials acquired from a supplier that will be used in the manufacture of goods; (2) work-in-process, which is partially completed goods at the end of the accounting period; and (3) finished goods, which are completed goods awaiting sale.

In managing inventory, the financial manager should:

1. Appraise the adequacy of the raw materials level, which depends on expected production, condition of equipment, and any seasonal considerations of business.

2. Forecast future movements in raw materials prices, so that if prices are expected to increase, additional material is purchased at the lower price.

3. Discard slow-moving products to reduce inventory carrying costs and improve cash flow.

4. Guard against inventory buildup, since it is associated with substantial carrying and opportunity costs.

5. Minimize inventory levels when liquidity and/or inventory financing problems exist.

6. Plan for a stock inventory balance that will guard against and cushion the possible loss of business from a material shortage.

7. Examine the quality of merchandise received. In this connection, the ratio of purchase returns to purchases should be examined. A sharp increase in the ratio indicates that a new supplier may be needed.

8. Keep a careful record of back orders. A high back order level indicates that less inventory balances are required. This is because back orders may be used as indicators of the production required, resulting in improved production planning and procurement. The trend in the ratio of the dollar amount of back orders to the average per-day sales will prove useful.

9. Appraise the acquisition and inventory control functions. Any problems must be identified and rectified. In areas where control is weak, inventory balances should be restricted.

10. Closely supervise warehouse and materials handling staff to guard against theft loss and to maximize efficiency.

11. Minimize the lead time in the acquisition, manufacturing, and distribution functions. The lead time in receiving goods is determined by dividing the value of outstanding orders by the average daily purchases. This ratio may indicate whether an increase in inventory stocking is required or whether the purchasing pattern should be altered.

12. Examine the time between raw materials input and the completion of production to see if production and engineering techniques can be implemented to hasten the production operation.

13. Examine the degree of spoilage.

14. Maintain proper inventory control, such as through the application of computer techniques and operations research.

The financial manager must also consider the risk associated with inventory. For example, technological, perishable, fashionable, flammable, and specialized goods usually have a high realization risk. The nature of the risk associated with the particular inventory item should be taken into account in computing the desired inventory level.

Inventory management involves a trade-off between the costs associated with keeping inventory versus the benefits of holding inventory. Higher inventory levels result in increased costs from storage, insurance, spoilage, and interest on borrowed funds needed to finance inventory acquisition. However, an increase in inventory lowers the possibility of lost sales from stockouts and the incidence of production slowdowns from inadequate inventory. Further, large volume purchases will result in greater purchase discounts. Inventory levels are also influenced by short-term interest rates. For example, as short-term interest rates increase, the optimum level of holding inventory will be reduced.

Inventory should be counted at regular, cyclic intervals because this provides the ability to check inventory on an ongoing basis as well as to reconcile the book and physical amounts. Cyclic counting has the following advantages:

1. It allows for an efficient use of a few full-time experienced counters throughout the year.

2. It enables the timely detection and correction of the causes of inventory error.

3. It does not require a plant shutdown, as does a year-end count.

4. It facilitates the modification of computer inventory programs if needed.

A quantity discount may be received when purchasing large orders. The discount serves as a reduction of the acquisition cost of materials.

EXAMPLE 4.19 A company purchases 1,000 units of an item having a list price of $10 each. The quantity discount is 5 percent. The net cost of the item is:

Acquisition cost (1,000 × $10)	$10,000
Less: Discount (0.05 × $10,000)	500
Net cost	$ 9,500

The average investment in inventory should be considered.

EXAMPLE 4.20 Savon Corporation places an order for 5,000 units at the beginning of the year. Each unit costs $10. The average investment is:

Average inventory[a]	2,500 units
Unit cost, $	×$10
Average investment	$25,000

$$^a \quad \frac{\text{Quantity }(Q)}{2} = \frac{5,000}{2}$$

The more frequently a company places an order, the lower will be the average investment.

Carrying and Ordering Costs

Inventory carrying costs include those for warehousing, handling, insurance, and property taxes. A provisional cost for spoilage and obsolescence should also be included in an analysis of inventory. In addition, the opportunity cost of holding inventory balances must be considered. Assuming that the carrying cost per unit is constant, then

$$\text{Carrying cost} = \frac{Q}{2} \times C$$

where $Q/2$ represents average quantity and C is the carrying cost per unit.

Inventory ordering costs are the costs of placing an order and receiving the merchandise. They include freight charges and the clerical costs to place an order. In the case of produced items, they also include the scheduling cost. The ordering cost per unit is assumed to be constant.

$$\text{Ordering cost} = \frac{S}{Q} \times P$$

where S = total usage

Q = quantity per order

P = cost of placing an order

The total inventory cost is therefore:

$$\frac{QC}{2} + \frac{SP}{C}$$

A trade-off exists between ordering and carrying costs. A greater order quantity will increase carrying costs but lower ordering costs.

Economic Order Quantity (EOQ)

The economic order quantity (EOQ) is the optimum amount of goods to order each time an order is placed so that total inventory costs are minimized.

$$\text{EOQ} = \sqrt{\frac{2SP}{C}}$$

The number of orders to be made for a period is the usage (S) divided by the EOQ.

EXAMPLE 4.21 Winston Corporation needs to know how frequently to place their orders. They provide the following information:

$$S = 500 \text{ units per month}$$
$$P = \$40 \text{ per order}$$
$$C = \$4 \text{ per unit}$$

$$\text{EOQ} = \sqrt{\frac{2SP}{C}} = \sqrt{\frac{2(500)(40)}{4}} = \sqrt{10,000} = 100 \text{ units}$$

The number of orders required each month is:

$$\frac{S}{\text{EOQ}} = \frac{500}{100} = 5$$

Therefore, an order should be placed about every 6 days (31/5).

EXAMPLE 4.22 Apex Appliance Store is determining its frequency of orders for toasters. Each toaster costs $15. The annual carrying costs are approximated at $200. The ordering cost is $10. Apex expects to sell 50 toasters each month. Its desired average inventory level is 40.

$$S = 50 \times 12 = 600$$
$$P = \$10$$
$$C = \frac{\text{purchase price} \times \text{carrying cost}}{\text{average investment}} = \frac{\$15 \times \$200}{40 \times \$15} = \$5$$

$$\text{EOQ} = \sqrt{\frac{2SP}{C}} = \sqrt{\frac{2(600)(10)}{5}} = \sqrt{\frac{12,000}{5}} = \sqrt{2,400} = 49 \text{ (rounded)}$$

The number of orders per year is:

$$\frac{S}{\text{EOQ}} = \frac{600}{49} = 12 \text{ orders (rounded)}$$

Apex Appliance should place an order about every 30 days (365/12).

During periods of inflation and tight credit, a company should be flexible in its inventory management policies. For example, its EOQ model will have to be modified to reflect rising costs.

Stockouts

Stockout of raw materials or work-in-process can result in a shutdown or slowdown in the production process. In order to avoid a stockout situation, a safety stock level should be maintained. Safety stock is the minimum inventory amount needed for an item, based on anticipated usage and the expected delivery time of materials. This cushion guards against unusual product demand or unexpected delivery problems.

EXAMPLE 4.23 Winston Corporation places an order when its inventory level reaches 210 rather than 180 units. Its safety stock is 30 units. In other words, the company expects to be stocked with 30 units when the new order is received.

The optimum safety stock level is the point where the increased carrying cost equals the opportunity cost associated with a potential stockout. The increased carrying cost is equal to the carrying cost per unit multiplied by the safety stock.

$$\text{Stockout cost} = \text{number of orders} \left(\frac{\text{usage}}{\text{order quantity}} \right) \times \text{stockout units}$$
$$\times \text{ unit stockout cost} \times \text{probability of a stockout}$$

EXAMPLE 4.24 Tristar Corporation uses 100,000 units annually. Each order placed is for 10,000 units. Stockout is 1,000 units; this amount is the difference between the maximum daily usage during the lead time less the reorder point, ignoring a safety stock factor. The stockout probability management wishes to take is 30 percent. The per-unit stockout cost is \$2.30. The carrying cost per unit is \$5. The inventory manager must determine (*a*) the stockout cost and (*b*) the amount of safety stock to keep on hand.

(*a*) $$\text{Stockout cost} = \frac{\text{usage}}{\text{order quantity}} \times \text{stockout units} \times \text{unit stockout cost} \times \text{probability of a stockout}$$

$$= \frac{100,000}{10,000} \times 1,000 \times \$2.30 \times 0.3 = \$6,900$$

(*b*) Let X = safety stock

$$\text{Stockout cost} = \text{carrying cost of safety stock}$$
$$\$6,900 = \$5X$$
$$1,380 \text{ units} = X$$

Economic Order Point (EOP)

The economic order point is the inventory level that signals the time to reorder merchandise at the EOQ amount. Safety stock is provided for in the computation.

$$\text{EOP} = SL + F\sqrt{S(\text{EOQ})(L)}$$

where L = the lead time
   F = the stockout acceptance factor

EXAMPLE 4.25 Blake Corporation provides the following data:

$$S = 2,000 \text{ units per month}$$
$$\text{EOQ} = 75 \text{ units}$$
$$L = \tfrac{1}{4} \text{ of a month}$$
$$F = 1.29, \text{ which represents the acceptable stockout level of 10 percent}$$
$$\text{EOP} = SL + F\sqrt{S(\text{EOQ})(L)} = (2,000)(\tfrac{1}{4}) + 1.29\sqrt{2,000(75)(\tfrac{1}{4})}$$
$$= 500 + 1.29\sqrt{37,500} = 500 + 1.29(193.6) = 750 \text{ (rounded)}$$

The financial manager should attempt to determine the inventory level that results in the greatest savings.

EXAMPLE 4.26 Frost Corporation is thinking of revising its inventory policy. The current inventory turnover is 16 times. Variable costs are 70 percent of sales. If inventory levels are increased, Frost anticipates additional sales generated and less of an incidence of inventory stockouts. The rate of return is 17 percent.

Actual and estimated sales and inventory turnover are as follows:

Sales	Turnover
$700,000	16
$780,000	14
$850,000	11
$940,000	7

Frost's financial manager can now compute the inventory level that will result in the highest net savings.

A	B	C	D	E	F
		Average Inventory	Opportunity Cost Associated with Additional	Additional	Net Savings
Sales	Turnover	(A ÷ B)	Inventory[a]	Profitability[b]	(E − D)
$700,000	16	$43,750			
$780,000	14	$55,714	$2,034	$24,000	$21,966
$850,000	11	$77,273	$3,665	$21,000	$17,335
$940,000	7	$134,286	$9,692	$27,000	$17,308

[a] Incremental average inventory balance × 0.17 (the rate of return)

[b] Incremental sales × 0.30 (contribution margin)

The best inventory level is 55,714 units, since the greatest savings result at this point.

ABC Inventory Control Method

The ABC method of inventory control requires the classification of inventory into one of three groups, A, B, or C. Group A items are most expensive, group B less expensive, and group C the least expensive. The higher the value of the inventory items, the more control should be exercised over them.

Inventory should be analyzed frequently when using the ABC method. The procedure for constructing an ABC analysis follows:

1. Separate each type of inventory, such as finished goods, work-in-process, and raw materials.
2. Calculate the annual dollar usage for each type of inventory by multiplying the unit cost times the expected future annual usage.
3. Rank each inventory type from high to low, based on annual dollar usage.
4. Classify the inventory as A, B, or C, based on the top 20 percent, the next 30 percent, and the last 50 percent valuation, respectively.
5. Tag the inventory with ABC classifications and record those classifications in the item inventory master records.

Figure 4-1 illustrates the ABC distribution.

Inventory Classification	Population (%)	$ Usage (%)
A	20	80
B	30	15
C	50	5

Fig. 4-1 ABC inventory distribution

The ABC analysis becomes a tool with which the materials manager checks the accuracy of his or her records. More time is spent checking A category items than B and C items. The financial manager should establish an audit program for those records and items that have the greatest impact on profitability based on the ABC analysis.

Review Questions

1. _____ equals current assets less current liabilities.

2. In managing working capital, one should consider the trade-off between _____ and _____ .

3. The financing of long-term assets with long-term debt is referred to as _____ .

4. Cash consists of _____ and _____ .

5. Cash held for emergency purposes is referred to as a(n) _____ balance.

6. Excess cash that will be needed in the near future should be temporarily invested in _____ securities.

7. The term _____ refers to funds retained by the bank on a loan made to the company.

8. The time required for a check to go from the maker to the payee is referred to as _____ .

9. The time needed for a check to clear is referred to as _____ .

10. A(n) _____ system is one in which a local bank picks up customer remissions from a post office box.

11. _____ is a system of collection in which a local bank receives funds and transfers them to a main concentration bank account.

12. One way to defer a cash payment is by the use of a(n) _____ , because the bank must first secure approval from the company before the instrument is paid.

13. The terms of a $1,000 sale are 3/20, net/40. If collection is received in 14 days, the amount received is $ _____ .

14. Partially completed merchandise at year-end is referred to as _____ inventory.

15. Inventory consisting of fashionable merchandise has high _____ risk.

16. _____ refers to the cost of holding inventory.

17. As the order size increases, carrying cost _____ and ordering cost _____ .

18. The optimum amount to order each time is referred to as the _____ .

19. The optimum inventory level requiring a reorder of goods is referred to as the _____ .

20. The _____ method requires that greater control be exercised over higher-valued merchandise.

Answers: (1) Net working capital; (2) risk, return; (3) hedging; (4) currency, demand deposits; (5) precautionary; (6) marketable; (7) compensating balance; (8) mail float; (9) deposit collection float; (10) lockbox; (11) Concentration banking; (12) draft; (13) 970; (14) work-in-process; (15) realization; (16) Carrying cost; (17) increases, decreases; (18) economic order quantity (EOQ); (19) economic order point (EOP); (20) ABC.

Solved Problems

4.1   **Net Working Capital.** Winston Corporation has the following selected assets and liabilities:

Cash	$15,000
Accounts receivable	$20,000
Inventory	$37,000
Land	$70,000
Building	$190,000
Goodwill	$26,000
Accounts payable	$13,000
Salaries payable	$7,000
Taxes payable	$19,000
Mortgage payable	$80,000
Common stock	$100,000
Retained earnings	$82,000

Determine the company's net working capital.

SOLUTION

CURRENT ASSETS		
Cash	$15,000	
Accounts receivable	20,000	
Inventory	37,000	$72,000
CURRENT LIABILITIES		
Accounts payable	$13,000	
Salaries payable	7,000	
Taxes payable	19,000	39,000
Net working capital		$33,000

4.2   Delay in Cash Receipt. Blake Corporation receives average daily cash receipts of $140,000. The finance manager has determined that the time period between the mailing of a check and its actual availability for corporate use is 4 days. What is the amount of cash being tied up because of the delay?

SOLUTION

$$4 \text{ days} \times \$140,000 = \$560,000$$

4.3 · Lockbox. It typically takes Lawrence Corporation 8 days to receive and deposit customer remissions. Lawrence is considering a lockbox system and anticipates that the system will reduce the float time to 5 days. Average daily cash receipts are $220,000. The rate of return is 10 percent.

(a) What is the reduction in cash balances associated with implementing the system? (b) What is the rate of return associated with the earlier receipt of the funds? (c) What should be the maximum monthly charge associated with the lockbox proposal?

SOLUTION

(a) $220,000 \times 3$ days = $660,000

(b) $0.10 \times \$660,000 = \$66,000$

(c) $\dfrac{\$66,000}{12} = \$5,500$

4.4   Lockbox. Doral Corporation is considering a lockbox arrangement that will cost $216,000 per year. Average daily collections are $450,000. As a result of the system, the float time will be reduced by 3 days. The rate of return is 14 percent. Should the lockbox arrangement be instituted?

SOLUTION

Cost	$216,000
Return on freed cash ($0.14 \times 3 \times \$450,000$)	189,000
Disadvantage of lockbox	$ 27,000

The lockbox should not be used.

4.5 **Dividing of Region.** Boston Corporation has an arrangement with XYZ Bank in which the bank handles $5 million a day in collections but requires a $420,000 compensating balance. The company is considering withdrawing from the arrangement and dividing its southern region so that two other banks will handle the business instead. Bank S will handle $3 million a day of collections and require a $450,000 compensating balance, and bank T will handle the other $2 million a day and require a compensating balance of $350,000. By dividing the southern region, collections will be accelerated by $\frac{1}{2}$ day. The rate of return is 17 percent. Should the southern region be divided?

SOLUTION

Accelerated cash inflow	
$5 million per day $\times \frac{1}{2}$ day	$2,500,000
Incremental compensating balance required	380,000
Increased cash flow	$2,120,000
Rate of return	×0.17
Net annual savings	$ 360,400

Yes, the southern region should be divided, as doing so will save the company $360,400 per year.

4.6 **Average Cash Balance.** Dane Company's weekly average cash balances are:

Week	Average Cash Balance
1	$15,000
2	19,000
3	12,000
4	17,000
Total	$63,000

(*a*) What is the monthly average cash balance? (*b*) Assuming an annual interest rate of 15 percent, what is the monthly rate of return earned on the average cash balance?

SOLUTION

(*a*)
$$\frac{\$63,000}{4} = \$15,750$$

(*b*)
$$\$15,750 \times (0.15 \div 12) = \$196.88$$

4.7 **Book Balance versus Bank Balance.** Company P writes checks averaging $30,000 per day that require 4 days to clear. By what amount will its book balance be less than its bank balance?

SOLUTION

$$\$30,000 \times 4 \text{ days} = \$120,000$$

4.8 **Opportunity Cost of Not Taking Discount.** What is the opportunity cost of not taking a discount when the terms are 2/20, net/45?

SOLUTION

$$\text{Opportunity cost} = \frac{\text{discount percent}}{100 - \text{discount percent}} \times \frac{360}{N} = \frac{2}{98} \times \frac{360}{25} = 29.4\%$$

4.9 **Optimal Cash Transaction Size.** Green Corporation anticipates a cash requirement of $1,000 over a 1-month period. It is expected that cash will be paid uniformly. The annual interest rate is 24 percent. The transaction cost of each borrowing or withdrawal is $30. (*a*) What is the optimal transaction size? (*b*) What is the average cash balance?

SOLUTION

(*a*) The optimum transaction size is:

$$Q = \sqrt{\frac{2FT}{i}} = \sqrt{\frac{2(30)(1,000)}{0.24 \div 12^a}} = \sqrt{\frac{60,000}{0.02}} = \$1,732.05$$

(*b*) The average cash balance is:

$$\frac{Q}{2} = \frac{\$1,732.05}{2} = \$866.03$$

---

^{a} Monthly interest rate $= \dfrac{0.24 \text{ annual interest rate}}{12 \text{ months}} = 0.02$

4.10 **Date of Cash Receipt.** The terms of sale are 3/20, net/45, May 1 dating. What is the last date the customer may pay in order to receive the discount?

SOLUTION

May 20.

4.11 **Average Investment in Accounts Receivable.** Milich Corporation sells on terms of net/90. Their accounts receivable are on average 20 days past due. If annual credit sales are $800,000, what is the company's average investment in accounts receivable?

SOLUTION

$$\frac{90+20}{360} \times \$800,000 = \$244,444$$

4.12 **Average Investment in Accounts Receivable.** The cost of product X is 30 percent of its selling price, and the carrying cost is 8 percent of selling price. Accounts are paid on average 60 days after sale. Sales per month average $25,000. What is the investment in accounts receivable?

SOLUTION

Accounts receivable $= 2$ months $\times$ \$25,000 sales $=$ \$50,000
Investment in accounts receivable $=$ \$50,000 $\times$ 0.38 $=$ \$19,000

4.13 **Average Investment in Accounts Receivable.** Levine Corporation has accounts receivable of $400,000. Its manufacturing cost approximates 35 percent of selling price. The before-tax profit margin is 16 percent, and the inventory carrying cost is 4 percent of the selling price. Sales commissions are 7 percent of sales. What is Levine's average investment in accounts receivable?

SOLUTION

Average investment in accounts receivable $=$ \$400,000(0.35 + 0.04 + 0.07) $=$ \$400,000(0.46) $=$ \$184,000

4.14   Average Investment in Accounts Receivable. Ajax Company's credit sales are $300,000, and the collection period is 90 days. Cost is 70 percent of selling price. Determine Ajax's average investment in accounts receivable.

SOLUTION

$$\text{Accounts receivable turnover} = \frac{360}{90} = 4$$

$$\text{Average accounts receivable} = \frac{\$300,000}{4} = \$75,000$$

$$\text{Average investment in accounts receivable} = \$75,000 \times 0.70 = \$52,500$$

4.15   Discount Policy. Stevens Company presents the following information:

Current annual credit sales:	$24,000,000
Collection period:	3 months
Terms:	net/30
Rate of return:	18%

The company is considering offering a 4/10, net/30 discount. It anticipates that 30 percent of its customers will take advantage of the discount. The collection period is expected to decrease to 2 months. Should the discount policy be implemented?

SOLUTION

Current average accounts receivable balance ($24,000,000/4)	$6,000,000
Average accounts receivable balance—after change in policy ($24,000,000/6)	4,000,000
Reduction in average accounts receivable	$2,000,000
Interest rate	×0.18
Rate of return	$ 360,000
Cost of discount (0.30 × $24,000,000 × 0.04)	$ 288,000
Advantage of discount policy ($360,000 − $288,000)	$ 72,000

Yes, Stevens Company should implement the discount policy.

4.16   Credit Policy. Nelson Corporation reports the following information:

Selling price per unit	$70
Variable cost per unit	$45
Fixed cost per unit	$15
Annual credit sales	400,000 units
Collection period	3 months
Rate of return	19%

The company is considering easing its credit standards. If it does, the following is expected to result: Sales will increase by 25 percent; collection period will increase to 4 months; bad debt losses are anticipated to be 4 percent on the incremental sales; and collection costs will increase by $34,000.

Should the proposed relaxation in credit standards be implemented?

SOLUTION

Incremental profitability:

Increased unit sales (400,000 × 0.25)	100,000
Contribution margin per unit ($70 − $45)	×$25
Incremental profit	$2,500,000

Increased bad debts:

Incremental dollar sales (100,000 × $70)	$7,000,000
Uncollectibility percentage	×0.04
Additional bad debts	$280,000

To determine the opportunity cost of the increased investment in accounts receivable, we first need to calculate the new average unit cost, as follows:

	Units	Unit Cost	Total Cost
Present	400,000	$60	$24,000,000
Increment	100,000	$45	4,500,000
Total	500,000		$28,500,000

$$\text{New average unit cost} = \frac{\$28,500,000}{500,000} = \$57$$

Additional cost:

Investment in average accounts receivable [(credit sales/turnover) × (unit cost/selling price)]		
After change in policy [($35,000,000/3) × ($57/$70)]		$9,500,000
Current [($28,000,000/4) × ($60/$70)]		6,000,000
Incremental		$3,500,000
Rate of return		×0.19
Opportunity cost		$ 665,000

Net advantage/disadvantage of proposal:

Additional profitability		$2,500,000
Less: Increased bad debts	$280,000	
Increased collection costs	34,000	
Opportunity cost	665,000	979,000
Net advantage		$1,521,000

Thus, the Nelson Corporation would benefit from relaxing its credit policy as proposed.

4.17 Credit Policy. Simon Corporation is evaluating a relaxation of its credit policy. At present, 70 percent of sales are on credit and there is a gross margin of 20 percent. Additional data are:

	Current	Anticipated
Sales	$500,000	$640,000
Credit sales	$410,000	$520,000
Collection expenses	3% of credit sales	4% of credit sales
Collection period	72 days	90 days

Using 360 days in a year, answer the following questions: (*a*) What is the change in gross profit associated with the proposal? (*b*) What is the incremental change in collection expenses? (*c*) What is the change in average accounts receivable?

SOLUTION

(*a*)

Incremental credit sales	$110,000
Gross profit rate	×0.20
Increase in gross profit	$ 22,000

(*b*)

Collection expenses with proposal (0.04 × $520,000)	$ 20,800
Collection expenses currently (0.03 × $410,000)	12,300
Increase in collection expenses	$ 8,500

(*c*) Average accounts receivable after change in policy are:

Credit sales/accounts receivable turnover ($520,000/4)	$130,000
Current average accounts receivable ($410,000/5)	82,000
Increase in average accounts receivable	$ 48,000

4.18 Sales Campaign. Jones Corporation is considering a sales campaign in which it will offer credit terms of 3/15, net/80. The finance manager expects that the collection period will increase from 90 days to 110 days. Information before and during the proposed campaign follows:

	% of Sales before Campaign	% of Sales during Campaign
Cash sales	20	10
Payment from		
1–15	35	25
16–120	45	65

The sales campaign is expected to raise sales from $5 million to $6 million. The gross profit rate is 30 percent and the rate of return is 16 percent. Sales discounts are given on cash sales.

Should the sales campaign be initiated?

SOLUTION

	Without Sales Campaign		With Sales Campaign	
Gross profit		$1,500,000		$1,800,000
Sales subject to discount				
$0.55 \times \$5,000,000$	$2,750,000			
$0.35 \times \$6,000,000$			$2,100,000	
Sales discount	×0.03	−82,500	×0.03	−63,000
Investment in average accounts receivable				
$(90/360) \times \$5,000,000 \times 0.7$	$ 875,000			
$(110/360) \times \$6,000,000 \times 0.7$			$1,283,333	
Rate of return	×0.16	−140,000	×0.16	−205,333
Net profit		$1,277,500		$1,531,667

The sales campaign should be implemented because it results in an incremental profit of $254,167.

4.19 Credit Policy. Wilder Corporation is considering granting credit to currently limited customers or no-credit customers. The following information is given:

Category	Bad Debt Percentage	Collection Period	Credit Terms	Incremental Annual Sales Accompanying Relaxation in Credit Standards
A	3%	20 days	Full	$250,000
B	6%	45 days	Restricted	$540,000
C	10%	90 days	No credit	$800,000

Gross profit approximates 12 percent of sales. The rate of return is 18 percent. Should credit be extended to categories B and C?

SOLUTION

	Category B	Category C
Gross profit		
$540,000 \times 0.12$	$64,800	
$800,000 \times 0.12$		$96,000
Less: Increased bad debts		
$540,000 \times 0.06$	−32,400	
$800,000 \times 0.10$		−80,000
Incremental investment in average accounts receivable		
$(45/360) \times 0.88 \times \$540,000$	$59,400	
$(90/360) \times 0.88 \times \$800,000$		$176,000
Rate of return	×0.18	×0.18
Opportunity cost	−10,692	−31,680
Net profit	$21,708	−$15,680

Credit should be extended only to category B.

4.20 **Materials Cost.** Grason Corporation purchases 3,000 units of a raw material at a list price of $5 each. The supplier offers a quantity discount of 4 percent. What is the material cost of the item?

SOLUTION

Acquisition cost (3,000 × $5)	$15,000
Less: Discount (0.04 × $15,000)	600
Net cost	$14,400

4.21 **Average Investment in Inventory.** West Corporation orders 4,000 units of a product at the beginning of the period for $7 each. What is West Corporation's average investment in inventory?

SOLUTION

Average inventory ($Q/2 = 4,000/2$)	2,000 units
Unit cost ($)	×7
Average investment	$14,000

4.22 **Ordering Cost.** Charles Corporation uses 8,500 units per year. Each order is for 200 units. The cost per order is $13. What is the total ordering cost for the year?

SOLUTION

$$\frac{8,500}{200} \times \$13 = \$552.50$$

4.23 **Economic Order Quantity.** Luster Corporation presents the following data: Usage is 400 units per month, cost per order is $20, and carrying cost per unit is $6.

Given these data, answer the following questions: (*a*) What is the economic order quantity? (*b*) How many orders are required each month? (*c*) How often should each order be placed?

SOLUTION

(*a*)
$$\text{EOQ} = \sqrt{\frac{2SP}{C}} = \sqrt{\frac{2(400)(20)}{6}} = \sqrt{\frac{16,000}{6}} = 52 \text{ (rounded)}$$

(*b*)
$$\frac{S}{\text{EOQ}} = \frac{400}{52} = 8 \text{ (rounded)}$$

(*c*)
$$\frac{31}{8} = \text{every 4 days}$$

4.24 **Stockout Cost.** Boston Corporation uses 30,000 units. Each order placed is for 1,500 units. The stockout units is 300. Management is willing to accept a stockout probability of 40 percent. The stockout cost per unit is $3.20. What is the total stockout cost?

SOLUTION

$$\text{Stockout cost} = \frac{\text{usage}}{\text{order quantity}} \times \text{stockout units} \times \text{unit stockout cost} \times \text{probability of stockout}$$

$$= \frac{30,000}{1,500} \times 300 \times \$3.20 \times 0.4 = \$7,680$$

4.25   Economic Order Point. Met Corporation reports the following data regarding one of its inventory items: Usage is 5,000 units per month, EOQ is 100 units, and lead time is $\frac{1}{2}$ month. The stockout acceptance factor is 1.29, which represents an acceptable stockout percentage of 10 percent.

Determine the economic order point.

SOLUTION

$$\begin{aligned}
EOP &= SL + F\sqrt{S(EOQ)(L)} \\
&= (5,000)(\tfrac{1}{2}) + 1.29\sqrt{5,000(100)(\tfrac{1}{2})} \\
&= 2,500 + 1.29\sqrt{250,000} = 2,500 + 1.29(500) = 3,145
\end{aligned}$$

4.26   Inventory Management. XYZ Appliance Store sells an average of 160 units per month. Each order the store places is for 300 units. The cost per unit is $5. The cost per order is $12. Carrying cost is $0.15 per dollar invested per year. The rate of return is 18 percent. The tax rate is 46 percent.

(a) What is the investment in average inventory? (b) What is the annual ordering cost? (c) What is the annual holding cost? (d) What is the opportunity cost of holding inventory? (e) What is the total cost of the inventory excluding the purchase price?

SOLUTION

(a)
$$\text{Average inventory} = \frac{Q}{2} = \frac{300}{2} = 150$$
$$\text{Investment in average inventory} = 150 \times \$5 = \$750$$

(b)
$$\text{Ordering cost} = \frac{S}{Q} \times P = \frac{160 \times 12}{300} \times \$12 = \$76.80$$

(c)
$$\text{Holding cost} = \text{carrying cost} \times \text{investment in average inventory}$$
$$= 0.15 \times \$750 = \$112.50$$

(d)
$$\text{Opportunity cost} = \text{rate of return} \times \text{investment in average inventory}$$
$$= 0.18 \times \$750 = \$135$$

(e)
$$\text{Inventory cost (excluding purchase price)}$$
$$= (100 - \text{tax rate}) \times (\text{ordering cost} + \text{holding cost}) + \text{opportunity cost}$$
$$= 0.54(\$76.80 + \$112.50) + \$135 = \$237.22$$

4.27   Optimum Inventory Level. Saft Corporation is considering changing its inventory policy. At present, the inventory turns over 12 times per year. Variable costs are 60 percent of sales. The rate of return is 21 percent. Sales and inventory turnover data follow:

Sales	Turnover
$800,000	12
$870,000	10
$950,000	7
$1,200,000	5

Determine the inventory level that results in the greatest net savings.

	A	B	C	D	E	F
			Average Inventory (A ÷ B)	Opportunity Cost Associated with Additional Inventory[a]	Additional Profitability[b]	Net Savings (E − D)
	Sales	Turnover				
	$800,000	12	$66,666			
	$870,000	10	$87,000	$4,270	$28,000	$23,730
	$950,000	7	$135,714	$10,230	$32,000	$21,770
	$1,200,000	5	$240,000	$21,900	$100,000	$78,100

[a] Incremental average inventory balance × 0.21.

[b] Incremental sales × 0.40

The inventory level that results in the greatest net savings is 240,000 units.

4.28 Lockbox System. Tunequip, Inc., is a wholesale distributor of specialized audio equipment, tapes, and records. Annual sales are projected at $27 million for the 19X1 fiscal year, and the average accounts receivable balance is estimated at $2.5 million. The average invoice size is $1,000. Customers pay their accounts by check, which are mailed to corporate headquarters in Florida.

The finance manager of Tunequip is examining the firm's cash handling techniques to find ways to reduce borrowing requirements and financing costs. One alternative under consideration is the establishment of a lockbox system to handle collections from customers in the western United States. Those customers are expected to account for $10.8 million of Tunequip's total projected sales in 19X1. Tunequip could acquire the use of the funds a day earlier if the western customers mailed their checks to a post office box in Utah. The Utah National Bank would process the payments mailed to the post office box; they would deposit the checks in Tunequip's account in Utah National, wire transfer the money to the Florida National Bank (Tunequip's primary bank), and send the payment information by mail. Utah National Bank's charge for operating the lockbox system would be a flat fee of $80 per month plus $0.10 for each paid invoice handled; in addition the Utah bank would require Tunequip to maintain a $5,000 minimum cash balance with the bank.

There would be no change in Tunequip's relationship with Florida National Bank. The finance manager estimates that Tunequip would be able to borrow funds from Florida National Bank during 19X1 at an interest rate of 9 percent.

(*a*) If Tunequip, Inc., established the lockbox system for its western customers, calculate (1) the annual cost of operating the lockbox system, and (2) the dollar amount of the change in the level of accounts receivable and the reduction in borrowing which will result from this system.

(*b*) What factors other than those referred to in (*a*) should Tunequip consider in its evaluation of the lockbox system?

(*c*) Do your calculations support the establishment of a lockbox system for Tunequip's western customers? Explain your answer. (CMA, adapted.)

SOLUTION

(*a*) (1)   The annual cost of operating the lockbox system is:

$$\text{Estimated number of invoices} = \frac{\text{western sales}}{\text{average invoice size}}$$

$$= \frac{\$10,800,000}{\$1,000/\text{invoice}} = 10,800 \text{ invoices}$$

Estimated handling fee ($10,800 \times \$0.10$)	$1,080
Fixed fee (12 months $\times$ $80)	960
Cost of compensating balance ($5,000 $\times$ 0.09)	450
Estimated annual operating cost	$2,490

(2)   The use of the lockbox will permit Tunequip to acquire the use of the funds 1 day earlier. This will have the effect of reducing the average accounts receivable by 1 day's sales and reduce the need for borrowing by the same amount. This amounts to $30,000 as is shown below.

$$\text{Reduction in average accounts receivable} = \frac{\text{western sales}}{\text{days in year}} = \frac{\$10,800,000}{360} = \$30,000$$

(*b*)   Other factors to be considered when changing to the lockbox system include the following: What is the cost of the wire transfers? Will there be a delay in recording receivables thus affecting customer attitudes? Will customers be upset because their lockbox checks will be cashed earlier? What is the impact of changes on costs in the main office? What other alternatives, such as tightening credit terms and slowing payments, of cash management can be used to reduce borrowing needs?

(*c*)   The financial manager makes the following recommendation:

Reduction in borrowing	$30,000
Interest rate	0.09
Annual savings	$ 2,700
Estimated annual operating cost	2,490
Estimated savings	$ 210

These projections give marginal support for the establishment of a lockbox because annual savings exceed costs by $210. However, the other items outlined in (*b*) should be considered in arriving at a final decision.

4.29   Credit Policy. The Heap Corporation finds itself with excess manufacturing capacity. The company has lost a portion of its share of the market over the past several years. This, in part, may be due to Heap having a more conservative credit policy than is common in the industry.

	Heap Corporation	Industry
Terms	2/10, net/30	2/10, net/60
Credit granted as percent of applicants by credit class		
A	100%	100%
B	100%	100%
C	25%	70%
D	11%	40%
E	2%	20%
F	0%	5%
Average collection period	30 days	60 days

The vice president for finance recommends that Heap Corporation relax its credit standards, with the expectation that sales and profitability will increase. Staff studies show that credit sales can be expected to increase to $92 million, bad debt losses will be approximately $2.4 million, inventory will need to be increased by $5.67 million, and average collection of accounts receivable will be 60 days. The 19X2 Heap income statement is given below.

Heap Corporation
Income Statement
(In Thousands of Dollars)
For Year Ended December 31, 19X2

Revenue		
Credit sales	$72	
Cash sales	8	$80
Costs and other charges		
Manufacturing expenses[a]	$57.4	
Administrative expenses[b]	3.0	
Selling expenses[c]	9.6	70
Net income before taxes		$10
Federal income tax		5
Net income		$ 5

[a] Materials and supplies	$10.0
Labor	40.0
Fixed overhead	7.4
	$57.4
[b] All fixed	$ 3.0
[c] Selling expenses	
Variable expense	$ 8.0
Bad debt loss estimate	1.6
	$ 9.6

(a) Estimate the accounts receivable balance at December 31, 19X2. (b) Assuming total assets at December 31, 19X2 equal 40 million dollars, (1) What is Heap Corporation's return on corporate assets? (2) What is the asset turnover? (c) What profit margin will Heap Corporation earn if the predictions are correct? (d) What return should be expected on corporate assets if the policy is adopted and the predictions are correct? (e) Will the company be better off financially if the proposed change in credit policy is made? Explain your answer. (CMA, adapted.)

SOLUTION

(a)

Credit sales	$72,000,000
Allowance for bad debts	$ 1,600,000
Net credit sales	$70,400,000
Average collection period	30 days
Accounts receivable turnover	12 times

$$\text{Net receivables balance, Dec. 31, 19X2} = \frac{\$70,400,000}{12} = \$5,866,667$$

(b) (1)
$$\text{Return on corporate assets} = \frac{\text{net income}}{\text{total assets}} = \frac{5,000,000}{40,000,000} = 12.5\%$$

(2)
$$\text{Asset turnover} = \frac{\text{sales}}{\text{assets}} = \frac{80,000,000}{40,000,000} = 2$$

(c)

Heap Corporation
Pro Forma Income Statement
(In Millions of Dollars)
For Year Ended Dec. 31, 19X3

Credit sales		$92.00	
Cash sales		8.00	$100.00
Manufacturing expense			
Materials and supplies	$12.50		
Labor	50.00		
Fixed overhead	7.40	$69.90	
Administrative expense		3.00	
Selling expense			
Variable	$10.00		
Bad debt loss estimate	2.40	12.40	85.30
Net income before taxes			$ 14.70
Federal income tax			7.35
Net income			$ 7.35

(d)

Total assets	
Prior assets	$40,000,000
Increase in receivables[a]	9,066,666
Increase in inventory	5,670,000
	$54,736,666

_____

[a]

$92,000,000	(credit sales)
2,400,000	(bad debt)
$89,600,000	(net credit sales)

$$\frac{360}{60} = 6 \quad \text{(receivables turnover)}$$

$$\frac{\$89,600,000}{6} = \$14,933,333$$

Change in receivables = $14,933,333 − $5,866,667 = $9,066,666

$$\text{Return on assets} = \frac{\$7,350,000}{\$54,736,666} = 13.4\%$$

(e) Since the overall return on assets has increased after the credit policy change, the company may be considered to be in better financial condition. However, it should be noted that the nature and cost of financing the current asset expansion has not been considered. If the incremental financing is available only at a comparatively high cost, the change in credit policy may not be desirable.

Chapter 5

Short-Term Financing

5.1 INTRODUCTION

This chapter discusses the advantages and disadvantages of the various short-term financing sources. "Short term" refers to financing that will be repaid in 1 year or less. Short-term financing may be used to meet seasonal and temporary fluctuations in a company's funds position as well as to meet permanent needs of the business. For example, short-term financing may be used to provide extra net working capital, finance current assets, or provide interim financing for a long-term project.

When compared to long-term financing, short-term financing has several advantages; for example, it is easier to arrange, it is less expensive, and it affords the borrower more flexibility. The drawbacks of short-term financing are that interest rates fluctuate more often, refinancing is frequently needed, and delinquent repayment may be detrimental to the credit rating of a borrower who is experiencing a liquidity problem.

The sources of short-term financing are trade credit, bank loans, bankers' acceptances, finance company loans, commercial paper, receivable financing, and inventory financing.

The merits of the different alternative sources of short-term financing are usually considered carefully before a firm borrows money. The factors bearing upon the selection of the source of short-term financing include:

1. Cost.
2. Effect on credit rating. Some sources of short-term financing may negatively affect the firm's credit rating.
3. Risk. The firm must consider the reliability of the source of funds for future borrowing.
4. Restrictions. Certain lenders may impose restrictions, such as requiring a minimum level of net working capital.
5. Flexibility. Certain lenders are more willing than others to work with the borrower, for example, to periodically adjust the amount of funds needed.
6. Expected money market conditions.
7. The inflation rate.
8. Corporate profitability and liquidity positions.
9. The stability of the firm's operations.

5.2 TRADE CREDIT

Trade credit (accounts payable) refers to balances owed to suppliers. It is a spontaneous financing source since it comes from normal business operations. Trade credit is the least expensive form of financing inventory. The benefits of trade credit are: It is readily available, since suppliers want business; collateral is not required; interest is typically not demanded or, if so, the amount is minimal; it is convenient; and trade creditors are frequently lenient in the event of corporate financial problems. A company having liquidity problems may stretch its accounts payable; however, among the disadvantages of doing so are the giving up of any cash discount offered and the probability of lowering the firm's credit rating.

EXAMPLE 5.1 Tristar Corporation purchases $475 worth of merchandise per day from suppliers. The terms of purchase are net/45, and the company pays on time. How much is Tristar's accounts payable balance?

$$\$475 \text{ per day} \times 45 \text{ days} = \$21,375$$

5.3 BANK LOANS

To be eligible for a bank loan, a company must have sufficient equity and good liquidity. When a short-term bank loan is taken, the debtor usually signs a note, which is a written statement that the borrower agrees to repay the loan at the due date. A note payable may be paid at maturity or in installments.

Bank loans are not spontaneous financing as is trade credit. Borrowers must apply for loans, and lenders must grant them. Without additional funds, a firm may have to restrict its plans; therefore, as a company's need for funds changes, it alters its borrowings from banks. One example is a self-liquidating (seasonal) loan which is used to pay for a temporary increase in accounts receivable or inventory. As soon as the assets realize cash, the loan is repaid.

Loans, of course, earn interest, and the prime interest rate is the lowest interest rate applied to short-term loans from a bank. Banks charge only their most creditworthy clients the prime rate; other borrowers are charged higher interest rates.

Bank financing may take any of the following forms:

1. Unsecured loans
2. Secured loans
3. Lines of credit
4. Installment loans

Unsecured Loans

Most short-term unsecured loans are self-liquidating. This kind of loan is recommended for use by companies with excellent credit ratings for financing projects that have quick cash flows. They are appropriate when the firm must have immediate cash and can either repay the loan in the near future or quickly obtain longer-term financing. The disadvantages of this kind of loan are that, because it is made for the short term, it carries a higher interest rate than a secured loan and payment in a lump sum is required.

Secured Loans

If a borrower's credit rating is deficient, the bank may lend money only on a secured basis, that is, with some form of collateral behind the loan. Collateral may take many forms including inventory, marketable securities, or fixed assets. In some cases, even though the company is able to obtain an unsecured loan, it may still give collateral in exchange for a lower interest rate.

Lines of Credit

Under a line of credit, the bank agrees to lend money to the borrower on a recurring basis up to a specified amount. Credit lines are typically established for a 1-year period and may be renewed annually. Construction companies often use such an arrangement because they usually receive only minimal payments from their clients during construction, being compensated primarily at the end of a job.

The advantages of a line of credit for a company are the easy and immediate access to funds during tight money market conditions and the ability to borrow only as much as needed and repay immediately when cash is available. The disadvantages relate to the collateral requirements and the additional financial information that must be presented to the bank. Also, the bank may place restrictions upon the company, such as a ceiling on capital expenditures or the maintenance of a minimum level of net working capital. Further, the bank will charge a commitment fee on the amount of the unused credit line.

When a company borrows under a line of credit, it may be required to maintain a deposit with the bank that does not earn interest. This deposit is referred to as a compensating balance and is stated as a percentage of the loan. The compensating balance effectively increases the cost of the loan. A compensating balance may also be placed on the unused portion of a line of credit, in which case the interest rate would be reduced.

EXAMPLE 5.2   A company borrows $200,000 and is required to keep a 12 percent compensating balance. It also has an unused line of credit in the amount of $100,000, for which a 10 percent compensating balance is required. What amount is the minimum balance that the business must maintain?

$$(\$200,000 \times 0.12) + (\$100,000 \times 0.10) = \$24,000 + \$10,000 = \$34,000$$

The bank may test a borrower's financial capability by requiring the borrower to "clean up," that is, repay the loan for a brief time during the year (e.g., for 1 month). A company that is unable to repay a short-term loan should probably finance with long-term funds. The payment shows the bank that the loan is actually seasonal rather than permanent financing.

Installment Loans

An installment loan requires monthly payments. When the principal on the loan decreases sufficiently, refinancing can take place at lower interest rates. The advantage of this kind of loan is that it may be tailored to satisfy a company's seasonal financing needs.

Computation of Interest

Interest on a loan may be paid either at maturity (ordinary interest) or in advance (discounting the loan). When interest is paid in advance, the proceeds from the loan are reduced and the effective (true) interest cost is increased.

EXAMPLE 5.3   Acme Company borrows $30,000 at 16 percent interest per annum and repays the loan 1 year hence. The interest paid is $30,000 \times 0.16 = \$4,800$. The effective interest rate is 16 percent.

EXAMPLE 5.4   Assume the same facts as in Example 5.3, except the note is discounted. The proceeds of this loan are smaller than in the previous example.

$$\text{Proceeds} = \text{principal} - \text{interest} = \$30,000 - \$4,800 = \$25,200$$

The true interest rate for this discounted loan is:

$$\text{Effective interest rate} = \frac{\text{interest}}{\text{proceeds}} = \frac{\$4,800}{\$25,000} = 19\%$$

EXAMPLE 5.5   Prestige Bank will give a company a 1-year loan at an interest rate of 20 percent payable at maturity, while Heritage Bank will lend on a discount basis at a 19 percent interest rate. Which bank charges the lowest effective rate?

$$\begin{array}{ll}
\text{Prestige Bank} & 20\% \\[2mm]
\text{Heritage Bank} & \dfrac{19\%}{81\%} = 23.5\%
\end{array}$$

The loan from Prestige Bank has the better interest rate.

When a loan has a compensating balance requirement associated with it, the proceeds received by the borrower are decreased by the amount of the balance. The compensating balance will increase the effective interest rate.

EXAMPLE 5.6   The effective interest rate associated with a 1-year, $600,000 loan that has a nominal interest rate of 19 percent, with interest due at maturity and requiring a 15 percent compensating balance is computed as follows:

$$\text{Effective interest rate (with compensating balance)} = \frac{\text{interest rate} \times \text{principal}}{\text{proceeds, \%} \times \text{principal}}$$

$$= \frac{0.19 \times \$600,000}{(1.00 - 0.15) \times \$600,000} = \frac{\$114,000}{\$510,000} = 22.4\%$$

EXAMPLE 5.7 Assume the same facts as in Example 5.6, except that the loan is discounted. The effective interest rate is:

$$\text{Effective interest rate (with discount)} = \frac{\text{interest rate} \times \text{principal}}{(\text{proceeds, \%} \times \text{principal}) - \text{interest}}$$

$$= \frac{0.19 \times \$600,000}{(0.85 \times \$600,000) - \$114,000} = \frac{\$114,000}{\$396,000} = 28.8\%$$

EXAMPLE 5.8 Jones Company has a line of credit in the amount of $400,000 from its bank, but it must maintain a compensating balance of 13 percent on outstanding loans and a compensating balance of 10 percent on the unused credit. The interest rate on the loan is 18 percent. The company borrows $275,000. What is the effective interest rate on the loan?

The required compensating balance is:

$0.13 \times \$275,000$	$35,750
$0.10 \times 125,000$	12,500
	$48,250

$$\text{Effective interest rate (with line of credit)} = \frac{\text{interest rate (on loan)} \times \text{principal}}{\text{principal} - \text{compensating balance}}$$

$$= \frac{0.18 \times \$275,000}{\$275,000 - \$48,250} = \frac{\$49,500}{\$226,750} = 21.8\%$$

On an installment loan, the effective interest rate computation is more involved. Assuming a 1-year loan is to be paid in equal monthly installments, the effective rate must be based on the average amount outstanding for the year. The interest to be paid is computed on the face amount of the loan.

EXAMPLE 5.9 A company borrows $40,000 at an interest rate of 10 percent to be paid in 12 monthly installments. The average loan balance is $40,000/2 = $20,000. The effective interest rate is $4,000/$20,000 = 20%.

EXAMPLE 5.10 Assume the same facts as in Example 5.9, except that the loan is discounted. The interest of $4,000 is deducted in advance so the proceeds received are $40,000 − $4,000 = $36,000. The average loan balance is $36,000/2 = $18,000. The effective interest rate is $4,000/$18,000 = 22.2%.

5.4 BANKERS' ACCEPTANCES

A banker's acceptance is a draft, drawn by an individual and accepted by a bank, that orders payment to a third party at a later date. The creditworthiness of the draft is of good quality because it has the backing of the bank, not the drawer. It is, in essence, a debt instrument created by the creditor out of a self-liquidating business transaction. Bankers' acceptances are often used to finance the shipment and handling of both domestic and foreign merchandise. Acceptances are classed as short-term financing because they typically have maturities of less than 180 days.

EXAMPLE 5.11 A United States oil refiner arranges with its United States commercial bank for a letter of credit to a Saudi Arabian exporter with whom the United States refiner has undertaken a transaction. The letter of credit provides the information regarding the shipment and states that the exporter can draw a time draft for a given amount on the United States bank. Because of the letter of credit, the exporter draws a draft on the bank and negotiates it with a local Saudi Arabian bank, receiving immediate payment. The Saudi Arabian bank sends the draft to the United States bank and when the latter accepts the draft, there is an acceptance to meet the obligation on the maturity date.

5.5 COMMERCIAL FINANCE COMPANY LOANS

When credit is unavailable from a bank, a company may have to go to a commercial finance company (e.g., CIT Financial). The finance company loan has a higher interest rate than a bank, and generally is secured. Typically, the amount of collateral placed will be greater than the balance of the loan. Collateral includes accounts receivable, inventories, and fixed assets. Commercial finance companies also finance the installment purchases of industrial equipment by firms. A portion of their financing is sometimes obtained through commercial bank borrowing at wholesale rates.

5.6 COMMERCIAL PAPER

Commercial paper can be issued only by companies possessing the highest credit ratings. Therefore, the interest rate is less than that of a bank loan, usually $\frac{1}{2}$ percent below prime. Commercial paper is unsecured and sold at a discount in the form of short-term promissory notes. The maturity date is usually less than 270 days, otherwise Securities and Exchange Commission (SEC) registration is needed. When a note is sold at a discount, it means that interest is immediately deducted from the face of the note by the creditor, but the debtor will pay the full face value. Commercial paper may be issued through a dealer or directly placed to an institutional investor.

The benefits of commercial paper are that no security is required, the interest rate is typically less than through bank or finance company borrowing, and the commercial paper dealer often offers financial advice. The drawbacks are that commercial paper can be issued only by large, financially sound companies, and commercial paper dealings relative to bank dealings are impersonal.

EXAMPLE 5.12 Travis Corporation's balance sheet appears below.

ASSETS		LIABILITIES AND STOCKHOLDERS' EQUITY	
Current assets	$ 540,000	Current liabilities	
Fixed assets	800,000	Notes payable to banks	$ 100,000
		Commercial paper	650,000
		Total current liabilities	$ 750,000
		Long-term liabilities	260,000
		Total liabilities	$1,010,000
		Stockholders' equity	330,000
		Total liabilities and	
Total assets	$1,340,000	stockholders' equity	$1,340,000

The amount of commercial paper issued by Travis is a high percentage of both its current liabilities, 86.7 percent ($650,000/$750,000), and its total liabilities, 64.4 percent ($650,000/$1,010,000). Probably Travis should do more bank borrowing because in the event of a money market squeeze, the company would find advantageous to have a working relationship with a bank.

EXAMPLE 5.13 Able Company sells $500,000 of commercial paper every 2 months at a 13 percent rate. There is a $1,000 placement cost each time. The percentage cost of the commercial paper is:

Interest ($500,000 × 0.13)	$65,000
Placement cost ($1,000 × 6)	6,000
Cost	$71,000

$$\text{Percentage cost of commercial paper} = \frac{\$71,000}{\$500,000} = 14.2\%$$

EXAMPLE 5.14 Ajax Corporation issues $300,000 worth of 18 percent, 90-day commercial paper. However, the funds are needed for only 70 days. The excess funds can be invested in securities earning 17 percent. The brokerage fee associated with the marketable security transaction is 1.5 percent. The dollar cost to the company in issuing the commercial paper is:

Interest expense	
[0.18 × $300,000 × (90/360)]	$13,500
Brokerage fee (0.015 × $300,000)	4,500
Total cost	$18,000
Less: Return on marketable securities	
[0.17 × $300,000 × (20/360)]	2,833
Net cost	$15,167

EXAMPLE 5.15 Charles Corporation anticipates it will need $500,000 cash for February 19X2 in order to purchase inventory. There are three ways to finance this purchase, as follows:

(a) Set up a 1-year credit line for $500,000. The bank requires a 1 percent commitment fee. The interest rate is 18 percent on borrowed funds. Funds are needed for 30 days.

(b) Do not take advantage of a 1/10, net/40 discount on a $500,000 credit purchase.

(c) Issue $500,000 of commercial paper for 30 days at 17 percent.

Which is the least expensive method of financing?

(a) Set up a credit line:

Commitment fee	
[0.01 × $500,000 × (11/12)]	$ 4,583
Interest [0.18 × $500,000 × (1/12)]	7,500
	$12,083

(b) Do not take advantage of discount:

$$0.01 × \$500,000 = \$5,000$$

(c) Issue commercial paper:

$$0.17 × \$500,000 × (1/12) = \$7,083$$

The financing with the least dollar cost is to not take the discount, as specified in (b).

5.7 RECEIVABLE FINANCING

The financing of accounts receivable can generally take place if:

1. Receivables are at a minimum of $25,000.
2. Sales are at a minimum of $250,000.
3. Individual receivables are at a minimum of $100.
4. Receivables apply to selling merchandise rather than rendering services.
6. Customers are financially strong.
7. Sales returns are not great.
8. Title to the goods is received by the buyer at shipment.

Receivable financing has several advantages, including avoiding the need for long-term financing and obtaining a recurring cash flow base. Accounts receivable financing has the drawback of high administrative costs when there are many small accounts. However, with the use of computers these costs can be curtailed.

Accounts receivable may be financed under either a factoring or assignment arrangement. *Factoring* refers to the outright sale of accounts receivable to a bank or finance company *without recourse*. The purchaser takes all credit and collection risks. The proceeds received by the selling company are equal to the face value of the receivables less the commission charge, which is typically 2 to 4 percent higher than the prime interest rate. The cost of the factoring arrangement is the factor's commission for credit investigation, interest on the unpaid balance of advanced funds, and a discount from the face value of the receivables where high credit risks exist. Remissions by customers are made directly to the factor.

The advantages of factoring include:

1. Immediate availability of cash
2. Reduction in overhead since the credit examination function is no longer required
3. Utilization of financial advice
4. Receipt of advances as needed on a seasonal basis
5. Strengthening of the balance sheet position

The drawbacks to factoring include both the high cost and the poor impression left with customers because of the change in ownership of the receivables. Also, factors may antagonize customers by their demanding methods of collecting delinquent accounts.

In an *assignment*, there is no transfer of the ownership of the accounts receivable. Receivables are given to a finance company *with recourse*. The finance company typically advances between 50 and 85 percent of the face value of the receivables in cash. The borrower is responsible for a service charge, interest on the advance, and any resulting bad debt losses. Customer remissions continue to be made directly to the company.

The assignment of accounts receivable has a number of advantages, including the immediate availability of cash, cash advances available on a seasonal basis, and avoidance of negative customer feelings. The disadvantages include the high cost, the continuance of the clerical function associated with accounts receivable, and the bearing of all credit risks.

The financial manager should be aware of the impact of a change in accounts receivable policy on the cost of financing receivables.

EXAMPLE 5.16 When accounts receivable are financed, the cost of financing may rise or fall under different conditions. For instance, (1) when credit standards are relaxed, costs increase; (2) when recourse for defaults is given to the finance company, costs decrease; and (3) when the minimum invoice amount of a credit sale is increased, costs decrease.

The finance manager should compute the costs of accounts receivable financing and select the least expensive alternative.

EXAMPLE 5.17 A factor will purchase Ryan Corporation's $120,000 per month accounts receivable. The factor will advance up to 80 percent of the receivables for an annual charge of 14 percent, and a 1.5 percent fee on receivables purchased. The cost of this factoring arrangement is:

Factor fee [0.015 × ($120,000 × 12)]	$21,600
Cost of borrowing [0.14 × ($120,000 × 0.8)]	13,440
Total cost	$35,040

EXAMPLE 5.18 Tristar Corporation needs $250,000 and is weighing the alternatives of arranging a bank loan or going to a factor. The bank loan terms are 18 percent interest, discounted, with a compensating balance of 20 percent required. The factor will charge a 4 percent commission on invoices purchased monthly, and the interest rate on the purchased invoices is 12 percent, deducted in advance. By using a factor, Tristar will save $1,000 monthly credit department costs, and uncollectible accounts estimated at 3 percent of the factored accounts receivable will not occur. Which is the better alternative for Tristar?

The bank loan which will net the company its desired $250,000 in proceeds is:

$$\frac{\text{Proceeds}}{100\% - (\text{percent deducted})} = \frac{\$250,000}{100\% - (18\% + 20\%)} = \frac{\$250,000}{1.0 - 0.38} = \frac{\$250,000}{0.62} = \$403,226$$

The effective interest rate associated with the bank loan is:

$$\text{Effective interest rate} = \frac{\text{interest rate}}{\text{proceeds, \%}} = \frac{0.18}{0.62} = 29.0\%$$

The amount of accounts receivable that should be factored to net the firm $250,000 is:

$$\frac{\$250,000}{1.0 - 0.16} = \frac{\$250,000}{0.84} = \$297,619$$

The total annual cost of the bank arrangement is:

Interest ($250,000 × 0.29)	$72,500
Additional cost of not using a factor:	
Credit costs ($1,000 × 12)	12,000
Uncollectible accounts ($297,619 × 0.03)	8,929
Total cost	$93,429

The effective interest rate associated with factoring accounts receivable is:

$$\text{Effective interest rate} = \frac{\text{interest rate}}{\text{proceeds, \%}} = \frac{12\%}{100\% - (12\% + 4\%)} = \frac{0.12}{0.84} = 14.3\%$$

The total annual cost of the factoring alternative is:

Interest ($250,000 × 0.143)	$35,750
Factoring ($297,619 × 0.04)	11,905
Total cost	$47,655

Factoring should be used since it will cost almost half as much as the bank loan.

EXAMPLE 5.19 System Corporation's factor charges a 3 percent fee per month. The factor lends the firm up to 75 percent of receivables purchased for an additional 1 percent per month. The company's credit sales are $400,000 per month. As a result of the factoring arrangement, the company saves $6,500 per month in credit costs and a bad debt expense of 2 percent of credit sales.

XYZ Bank has offered an arrangement where it will lend the firm up to 75 percent of the receivables. The bank will charge 2 percent per month interest plus a 4 percent processing charge on receivable lending.

The collection period is 30 days. If System Corporation borrows the maximum allowed per month, should the firm stay with the factor or switch to XYZ Bank?

Cost of factor:

Purchased receivables (0.03 × $400,000)	$12,000
Lending fee (0.01 × $300,000)	3,000
Total cost	$15,000

Cost of bank financing:

Interest (0.02 × $300,000)	$ 6,000
Processing charge (0.04 × $300,000)	12,000
Additional cost of not using the factor:	
Credit costs	6,500
Bad debts (0.02 × $400,000)	8,000
Total cost	$32,500

System Corporation should stay with the factor.

EXAMPLE 5.20 Davis Company is considering a factoring arrangement. The company's sales are $2,700,000, accounts receivable turnover is 9 times, and a 17 percent reserve on accounts receivable is required by the factor. The factor's commission charge on average accounts receivable payable at the point of receivable purchase is 2.0 percent. The factor's interest charge is 16 percent on receivables after subtracting the commission charge and reserve. The interest charge reduces the advance. What is the annual effective cost under the factoring arrangement?

$$\text{Average accounts receivable} = \frac{\text{credit sales}}{\text{turnover}} = \frac{\$2,700,000}{9} = \$300,000$$

Davis will receive the following amount by factoring its accounts receivable:

Average accounts receivable	$300,000
Less: Reserve ($300,000 × 0.17)	−51,000
Commission ($300,000 × 0.02)	−6,000
Net prior to interest	$243,000
Less: Interest [$243,000 × (16%/9)]	4,320
Proceeds received	$238,680

The annual cost of the factoring arrangement is:

Commission ($300,000 × 0.02)	$ 6,000
Interest [$243,000 × (16%/9)]	4,320
Cost each 40 days (360/9)	$10,320
Turnover	×9
Total annual cost	$92,880

The annual effective cost under the factoring arrangement based on the amount received is:

$$\frac{\text{Annual cost}}{\text{Average amount received}} = \frac{\$92,880}{\$238,680} = 38.9\%$$

5.8 INVENTORY FINANCING

Financing inventory typically occurs when a company has fully used its borrowing capacity on receivables. Inventory financing requires the existence of marketable, nonperishable, and standardized goods that have quick turnover. The merchandise should not be subject to rapid obsolescence. Good collateral inventory is that which can be marketed apart from the borrower's marketing organization. Inventory financing should take into account the price stability of the inventory and the expenses associated with selling it.

In the case of marketable inventory, the advance is high. In general, the financing of raw materials and finished goods is about 75 percent of their value. The interest rate approximates 3 to 5 points (i.e., 3 to 5 percent) over prime.

The disadvantages of inventory financing include the high interest rate and the restrictions on some of the company's inventory.

The vehicles of inventory financing include a floating (blanket) lien, warehouse receipt, and trust receipt. In the case of a *floating lien*, the creditor's security lies in the aggregate inventory rather than in its components. Even though the borrower sells and restocks, the lender's security interest continues. With a *warehouse receipt*, the lender receives an interest in the borrower's inventory stored at a public warehouse; however, the fixed costs of this arrangement are quite high. There may be a field warehouse arrangement where the warehouser sets up a secured area directly at the debtor's location. The debtor has access to the goods but must continually account for them. With a *trust receipt* loan, the creditor has title to given goods but releases them to the borrower to sell on the creditor's behalf. As goods are sold, the borrower remits the funds to the lender. A good example of trust receipt use is in automobile dealer financing. The drawback of the trust receipt arrangement is that a trust receipt must be given for specific items.

A collateral certificate may be issued by a third party to the lender guaranteeing the existence of pledged inventory. The advantage of a collateral certificate is flexibility since merchandise does not have to be segregated or possessed by the lender.

EXAMPLE 5.21 Jackson Corporation wishes to finance its $500,000 inventory. Funds are needed for 3 months. A warehouse receipt loan may be taken at 16 percent with a 90 percent advance against the inventory's value. The warehousing cost is $4,000 for the 3-month period. The cost of financing the inventory is:

Interest $[0.16 \times 0.90 \times \$500,000 \times (3/12)]$	$18,000
Warehousing cost	4,000
Total cost	$22,000

EXAMPLE 5.22 Hardy Corporation has been showing growth in its operations but is currently experiencing liquidity problems. Six large financially sound companies are Hardy customers, being responsible for 75 percent of Hardy's sales. On the basis of the following information for 19X1, would Hardy Corporation be able to borrow on receivables or inventory?

Balance sheet data are as follows:

ASSETS

Current assets

Cash	$ 27,000	
Receivables	380,000	
Inventory (consisting of 55% of work-in-process)	320,000	
Total current assets		$727,000
Fixed assets		250,000
Total assets		$977,000

LIABILITIES AND STOCKHOLDERS' EQUITY

Current liabilities

Accounts payable	$260,000	
Loans payable	200,000	
Accrued expenses	35,000	
Total current liabilities		$495,000
Bonds payable		110,000
Total liabilities		$605,000
Stockholders' equity		
Common stock	$250,000	
Retained earnings	122,000	
Total stockholders' equity		372,000
Total liabilities and stockholders' equity		$977,000

Selected income statement data are as follows:

Sales	$1,800,000
Net income	$130,000

Receivable financing can be expected since a high percentage of sales are made to only six large financially healthy firms. Receivables will therefore show good collectibility. It is also easier to control a few large customer accounts.

Inventory financing is not likely, due to the high percentage of partially completed items. Lenders are reluctant to finance inventory when a large work-in-process balance exists since the goods will be difficult to further process and sell by lenders.

5.9 OTHER ASSETS

Assets other than inventory and receivables may be used as security for short-term bank loans such as real estate, plant and equipment, cash surrender value of life insurance policies, and securities. Also, lenders are usually willing to advance a high percentage of the market value of bonds. The owner's personal assets may be pledged when the company's financial position is very weak. In addition, loans may be made based on a guaranty of a third party.

Review Questions

1. Short-term financing refers to the issuance of debt having a maturity of less than _____ .

2. Short-term financing makes the borrower more susceptible to _____ fluctuations.

3. The least expensive source of short-term financing is _____ .

4. Accounts payable is a(n) _____ financing source.

5. Accounts payable should not be stretched too far because of a possible reduction in the firm's _____ .

6. A note payable may be payable at _____ or in _____ .

7. _____ loans are those in which the loan is paid as soon as the financed assets realize cash.

8. The rate charged by banks to their best clients is called the _____ interest rate.

9. _____ loans require no collateral.

10. When a(n) _____ is given, the bank agrees to lend the borrower money on a continual basis up to a given amount.

11. A(n) _____ refers to the deposit, which does not earn interest, that a company must maintain at the bank as collateral for a loan.

12. In a(n) _____ loan, monthly payments are required.

13. Interest on a loan may be paid at _____ or _____ .

14. When a loan is discounted, the _____ interest rate will be higher.

15. A(n)_____ is a draft drawn by an individual and accepted by the bank requiring future payment to a third party.

16. The interest rate on _____ is less than the interest rate on a bank loan.

17. The outright sale of accounts receivable to a third party is called _____ .

18. In a(n) _____, accounts receivable are transferred to a third party with recourse.

19. In the case of inventory financing, a(n) _____ lien applies to the aggregate inventory rather than the components.

20. In a(n) _____ loan, the creditor has title to goods but releases them to the borrower to sell on the creditor's behalf.

Answers: (1) 1 year; (2) interest rate; (3) trade credit; (4) spontaneous; (5) credit rating; (6) maturity, installments; (7) Self-liquidating; (8) prime; (9) Unsecured; (10) line of credit; (11) compensating balance; (12) installment; (13) maturity, in advance; (14) effective; (15) bankers' acceptance; (16) commercial paper; (17) factoring; (18) assignment; (19) floating (blanket); (20) trust receipt.

Solved Problems

5.1 Accounts Payable. James Corporation purchases $750 per day from suppliers on terms of net/30. Determine the accounts payable balance.

SOLUTION

$$\$750 \text{ per day} \times 30 \text{ days} = \$22,500$$

5.2 Compensating Balance. Carl Corporation borrows $150,000 from a bank. A 10 percent compensating balance is required. What is the amount of the compensating balance?

SOLUTION

$$\$150,000 \times 0.10 = \$15,000$$

5.3 Compensating Balance. Wilson Company borrows $500,000 from the bank and is required to maintain a 15 percent compensating balance. Further, Wilson has an unused line of credit of $200,000, with a required 11 percent compensating balance. What is the total required compensating balance the firm must maintain?

SOLUTION

$$(\$500,000 \times 0.15) + (\$200,000 \times 0.11) = \$97,000$$

5.4   **Effective Interest Rate.** Charles Corporation borrows $70,000 at 19 percent annual interest. Principal and interest is due in 1 year. What is the effective interest rate?

SOLUTION

The effective interest rate is 19 percent.

5.5   **Proceeds of Loan.** Assume the same information as in Problem 5.4, except that interest is deducted in advance. (*a*) What is the amount of proceeds the company will receive at the time of the loan? (*b*) What is the effective interest rate?

SOLUTION

(*a*)
$$\text{Interest} = \$70,000 \times 0.19 = \$13,300$$

$$\text{Proceeds} = \text{principal} - \text{interest} = \$70,000 - \$13,300 = \$56,700$$

(*b*)
$$\text{Effective interest rate} = \frac{\text{interest}}{\text{proceeds}} = \frac{\$13,300}{\$56,700} = 23.5\%$$

5.6   **Interest Cost.** Ajax Corporation is deciding which of two banks to borrow from on a 1-year basis. Bank A charges an 18 percent interest rate payable at maturity. Bank B charges a 17 percent interest rate on a discount basis. Which loan is cheaper?

SOLUTION

$$
\begin{array}{ll}
\text{Bank A} & 18\% \\
\text{Bank B} & \dfrac{17\%}{83\%} = 20.5\%
\end{array}
$$

Ajax should borrow from bank A since the effective interest rate is lower.

5.7   **Effective Interest Rate.** Tech Corporation takes out a $70,000 loan having a nominal interest rate of 22 percent payable at maturity. The required compensating balance is 12 percent. What is the effective interest rate?

SOLUTION

$$\text{Effective interest rate} = \frac{\text{interest rate}}{\text{proceeds, \%}} = \frac{0.22}{1.00 - 0.12} = \frac{0.22}{0.88} = 25\%$$

5.8   **Effective Interest Rate.** Assume the same information as in Problem 5.7 except that interest is payable in advance. What is the effective interest rate?

SOLUTION

$$\text{Effective rate} = \frac{\text{interest rate}}{\text{proceeds, \%}} = \frac{0.22}{0.88 - 0.22} = \frac{0.22}{0.66} = 33.3\%$$

5.9   **Effective Interest Rate and Compensating Balance.** Wilson Corporation has a credit line of $800,000. The compensating balance requirement on outstanding loans is 14 percent, and 8 percent on the unused credit line. The company borrows $500,000 at a 20 percent interest rate. (*a*) What is the required compensating balance? (*b*) What is the effective interest rate?

SOLUTION

(a)   The required compensating balance is:

Loan $0.14 \times \$500,000$	$70,000
Unused credit $0.08 \times \$300,000$	24,000
	$94,000

(b) $$\text{Effective interest rate} = \frac{\text{interest}}{\text{proceeds}} = \frac{0.20 \times \$500,000}{\$500,000 - \$94,000} = \frac{\$100,000}{\$406,000} = 24.6\%$$

5.10   Average Loan Balance. Wise Corporation borrows $70,000 payable in 12 monthly installments. The interest rate is 15 percent. (a) What is the average loan balance? (b) What is the effective interest rate?

SOLUTION

(a) $$\text{Average loan balance} = \frac{\$70,000}{2} = \$35,000$$

(b) $$\text{Effective interest rate} = \frac{0.15 \times \$70,000}{\$35,000} = \frac{\$10,500}{\$35,000} = 30\%$$

5.11   Average Loan Balance. Assume the same information as in Problem 5.10, except that the loan is on a discount basis. (a) What is the average loan balance? (b) What is the effective interest rate?

SOLUTION

(a) $$\text{Proceeds} = \$70,000 - \$10,500 = \$59,500$$

$$\text{Average loan balance} = \frac{\$59,500}{2} = \$29,750$$

(b) $$\text{Effective interest rate} = \frac{\$10,500}{\$29,750} = 35.3\%$$

5.12   Commercial Paper. Boston Corporation's balance sheet follows:

ASSETS

Current assets	$ 700,000
Fixed assets	1,600,000
Total assets	$2,300,000

LIABILITIES AND STOCKHOLDERS' EQUITY

Current liabilities	
Bank loans payable	$ 500,000
Commercial paper	100,000
Total current liabilities	$ 600,000
Long-term liabilities	300,000
Total liabilities	$ 900,000
Stockholders' equity	1,400,000
Total liabilities and stockholders' equity	$2,300,000

The company has an excellent credit rating and can issue additional commercial paper if it wishes. Should Boston Corporation issue additional commercial paper?

SOLUTION

Yes. Commercial paper is a low percentage of current liabilities, 16.7 percent ($100,000/$600,000), and of total liabilities, 11.1 percent ($100,000/$900,000). Since the cost of commercial paper is less than a bank loan and since the percentage of commercial paper to total debt financing is low, additional commercial paper should be issued.

5.13   Cost of Commercial Paper. Nelson Corporation issues $800,000 of commercial paper every 3 months at a 16 percent rate. Each issuance involves a placement cost of $2,000. What is the annual percentage cost of the commercial paper?

SOLUTION

Interest ($800,000 × 0.16)	$128,000
Placement cost ($2,000 × 4)	8,000
Total cost	$136,000

$$\text{Cost of commercial paper} = \frac{\$136,000}{\$800,000} = 17.0\%$$

5.14   Cost of Commercial Paper. Cho Corporation issues $500,000, 20 percent, 120-day commercial paper. However, the funds are needed for only 90 days. The excess funds can be invested in securities earning 19 percent. The brokerage fee for the marketable security transaction is 1.0 percent. What is the net cost to the company for issuing the commercial paper?

SOLUTION

Interest [0.20 × $500,000 × (120/360)]	$33,333
Brokerage fee (0.01 × $500,000)	5,000
Total cost	$38,333
Less: Return on marketable securities	
[0.19 × $500,000 × (30/360)]	7,917
Net cost	$30,416

5.15   Financing Strategy. Johnson Company expects that it will need $600,000 cash for March 19X2. Possible means of financing are: (*a*) Establish a 1-year credit line for $600,000. The bank requires a 2 percent commitment fee. The interest rate is 21 percent. Funds are needed for 30 days. (*b*) Fail to take a 2/10, net/40 discount on a $600,000 credit purchase. (*c*) Issue $600,000, 20 percent commercial paper for 30 days. Which financing strategy should be selected?

SOLUTION

(*a*)   The credit line cost is:

Commitment fee [0.02 × $600,000 × (11/12)]	$11,000
Interest [0.21 × $600,000 × (1/12)]	10,500
Total cost	$21,500

(*b*)   The cost of not taking discount is:

$$0.02 \times \$600,000 = \$12,000$$

(c)   The cost of commercial paper is:

$$0.20 \times \$600,000 \times \tfrac{1}{12} = \$10,000$$

Strategy (c) is best since issuance of commercial paper involves the least cost.

5.16   Cost of Accounts Receivable Financing. What is the effect of each of the following situations on the cost of accounts receivable financing? (a) A more thorough credit check is undertaken. (b) Receivables are sold without recourse. (c) The minimum invoice amount for a credit sale is decreased. (d) Credit standards are tightened.

SOLUTION

(a) Decrease   (c) Increase

(b) Increase   (d) Decrease

5.17   Cost of Factoring. Drake Company is contemplating factoring its accounts receivable. The factor will acquire $250,000 of the company's accounts receivable every 2 months. An advance of 75 percent is given by the factor on receivables at an annual charge of 18 percent. There is a 2 percent factor fee associated with receivables purchased. What is the cost of the factoring arrangement?

SOLUTION

Factor fee $(0.02 \times \$250,000 \times 6)$	$30,000
Cost of advance $(0.18 \times \$250,000 \times 0.75)$	33,750
Total cost	$63,750

5.18   Bank versus Factor. Forest Corporation needs $400,000 additional financing. The company is considering the choice of financing with a bank or a factor. The bank loan carries a 20 percent interest rate on a discount basis with a required compensating balance of 16 percent. The factor charges a 3 percent commission on invoices purchased monthly. The interest rate associated with these invoices is 11 percent with interest deductible in advance. If a factor is used, there will be a monthly savings of $1,500 per month in credit department costs. Further, an uncollectible accounts expense of 2 percent on the factored receivables will not exist.

(a) What amount of principal must the company borrow from the bank to receive $400,000 in proceeds? (b) What amount of accounts receivable must be factored to net the firm $400,000? (c) What is the effective interest rate on the bank loan? (d) What is the total annual cost of the bank arrangement? (e) What is the effective interest rate associated with the factoring arrangement? (f) What is the total annual cost of factoring?

SOLUTION

(a)
$$\frac{\text{Principal}}{\text{Proceeds}} = \frac{1.00}{1.00 - (0.20 + 0.16)}$$

$$\frac{\text{Principal}}{\$400,000} = \frac{1}{1 - 0.36} = \frac{\$400,000}{1.0 - 0.36} = \frac{\$400,000}{0.64} = \$625,000$$

(b)
$$\text{Accounts receivables to factor} = \frac{\$400,000}{1.0 - 0.14} = \frac{\$400,000}{0.86} = \$465,116$$

(c)
$$\text{Effective interest rate of bank loan} = \frac{\text{interest rate}}{\text{proceeds, \%}} = \frac{0.20}{0.64} = 31.3\%$$

(d)   The cost of the bank loan is:

Interest ($400,000 × 0.313)	$125,200
Credit costs ($1,500 × 12)	18,000
Uncollectible accounts ($465,116 × 0.02)	9,302
Total annual cost	$152,502

(e)   The effective interest rate of factoring is:

$$\frac{0.11}{0.86} = 12.8\%$$

(f)   The cost of factoring is:

Interest ($400,000 × 0.128)	$51,200
Factoring ($465,116 × 0.03)	13,953
Total annual cost	$65,153

5.19   **Bank versus Factor.** Wayne Corporation's factor charges a 4 percent monthly fee. The factor lends Wayne up to 85 percent of receivables purchased for an additional $1\frac{1}{2}$ percent per month. The monthly credit sales are $350,000. With the factoring arrangement, there is a savings in corporate credit checking costs of $4,200 per month and in bad debts of 3 percent on credit sales.

Trust Bank has offered to lend Wayne up to 85 percent of the receivables, at an interest charge of 2.5 percent per month plus a 5 percent processing charge on receivable lending.

The collection period is 30 days, and Wayne borrows the maximum amount permitted each month. Should Wayne Corporation accept the bank's offer?

SOLUTION

Cost of factor:

Purchased receivables (0.04 × $350,000)	$14,000
Lending fee (0.015 × $350,000 × 0.85)	4,463
Total cost	$18,463

Cost of bank financing:

Interest (0.025 × $350,000 × 0.85)	$ 7,438
Processing charge (0.05 × $350,000 × 0.85)	14,875
Additional cost of not using factor	
Credit costs	4,200
Bad debts (0.03 × $350,000)	10,500
Total cost	$37,013

Wayne Corporation should stay with the factor, since the cost of the bank's offer is more than twice the cost of factoring.

5.20   **Factoring Accounts Receivable.** Grafton Corporation is considering factoring its accounts receivable. Its sales are $3,600,000, and accounts receivable turnover is two times. The factor requires (1) an 18 percent reserve on accounts receivable, (2) a commission charge of 2.5 percent on average accounts receivable, payable when receivables are purchased, and (3) an interest charge of 19 percent on receivables after deducting the commission charge and reserve. The interest charge reduces the advance.

Given the facts, answer the following questions: (*a*) What is the average accounts receivable? (*b*) How much will Grafton receive by factoring its accounts receivable? (*c*) What is the annual cost of the factoring arrangement? (*d*) What is the effective annual cost of factoring?

SOLUTION

(*a*)
$$\text{Average accounts receivable} = \frac{\text{credit sales}}{\text{turnover}} = \frac{\$3,600,000}{2} = \$1,800,000$$

(*b*)   The proceeds from factoring are:

Average accounts receivable	$1,800,000
Less: Reserve ($1,800,000 × 0.18)	−324,000
Commission ($1,800,000 × 0.025)	−45,000
Net prior to interest	$1,431,000
Less: Interest [$1,431,000 × (19%/2)]	135,945
Proceeds received	$1,295,055

(*c*)   The cost of factoring is:

Commission ($1,800,000 × 0.025)	$ 45,000
Interest [$1,431,000 × (19%/2)]	135,945
Cost each 180 days (360/2)	$180,945
Turnover	×2
Total annual cost	$361,890

(*d*)
$$\text{Effective annual cost of factoring} = \frac{\text{annual cost}}{\text{average amount received}} = \frac{\$361,890}{\$1,295,055} = 27.9\%$$

5.21   Financing Cost of Inventory. Blake Company desires to finance its $300,000 inventory. Funds are required for 4 months. Under consideration is a warehouse receipt loan at an annual interest rate of 17 percent, with an 85 percent advance against the inventory's value. The warehousing cost is $5,000 for the 4-month period. Determine the financing cost.

SOLUTION

Interest [0.17 × 0.85 × $300,000 × (4/12)]	$14,450
Warehousing cost	5,000
Total cost	$19,450

5.22   Receivable Financing or Inventory Financing. Large Corporation has liquidity problems. Most of its sales are made to small customer accounts. Relevant balance sheet data for 19X1 are:

ASSETS

Current assets		
Cash	$ 35,000	
Receivables	410,000	
Inventory (primarily consisting of finished goods and raw materials)	360,000	
Total current assets		$ 805,000
Fixed assets		600,000
Total assets		$1,405,000

LIABILITIES AND STOCKHOLDERS' EQUITY

Current liabilities		
Accounts payable	$350,000	
Loans payable	320,000	
Accrued expenses	56,000	
Total current liabilities		$ 726,000
Bonds payable		225,000
Total liabilities		$ 951,000
Stockholders' equity		
Common stock	$300,000	
Retained earnings	154,000	
Total stockholders' equity		454,000
Total liabilities and stockholders' equity		$1,405,000

Relevant income statement data are:

Sales	$2,400,000
Net income	$480,000

Given the balance sheet and income statement data, (*a*) Is receivable financing likely? (*b*) Is inventory financing likely?

SOLUTION

(*a*) No, receivable financing is not likely since receivables are made to many small customer accounts. Control over receivables will therefore be a problem. (*b*) Yes, inventory financing is likely since inventory consists of a large proportion of finished goods and raw materials which are readily salable.

5.23 **Cost of Issuing the Commercial Paper.** Cartele, Inc., will need $4 million over the next year to finance its short-term requirements. The company is considering financing alternatives—bank financing and the sale of commercial paper.

Addison Union Bank is willing to loan Cartele the necessary funds providing the company maintains a 20 percent compensating balance. The effective cost of the bank loan, considering the compensating balance requirement, is 10.4 percent on a pretax basis.

Under the other alternative Cartele would sell $4 million of 90-day maturity commercial paper every 3 months. The commercial paper will carry a rate of $7\frac{3}{4}$ percent; the interest rate is expected to remain at this level throughout the year. The commercial paper dealer's fee to place the issue would be a one-time charge of $\frac{1}{8}$ percent. The commercial paper dealer will require Cartele to establish a $400,000 compensating balance.

Management prefers the flexibility of bank financing. However, if the cost of bank financing should exceed the cost of the commercial paper by more than 1 percent, Cartele plans to issue the commercial paper.

(*a*) Calculate the effective cost on a pretax basis of issuing the commercial paper and, based solely upon your cost calculations, recommend the method of financing Cartele, Inc., should select. (*b*) Identify the characteristics Cartele should possess in order to deal regularly in the commercial paper market. (CMA, adapted.)

SOLUTION

(*a*)
$$\text{Cost of commercial paper} = \frac{\text{costs incurred by using commercial paper}}{\text{net funds available from commercial paper}}$$

The cost of commercial paper in the first quarter is:

Cost of issuing commercial paper		
Interest ($4,000,000 × 0.0775 × $\frac{1}{4}$)		$ 77,500
Placement fee ($4,000,000 × 0.00125)		5,000
1st-quarter cost		$ 82,500

Funds available for use		
Funds raised		$4,000,000
Less: Compensating balance	$400,000	
Interest and placement	82,500	482,500
Net funds available in the 1st quarter		$3,517,500

$$\text{Cost of commercial paper in the 1st quarter} = \frac{\$82,500}{\$3,517,500} = 2.345\%$$

Cost of issuing commercial paper per quarter		
Interest ($4,000,000 × 0.0775 × $\frac{1}{4}$)		$ 77,500

Funds available for use		
Funds raised		$4,000,000
Less: Compensating balance	$400,000	
Interest	77,500	477,500
Net funds available per quarter		$3,522,500

$$\text{Cost of commercial paper per quarter} = \frac{\$77,500}{\$3,522,500} = 2.20\%$$

The total annual effective cost of commercial paper is:

Effective cost = 1st-qtr. cost + 3(cost per quarter – for 2d, 3d, 4th qtrs.)

= 0.02345 + 3(0.02200) = 0.02345 + 0.06600 = 0.089545 = 8.95%

Cartele, Inc., should choose commercial paper because the cost of bank financing (10.4 percent) exceeds the cost of commercial paper (8.95 percent) by greater than 1 percent.

(b) The characteristics Cartele, Inc., should possess in order to deal regularly in the commercial paper market include the following:

1. Have a prestigious reputation, be financially strong, and have a high credit rating.

2. Have flexibility to arrange for large amounts of funds through regular banking channels.

3. Have large and frequently recurring short-term or seasonal needs for funds.

4. Have the ability to deal in large denominations of funds for periods of 1 to 9 months and be willing to accept the fact that commercial paper cannot be paid prior to maturity.

5.24 Establishing a Line of Credit. Luther Company produces and sells a complete line of infant and toddler toys. Its sales, characteristic of the entire toy industry, are very seasonal. The company offers favorable credit to those customers who will place their Christmas orders early and who will accept a shipment schedule arranged to fit the production schedules of Luther. The customer must place orders by May 15 and be willing to accept shipments beginning August 15; Luther guarantees shipment no later than October 15. Customers willing to accept these conditions are not required to pay for their Christmas purchases until January 30.

The suppliers of the raw materials used by Luther in the manufacture of toys offer more normal credit terms. The usual terms for the raw materials are 2/10, net/30. Luther Company makes payment within the 10-day discount period during the first 6 months of the year; however, in the summer and fall, it does not even meet the 30-day terms. The company regularly pays invoices for raw materials 80 to 90 days after the invoice date during this latter period. Suppliers have come to accept this pattern because it has existed for many years. In addition, this payment pattern has not affected Luther's credit rating or ability to acquire the necessary raw materials.

Luther recently hired a new financial vice president. He feels quite uncomfortable with the unusually large accounts receivable and payable balances in the fall and winter and with the poor payment practice of Luther. He would like to consider alternatives to the present method of financing the accounts receivable.

One proposal being considered is to establish a line of credit at a local bank. The company could then draw against this line of credit in order to pay the invoices within the 10-day discount period and pay off the debt in February when the accounts receivable are collected. The effective interest rate for this arrangement would be 12 percent.

(a) Would establishing a line of credit reduce Luther's cost of doing business? Support your answer with appropriate calculations. (b) Would long-term financing (debt and common stock) be a sound alternative means of financing Luther's generous accounts receivable terms? (CMA, adapted.)

SOLUTION

(a) No, the line of credit alternative would not reduce Luther Company's cost of doing business. The cost of not taking the cash discount is calculated as follows:

$$\text{Cost} = \frac{\text{discount percent}}{(1.00 - \text{discount percent})} \times \frac{360}{\text{payment date} - \text{discount period}}$$

If Luther pays its invoices within 80 days, the cost of the cash discount forgone is 10.5 percent as shown below.

$$\text{Cost} = \frac{0.02}{(1.00 - 0.02)} \times \frac{360}{(80 - 10)} = \frac{0.02}{0.98} \times \frac{360}{70} = 10.5\%$$

Therefore, given the assumptions that Luther Company's credit rating or supply sources would not suffer due to late payment, the cost of the trade credit and forgoing the cash discount is lower than the 12 percent effective cost of the line of credit arrangement that would be used to take advantage of the 2 percent cash discounts.

(b) No, long-term financing is not an appropriate financing alternative to either the present method or the proposed line of credit for Luther Company.

Luther's financing need is primarily short-term and seasonal. If long-term financing is employed, Luther would probably have excess funds for 6 months of each year. The use of long-term financing to meet seasonal needs usually is impractical and can affect the company's profits and financing flexibility adversely. Generally, the matching of asset lives and liability maturity provides less risk because the return on and proceeds from the sale of the assets provide the funds necessary to pay off the debt when due. For example, noncurrent assets should be financed with long-term debt rather than short-term obligations.

5.25 Costs of Alternative Sources of Short-Term Financing. On March 1, 19X1, National Corporation purchased $100,000 worth of inventory on credit with terms of 1/20, net/60. In the past, National has always followed the policy of making payment 1 month (30 days) after the goods are purchased.

A new member of National's staff has indicated that the company she had previously worked for never passed up its cash discounts, and she wonders if that is not a sound policy. She has also pointed out to National that if it does not take advantage of the cash discount, it should wait the entire 60-day period to pay the full bill rather than paying within 30 days.

If National were to take advantage of the discount and pay the bill on March 20 rather than on March 30, the firm would have to borrow the necessary funds for the 10 extra days. National's borrowing terms with a local bank are estimated to be at $8\frac{1}{2}$ percent (annual rate), with a 15 percent compensating balance for the term of the loan. Most members of National's staff feel that it makes little sense to take out an $8\frac{1}{2}$ percent loan with a compensating balance of 15 percent in order to save 1 percent on its $100,000 by paying the account 10 days earlier than it had planned.

(a) Just in terms of true interest cost, would it be to National's advantage to take the 1 percent discount by paying the bill 10 days earlier than usual if to do this it borrowed the necessary amount on the above-mentioned terms? (b) If National ordinarily paid 60 days after purchase (instead of 30 days); would the company benefit by taking the discount if it had to borrow the money on the above-mentioned terms? (c) Compare your answers to (a) and (b) and explain what makes the discount more (less) desirable under the conditions stated in (b) than in (a). (CMA, adapted.)

SOLUTION

(a) The cost of not paying by the twentieth day is $1,000. The company pays on the thirtieth day; thus, it is paying $1,000 to borrow $99,000 for 10 days. The annual interest cost is:

$$\frac{\$1,000}{\$99,000} \times \frac{360}{10} = 36.36\%$$

It would be necessary to borrow $116,471 from the bank to satisfy the 15 percent compensating balance and pay $99,000 to the suppliers ($99,000 ÷ 0.85). The interest charges for the 10-day period would be $116,471 × 0.085 × 10/360 = $275.00. The interest rate on the $99,000 would be:

$$\frac{\$275}{\$99,000} \times \frac{360}{10} = 10.00\%$$

It is to National's advantage to borrow from the bank in order to earn the discount.

(b) Waiting 40 days past the discount date to pay the bill changes the annual interest cost of the discount to 9.09 percent.

$$\frac{\$1,000}{\$99,000} \times \frac{360}{40} = 9.09\%$$

The interest charges at the bank would be $116,471 × 0.085 × 40/360 = $1,100.
The interest rate on the $99,000 would be:

$$\frac{\$1,100}{\$99,000} \times \frac{360}{40} = 10.00\%$$

It is not in National's best interest to borrow from the bank in this case.

(c) The reason the borrowing alternative is no longer desirable in (b) is the change in the number of days that the borrowing covers. The $1,000 discount is a fixed charge for the 40-day period; it is unchanged by the number of days that lapse between the twentieth day and the day of payment. However, the interest charges vary with the number of days. Changing the borrowing period from 10 to 40 days increases the interest charges from $275 to $1,100.

5.26   Factoring. The Jackson Company has been negotiating with the Wright Bank with the hope of finding a cheaper source of funds than their current factoring arrangements. Forecasts indicate that, on average, they will need to borrow $180,000 per month this year—which is approximately 30 percent more than they have been borrowing on their receivables during the past year. Sales are expected to average $900,000 per month, of which 70 percent are on credit.

As an alternative to the present arrangements, Wright Bank has offered to lend the company up to 75 percent of the face value of the receivables shown on the schedule of accounts. The bank would charge 15 percent per annum interest plus a 2 percent processing charge per dollar of receivables assigned to support the loans. Jackson Company extends terms of net 30 days, and all customers who pay their bills do so by the 30th of the month.

The company's present factoring arrangement costs them a $2\frac{1}{2}$ percent factor fee plus an additional $1\frac{1}{2}$ percent per month on advances up to 90 percent of the volume of credit sales. Jackson Company saves $2,500 per month that would be required to support a credit department and a $1\frac{3}{4}$ percent bad debt expense on credit sales.

(a) Calculate the expected monthly cost of the bank financing proposal. (b) Calculate the expected monthly cost of factoring. (c) Discuss three advantages of factoring. (d) Discuss three disadvantages of factoring. (e) Would you recommend that the firm discontinue or reduce its factoring arrangement in favor of Wright Bank's financing plan? Explain your answer. (CMA, adapted.)

SOLUTION

(a) The expected monthly cost of bank financing is the sum of the interest cost, processing cost, bad debt expense, and credit department cost. The calculations are as follows:

Interest [$(0.15/12) \times \$180,000$]	$ 2,250
Processing [$0.02 \times (\$180,000/0.75)$]	4,800
Additional cost of not using factor:	
Credit department	2,500
Bad debt expense	
($0.0175 \times 0.7 \times \$900,000$)	11,025
Expected monthly cost of bank financing	$20,575

(b) The expected monthly cost of factoring is the sum of the interest cost and the factor cost. The calculations are as follows:

Interest ($0.015 \times \$180,000$)	$ 2,700
Factor ($0.025 \times 0.7 \times \$900,000$)	15,750
Expected monthly cost of factoring	$18,450

(c) The following are possible advantages of factoring: (1) Using a factor eliminates the need to carry a credit department. (2) Factoring is a flexible source of financing because as sales increase, the amount of readily available financing increases. (3) Factors specialize in evaluating and diversifying credit risks.

(d) The following are possible disadvantages of factoring: (1) The administrative costs may be excessive when invoices are numerous and relatively small in dollar amount. (2) Factoring removes one of the most liquid of the firm's assets and weakens the position of creditors. It may mar the firm's credit rating and increase the cost of other borrowing arrangements. (3) Customers could react unfavorably to a firm's factoring their accounts receivable.

(e) Based upon the calculations in parts (a) and (b), the factoring arrangement should be continued. The disadvantages of factoring are relatively unimportant in this case, especially since Jackson Company has been using the factor in the past. Before arriving at a final decision, the other services offered by the factor and bank would have to be evaluated, as well as the margin of error inherent in the estimation of the source data used in the calculations for parts (a) and (b). The additional borrowing capacity needed by Jackson Company is irrelevant because the firm needs only $180,000, the bank will loan $472,500 ($900,000 \times 0.70 \times 0.75$), and the factor will lend $567,000 ($900,000 \times 0.70 \times 0.90$).

Examination I

1. What are the principal functions of the financial manager?

2. Charles Corporation reports the following for 19X1:

Accounts receivable—Jan. 1	$100,000
Accounts receivable—Dec. 31	$150,000
Inventory—Jan. 1	$40,000
Inventory—Dec. 31	$55,000
Net credit sales	$800,000
Cost of goods sold	$450,000

Compute: (*a*) accounts receivable turnover, (*b*) collection period, (*c*) inventory turnover, (*d*) age of inventory, and (*e*) operating cycle.

3. Column A lists the name of a ratio and column B indicates how the ratio is computed. For each ratio name given in column A identify the ratio computation from column B.

Column A		**Column B**
(1) Profit margin	(*a*)	$\dfrac{\text{Net income} - \text{preferred dividends}}{\text{common stock outstanding}}$
(2) Dividend payout	(*b*)	$\dfrac{\text{Market price per share}}{\text{Earnings per share}}$
(3) Earnings per share	(*c*)	$\dfrac{\text{Net income}}{\text{Sales}}$
(4) Dividend yield	(*d*)	$\dfrac{\text{Dividends per share}}{\text{Earnings per share}}$
(5) Quick ratio	(*e*)	$\dfrac{\text{Current assets}}{\text{Current liabilities}}$
(6) Interest coverage	(*f*)	$\dfrac{\text{Cash} + \text{marketable securities} + \text{accounts receivable}}{\text{Current liabilities}}$
(7) Current ratio	(*g*)	$\dfrac{\text{Dividends per share}}{\text{Market price per share}}$
(8) Price/earnings ratio	(*h*)	$\dfrac{\text{Income before interest and taxes}}{\text{Interest expense}}$

4. Indicate how each of the following transactions would be reported in the statement of changes in financial position by placing an X in the appropriate column.

		Listed as a Source	Listed as an Application	Disclosed as a Material Noncurrent Transaction	Not Reported
(a)	Purchased land				
(b)	Sold an auto at book value				
(c)	Declared a stock dividend				
(d)	Appropriated retained earnings				
(e)	Issued common stock for equipment				

5. Sales terms call for a 2 percent discount if paid within the first 10 days of the month after sale. Based on prior experience, 70 percent of the sales are collected within the discount period, 20 percent are collected by the end of the month after sale, 8 percent are collected in the following month, and 2 percent are uncollectible. Actual sales for October and November are $10,000 and $20,000, respectively. Compute the cash collections forecast for December.

6. Wise Corporation is considering entering into a lockbox arrangement which will have a yearly cost of $115,000. Average daily collections are $380,000. The lockbox system will reduce float time by 2 days. The rate of return is 16 percent. Should the lockbox system be implemented?

7. Geller Corporation provides the following data:

Current annual credit sales	$30,000,000
Collection period	2 months
Terms	net/30
Rate of return	15%

   The business is considering offering a 3/10, net/30 discount. It is expected that 25 percent of the customers will take advantage of the discount. The collection period is anticipated to decrease to 1 month. Is it financially feasible to implement the discount policy?

8. William Company provides the following information: Usage is 300 units per month, cost per order is $15, and carrying cost per unit is $8.
   Determine: (a) economic order quantity, (b) the number of orders required each month, and (c) the number of days that should elapse between orders.

9. What is the opportunity cost of not taking a discount when the terms are 4/10, net/60?

10. Scott Corporation makes an $80,000 loan having a nominal interest rate of 18 percent. Interest is payable in advance and there is a required compensating balance of 10 percent. What is the effective interest rate of the loan?

11. Remsen Corporation's factor charges a 5 percent monthly fee. It lends Remsen up to 90 percent of receivables purchased for an additional 2 percent per month. Monthly credit sales are $400,000. With the factoring arrangement, there is a savings in corporate credit checking costs of $3,600 per month and in bad debts of 3.5 percent on credit sales.
   Service Bank offers to lend the company up to 90 percent of the receivables. The bank's interest charge will be 2.5 percent per month plus a 4 percent processing charge on receivable lending. The collection period is 30 days, and the company borrows the maximum allowed each month.
   Is it less expensive to finance with the factor or bank?

Answers to Examination I

1. The prime functions of the financial manager are: (*a*) obtaining financing, (*b*) investing funds, (*c*) managing assets, (*d*) paying out the appropriate amount of dividends, and (*e*) financial forecasting.

2. (*a*)
$$\text{Accounts receivable turnover} = \frac{\text{net credit sales}}{\text{average accounts receivable}} = \frac{\$800,000}{\$125,000} = 6.4 \text{ times}$$

(*b*)
$$\text{Collection period} = \frac{365}{\text{accounts receivable turnover}} = \frac{365}{6.4} = 57 \text{ days}$$

(*c*)
$$\text{Inventory turnover} = \frac{\text{cost of goods sold}}{\text{average inventory}} = \frac{\$450,000}{\$47,500} = 9.47 \text{ times}$$

(*d*)
$$\text{Age of inventory} = \frac{365}{\text{inventory turnover}} = \frac{365}{9.47} = 38.5 \text{ days}$$

(*e*) The operating cycle is:

Collection period	57.0 days
Age of inventory	38.5 days
Operating cycle	95.5 days

3. (1) (*c*); (2) (*d*); (3) (*a*); (4) (*g*); (5) (*f*); (6) (*h*); (7) (*e*); (8) (*b*).

4.

		Listed as a Source	Listed as an Application	Disclosed as a Material Noncurrent Transaction	Not Reported
(*a*)	Purchased land		X		
(*b*)	Sold an auto at book value	X			
(*c*)	Declared a stock dividend				X
(*d*)	Appropriated retained earnings				X
(*e*)	Issued common stock for equipment			X	

5. The cash collections forecast for December is:

October sales ($10,000 × 0.08)		$ 800
November sales		
Discount ($20,000 × 0.70 × 0.98)	$13,720	
No discount ($20,000 × 0.20)	4,000	17,720
Total cash collections		$18,520

6. The proposed lockbox arrangement for Wise Corporation is:

Cost	$115,000
Return on freed cash (0.16 × 2 × $380,000)	121,600
	$ 6,600

The lockbox system would save the company $6,600 and should be implemented.

7.

Current average accounts receivable balance ($30,000,000/6)	$5,000,000
Average accounts receivable balance—after change in policy ($30,000,000/12)	2,500,000
Reduction in average accounts receivable	$2,500,000
Rate of return	×0.15
Dollar return	$ 375,000
Cost of discount (0.25 × $30,000,000 × 0.03)	$ 225,000
Advantage to discount policy ($375,000 − $225,000)	$ 150,000

The discount policy is financially feasible.

8. (*a*)
$$EOQ = \sqrt{\frac{2SP}{C}} = \sqrt{\frac{2(300)(15)}{8}} = \sqrt{\frac{9,000}{8}} = 34 \text{ (rounded)}$$

(*b*)
$$\frac{S}{EOQ} = \frac{300}{34} = 9 \text{ (rounded)}$$

(*c*)
$$\frac{31}{9} = \text{every 3 days (rounded)}$$

9.
$$\text{Opportunity cost of not taking discount} = \frac{\text{discount percent}}{100 - \text{discount percent}} \times \frac{360}{N} = \frac{4}{96} \times \frac{360}{50} = 30.0\%$$

10.
$$\text{Effective interest rate} = \frac{\text{interest rate} \times \text{principal}}{(\text{proceeds, \%} \times \text{principal}) - \text{interest}}$$
$$= \frac{18\% \times \$80,000}{(90\% \times \$80,000) - \$14,400} = \frac{\$14,400}{\$57,600} = 25\%$$

11. The cost of financing with a factor is:

Purchased receivable (0.05 × $400,000)	$20,000
Lending fee (0.02 × $400,000 × 0.90)	7,200
Total cost	$27,200

The cost of financing with a bank is:

Interest (0.025 × $400,000 × 0.90)	$ 9,000
Processing charge (0.04 × $400,000 × 0.90)	14,400
Additional cost of not using factor	
Credit costs	3,600
Bad debts (0.035 × $400,000)	14,000
Total cost	$41,000

It is less expensive to use the factor.

Chapter 6

Time Value of Money

6.1 INTRODUCTION

Time value of money is a critical consideration in financial and investment decisions. For example, *compound interest* calculations are needed to determine future sums of money resulting from an investment. Discounting, or the calculation of *present value*, which is inversely related to compounding, is used to evaluate future cash flow associated with capital budgeting projects. There are plenty of applications of time value of money in finance. The chapter discusses the concepts, calculations, and applications of future values and present values.

6.2 FUTURE VALUES—COMPOUNDING

A dollar in hand today is worth more than a dollar to be received tomorrow because of the interest it could earn from putting it in a savings account or placing it in an investment account. Compounding interest means that interest earns interest. For the discussion of the concepts of compounding and time value, let us define:

F_n = future value = the amount of money at the end of year n

P = principal

i = annual interest rate

n = number of years

Then,

F_1 = the amount of money at the end of year 1

= principal and interest = $P + iP = P(1 + i)$

F_2 = the amount of money at the end of year 2

= $F_1(1 + i) = P(1 + i)(1 + i) = P(1 + i)^2$

The future value of an investment compounded annually at rate i for n years is

$$F_n = P(1 + i)^n = P \cdot \text{FVIF}_{i,n}$$

where $\text{FVIF}_{i,n}$ is the future value interest factor for $1 and can be found in Appendix A.

EXAMPLE 6.1 George Jackson placed $1,000 in a savings account earning 8 percent interest compounded annually. How much money will he have in the account at the end of 4 years?

$$F_n = P(1 + i)^n$$
$$F_4 = \$1,000(1 + 0.08)^4$$

From Appendix A, the FVIF for 4 years at 8 percent is 1.3605. Therefore,

$$F_4 = \$1,000(1.3605) = \$1,360.50$$

EXAMPLE 6.2 Rachael Kahn invested a large sum of money in the stock of TLC Corporation. The company paid a $3 dividend per share. The dividend is expected to increase by 20 percent per year for the next 3 years. She wishes to project the dividends for years 1 through 3.

$$F_n = P(1 + i)^n$$
$$F_1 = \$3(1 + 0.2)^1 = \$3(1.2000) = \$3.60$$
$$F_2 = \$3(1 + 0.2)^2 = \$3(1.4400) = \$4.32$$
$$F_3 = \$3(1 + 0.2)^3 = \$3(1.7280) = \$5.18$$

Intrayear Compounding

Interest is often compounded more frequently than once a year. Banks, for example, compound interest quarterly, daily, and even continuously. If interest is compounded m times a year, then the general formula for solving for the future value becomes

$$F_n = P \left(1 + \frac{i}{m}\right)^{n \cdot m} = P \cdot \text{FVIF}_{i/m, n \cdot m}$$

The formula reflects more frequent compounding $(n \cdot m)$ at a smaller interest rate per period (i/m). For example, in the case of semiannual compounding $(m = 2)$, the above formula becomes

$$F_n = P \left(1 + \frac{i}{2}\right)^{n \cdot 2} = P \cdot \text{FVIF}_{i/2, n \cdot 2}$$

As m approaches infinity, the term $(1 + i/m)^{n \cdot m}$ approaches $e^{i \cdot n}$, where e is approximately 2.71828, and F_n becomes

$$F_n = P \cdot e^{i \cdot n}$$

The future value increases as m increases. Thus, continuous compounding results in the maximum possible future value at the end of n periods for a given rate of interest.

EXAMPLE 6.3 Assume that $P = \$100$, $i = 12\%$ and $n = 3$ years. Then for

Annual compounding $(m = 1)$: $F_3 = \$100(1 + 0.12)^3 = \$100(1.404)^3 = \$140.49$

Semiannual compounding $(m = 2)$: $F_3 = \$100 \left(1 + \dfrac{0.12}{2}\right)^{3 \cdot 2}$

$$= \$100(1 + 0.06)^6 = \$100(1.4185) = \$141.85$$

Quarterly compounding $(m = 4)$: $F_3 = \$100 \left(1 + \dfrac{0.12}{4}\right)^{3 \cdot 4} = \$100(1 + 0.03)^{12}$

$$= \$100(1.4257) = \$142.57$$

Monthly compounding $(m = 12)$: $F_3 = \$100 \left(1 + \dfrac{0.12}{12}\right)^{3 \cdot 12}$

$$= \$100(1 + 0.01)^{36} = \$100(1.4307) = \$143.07$$

Continuous compounding $(e^{i \cdot n})$: $F_3 = \$100 \cdot e^{(0.12 \cdot 3)} = \$100(2.71828)^{0.36}$

$$= \$100(1.4333) = \$143.33$$

Future Value of an Annuity

An *annuity* is defined as a series of payments (or receipts) of a fixed amount for a specified number of periods. Each payment is assumed to occur at the *end* of the period. The future value of an annuity is a compound annuity which involves depositing or investing an equal sum of money at the end of each year for a certain number of years and allowing it to grow.

Let S_n = the future value of an n-year annuity

A = the amount of an annuity

Then we can write

$$\begin{aligned} S_n &= A(1+i)^{n-1} + A(1+i)^{n-2} + \cdots + A(1+i)^0 \\ &= A[(i+i)^{n-1} + (1+i)^{n-2} + \cdots + (1+i)^0] \\ &= A \cdot \sum_{t=0}^{n-1} (1+i)^t + A \cdot \text{FVIFA}_{i,n} \end{aligned}$$

where $\text{FVIFA}_{i,n}$ represents the future value interest factor for an n-year annuity compounded at i percent and can be found in Appendix B.

EXAMPLE 6.4 Jane Oak wishes to determine the sum of money she will have in her savings account at the end of 6 years by depositing $1,000 at the end of each year for the next 6 years. The annual interest rate is 8 percent. The $\text{FVIFA}_{8\%, 6\,\text{years}}$ is given in Appendix B as 7.336. Therefore,

$$S_6 = \$1,000(\text{FVIFA}_{8,6}) = \$1,000(7.336) = \$7,336$$

6.3 PRESENT VALUE—DISCOUNTING

Present value is the present worth of future sums of money. The process of calculating present values, or *discounting*, is actually the opposite of finding the compounded future value. In connection with present value calculations, the interest rate i is called the *discount rate*.

Recall that

$$F_n = P(1 + i)^n$$

Therefore,

$$P = \frac{F_n}{(1 + i)^n} = F_n \left[\frac{1}{(1 + i)^n} \right] = F_n \cdot \text{PVIF}_{i,n}$$

Where $\text{PVIF}_{i,n}$ represents the present value interest factor for $1 and is given in Appendix C.

EXAMPLE 6.5 Ron Jaffe has been given an opportunity to receive $20,000 6 years from now. If he can earn 10 percent on his investments, what is the most he should pay for this opportunity? To answer this question, one must compute the present value of $20,000 to be received 6 years from now at a 10 percent rate of discount. F_6 is $20,000, i is 10 percent, which equals 0.1, and n is 6 years. $\text{PVIF}_{10,6}$ from Appendix C is 0.5645.

$$P = \$20,000 \left[\frac{1}{(1 + 0.1)^6} \right] = \$20,000(\text{PVIF}_{10,6}) = \$20,000(0.5645) = \$11,290$$

This means that Ron Jaffe, who can earn 10 percent on his investment, could be indifferent to the choice between receiving $11,290 now or $20,000 6 years from now since the amounts are time equivalent. In other words, he could invest $11,290 today at 10 percent and have $20,000 in 6 years.

Present Value of Mixed Streams of Cash Flows

The present value of a series of mixed payments (or receipts) is the sum of the present value of each individual payment. We know that the present value of each individual payment is the payment times the appropriate PVIF.

EXAMPLE 6.6 Candy Parker has been offered an opportunity to receive the following mixed stream of revenue over the next 3 years:

Year	Revenue
1	$1,000
2	$2,000
3	$500

If she must earn a minimum of 6 percent on her investment, what is the most she should pay today? The present value of this series of mixed streams of revenue is as follows:

Year	Revenue ($)	× PVIF	= Present Value
1	1,000	0.943	$ 943
2	2,000	0.890	1,780
3	500	0.840	420
			$3,143

Present Value of an Annuity

Interest received from bonds, pension funds, and insurance obligations all involve annuities. To compare these financial instruments, we need to know the present value of each. The present value of an annuity (P_n) can be found by using the following equation:

$$P_n = A \cdot \frac{1}{(1+i)^1} + A \cdot \frac{1}{(1+i)^2} + \cdots + A \cdot \frac{1}{(1+i)^n}$$

$$= A \left[\frac{1}{(1+i)^1} + \frac{1}{(1+i)^2} + \cdots + \frac{1}{(1+i)^n} \right]$$

$$= A \cdot \sum_{t=1}^{n} \frac{1}{(1+i)^t} = A \cdot \text{PVIFA}_{i,n}$$

where $\text{PVIFA}_{i,n}$ represents the appropriate value for the present value interest factor for a $1 annuity discounted at i percent for n years and is found in Appendix D.

EXAMPLE 6.7   Assume that the revenues in Example 6.6 form an annuity of $1,000 for 3 years. Then the present value is

$$P_n = A \cdot \text{PVIFA}_{i,n}$$
$$P_3 = \$1,000(\text{PVIFA}_{6,3}) = \$1,000(2.6730) = \$2,673$$

Perpetuities

Some annuities go on forever. Such annuities are called *perpetuities*. An example of a perpetuity is preferred stock which yields a constant dollar dividend indefinitely. The present value of a perpetuity is found as follows:

$$\text{Present value of a perpetuity} = \frac{\text{receipt}}{\text{discount rate}} = \frac{A}{i}$$

EXAMPLE 6.8   Assume that a perpetual bond has an $80-per-year interest payment and that the discount rate is 10 percent. The present value of this perpetuity is:

$$P = \frac{A}{i} = \frac{\$80}{0.10} = \$800$$

6.4   APPLICATIONS OF FUTURE VALUES AND PRESENT VALUES

Future and present values have numerous applications in financial and investment decisions, which will be discussed throughout the book. Five of these applications are presented below.

Deposits to Accumulate a Future Sum (or Sinking Fund)

An individual might wish to find the annual deposit (or payment) that is necessary to accumulate a future sum. To find this future amount (or sinking fund) we can use the formula for finding the future value of an annuity.

$$S_n = A \cdot \text{FVIFA}_{i,n}$$

Solving for A, we obtain:

$$\text{Sinking fund amount} = A = \frac{S_n}{\text{FVIFA}_{i,n}}$$

EXAMPLE 6.9   Mary Czech wishes to determine the equal annual end-of-year deposits required to accumulate $5,000 at the end of 5 years when her son enters college. The interest rate is 10 percent. The annual deposit is:

$$S_5 = \$5,000$$
$$\text{FVIFA}_{10,5} = 6.1051 \quad \text{(from Appendix B)}$$
$$A = \frac{\$5,000}{6.1051} = \$818.99 \cong \$819$$

In other words, if she deposits \$819 at the end of each year for 5 years at 10 percent interest, she will have accumulated \$5,000 at the end of the fifth year.

Amortized Loans

If a loan is to be repaid in equal periodic amounts, it is said to be an *amortized loan*. Examples include auto loans, mortgage loans, and most commercial loans. The periodic payment can easily be computed as follows:

$$P_n = A \cdot \text{PVIFA}_{i,n}$$

Solving for A, we obtain: $\text{Amount of loan} = A = \dfrac{P_n}{\text{PVIFA}_{i,n}}$

EXAMPLE 6.10 Jeff Balthness has a 40-month auto loan of \$5,000 at a 12 percent annual interest rate. He wants to find out the monthly loan payment amount.

$$i = 12\% \div 12 \text{ months} = 1\%$$
$$P_{40} = \$5,000$$
$$\text{PVIFA}_{1,40} = 32.8347 \quad \text{(from Appendix D)}$$

Therefore, $A = \dfrac{\$5,000}{32.8347} = \$152.28$

So, to repay the principal and interest on a \$5,000, 12 percent, 40-month loan, Jeff Balthness has to pay \$152.28 a month for the next 40 months.

EXAMPLE 6.11 Assume that a firm borrows \$2,000 to be repaid in three equal installments at the end of each of the next 3 years. The bank wants 12 percent interest. Compute the amount of each payment.

$$P_3 = \$2,000$$
$$\text{PVIFA}_{12,3} = 2.4018$$

Therefore, $A = \dfrac{\$2,000}{2.4018} = \$832.71$

Each loan payment consists partly of interest and partly of principal. The breakdown is often displayed in a *loan amortization schedule*. The interest component is largest in the first period and subsequently declines, whereas the principal portion is smallest in the first period and increases thereafter, as shown in the following example.

EXAMPLE 6.12 Using the same data as in Example 6.11, we set up the following amortization schedule:

Year	Payment	Interest	Repayment of Principal	Remaining Balance
1	\$832.71	\$240.00 [a]	\$592.71	\$1,407.29
2	\$832.71	\$168.88	\$663.83	\$743.46
3	\$832.68 [b]	\$89.22	\$743.46 [c]	

[a] Interest is computed by multiplying the loan balance at the beginning of the year by the interest rate. Therefore, interest in year 1 is \$2,000(0.12) = \$240; in year 2 interest is \$1,407.29(0.12) = \$168.88; and in year 3 interest is \$743.46(0.12) = \$89.22. All figures are rounded.

[b] Last payment is adjusted downward.

[c] Not exact because of accumulated rounding errors.

Annual Percentage Rate (APR)

Different types of investments use different compounding periods. For example, most bonds pay interest semiannually; banks generally pay interest quarterly. If an investor wishes to compare investments with different compounding periods, he or she needs to put them on a common basis. The *annual percentage rate* (APR), or effective annual rate, is used for this purpose and is computed as follows:

$$APR = \left(1 + \frac{r}{m}\right)^m - 1.0$$

where r = the stated, nominal or quoted rate and m = the number of compounding periods per year.

EXAMPLE 6.13   If the nominal rate is 6 percent, compounded *quarterly*, the APR is

$$APR = \left(1 + \frac{r}{m}\right)^m - 1.0 = \left(1 + \frac{0.06}{4}\right)^4 - 1.0 = (1.015)^4 - 1.0 = 1.0614 - 1.0 = 0.0614 = 6.14\%$$

This means that if one bank offered 6 percent with quarterly compounding, while another offered 6.14 percent with annual compounding, they would both be paying the same effective rate of interest.

Rates of Growth

In finance, it is necessary to calculate the *compound annual interest rate*, or rate of growth, associated with a stream of earnings.

EXAMPLE 6.14   Assume that the Geico Company has earnings per share of $2.50 in 19X1, and 10 years later the earnings per share has increased to $3.70. The compound annual rate of growth of the earnings per share can be computed as follows:

$$F_n = P \cdot FVIF_{i,n}$$

Solving this for FVIF, we obtain:

$$FVIF_{i,n} = \frac{F_n}{P}$$

$$FVIF_{i,10} = \frac{\$3.70}{\$2.50} = 1.48$$

From Appendix A an FVIF of 1.48 at 10 years is at $i = 4\%$. The compound annual rate of growth is therefore 4 percent.

Bond Values

Bonds call for the payment of a specific amount of interest for a stated number of years *and* the repayment of the face value at the bond's maturity. Thus, a bond represents an annuity plus a lump sum. Its value is found as the present value of this payment stream. The interest is usually paid semiannually.

$$V = \sum_{t=1}^{n} \frac{I}{(1+r)^t} + \frac{M}{(1+r)^n}$$

$$= I(PVIFA_{r,n}) + M(PVIF_{r,n})$$

where I = interest payment per period

M = par value, or maturity value, usually $1,000

r = investor's required rate of return

n = number of periods

This topic is covered in more detail in Chapter 7, "Risk, Return, and Valuation."

EXAMPLE 6.15 Assume there is a 10-year bond with a 10 percent coupon, paying interest semiannually and having a face value of $1,000. Since interest is paid semiannually, the number of periods involved is 20 and the semiannual cash inflow is $100/2 = $50.

Assume that investors have a required rate of return of 12 percent for this type of bond. Then, the present value (V) of this bond is:

$$V = \$50(\text{PVIFA}_{6,20}) + \$1,000(\text{PVIF}_{6,20})$$
$$= \$50(11.4699) + \$1,000(0.3118) = \$573,50 + \$311.80 = \$885.30$$

Note that the required rate of return (12 percent) is higher than the coupon rate of interest (10 percent), and so the bond value (or the price investors are willing to pay for this particular bond) is less than its $1,000 face value.

Review Questions

1. _____ is a critical consideration in many financial and investment decisions.

2. The process of determining present value is often called _____ and is the reverse of the _____ process.

3. $F_n = P(1 + i/m)^{n \cdot m}$ is a general formula used for _____.

4. _____ results in the maximum possible future value at the end of n periods for a given rate of interest.

5. A(n) _____ is a series of payments (or receipts) of a fixed amount for a specified number of periods.

6. The _____, or effective annual rate, is used to compare investments with different _____ on a common basis.

7. The present value of a mixed stream of payments (or receipts) is the _____ of present values of _____.

8. A(n) _____ is an annuity in which payments go on forever.

9. The _____ is the annual deposit (or payment) of an amount that is necessary to accumulate a specified future sum.

10. If a loan is to be repaid in equal periodic amounts, it is said to be a(n) _____.

Answers: (1) Time value of money; (2) discounting, compounding; (3) intrayear compounding; (4) Continuous compounding; (5) annuity; (6) annual percentage rate (APR), compounding periods; (7) sum, the individual payments; (8) perpetuity; (9) sinking fund; (10) amortized loan.

Solved Problems

6.1   **Future Value.** Compute the future values of (a) an initial $2,000 compounded annually for 10 years at 8 percent; (b) an initial $2,000 compounded annually for 10 years at 10 percent; (c) an annuity of $2,000 for 10 years at 8 percent; and (d) an annuity of $2,000 for 10 years at 10 percent.

SOLUTION

(a)   To find the future value of an investment compounded annually, use:

$$F_n = P(1 + i)^n = P \cdot \text{FVIF}_{i,n}$$

In this case, $P = \$2,000$, $i = 8\%$, $n = 10$, and $\text{FVIF}_{8\%, 10\,\text{yr}} = 2.1589$. Therefore,

$$F_{10} = \$2,000(1 + 0.08)^{10} = \$2,000(2.1589) = \$4,317.80$$

(b) $$F_n = P(1 + i)^n = P \cdot \text{FVIF}_{i,n}$$

Here $P = \$2,000$, $i = 10\%$, $n = 10$, and $\text{FVIF}_{10,10} = 2.5937$. Therefore,

$$F_{10} = \$2,000(1 + 0.10)^{10} = \$2,000(2.5937) = \$5,187.40$$

(c)   For the future value of an annuity, use:

$$S_n = A \cdot \text{FVIFA}_{i,n}$$

In this case $A = \$2,000$, $i = 8\%$, $n = 10$, and $\text{FVIFA}_{8\%, 10\,\text{yr}} = 14.486$. Therefore,

$$S_{10} = \$2,000(14.486) = \$28,972$$

(d) $$S_n = A \cdot \text{FVIFA}_{i,n}$$

Here, $A = \$2,000$, $i = 10\%$, and $\text{FVIFA}_{10,10} = 15.937$. Therefore,

$$S_{10} = \$2,000(15.937) = \$31,874$$

6.2   **Intrayear Compounding.** Calculate how much you would have in a savings account 5 years from now if you invest $1,000 today, given that the interest paid is 8 percent compounded (a) annually, (b) semiannually, (c) quarterly, and (d) continuously.

SOLUTION

A general formula for intrayear compounding is:

$$F_n = P(1 + i/m)^{n \cdot m} = P \cdot \text{FVIF}_{i/m, n \cdot m}$$

For this problem $P = \$1,000$ and $n = 5$ years.

(a)   When $m = 1$, $i = 8\%$, and $\text{FVIF}_{(8\%/1), 5 \cdot 1} = 1.4693$,

$$F_5 = \$1,000 \left(1 + \frac{0.08}{1}\right)^{5 \cdot 1} = \$1,000(1.4693) = \$1,469.30$$

(b)   When $m = 2$ and $\text{FVIF}_{(8\%/2), 5 \cdot 2} = \text{FVIF}_{4,10} = 1.4802$,

$$F_5 = \$1,000(1.4802) = \$1,480.20$$

(c) $m = 4$ and $\text{FVIF}_{(8\%/4), 5 \cdot 4} = \text{FVIF}_{2,20} = 1.4859$,

$$F_5 = \$1,000(1.4859) = \$1,485.90$$

(d)   For continuous compounding, use:

$$F_n = P \cdot e^{i \cdot n}$$

$$F_5 = \$1,000(2.71828)^{0.08 \cdot 5} = \$1,000(2.71828)^{0.4}$$

$$= \$1,000(1.4918) = \$1,491.80$$

6.3   **Present Value.** Calculate the present value, discounted at 10 percent, of receiving: (*a*) $800 at the end of year 4, (*b*) $200 at the end of year 3 and $300 at the end of year 5, (*c*) $500 at the end of year 4 and $300 at the end of year 6, and (*d*) $500 a year for the next 10 years.

SOLUTION

(*a*)
$$P = F_n \left[\frac{1}{(1+i)^n} \right] = F_n \cdot \text{PVIF}_{i,n}$$

Here $n = 4$, $F_4 = \$800$, and $i = 10\%$.

$$\text{PVIF}_{10,4} = 0.6830$$
$$P = \$800(0.6830) = \$546.40$$

(*b*)
$$P = \$200(\text{PVIF}_{10,3}) + \$300(\text{PVIF}_{10,5})$$
$$= \$200(0.7513) + \$300(0.6209) = \$150.26 + \$186.27 = \$336.53$$

(*c*)
$$P = \$500(\text{PVIF}_{10,4}) + \$300(\text{PVIF}_{10,6}) = \$500(0.6830) + \$300(0.5645)$$
$$= \$341.50 + \$169.35 = \$510.85$$

(*d*)   For the present value of an annuity, use:

$$P_n = A \cdot \text{PVIFA}_{i,n}$$

Here $A = \$500$, $n = 10$, and $i = 10\%$. Therefore,

$$P_{10} = \$500(\text{PVIFA}_{10,10}) = \$500(6.1446) = \$3,072.30$$

6.4   **Present Value.** Calculate the present value of the following future cash inflows discounted at 10 percent: (*a*) $1,000 a year for years 1 through 10; (*b*) $1,000 a year for years 5 through 10; and (*c*) $1,000 a year for years 1 through 3, nothing in years 4 through 5, then $2,000 a year for years 6 through 10.

SOLUTION

(*a*)
$$P_n = A \cdot \text{PVIFA}_{i,n}$$

Here $A = \$1,000$, $i = 10\%$, and $n = 10$ years. Therefore,

$$P_{10} = \$1,000(\text{PVIFA}_{10,10}) = \$1,000(6.1446) = \$6,144.60$$

(*b*)
$$P = \$1,000(\text{PVIFA}_{10,10}) - \$1,000(\text{PVIFA}_{10,4})$$
$$= \$1,000(6.1446) - \$1,000(3.1699) = \$6,144.60 - \$3,169.90 = \$2,974.70$$

This type of annuity is called a *deferred annuity*.

(*c*)
$$P = \$1,000(\text{PVIFA}_{10,3}) + [\$2,000(\text{PVIFA}_{10,10}) - \$2,000(\text{PVIFA}_{10,5})]$$
$$= \$1,000(2.4869) + [\$2,000(6.1446) - \$2,000(3.7908)]$$
$$= \$2,486.90 + [\$12,289.2 - \$7,581.60] = \$2,466.90 + \$4,707.60 = \$7,194.5$$

6.5   **Present Value.** Your favorite uncle has offered you the choice of the following options. He will give you either $2,000 1 year from now or $3,000 4 years from now. Which would you choose if the discount rate is (*a*) 10 percent? (*b*) 20 percent?

SOLUTION

$$P = F_n \cdot \text{PVIF}_{i,n}$$

(*a*)   Option 1: $2,000 one year from now. In this case $i = 10\%$, $n = 1$, $F_1 = \$2,000$, and $\text{PVIF}_{10,1} = 0.9091$. Therefore,

$$P = \$2,000(0.9091) = \$1,818.20$$

Option 2: $3,000 four years from now. In this case $i = 10\%$, $n = 4$, $F_4 = \$3,000$, and $\text{PVIF}_{10,4} = 0.6830$. Therefore,

$$P = \$3,000(0.6830) = \$2,049$$

At 10 percent, the best choice is $3,000 four years from now.

(b) Option 1: $2,000 one year from now. In this case $i = 20\%$, $n = 1$, $F_1 = \$2,000$, and $\text{PVIF}_{20,1} = 0.8333$. Therefore,

$$P = \$2,000(0.8333) = \$1,666.60$$

Option 2: $3,000 four years from now. In this case $i = 20\%$, $n = 4$, $F_4 = \$3,000$, and $\text{PVIF}_{20,4} = 0.4823$. Therefore,

$$P = \$3,000(0.4823) = \$1,446.9$$

At 20 percent, the best choice is $2,000 one year from now.

6.6   **Present value.** A 55-year-old executive will retire at age 65 and expects to live to age 75. Assuming a 10 percent rate of return, calculate the amount he must have available at age 65 in order to receive $10,000 annually from retirement until death. (CFA, adapted.)

SOLUTION

This problem involves finding the present value of an annuity. The executive must have $61,446 available at age 65, calculated as follows:

$$P_n = A \cdot \text{PVIFA}_{i,n}$$

Here $A = \$10,000$, $n = 10$, $i = 10\%$, and $\text{PVIFA}_{10,10} = 6.1446$. Therefore,

$$P_{10} = \$10,000(6.1446) = \$61,446$$

6.7   **Present Value.** Your father is about to retire. His firm has given him the option of retiring with a lump sum of $20,000 or an annuity of $2,500 for 10 years. Which is worth more now, if an interest rate of 6 percent is used for the annuity?

SOLUTION

$$P_n = A \cdot \text{PVIF}_{i,n}$$

Here $A = \$2,500$, $i = 6\%$, $n = 10$, and $\text{PVIFA}_{6,10} = 7.3601$. Therefore,

$$P_{10} = \$2,500(\text{PVIFA}_{6,10}) = \$2,500(7.3601) = \$18,400.25$$

The lump sum of $20,000 is worth more now.

6.8   **Perpetuities.** What is the present value of a perpetuity of $80 per year if the discount rate is 11 percent.

SOLUTION

$$\text{The present value of a perpetuity} = \frac{A}{i} = \frac{\$80}{11\%} = \$727.27$$

6.9   **Deposits Required.** If you need $6,000 5 years from now, how much of a deposit must you make in your savings account each year, assuming an 8 percent annual interest rate?

SOLUTION

Solving $S_n = A \cdot \text{FVIFA}_{i,n}$ for A yields:

$$A = \frac{S_n}{\text{FVIFA}_{i,n}}$$

In this problem $S_5 = \$6,000$, $i = 8\%$, $n = 5$, and $\text{FVIFA}_{8,5} = 5.8666$. Therefore,

$$A = \frac{\$6,000}{5.8666} = \$1,022.74$$

6.10 **Sinking Fund.** A \$1 million bond issue is outstanding. Assume deposits earn 8 percent per annum. Calculate the amount to be deposited to a sinking fund each year in order to accumulate enougn money to retire the entire \$1 million issue at the end of 20 years. (CFA, adapted.)

SOLUTION

$$A = \frac{S_n}{\text{FVIFA}_{i,n}}$$

In this problem, $S_{20} = \$1,000,000$ and $\text{FVIFA}_{8,20} = 45.762$. Therefore,

$$A = \frac{\$1,000,000}{45.762} = \$21,852.19$$

6.11 **Loan Amortization.** You have applied for a home mortgage of \$75,000 to finance the purchase of a new home for 30 years. The bank requires a 14 percent interest rate. What will be annual payment?

SOLUTION

Solving $P_n = A \cdot \text{PVIFA}_{i,n}$ for A yields:

$$A = \frac{P_n}{\text{PVIFA}_{i,n}}$$

Here $P_{30} = \$75,000$ and $\text{PVIFA}_{14,30} = 7.0027$. Therefore,

$$A = \frac{\$75,000}{7.0027} = \$10,710.16$$

6.12 **Loan Amortization.** A commercial bank is willing to make you a loan of \$10,000. The bank wants a 12 percent interest rate and requires five equal annual payments to repay both interest and principal. What will be the dollar amount of the annual payment?

SOLUTION

$$A = \frac{P_n}{\text{PVIFA}_{i,n}}$$

Here $P_5 = \$10,000$ and $\text{PVIFA}_{12,5} = 3.6048$. Therefore,

$$A = \frac{\$10,000}{3.6048} = \$2,774.08$$

6.13 **Loan Amortization Schedule.** Set up an amortization schedule for a \$5,000 loan to be repaid in equal installments at the end of each of the next 3 years. The interest rate is 15 percent.

SOLUTION

First, find the amount of equal installment by using the following formula:

$$A = \frac{P_n}{\text{PVIFA}_{i,n}}$$

In this problem $P_3 = \$5,000$ and $\text{PVIFA}_{15,3} = 2.2832$. Therefore,

$$A = \frac{\$5,000}{2.2832} = \$2,189.91$$

The amortization schedule is as follows:

Year	Payment	Interest [a]	Repayment of Principal	Remaining Balance
1	\$2,189.91	\$750	\$1,439.91	\$3,560.09
2	\$2,189.91	\$534.01	\$1,655.90	\$1,904.19
3	\$2,189.82 [b]	\$285.63	\$1.904.19 [c]	

[a] Interest is computed by multiplying the loan balance at the beginning of the year by the interest rate. Therefore, interest in year 1 is $\$5,000(0.15) = \$750$; in year 2 interest $\$3,560.09(0.15) = \$534.01$; etc.

[b] Last payment is adjusted downward.

[c] Not exact because of accumulated rounding errors.

6.14 **Annual Percentage Rate (APR).** Suppose that a company borrows \$20,000 for 1 year at a stated rate of interest of 9 percent. What is the annual percentage rate (APR) if interest is paid to the lender (*a*) annually? (*b*) semiannually? (*c*) quarterly?

SOLUTION

$$\text{APR} = \left(1 + \frac{r}{m}\right)^m - 1.0$$

In this problem $r = 9\% = 0.09$.

(*a*) If interest is paid at the end of the year, $m = 1$ and

$$\text{APR} = \left(1 + \frac{0.09}{1}\right)^1 - 1.0 = 1.09 - 1.0 = 0.09 = 9.0\%$$

(*b*) If interest is paid at the end of each 6-month period, $m = 2$ and

$$\text{APR} = \left(1 + \frac{0.09}{2}\right)^2 - 1.0 = (1.045)^2 - 1.0$$
$$= 1.092 - 1.0 = 0.092 = 9.2\%$$

(*c*) If interest is paid at the end of each quarter, $m = 4$ and

$$\text{APR} = \left(1 + \frac{0.09}{4}\right)^4 - 1.0 = (1.0225)^4 - 1.0$$
$$= 1.093 - 1.0 = 0.093 = 9.3\%$$

More frequent payment of interest increases the effective annual cost paid by the company.

6.15 **Rate of Growth.** If a firm's earnings increase from \$3.00 per share to \$4.02 over a 6-year period, what is the rate of growth?

SOLUTION

Solving $F_n = P \cdot \text{FVIF}_{i,n}$ for FVIF yields:

$$\text{FVIF}_{i,n} = \frac{F_n}{P}$$

Here, $P = \$3.00$ and $F_6 = \$4.02$. Therefore,

$$\text{FVIF}_{i,6} = \frac{\$4.02}{\$3.00} = 1.340$$

From Appendix A, an FVIF of 1.340 at 6 years is at $i = 5\%$. The rate of growth of earnings is therefore 5 percent.

6.16   Annual Rate of Interest. You borrowed \$20,000, to be repaid in 12 monthly installments of \$1,891.20. What is the annual interest rate?

SOLUTION

Solving $P_n = A \cdot \text{PVIFA}_{i,n}$ for PVIFA yields:

$$\text{PVIFA}_{i,n} = \frac{P_n}{A}$$

In this problem $P_{12} = \$20,000$ and $A = \$1,891.20$. Therefore,

$$\text{PVIFA}_{i,12} = \frac{\$20,000}{\$1,891.20} = 10.5753$$

From Appendix D, a PVIFA of 10.5753 for 12 periods is at $i = 2\%$. The annual interest rate is therefore $2\% \times 12 = 24\%$.

6.17   Bond Values. What amount should an investor be willing to pay for a \$1,000, 5-year United States government bond which pays \$50 interest semiannually and is sold to yield 8 percent?

SOLUTION

The semiannual interest is 4 percent. The value of the bond is:

$$\begin{aligned} V &= I(\text{PVIFA}_{r,n}) + M(\text{PVIF}_{r,n}) \\ &= \$50(\text{PVIFA}_{4,10}) + \$1,000(\text{PVIF}_{4,10}) \\ &= \$50(8.1109) + \$1,000(0.6756) = \$405.55 + \$675.60 = \$1,081.15 \end{aligned}$$

6.18   Bond Values. Calculate the value of a bond with a face value of \$1,000, a coupon interest rate of 8 percent paid semiannually, and a maturity of 10 years. Assume the following discount rates: (a) 6 percent, (b) 8 percent, and (c) 10 percent.

SOLUTION

$$\text{Semiannual interest} = \frac{8\%(\$1,000)}{2} = \$40$$

$$\text{Number of periods} = 10 \times 2 = 20 \text{ periods}$$

(a)
$$\begin{aligned} V &= I(\text{PVIA}_{r,n}) + M(\text{PVIF}_{r,n}) \\ &= \$40(\text{PVIFA}_{3,20}) + \$1,000(\text{PVIF}_{3,20}) \\ &= \$40(14.8775) + \$1,000(0.5537) = \$595.10 + \$553.7 = \$1,148.80 \end{aligned}$$

(b)
$$\begin{aligned} V &= \$40(\text{PVIFA}_{4,20}) + \$1,000(\text{PVIF}_{4,20}) \\ &= \$40(13.5903) + \$1,000(0.4564) = \$543.61 + \$456.40 = \$1,000 \text{ (rounded)} \end{aligned}$$

(c)
$$\begin{aligned} V &= \$40(\text{PVIFA}_{5,20}) + \$1,000(\text{PVIF}_{5,20}) \\ &= \$40(12.4622) + \$1,000(0.3769) = \$498.49 + \$376.90 = \$875.37 \end{aligned}$$

Chapter 7

Risk, Return, and Valuation

7.1 RISK DEFINED

Risk (or uncertainty) refers to the variability of expected returns associated with a given investment. Risk, along with the concept of return, is a key consideration in investment and financial decisions. This chapter will discuss procedures for measuring risk and investigate the relationship between risk, returns, and security valuation.

Probability Distributions

Probabilities are used to evaluate the risk involved in a security. The *probability* of an event taking place is defined as the chance that the event will occur. It may be thought of as the percentage chance of a given outcome.

EXAMPLE 7.1 A weather forecaster may state, "There is a 30 percent chance of rain tomorrow and a 70 percent chance of no rain." Then we could set up the following probability distribution:

Outcome	Probability
Rain	30% = 0.3
No rain	70% = 0.7
	100% = 1.00

Expected Rate of Return

Expected rate of return ($\bar{r}$) is the weighted average of possible returns from a given investment, weights being probabilities. Mathematically,

$$\bar{r} = \sum_{i=1}^{n} r_i p_i$$

where r_i = ith possible return
p_i = probability of the ith return
n = number of possible returns

EXAMPLE 7.2 Consider the possible rates of return that you might earn next year on a $50,000 investment in stock A or on a $50,000 investment in stock B, depending upon the states of the economy: recession, normal, and prosperity.

For stock A:

State of Economy	Return (r_i)	Probability (p_i)
Recession	−5%	0.2
Normal	20%	0.6
Prosperity	40%	0.2

For stock B:

State of Economy	Return (r_i)	Probability (p_i)
Recession	10%	0.2
Normal	15%	0.6
Prosperity	20%	0.2

178

Then the expected rate of return ($\bar{r}$) for stock A is computed as follows:

$$\bar{r} = \sum_{i=1}^{n} r_i p_i = (-5\%)(0.2) + (20\%)(0.6) + (40\%)(0.2) = 19\%$$

Stock B's expected rate of return is:

$$\bar{r} = (10\%)(0.2) + (15\%)(0.6) + 20\%(0.2) = 15\%$$

Measuring Risk: The Standard Deviation

The standard deviation (σ), which is a measure of dispersion of the probability distribution, is commonly used to measure risk. The smaller the standard deviation, the tighter the probability distribution and, thus, the lower the risk of the investment.

Mathematically,

$$\sigma = \sqrt{\sum_{i=1}^{n} (r_i - \bar{r})^2 p_i}$$

To calculate σ, take the following steps:

Step 1. Compute the expected rate of return ($\bar{r}$).

Step 2. Subtract each possible return from $\bar{r}$ to obtain a set of deviations ($r_i - \bar{r}$).

Step 3. Square each deviation, multiply the squared deviation by the probability of occurrence for its respective return, and sum these products to obtain the *variance* (σ^2):

$$\sigma^2 = \sum_{i=1}^{n} (r_i - \bar{r})^2 p_i$$

Step 4. Finally, take the square root of the variance to obtain the standard deviation (σ).

To follow this step-by-step approach, it is convenient to set up a table.

EXAMPLE 7.3 Using the data given in Example 7.2, compute the standard deviation for each stock and set up the tables as follows for stock A:

Return (r_i) (%)	Probability (p_i)	Step 1 $r_i p$ (%)	Step 2 $(r_i - \bar{r})$ (%)	$(r_i - \bar{r})^2$	Step 3 $(r_i - \bar{r})^2 p_i$ (%)
-5	0.2	-1	-24	576	115.2
20	0.6	12	1	1	0.6
40	0.2	8	21	441	88.2
		$\bar{r} = 19$			$\sigma^2 = 204$

Knowing $\sigma^2 = 204$, we proceed with Step 4 and

$$\sigma = \sqrt{204} = 14.28\%$$

For stock B:

Return (r_i) (%)	Probability (p_i)	Step 1 $r_i p_i$ (%)	Step 2 $(r_i - \bar{r})$ (%)	$(r_i - \bar{r})^2$	Step 3 $(r_i - \bar{r})^2 p_i$ (%)
10	0.2	2	-5	25	5
15	0.6	9	0	0	0
20	0.2	4	5	25	5
		$\bar{r} = 15$			$\sigma^2 = 10$

Knowing $\sigma^2 = 10$, we take Step 4 and

$$\sigma = \sqrt{10} = 3.16\%$$

Statistically, if the probability distribution is *normal*, 68 percent of the returns will lie in ± 1 standard deviation, 95 percent of all observations will lie between ± 2 standard deviations, and 99 percent of all observations will lie between ± 3 standard deviations of the expected value.

EXAMPLE 7.4   Using the results from Example 7.3,

	Stock A	Stock B
Expected return ($\bar{r}$)	19%	15%
Standard deviation (σ)	14.28%	3.16%

For stock A, there is a 68 percent probability that the actual return will be in the range of 19 percent plus or minus 14.28 percent or from 4.72 percent to 33.28 percent. Since the range is so great, stock A is risky; it is likely to either fall far below its expected rate of return or far exceed the expected return. For stock B, the 68 percent range is 15 percent plus or minus 3.16 percent or from 11.84 percent to 18.16 percent. With such a small σ, there is only a small probability that stock B's return will be far less or greater than expected; hence, stock B is not very risky.

Measure of Relative Risk: Coefficient of Variation

One must be careful when using the standard deviation to compare risk since it is only an absolute measure of dispersion (risk) and does not consider the dispersion of outcomes in relationship to an expected value (return). Therefore, when comparing securities that have different expected returns, use the coefficient of variation. The coefficient of variation is computed simply by dividing the standard deviation for a security by expected value: $\sigma/\bar{r}$. The higher the coefficient, the more risky the security.

EXAMPLE 7.5   Again, using the results from Example 7.3:

	Stock A	Stock B
$\bar{r}$	19%	15%
σ	14.28%	3.16%
$\sigma/\bar{r}$	0.75%	0.21%

Although stock A is expected to produce a considerably higher return than stock B, stock A is overall more risky than stock B, based on the computed coefficient variation.

Types of Risk

The various risks that must be considered when making financial and investment decisions are as follows:

1. *Business risk* is caused by fluctuations of earnings before interest and taxes (operating income). Business risk depends on variability in demand, sales price, input prices, and amount of operating leverage.

2. *Liquidity risk* represents the possibility that an asset may not be sold on short notice for its market value. If an asset must be sold at a high discount, then it is said to have a substantial amount of liquidity risk.

3. *Default risk* is the risk that a borrower will be unable to make interest payments or principal repayments on debt. For example, there is a great amount of default risk inherent in the bonds of a company experiencing financial difficulty.

4. *Market risk* is the risk that a stock's price will change due to changes in the stock market atmosphere as a whole since prices of all stocks are correlated to some degree with broad swings in the stock market.

5. *Interest rate risk* is the risk resulting from fluctuations in the value of an asset as interest rates change. For example, if interest rates rise (fall), bond prices fall (rise).

6. *Purchasing power risk* is the risk that a rise in price will reduce the quantity of goods that can be purchased with a fixed sum of money.

7.2 PORTFOLIO RISK AND CAPITAL ASSET PRICING MODEL (CAPM)

Most financial assets are not held in isolation; rather, they are held as parts of portfolios. Therefore, risk-return analysis (discussed in Section 7.1) should not be confined to single assets only. It is important to look at portfolios and the gains from diversification. What is important is the return on the portfolio, not just the return on one asset, and the portfolio's risk.

Portfolio Return

The expected return on a portfolio (r_p) is simply the weighted average return of the individual assets in the portfolio, the weights being the fraction of the total funds invested in each asset:

$$r_p = w_1 r_1 + w_2 r_2 + \cdots + w_n r_n = \sum_{j=1}^{n} w_j r_j$$

where r_j = expected return on each individual asset
         w_j = fraction for each respective asset investment
         n = number of assets in the portfolio

$$\sum_{j=1}^{n} w_j = 1.0$$

EXAMPLE 7.6 A portfolio consists of assets A and B. Asset A makes up one-third of the portfolio and has an expected return of 18 percent. Asset B makes up the other two-thirds of the portfolio and is expected to earn 9 percent. What is the expected return on the portfolio?

Asset	Return (r_j)	Fraction (w_j)	$w_j r_j$
A	18%	$\frac{1}{3}$	$\frac{1}{3} \times 18\% = 6\%$
B	9%	$\frac{2}{3}$	$\frac{2}{3} \times 9\% = \underline{\ 6\%}$
			$r_p = \underline{\underline{12\%}}$

Portfolio Risk

Unlike returns, the risk of a portfolio (σ_p) is not simply the weighted average of the standard deviations of the individual assets in the contribution, for a portfolio's risk is also dependent on the correlation coefficients of its assets. The correlation coefficient (ρ) is a measure of the degree to which two variables "move" together. It has a numerical value that ranges from −1.0 to 1.0. In a two-asset (A and B) portfolio, the portfolio risk is defined as:

$$\sigma_p = \sqrt{w_A^2 \sigma_A^2 + w_B^2 \sigma_B^2 + 2 w_A w_B \cdot \rho_{AB} \sigma_A \sigma_B}$$

where σ_A and σ_B = standard deviations of assets A and B, respectively

w_A and w_B = weights, or fractions, of total funds invested in assets A and B

ρ_{AB} = the correlation coefficient between assets A and B

Portfolio risk can be minimized by *diversification*, or by combining assets in an appropriate manner. The degree to which risk is minimized depends on the correlation between the assets being combined. For example, by combining two *perfectly negative* correlated assets ($\rho = -1$), the overall portfolio riks can be completely eliminated. Combining two *perfectly positive* correlated assets ($\rho = +1$) does nothing to help reduce risk. (See Example 7.7.) An example of the latter might be ownership of two automobile stocks or two housing stocks.

EXAMPLE 7.7   Assume the following:

Asset	σ	w
A	20%	$\frac{1}{3}$
B	10%	$\frac{2}{3}$

The portfolio risk then is:

$$\sigma_p = \sqrt{w_A^2 \sigma_A^2 + w_B^2 \sigma_B^2 + 2 w_A w_B \cdot \rho_{AB} \sigma_A \sigma_B}$$
$$= \sqrt{(\tfrac{1}{3})^2 (0.2)^2 + (\tfrac{2}{3})^2 (0.1)^2 + 2\rho_{AB}(\tfrac{1}{3})(\tfrac{2}{3})(0.2)(0.1)}$$
$$= \sqrt{0.0089 + 0.0089 \rho_{AB}}$$

(a)   Now assume that the correlation coefficient between A and B is +1 (a perfectly positive correlation). This means that when the value of asset A increases in response to market conditions, so does the value of asset B, and it does so at exactly the same rate as A. The portfolio risk when $\rho = +1$ then becomes:

$$\sigma_p = \sqrt{0.0089 + 0.0089 \rho_{AB}} = \sqrt{0.0089 + 0.0089(1)} = \sqrt{0.0178} = 0.1334 = 13.34\%$$

(b)   If $\rho = 0$, the assets lack correlation and the portfolio risk is simply the risk of the expected returns on the assets, i.e., the weighted average of the standard deviations of the individual assets in the portfolio. Therefore, when $\rho_{AB} = 0$, the portfolio risk for this example is:

$$\sigma_p = \sqrt{0.0089 + 0.089 \rho_{AB}} = \sqrt{0.0089 + 0.0089(0)} = \sqrt{0.0089} = 0.0943 = 9.43\%$$

(c)   If $\rho = -1$ (a perfectly negative correlation coefficient), then as the price of A rises, the price of B declines at the very same rate. In such a case, risk would be completely eliminated. Therefore, when $\rho_{AB} = -1$, the portfolio risk is

$$\sigma_p = \sqrt{0.0089 + 0.0089 \rho_{AB}} = \sqrt{0.0089 + 0.0089(-1)} = \sqrt{0.0089 - 0.0089} = \sqrt{0} = 0$$

When we compare the results of (a), (b), and (c), we see that a positive correlation between assets increases a portfolio's risk above the level found at zero correlation, while a perfectly negative correlation eliminates that risk.

EXAMPLE 7.8   To illustrate the point of diversification, assume the data on the following three securities are as follows:

Year	Security X (%)	Security Y (%)	Security Z (%)
19X1	10	50	10
19X2	20	40	20
19X3	30	30	30
19X4	40	20	40
19X5	50	10	50
r_j	30	30	30
σ_p	14.14	14.14	14.14

Note here that securities X and Y have a perfectly negative correlation, and securities X and Z have a perfectly positive correlation. Notice what happens to the portfolio risk when X and Y, and X and Z are combined. Assume that funds are split equally between the two securities in each portfolio.

Year	Portfolio XY (50%–50%)	Portfolio XZ (50%–50%)
19X1	30	10
19X2	30	20
19X3	30	30
19X4	30	40
19X5	30	50
r_p	30	30
σ_p	0	14.14

Again, see that the two perfectly negative correlated securities (XY) result in a zero overall risk.

Capital Asset Pricing Model (CAPM)

A security risk consists of two components—diversifiable risk and nondiversifiable risk. *Diversifiable risk*, sometimes called *controllable risk* or *unsystematic risk*, represents the portion of a security's risk that can be controlled through diversification. This type of risk is unique to a given security. Business, liquidity, and default risks fall into this category. *Nondiversifiable risk*, sometimes referred to as *noncontrollable risk* or *systematic risk*, results from forces outside of the firm's control and is therefore not unique to the given security. Purchasing power, interest rate, and market risks fall into this category. Nondiversifiable risk is assessed relative to the risk of a diversified portfolio of securities, or the *market portfolio*. This type of risk is measured by the *beta* coefficient.

The capital asset pricing model (CAPM) relates the risk measured by beta to the level of expected or required rate of return on a security. The model, also called the security market line (SML), is given as follows:

$$r_j = r_f + b(r_m - r_f)$$

where r_j = the expected (or required) return on security j
r_f = the risk-free security (such as a T-bill)
r_m = the expected return on the market portfolio (such as Standard & Poor's 500 Stock Composite Index or Dow Jones 30 Industrials)
b = beta, an index of nondiversifiable (noncontrollable, systematic) risk

The key component in the CAPM, beta (b), is a measure of the security's volatility relative to that of an average security. For example: b = 0.5 means the security is only half as volatile, or risky, as the average security; b = 1.0 means the security is of average risk; and b = 2.0 means the security is twice as risky as the average risk.

The whole term $b(r_m - r_f)$ represents the risk premium, the additional return required to compensate investors for assuming a given level of risk.

Thus, in words, the CAPM (or SML) equation shows that the required (expected) rate of return on a given security (r_j) is equal to the return required for securities that have no risk (r_f) plus a risk premium required by investors for assuming a given level of risk. The higher the degree of systematic risk (b), the higher the return on a given security demanded by investors.

EXAMPLE 7.9 Assuming that the risk-free rate (r_f) is 8 percent, and the expected return for the market (r_m) is 12 percent, then if

b = 0 (risk-free security)	$r_j = 8\% + 0(12\% - 8\%) = 8\%$
b = 0.5	$r_j = 8\% + 0.5(12\% - 8\%) = 10\%$
b = 1.0 (market portfolio)	$r_j = 8\% + 1.0(12\% - 8\%) = 12\%$
b = 2.0	$r_j = 8\% + 2.0(12\% - 8\%) = 16\%$

7.3 BOND AND STOCK VALUATION

The process of determining security valuation involves finding the present value of an asset's expected future cash flows using the investor's required rate of return. Thus, the basic security valuation model can be defined mathematically as follows:

$$V = \sum_{t=1}^{n} \frac{C_t}{(1+r)^t}$$

where V = intrinsic value or present value of an asset

C_t = expected future cash flows in period $t = 1, \ldots, n$

r = investor's required rate of return

Bond Valuation

The valuation process for a bond requires a knowledge of three basic elements: (1) the amount of the cash flows to be received by the investor, which is equal to the periodic interests to be received and the par value to be paid at maturity; (2) the maturity date of the loan; and (3) the investor's required rate of return.

Incidentally, the periodic interest can be received annually or semiannually. The value of a bond is simply the present value of these cash flows. Two versions of the bond valuation model are presented below:

If the interest payments are made annually, then

$$V = \sum_{t=1}^{n} \frac{I}{(1+r)^t} + \frac{M}{(1+r)^n} = I(\text{PVIFA}_{r,n}) + M(\text{PVIF}_{r,n})$$

where I = interest payment each year = coupon interest rate × par value

M = par value, or maturity value, typically \$1,000

r = investor's required rate of return

n = number of years to maturity

PVIFA = present value interest factor of an annuity of \$1 (which can be found in Appendix D)

PVIF = present value interest factor of \$1 (which can be found in Appendix C)

EXAMPLE 7.10   Consider a bond, maturing in 10 years and having a coupon rate of 8 percent. The par value is \$1,000. Investors consider 10 percent to be an appropriate required rate of return in view of the risk level associated with this bond. The annual interest payment is \$80(8% × \$1,000). The present value of this bond is:

$$V = \sum_{t=1}^{n} \frac{I}{(1+r)^t} + \frac{M}{(1+r)^n} = I(\text{PVIFA}_{r,n}) + M(\text{PVIF}_{r,n})$$

$$= \sum_{t=1}^{10} \frac{\$80}{(1+0.1)^t} + \frac{\$1,000}{(1+0.1)^{10}} = \$80(\text{PVIFA}_{10\%,10}) + \$1,000(\text{PVIF}_{10\%,10})$$

$$= \$80(6.1446) + \$1,000(0.3855) = \$491.57 + \$385.50 = \$877.07$$

If the interest is paid *semiannually*, then

$$V = \sum_{t=1}^{2n} \frac{I/2}{(1+r/2)^t} + \frac{M}{(1+r/2)^{2n}} = \frac{I}{2}(\text{PVIFA}_{r/2,2n}) + M(\text{PVIF}_{r/2,2n})$$

EXAMPLE 7.11   Assume the same data as in Example 7.10, except the interest is paid semiannually.

$$V = \sum_{t=1}^{2n} \frac{I/2}{(1+r/2)^t} + \frac{M}{(1+r/2)^{2n}} = \frac{I}{2}(\text{PVIFA}_{r/2,2n}) + M(\text{PVIF}_{r/2,2n})$$

$$= \sum_{t=1}^{20} \frac{\$40}{(1+0.05)^t} + \frac{\$1,000}{(1+0.05)^{20}}$$

$$= \$40(\text{PVIFA}_{5\%,20}) + \$1,000(\text{PVIF}_{5\%,20}) = \$40(12.4622) + \$1,000(0.3769) = \$498.49 + \$376.90 = \$875.39$$

Common Stock Valuation

Like bonds, the value of a common stock is the present value of all future cash inflows expected to be received by the investor. The cash inflows expected to be received are dividends and the future price at the time of the sale of the stock. For an investor holding a common stock for only 1 year, the value of the stock would be the present value of both the expected cash dividend to be received in 1 year (D_1) and the expected market price per share of the stock at year-end (P_1). If r represents an investor's required rate of return, the value of common stock (P_0) would be:

$$P_0 = \frac{D_1}{(1+r)^1} + \frac{P_1}{(1+r)^1}$$

EXAMPLE 7.12   Assume an investor is considering the purchase of stock A at the beginning of the year. The dividend at year-end is expected to be \$1.50, and the market price by the end of the year is expected to be \$40. If the investor's required rate of return is 15 percent, the value of the stock would be:

$$P_0 = \frac{D_1}{(1+r)^1} + \frac{P_1}{(1+r)^1} = \frac{\$1.50}{(1+0.15)} + \frac{\$40}{(1+0.15)} = \$1.50(0.870) + \$40(0.870) = \$1.31 + \$34.80 = \$36.11$$

Since common stock has no maturity date and is held for many years, a more general, multiperiod model is needed. The general common stock valuation model is defined as follows:

$$P_0 = \sum_{t=1}^{\infty} \frac{D_t}{(1+r)^t}$$

There are three cases of growth in dividends. They are (1) zero growth, (2) constant growth, and (3) nonconstant, or supernormal, growth.

In the case of zero growth, if

$$D_0 = D_1 = \cdots = D_\infty$$

then the valuation model

$$P_0 = \sum_{t=1}^{\infty} \frac{D_t}{(1+r)^t}$$

reduces to the formula:

$$P_0 = \frac{D_1}{r}$$

EXAMPLE 7.13   Assuming D equals \$2.50 and r equals 10 percent, then the value of the stock is:

$$P_0 = \frac{\$2.50}{0.1} = \$25$$

In the case of constant growth, if we assume that dividends grow at a constant rate of g every year [i.e., $D_t = D_0(1+g)^t$], then the above model is simplified to:

$$P_0 = \frac{D_1}{r-g}$$

This formula is known as the *Gordon growth model*.

EXAMPLE 7.14   Consider a common stock that paid a \$3 dividend per share at the end of the last year and is expected to pay a cash dividend every year at a growth rate of 10 percent. Assume the investor's required rate of return is 12 percent. The value of the stock would be:

$$D_1 = D_0(1 + g) = \$3(1 + 0.10) = \$3.30$$

$$P_0 = \frac{D_1}{r - g} = \frac{\$3.30}{0.12 - 0.10} = \$165$$

Finally, consider the case of nonconstant, or supernormal, growth. Firms typically go through life cycles, during part of which their growth is faster than that of the economy and then falls sharply. The value of stock during such supernormal growth can be found by taking the following steps: (1) Compute the dividends during the period of supernormal growth and find their present value; (2) find the price of the stock at the end of the supernormal growth period and compute its present value; and (3) add these two PV figures to find the value (P_0) of the common stock.

EXAMPLE 7.15 Consider a common stock whose dividends are expected to grow at a 25 percent rate for 2 years, after which the growth rate is expected to fall to 5 percent. The dividend paid last period was $2. The investor desires a 12 percent return. To find the value of this stock, take the following steps:

1. Compute the dividends during the supernormal growth period and find their present value. Assuming D_0 is $2, g is 15 percent, and r is 12 percent:

$$D_1 = D_0(1 + g) = \$2(1 + 0.25) = \$2.50$$

$$D_2 = D_0(1 + g)^2 = \$2(1.563) = \$3.125$$

or

$$D_2 = D_1(1 + g) = \$2.50(1.25) = \$3.125$$

$$\text{PV of dividends} = \frac{D_1}{(1 + r)^1} + \frac{D^2}{(1 + r)^2} = \frac{\$2.50}{(1 + 0.12)} + \frac{\$3.125}{(1 + 0.12)^2}$$

$$= \$2.50(\text{PVIF}_{12\%,1}) + \$3.125(\text{PVIF}_{12\%,2})$$

$$= \$2.50(0.8929) + \$3.125(0.7972) = \$2.23 + \$2.49 = \$4.72$$

2. Find the price of the stock at the end of the supernormal growth period. The dividend for the third year is:

$$D_3 = D_2(1 + g'), \text{ where } g' = 5\%$$

$$= \$3.125(1 + 0.05) = \$3.28$$

The price of the stock is therefore:

$$P_2 = \frac{D_3}{r - g'} = \frac{\$3.28}{0.12 - 0.05} = \$46.86$$

$$\text{PV of stock price} = \$46.86(\text{PVIF}_{12\%,2}) = \$46.86(0.7972) = \$37.36$$

3. Add the two PV figures obtained in steps 1 and 2 to find the value of the stock.

$$P_0 = \$4.72 + \$37.36 = \$42.08$$

Expected Rate of Return on a Bond: Yield to Maturity

The expected rate of return on a bond, better known as the bond's *yield to maturity*, is computed by solving the following equation (the bond valuation model) for r:

$$V = \sum_{t=1}^{n} \frac{I}{(1 + r)^t} + \frac{M}{(1 + r)^n} = I(\text{PVIFA}_{r,n}) + M(\text{PVIF}_{r,n})$$

where V is the market price of the bond.

Finding the bond's yield, r, involves trial and error. It is best explained by example.

EXAMPLE 7.16 Suppose you were offered a 10-year, 8 percent coupon, $1,000 par value bond at a price of $877.07. What rate of return could you earn if you bought the bond and held it to maturity? Recall that in Example 7.10 the value of the bond, $877.07, was obtained using the required rate of return of 10 percent. Compute this bond's yield to see if it is 10 percent.

First, set up the bond valuation model:

$$V = \$877.07 = \sum_{t=1}^{10} \frac{\$80}{(1+r)^t} + \frac{\$1,000}{(1+r)^{10}}$$

$$= \$80(\text{PVIFA}_{r,10}) + \$1,000(\text{PVIF}_{r,10})$$

Since the bond is selling at a discount under the par value (\$877.07 versus \$1,000), the bond's yield is above the going coupon rate of 8 percent. Therefore, try a rate of 9 percent. Substituting factors for 9 percent in the equation, we obtain:

$$V = \$80(6.4177) + \$1,000(0.4224) = \$513.42 + \$422.4 = \$935.82$$

The calculated bond value, \$935.82, is *above* the actual market price of \$877.07, so the yield is *not* 9 percent. To lower the calculated value, the rate must be *raised*. Trying 10 percent, we obtain:

$$V = \$80(6.1446) + \$1,000(0.3855) = \$491.57 + \$385.50 = \$877.07$$

This calculated value is exactly equal to the market price of the bond; thus, *10 percent* is the bond's yield to maturity.

The formula that can be used to find the *approximate* yield to maturity on a bond is:

$$\text{Yield} = \frac{I + (M - V)/n}{(M + V)/2}$$

where I = dollars of interest paid per year
        M = the par value, typically \$1,000 per share
        V = a bond's value
        n = number of years to maturity

This formula can also be used to obtain a starting point for the trial-and-error method discussed in Example 7.16.

EXAMPLE 7.17   Using the same data as in Example 7.16 and the shortcut method, the rate of return on the bond is:

$$\text{Yield} = \frac{I + (M - V)/n}{(M + V)/2} = \frac{\$80 + (\$1,000 - \$877.60)/10}{(\$1,000 + \$877.60)/2} = \frac{\$80 + \$12.24}{\$938.80} = \frac{\$92.24}{\$938.80} = 9.8\%$$

which is very close to the exact rate of 10 percent.

Expected Rate of Return on Common Stock

The formula for computing the expected rate of return on common stock can be derived easily from the valuation models.

The single-period return formula is derived from:

$$P_0 = \frac{D_1}{(1+r)} + \frac{P_1}{(1+r)}$$

Solving for r gives:

$$r = \frac{D_1 + (P_1 - P_0)}{P_0}$$

In words,

$$\text{Rate of return} = \frac{\text{dividends} + \text{capital gain}}{\text{beginning price}}$$

$$= \text{dividend yield} + \text{capital gain yield}$$

EXAMPLE 7.18 Consider a stock that sells for $50. The company is expected to pay a $3 cash dividend at the end of the year, and the stock's market price at the end of the year is expected to be $55 a share. Thus, the expected return would be:

$$r = \frac{D_1 + (P_1 - P_0)}{P_0} = \frac{\$3.00 + (\$55 - \$50)}{\$50} = \frac{\$3.00 + \$5.00}{\$50} = 16\%$$

or:

$$\text{Dividend yield} = \frac{\$3.00}{\$50} = 6\%$$

$$\text{Capital gain yield} = \frac{\$5.00}{\$50} = 10\%$$

$$r = \text{dividend yield} + \text{capital gain yield}$$
$$= 6\% + 10\% = 16\%$$

Assuming a constant growth in dividend, the formula for the expected rate of return on an investment in stock can be derived as follows:

$$P_0 = \frac{D_1}{r - g}$$

$$r = \frac{D_1}{P_0} + g$$

EXAMPLE 7.19 Suppose that ABC Company's dividend per share was $4.50, expected to grow at a constant rate of 6 percent. The current market price of the stock is $30. Then the expected rate of return is:

$$r = \frac{D_1}{P_0} + g = \frac{\$4.50}{\$30} + 6\% = 15\% + 6\% = 21\%$$

Review Questions

1. _____ refers to the variability of _____ associated with a given investment.

2. Expected rate of return is the _____ of possible returns from a given investment, with the weights being _____ .

3. The smaller the standard deviation, the "tighter" the _____ and, thus, the lower the _____ of the investment.

4. The higher the coefficient of _____, the greater the risk of the security.

5. _____ depends on _____ in demand, sales price, input prices, and so on.

6. _____ refers to the change in a stock's price that results from changes in the stock market as a whole.

7. Total risk is the sum of _____ and _____ .

8. Portfolio risk can be reduced by _____.

9. $\rho_{AB} = -1.0$ means that assets A and B have a(n)_____.

10. The_____, or _____, equation shows that the required rate of return on a security is equal to the risk-free rate plus _____.

11. The valuation process involves finding the _____ of an asset's expected future cash flows using the investor's required rate of return.

12. The expected rate of return on a stock is the sum of _____ yield and_____ yield.

13. The _____ computes the value of a common stock when dividends are expected to grow at a constant rate.

14. The three cases of dividend growth are: _____, _____, and _____.

15. The one-period return on stock investment is dividends plus_____, divided by the beginning price.

16. _____ is an index of systematic risk.

Answers: (1) Risk, expected return (or earnings); (2) weighted average, probabilities; (3) probability distribution, risk; (4) variation; (5) Business risk, variability; (6) Market risk; (7) unsystematic risk, systematic risk; (8) diversification; (9) perfectly negative correlation; (10) capital asset pricing model (CAPM), security market line (SML), a risk premium; (11) present value; (12) dividend, capital gain; (13) Gordon growth model; (14) zero growth, constant growth, supernormal growth; (15) capital gain; (16) Beta.

Solved Problems

7.1   Expected Return and Standard Deviation. Assuming the following probability distribution of the possible returns, calculate the expected return ($\bar{r}$) and the standard deviation (σ) of the returns.

Probability (p_i)	Return (r_i)
0.1	−20%
0.2	5%
0.3	10%
0.4	25%

SOLUTION

$$\bar{r} = \sum r_i p_i$$

$$\sigma = \sqrt{\sum (r_i - \bar{r})^2 p_i}$$

It is convenient to set up the following table:

r_i (%)	p_i	$r_i p_i$ (%)	$(r_i - \bar r)$ (%)	$(r_i - \bar r)^2$	$(r_i - \bar r)^2 p_i$ (%)
−20	0.1	−2	−32	1,024	102.4
5	0.2	1	−7	49	9.8
10	0.3	3	−2	4	1.2
25	0.4	10	13	169	67.6
		$\bar r = 12$			$\sigma^2 = 181$

Since $\sigma^2 = 181$, $\sigma = \sqrt{181} = 13.45\%$.

7.2   **Return and Measures of Risk.** Stocks A and B have the following probability distributions of possible future returns:

Probability (p_i)	A (%)	B (%)
0.1	−15	−20
0.2	0	10
0.4	5	20
0.2	10	30
0.1	25	50

(*a*) Calculate the expected rate of return for each stock and the standard deviation of returns for each stock. (*b*) Calculate the coefficient of variation. (*c*) Which stock is less risky? Explain.

SOLUTION

(*a*)   For stock A:

r_i (%)	p_i	$r_i p_i$ (%)	$(r_i - \bar r)$ (%)	$(r_i - \bar r)^2$	$(r_i - \bar r)^2 p_i$ (%)
−15	0.1	−1.5	−20	400	40
0	0.2	0	−5	25	5
5	0.4	2	0	0	0
10	0.2	2	5	25	5
25	0.1	2.5	20	400	40
		$\bar r = 5.0$			$\sigma^2 = 90$

Since $\sigma^2 = 90$, $\sigma = \sqrt{90} = 9.5\%$.
For stock B:

r_i (%)	p_i	$r_i p_i$ (%)	$(r_i - \bar r)$ (%)	$(r_i - \bar r)^2$	$(r_i - \bar r)^2 p_i$ (%)
−20	0.1	−2	−39	1,521	152.1
10	0.2	2	−9	81	16.2
20	0.4	8	1	1	0.4
30	0.2	6	11	121	24.2
50	0.1	5	31	961	96.1
		$\bar r = 19$			$\sigma^2 = 289$

Since $\sigma^2 = 289$, $\sigma = \sqrt{289} = 17\%$.

(b) The coefficient of variation is $\sigma/\bar{r}$. Thus, for stock A:

$$\frac{9.5\%}{5\%} = 1.9$$

For stock B:

$$\frac{17.0\%}{19\%} = 0.89$$

(c) Stock B is less risky than stock A since the coefficient of variation (a measure of relative risk) is smaller for stock B.

7.3   Absolute and Relative Risk. Ken Parker must decide which of two securities is best for him. By using probability estimates, he computed the following statistics:

Statistic	Security X	Security Y
Expected return ($\bar{r}$)	12%	8%
Standard deviation (σ)	20%	10%

(a) Compute the coefficient of variation for each security, and (b) explain why the standard deviation and coefficient of variation give different rankings of risk. Which method is superior and why?

SOLUTION

(a) For the X coefficient of variation ($\sigma/\bar{r}$) is $20/12 = 1.67$. For Y it is $10/8 = 1.25$.

(b) Unlike the standard deviation, the coefficient of variation considers the standard deviation of securities relative to their average return. The coefficient of variation is therefore the more useful measure of relative risk. The lower the coefficient of variation, the less risky the security relative to the expected return. Thus, in this problem, security Y is relatively less risky than security X.

7.4   Diversification Effects. The securities of firms A and B have the expected return and standard deviations given below; the expected correlation between the two stocks (ρ_{AB}) is 0.1.

	$\bar{r}$	σ
A	14%	20%
B	9%	30%

Compute the return and risk for each of the following portfolios: (a) 100 percent A, (b) 100 percent B, (c) 60 percent A–40 percent B, and (d) 50 percent A–50 percent B.

SOLUTION

(a)   100 percent A: $\bar{r} = 14\%$; $\sigma = 20\%$; $\sigma/\bar{r} = \dfrac{20}{14} = 1.43$

(b)   100 percent B: $\bar{r} = 9\%$; $\sigma = 30\%$; $\sigma/\bar{r} = \dfrac{30}{9} = 3.33$

(c) 60 percent A − 40 percent B:

$$r_p = w_A r_A + w_B r_B = (0.6)(14\%) + (0.4)(9\%) = 12\%$$

$$\sigma_p = \sqrt{w_A^2 \sigma_A^2 + w_B^2 \sigma_B^2 + 2 w_A w_B \rho_{AB} \sigma_A \sigma_B}$$

$$= \sqrt{(0.6)^2(0.2)^2 + (0.4)^2(0.3)^2 + 2(0.6)(0.4)\rho_{AB}(0.2)(0.3)}$$

$$= \sqrt{0.0144 + 0.0144 + 0.0288\rho_{AB}} = \sqrt{0.0288 + 0.0288(0.1)} = \sqrt{0.03168} = 0.1780 = 17.8\%$$

(d)   50 percent A–50 percent B:

$$r_p = (0.5)(14\%) + (0.5)(9\%) = 11.5\%$$

$$\sigma_P = \sqrt{(0.5)^2(0.2)^2 + (0.5)^2(0.3)^2 + 2(0.5)(0.5)\rho_{AB}(0.2)(0.3)}$$

$$= \sqrt{0.01 + 0.0225 + 0.03\rho_{AB}} = \sqrt{0.0325 + 0.03\rho_{AB}}$$

$$= \sqrt{0.0325 + 0.03(0.1)} = \sqrt{0.0355} = 0.1884 = 18.84\%$$

7.5   Diversification Effects. Use the same facts as for Problem 7.4, except for this problem assume the expected correlation between the two stocks (ρ_{AB}) = −1.0.

SOLUTION

(a) and (b)   The answers are the same as in Problem 7.4.

(c) $$r_p = 12\%$$

$$\sigma_p = \sqrt{0.0288 + 0.0288(-1.0)} = \sqrt{0} = 0\%$$

(d) $$r_p = 11.5\%$$

$$\sigma_p = \sqrt{0.0325 + 0.03(-1.0)} = \sqrt{0.0025} = 0.05 = 5\%$$

7.6   Beta and Expected Return. Assume that the risk-free rate of return is 8 percent, the required rate of return on the market is 13 percent, and stock X has a beta coefficient of 1.5. (a) What is stock X's required rate of return? (b) What if the beta increases to 2? (c) What if the risk-free rate decreases to 6 percent, assuming the beta is still 1.5?

SOLUTION

$$r = r_f + b(r_m - r_f)$$

(a) $$r = 8\% + 1.5(13\% - 8\%) = 8\% + 1.5(5\%) = 15.5\%$$

(b) $$r = 8\% + 2(13\% - 8\%) = 8\% + 10\% = 18\%$$

(c) $$r = 6\% + 1.5(13\% - 6\%) = 6\% + 10.5 = 16.5\%$$

7.7   Required Rate of Return and Beta. Moe Corporation is considering several securities. The rate on Treasury bills is currently 8.25 percent, and the expected return for the market is 11.5 percent. What should be the required rates of return for each security?

Security	Beta
A	1.15
B	0.85
C	1.00
D	1.50

SOLUTION

Security	r_f (%)	+	$b[r_m (\%) - r_f (\%)]$	=	r (%)
A	8.25		$(1.15)(11.5 - 8.25)$		11.9875
B	8.25		$(0.85)(11.5 - 8.25)$		11.0125
C	8.25		$(1.00)(11.5 - 8.25)$		11.5
D	8.25		$(1.50)(11.5 - 8.25)$		13.125

7.8   CAPM. If Treasury bills yield 10 percent, and Alpha Company's expected return for next year is 18 percent and its beta is 2, what is the market's expected return for next year? Assume the capital asset pricing model (CAPM) applies and everything is in equilibrium.

SOLUTION

$$r = r_f + b(r_m - r_f)$$
$$18\% = 10\% + 2(r_m - 10\%)$$
$$0.18 = 0.1 + 2r_m - 0.2$$
$$0.28 = 2r_m$$
$$r_m = \frac{0.28}{2} = 0.14 = 14\%$$

7.9   Beta. Assuming the CAPM applies, if the market's expected return is 13 percent, the risk-free rate is 8 percent, and stock A's required rate of return is 16 percent, what is the stock's beta coefficient?

SOLUTION

$$r = r_f + b(r_m - r_f)$$
$$16\% = 8\% + b(13\% - 8\%)$$
$$0.16 = 0.08 + b(0.05)$$
$$0.08 = b(0.05)$$
$$b = 1.6$$

7.10   Security Market Line (SML). The risk-free rate is 7 percent, and the expected return on the market portfolio is 12 percent. (*a*) What is the equation for the security market line (SML)? (*b*) Graph the SML.

SOLUTION

(*a*)   The SML equation is:

$$r = r_f + b(r_m - r_f) = 7\% + b(12\% - 7\%) = 7\% + b(5\%)$$

(*b*)   See Fig. 7-1.

7.11   CAPM. Assume the following: the risk-free rate is 8 percent, and the market portfolio expected return is 12 percent.

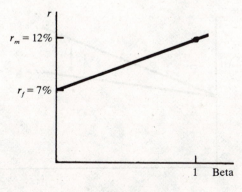

Fig. 7-1

Portfolio	Beta
A	0.6
B	1.0
C	1.4

(*a*) Calculate for each of the three portfolios the expected return consistent with the capital asset pricing model. (*b*) Show graphically the expected portfolio returns in (*a*). (*c*) Indicate what would happen to the capital market line if the expected return on the market portfolio were 10 percent. (CFA, adapted.)

SOLUTION

(*a*)
Portfolio A: $r = 8\% + 0.6(12\% - 8\%) = 10.4\%$
Portfolio B: $r = 8\% + 1.0(12\% - 8\%) = 12.0\%$
Portfolio C: $r = 8\% + 1.4(12\% - 8\%) = 13.6\%$

(*b*) See Fig. 7-2.

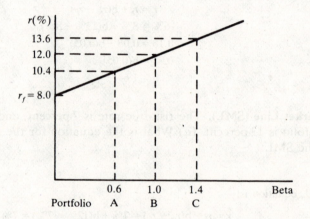

Fig. 7-2

(*c*) A lower expected return for the market portfolio would change the slope of the market line downward, as is shown in Fig. 7-3.

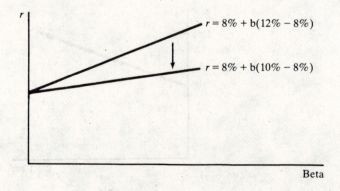

Fig. 7-3

7.12 CAPM. During a 5-year period, the relevant results for the aggregate market are that the r_f (risk-free rate) is 8 percent and the r_m (return on market) is 14 percent. For that period, the results of four portfolio managers are as follows:

Portfolio Manager	Average Return (%)	Beta
A	13	0.80
B	14	1.05
C	17	1.25
D	13	0.90

(*a*) Calculate the expected rate of return for each portfolio manager and compare the actual returns with the expected returns. (*b*) Based upon your calculations, select the manager with the best performance. (*c*) What are the critical assumptions in the capital asset pricing model (CAPM)? What are the implications of relaxing these assumptions? (CFA, adapted.)

SOLUTION

(*a*) Use the CAPM equation:

$$r_j = r_f + b(r_m - r_f)$$

The expected rates of return are as follows:

Portfolio Manager	Average Return (%)	Expected Return (%)	Actual Return (%)	Difference between Actual and Expected Returns (%)
A	13	$r_A = 8\% + 0.80(14\% - 8\%) = 12.8$	13	+0.2
B	14	$r_B = 8\% + 1.05(14\% - 8\%) = 14.3$	14	−0.3
C	17	$r_C = 8\% + 1.25(14\% - 8\%) = 15.5$	17	+1.5
D	13	$r_D = 8\% + 0.90(14\% - 8\%) = 13.4$	13	−0.4

(*b*) Portfolio managers A and C did better than expected, since A exceeded the expected return by 1.56 percent (0.2% ÷ 12.8%) and C bettered the expected return by 9.68 percent (1.5% ÷ 15.5%). C therefore showed the best performance.

(*c*) The critical assumptions in CAPM are perfect capital markets and homogeneous expectations.

Relaxation of the perfect capital markets assumption results in limitations to the effectiveness of predicting and computing expected return on stock. Certain securities may have values and expected returns that are not entirely explained by the security market line. Residual risk may be important, particularly where bankruptcy costs are significant. When expectations of market participants are not homogeneous, each investor has his or her own capital market line. The important thing to stress, however, is that in market equilibrium, there still will exist an implied risk-return trade-off for securities where risk is represented by the undiversifiable risk, as opposed to the total risk of the security.

7.13 Value of Bond. Trooper Corporation has a bond issue with a coupon rate of 10 percent per year and 5 years remaining until maturity. The par value of the bond is $1,000. What is the value of the bond when the going rate of interest is (*a*) 6 percent, (*b*) 10 percent, and (*c*) 12 percent? The bond pays interest annually.

SOLUTION

$$\text{Annual interest} = 10\% \times \$1,000 = \$100$$

$$V = \sum_{t=1}^{n} \frac{I}{(1+r)^t} + \frac{M}{(1+r)^n} = \frac{\$100}{(1+r)^1} + \frac{\$100}{(1+r)^2} + \cdots + \frac{\$100}{(1+r)^5} + \frac{\$1,000}{(1+r)^5}$$

$$= \$100(\text{PVIFA}_{r,n}) + \$1,000(\text{PVIF}_{r,n})$$

(a)   Value $= \$100(\text{PVIFA}_{6\%,5}) + \$1{,}000(\text{PVIF}_{6\%,5})$

$= \$100(4.2124) + \$1{,}000(0.7473) = \$421.24 + \$747.30 = \$1{,}168.54$

(b)   Value $= \$100(\text{PVIFA}_{10\%,5}) + \$1{,}000(\text{PVIF}_{10\%,5})$

$= \$100(3.7908) + \$1{,}000(0.6209) = \$379.08 + \$620.90 = \$999.98$

(c)   Value $= \$100(\text{PVIFA}_{12\%,5}) + \$1{,}000(\text{PVIF}_{12\%,5})$

$= \$100(3.6048) + \$1{,}000(0.5674) = \$360.48 + \$567.40 = \$927.88$

7.14   Value of Bond. Assume the same data and questions as in Problem 7.13, except that in this problem, the bond pays interest semiannually.

SOLUTION

$$\text{Semiannual interest} = \frac{\$100}{2} = \$50$$

$$\text{Number of periods} = 5 \text{ years} \times 2 = 10 \text{ periods}$$

$$V = \sum_{t=1}^{2n} \frac{I/2}{(1+r/2)^t} + \frac{M}{(1+r/2)^{2n}}$$

$$= \frac{\$50}{(1+r/2)} + \frac{\$50}{(1+r/2)^2} \cdots \frac{\$50}{(1+r/2)^{10}} + \frac{\$1{,}000}{(1+r/2)^{10}}$$

$$= \$50(\text{PVIFA}_{r/2,10}) + \$1{,}000(\text{PVIF}_{r/2,10})$$

(a) $V = \$50(\text{PVIFA}_{3\%,10}) + \$1{,}000(\text{PVIF}_{3\%,10})$

$= \$50(8.5302) + \$1{,}000(0.7441) = \$426.51 + \$744.10 = \$1{,}170.61$

(b) $V = \$50(\text{PVIFA}_{5\%,10}) + \$1{,}000(\text{PVIF}_{5\%,10})$

$= \$50(7.7217) + \$1{,}000(0.6139) = \$386.09 + \$613.90 = \$999.99$

(c) $V = \$50(\text{PVIFA}_{6\%,10}) + \$1{,}000(\text{PVIF}_{6\%,10})$

$= \$50(7.3601) + \$1{,}000(0.5584) = \$368.01 + \$558.40 = \$926.41$

7.15   Stock Valuation—Single Period. Mary Czech is considering the purchase of stock X at the beginning of the year. The dividend at year-end is expected to be $3.25, and the market price by the end of the year is expected to be $25. If she requires a rate of return of 12 percent, what is the value of the stock?

SOLUTION

$$P_0 = \frac{D_1}{(1+r)} + \frac{P_1}{(1+r)} = \frac{\$3.25}{(1+0.12)} + \frac{\$25}{(1+0.12)}$$

$$= \$3.25(0.893) + \$25(0.893) = \$2.90 + \$22.33 = \$25.23$$

7.16   Stock Valuation—Finite Periods. The Ohm Company paid a $2.50 dividend per share at the end of the year. The dividend is expected to grow by 10 percent each year for the next 3 years, and the stock's market price per share is expected to be $50 at the end of the third year. Investors require a rate of return of 14 percent. At what price per share should the Ohm stock sell?

SOLUTION

$$P_0 = \sum_{t=1}^{3} \frac{D_t}{(1+r)^t} + \frac{P_3}{(1+r)^3}$$

Note that
$$D_0 = \$2.50$$
$$D_1 = \$2.50(1 + 0.10) = \$2.50(1.10) = \$2.75$$
$$D_2 = \$2.50(1 + 0.10)^2 = \$2.50(1.21) = \$3.03$$
$$D_3 = \$2.50(1 + 0.10)^3 = \$2.50(1.331) = \$3.33$$

$$P_0 = \frac{\$2.75}{(1 + 0.14)} + \frac{\$3.03}{(1 + 0.14)^2} + \frac{\$3.33}{(1 + 0.14)^3} + \frac{\$50}{(1 + 0.14)^3}$$
$$= \$2.75(0.877) + \$3.03(0.770) + \$3.33(0.675) + \$50(0.675)$$
$$= \$2.41 + \$2.33 + \$2.25 + \$33.75 = \$40.74$$

The stock should sell for \$40.74 per share.

7.17   Stock Valuation—No Growth in Dividends. Susan O'Reilly invests in a stock of company X which expects no growth in dividends. The company paid a \$2.75 dividend per share. If Susan requires a rate of return of 10 percent, what would be the value of the stock?

SOLUTION

If $D_0 = D_1 = D_2 = \cdots = D_\infty$, then

$$P_0 = \frac{D}{r}$$

Therefore,

$$P_0 = \frac{\$2.75}{0.1} = \$27.50$$

7.18   The Gordon Dividend Growth Model. Develop the Gordon growth model, assuming constant growth of dividends, i.e., $D_t = D_0(1 + g)^t$.

SOLUTION

Since $D_t = D_0(1 + g)^t$

$$P_0 = \frac{D_0(1 + g)}{(1 + r)} + \frac{D_0(1 + g)^2}{(1 + r)^2} + \cdots + \frac{D_0(1 + g)^\infty}{(1 + r)^\infty}$$

If both sides of this expression are multiplied by $(1 + r)/(1 + g)$ and then this is subtracted from the product, the result is:

$$\frac{P_0(1 + r)}{(1 + g)} - P_0 = D_0 - \frac{D_0(1 + g)^\infty}{(1 + r)^\infty}$$

If $r > g$, which should normally be true, the term on the far right-hand side approaches zero. As a result,

$$\frac{P_0(1 + r)}{(1 + g)} - P_0 = D_0$$

$$P_0\left(\frac{1 + r}{1 + g}\right) - P_0\left(\frac{1 + g}{1 + g}\right) = D_0$$

$$P_0\left[\frac{(1 + r) - (1 + g)}{(1 + g)}\right] = D_0$$

$$P_0(r - g) = D_0(1 + g)$$

If we assume dividends grow at a constant rate g, then

$$D_t = D_0(1 + g)^t \qquad \text{and} \qquad t = 1$$

and

$$P_0 = \frac{D_1}{r - g}$$

7.19 **Stock Valuation.** Investors require a rate of return of 12 percent. At what price will the stock sell if the next expected dividend D_1 is $1 per share and investors expect the dividends and earnings to grow (a) at 8 percent, (b) at 10 percent, (c) at 12 percent, and (d) at 14 percent?

SOLUTION

$$P_0 = \frac{D_1}{r - g}$$

(a)

$$P_0 = \frac{\$1}{0.12 - 0.08} = \$25$$

(b)

$$P_0 = \frac{\$1}{0.12 - 0.1} = \$50$$

(c)

$$P_0 = \frac{\$1}{0.12 - 0.12} = \text{undefined}$$

The formula is invalid since a necessary condition is $r > g$.

(d)

$$P_0 = \frac{\$1}{0.12 - 0.14} = \text{undefined}$$

7.20 **Beta and Stock Valuation.** The risk-free rate is 6 percent, the required rate of return on the market is 12 percent, and stock A has a beta coefficient of 1.2. If the dividend expected during the coming year is $2 and the growth rate of dividends and earnings is 7 percent, at what price should stock A sell?

SOLUTION

$$r = r_f + b(r_m - r_f) = 6\% + 1.2(12\% - 6\%) = 6\% + 7.2\% = 13.2\%$$

Therefore,

$$P_0 = \frac{D_1}{r - g} = \frac{\$2}{13.2\% - 7\%} = \frac{\$2}{0.062} = \$32.26$$

7.21 **Stock Valuation.** Investors require a 20 percent per year return on the stock of M Company. Yesterday M Company paid a $2 dividend (dividends are paid annually). The dividend is expected to grow 30 percent per year for the next 2 years and at 8 percent year thereafter. At what price should the stock sell?

SOLUTION

$$D_0 = \$2$$
$$D_1 = \$2(1 + 0.3) = \$2.60$$
$$D_2 = \$2(1 + 0.3)^2 = \$2(1.69) = \$3.38$$
$$D_3 = \$3.38(1 + 0.08) = \$3.65$$

Present value of dividends for the first 2 years are:

$$\frac{\$2.60}{(1 + 0.2)} + \frac{\$3.38}{(1 + 0.2)^2} = \$2.60(\text{PVIF}_{20\%,1}) + \$3.38(\text{PVIF}_{20\%,2})$$

$$= \$2.60(0.8333) + \$3.38(0.6944) = \$2.17 + \$2.35 = \$4.52$$

Find P_2:

$$P_2 = \frac{D_3}{r - g} = \frac{\$3.65}{0.2 - 0.08} = \$30.42$$

Present value of $30.42 is:

$$\frac{\$30.42}{(1+0.2)^2} = \$30.42(\text{PVIF}_{20\%,2}) = \$30.42(0.6944) = \$21.12$$

Add these two PV figures to obtain P_0:

$$P_0 = \$4.52 + \$21.12 = \$25.64$$

7.22 **Stock Valuation.** Investors require a 10 percent per year return on the stock of the Take-Two Corporation, which anticipates a nonconstant growth pattern for dividends. The company paid a $2 per share dividend. The dividend is expected to grow by 15 percent per year until the end of year 4 (i.e., for the next 3 years) and 7 percent thereafter.

(a) Project dividends for years 1 through 4. (b) Compute the present value of the dividends in part (a). (c) Project the dividend for the fifth year (D_5). (d) Find the present value of all future dividends beginning with the fifth year's dividend. The present value you find will be at the end of the fourth year. Use the formula $P_4 = D_5/(r-g)$. (e) Discount back the value found in part (d) for 4 years at 10 percent. (f) Determine the value of the stock P_0.

SOLUTION

(a)
$$D_0(\text{given}) = \$2$$
$$D_1 = \$2(1+0.15) = \$2.30$$
$$D_2 = \$2.30(1+0.15) = \$2.65$$
$$D_3 = \$2.65(1+0.15) = \$3.05$$
$$D_4 = \$3.05(1+0.15) = \$3.51$$

(b)   PV of dividends $= \dfrac{\$2.30}{(1+0.1)} + \dfrac{\$2.65}{(1+0.1)^2} + \dfrac{\$3.05}{(1+0.1)^3} + \dfrac{\$3.51}{(1+0.1)^4}$

$$= \$2.30(\text{PVIF}_{10\%,1}) + \$2.65(\text{PVIF}_{10\%,2}) + \$3.05(\text{PVIF}_{10\%,3}) + \$3.51(\text{PVIF}_{10\%,4})$$

$$= \$2.30(0.9091) + \$2.65(0.8264) + \$3.05(0.7513) + \$3.51(0.6830)$$

$$= \$2.09 + \$2.19 + \$2.29 + \$2.40 = \$8.97$$

(c)
$$D_5 = \$3.51(1+0.15) = \$4.04$$

(d)
$$P_4 = \frac{D_5}{r-g} = \frac{\$4.04}{0.1-0.07} = \frac{\$4.04}{0.03} = \$134.67$$

(e)   Therefore, $\dfrac{\$134.67}{(1+0.1)^4} = \$134.67(\text{PVIF}_{10\%,4}) = \$134.67(0.6830) = \$91.98$

(f)   The value of the stock, P_0, is:

$$P_0 = \$8.97 + \$91.98 = \$100.95$$

7.23 **Stock Valuation.** On December 31, 19X2, the shares of Amacom, Inc., closed at $20. The company subsequently paid a year-end dividend in each of the years 19X3 through 19X7 as follows:

19X3:	$1.00	19X6:	$1.25
19X4:	$1.00	19X7:	$1.25
19X5:	$1.10		

Suppose you had purchased a share of Amacom stock on December 31, 19X2. Find the price at which you must sell your share at 19X7 year-end in order to realize an annual compounded total rate of return of 10 percent on your initial investment (before commissions and taxes). (CFA, adapted.)

SOLUTION

$$P_0 = \sum_{t=1}^{5} \frac{D_t}{(1+r)^t} + \frac{P_5}{(1+r)^5}$$

Substituting the value given yields:

$$\$20 = \sum_{t=1}^{5} \frac{D_t}{(1+0.1)^t} + \frac{P_5}{(1+0.1)^5}$$

First compute the present value of dividends for the years 19X3 through 19X7.

$$\frac{\$1.00}{(1+0.1)^1} + \frac{\$1.00}{(1+0.1)^2} + \frac{\$1.10}{(1+0.1)^3} + \frac{\$1.25}{(1+0.1)^4} + \frac{\$1.25}{(1+0.1)^5}$$

$$= \$1.00(0.9091) + \$1.00(0.8264) + \$1.10(0.7513) + \$1.25(0.6830) + \$1.25(0.6209)$$

$$= \$0.91 + \$0.83 + \$0.83 + \$0.85 + \$0.78 = \$4.20$$

Therefore,

$$\$20 = \$4.20 + \frac{P_5}{(1+0.1)^5}$$

$$\$20 = \$4.20 + P_5(\text{PVIF}_{10\%,5})$$

$$\$20 = \$4.20 + P_5(0.6209)$$

$$P_5(0.6209) = \$20 - \$4.20$$

$$P_5(0.6209) = \$15.80$$

$$P_5 = \frac{\$15.80}{0.6209} = \$25.45$$

7.24 **Yield to Maturity.** The Rite Company's bonds have 3 years remaining until maturity. Interest is paid annually, the bonds have a $1,000 par value, and the coupon interest rate is 10 percent. What is the yield to maturity at a current market price of (*a*) $1,052, (*b*) $1,000, and (*c*) $935?

SOLUTION

$$\text{Annual interest} = \$100 \qquad (10\% \times \$1,000)$$

$$V = \sum_{t=1}^{n} \frac{I}{(1+r)^t} + \frac{M}{(1+r)^n}$$

$$= I(\text{PVIFA}_{r,n}) + M(\text{PVIF}_{r,n})$$

(*a*)

$$\$1,052 = \frac{\$100}{(1+r)^1} + \frac{\$100}{(1+r)^2} + \cdots + \frac{\$100}{(1+r)^3} + \frac{\$1,000}{(1+r)^3}$$

$$\$1,052 = \$100(\text{PVIFA}_{r,3}) + \$1,000(\text{PVIF}_{r,3})$$

Since the bond is selling above par value, the bond's yield is below the coupon rate of 10 percent. At $r = 8\%$:

$$V = \$100(2.5771) + \$1,000(0.7938) = \$257.71 + \$793.80 = \$1,051.51$$

Therefore, the annual yield to maturity of the bond is 8 percent.

Alternatively, the shortcut formula yields:

$$\text{Yield to maturity of a bond} = \frac{I + (M - V)/n}{(M + V)/2}$$

$$= \frac{\$100 + (\$1,000 - \$1,052)/3}{(\$1,000 + \$1,052)/2} = \frac{\$82.67}{\$1,026} = 8.05\%$$

(b)
$$\$1,000 = \$100(PVIFA_{r,3}) + \$1,000(PVIF_{r,3})$$

Since the bond is selling at par value, the bond's yield should be the same as the coupon rate. At $r = 10\%$:

$$V = \$100(2.4869) + \$1,000(0.7513) = \$248.69 + \$751.30 = \$999.99$$

Or, using the shortcut formula:

$$\text{Yield} = \frac{\$100 + (\$1,000 - \$1,000)/3}{(\$1,000 + \$1,000)/2} = \frac{\$100}{\$1,000} = 10\%$$

(c)
$$\$935 = \$100(PVIFA_{r,3}) + \$1,000(PVIFA_{r,3})$$

Since the bond is selling at a discount under the par value, the bond's yield is above the going coupon rate of 10 percent. At $r = 12\%$:

$$V = \$100(2.4018) + \$1,000(0.7118) = \$240.18 + \$711.80 = \$951.98$$

At 10 percent, the bond's value is above the actual market value of \$935, so we must raise the rate. At $r = 13\%$:

$$V = \$100(2.361) + \$1,000(0.693) = \$236.10 + \$693 = \$929.10$$

Since the bond value of \$935 falls between 12 percent and 13 percent, find the yield by interpolation, as follows:

	Bond Value	
12%	\$951.18	\$951.18
True yield	935.00	
13%		929.10
Difference	\$ 16.18	\$ 22.08

$$\text{Yield} = 12\% + \frac{16.18}{22.08}(1\%) = 12\% + 0.73(1\%) = 12.73\%$$

Alternatively, using the shortcut method:

$$\text{Yield} = \frac{\$100 + (\$1,000 - \$935)/3}{(\$1,000 + \$935)/2} = \frac{\$121.67}{\$967.5} = 12.58\%$$

7.25 Yield to Maturity. Assume a bond has 4 years remaining until maturity and that it pays interest semiannually (the most recent payment was yesterday). (a) What is the yield to maturity of the bond if its maturity value is \$1,000, its coupon yield is 8 percent, and it currently sells for \$821? (b) What if it currently sells for \$1,070?

SOLUTION

$$V = \sum_{t=1}^{2n} \frac{I/2}{(1 + r/2)^t} + \frac{M}{(1 + r/2)^{2n}}$$
$$= I/2(PVIFA_{r/2,2n}) + M(PVIF_{r/2,2n})$$

(a)
$$\text{Semiannual interest} = \frac{8\%(\$1,000)}{2} = \$40$$

$$\$821 = \frac{\$40}{(1 + r/2)^1} + \frac{40}{(1 + r/2)^2} + \cdots + \frac{40}{(1 + r/2)^8} + \frac{\$1,000}{(1 + r/2)^8}$$

$$\$821 = \$40(PVIFA_{r/2,8}) + \$1,000(PVIF_{r/2,8})$$

By trial and error, we find that when $r/2 = 7\%$:

$$V = \$40(5.9713) + \$1,000(0.5820) = \$238.85 + \$582 = \$820.85$$

Therefore, the annual yield is $7\% \times 2 = 14\%$.

Using the shortcut formula:

$$\text{Yield} = \frac{I + (M - V)/n}{(M + V)/2} = \frac{\$80 + (\$1,000 - \$821)/4}{(\$1,000 + \$821)/2} = \frac{\$124.75}{\$910.5} = 13.7\%$$

(b)

$$\$1,070 = \frac{\$40}{(1 + r/2)^1} + \frac{40}{(1 + r/2)^2} + \cdots + \frac{40}{(1 + r/2)^8} + \frac{\$1,000}{(1 + r/2)^8}$$

$$\$1,070 = \$40(\text{PVIFA}_{r/2,8}) + \$1,000(\text{PVIF}_{r/2,8})$$

By trial and error, we get the semiannual interest of 3 percent:

$$V = \$40(7.0197) + \$1,000(0.7894) = \$280.79 + \$789.40 = \$1,070.19$$

Therefore, the annual yield is $3\% \times 2 = 6\%$.

Alternatively, using the shortcut method:

$$\text{Yield} = \frac{\$80 + (\$1,000 - \$1,070)/4}{(\$1,000 + \$1,070)/2} = \frac{\$62.5}{\$1,035} = 6\%$$

7.26   Yield of a Note. You can buy a note at a price of $13,500. If you buy the note, you will receive 10 annual payments of $2,000, the first payment to be made immediately. What rate of return, or yield, does the note offer?

SOLUTION

$$V = \sum_{t=1}^{n} \frac{C_t}{(1 + r)^t}$$

$$\$13,500 = \$2,000 + \frac{\$2,000}{(1 + r)^1} + \frac{\$2,000}{(1 + r)^2} + \cdots + \frac{\$2,000}{(1 + r)^9}$$

$$\$13,500 = \$2,000(1 + \text{PVIFA}_{r,9})$$

$$(1 + \text{PVIFA}_{r,9}) = \frac{\$13,500}{\$2,000} = 6.75$$

$\text{PVIFA}_{r,9} = 6.75 - 1 = 5.75$, which is very close to 10 percent as found in Appendix D.

7.27   Expected Return on Stock Investment. You are considering the purchase of a share of stock in a firm for $40. The company is expected to pay a $2.50 dividend at the end of the year, and its market price after the payment of the dividend is expected to be $45 a share. What is the expected return on the investment in this stock?

SOLUTION

$$r = \frac{\text{dividends} + (\text{ending price} - \text{beginning price})}{\text{beginning price}} = \frac{D_1 + (P_1 - P_0)}{P_0}$$

$$= \frac{\$2.50 + (\$45 - \$40)}{\$40} = 18.75\%$$

Alternatively, we set the current market price equal to the present value of the dividend, plus the expected market price, as follows:

$$\$40 = \frac{\$2.50}{(1 + r)} + \frac{\$45}{(1 + r)}$$

Solving this equation for r:

$$\$40(1 + r) = \$2.50 + \$45$$

$$1 + r = \frac{\$2.50 + \$45}{\$40}$$

$$r = \frac{\$2.50 + \$45}{\$40} - 1 = \frac{\$47.50}{40} - 1 = 1.1875 - 1 = 18.75\%$$

7.28 **Expected Return on Stock Investment.** Tom Laboratory's common stock is currently selling at $60 per share. The next annual dividend is expected to be $3 per share, and the earnings, dividends, and stock prices are expected to grow at a rate of (*a*) 0 percent, (*b*) 4 percent, and (*c*) 6 percent. What is the expected total return in each case from the purchase of the common stock?

SOLUTION

$$r = \frac{D_1}{P_0} + g$$

(*a*) $$r = \frac{\$3}{\$60} + 0 = 5\%$$

(*b*) $$r = \frac{\$3}{\$60} + 4\% = 5\% + 4\% = 9\%$$

(*c*) $$r = \frac{\$3}{\$60} + 6\% = 5\% + 6\% = 11\%$$

7.29 **Dividend Yield and Capital Gain Yield.** N Company's last dividend, D_0, was $1. Earnings and dividends are expected to grow at a 5 percent rate. The required rate of return on the stock is 13 percent. The current stock price is $25. What is the expected dividend yield and expected capital gains yield for the coming year?

SOLUTION

$$\text{Dividend yield} = \frac{\$1.00(1 + 0.05)}{\$25} = \frac{\$1.05}{\$25} = 4.2\%$$

$$\text{Capital gain yield} = \text{rate of return} - \text{dividend yield} = 13\% - 4.2\% = 8.8\%$$

Chapter 8

Capital Budgeting
(Including Leasing)

8.1 CAPITAL BUDGETING DECISIONS DEFINED

Capital budgeting is the process of making long-term planning decisions for investments. There are typically two types of investment decisions: (1) selection decisions concerning proposed projects (for example, investments in long-term assets such as property, plant, and equipment, or resource commitments in the form of new product development, market research, re-funding of long-term debt, introduction of a computer, etc.); and (2) replacement decisions (for example, replacement of existing facilities with new facilities).

8.2 MEASURING CASH FLOWS

The *incremental* (or relevant) after-tax cash flows that occur with an investment project are the ones that are measured. In general the cash flows of a project fall into the following three categories: (1) the initial investment, (2) the incremental (relevant) cash inflows over the life of the project, and (3) the terminal cash flow.

Initial Investment

The initial investment (I) is the initial cash outlay necessary to purchase the asset and put it in operating order. It is determined as follows:

$$\text{Initial investment} = \text{cost of asset} + \text{installation cost} - \frac{\text{proceeds from}}{\text{sale of old asset}} \pm \frac{\text{taxes on sale}}{\text{of old asset}}$$

The proceeds from the sale of old assets are subject to some type of tax. There are four possibilities:

1. The asset is sold for more than its initial cost.

2. The asset is sold for more than its book value but less than its initial cost.

3. The asset is sold for its book value.

4. The asset is sold for less than its book value.

EXAMPLE 8.1 Assume that an asset has a book value of $60,000 and initially cost $100,000. Assume further that the firm's ordinary marginal tax rate is 46 percent, and the tax rate on long-term capital gains is 28 percent. Consider each of the four possible tax situations dealing with the sale of the old asset.

1. Suppose that the old asset is sold for $120,000. The total gain, which is the difference between the selling price and the book value, is split into two types and each is taxed differently. The amount by which the selling price exceeds the initial cost is considered a *capital gain* and is subject to the long-term gain tax rate. The amount by which the initial price exceeds the book value is considered *recapture of depreciation* and is taxed at the ordinary rate. The total gain of $60,000 (i.e., $120,000 − $60,000) is split into the capital gain and recapture of depreciation as follows:

    $$\underbrace{(\$120,000 - \$100,000)}_{\text{Capital gain}} + \underbrace{(\$100,000 - \$60,000)}_{\text{Recapture of depreciation}}$$

The tax on the total gain is then calculated as follows:

Capital gains tax	
($120,000 − $100,000)(0.28)	$ 5,600
Recapture of depreciation	
($100,000 − $60,000)(0.46)	18,400
Total tax	$24,000

2. The old asset is sold for $80,000. In this case, the total gain is simply recapture of depreciation and taxed at the ordinary rate. Therefore,

$$($80,000 − $60,000)(0.46) = $9,200$$

3. The old asset is sold for $60,000. In this case, no taxes result since there is neither a gain nor a loss on the sale.

4. The old asset is sold for $50,000. In this case there is a loss, which results in tax savings. The tax savings are as follows:

$$($60,000 − $50,000)(0.46) = $4,600$$

Taxes on the gain from the sale of an old asset or the tax savings on a loss must be considered when determining the amount of the initial investment of a new asset.

EXAMPLE 8.2 XYZ Corporation is considering the purchase of a new machine for $250,000, which will be depreciated on a straight-line basis over 5 years with no salvage value. In order to put this machine in operating order, it is necessary to pay installation charges of $50,000. The new machine will replace an existing machine, purchased 3 years ago at a cost of $240,000, that is depreciated on a straight-line basis (with no salvage value) over its 8-year life (i.e., $30,000 per year depreciation). The old machine can be sold for $255,000 to a scrap dealer. The company is in the 46 percent tax bracket, and long-term capital gains are taxed at a rate of 28 percent.

The key calculation of the initial investment is the taxes on the sale of the old machine. The total gain, which is the difference between the selling price and the book value, is $105,000 ($255,000 − $150,000). The tax on this $105,000 total gain is computed as follows:

Capital gain tax	
($255,000 − $240,000)(0.28)	$ 4,200
Recapture of depreciation	
($240,000 − $150,000)(0.46)	41,400
Total tax	$45,600

Therefore, the amount of initial investment is:

Purchase price of the machine	$250,000
+ Installation cost	50,000
− Proceeds from sales of old machine	255,000
+ Taxes on sale of old machine	45,600
Initial investment	$ 90,600

Incremental (Relevant) Cash Inflows

The relevant cash inflows over a project's expected life involve the incremental after-tax cash flows resulting from increased revenues and/or savings in cash operating costs. Cash flows are not the same as accounting income, which is not usually available for paying the firm's bills. The differences between accounting income and cash flows are such noncash charges as depreciation expense and amortization expense.

The computation of relevant or incremental cash inflows after taxes involves the following two steps:

1. Compute the after-tax cash flows of each proposal by adding back any noncash charges, which are deducted as expenses on the firm's income statement, to net profits (earnings) after taxes; that is:

    After-tax cash inflows = net profits (or earnings) after taxes + depreciation

2. Subtract the cash inflows after taxes resulting from use of the old asset from the cash inflows generated by the new asset to obtain the relevant (incremental) cash inflows after taxes.

EXAMPLE 8.3 XYZ Corporation has provided its revenues and cash operating costs (excluding depreciation) for the old and the new machine, as follows:

	Annual		**Net Profits before Depreciation and Taxes**
	Revenue	**Cash Operating Costs**	
Old machine	$150,000	$70,000	$80,000
New machine	$180,000	$60,000	$120,000

Recall from Example 8.2 that the annual depreciation of the old machine and the new machine will be $30,000 and $50,000, respectively.

To arrive at net profits after taxes, we first have to deduct depreciation expenses from the net profits before depreciation and taxes, as follows:

	Net Profits after Taxes	**Add Depreciation**	**After-Tax Cash Inflows**
Old machine	($80,000 − $30,000)(1 − 0.46) = $27,000	$30,000	$57,000
New machine	($120,000 − $50,000)(1 − 0.46) = $37,800	$50,000	$87,800

Subtracting the after-tax cash inflows of the old machine from the cash inflows of the new machine results in the relevant, or incremental, cash inflows for each year.

Therefore, in this example, the relevant or incremental cash inflows for each year are $87,800 − $57,000 = $30,800.

Alternatively, the incremental cash inflows after taxes can be computed, using the following simple formula:

After-tax *incremental* cash inflows = (increase in revenues)(1 − tax rate)

− (increase in cash charges)(1 − tax rate)

+ (increase in depreciation expenses)(tax rate)

EXAMPLE 8.4 Using the data in Example 8.3, after-tax incremental cash inflows for each year are:

Increase in revenue × (1 − tax rate):	
($180,000 − $150,000)(1 − 0.46)	$16,200
− Increase in cash charges × (1 − tax rate):	
($60,000 − $70,000)(1 − 0.46)	−(−5,400)
+ Increase in depreciation expense ×	
tax rate: ($50,000 − $30,000)(0.46)	9,200
	$30,800

Terminal Cash Flow

Cash flows associated with a project's termination generally include the disposal value of the project plus or minus any taxable gains or losses associated with its sale. The way in which to compute these gains or losses is very similar to the method for computing the taxes on the sale of an old asset. In most cases, the disposal value at the end of the project's useful life results in a taxable gain since its book value (or undepreciated value) is usually zero.

8.3 CAPITAL BUDGETING TECHNIQUES

Several methods of evaluating investment projects are as follows:

1. Payback period
2. Accounting rate of return (ARR)
3. Net present value (NPV)
4. Internal rate of return (IRR)
5. Profitability index (or benefit/cost ratio)

The NPV method and the IRR method are called discounted cash flow (DCF) methods. Each of these methods is discussed below.

Payback Period

The payback period measures the length of time required to recover the amount of initial investment. It is computed by dividing the initial investment by the cash inflows through increased revenues or cost savings.

EXAMPLE 8.5 Assume:

Cost of investment	$18,000
Annual after-tax cash savings	$3,000

Then, the payback period is:

$$\text{Payback period} = \frac{\text{initial investment cost}}{\text{increased revenues or lost savings}} = \frac{\$18,000}{\$3,000} = 6 \text{ years}$$

Decision rule: Choose the project with the shorter payback period. The rationale behind this choice is: The shorter the payback period, the less risky the project, and the greater the liquidity.

EXAMPLE 8.6 Consider two projects whose after-tax cash inflows are not even. Assume each project costs $1,000.

	Cash Inflow	
Year	**A ($)**	**B ($)**
1	100	500
2	200	400
3	300	300
4	400	100
5	500	
6	600	

When cash inflows are not even, the payback period has to be found by trial and error. The payback period of project A is ($1,000 = $100 + $200 + $300 + $400) 4 years. The payback period of project B is ($1,000 = $500 + $400 + $100):

$$2 \text{ years} + \frac{\$100}{\$300} = 2\tfrac{1}{3} \text{ years}$$

Project B is the project of choice in this case, since it has the shorter payback period.

The *advantages* of using the payback period method of evaluating an investment project are that (1) it is simple to compute and easy to understand, and (2) it handles investment risk effectively.

The *shortcomings* of this method are that (1) it does not recognize the time value of money, and (2) it ignores the impact of cash inflows received after the payback period; essentially, cash flows after the payback period determine profitability of an investment.

Accounting Rate of Return

Accounting rate of return (ARR) measures profitability from the conventional accounting standpoint by relating the required investment—or sometimes the average investment—to the future annual net income.

Decision rule: Under the ARR method, choose the project with the higher rate of return.

EXAMPLE 8.7   Consider the following investment:

Initial investment	$6,500
Estimated life	20 years
Cash inflows per year	$1,000
Depreciation per year (using straight line)	$325

The accounting rate of return for this project is:

$$\text{ARR} = \frac{\text{net income}}{\text{investment}} = \frac{\$1,000 - \$325}{\$6,500} = 10.4\%$$

If *average* investment (usually assumed to be one-half of the original investment) is used, then:

$$\text{ARR} = \frac{\$1,000 - \$325}{\$3,250} = 20.8\%$$

The *advantages* of this method are that it is easily understandable, simple to compute, and recognizes the profitability factor.

The *shortcomings* of this method are that it fails to recognize the time value of money, and it uses accounting data instead of cash flow data.

Net Present Value

Net present value (NPV) is the excess of the present value (PV) of cash inflows generated by the project over the amount of the initial investment (I):

$$\text{NPV} = \text{PV} - \text{I}$$

The present value of future cash flows is computed using the so-called cost of capital (or minimum required rate of return) as the discount rate. In the case of an annuity, the present value would be

$$\text{PV} = \text{A} \cdot \text{PVIFA}$$

where A is the amount of the annuity. The value of PVIFA is found in Appendix D.

Decision rule: If NPV is positive, accept the project. Otherwise reject it.

EXAMPLE 8.8   Consider the following investment:

Initial investment	$12,950
Estimated life	10 years
Annual cash inflows	$3,000
Cost of capital (minimum required rate of return)	12%

Present value of the cash inflows is

$$PV = A \cdot PVIFA = \$3,000 \times PVIFA_{12\%,10}$$

$= \$3,000\,(5.6502)$	$16,950.60
Initial investment (I)	12,950.00
Net present value (NPV = PV − I)	$ 4,000.60

Since the NPV of the investment is positive, the investment should be accepted.

The *advantages* of the NPV method are that it obviously recognizes the time value of money and it is easy to compute whether the cash flows form an annuity or vary from period to period.

Internal Rate of Return

Internal rate of return (IRR) is defined as the rate of interest that equates I with the PV of future cash inflows. In other words, at IRR,

$$I = PV$$

or

$$NPV = 0$$

Decision rule: Accept the project if the IRR exceeds the cost of capital. Otherwise, reject it.

EXAMPLE 8.9   Assume the same data given in Example 8.8, and set the following equality (I = PV):

$$\$12,950 = \$3,000 \times PVIFA$$

$$PVIFA = \frac{\$12,950}{\$3,000} = 4.317$$

which stands somewhere between 18 percent and 20 percent in the 10-year line of Appendix D. The interpolation follows:

	PV Factor	
18%	4.494	4.494
IRR	4.317	
20%		4.192
Difference	0.177	0.302

Therefore,

$$IRR = 18\% + \frac{0.177}{0.302}\,(20\% - 18\%)$$

$$= 18\% + 0.586(2\%) = 18\% + 1.17\% = 19.17\%$$

Since the IRR of the investment is greater than the cost of capital (12 percent), accept the project.

The *advantage* of using the IRR method is that it does consider the time value of money and, therefore, is more exact and realistic than the ARR method.

The *shortcomings* of this method are that (1) it is time-consuming to compute, especially when the cash inflows are not even, although most business calculators have a program to calculate IRR, and (2) it fails to recognize the varying sizes of investment in competing projects and their respective dollar profitabilities.

When cash inflows are not even, IRR is computed by the trial and error method, as follows:

1. Compute NPV at cost of capital, denoted here as r_1.

2. See if NPV is positive or negative.

3. If NPV is positive, then pick another rate (r_2) much higher than r_1. If NPV is negative, then pick another rate (r_2) much smaller than r_1. The true IRR, at which NPV = 0, must lie somewhere in between these two rates.

4. Compute NPV using r_2.

5. Interpolate to get the exact rate.

EXAMPLE 8.10   Consider the following investment whose cash flows are different from year to year:

Year	After-Tax Cash Inflows ($)
1	1,000
2	2,500
3	1,500

Assume that the amount of initial investment is $3,000 and the cost of capital is 14 percent.

1. NPV at 14 percent:

Year	Cash Inflow ($)	PV Factor at 14%	Total PV ($ Rounded)
1	1,000	0.8772	877
2	2,500	0.7695	1,924
3	1,500	0.6750	1,013
			3,814

Therefore,

$$NPV = \$3,814 - \$3,000 = \$814$$

2. We see that NPV = $813 is positive at $r_1 = 14\%$.

3. Pick, say, 30 percent to play safe as r_2.

4. Computing NPV at $r_2 = 30\%$:

Year	Cash Inflow ($)	PV Factor at 30%	Total PV ($ Rounded)
1	1,000	0.7694	769
2	2,500	0.5921	1,480
3	1,500	0.4558	684
			2,933

Therefore,

$$NPV = \$2,933 - \$3,000 = -\$67$$

5. Interpolate:

		NPV
14%	$814	$814
IRR	0	
30%		$-(-67)$
Difference	$\underline{\underline{\$814}}$	$\underline{\underline{\$881}}$

Therefore,

$$\text{IRR} = 14\% + \frac{\$814}{\$881}(30\% - 14\%) = 14\% + 0.924(16\%) = 14\% + 14.78\% = 28.78\%$$

Profitability Index (Benefit/Cost Ratio)

The profitability index is the ratio of the total PV of future cash inflows to the initial investment, that is, PV/I. This index is used as a means of ranking projects in descending order of attractiveness. If the profitability index is greater than 1, then accept the project.

Decision rule: If the profitability index is greater than 1, then accept the project.

EXAMPLE 8.11   Using the data in Example 8.8, the profitability index is

$$\frac{\text{PV}}{\text{I}} = \frac{\$16,950}{\$12,950} = 1.31$$

Since this project generates $1.31 for each dollar invested (i.e., its profitability index is greater than 1), accept the project.

8.4 MUTUALLY EXCLUSIVE INVESTMENTS

A project is said to be *mutually exclusive* if the acceptance of one project automatically excludes the acceptance of one or more other projects. In the case where one must choose between mutually exclusive investments, the NPV and IRR methods may result in contradictory indications. The conditions under which contradictory rankings can occur are:

1. Projects that have different life expectancies.
2. Projects that have different sizes of investment.
3. Projects whose cash flows differ over time. For example, the cash flows of one project increase over time, while those of another decrease.

The contradictions result from different assumptions with respect to the reinvestment rate on cash flows from the projects.

1. The NPV method discounts all cash flows at the cost of capital, thus implicitly assuming that these cash flows can be reinvested at this rate.
2. The IRR method implies a reinvestment rate at IRR. Thus, the implied reinvestment rate will differ from project to project.

The NPV method generally gives correct ranking, since the cost of capital is a more realistic reinvestment rate.

EXAMPLE 8.12   Assume the following:

			Cash Flows			
	0	**1**	**2**	**3**	**4**	**5**
A	(100)	120				
B	(100)					201.14

Computing IRR and NPV at 10 percent gives the following different rankings:

	IRR	NPV at 10%
A	20%	9.01
B	15%	24.90

The NPVs plotted against the appropriate discount rates form a graph called a NPV profile (Fig. 8-1).

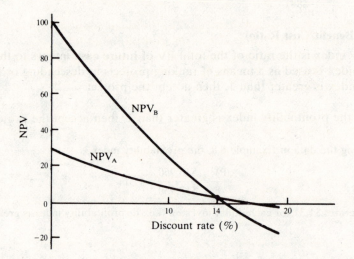

Fig. 8-1 NPV profile

At a discount rate larger than 14 percent, A has a higher NPV than B. Therefore, A should be selected. At a discount rate less than 14 percent, B has the higher NPV than A, and thus should be selected. The correct decision is to select the project with the higher NPV, since the NPV method assumes a more realistic reinvestment rate, that is, the cost of capital.

8.5 CAPITAL RATIONING

Many firms specify a limit on the overall budget for capital spending. *Capital rationing* is concerned with the problem of selecting the mix of acceptable projects that provides the *highest overall NPV*. The profitability index is used widely in ranking projects competing for limited funds.

EXAMPLE 8.13 A company with a fixed budget of $250,000 needs to select a mix of acceptable projects from the following:

Projects	I ($)	PV ($)	NPV ($)	Profitability Index	Ranking
A	70,000	112,000	42,000	1.6	1
B	100,000	145,000	45,000	1.45	2
C	110,000	126.500	16,500	1.15	5
D	60,000	79,000	19,000	1.32	3
E	40,000	38,000	−2,000	0.95	6
F	80,000	95,000	15,000	1.19	4

The ranking resulting from the profitability index shows that the company should select projects A, B, and D:

	I	PV
A	$ 70,000	$112,000
B	100,000	145,000
D	60,000	79,000
	$230,000	$336,000

Therefore,

$$NPV = \$336,000 - \$230,000 = \$106,000$$

Unfortunately, the profitability index method has some limitations. One of the more serious is that it breaks down whenever more than one resource is rationed.

A more general approach to solving capital rationing problems is the use of *mathematical* (or *zero-one*) *programming*.[1] Here the objective is to select the mix of projects that maximizes the NPV subject to a budget constraint.

EXAMPLE 8.14   Using the data given in Example 8.13 set up the problem as a mathematical programming problem. First label project A as X_1, B as X_2, and so on; the problem can be stated as follows: Maximize

$$NPV = \$42,000X_1 + \$45,000X_2 + \$16,500X_3 + \$19,000X_4 - \$2,000X_5 + \$15,000X_6$$

subject to

$$\$70,000X_1 + \$100,000X_2 + \$110,000X_3 + \$60,000X_4 + \$40,000X_5 + \$80,000X_6 \leqq \$250,000$$

$$X_i = 0, 1 \quad (i = 1, 2, \ldots, 6)$$

Using the mathematical program solution routine, the solution to this problem is:

$$X_1 = 1, \qquad X_2 = 1, \qquad X_4 = 1$$

and the NPV is $106,000. Thus, projects A, B, and D should be accepted.

8.6   CAPITAL BUDGETING DECISIONS AND THE ACCELERATED COST RECOVERY SYSTEM (ACRS)

Although the traditional depreciation methods described in the previous section still can be used for computing depreciation for book purposes, 1981 saw a new way of computing depreciation deductions for tax purposes. The new rule is called the accelerated cost recovery system (ACRS) rule. Effective for assets placed into service after January 1, 1981, the rule is characterized as follows:

1. It abandons the concept of useful life, places the assets into one of five property classes, and computes depreciation deductions, based on an allowable percentage of the asset's original cost. (See Tables 8-1 and 8-2.)

2. It is not necessary to consider the salvage value of an asset in computing depreciation.

3. The company may elect to use the straight-line method. In such a case, the company may elect to use asset lives greater than those shown in the five basic classes, as shown in Table 8-3.

The straight-line option must follow what is called the *half-year convention*. This means that the company can deduct only half of the regular straight-line depreciation amount in the first year.

---

[1] A comprehensive treatment of the problem appears in H. Martin Weingartner, "Capital Budgeting of Interrelated Projects—Survey and Synthesis," *Management Science*, vol. 12, March 1966, pp. 485–516.

Table 8-1.   **Accelerated Cost Recovery System—Classification of Assets**

Class	Types of Assets
3-year property	Includes automobiles, light-duty trucks, equipment used in research and development, and certain special tools
5-year property	Includes all other items of machinery and equipment used in a business that do not fall into the 3-year property class
10-year property	Includes mostly public utility property (with an 18- to 25-year useful life), and certain limited real property such as theme parks
15-year property	Includes all public utility property other than that in the 10-year property class
15-year property	Includes all depreciable real property used in a business, other than that included in the 10-year property class

Table 8-2.   **Accelerated Cost Recovery System Tables by Property Class**

Taxable Year	Property Class				
	3-Year (%)	5-Year (%)	10-year (%)	15-year Utility Property (%)	15-year Real Property (%)
1	25	15	8	5	12
2	38	22	14	10	10
3	37	21	12	9	9
4		21	10	8	8
5		21	10	7	7
6			10	7	6
7			9	6	6
8			9	6	6
9			9	6	6
10			9	6	5
11				6	5
12				6	5
13				6	5
14				6	5
15				6	5

Table 8-3.   **Accelerated Cost Recovery System—The Straight-Line Depreciation Option**

Property	Optional Periods for Straight-Line Depreciation
3-year	3, 5, or 12 years
5-year	5, 12, or 25 years
10-year	10, 25, or 35 years
15-year	15, 35, or 45 years

EXAMPLE 8.15 Assume that a machine falls under the 3-year property class and cost $3,000 initially. Using the straight-line option under ACRS, the company would deduct only $500 depreciation in the first year and the fourth year ($3,000 ÷ 3 = $1,000; $1,000 × $\frac{1}{2}$ = $500).

Year	Depreciation
1	$ 500
2	1,000
3	1,000
4	500
	$3,000

Investment Tax Credit (ITC)

Investment tax credit (ITC) is a direct reduction of income taxes and is taken in the year in which an asset is first placed into service. The percentages depend on the age classes as follows:

Property Class	ITC for the Reduced Basis Cost	ITC for the Full Basis Cost
3-year	4%	6%
5-, 10-, 15-year	8%	10%

The company generally must decide either to reduce the basis (cost) of the asset by 50 percent of the ITC *or* to reduce the amount of ITC by 2 percentage points.

EXAMPLE 8.16 A machine costs $1,000. Annual cash inflows are expected to be $500. The machine will be depreciated using the ACRS rule and will fall under the 3-year property class. The cost of capital after taxes is 8 percent. The estimated life of the machine is 3 years. The tax rate is 40 percent. The investment tax credit the company elected to take is the reduced 4 percent. Annual depreciation deductions under the ACRS rule are:

Year	Cost	ACRS	Depreciation
1	$1,000	25%	$ 250
2	$1,000	38%	380
3	$1,000	37%	370
			$1,000

After-tax cash inflows are then computed as follows:

	Year 1	Year 2	Year 3
Cash inflows	$500	$500	$500
Depreciation	250	380	370
Net profits before tax	$250	$120	$130
Tax (40%)	100	48	52
Net profits after tax	$150	$ 72	$ 78
Depreciation	250	380	370
After-tax cash inflows	$400	$452	$448

The NPV of the new investment is computed as follows:

Year	Cash Flow ($)	PV of $1 at 8%	NPV ($)
0	(1,000)	1.000	(1,000)
1	400	0.926	370
	40[a]	0.926	37
2	452	0.857	387
3	448	0.794	356
			150

[a] The investment tax credit of $40 ($1,000 × 4%) is assumed to be taken in year 1 in which the machine is first placed in service.

Since NPV is positive (i.e., $150), the machine should be bought.

8.7 LEASING

Leasing provides an alternative to purchasing an asset in order to acquire its services without directly incurring any fixed debt obligation. There are two basic types of leases available to the business firm:

1. *An operating lease* is basically a short-term lease. It is cancelable at the option of the firm leasing the asset (the lessee). Such leases are commonly used for leasing such items as computer hardware, cash registers, vehicles, and equipment.

2. *A financial (capital) lease* is a longer-term lease than an operating lease. It constitutes a noncancelable contractual commitment on the part of the lessee to make a series of payments to the firm that actually owns the asset (the lessor) for the use of the asset.

Accounting for Leases

Prior to 1977, most financial (capital) leases were not included in the balance sheets of the lessee. Instead, they were reported in the footnotes of the balance sheet. However, in November 1976, the Financial Accounting Standards Board (FASB), which is a part of the Americal Institute of Certified Public Accountants, issued a statement that requires any lease meeting one or more of the following criteria[2] to be included in the body of the balance sheet of the lessor.

1. The lease transfers ownership of the property to the lessee by the end of the lease term.

2. The lease contains a bargain repurchase option.

3. The lease term is equal to 75 percent or more of the estimated economic life of the leased property.

4. The present value of the minimum lease payments equals or exceeds 90 percent of the excess of the fair value of the property over any related investment tax credit retained by the lessor.

The Lease-Purchase Decision

The lease-purchase decision is a decision that commonly confronts firms considering the acquisition of new assets. It is a hybrid capital budgeting decision which forces a company to compare the leasing and purchasing alternatives. To make an intelligent decision, an *after-tax, cash outflow, present value* comparison is needed. There are special steps to take when making this comparison.

---

[2] Financial Accounting Standards Board, *Statement of Accounting Standards No. 13*, "Accounting for Leases," November 1976, Stamford, Conn.

When considering a lease, take the following steps:

1. Find the annual lease payment. Since the annual lease payment is typically made in advance, the formula to be used is:

$$\text{Amount of lease} = A + A(\text{PVIFA}_{i,n-1}) \qquad \text{or} \qquad A = \frac{\text{amount of lease}}{1 + \text{PVIFA}_{i,n-1}}$$

Notice we use $n-1$ rather than n.

2. Find the after-tax cash outflows.

3. Find the present value of the after-tax cash outflows.

When considering a purchase, take the following steps:

1. Find the annual loan amortization by using:

$$A = \frac{\text{amount of loan for the purchase}}{\text{PVIFA}_{i,n}}$$

This step may not be necessary since this amount is usually available.

2. Calculate the interest. The interest is segregated from the principal in each of the annual loan payments because only the interest is tax-deductible.

3. Find the cash outflows by adding interest and depreciation (plus any maintenance costs), and then compute the after-tax outflows.

4. Find the present value of the after-tax cash outflows, using Appendix C.

EXAMPLE 8.17 A firm has decided to acquire an asset costing $100,000 that has an expected life of 5 years, after which the asset is not expected to have any residual value. The asset can be purchased by borrowing or it can be leased. If leasing is used, the lessor requires a 12 percent return. As is customary, lease payments are to be made in advance, that is, at the end of the year prior to each of the 10 years. The tax rate is 50 percent and the firm's cost of capital, or after-tax cost of borrowing, is 8 percent.

First compute the present value of the after-tax cash outflows associated with the leasing alternative.

1. Find the annual lease payment:

$$A = \frac{\text{amount of lease}}{1 + \text{PVIFA}_{i,n-1}}$$

$$= \frac{\$100,000}{1 + \text{PVIFA}_{12\%,4\text{ years}}} = \frac{\$100,000}{1 + 3.3073} = \frac{\$100,000}{4.3073} = \$23,216 \text{ (rounded)}$$

Steps 2 and 3 can be done in the same schedule, as follows:

Year	(1) Lease Payment ($)	(2) Tax Savings ($)	(3) = (1) − (2) After-Tax Cash Outflow ($)	(4) PV at 8%	(5) = (3) × (4) PV of Cash Outflow ($, Rounded)
0	23,216		23,216	1.000	23,216
1–4	23,216	11,608[a]	11,608	3.3121[b]	38,447
5		11,608	(11,608)	0.6806[a]	(7,900)
					53,763

---

[a] $23,216 × 50%

[b] From Appendix D.

[c] From Appendix C.

If the asset is purchased, the firm is assumed to finance it entirely with a 10 percent unsecured term loan. Straight-line depreciation is used with no salvage value. Therefore, the annual depreciation is $20,000 ($100,000/5 years). In this alternative, first find the annual loan payment by using:

$$A = \frac{\text{amount of loan}}{\text{PVIFA}_{i,n}}$$

$$= \frac{\$100,000}{\text{PVIFA}_{10\%,5 \text{ years}}} = \frac{\$100,000}{3.7906} = \$26,381 \text{ (rounded)}$$

2. Calculate the interest by setting up a loan amortization schedule.

Year	(1) Loan Payment ($)	(2) Beginning-of-Year Principal ($)	(3) = (2)(10%) Interest ($)	(4) = (1) − (3) Principal ($)	(5) = (2) − (4) End-of-Year Principal ($)
1	26,381	100,000	10,000	16,381	83,619
2	26,381	83,619	8,362	18,019	65,600
3	26,381	65,600	6,560	19,821	45,779
4	26,381	45,779	4,578	21,803	23,976
5	26,381	23,976[a]	2,398	23,983[a]	

[a] Because of rounding errors, there is a slight difference between (2) and (4).

Steps 3 (cash outflows) and 4 (present values of those outflows) can be done as follows:

Year	(1) Loan Payment ($)	(2) Interest ($)	(3) Depreciation ($)	(4) = (2) + (3) Total Deductions ($)	(5) = (4)(50%) Tax Savings ($)	(6) = (1) − (5) Cash Outflow($)	(7) PV at 8%	(8) = (6) × (7) PV of Cash Outflow ($)
1	26,381	10,000	20,000	30,000	15,000	11,381	0.9259	10,538
2	26,381	8,362	20,000	28,362	14,181	12,200	0.8573	10,459
3	26,381	6,560	20,000	26,560	13,280	13,101	0.7938	10,400
4	26,381	4,578	20,000	24,578	12,289	14,092	0.7350	10,358
5	26,381	2,398	20,000	22,398	11,199	15,182	0.6806	10,333
								52,088

The sum of the present values of the cash outflows for leasing and purchasing by borrowing shows that purchasing is preferable because the PV of borrowing is less than the PV of leasing ($52,088 versus $53,763). The *incremental* savings would be $1,675 ($53,763 − $52,088).

Review Questions

1. The initial investment is _____ plus installation cost minus _____ plus or minus _____.

2. The total gain is split into _____ and _____. These breakdowns are subject to _____ tax rates.

3. After-tax cash inflows equal net profits after taxes plus _____.

4. The NPV method and the IRR method are called _____ methods.

5. _____ is the process of making _____ decisions.

6. _____ is the _____ divided by the cash inflow through increased revenues or cash savings in operating expenses.

7. The shorter the _____, the less risky the project and the greater the _____.

8. Accounting rate of return does not recognize the _____.

9. Internal rate of return is the rate at which _____ equals _____.

10. Accept the investment if its IRR exceeds _____.

11. IRR is difficult to compute when the cash flows are _____.

12. In _____, the NPV and the IRR methods may produce _____.

13. _____ is used widely in ranking the investments competing for limited funds.

14. The _____ method discounts all cash flows at the _____, thus implicitly assuming that these cash flows can be reinvested at this rate.

15. ACRS rules abandon the concept of _____.

16. _____ is taken in the year in which an asset is first placed into service.

17. The straight-line depreciation method with _____ allows the company to deduct only half of the regular straight-line deduction amount in the _____ year.

18. Immediate disposal of an old machine usually results in _____ that is fully deductible from current income for tax purposes.

19. The FASB requires firms to _____ certain financial (capital) leases and to restate their _____.

20. Lease payments represent a desired rate of return to the _____.

Answers: (1) cost (purchase price) of the asset, the proceeds from sale of the old asset, taxes on the sale of old asset; (2) a capital gain, recapture of depreciation, different; (3) depreciation; (4) discounted cash flow (DCF); (5) Capital budgeting, long-term investment; (6) Payback period, initial amount of investment; (7) payback period, liquidity; (8) time value of money; (9) present value of cash inflows, the initial investment; (10) the cost of capital; (11) not even; (12) mutually exclusive investments, conflicting rankings; (13) Profitability index (or benefit/cost ratio); (14) NPV, cost of capital; (15) useful life; (16) Investment tax credit (ITC); (17) the half-year convention, first; (18) a loss; (19) capitalize, balance sheets; (20) lessor.

Solved Problems

8.1   **Capital Gain (Loss) and Recapture of Depreciation.** For each of the following cases, compute the total taxes resulting from the sale of the asset. Assume a 28 percent long-term capital gains tax and a 46 percent ordinary tax rate. The asset was purchased for $75,000 3 years ago and has a book value (undepreciated value) of $40,000. (*a*) The asset is sold for $80,000. (*b*) The asset is sold for $70,000. (*c*) The assset is sold for $40,000. (*d*) The asset is sold for $38,000.

SOLUTION

(*a*)
$$\text{Total gain} = \text{selling price} - \text{book value}$$
$$= \$80,000 - \$40,000 = \$40,000$$

which is split into:

Capital gain ($80,000 − $75,000)	$ 5,000
Recapture of depreciation ($75,000 − $40,000)	35,000
	$40,000

Total taxes are:

Capital gain ($5,000 × 0.28)	$ 1,400
Recapture of depreciation ($35,000 × 0.46)	16,100
	$17,500

(*b*)   No capital gain.

Recapture of depreciation:	$70,000 − $40,000 = $30,000
Tax:	$30,000 × 0.46 = $13,800

(*c*)   No tax.

(*d*)   Loss: $38,000 − $40,000 = $2,000

Tax saving: $2,000 × 0.46 = $920

8.2   **Calculation of Initial Investment.** A firm is considering replacing an old machine with another. The new machine costs $90,000 plus $10,000 to install. For each of the four cases given in Problem 8.1, calculate the initial investment of the replacement.

SOLUTION

	(*a*)	(*b*)	(*c*)	(*d*)
Cost of new machine	$90,000	$90,000	$90,000	$90,000
+ Installation cost	10,000	10,000	10,000	10,000
− Proceeds from sale of old machine	80,000	70,000	40,000	38,000
+ Taxes on sale of old machine	17,500	13,800	0	(920)
Initial investment	$37,500	$43,800	$60,000	$61,080

8.3   **Incremental Cash Inflows.** National Bottles Corporation is contemplating the replacement of one of its bottling machines with a new one that will increase revenue from $25,000 to $31,000 per year and reduce cash operating costs from $12,000 to $10,000 per year. The new machine will cost $48,000 and have an estimated life of 10 years with no salvage value. The firm uses straight-line depreciation and is subject to a 46 percent tax rate. The old machine has been fully depreciated and has no salvage value. What is the incremental (relevant) cash inflows generated by the replacement?

SOLUTION

$$\text{Annual depreciation of the new machine} = \frac{\text{cost}}{\text{expected life}}$$

$$= \frac{\$48,000}{10} = \$4,800 \text{ per year}$$

	Annual		**Net Profits before**
	Revenue	**Cash Operating Costs**	**Depreciation and Taxes**
Old	$25,000	$12,000	$13,000
New	$31,000	$10,000	$21,000

Net profits after taxes and after-tax cash inflows for both machines are computed as follows:

	Net Profits after Taxes	**Add Depreciation**	**After-Tax Cash Inflows**
Old	($13,000 − 0)(1 − 0.46) = $7,020	$0	$7,020
New	($21,000 − $4,800)(1 − 0.46) = $8,748	$4,800	$13,548

Therefore, the relevant incremental cash inflows for each year are:

$$\$13,548 - \$7,020 = \$6,528$$

Alternatively, use the shortcut formula, as follows:

Increase in revenue × (1 − tax rate):	
($31,000 − $25,000)(1 − 0.46)	$3,240
− Increase in cash charges × (1 − tax rate):	
($10,000 − $12,000)(1 − 0.46)	−(−1,080)
+ Increase in depreciation × tax rate:	
($4,800 − 0)(0.46)	2,208
After-tax cash inflows	$6,528

8.4   Basic Evaluation Methods. The following data are given for the Alright Aluminum Company:

Initial cost of proposed equipment	$75,000
Estimated useful life	7 years
Estimated annual savings in cash operating expenses	$18,000
Predicted residual value at the end of the useful life	$3,000
Cost of capital	12%

Compute the (a) payback period, (b) present value of estimated annual savings, (c) present value of estimated residual value, (d) total present value of estimated cash inflows, (e) net present value (NPV), and (f) internal rate of return (IRR).

SOLUTION

(a)
$$\text{Payback period} = \frac{\text{initial investment}}{\text{annual savings}} = \frac{\$75,000}{\$18,000} = 4.167 \text{ years}$$

(b)
$$PV = A \times PVIFA_{12\%,7\,\text{years}} = \$18,000 \times 4.5638 = \$82,148 \text{ (rounded)}$$

(c)
$$PV = \$3,000 \times PVIF_{12\%,7\,\text{years}} = \$3,000 \times 0.4523 = \$1,357 \text{ (rounded)}$$

(d)
$$\text{Total PV} = \$82,148 + \$1,357 = \$83,505$$

(e)
$$\text{NPV} = PV - I = \$83,505 - \$75,000 = \$8,505$$

(f) At IRR, I = PV. Thus,

$$\$75,000 = \$18,000 \times PVIFA_{r,7}$$

$$PVIFA_{r,7} = \frac{\$75,000}{\$18,000} = 4.1667$$

which is somewhere between 14 percent and 15 percent in the 7-year line.
Using interpolation,

	PVIFA	
14%	4.2883	4.2883
True rate	4.1667	
15%		4.1604
Difference	0.1216	0.1279

$$\text{IRR} = 14\% + \frac{4.2883 - 4.1667}{4.2883 - 4.1604}(15\% - 14\%)$$

$$= 14\% + \frac{0.1216}{0.1279}(1\%) = 14\% + 0.95\% = 14.95\%$$

8.5 Payback Period and ARR. The John-in-the-Box Store is a fast food restaurant chain. Potential franchisees are given the following revenue and cost information:

Building and equipment	$490,000
Annual revenue	$520,000
Annual cash operating costs	$380,000

The building and equipment have a useful life of 20 years. The straight-line method for depreciation is used. The income tax is 40 percent. Given these facts, (a) What is the payback period? (b) What is the accounting rate of return?

SOLUTION

$$\text{Net profits before depreciation and taxes} = \$520,000 - \$380,000 = \$140,000$$

$$\text{Annual depreciation} = \frac{\$490,000}{20 \text{ years}} = \$24,500$$

Therefore,

$$\text{Net profit after taxes} = (\$140,000 - \$24,500)(1 - 0.4) = \$69,300$$

$$\text{After-tax cash inflows} = \$69,300 + \$24,500 = \$93,800$$

(a)
$$\text{Payback period} = \frac{\text{Initial investment}}{\text{annual cash flow}} = \frac{\$490,000}{\$93,800} = 5.22 \text{ years}$$

(b) $$\text{Accounting rate of return} = \frac{\text{net income}}{\text{investment}} = \frac{\$69,300}{\$490,000} = 14.14\%$$

or using average investment in the denominator gives:

$$\text{ARR} = \frac{\$69,300}{\$490,000/2} = 28.28\%$$

8.6   Basic Evaluation Methods. The Rango Company is considering a capital investment for which the initial outlay is $20,000. Net annual cash inflows (before taxes) are predicted to be $4,000 for 10 years. Straight-line depreciation is to be used, with an estimated salvage value of zero. Ignore income taxes. Compute the (a) payback period; (b) accounting rate of return (ARR); (c) net present value (NPV), assuming a cost of capital (before tax) of 12 percent; and (d) internal rate of return (IRR).

SOLUTION

(a) $$\text{Payback period} = \frac{\text{initial investment}}{\text{annual cash flow}} = \frac{\$20,000}{\$4,000/\text{year}} = 5 \text{ years}$$

(b) $$\text{Accounting rate of return (ARR)} = \frac{\text{net income}}{\text{initial investment}}$$

$$\text{Depreciation} = \frac{\$20,000}{10 \text{ years}} = \$2,000/\text{year}$$

$$\text{Accounting rate of return} = \frac{(\$4,000 - \$2,000)/\text{year}}{\$20,000} = 0.10 = 10\%$$

(c)   Net present value (NPV) = PV of cash inflows [discounted at the cost of capital (12%)]
            − initial investment

$$\$4,000 \times (\text{PVIFA}_{12\%,10}) - \$20,000 = \$4,000(5.6502) - \$20,000 = \$2,600.80$$

(d)   Internal rate of return (IRR) is the rate which equates the amount invested with the present value of cash inflows generated by the project.

$$\$20,000 = \$4,000(\text{PVIFA}_{r,10})$$

$$\text{PVIFA}_{r,10} = \frac{\$20,000}{\$4,000} = 5$$

which is between 15 percent and 16 percent in Appendix D. Using interpolation,

	PVIFA	
15%	5.0188	5.0188
True rate	5.0000	
16%		4.8332
Difference	0.0188	0.1856

$$\text{IRR} = 15\% + \left(\frac{5.0188 - 5.0000}{5.0188 - 4.8332}\right)(16\% - 15\%) = 15\% + \frac{0.0188}{0.1856}(1\%)$$

$$= 15\% + 0.101\% = 15.101\%$$

8.7   Basic Capital Budgeting Decisions. Consider an investment which has the following cash flows:

Year	Cash Flow ($)
0	(31,000)
1	10,000
2	20,000
3	10,000
4	10,000
5	5,000

(a) Compute the (1) payback period, (2) net present value (NPV) at 14 percent cost of capital, and (3) internal rate of return (IRR).

(b) Based on (2) and (3) in part (a), make a decision about the investment. Should it be accepted or not?

SOLUTION

(a) (1) The payback period is computed as follows:

		Recovery of Initial Outlay		
Year	Cash Flow	Needed	Balance	Payback Period
1	$10,000	$31,000	$21,000	1.00
2	$20,000	$21,000	$1,000	1.00
3	$10,000	$1,000		0.10
				2.1 [a]

[a] Payback period in years.

(2) NPV is computed as follows:

Year	Cash Flow ($)	PV Factor at 14%	PV ($)
0	(31,000)	1.000	(31,000)
1	10,000	0.8772	8,772
2	20,000	0.7695	15,390
3	10,000	0.6750	6,750
4	10,000	0.5921	5,921
5	5,000	0.5194	2,597
		NPV	8,430

(3) By definition, IRR is the rate at which PV = I or NPV = 0. From part (2), NPV at 14% = $8,430. Try 30 percent to determine what happens to NPV.

Year	Cash Flow ($)	PV Factor at 30%	PV ($)
0	(31,000)	1.000	(31,000)
1	10,000	0.7694	7,694
2	20,000	0.5921	11,842
3	10,000	0.4558	4,558
4	10,000	0.3509	3,509
5	5,000	0.2702	1,351
			(2,046)

True IRR is somewhere between 14 percent and 30 percent. Use interpolation to determine the amount.

		NPV
14%	$8,430	$ 8,430
True rate	0	
30%		$-(-2,046)$
Difference	$8,430	$10,476

Therefore,

$$\text{IRR} = 14\% + \frac{\$8,430}{\$8,430 - (-\$2,046)}(30\% - 14\%)$$

$$= 14\% + \frac{\$8,430}{\$10,476}(16\%) = 14\% + 12.875\% = 26.875\%$$

(b) Under the NPV method, accept the project since the NPV is positive ($8,430). Under the IRR method, accept the project since the IRR of 26.875 percent exceeds the cost of capital of 14 percent.

8.8   **Comprehensive Capital Budgeting Decision.** The Chellin Company purchased a special machine 1 year ago at a cost of $12,000. At that time the machine was estimated to have a useful life of 6 years and no salvage value. The annual cash operating cost is approximately $20,000. A new machine has just come on the market which will do the same job but with an annual cash operating cost of only $17,000. This new machine costs $21,000 and has an estimated life of 5 years with zero salvage value. The old machine can be sold for $10,000 to a scrap dealer. Straight-line depreciation is used, and the company's income tax rate is 40 percent.

Assuming a cost of capital of 8 percent after taxes, calculate (a) the initial investment, (b) the incremental cash inflow after taxes, (c) the NPV of the new investment, and (d) the IRR on the new investment.

SOLUTION

(a) The initial investment is:

Cost of new machine	$21,000
− Proceeds from sale of old machine	10,000
	$11,000

Since the selling price ($10,000) is the same as the book value ($12,000 − $2,000 = $10,000), no taxable gain or loss results.

(b) The incremental cash inflow may be computed by using the shortcut formula:

Annual cash savings	
$[\$3,000 \times (1 - 0.4)]$	$1,800
+ Increase in depreciation × tax rate	
$[(\$4,200 - \$2,000)(0.4)]$	880
After-tax cash inflow	$2,680

(c) $$\text{NPV} = \text{PV} - \text{I}$$
$$= \$2,680(\text{PVIFA}_{8,5}) - \$11,000 = \$2,680(3.9927) - \$11,000$$
$$= \$10,700 - \$11,000 = -\$300 \text{ (rounded)}$$

(d)   IRR is the rate at which I = PV. Thus,

$$I = PV$$
$$\$11,000 = \$2,680 \text{ PVIFA}_{r,5 \text{ years}}$$
$$\text{PVIFA}_{r,5} = \frac{\$11,000}{\$2,680} = 4.1045$$

which is about 7 percent in the 5-year line of Appendix D.

8.9   Supplying Missing Data. Fill in the blanks for each of the following independent cases. Assume in all cases the investment has a useful life of 10 years.

Annual Cash Inflow	Investment	Cost of Capital	IRR	NPV
$100,000	$449,400	14%	(a)	(b)
$70,000	(c)	14%	20%	(d)
(e)	$200,000	(f)	14%	$35,624
(g)	$300,000	12%	(h)	$39,000

SOLUTION

(a)
$$I = PV$$
$$\$449,400 = \$100,000 \text{ PVIFA}_{r,10}$$
$$\text{PVIFA}_{r,10} = \frac{\$449,400}{\$100,000} = 4.494$$

From Appendix D, the present value factor of 4.494 at 10 years gives a rate of 18%.

(b)
$$NPV = PV - I$$
$$= \$100,000 \text{ PVIFA}_{14,10} - \$449,400$$
$$= \$100,000(5.2161) - \$449,400 = \$521,610 - \$449,400 = \$72,210$$

(c)
$$I = PV$$
$$= \$70,000 \text{ PVIFA}_{20,10} = \$70,000(4.1925) = \$293,475$$

(d)
$$NPV = PV - I$$
$$= \$70,000 \text{ PVIFA}_{14,10} - \$293,475$$
$$= \$70,000(5.2161) - \$293,475 = \$365,127 - \$293,475 = \$71,652$$

(e)   At IRR = 14%, PV = I.

$$\text{Cash inflow} \times \text{PVIFA}_{14,10} = \text{investment}$$
$$\text{Cash inflow} = \frac{\text{investment}}{\text{PVIFA}_{14,10}} = \frac{\$200,000}{5.2161} = \$38,343 \text{ (rounded)}$$

(f)
$$NPV = PV - I$$
$$\$35,624 = PV - \$200,000$$
$$\$35,624 + \$200,000 = PV = \text{cash inflow (PVIFA}_{r,10})$$
$$\$235,624 = \$38,343 \text{ PVIFA}_{r,10}$$
$$\frac{\$235,624}{\$38,343} = \text{PVIFA}_{r,10}$$
$$6.1451 = \text{PVIFA}_{r,10}$$

Since this is the present value factor for 10 percent at 10 years, the cost of capital is 10 percent.

(g)
$$PV = NPV + 1$$

$$\text{Cash inflow (PVIFA}_{12,10}) = NPV + I = \$39,000 + \$300,000 = \$339,000$$

$$\text{Cash inflow} = \frac{\$339,000}{\text{PVIFA}_{12,10}} = \frac{\$339,000}{5.6502} = \$59,998 \text{ (rounded)}$$

(h)
$$I = PV$$

$$\$300,000 = \$59,998 \, \text{PVIFA}_{r,10}$$

$$\text{PVIFA}_{r,10} = \frac{\$300,000}{\$59,998} = 5.0002$$

Since this PVIFA value is about halfway between 15 percent and 16 percent at 10 years, IRR is estimated at about 15.5 percent.

8.10   NPV Analysis. Kim Corporation invested in a 4-year project. Kim's cost of capital is 8 percent. Additional information on the project follows:

Year	After-Tax Cash Inflow	Present Value of $1 at 8%
1	$2,000	0.926
2	$2,200	0.857
3	$2,400	0.794
4	$2,600	0.735

Assuming a NPV of $700, what was the initial investment?

SOLUTION

Year	Cash Inflow	PV	Total PV
1	$2,000	0.926	$1,852
2	$2,200	0.857	1,885
3	$2,400	0.794	1,906
4	$2,600	0.735	1,911
			$7,554

$$NPV = PV - I$$
$$I = PV - NPV$$
$$= \$7,554 - \$700 = \$6,854$$

8.11   IRR. XYZ, Inc., invested in a machine with a useful life of 6 years and no salvage value. The machine was depreciated using the straight-line method and it was expected to produce annual cash inflow from operations, net of income taxes, of $2,000. The present value of an ordinary annuity of $1 for six periods at 10 percent is 4.3553. The present value of $1 for six periods at 10 percent is 0.5645. Assuming that XYZ used an internal rate of return of 10 percent, what was the amount of the original investment?

SOLUTION

By definition, at IRR, PV = I or NPV = 0.
To obtain the amount of initial investment find the present value of $2,000 a year for 6 periods.

$$PV = \$2,000 \times 4.3553 = \$8,710.60$$

8.12   Ranking. Data relating to three investment projects are given below.

	A	**B**	**C**
Investment (I)	$30,000	$20,000	$50,000
Useful life	10 years	4 years	20 years
Annual cash savings	$6,207	$7,725	$9,341

Rank the projects according to their attractiveness using the (*a*) payback period, (*b*) IRR, and (*c*) NPV at 14 percent cost of capital.

SOLUTION

(*a*)

$$\text{Payback period} = \frac{\text{initial investment}}{\text{increased revenue or savings}}$$

Project	Payback Period	Rank
A	$\dfrac{\$30,000}{\$6,207} = 4.833$ years	2
B	$\dfrac{\$20,000}{\$7,725} = 2.588$ years	1
C	$\dfrac{\$50,000}{\$9,341} = 5.353$ years	3

(*b*)   The IRR ranking is:

Project	Closest Rate[a]	Rank
A	16%	3
B	20%	1
C	18%	2

[a] $PV = I$

Cash inflow $\times$ PVIFA $= I$

$$PVIFA = \frac{I}{\text{Cash inflow}}$$

For A: $PVIFA_{r,10} = \dfrac{\$30,000}{\$6,207} = 4.8333$

For B: $PVIFA_{r,4} = \dfrac{\$20,000}{\$7,725} = 2.589$

For C: $PVIFA_{r,20} = \dfrac{\$50,000}{\$9,341} = 5.3527$

(*c*)   NPV at 14 percent is:

Project	Annual Savings	PV Factor	Total PV	I	NPV (PV − I)	Rank
A	$6,207	5.2161	$32,376	$30,000	$2,376	3
B	$7,725	2.9137	$22,508	$20,000	$2,508	2
C	$9,341	6.6231	$61,866	$50,000	$11,866	1

8.13 Capital Rationing. Rand Corporation is considering five different investment opportunities. The company's cost of capital is 12 percent. Data on these opportunities under consideration are given below.

Project	Investment ($)	PV at 12% ($)	NPV ($)	IRR (%)	Profitability Index (Rounded)
1	35,000	39,325	4,325	16	1.12
2	20,000	22,930	2,930	15	1.15
3	25,000	27,453	2,453	14	1.10
4	10,000	10,854	854	18	1.09
5	9,000	8,749	(251)	11	0.97

Based on these data, (*a*) rank these five projects in the descending order of preference, according to NPV, IRR, and profitability index (or benefit/cost ratio). (*b*) Which ranking would you prefer? (*c*) Based on your answer to part (*b*), which projects would you select if $55,000 is the limit to be spent?

SOLUTION

(*a*)

	Order of Preference		
Project	NPV	IRR	Profitability Index
1	1	2	2
2	2	3	1
3	3	4	3
4	4	1	4
5	5	5	5

(*b*) The profitability index approach is generally considered the most dependable method of ranking projects competing for limited funds. It is an index of relative attractiveness, measured in terms of how much is returned for each dollar invested.

(*c*) Based on the answer in part (*b*), choose projects (2) and (1), for which the combined NPV would be $7,255 ($2,930 + $4,325) with the limited budget of $55,000.

8.14 Capital Rationing and Mathematical Programming. Express the capital rationing problem given in Problem 8.13 as a mathematical programming problem.

SOLUTION

Labeling project (1) as X_1, project (2) as X_2, and so on, the problem can be stated as follows:
Maximize

$$NPV = \$4,325X_1 + \$2,930X_2 + \$2,453X_3 + \$854X_4 - \$251X_5$$

subject to

$$\$35,000X_1 + \$20,000X_2 + \$25,000X_3 + \$10,000X_4 + \$9,000X_5 \leq \$55,000$$
$$X_i = 0,1 \quad (i = 1, 2, \ldots, 5)$$

8.15 NPV Analysis. In Problem 8.3, should National Bottles Corporation buy the new machine? Base your answer on the NPV method, assuming that the cost of capital is 8 percent after taxes.

SOLUTION

From Problem 8.3,

$$I = \$48,000$$
$$n = 10 \text{ years}$$
$$A = \$6,528/\text{year}$$

Therefore,

$$NPV = PV - I = A \cdot PVIFA - I$$
$$= \$6,528(6.7101) - \$48,000 = \$43,804 - \$48,000 = -\$4,196 \text{ (rounded)}$$

National Bottles Corporation should not purchase the machine, because the NPV is negative.

8.16 **Computerized Bookkeeping System and NPV Analysis.** Zeta Corporation is contemplating the purchase of a minicomputer in order to reduce the cost of its data processing operations. Currently, the manual bookkeeping system in use involves the following annual cash expenses:

Salaries	$84,000
Payroll taxes and fringe benefits	24,000
Forms and supplies	6,000
	$114,000

The present equipment is fully depreciated and has no salvage value. The cost of the computer, including installation and software, is $100,000. This entire amount is depreciable for income tax purposes on a double declining basis at the rate of 20 percent per annum.

Annual costs of the computerized bookkeeping system are estimated and given below.

Salaries	$40,000
Payroll taxes and fringe benefits	8,000
Forms and supplies	6,000
	$54,000

The computer is expected to be obsolete in 3 years, at which time its salvage value is $10,000.

(a) Compute after-tax-cash savings. Assume a 40 percent tax rate. (b) Decide whether or not to purchase the computer, using the NPV method. Assume a cost of capital of 10 percent after taxes.

SOLUTION

(a)

Annual cash expenses of the manual system		$114,000
Annual cash expenses of computerized bookkeeping		54,000
Annual cash savings		$ 60,000

Double-declining-balance method:

Year 1	$20,000	($100,000 × 20%)
Year 2	16,000	($80,000 × 20%)
Year 3	12,800	($64,000 × 20%)
	$48,800	

Therefore, after-tax cash savings are computed as follows:

	Year 1	Year 2	Year 3
Annual cash savings	$60,000	$60,000	$60,000
Depreciation	20,000	16,000	12,800
Net profits before tax	$40,000	$44,000	$47,200
Tax (40%)	16,000	17,600	18,880
Net profits after tax	$24,000	$26,400	$28,320
Depreciation	20,000	16,000	12,800
After-tax cash inflow	$44,000	$42,400	$41,120

(b)

Year	After-Tax Cash Inflow ($)	PV of $1 at 10%	Total PV ($, Rounded)
1	44,000	0.9091	40,000
2	42,400	0.8264	35,039
3	41,120	0.7513	30,893
	10,000 [a]	0.7513	7,513
	16,480 [b]	0.7513	12,381
			125,826

[a] Salvage.

[b] $16,480 is the tax savings from the loss on the disposal of the computer at the end of year 3, computed as follows:

Salvage value	$ 10,000
Book value ($100,000 − $48,800)	51,200
Loss on disposal	$(41,200)
Tax (40%)	
Tax savings (0.4 × $41,200)	$ 16,480

8.17 Computerized Bookkeeping System and NPV Analysis. Rework Problem 8.16 using the sum-of-years'-digits method of depreciation for the computer.

SOLUTION

(a) The sum-of-years'-digits depreciation is:

Year	Rate	Depreciation	
1	3/6	$ 50,000	($100,000 × 3/6)
2	2/6	33,333	($100,000 × 2/6)
3	1/6	16,667	($100,000 × 1/6)
		$100,000	

Therefore, after-tax cash savings are computed as follows:

	Year 1	Year 2	Year 3
Annual cash savings	$60,000	$60,000	$60,000
Depreciation	50,000	33,333	16,667
Net profits before tax	$10,000	$26,667	$43,333
Tax (40%)	4,000	10,667	17,333
Net profits after tax	$ 6,000	$16,000	$26,000
Depreciation	50,000	33,333	16,667
After-tax cash inflow	$56,000	$49,333	$42,667

(b)

Year	After-Tax Cash Inflow ($)	PV of $1	Total PV ($, Rounded)
1	56,000	0.9091	50,910
2	49,333	0.8264	40,769
3	42,667	0.7513	32,056
	6,000 [a]	0.7513	4,508
			128,243

[a] The $6,000 cash inflow is computed as follows:

Salvage value	$10,000
Book value	0
Gain	$10,000
Tax (40%)	4,000
After-tax gain	$ 6,000

$$NPV = PV - I$$
$$= \$128,243 - \$100,000 = \$28,243$$

Since NPV is positive, the company should purchase the computer, replacing the manual bookkeeping system.

8.18 **Replacement Decision.** Wisconsin Products Company manufactures several different products. One of the firm's principal products sells for $20 per unit. The sales manager of Wisconsin Products has stated repeatedly that he could sell more units of this product if they were available. In an attempt to substantiate his claim the sales manager conducted a market research study last year at a cost of $44,000 to determine potential demand for this product. The study indicated that Wisconsin Products could sell 18,000 units of this product annually for the next 5 years.

The equipment currently in use has the capacity to produce 11,000 units annually. The variable production costs are $9 per unit. The equipment has a book value of $60,000 and a remaining useful life of 5 years. The salvage value of the equipment is negligible now and will be zero in 5 years.

A maximum of 20,000 units could be produced annually on new machinery. The new equipment costs $300,000 and has an estimated useful life of 5 years, with no salvage value at the end of 5 years. Wisconsin Product's production manager has estimated that the new equipment, if purchased, would provide increased production efficiencies that would reduce the variable production costs to $7 per unit.

Wisconsin Products Company uses straight-line depreciation on all its equipment for tax purposes. The firm is subject to a 40 percent tax rate, and its after-tax cost of capital is 15 percent.

The sales manager felt so strongly about the need for additional capacity that he attempted to prepare an economic justification for the equipment although this was not one of his responsibilities. His analysis, presented below and on the next page, disappointed him because it did not justify acquisition of the equipment.

He computed the required investment as follows:

Purchase price of new equipment		$300,000
Disposal of existing equipment		
Loss on disposal	$60,000	
Less tax benefit (40%)	24,000	36,000
Cost of market research study		44,000
Total investment		$380,000

He computed the annual returns as follows:

Contribution margin from product	
Using the new equipment	
[18,000 × ($20 − $7)]	$234,000
Using the existing equipment	
[11,000 × ($20 − $9)]	121,000
Increase in contribution margin	$113,000
Less depreciation	60,000
Increase in before-tax income	$ 53,000
Income tax (40%)	21,200
Increase in income	$ 31,800
Less 15% cost of capital on the additional investment required (0.15 × $380,000)	57,000
Net annual return on proposed investment in new equipment	$ (25,200)

The controller of Wisconsin Products Company plans to prepare a discounted cash flow analysis for this investment proposal. The controller has asked you to prepare corrected calculations of (a) the required investment in the new equipment and (b) the recurring annual cash flows. Explain why your corrected calculations differ from the original analysis prepared by the sales manager. (c) Calculate the net present value of the proposed investment in the new equipment.

SOLUTION

(a)   The initial investment is:

Purchase price of new equipment	$300,000
− Tax savings from loss on disposal[a]	24,000
	$276,000

---

[a] Tax savings are computed as follows:

$$\text{Loss} = \text{selling price} - \text{book value}$$
$$= (\$0 - \$60,000) = \$60,000$$

Tax rate	0.4
Tax savings	$24,000

(b)   Using the shortcut method; the annual cash flows are computed by first determining the increased cash flows resulting from change in contribution margin:

Using new equipment	
[18,000 ($20 − $7)]^a	$234,000
Using existing equipment	
[11,000 ($20 − $9)]	121,000
Increased cash flows	$113,000
Taxes (0.40 × $113,000)	45,200
Increased cash flows after taxes	$ 67,800

Next, compute the increase in depreciation:

Depreciation on new equipment		
($300,000 ÷ 5)	$60,000	
Depreciation on existing equipment		
($60,000 ÷ 5)	12,000	
Increased depreciation charge	$48,000	
Tax rate	0.4	
		19,200
Recurring annual cash flows		$ 87,000

---

^{a} The new equipment is capable of producing 20,000 units, but Wisconsin Products can sell only 18,000 units annually.

The sales manager made several errors in his calculations of required investment and annual cash flows.

Concerning the required investment, the sales manager made two errors: First, the cost of the market research study ($44,000) is a sunk cost because it was incurred last year and will not change regardless of whether the investment is made or not. Second, the loss on the disposal of the existing equipment does not result in an actual cash cost as shown by the sales manager. The loss on disposal results in a reduction of taxes which reduces the cost of the new equipment.

In computing the annual cash flows, the sales manager made three errors: First, he considered only the depreciation on the new equipment rather than just the additional depreciation which would result from the acquisition of the new equipment. Second, he failed to consider that the depreciation is a noncash expenditure which provides a tax shield. Third, the sales manager's use of the discount rate (i.e., cost of capital) was incorrect. The discount rate should be used to reduce the value of future cash flows to their current equivalent at time period zero.

(c) $$NPV = PV - I = \text{cash flow } (PVIFA_{15,5}) - I$$
$$= (\$87,000 \times 3.3522) - \$276,000 = \$291,641 - \$276,000 = \$15,641$$

8.19   Mutually Exclusive Investments. The Wan-Ki Manufacturing Company must decide between investment projects A and B, which are mutually exclusive. The data on these projects are as follows (in thousands of dollars):

Cash Flows, per Year

Project	0	1	2	3	4
A	(100)	$120.000			
B	(100)				$193.80

(a) For each project, compute the NPV at 12 percent cost of capital, and the IRR. (b) Explain why the rankings conflict. Recommend which project should be chosen.

SOLUTION

(a) The NPV at 12 percent is:

Project	Cash Inflow	PV at $1[a]	PV	NPV (PV − I)
A	$120.00	0.8929	$107.15	$7.15
B	$193.80	0.6355	$123.16	$23.16

[a] $PVIF_{12,1}$ for A and $PVIF_{12,4}$ for B; both from Appendix C.

The IRR is:

Project	I/Cash Flow	PVIF	IRR
A	$\dfrac{\$100}{\$120.00} = 0.8333$ (at 1 year)		20%
B	$\dfrac{\$100}{\$193.80} = 0.516$ (at 4 years)		18%

(*b*) The conflicting ranking results from different assumptions regarding the reinvestment rate on the cash inflows released by the project. The NPV method assumes the cost of capital (12 percent in this problem) as the rate for reinvestment, whereas the IRR method assumes the cash inflows are reinvested at their own internal rate of return (20 percent in the case of project A). The use of NPV for ranking mutually exclusive investments is recommended since the cost of capital is a more realistic reinvestment rate. Therefore, project B should be chosen.

8.20 NPV, IRR, and Mutually Exclusive Investments. The Bitter Almond Company was confronted with the two mutually exclusive investment projects, A and B, which have the following after-tax cash flows:

	Cash Flows, per Year ($)				
Project	0	1	2	3	4
A	(12,000)	5,000	5,000	5,000	5,000
B	(12,000)				25,000

Based on these cash flows: (*a*) Calculate each project's NPV and IRR. (Assume that the firm's cost of capital after taxes is 10 percent.) (*b*) Which of the two projects would be chosen according to the IRR criterion? (*c*) How can you explain the differences in rankings given by the NPV and IRR methods in this case?

SOLUTION

(*a*) The NPV for project A is:

Year	Cash (Outflow) or Inflow	Present Value of $1 at 10%	Net Present Value of Cash Flow
0	$(12,000)	1.000	$(12,000)
1–4	$5,000	3.1699	15,850
			$ 3,850

The NPV for project B is:

Year	Cash (Outflow) or Inflow	Present Value of $1 at 10%	Net Present Value of Cash Flow
0	$(12,000)	1.000	$(12,000)
4	$25,000	0.6830	17,075
			$ 5,075

The IRR for project A is:

$$\$12{,}000 = \$5{,}000 \ (\text{PVIFA}_{r,4})$$

$$\text{PVIFA}_{r,4} = \frac{\$12{,}000}{\$5{,}000} = 2.4$$

Using interpolation:

	PV	
24%	2.4043	2.4043
True rate	2.4000	
28%		2.2410
Difference	0.0043	0.1633

$$\text{IRR} = 24\% + \frac{0.0043}{0.1633}\,(4\%) = 24\% + 0.11\% = 24.11\%$$

The IRR for project B is:

Year	Cash (Outflow) Inflow	Present Value of $1 at 20%	Net Present Value of Cash Flow	Present Value of $1 at 22%	Net Present Value of Cash Flow
0	$(12,000)	1.000	$(12,000)	1.000	$(12,000)
4	$25,000	0.4823	12,058	0.4526[a]	11,315
			$ 58		$ (685)

	NPV	
20%	$50	$ 50
True rate	0	
22%		− (−685)
Difference	$50	$735

$$\text{IRR} = 20\% + \frac{\$50}{\$735}\,(2\%) = 20\% + 0.14\% = 20.14\$$$

(b) In summary,

Projects	NPV	IRR
A	$3,850	24.11%
B	$5,075	20.14%

Under the NPV method, choose B over A. Under the IRR method, choose A over B.

(c) The decision of which project to choose hinges on assumptions made about reinvestment of cash inflow. Theory suggests resorting to the NPV method because the cost of capital reinvestment assumption implicit in this method is considered to be a more realistic assumption than the IRR, where a reinvestment at the IRR is assumed. Therefore, choose B rather than A, using the NPV ranking.

8.21 Capital Budgeting Under ACRS Rule. A firm is considering the purchase of an automatic machine for $6,200. The machine has an installation cost of $800 and zero salvage value at the end of its expected life of 5 years. The machine is depreciated using the ACRS rule; the machine is considered to be a 3-year property and therefore allowed a 4 percent investment tax credit. Expected cash savings before tax is $3,000 per year over the 5 years. The firm is in the 40 percent tax bracket. The firm has determined the cost of capital (or minimum required rate of return) of 10 percent after taxes. Use the NPV method to determine if the firm should purchase the machine. Assume the machine is put into service in year 1.

SOLUTION

First, compute annual depreciation deductions under the ACRS rule, as follows:

Year	Cost	ACRS	Depreciation
1	$7,000	25%	$1,750
2	$7,000	38%	2,660
3	$7,000	37%	2,590
			$7,000

After-tax cash inflows are:

	Year 1	Year 2	Year 3	Year 4	Year 5
Cash inflows	$3,000	$3,000	$3,000	$3,000	$3,000
Depreciation	1,750	2,660	2,590		
Net profits before tax	$1,250	$ 340	$ 410	$3,000	$3,000
Tax (40%)	500	136	164	1,200	1,200
Net profits after tax	$ 750	$ 204	$ 246	$1,800	$1,800
Depreciation	1,750	2,660	2,590		
After-tax cash inflow	$2,500	$2,864	$2,836	$1,800	$1,800

The NPV is computed as follows:

Year	Cash Flow ($)	PV of $1 at 10%	NPV ($, Rounded)
0	(7,000)	1.000	(7,000)
1	2,500	0.9091	2,273
	280[a]	0.9091	255
2	2,864	0.8264	2,367
3	2,836	0.7513	2,131
4	1,800	0.6830	1,229
5	1,800	0.6209	1,118
			2,373

[a] The investment tax credit is $7,000 × 4% = $280.

Since the NPV is $2,373 and is positive, the firm should purchase the machine.

8.22 Annual Lease Payments. Fairchild Leasing Company is setting up a capital lease with Gemi Trucking, Inc. The lease will cover a $36,000 delivery truck. The terms of the lease call for a 12 percent return to the truck lessor. The lease is to run for 5 years.

Based on these data, determine (*a*) the annual lease payment and (*b*) the annual lease payment if the lessor desires 10 percent on its lease.

SOLUTION

(a)
$$\text{Annual lease payment} = A = \frac{\text{amount}}{\text{PVIFA}_{12\%,5}} = \frac{\$36,000}{3.6048} = \$9,987 \text{ (rounded)}$$

(b)
$$A = \frac{\$36,000}{\text{PVIFA}_{10\%,5}} = \frac{\$36,000}{3.7908} = \$9,497 \text{ (rounded)}$$

8.23 Annual Lease Payments. Star Wars Leasing, Inc., is setting up a financial lease covering a $36,000 truck. The lease arrangement requires beginning-of-year payments and the life of the lease is 5 years. The company wants equal annual lease payments that will allow it to earn 12 percent on its investment.

Based on these data, determine (a) the annual lease payment and (b) the annual lease payment if the desired rate of return is only 10 percent.

SOLUTION

(a) Since the lease payment is made in advance, the straightforward application of the formula (i.e., A = amount/PVIFA) does not work. The equation can be set up as follows:

$$\$36,000 = A + A \cdot \text{PVIFA}_{12\%,4}$$
$$\$36,000 = A(1 + \text{PVIFA}_{12\%,4})$$
$$A = \frac{\$36,000}{1 + \text{PVIFA}_{12\%,4}} = \frac{\$36,000}{1 + 3.0373} = \frac{\$36,000}{4.0373} = \$8,917 \text{ (rounded)}$$

(b)
$$A = \frac{\$36,000}{1 + \text{PVIFA}_{10\%,4}} = \frac{\$36,000}{1 + 3.1699} = \frac{\$36,000}{4.1699} = \$8,633 \text{ (rounded)}$$

8.24 Lease versus Purchase Decision. Carter Company wishes to expand its productive capacity. In order to do so it must acquire a new tractor costing $40,000. The machine can be purchased or leased. The firm is in the 40 percent tax bracket and its after-tax cost of debt is currently 6 percent.

If the firm purchased the machine, the purchase would be totally financed with a 10 percent loan requiring equal annual end-of-year payments over 5 years. The machine would be depreciated straight-line over its 5-year life. A salvage value of zero is anticipated. The life of a lease would be 5 years. The lessor intends to charge equal annual lease payments that will enable it to earn 15 percent on its investment. In doing the following calculations, round your answers to the nearest dollar.

(a) Calculate the annual lease payment required in order to give the lessor its desired return. (b) Calculate the annual loan payment paying 10 percent interest. (c) Determine the after-tax cash outflows associated with each alternative. (d) Find the present value of the after-tax cash outflows using the after-tax cost of debt. (e) Which alternative (i.e., lease or purchase) would you recommend? Why?

SOLUTION

(a)
$$\text{Annual lease payment} = A = \frac{\$40,000}{\text{PVIFA}_{15\%,5}} = \frac{\$40,000}{3.3522} = \$11,932$$

(b)
$$\text{Annual loan payment} = A = \frac{\$40,000}{\text{PVIFA}_{10\%,5}} = \frac{\$40,000}{3.7908} = \$10,552$$

(c) and (d) Data pertaining to a lease agreement are as follows:

Year	Payment	After-Tax Cost	PV Factor at 6%	PV of Outflow
1–5	$11,932	$7,159	4.2124	$30,157

Data pertaining to a purchase agreement are as follows:

Year	Payment ($)	Interest ($)	Principal ($)	Balance ($)	Depreciation ($)
1	10,552	4,000	6,552	33,448	8,000
2	10,552	3,345	7,207	26,241	8,000
3	10,552	2,624	7,928	18,313	8,000
4	10,552	1,831	8,721	9,592	8,000
5	10,552	959	9,593		8,000

Year	Total ($) (Interest + Dep.)	Tax Savings ($)	After-Tax Cash Outflow ($)	PV Factor at 6%	PV of Outflow
1	12,000	4,800	5,752	0.9434	$ 5,426
2	11,345	4,538	6,014	0.8900	5.352
3	10,624	4,250	6,302	0.8396	5,291
4	9,831	3,932	6,620	0.7921	5,244
5	8,959	3,584	6,968	0.7473	5,207
					$26,520

(e) The purchase alternative is preferable because the PV of the purchase cash outflow is less than the PV of the lease cash outflow.

8.25 Lease versus Purchase Decision. Sanchez Co. is considering a capital lease providing additional warehouse space for its department stores. The price of the facility is $330,000. The leasing arrangement requires beginning-of-year payments which, for tax purposes, cannot be deducted until the end of the year. The life of the lease is 5 years and the facility has zero expected salvage value. The lessor wants a 5 percent return on its lease. Assume that the firm is in the 40 percent tax bracket and its after-tax cost of debt is currently 7 percent. Find the present value of the after-tax cash outflows using the after-tax cost of debt as the discount rate. Round your answer to the nearest dollar.

SOLUTION

$$\text{Annual lease payment (for the beginning-of-year payment situation)} = \frac{\$330,000}{1 + \text{PVIFA}_{15\%,4}}$$

$$= \frac{\$330,000}{1 + 2.8550} = \frac{\$330,000}{3.8550} = \$85,603$$

Year	Payment	Tax Savings	After-Tax Cost	PV at 7%	PV of Cash Outflow
0	$85,603	0	$85,603	0.9346	$ 80,005
1–4	$85,603	$34,241	$51,362	3.3872	173,973
5		$34,241	($34,241)	0.7130	(24,414)
					$229,564

8.26 **Lease versus Purchase Decision.** The Marijay Co. has selected a machine that will produce substantial cost savings over the next 5 years. The company can acquire the machine by outright purchase for $240,000 or a lease arrangement from the manufacturer.

Marijay could obtain a 5-year loan from a local bank to pay for the outright purchase. The bank would charge interest at an annual rate of 10 percent on the outstanding balance of the loan and require Marijay to maintain a compensating balance equal to 20 percent of the outstanding balance of the loan. The principal would be paid in five equal installments, and each annual payment of principal and interest would be due at the end of each year. In addition to borrowing the amount needed to purchase the machine, Marijay would have to obtain a loan to cover the compensating balance required by the local bank.

A local financier and investor heard of Marijay's need and offered them an unusual proposition. She would advance the company $240,000 to purchase the machine if the company would agree to pay her a lump sum of $545,450 at the end of 5 years.

The capital lease offered by the manufacturer would allow all the tax benefits of ownership to accrue to Marijay. The title to the machine would be transferred to Marijay at the end of the 5 years at no cost. The manufacturer would be responsible for maintenance of the machine and has included $8,000 per year in the lease payment to cover the maintenance cost. Marijay would pay $70,175 to the manufacturer at the beginning of each year for the 5-year period.

(*a*) Calculate the before-tax interest rate for each of the three alternatives.

(*b*) Without prejudice to your answer to (*a*), what arguments would you present to justify a lease financing alternative even if that arrangement turned out to have a higher interest cost than a regular loan?

(*c*) Compare the relative effect that the three financing alternatives would have on Marijay's current ratio at the end of the first year. (CMA, adapted.)

SOLUTION

(*a*)   The before-tax interest rates of return for each of the three alternatives are shown below.
    For a local financier

$$\text{PVIF}_{r,5} = \frac{\text{principal}}{\text{total payment}} = \frac{\$240,000}{\$545,450} = 0.44$$

The before-tax interest rate is 18 percent, which is determined by finding the rate for a PVIF of 0.44 for year 5 in Appendix C.
    For a lease:

Annual payment for leasing = $70,175 yearly payment − $8,000 maintenance = $62,175

To find the principal, subtract the first annual payment from the price of the machine, since this payment is made at the *beginning* of the year. Therefore,

$$\text{PVIFA}_{r,4} = \frac{\text{principal}}{\text{annual payment}}$$
$$= \frac{\$240,000 - \$62,175}{\$62,175} = 2.8601$$

From Appendix D, the before-tax interest rate is 15 percent for a PVIFA of 2.8601 at 4 years (4 years, not 5, since payments are made at the beginning of each year).
    For a purchase:

Beginning of Year	Principal Borrowed ($) [a]	Compensating Balance (20%) ($)	(1) Principal for Use (80%) ($)	(2) Interest (10%) on Borrowings ($)	(2 ÷ 1) Effective Rate (%)
1	300,000	60,000	240,000	30,000	$12\frac{1}{2}$
2	240,000	48,000	192,000	24,000	$12\frac{1}{2}$
3	180,000	36,000	144,000	18,000	$12\frac{1}{2}$
4	120,000	24,000	96,000	12,000	$12\frac{1}{2}$
5	60,000	12,000	48,000	60,000	$12\frac{1}{2}$

[a] One-fifth of loan repaid each year at the end of the year.

(b) Arguments justifying leases are as follows: The commitment for maintenance is limited, the cash budgeting impact of maintenance is known, manufacturer may exchange the machine for improved model at reduced rates, and financing alternatives are expanded.

(c) The effect on the current ratio at the end of the first year differs according to the financing alternative. For the financier there is no effect because the entire transaction is recorded as a long-term debt and there is no current asset or current liability until the end of the fourth year. With a loan, the current ratio will be lower than with the financier arrangement because there will be net cash outlays in the first year and a current liability recorded at the end of the first year. If a lease is chosen, the current ratio will be lower than both prior alternatives. There will be a greater net cash outlay in the first year and a larger current liability recorded at the end of the first year.

Chapter 9

Capital Budgeting Under Risk

9.1 INTRODUCTION

Risk analysis is important in making capital investment decisions because of the large amount of capital involved and the long-term nature of the investments being considered. The higher the risk associated with a proposed project, the greater the rate of return that must be earned on the project to compensate for that risk.

9.2 MEASURES OF RISK

Risk, a measure of the dispersion around a probability distribution, is defined as the variability of cash flow around the expected value. Risk can be measured in either *absolute* or *relative* terms. First, the *expected value*, $\bar{A}$, is

$$\bar{A} = \sum_{i=1}^{n} A_i p_i$$

where
A_i = the value of the ith possible outcome
p_i = the probability that the ith outcome will occur
n = the number of possible outcomes

Then, the absolute risk is measured by the *standard deviation*:

$$\sigma = \sqrt{\sum_{i=1}^{n} (A_i - \bar{A})^2 p_i}$$

The relative risk is measured by the *coefficient of variation*, which is $\sigma/\bar{A}$. (These three statistics were also discussed in Chapter 7.)

EXAMPLE 9.1 The ABC Corporation is considering investment in one of two mutually exclusive projects. Depending on the state of the economy, the projects would provide the following cash inflows in each of the next 5 years:

State	Probability	Proposal A	Proposal B
Recession	0.3	$1,000	$500
Normal	0.4	$2,000	$2,000
Boom	0.3	$3,000	$5,000

To compute the expected value ($\bar{A}$), the standard deviation (σ), and the coefficient of variation, it is convenient to set up the following tables:

For proposal A:

A_i ($)	p_i	$A_i p_i$ ($)	$(A_i - \bar{A})$ ($)	$(A_i - \bar{A})^2$ ($)
1,000	0.3	300	−1,000	1,000,000
2,000	0.4	800	0	0
3,000	0.3	900	1,000	1,000,000
		$\bar{A} = 2,000$		$\sigma^2 = 2,000,000$

242

Since $\sigma^2 = 2,000,000$, $\sigma = 1,414$. Thus

$$\frac{\sigma}{\bar{A}} = \frac{\$1,414}{\$2,000} = 0.71$$

For proposal B:

A_i ($)	p_i	$A_i p_i$ ($)	$(A_i - \bar{A})$ ($)	$(A_i - \bar{A})^2$ ($)
500	0.3	150	−1,950	3,802,500
2,000	0.4	800	−450	202,500
5,000	0.3	1,500	2,550	6,502,500
		2,450		$\sigma^2 = 10,507,500$

Since $\sigma^2 = 10,507,500$, $\sigma = \$3,242$. Thus

$$\frac{\sigma}{\bar{A}} = \frac{\$3,242}{\$2,450} = 1.32$$

Therefore, proposal A is relatively less risky than proposal B, as indicated by the lower coefficient of variation.

9.3 RISK ANALYSIS IN CAPITAL BUDGETING

Since different investment projects involve different risks, it is important to incorporate risk into the analysis of capital budgeting. There are several methods for incorporating risk, including:

1. Probability distributions
2. Risk-adjusted discount rate
3. Certainty equivalent
4. Simulation
5. Sensitivity analysis
6. Decision trees (or probability trees)

Probability Distributions

Expected values of a probability distribution may be computed. Before any capital budgeting method is applied, compute the expected cash inflows, or in some cases, the expected life of the asset.

EXAMPLE 9.2 A firm is considering a $30,000 investment in equipment that will generate cash savings from operating costs. The following estimates regarding cash savings and useful life, along with their respective probabilities of occurrence, have been made:

Annual Cash Savings		Useful Life	
$6,000	0.2	4 years	0.2
$8,000	0.5	5 years	0.6
$10,000	0.3	6 years	0.2

Then, the expected annual saving is:

$$
\begin{aligned}
\$6,000(0.2) &= \quad\$1,200 \\
\$8,000(0.5) &= \quad 4,000 \\
\$10,000(0.3) &= \quad \underline{3,000} \\
&= \quad \underline{\$8,200}
\end{aligned}
$$

The expected useful life is:

$$4(0.2) = 0.8$$
$$5(0.6) = 3.0$$
$$6(0.2) = \underline{1.2}$$
$$\underline{5 \text{ years}}$$

The expected NPV is computed as follows (assuming a 10 percent cost of capital):

$$NPV = PV - I = \$8,200(PVIFA_{10\%,5}) - \$30,000$$
$$= \$8,200(3.7908) - \$30,000 = \$31,085 - \$30,000 = \$1,085$$

The expected IRR is computed as follows: By definition, at IRR,

$$I = PV$$
$$\$30,000 = \$8,200(PVIFA_{v,5})$$
$$PVIFA_{v,5} = \frac{\$30,000}{\$8,200} = 3.6585$$

which is about halfway between 10 percent and 12 percent in Appendix D, so that we can estimate the rate to be ~11 percent. Therefore, the equipment should be purchased, since (1) NPV = \$1,085, which is positive, and/or (2) IRR = 11 percent, which is greater than the cost of capital of 10 percent.

Risk-Adjusted Discount Rate

This method of risk analysis adjusts the cost of capital (or discount rate) upward as projects become riskier. Therefore, by increasing the discount rate from 10 percent to 15 percent, the expected cash flow from the investment must be relatively larger or the increased discount rate will generate a negative NPV, and the proposed acquisition/investment would be turned down.

The use of the risk-adjusted discount rate is based on the assumption that investors demand higher returns for riskier projects. The expected cash flows are discounted at the risk-adjusted discount rate and then the usual capital budgeting criteria such as NPV and IRR are applied.

EXAMPLE 9.3 A firm is considering an investment project with an expected life of 3 years. It requires an initial investment of \$35,000. The firm estimates the following data in each of the next 3 years:

After-Tax Cash Inflow	Probability
−\$5,000	0.2
\$10,000	0.3
\$30,000	0.3
\$50,000	0.2

Assuming a risk-adjusted required rate of return (after taxes) of 20 percent is appropriate for the investment projects of this level of risk, compute the risk-adjusted NPV.

First,

$$\bar{A} = -\$5,000(0.2) + \$10,000(0.3) + \$30,000(0.3) + \$50,000(0.2) = \$21,000$$

The expected NPV = \$21,000(PVIFA_{20\%,3}) - \$35,000

$$= \$21,000(2.1065) - \$35,000 = \$44,237 - \$35,000 = \$9,237$$

Certainty Equivalent

The certainty equivalent approach to risk analysis is drawn directly from the concept of utility theory. This method forces the decision maker to specify at what point the firm is *indifferent* to the choice between a certain sum of money and the expected value of a risky sum.

Once certainty equivalent coefficients are obtained, they are multiplied by the original cash flow to obtain the equivalent certain cash flow. Then, the accept-or-reject decision is made, using the normal capital budgeting criteria. The risk-free rate of return is used as the discount rate under the NPV method and as the cutoff rate under the IRR method.

EXAMPLE 9.4   XYZ, Inc., with a 14 percent cost of capital after taxes is considering a project with an expected life of 4 years. The project requires an initial certain cash outlay of $50,000. The expected cash inflows and certainty equivalent coefficients are as follows:

Year	After-Tax Cash Flow ($)	Certainty Equivalent Coefficient
1	10,000	0.95
2	15,000	0.80
3	20,000	0.70
4	25,000	0.60

The risk-free rate of return is 5 percent; compute the NPV and IRR.
The equivalent certain cash inflows are obtained as follows:

Year	After-Tax Cash Inflow ($)	Certainty Equivalent Coefficient	Equivalent Certain Cash Inflow ($)	PV at 5%	PV ($)
1	10,000	0.95	9,500	0.9524	9,048
2	15,000	0.80	12,000	0.9070	10,884
3	20,000	0.70	14,000	0.8638	12,093
4	25,000	0.60	15,000	0.8227	12,341
					44,366

$$\text{NPV} = \$44,366 - \$50,000 = -\$5,634$$

By trial and error, we obtain 4 percent as the IRR. Therefore, the project should be rejected, since (1) NPV = −5,634, which is negative and/or (2) IRR = 4 percent is less than the risk-free rate of 5 percent.

Simulation

This risk analysis method is frequently called the Monte Carlo simulation. It requires that a probability distribution be constructed for each of the important variables affecting the project's cash flows. Since a computer is used to generate many results using random numbers, project simulation is expensive.

Sensitivity Analysis

Forecasts of many calculated NPVs under various alternative functions are compared to see how sensitive NPV is to changing conditions. It may be found that a certain variable or group of variables, once their assumptions are changed or relaxed, drastically alters the NPV. This results in a much riskier asset than was originally forecast.

Decision Trees

Some firms use decision trees (probability trees) to evaluate the risk of capital budgeting proposals. A decision tree is a graphical method of showing the sequence of possible outcomes. A capital budgeting tree would show the cash flows and NPV of the project under different possible circumstances. The decision tree method has the following advantages: (1) It visually lays out all the possible outcomes of the proposed project and makes management aware of the adverse possibilities, and (2) the conditional nature of successive years' cash flows can be expressly depicted. The primary disadvantage is that most problems are too complex to permit a year-by-year depiction. For example, for a 3-year project with three possible outcomes following each year, there are 27 paths. For a 10-year project (again with three possible outcomes following each year) there will be about 60,000 paths.

EXAMPLE 9.5 A firm has an opportunity to invest in a machine which will last 2 years, initially cost $125,000, and has the following estimated possible after-tax cash inflow pattern: In year 1, there is a 40 percent chance that the after-tax cash inflow will be $45,000, a 25 percent chance that it will be $65,000, and a 35 percent chance that it will be $90,000. In year 2, the after-tax cash inflow possibilities depend on the cash inflow that occurs in year 1; that is, the year 2 after-tax cash inflows are *conditional probabilities*. Assume that the firm's after-tax cost of capital is 12 percent. The estimated conditional after-tax cash inflows (ATCI) and probabilities are given below.

If ATCI$_1$ = $45,000		If ATCI$_1$ = $65,000		If ATCI$_1$ = $90,000	
ATCI$_2$ ($)	Probability	ATCI$_2$ ($)	Probability	ATCI$_2$ ($)	Probability
30,000	0.3	80,000	0.2	90,000	0.1
60,000	0.4	90,000	0.6	100,000	0.8
90,000	0.3	100,000	0.2	110,000	0.1

Then the decision tree which shows the possible after-tax cash inflow in each year, including the conditional nature of the year 2 cash inflow and its probabilities, can be depicted as follows:

^{a} $\text{NPV} = \text{PV} - \text{I} = \dfrac{\$45,000}{(1+0.12)} + \dfrac{\$30,000}{(1+0.12)^2} - \$125,000$

$\qquad = \$45,000(\text{PVIF}_{12\%,1}) + \$30,000(\text{PVIF}_{12\%,2}) - \$125,000$

$\qquad = \$45,000(0.893) + \$30,000(0.797) - \$125,000 = \$40,185 + \$23,910 - \$125,000 = -\$60,905$

^{b} Joint probability = $(0.4)(0.3) = 0.120$

The last column shows the calculation of expected NPV, which is the weighted average of the individual path NPVs where the weights are the path probabilities. In this example, the expected NPV of the project is −$1,330, and the project should be rejected.

9.4 CORRELATION OF CASH FLOWS OVER TIME

When cash inflows are independent from period to period, it is fairly easy to measure the overall risk of an investment proposal. In some cases, however, especially with the introduction of a new product, the cash flows experienced in early years affect the size of the cash flows in later years. This is called the *time dependence of cash flows*, and it has the effect of increasing the risk of the project over time.

EXAMPLE 9.6 Janday Corporation's after-tax cash inflows (ATCI) are time-dependent, so that year 1 results (ATCI$_1$) affect the flows in year 2 (ATCI$_2$) as follows:

If ATCI$_1$ is $8,000 with a 40 percent probability, the distribution for ATCI$_2$ is:

0.3	$5,000
0.5	$10,000
0.2	$15,000

If ATCI$_1$ is $15,000 with a 50 percent probability, the distribution for ATCI$_2$ is:

0.3	$10,000
0.6	$20,000
0.1	$30,000

If ATCI$_1$ is $20,000 with a 10 percent chance, the distribution for ATCI$_2$ is:

0.1	$15,000
0.8	$40,000
0.1	$50,000

The project requires an initial investment of $20,000, and the risk-free rate of capital is 10 percent.

The company uses the expected NPV from decision tree analysis to determine whether the project should be accepted. The analysis is as follows:

Time 0	Time 1	Time 2	NPV at 10%	Joint Probability	Expected NPV
		0.3 $5,000	−$8,595 [a]	0.12 [b]	−$1,031
	$8,000	0.5 $10,000	−$4,463	0.20	−893
		0.2 $15,000	−$331	0.08	−26
		0.3 $10,000	$1,901	0.15	285
−$20,000	$15,000	0.6 $20,000	$10,165	0.30	3,050
		0.1 $30,000	$18,429	0.05	921
		0.1 $15,000	$10,576	0.01	106
	$20,000	0.8 $40,000	$31,238	0.08	2,499
		0.1 $50,000	$39,502	0.01	395
				1.00	$5,306

[a]   NPV = PV − I = $8,000 PVIF$_{10,1}$ + $5,000 PVIF$_{10,2}$ − $20,000

= $8,000(0.9091) + $5,000(0.8264) − $20,000 = −$8,595

[b]   Joint probability of the first path = (0.4)(0.3) = 0.12

Since the NPV is positive ($5,306), Janday Corporation should accept the project.

9.5 NORMAL DISTRIBUTION AND NPV ANALYSIS: STANDARDIZING THE DISPERSION

With the assumption of *independence* of cash flows over time, the expected NPV would be

$$NPV = PV - I$$

$$= \sum_{t=1}^{n} \frac{\bar{A}_t}{(1+r)^t} - I$$

The standard deviation of NPVs is

$$\sigma = \sqrt{\sum_{t=1}^{n} \frac{\sigma_t^2}{(1+r)^{2t}}}$$

The expected value ($\bar{A}$) and the standard deviation (σ) give a considerable amount of information by which to assess the risk of an investment project. If the probability distribution is *normal*, some probability statement regarding the project's NPV can be made. For example, the probability of a project's NPV providing an NPV of less or greater than zero can be computed by standardizing the normal variate x as follows:

$$z = \frac{x - \text{NPV}}{\sigma}$$

where x = the outcome to be found

NPV = the expected NPV

z = the standardized normal variate whose probability value can be found in Appendix E.

EXAMPLE 9.7   Assume an investment with the following data:

	Period 1	Period 2	Period 3
Expected cash inflow ($\bar{A}$)	$5,000	$4,000	$3,000
Standard deviation (σ)	$1,140	$1,140	$1,140

Assume that the firm's cost of capital is 8 percent and the initial investment is $9,000. Then the expected NPV is:

$$\begin{aligned}
\text{NPV} &= \text{PV} - \text{I} \\
&= \frac{\$5,000}{(1+0.08)} + \frac{\$4,000}{(1+0.08)^2} + \frac{\$3,000}{(1+0.08)^3} - \$9,000 \\
&= \$5,000(\text{PVIF}_{8,1}) + \$4,000(\text{PVIF}_{8,2}) + \$3,000(\text{PVIF}_{8,3}) - \$9,000 \\
&= \$5,000(0.9259) + \$4,000(0.8573) + \$3,000(0.7938) - \$9,000 \\
&= \$4,630 + \$3,429 + \$2,381 - \$9,000 = \$1,440
\end{aligned}$$

The standard deviation about the expected NPV is

$$\begin{aligned}
\sigma &= \sqrt{\sum_{t=1}^{n} \frac{\sigma_t^2}{(1+r)^{2t}}} \\
&= \sqrt{\frac{\$1,140^2}{(1+0.08)^2} + \frac{\$1,140^2}{(1+0.08)^4} + \frac{\$1,140^2}{(1+0.08)^6}} \\
&= \sqrt{\$2,888,411} = \$1,670
\end{aligned}$$

The probability that the NPV is less than zero is then:

$$\begin{aligned}
z &= \frac{x - \text{NPV}}{\sigma} \\
&= \frac{0 - \$1,440}{\$1,670} = -0.862
\end{aligned}$$

The area of normal distribution that is z standard deviations to the left or right of the mean may be found in Appendix E. A value of z equal to -0.862 falls in the area between 0.1949 and 0.1922 in Appendix E. Therefore, there is approximately a 19 percent chance that the project's NPV will be zero or less. Putting it another way, there is a 19 percent chance that the IRR of the project will be less than the risk-free rate.

9.6 PORTFOLIO RISK AND THE CAPITAL ASSET PRICING MODEL (CAPM)

Portfolio considerations play an important role in the overall capital budgeting process. Through diversification, a firm can stabilize earnings, reduce risk, and thereby increase the market price of the firm's stock.

Beta Coefficient

The capital asset pricing model (CAPM) can be used to determine the appropriate cost of capital. The NPV method uses the cost of capital as the rate to discount future cash flows. The IRR method uses the cost of capital as the cutoff rate. The required rate of return, or cost of capital according to the CAPM, or security market line (SML), is equal to the risk-free rate of return (r_f) plus a risk premium equal to the firm's beta coefficient (b) times the market risk premium ($r_m - r_f$):

$$r_j = r_f + b(r_m - r_f)$$

EXAMPLE 9.8 A project has the following projected cash flows:

Year 0	Year 1	Year 2	Year 3
$(400)	$300	$200	$100

The estimated beta for the project is 1.5. The market return is 12 percent, and the risk-free rate is 6 percent. Then the firm's cost of capital, or required rate of return is:

$$r_j = r_f + b(r_m - r_f) = 6\% + 1.5(12\% - 6\%) = 15\%$$

The project's NPV can be computed using 15 percent as the discount rate:

Year	Cash Flow ($)	PV at 15%	PV ($)
0	(400)	1.000	(400)
1	300	0.870	261
2	200	0.756	151
3	100	0.658	66
			78 [a]

[a] NPV.

The project should be accepted since its NPV is positive, that is, $78. Also, the project's IRR can be computed by trial and error. It is almost 30 percent, which exceeds the cost of capital of 15 percent. Therefore, by that standard also the project should be accepted.

Calculation of Beta Coefficient

In measuring an asset's systematic risk, beta, an indication is needed of the relationship between the asset's returns and the market returns (such as returns on the Standard & Poor's 500 Stock Composite Index or Dow Jones 30 Industrials). This relationship can be statistically computed by determining the regression coefficient between asset and market returns. The method is presented below.

$$b = \frac{\text{Cov}(r_j, r_m)}{\sigma_m^2}$$

where $\text{Cov}(r_j, r_m)$ is the covariance of the returns of the assets with the market returns, and σ_m^2 is the variance (standard deviation squared) of the market returns.

An easier way to compute beta is to determine the slope of the least-squares linear regression line $(r_j - r_f)$, where the excess return of the asset $(r_j - r_f)$ is regressed against the excess return of the market portfolio $(r_m - r_f)$. The formula for b is:

$$b = \frac{\sum MK - n\bar{M}\bar{K}}{\sum M^2 - n\bar{M}^2}$$

where $M = (r_m - r_f)$
        $K = (r_j - r_f)$
        n = number of years
        $\bar{M}$ = average of M
        $\bar{K}$ = average of K

EXAMPLE 9.9   Compute the beta coefficient, b, using the following data for stock x and the market portfolio:

Historic Rates of Return

Year	r_j (%)	r_m (%)
19X1	−5	10
19X2	4	8
19X3	7	12
19X4	10	20
19X5	12	15

Assume that the risk-free rate is 6 percent. For easy computation, it is convenient to set up the following table:

Year	Stock Return, r_j	Market Return, r_m	Risk-free Rate, r_f	$(r_j - r_f) = K$	$(r_m - r_f) = M$	M^2	MK
19X1	−0.05	0.10	0.06	−0.11	0.04	0.0016	−0.0044
19X2	0.04	0.08	0.06	−0.02	0.02	0.0004	−0.0004
19X3	0.07	0.12	0.06	0.01	0.06	0.0036	0.0006
19X4	0.10	0.20	0.06	0.04	0.14	0.0196	0.0056
19X5	0.12	0.15	0.06	0.06	0.09	0.0081	0.0054
				−0.02	0.35	0.0333	0.0068

$$\bar{K} = -0.004 \qquad \bar{M} = 0.07$$

Therefore, beta is:

$$b = \frac{\sum MK - n\bar{M}\bar{K}}{\sum M^2 - n\bar{M}^2} = \frac{0.0068 - (5)(-0.004)(0.07)}{0.0333 - (5)(0.07)^2} = \frac{0.0082}{0.0088} = 0.93$$

Review Questions

1. _____ is important in the capital budgeting process.

2. Risk can be measured in either _____ or _____ terms.

3. The use of _____ is based on the concept that investors demand _____ for riskier projects.

4. The certainty equivalent approach is directly drawn from the concept of _____ .

5. Under the certainty equivalent approach, _____ is used as the discount rate under the NPV method and as the cutoff rate under the IRR method.

6. Simulation is often called _____ simulation.

7. _____ attempts to determine how sensitive NPV or IRR is to changing conditions.

8. A(n) _____ is a graphical exposition of the _____ of possible outcomes.

9. If the probability distribution is _____ , the expected value and the _____ may be used to compute the probability of a project's providing an NPV of less or greater than zero.

10. The required rate of return on a company's security is equal to the _____ plus a _____ .

11. Riskier projects should be evaluated with a higher discount rate, called a _____ .

12. An easier way to determine beta is to determine the _____ of the least-squares linear regression line, where the _____ of the security is regressed against the _____ of the _____ .

13. Relative risk is measured by the _____ .

14. _____ is an index of _____ risk.

Answers: (1) Risk analysis; (2) absolute, relative; (3) risk-adjusted rates of return, higher returns; (4) utility theory; (5) the risk-free rate; (6) Monte Carlo; (7) Sensitivity analysis; (8) decision tree (or probability tree), sequence; (9) normal, standard deviation; (10) risk-free rate, risk premium; (11) risk-adjusted discount rate; (12) slope, excessive return, excessive return, market portfolio; (13) coefficient of variation; (14) Beta, systematic (noncontrollable, nondiversifiable).

Solved Problems

9.1 **Expected Value and Standard Deviation.** The Lendel Company is considering investment in one of two mutually exclusive projects. They have the following cash inflows for each of the next 3 years:

	Cash Inflows ($)	
Probability	Project A	Project B
0.10	3,000	3,000
0.25	3,500	4,000
0.30	4,000	5,000
0.25	4,500	6,000
0.10	5,000	7,000

Calculate (*a*) the expected value (expected cash inflow) of each project, (*b*) the standard deviation of each project, and (*c*) the coefficient of variation. (*d*) Which project has the greater degree of risk? Why?

SOLUTION

(*a*) and (*b*)
$$\bar{A} = \sum_{i=1}^{n} A_i p_i \qquad \sigma = \sqrt{\sum_{i=1}^{n} (A_i - \bar{A})^2 p_i}$$

For project A:

A_i (\$)	p_i	$A_i p_i$ (\$)	$A_i - \bar{A}$ (\$)	$(A_i - \bar{A})^2$ (\$)	$(A_i - \bar{A})^2 p_i$
3,000	0.10	300	−1,000	1,000,000	100,000
3,500	0.25	875	−500	250,000	62,500
4,000	0.30	1,200	0	0	0
4,500	0.25	1,125	500	250,000	62,500
5,000	0.10	500	1,000	1,000,000	100,000
		$\bar{A} = 4,000$			$\sigma^2 = 325,000$

Since $\sigma^2 = 325{,}000$, $\sigma = \$570.09$.

For project B:

A_i (\$)	p_i	$A_i p_i$ (\$)	$(A_i - \bar{A})$ (\$)	$(A_i - \bar{A})^2$ (\$)	$(A_i - \bar{A})^2 p_i$ (\$)
3,000	0.10	300	−2,000	4,000,000	400,000
4,000	0.25	1,000	−1,000	1,000,000	250,000
5,000	0.30	1,500	0	0	0
6,000	0.25	1,500	1,000	1,000,000	250,000
7,000	0.10	700	2,000	4,000,000	400,000
		$\bar{A} = 5,000$			$\sigma^2 = 1,300,000$

Since $\sigma^2 = 1{,}300{,}000$, $\sigma = \$1{,}140.18$.

(*c*) The coefficient of variation is:

	A	**B**
$\dfrac{\sigma}{\bar{A}}$	$\dfrac{\$570.09}{\$4,000} = 0.14$	$\dfrac{\$1,140.18}{\$5,000} = 0.23$

(*d*) Project B is riskier, since it has the greater coefficient of variation (i.e., 0.23 versus 0.14).

9.2   Coefficient of Variation. McEnro wishes to decide between two projects, X and Y. By using probability estimates, he has determined the following statistics:

	Project X	Project Y
Expected NPV	\$35,000	\$20,000
σ	\$22,000	\$20,000

(*a*) Compute the coefficient of variation for each project, and (*b*) explain why σ and the coefficient of variation give different rankings of risk. Which method is better?

SOLUTION

(a)

	Project X	**Project Y**
$\sigma/\bar{A}$	$\dfrac{\$22,000}{35,000} = 0.63$	$\dfrac{\$20,000}{20,000} = 1.00$

(b) The coefficient of variation is a superior measure of risk because it is a relative measure, giving the degree of dispersion relative to the expected value.

9.3   NPV Analysis Under Risk. The Connors Company is considering a $60,000 investment in a machine that will reduce operating costs. The following estimates regarding cash savings, along with their probabilities of occurrence, have been made:

\multicolumn{2}{c}{**Annual Cash Savings**}	\multicolumn{2}{c}{**Useful Life**}
Event	**Probability**	**Event**	**Probability**
$20,000	0.30	9 years	0.40
$14,000	0.30	8 years	0.40
$12,000	0.40	6 years	0.20

(a) Compute the expected annual cash savings and useful life. Determine whether the machine should be purchased, using the NPV method.

(b) The company wishes to see whether the machine would be a good investment if each of its most pessimistic estimates, but not both at the same time, came true. Determine whether the investment would be desirable if (1) the useful life is the the expected value computed in part (a), and annual cash flows are only $12,000; (2) the annual cash flows are equal to the expected value computed in part (a) and the useful life is only 6 years.

SOLUTION

(a)   Determination of expected annual cash savings is:

Event (A_i)	**Probabilities (p_i)**	**Expected Value**
$20,000	0.30	$ 6,000
$14,000	0.30	4,200
$12,000	0.40	4,800
	1.00	$15,000

Determination of useful life is:

Event	**Probability**	**Useful Life**
9 years	0.40	3.6 years
8 years	0.40	3.2 years
6 years	0.20	1.2 years
	1.00	8.0 years

Expected annual cash savings	$15,000
Present value factor for 8-year annuity at 16%	×4.344
Present value of future flows (PV)	$65,160
Less cost of machine (I)	60,000
Net present value (NPV)	$ 5,160

The purchase of the machine would appear to be wise because of its positive net present value.

(b) (1) The present value of the future cash savings ($52,128) is less than the purchase price ($60,000) and the machine should not be purchased.

Annual cash savings, pessimistic estimate	$12,000
Present value factor, 8-year annuity at 16%	4.344
Present value of future cash flows	$52,128

(2) The present value of the future cash savings ($55,275) is less than the purchase price ($60,000) and the machine should not be purchased.

Annual cash savings, expected value	$15,000
Present value factor, 6-year annuity at 16%	3.685
Present value of future cash flows	$55,275

9.4   Expected NPV and Risk. The administrator of ABC Hospital is considering the purchase of new operating room equipment at a cost of $7,500. The surgical staff has furnished the following estimates of useful life and cost savings. Each useful life estimate is independent of each cost savings estimate.

Years of Estimated Useful Life	Probability of Occurrence	Estimated Cost Savings	Probability of Occurrence
4	0.25	$1,900	0.30
5	0.50	$2,000	0.40
6	0.25	$2,100	0.30
	1.00		1.00

Calculate (a) the expected net present value, allowing ιur risk and uncertainty and using a 10 percent discount rate, and (b) the standard deviation and coefficient of variation for the present value calculations of estimated cost savings before deducting the investment.

SOLUTION

(a)

(1)	(2)	(3)	(4)	(5)	(6)	(7)	(8)
Estimated Useful Life		Estimated Cost Savings		Combined Probability	Present Value	Present Value ($) (Conditional Value)	Expected Present Value ($)
Years	Probability	$	Probability	(2) × (4)	Factor 10%	(3) × (6)	(5) × (7)
	0.25	1,900	0.30	0.075	3.170	6,023	452
4	0.25	2,000	0.40	0.100	3.170	6,340	634
	0.25	2,100	0.30	0.075	3.170	6,657	499
	0.50	1,900	0.30	0.150	3.791	7,203	1,080
5	0.50	2,000	0.40	0.200	3.791	7,582	1,516
	0.50	2,100	0.30	0.150	3.791	7,961	1,194
	0.25	1,900	0.30	0.075	4.355	8,275	621
6	0.25	2,000	0.40	0.100	4.355	8,710	871
	0.25	2,100	0.30	0.075	4.355	9,146	686
				1.000			7,553

Total expected present value	$7,553
Less investment in equipment	7,500
Expected net present value	$ 53

(b)

(1) Present Value (\$) (Conditional Value)	(2) Difference from Expected Value (\$) (\$7,553)	(3) (2) Squared (\$)	(4) Probability	(5) (3) × (4) (\$)
6,023	−1,530	2,340,900	0.075	175,568
6,340	−1,213	1,471,369	0.100	147,137
6,657	−896	802,816	0.075	60,211
7,203	−350	122,500	0.150	18,375
7,582	29	841	0.200	168
7,961	408	166,464	0.150	24,970
8,275	722	521,284	0.075	39,096
8,710	1,157	1,338,649	0.100	133,865
9,146	1,593	2,537,649	0.075	190,324

$$\sigma^2 = \underline{\$789,714}$$

$$\sigma = \sqrt{\$789,714} = \$889$$

$$\text{Coefficient of variation} = \frac{\sigma}{\bar{A}} = \frac{\$889}{\$7,553} = 0.12$$

9.5 Risk-Adjusted NPV and Decision. Vilas Corporation is considering two mutually exclusive projects, both of which require an initial investment of \$4,500 and an expected life of 10 years. The probability distribution for the cash inflows are as follows (for years 1 through 10):

Project A		Project B	
Cash Inflow	Probability	Cash Inflow	Probability
\$ 700	0.10	\$ 550	0.2
900	0.80	800	0.3
1,000	0.10	1,000	0.3
		1,400	0.2

The company has decided that the project with higher relative risk should have a required rate of return of 16 percent, whereas the less risky project's required rate of return should be 14 percent.

Compute (a) the coefficient of variation as a measure of relative risk, and (b) the risk-adjusted NPV of each project. Which project should be chosen? (c) What factors other than NPV should be considered when deciding between these two projects?

SOLUTION

(a)	For project A:

$$\bar{A} = \sum_{i=1}^{n} A_i p_i = \$700(0.1) + \$900(0.8) + \$1,000(0.1)$$

$$= \$70 + \$720 + \$100 = \$890$$

$$\sigma = \sqrt{\sum_{i=1}^{n}(A_i - \bar{A})^2 p_i} = \sqrt{(\$700 - \$890)^2(0.1) + (\$900 - \$890)^2(0.8) + (\$1,000 - \$890)^2(0.1)}$$

$$= \sqrt{\$3,610 + \$80 + \$1,210} = \sqrt{\$4,900} = \$70$$

$$\frac{\sigma}{\bar{A}} = \frac{\$70}{\$890} = 0.079$$

For project B:

$$\bar{A} = \$550(0.2) + \$800(0.3) + \$1,000(0.3) + \$1,400(0.2)$$
$$= \$110 + \$240 + \$300 + \$280 = \$930$$

$$\sigma = \sqrt{(\$550 - \$930)^2(0.2) + (\$800 - \$930)^2(0.3) + (\$1,000 - \$930)^2(0.3) + (\$1,400 - \$930)^2(0.2)}$$

$$= \sqrt{\$28,880 + \$5,070 + \$1,470 + \$44,180} = \sqrt{\$79,600} = \$282.13$$

$$\frac{\sigma}{\bar{A}} = \frac{\$282.13}{\$930} = 0.30$$

(b) Project A is relatively less risky than project B. Therefore, project A's expected cash inflow is discounted at 14 percent, while project B's expected cash inflow is discounted at 16 percent.

For project A:

$$\text{Expected NPV} = \text{PV} - \text{I} = \$890(\text{PVIFA}_{14\%,10}) - \$4,500 = \$890(5.216) - \$4,500$$
$$= \$4,642.24 - \$4,500 = \$142.24$$

For project B:

$$\text{Expected NPV} = \$930(\text{PVIFA}_{16\%,10}) - \$4,500 = \$930(4.833) - \$4,500$$
$$= \$4,494.69 - \$4,500 = -\$5.31$$

Because project A has a positive NPV, project A should be chosen.

(c) The company should also consider the potential diversification effect associated with these projects. If the project's cash inflow patterns are negatively correlated with those of the company, the overall risk of the company may be significantly reduced.

9.6   Risk-Adjusted NPV. Kyoto Laboratories, Inc., is contemplating a capital investment project with an expected useful life of 10 years that requires an initial cash outlay of $225,000. The company estimates the following data:

Annual Cash Inflows ($)	Probabilities
0	0.10
50,000	0.20
65,000	0.40
70,000	0.20
90,000	0.10

(a) Assuming a risk-adjusted required rate of return of 25 percent is appropriate for projects of this level of risk, calculate the risk-adjusted NPV of the project. (b) Should the project be accepted?

SOLUTION

(a) $$\bar{A} = \sum_{i=1}^{n} A_i p_i = \$0(0.10) + \$50,000(0.2) + \$65,000(0.4) + \$70,000(0.2) + \$90,000(0.1)$$
$$= \$0 + \$10,000 + \$26,000 + \$14,000 + \$9,000 = \$59,000$$

$$\text{Expected NPV} = \text{PV} - \text{I}$$

$$= \$59,000 (\text{PVIFA}_{25\%,10}) - \$225,000 = \$210,689 - \$225,000 = -\$14,311$$

(b) Reject the project, since the expected NPV is negative.

9.7 **Certainty Equivalent NPV.** Rush Corporation is considering the purchase of a new machine that will last 5 years and require a cash outlay of $300,000. The firm has a 12 percent cost of capital rate and its after-tax risk-free rate is 9 percent. The company has expected cash inflows and certainty equivalents for these cash inflows, as follows:

Year	After-Tax Cash Inflows ($)	Certainty Equivalent
1	100,000	1.00
2	100,000	0.95
3	100,000	0.90
4	100,000	0.80
5	100,000	0.70

Calculate (a) the unadjusted NPV, and (b) the certainty equivalent NPV. (c) Determine if the machine should be purchased.

SOLUTION

(a)
$$NPV = PV - I = \$100,000(PVIFA_{12\% 5}) - \$200,000$$
$$= \$100,000(3.605) - \$300,000 = \$360,500 - \$300,000 = \$60,500$$

(b)

Year	After-Tax Cash Inflows ($)	Certainty Equivalents	Certain Cash Inflows ($)	PV at 9%	PV ($)
1	100,000	1.00	100,000	0.917	91,700
2	100,000	0.95	95,000	0.842	79,990
3	100,000	0.90	90,000	0.772	69,480
4	100,000	0.80	80,000	0.708	56,640
5	100,000	0.70	70,000	0.650	45,500
					343,310

Certainty equivalent NPV = $343,310 - $300,000 = $43,310

(c) Because of a positive NPV, the machine should be purchased.

9.8 **Decision Tree.** The Summerall Corporation wishes to introduce one of two products to the market this year. The probabilities and present values of projected cash inflows are given below.

Products	Initial Investment ($)	PV of Cash Inflows ($)	Probabilities
A	225,000		1.00
		450,000	0.4
		200,000	0.5
		-100,000	0.1
B	80,000		1.00
		320,000	0.2
		100,000	0.6
		-150,000	0.2

(a) Construct a decision tree to analyze the two products. (b) Which product would you introduce? Comment on your decision.

SOLUTION

(*a*)

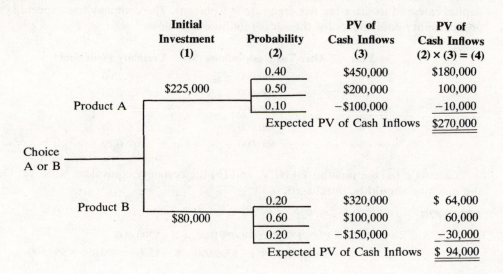

	Initial Investment (1)	Probability (2)	PV of Cash Inflows (3)	PV of Cash Inflows (2) × (3) = (4)
		0.40	$450,000	$180,000
Product A	$225,000	0.50	$200,000	100,000
		0.10	−$100,000	−10,000
			Expected PV of Cash Inflows	$270,000
Product B	$80,000	0.20	$320,000	$ 64,000
		0.60	$100,000	60,000
		0.20	−$150,000	−30,000
			Expected PV of Cash Inflows	$ 94,000

For product A:

$$\text{Expected NPV} = \text{expected PV} - I = \$270,000 - \$225,000 = \$45,000$$

For product B:

$$\text{Expected NPV} = \$94,000 - \$80,000 = \$14,000$$

(*b*) Based on the expected NPV, choose product A over product B, however, this analysis fails to recognize the risk factor in project analysis.

9.9   Dependent Cash Inflows and Expected NPV. The Newcome Corporation has determined that its after-tax cash inflow (ATCI) distributions are not independent. Further, the company has estimated that the year 1 results (ATCI_1) will affect the year 2 flows (ATCI_2) as follows:
  If $\text{ATCI}_1 = \$40,000$ with a 30 percent chance, the distribution for ATCI_2 is:

0.2	$20,000
0.6	$50,000
0.2	$80,000

If $\text{ATCI}_1 = \$60,000$ with a 40 percent chance, the distribution for ATCI_2 is:

0.3	$70,000
0.4	$80,000
0.3	$90,000

If $\text{ATCI}_1 = \$80,000$ with a 30 percent chance, the distribution for ATCI_2 is:

0.1	$80,000
0.8	$100,000
0.1	$120,000

Assume that the project's initial investment is $100,000.

(*a*) Set up a decision tree to depict the above cash flow possibilities, and calculate an expected NPV for each 2-year possibility using a risk-free rate of 15 percent. (*b*) Determine if the project should be accepted.

SOLUTION

(*a*)

Time 0	Time 1		Time 2	NPV at 10%	Joint Probability	Expected NPV
		0.2	$20,000	−$50,080 [a]	0.06 [b]	$−3,005
	$40,000	0.6	$50,000	−$27,400	0.18	−4,912
		0.2	$80,000	−$4,720	0.06	−283
		0.3	$70,000	$5,120	0.12	614
−$100,000 0.4	$60,000	0.4	$80,000	$12,680	0.16	2,029
0.3		0.3	$90,000	$20,240	0.12	2,428
0.3		0.1	$80,000	$30,080	0.03	902
	$80,000	0.8	$100,000	$45,200	0.24	10,848
		0.1	$120,000	$60,320	0.03	1,810
					1.00	$10,431

[a] $\text{NPV} = \text{PV} - I = \dfrac{\$40,000}{(1+0.15)} + \dfrac{\$20,000}{(1+0.15)^2} - \$100,000$

$= \$40,000(\text{PVIF}_{15\%,1}) + \$20,000(\text{PVIF}_{15\%,2}) - \$100,000$

$= \$40,000(0.87) + \$20,000(0.756) - \$100,000 = \$34,800 + \$15,120 - \$100,000 = -\$50,080$

[b] Joint probability of the first path = (0.3)(0.2) = 0.06

The expected NPV is $10,431.

(*b*)   Accept the project, since the expected NPV is positive.

9.10   Decision Tree Analysis. The Drysdale Corporation is contemplating the development of a new product. The initial investment required to purchase the necessary equipment is $200,000. There is a 60 percent chance that demand will be high in year 1. If it is high, there is an 80 percent chance that it will continue high indefinitely. If demand is low in year 1, there is a 60 percent chance that it will continue to be low indefinitely. If demand is high, forecasted cash inflow (before taxes) is $90,000 a year; if demand is low, forecasted cash inflow is $30,000 a year.

The corporate income tax rate is 40 percent. The company uses straight-line depreciation and will depreciate the equipment over 10 years with no salvage value.

(*a*) Determine the after-tax cash inflows. (*b*) Set up a decision tree representing all possible outcomes, and compute the expected NPV using a 10 percent risk-free rate of return.

SOLUTION

(*a*)   First, compute the annual depreciation.

$$\text{Depreciation} = \text{price/useful life} = \frac{\$200,000}{10 \text{ years}} = \$20,000/\text{year}$$

$$\text{After-tax cash inflow} = \text{after-tax net profits} + \text{depreciation}$$

Therefore, when demand is high:

$$\text{After-tax cash inflow} = (\$90,000 - \$20,000)(1 - 0.4) + \$20,000 = \$62,000$$

When demand is low:

$$\text{After-tax cash inflow} = (\$30,000 - \$20,000)(1 - 0.4) + \$20,000 = \$26,000$$

(b)

Time 0	Time 1	Times 2–10	NPV at 10%	Joint Probability	Expected NPV

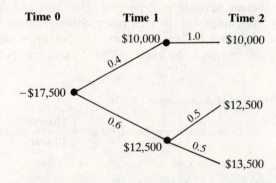

$$^a NPV = PV - I = \frac{\$62,000}{(1+0.1)} + \frac{\$62,000}{(1+0.1)^2} + \cdots + \frac{\$62,000}{(1+0.1)^{10}} - \$200,000$$

$$= \$62,000(PVIF_{10\%,1}) + \$62,000(PVIFA_{10\%,10} - PVIFA_{10\%,1}) - \$200,000$$

$$= \$62,000(0.909) + \$62,000(6.145 - 0.909) - \$200,000$$

$$= \$56,358 + \$324,632 - \$200,000 = \$180,990$$

^{b} Joint probability = (0.6)(0.8) = 0.48

The expected NPV is $100,042.

9.11   Decision Tree Analysis and Expected IRR. The NFL Systems, Inc., is considering the purchase of a minicomputer using the following decision tree:

(a) Complete the decision tree by computing IRR, joint probability, and the expected IRR (round to the nearest whole percent of IRR). (b) Should this computer be purchased? (Assume the company's cost of capital is 16 percent.)

SOLUTION

(a)

Time 0	Time 1	Time 2	IRR	Joint Probability	Expected IRR
	$10,000 1.0	$10,000	9% ^{a}	0.4 ^{b}	3.6
−$17,500 0.4					
0.6	0.5 $12,500	$12,500	25%	0.30	7.5
	$12,500 0.5	$13,500	30% ^{c}	0.30	9.0
				1.00	20.1%

---

^{a} By definition, at IRR, I = PV.
   Thus,

$$\$17,500 = \$10,000(\text{PVIFA}_{r,2})$$

$$\text{PVIFA}_{r,2} = \frac{\$17,500}{\$10,000} = 1.75$$

From Appendix D this value is close to 9 percent.

^{b} Joint probability = (0.4)(1.0) = 0.4

^{c} I = PV($17,500) = $12,500(PVIF$_{r,1}$) + $13,500(PVIF$_{r,2}$)
   By trial and error, IRR is approximately 30 percent. In other words, at $r = 30$ percent:

$$I = PV$$
$$= \$12,500(0.769) + \$13,500(0.592) = \$9,613 + \$7,992 = \$17,605$$

(b) The expected IRR is 20.1 percent, which exceeds the cost of capital of 16 percent. Therefore, the computer should be purchased.

9.12 Normal Distribution and NPV Analysis. The probability distribution of possible NPVs for project A has an expected cash inflow of $30,000 and a standard deviation of $15,000. Assuming a normal distribution, compute the probability that (a) the NPV will be zero or less, (b) the NPV will be greater than $45,000; and (c) the NPV will be less than $7,500.

SOLUTION

The standardized normal variate is:

$$z = \frac{x - \text{NPV}}{\sigma}$$

(a) For NPV of zero or less:

$$z = \frac{0 - \$30,000}{\$15,000} = -2$$

From Appendix E, $z = \pm 2$ corresponds to a probability of 0.0228 or 2.28 percent.

(b) For NPV of $45,000 or more:

$$z = \frac{\$45,000 - \$30,000}{\$15,000} = 1.0$$

From Appendix E, the probability for this value of z is 15.77 percent.

(c) For NPV of $7,500 or less:

$$z = \frac{\$7,500 - \$30,000}{\$15,000} = -1.5$$

From Appendix E, the probability for $z = \pm 1.5$ is 6.68 percent.

9.13 Normal Distribution and NPV Analysis. The Halo Shipping Company is considering an investment in a project that requires an initial investment of $6,000, with a projected after-tax cash inflow generated over the next 3 years as follows:

Period 1		Period 2		Period 3	
Probability	Cash Flow ($)	Probability	Cash Flow ($)	Probability	Cash Flow ($)
0.10	1,000	0.2	1,000	0.3	1,000
0.30	2,000	0.4	2,000	0.4	2,000
0.20	3,000	0.3	3,000	0.1	3,000
0.40	4,000	0.1	4,000	0.2	4,000

Assume that probability distributions are independent and the after-tax risk-free rate of return is 6 percent. Calculate (a) the expected NPV of the project, (b) the standard deviation of the expected NPV, (c) the probability that the NPV will be zero or less (assume that the probability distribution is normal and continuous), (d) the probability that the NPV will be greater than zero, and (e) the probability that the NPV will be greater than the expected value.

SOLUTION

(a)

Period 1	Period 2	Period 3
$1,000(0.1) = \$ \ 100$	$1,000(0.2) = \$ \ 200$	$1,000(0.3) = \$ \ 300$
$2,000(0.3) = \ \ \ \ 600$	$2,000(0.4) = \ \ \ \ 800$	$2,000(0.4) = \ \ \ \ 800$
$3,000(0.2) = \ \ \ \ 600$	$3,000(0.3) = \ \ \ \ 900$	$3,000(0.1) = \ \ \ \ 300$
$4,000(0.4) = \underline{\ 1,600}$	$4,000(0.1) = \underline{\ \ \ 400}$	$4,000(0.2) = \underline{\ \ \ 800}$
$\$2,900$	$\$2,300$	$\$2,200$

$$\text{NPV} = \text{PV} - \text{I}$$

$$= \frac{\$2,900}{(1+0.06)} + \frac{\$2,300}{(1+0.06)^2} + \frac{\$2,200}{(1+0.06)^3} - \$6,000$$

$$= \$2,900(\text{PVIF}_{6\%,1}) + \$2,300(\text{PVIF}_{6\%,2}) + \$2,200(\text{PVIF}_{6\%,3}) - \$6,000$$

$$= \$2,900(0.943) + \$2,300(0.89) + \$2,200(0.84) - \$6,000$$

$$= \$2,735 + \$2,047 + \$1,848 - \$6,000 = \$6,630 - \$6,000 = \$630$$

(b) Calculations for standard deviation of NPV are as follows:

For period 1:

A	p	$(A - \bar{A})$	$(A - \bar{A})^2$	$(A - \bar{A})^2 p$
$1,000	0.1	$-$1,900	$3,610,000	$ 361,000
$2,000	0.3	$-$900	$810,000	243,000
$3,000	0.2	$100	$10,000	2,000
$4,000	0.4	$1,100	$1,210,000	484,000
				$1,090,000 [a]
				$ 1,044 [b]

[a] $1,090,000 = \sigma^2$

[b] $1,044 = \sigma$

For period 2:

A ($)	p	$(A - \bar{A})$ ($)	$(A - \bar{A})^2$ ($)	$(A - \bar{A})^2 p$ ($)
1,000	0.2	$-1,300$	1,690,000	338,000
2,000	0.4	-300	90,000	36,000
3,000	0.3	700	490,000	147,000
4,000	0.1	1,700	2,890,000	289,000
			$\sigma^2 =$	810,000
			$\sigma = \$$	800

For period 3:

A ($)	p	$(A - \bar{A})$ ($)	$(A - \bar{A})^2$ ($)	$(A - \bar{A})^2 p$ ($)
1,000	0.3	$-1,200$	1,440,000	432,000
2,000	0.4	-200	40,000	16,000
3,000	0.1	800	640,000	64,000
4,000	0.2	1,800	3,240,000	648,000
			$\sigma^2 =$	1,160,000
			$\sigma = \$$	1,077

The standard deviation of the expected NPV is:

$$\sigma_{\text{NPV}} = \sqrt{\frac{(\$1,044)^2}{(1 + 0.06)^2} + \frac{(\$900)^2}{(1 + 0.06)^4} + \frac{(\$1,077)^2}{(1 + 0.06)^6}}$$

$$= \sqrt{\$970,039 + \$642,857 + \$727,776} = \sqrt{\$2,340,672} = \$1,530$$

(c)
$$z = \frac{x - \text{NPV}}{\sigma} = \frac{0 - \$630}{\$1,530} = -0.41176$$

From the normal distribution table Appendix E, this value of z gives a probability of 0.3409, or approximately a 34 percent chance that NPV will be zero or less.

(d) The probability of the NPV being greater than zero is the compliment of 34 percent, or 66 percent.

(e)
$$z = \frac{\$630 - \$630}{\$1,530} = 0$$

Reading from Appendix E, at $z = 0$, there is 50 percent probability that the NPV will be greater than the expected value.

9.14 **Portfolio Effects.** The projected cash inflows of three projects—X, Y, and Z—for the period 19X1 to 19X5 are given below.

Year	Project X	Project Y	Project Z
19X1	$2,000	$6,000	$1,000
19X2	$3,000	$4,000	$2,000
19X3	$4,000	$3,000	$3,000
19X4	$5,000	$2,000	$3,000
19X5	$7,000	$1,000	$6,000

	Project X	Project Y	Project Z
$\bar{A}$	$4,200	$3,200	$3,000
σ	$3,847	$3,847	$3,742

(*a*) Calculate the expected cash inflows and standard deviation of cash inflows for project combinations XY and XZ, and (*b*) determine the portfolio effects of the above combinations of projects upon the portfolio risk.

SOLUTION

Since the probabilities associated with the cash inflows are not given (in fact, their cash inflows are equally likely), the formulas for $\bar{A}$ and σ are

$$\bar{A} = \sum A_i/n \qquad \text{and} \qquad \sigma = \sqrt{\sum_{i=1}^{n} (A_i - \bar{A})^2/n}$$

where *n* is the number of terms.

(*a*) For projects XY:

Cash Inflow (A) ($)	($A - \bar{A}$) ($)	($A - \bar{A}$)^2 ($)
8,000	600	360,000
7,000	−400	160,000
7,000	−400	160,000
7,000	−400	160,000
8,000	600	360,000
37,000		1,200,000

$$\bar{A} = \frac{\$37,000}{5} = \$7,400$$

$$\sigma^2 = \frac{\$1,200,000}{5} = \$240,000$$

Thus

$$\sigma = \$490$$

For projects XZ:

Cash Inflow (A) ($)	($A - \bar{A}$) ($)	($A - \bar{A}$)^2 ($)
3,000	−4,200	17,640,000
5,000	−2,200	4,840,000
7,000	−200	40,000
8,000	800	640,000
13,000	5,800	33,640,000
36,000		56,800,000

$$\bar{A} = \frac{\$36,000}{5} = \$7,200$$

$$\sigma^2 = \frac{56,800,000}{5} = \$11,360,000$$

Thus

$$\sigma = \$3,370$$

(b) The greatest reduction in overall risk occurs when the portfolio combines projects which are negatively correlated such as projects XY (i.e., $\sigma_{XY} = \$490$).

9.15 **CAPM and Capital Budgeting Decision.** The Taylor Corporation is evaluating some new capital budgeting projects. Their evaluation method involves comparing each project's risk-adjusted return obtained from the capital asset pricing model (CAPM) with the project's average rate of return. The following data are provided:

Projects	Beta
A	−0.5
B	0.8
C	1.2
D	2.0

Possible rates of return and associated probabilities are:

	Rates of return (%)		
	(0.4)	(0.5)	(0.1)
A	4	2	5
B	2	6	12
C	10	15	20
D	−8	25	50

Assume that the risk-free rate of return is 6 percent and the market rate of return is 12 percent. Which projects should be selected?

SOLUTION

Use the CAPM equation to compute:

Projects	$r = r_f + b(r_m - r_f)$
A	$r_A = 6\% + (-0.5)(12\% - 6\%) = 3\%$
B	$r_B = 6\% + (0.8)(12\% - 6\%) = 10.8\%$
C	$r_C = 6\% + (1.2)(12\% - 6\%) = 13.2\%$
D	$r_D = 6\% + (2.0)(12\% - 6\%) = 18\%$

Average rates of return are:

Projects	
A	$4(0.4) + 2(0.5) + 5(0.1) = 3.1\%$
B	$2(0.4) + 6(0.5) + 12(0.1) = 5\%$
C	$10(0.4) + 15(0.5) + 20(0.1) = 13.5\%$
D	$-8(0.4) + 25(0.5) + 50(0.1) = 14.3\%$

Projects A and C should be selected, since their average rates of return exceed the required rates of return provided by the CAPM equation.

9.16 **Beta and NPV Analysis.** The risk-free rate is 5 percent and the expected return on the market portfolio is 13 percent. On the basis of the CAPM, answer the following questions: (*a*) What is the risk premium on the market? (*b*) What is the required rate of return on an investment with a beta equal to 1.2? (*c*) If an investment with a beta of 0.6 offers an expected return of 8.5 percent, does it have a positive NPV? (*d*) If the market expects a return of 12.5 percent from stock A, what is its beta?

SOLUTION

(*a*) $$\text{Risk premium} = (r_m - r_f) = 13\% - 5\% = 8\%$$

(*b*) $$r_j = r_f + b(r_m - r_f)$$
$$= 5\% + 1.2(13\% - 5\%) = 5\% + 9.6\% = 14.6\%$$

(*c*) The answer is no.

$$r_j = 5\% + 0.6(13\% - 5\%) = 9.8\%$$

Since the required rate of return is 9.8 percent and the expected return from the investment is only 8.5 percent, the project produces a negative NPV.

(*d*) $$r_j = r_f + b(r_m - r_f)$$
$$12.5\% = 5\% + b(13\% - 5\%)$$
$$b = 0.9375$$

9.17 **Beta and NPV Analysis.** A project has the following forecasted cash flows (in thousands of dollars):

Year 0	Year 1	Year 2	Year 3
($100)	$30	$50	$90

The estimated project beta is 2.0. The market return is 13 percent, and the Treasury bill yield is 6 percent. Compute (*a*) the project's cost of capital and (*b*) the project's NPV.

SOLUTION

(*a*) The project's cost of capital is:
$$r = r_f + b(r_m - r_f)$$
$$= 6\% + 2.0(13\% - 6\%) = 6\% + 14\% = 20\%$$

(*b*) The project's NPV is:

Year	Cash Flow ($)	PV at 20%	PV ($)
0	(100)	1.000	(100)
1	30	0.833	25
2	50	0.694	35
3	90	0.579	52
		NPV =	12

9.18 Calculation of Beta Using Regression Analysis. You are given the following data for stock A and the market portfolio:

	Historic Rates of Return	
Year	r_j (%)	r_m (%)
19X0	1	−2
19X1	3	7
19X2	14	20
19X3	18	30

Assuming that the risk-free rate is 4 percent, compute (a) the beta coefficient and (b) the required rate of return to be used for capital budgeting decisions in 19X4 when the market rate of return is expected to be 18 percent?

SOLUTION

(a)

Year	Stock Return, r_j	Market Return, r_m	Risk-Free Rate, r_f	Excess Stock Return, $(r_j - r_f) = K$	Excess Market Return, $(r_f - r_m) = M$	M^2	Cross Product MK
19X0	0.01	−0.02	0.04	−0.03	0.06	0.0036	−0.0018
19X1	0.03	0.07	0.04	−0.01	−0.03	0.0009	0.0003
19X2	0.14	0.2	0.04	0.10	−0.16	0.0256	−0.016
19X3	0.18	0.3	0.04	0.14	−0.26	0.0676	−0.0364
				0.2	−0.39	0.0977	−0.0539

$$\bar{K} = 0.05$$

$$\bar{M} = -0.0975$$

$$b = \frac{\sum MK - n\bar{M}\bar{K}}{\sum M^2 - n\bar{M}^2} = \frac{-0.0539 - (4)(-0.0975)(0.05)}{0.0977 - (4)(-0.0975)^2} = \frac{-0.0344}{-0.0597} = 0.59$$

(b)

$$r_j = r_f + b(r_m - r_f)$$

$$= 4\% + (0.59)(18\% - 4\%) = 12.26\%$$

Therefore, the 19X4 risk-adjusted rate of return that is required for capital budgeting projects is 16.18 percent.

Chapter 10

Cost of Capital

10.1 COST OF CAPITAL DEFINED

Cost of capital is defined as the rate of return that is necessary to maintain the market value of the firm (or price of the firm's stock). Managers must know the cost of capital, often called the *minimum required rate of return* in (1) making capital budgeting decisions, (2) helping to establish the optimal capital structure, and (3) making decisions such as leasing, bond refunding, and working capital management. The cost of capital is computed as a weighted average of the various capital components, which are items on the right-hand side of the balance sheet such as debt, preferred stock, common stock, and retained earnings.

10.2 COMPUTING INDIVIDUAL COSTS OF CAPITAL

Each element of capital has a component cost that is identified by the following:

k_i = before-tax cost of debt

$k_d = k_i(1 - t)$ = after-tax cost of debt, where t = tax rate

k_p = cost of preferred stock

k_s = cost of retained earnings (or internal equity)

k_e = cost of external equity, or cost of issuing new common stock

k_o = firm's overall cost of capital, or a weighted average cost of capital

Cost of Debt

The before-tax cost of debt can be found by determining the internal rate of return (or yield to maturity) on the bond cash flows, which was discussed in detail in Chapter 7. However, the following shortcut formula may be used for *approximating* the yield to maturity on a bond:

$$k_i = \frac{I + (M - V)/n}{(M + V)/2}$$

where I = annual interest payments in dollars

M = par value, usually \$1,000 per bond

V = value or net proceeds from the sale of a bond

n = term of the bond in years

Since the interest payments are tax-deductible, the cost of debt must be stated on an after-tax basis. The after-tax cost of debt is:

$$k_d = k_i(1 - t)$$

where t is the tax rate.

EXAMPLE 10.1 Assume that the Carter Company issues a \$1,000, 8 percent, 20-year bond whose net proceeds are \$940. The tax rate is 40 percent. Then, the before-tax cost of debt, k_i, is:

$$k_i = \frac{I + (M - V)/n}{(M + V)/2}$$

$$= \frac{\$80 + (\$1,000 - \$940)/20}{(\$1,000 + \$940)/2} = \frac{\$83}{\$970} = 8.56\%$$

Therefore, the after-tax cost of debt is:

$$k_d = k_i(1-t)$$
$$= 8.56\%(1-0.4) = 5.14\%$$

Cost of Preferred Stock

The cost of preferred stock, k_p, is found by dividing the annual preferred stock dividend, d_p, by the net proceeds from the sale of the preferred stock, p, as follows:

$$k_p = \frac{d_p}{p}$$

Since preferred stock dividends are not a tax-deductible expense, these dividends are paid out after taxes. Consequently, no tax adjustment is required.

EXAMPLE 10.2 Suppose that the Carter Company has preferred stock that pays a \$13 dividend per share and sells for \$100 per share in the market. The flotation (or underwriting) cost is 3 percent, or \$3 per share. Then the cost of preferred stock is:

$$k_p = \frac{d_p}{p}$$
$$= \frac{\$13}{\$97} = 13.4\%$$

Cost of Equity Capital

The cost of common stock, k_e, is generally viewed as the rate of return investors require on a firm's common stock. Three techniques for measuring the cost of common stock equity capital are available: (1) the Gordon's growth model, (2) the capital asset pricing model (CAPM) approach, and (3) the bond plus approach.

The Gordon's Growth Model. The Gordon's model was discussed in detail in Chapter 7. The model is:

$$P_0 = \frac{D_1}{r-g}$$

where P_0 = value of common stock
   D_1 = dividend to be received in 1 year
   r = investor's required rate of return
   g = rate of growth (assumed to be constant over time)

Solving the model for r results in the formula for the cost of common stock:

$$r = \frac{D_1}{P_0} + g \qquad \text{or} \qquad k_e = \frac{D_1}{P_0} + g$$

Note that the symbol r is changed to k_e to show that it is used for the computation of cost of capital.

EXAMPLE 10.3 Assume that the market price of the Carter Company's stock is \$40. The dividend to be paid at the end of the coming year is \$4 per share and is expected to grow at a constant annual rate of 6 percent. Then the cost of this common stock is:

$$k_e = \frac{D_1}{P_0} + g = \frac{\$4}{\$40} + 6\% = 16\%$$

The cost of *new* common stock, or external equity capital, is higher than the cost of existing common stock because of the flotation costs involved in selling the new common stock.

If f is flotation cost in percent, the formula for the cost of new common stock is:

$$k_e = \frac{D_1}{P_0(1-f)} + g$$

EXAMPLE 10.4 Assume the same data as in Example 10.3, except the firm is trying to sell new issues of stock A and its flotation cost is 10 percent. Then:

$$k_e = \frac{D_1}{P_0(1-f)} + g$$

$$= \frac{\$4}{\$40(1-0.1)} + 6\% = \frac{\$4}{\$36} + 6\% = 11.11\% + 6\% = 17.11\%$$

The CAPM Approach. An alternative approach to measuring the cost of common stock is to use the CAPM, which involves the following steps:

1. Estimate the risk-free rate, r_f, generally taken to be the United States Treasury bill rate.
2. Estimate the stock's beta coefficient, b, which is an index of systematic (or nondiversifiable market) risk.
3. Estimate the rate of return on the market portfolio such as the Standard & Poor's 500 Stock Composite Index or Dow Jones 30 Industrials.
4. Estimate the required rate of return on the firm's stock, using the CAPM (or SML) equation:

$$k_e = r_f + b(r_m - r_f)$$

Again, note that the symbol r_j is changed to k_e.

EXAMPLE 10.5 Assuming that r_f is 7 percent, b is 1.5, and r_m is 13 percent, then:

$$k_e = r_f + b(r_m - r_f) = 7\% + 1.5(13\% - 7\%) = 16\%$$

This 16 percent cost of common stock can be viewed as consisting of a 7 percent risk-free rate plus a 9 percent risk premium, which reflects that the firm's stock price is 1.5 times more volatile than the market portfolio to the factors affecting nondiversifiable, or systematic, risk.

The Bond Plus Approach. Still another simple but useful approach to determining the cost of common stock is to add a *risk premium* to the firm's own cost of long-term debt, as follows:

$$k_e = \text{long-term bond rate} + \text{risk premium}$$
$$= k_i(1-t) + \text{risk premium}$$

A risk premium of about 4 percent is commonly used with this approach.

EXAMPLE 10.6 Using the data found in Example 10.1, the cost of common stock using the bond plus approach is:

$$k_e = \text{long-term bond rate} + \text{risk premium}$$
$$= k_i(1-t) + \text{risk premium}$$
$$= 5.14\% + 4\% = 9.14\%$$

Cost of Retained Earnings

The cost of retained earnings, k_s, is closely related to the cost of existing common stock, since the cost of equity obtained by retained earnings is the same as the rate of return investors require on the firm's common stock. Therefore,

$$k_e = k_s$$

10.3 MEASURING THE OVERALL COST OF CAPITAL

The firm's overall cost of capital is the weighted average of the individual capital costs, with the weights being the proportions of each type of capital used. Let k_o be the overall cost of capital.

$$k_o = \sum \begin{pmatrix} \% \text{ of total capital} & \text{cost of capital} \\ \text{structure supplied by} \times & \text{for each source} \\ \text{each type of capital} & \text{of capital} \end{pmatrix}$$

$$= w_d \cdot k_d + w_p \cdot k_p + w_e \cdot k_e + w_s \cdot k_s$$

where w_d = % of total capital supplied by debt
w_p = % of total capital supplied by preferred stock
w_e = % of total capital supplied by external equity
w_s = % of total capital supplied by retained earnings (or internal equity)

The weights can be historical, target, or marginal.

Historical Weights

Historical weights are based on a firm's existing capital structure. The use of these weights is based on the assumption that the firm's existing capital structure is optimal and therefore should be maintained in the future. Two types of historical weights can be used—book value weights and market value weights.

Book Value Weights. The use of book value weights in calculating the firm's weighted cost of capital assumes that new financing will be raised using the same method the firm used for its present capital structure. The weights are determined by dividing the book value of each capital component by the sum of the book values of all the long-term capital sources. The computation of overall cost of capital is illustrated in the following example.

EXAMPLE 10.7 Assume the following capital structure for the Carter Company:

Mortgage bonds ($1,000 par)	$20,000,000
Preferred stock ($100 par)	5,000,000
Common stock ($40 par)	20,000,000
Retained earnings	5,000,000
Total	$50,000,000

The book value weights and the overall cost of capital are computed as follows:

Source	Book Value	Weights	Cost	Weighted Cost
Debt	$20,000,000	40%	5.14%	2.06%
Preferred stock	5,000,000	10	13.40%	1.34
Common stock	20,000,000	40	17.11%	6.84
Retained earnings	5,000,000	10	16.00%	1.60
Totals	$50,000,000	100%		11.84%

Overall cost of capital = k_o = 11.84%

Market Value Weights. Market value weights are determined by dividing the market value of each source by the sum of the market values of all sources. The use of market value weights for computing a firm's weighted average cost of capital is theoretically more appealing than the use of book value weights because the market values of the securities closely approximate the actual dollars to be received from their sale.

EXAMPLE 10.8 In addition to the data from Example 10.7, assume that the security market prices are as follows:

$$\text{Mortgage bonds} = \$1,100 \text{ per bond}$$
$$\text{Preferred stock} = \$90 \text{ per share}$$
$$\text{Common stock} = \$80 \text{ per share}$$

The firm's number of securities in each category is:

$$\text{Mortgage bonds} = \frac{\$20,000,000}{\$1,000} = 20,000$$

$$\text{Preferred stock} = \frac{\$5,000,000}{\$100} = 50,000$$

$$\text{Common stock} = \frac{\$20,000,000}{\$40} = 500,000$$

Therefore, the market value weights are:

Source	Number of Securities	Price	Market Value
Debt	20,000	$1,100	$22,000,000
Preferred stock	50,000	$90	4,500,000
Common stock	500,000	$80	40,000,000
			$66,500,000

The $40 million common stock value must be split in the ratio of 4 to 1 (the $20 million common stock versus the $5 million retained earnings in the original capital structure), since the market value of the retained earnings has been impounded into the common stock.

The firm's cost of capital is as follows:

Source	Market Value	Weights	Cost	Weighted Average
Debt	$22,000,000	33.08%	5.14%	1.70%
Preferred stock	4,500,000	6.77	13.40%	0.91
Common stock	32,000,000	48.12	17.11%	8.23
Retained earnings	8,000,000	12.03	16.00%	1.92
	$66,500,000	100.00%		12.76%

Overall cost of capital = $k_o = 12.76\%$

Target Weights

If the firm has determined the capital structure it believes most consistent with its goal, the use of that capital structure and associated weights is appropriate.

Marginal Weights

The use of marginal weights involves weighting the specific costs of various types of financing by the percentage of the total financing expected to be raised using each method. In using target weights, the firm is concerned with what it believes to be the optimal capital structure or target percentage. In using marginal weights, the firm is concerned with the *actual* dollar amounts of each type of financing to be needed for a given investment project.

EXAMPLE 10.9 The Carter Company is considering raising $8 million for plant expansion. Management estimates using the following mix for financing this project:

Debt	$4,000,000	50%
Common stock	2,000,000	25
Retained earnings	2,000,000	25
	$8,000,000	100%

The company's cost of capital is computed as follows:

Source	Marginal Weights	Cost	Weighted Cost
Debt	50%	5.14%	2.57%
Common stock	25	17.11%	4.28
Retained earnings	25	16.00%	4.00
	100%		10.85%

Overall cost of capital = k_o = 10.85%

10.4 LEVEL OF FINANCING AND THE MARGINAL COST OF CAPITAL (MCC)

Because external equity capital has a higher cost than retained earnings due to flotation costs, the weighted cost of capital increases for each dollar of new financing. Therefore, lower-cost capital sources are used first. In fact, the firm's cost of capital is a function of the size of its total investment. A schedule or graph relating the firm's cost of capital to the level of new financing is called the *weighted marginal cost of capital* (*MCC*). Such a schedule is used to determine the discount rate to be used in the firm's capital budgeting process. The steps to be followed in calculating the firm's marginal cost of capital are summarized below.

1. Determine the cost and the percentage of financing to be used for each source of capital (debt, preferred stock, common stock equity).

2. Compute the break points on the MCC curve where the weighted cost will increase. The formula for computing the break points is:

$$\text{Break point} = \frac{\text{maximum amount of the lower-cost source of capital}}{\text{percentage financing provided by the source}}$$

3. Calculate the weighted cost of capital over the range of total financing between break points.

4. Construct a MCC schedule or graph that shows the weighted cost of capital for each level of total new financing. This schedule will be used in conjunction with the firm's available investment opportunities schedule (IOS) in order to select the investments. As long as a project's IRR is greater than the marginal cost of new financing, the project should be accepted. Also, the point at which the IRR intersects the MCC gives the optimal capital budget.

Example 10.10 illustrates the procedure for determining a firm's weighted cost of capital for each level of new financing and how a firm's investment opportunity schedule (IOS) is related to its discount rate.

EXAMPLE 10.10 A firm is contemplating three investment projects, A, B, and C, whose initial cash outlays and expected IRR are shown below. IOS for these projects is:

Project	Cash Outlay	IRR
A	$2,000,000	13%
B	$2,000,000	15%
C	$1,000,000	10%

If these projects are accepted, the financing will consist of 50 percent debt and 50 percent common stock. The firm should have $1.8 million in earnings available for reinvestment (internal common). The firm will consider only the effects of increases in the cost of common stock on its marginal cost of capital.

1. The costs of capital for each source of financing have been computed and are given below:

Source	Cost
Debt	5%
Common stock ($1.8 million)	15%
New common stock	19%

If the firm uses only internally generated common stock, the weighted cost of capital is:

$$k_o = \sum \text{percentage of the total capital structure supplied by each source of capital}$$

$$\times \text{cost of capital for each source}$$

In this case the capital structure is composed of 50 percent debt and 50 percent internally generated common stock. Thus,

$$k_o = (0.5)5\% + (0.5)15\% = 10\%$$

If the firm uses only new common stock, the weighted cost of capital is:

$$k_o = (0.5)5\% + (0.5)19\% = 12\%$$

Range of Total New Financing (In Millions of Dollars)	Type of Capital	Proportion	Cost	Weighted Cost
$0–$3.6	Debt	0.5	5%	2.5%
	Internal common	0.5	15%	7.5
				10.0%
$3.6 and up	Debt	0.5	5%	2.5%
	New common	0.5	19%	9.5
				12.0%

2. Next compute the break point, which is the level of financing at which the weighted cost of capital increases.

$$\text{Break point} = \frac{\text{maximum amount of source of the lower cost source of capital}}{\text{percentage financing provided by the source}}$$

$$= \frac{\$1,800,000}{0.5} = \$3,600,000$$

3. That is, the firm may be able to finance $3.6 million in new investments with internal common stock and debt without having to change the current mix of 50 percent debt and 50 percent common stock. Therefore, if the total financing is $3.6 million or less, the firm's cost of capital is 10 percent.

4. Construct the MCC schedule on the IOS graph to determine the discount rate to be used in order to decide in which project to invest and to show the firm's optimal capital budget. See Fig. 10-1.

The firm should continue to invest up to the point where the IRR equals the MCC. From the graph in Fig. 10-1, note that the firm should invest in projects B and A, since each IRR exceeds the marginal cost of capital. The firm should reject project C since its cost of capital is greater than the IRR. The optimal capital budget is $4 million, since this is the sum of the cash outlay required for projects A and B.

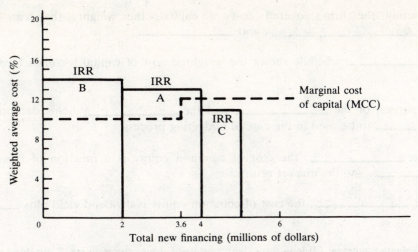

Fig. 10-1 MCC schedule and IOS graph

Review Questions

1. The firm's cost of capital is calculated as a(n) _____ of the costs of the various types of financing.

2. Capital components on the right-hand side of the firm's balance sheet are _____ , _____ , _____ and _____ .

3. There are three techniques for measuring the cost of common stock. They are _____ , _____ , and _____ .

4. The cost of capital, often called the _____ , is used in (1) making _____ decisions, (2) helping to establish the _____ , and (3) making such decisions as _____ , bond financing, and working capital management.

5. The after-tax cost of debt is k_i times _____ .

6. The _____ is found by dividing the annual _____ dividend by the net proceeds from sale.

7. No tax adjustments are necessary for the computation of the costs of _____ and preferred stock.

8. The cost of _____ is higher than the cost of common stock because of _____ involved in its sale.

9. The _____ approach to determining the cost of common stock is to add a _____ to the firm's own cost of long-term debt.

10. Two types of historical weights are used: _____ and _____ .

11. In computing the firm's overall cost of capital, the weights that can be used are
   _____, _____, and _____.

12. The _____ schedule shows the weighted cost of capital for each level of total new
   financing.

13. The comparison of the _____ and the _____ helps determine the firm's
   _____ to be used in the capital budgeting process.

14. Using the _____, the cost of common equity is a function of the risk-free rate,
   _____, and the market return.

15. Using the _____, the cost of common equity is dividend yield plus _____.

Answers: (1) weighted average; (2) long-term debt, preferred stock, common stock, retained earnings; (3) the
Gordon's growth model approach, the CAPM approach, the bond plus approach; (4) required rate of return,
capital budgeting, optimal capital structure, leasing; (5) (1 − tax rate); (6) cost of preferred stock, preferred stock;
(7) common stock (equity); (8) new common stock, flotation costs; (9) bond plus, risk premium; (10) book value,
market value (11) historical, target, marginal; (12) marginal cost of capital (MCC); (13) MCC, investment
opportunity schedule (IOS), optimal capital budget; (14) CAPM, beta; (15) Gordon's growth model, growth rate
in earnings and dividends.

Solved Problems

10.1   Cost of Debt. Calculate the after-tax cost of debt under each of the following cases: (*a*) the
interest rate is 10 percent, and the tax rate is 40 percent; (*b*) the interest rate is 11 percent, and
the tax rate is 50 percent.

SOLUTION

$$k_d = k_i(1 - t)$$

(*a*) $$k_d = 10\%(1 - 0.4) = 6\%$$

(*b*) $$k_d = 11\%(1 - 0.5) = 5.5\%$$

10.2   Cost of Bonds. XYZ Company has bonds outstanding with 7 years left before maturity. The
bonds are currently selling for $800 per $1,000 face value. The interest is paid annually at a
rate of 12 percent. The firm's tax rate is 40 percent. Calculate the after-tax cost of debt using
(*a*) the regular method, and (*b*) the shortcut method.

SOLUTION

(*a*)   Using the regular method, the yield to maturity is:

$$V = \sum_{t=1}^{n} \frac{I}{(1 + r)^t} + \frac{M}{(1 + r)^n}$$

$$= I(\text{PVIFA}_{r,n}) + M(\text{PVIF}_{r,n})$$

$$\$800 = \$120(\text{PVIFA}_{r,7}) + \$1,000(\text{PVIF}_{r,7})$$

At 17%,

$$V = \$120(3.9215) + \$1,000(0.3338) = \$470.58 + \$333.80 = \$804.38$$

which is close enough to $800; therefore, the yield to maturity or before-tax cost of debt is 17 percent.

The after-tax cost of debt is computed as:

$$k_d = k_i(1 - t)$$
$$= 17\%(1 - 0.4) = 10.2\%$$

(b) Using the shortcut method:

$$k_i = \frac{I + [(M - V)/n]}{(M + V)/2} = \frac{\$120 + [(\$1,000 - \$800)/7]}{(\$1,000 + \$800)/2} = \frac{\$120 + \$28.57}{\$900} = 16.51\%$$

Therefore, the after-tax cost of debt is computed as:

$$k_d = 16.51\%(1 - 0.4) = 9.91\%$$

10.3   Cost of Bonds. Assume the same data as in Problem 10.2, but now assume the interest is paid semiannually. Calculate the after-tax cost of debt, using (a) the regular method, and (b) the shortcut method.

SOLUTION

(a) Since the interest is paid semiannually, the interest payment is $120 \div 2 = \$60$ and the number of periods is 14. Using the regular method gives:

$$V = I(\text{PVIFA}_{r,n}) + M(\text{PVIF}_{r,n})$$
$$\$800 = \$60(\text{PVIFA}_{i,14}) + \$1,000(\text{PVIF}_{i,14})$$

To arrive at a value of $800, first try 8 percent:

$$V = \$60(8.2442) + \$1,000(0.3405) = \$494.65 + \$340.50 = \$835.15$$

Since this is too high, try 9 percent:

$$V = \$60(7.7862) + \$1,000(0.2992) = \$467.17 + \$299.20 = \$766.37$$

Since this value is too low, the cost of debt is somewhere between 8 percent and 9 percent. Using the interpolation:

	8%	9%
PV	$835.15	$835.15
True rate	800.00	
PV		766.37
Difference	$ 35.15	$ 68.78

$$\text{True rate} = 8\% + \frac{\$35.15}{\$68.78}(1\%) = 8\% + 0.51 = 8.51\%$$

$$\text{Annual rate} = 8.51\% \times 2 = 17.02\%$$

Therefore, the after-tax cost of debt is computed as:

$$k_d = k_i(1 - t) = 17.02\%(1 - 0.4) = 10.21\%$$

(b) Using the shortcut method:

$$k_i = \frac{\$60 + [(\$1,000 - \$800)/14]}{(\$1,000 + \$800)/2} = \frac{\$60 + \$14.29}{\$900} = 8.25\%$$

$$\text{Annual rate} = 8.25\% \times 2 = 16.5\%$$

Therefore, the after-tax cost of debt is computed as:

$$k_d = 16.5\%\,(1 - 0.4) = 9.9\%$$

10.4 Cost of Preferred Stock. In its capital structure, ABC Corporation has preferred stock paying a dividend of $5 per share and selling for $23. The company's tax rate is 40 percent. Calculate (a) the before-tax cost of preferred stock, and (b) the after-tax cost of preferred stock.

SOLUTION

(a) The before-tax cost of preferred stock is:

$$k_p = \frac{d_p}{p} = \frac{\$5}{\$23} = 21.7\%$$

(b) The same as the above, since preferred stock dividends are not a tax-deductible expense and are therefore paid out after taxes.

10.5 Cost of Retained Earnings. Plato Company's common stock is selling for $50. Last year's dividend was $4.8 per share. Compute the cost of retained earnings (or internal equity) if both earnings and dividends are expected to grow at (a) zero percent and (b) a constant rate of 9 percent.

SOLUTION

(a)
$$D_1 = D_0(1 + g) = \$4.8(1 + 0) = \$4.8$$

$$k_s = \frac{D_1}{P_0} = \frac{\$4.8}{\$50} = 9.6\%$$

(b)
$$D_1 = D_0(1 + g) = \$4.8(1 + 0.09) = \$5.232$$

$$k_s = \frac{D_1}{P_0} + g = \frac{\$5.232}{\$50} + 9\% = 10.5 + 9\% = 19.5\%$$

10.6 Cost of Retained Earnings (or Internal Equity). Epsilon Company's last annual dividend was $4 per share, and both earnings and dividends are expected to grow at a constant rate of 8 percent. The stock now sells for $50 per share. The company's beta coefficient is 1.5. The return of a market portfolio is 12 percent, and the risk-free rate is 8 percent. The company's A-rated bonds are yielding 12 percent. Calculate the cost of retained earnings (or internal equity) using (a) the Gordon's growth model, (b) the bond plus method, and (c) the capital asset pricing model.

SOLUTION

(a) For the Gordon's growth model:

$$D_1 = D_0(1 + g) = \$4.00(1 + 0.08) = \$4.32$$

$$k_s = \frac{D_1}{P_0} + g = \frac{\$4.32}{\$50} + 8\% = 8.64\% + 8\% = 16.64\%$$

(b) k_s = bond yield + risk premium = 12% + ~4% = 16%

For the bond plus method, a risk premium of about 4 percent is commonly used:

(c)   For the CAPM:

$$k_s = r_f + b(r_m - r_f) = 8\% + 1.5(12\% - 8\%) = 8\% + 6\% = 14\%$$

10.7   **Cost of New Common Stock.** Assume the data given in Problem 10.5 is for new stock. Compute the cost of new common stock (or external equity). Assume there is a 10 percent flotation cost associated with issuing new common stock.

SOLUTION

(a) $$D_1 = D_0(1 + g) = \$4.80(1 + 0) = \$4.80$$

$$k_e = \frac{D_1}{P_0(1-f)} + g = \frac{\$4.80}{\$50(1-0.1)} + 0 = \frac{\$4.80}{\$45} = 10.67\%$$

(b) $$D_1 = D_0(1 + g) = \$4.80(1 + 0.09) = \$5.232$$

$$k_e = \frac{D_1}{P_0(1-f)} = g = \frac{\$5.232}{\$50(1-0.1)} + 9\%$$

$$= \frac{\$5.232}{\$45} + 9\% = 11.63\% + 9\% = 20.63\%$$

10.8   **Costs of Retained Earnings and New Common Stock.** Armon Brothers, Inc., is attempting to evaluate the costs of internal and external common equity. The company's stock is currently selling for $62.50 per share. The company expects to pay $5.42 per share at the end of the year. The dividends for the past 5 years are given below:

Year	Dividend
19X5	$5.17
19X4	$4.92
19X3	$4.68
19X2	$4.46
19X1	$4.25

The company expects to net $57.50 per share on a new share after flotation costs. Calculate (a) the growth rate of dividends, (b) the flotation cost (in percent), (c) the cost of retained earnings (or internal equity), and (d) the cost of new common stock (or external equity).

SOLUTION

(a) $$\$5.17 = \$4.25(\text{FVIF}_{i,r \text{ yrs}})$$

$$\text{FVIF}_{i,4 \text{ yrs}} = \frac{\$5.17}{\$4.25} = 1.216$$

From Appendix A, we obtain 5 percent from the 4-year line.
    Alternatively,

$$\$5.42 = \$4.25(\text{FVIF}_{i,5 \text{ yrs}})$$

$$\text{FVIF}_{i,5 \text{ yrs}} = \frac{\$5.42}{\$4.25} = 1.276$$

From Appendix A, obtain 5 percent in the 5-year line.

(b) The flotation cost percentage is calculated as follows:

$$\frac{\$62.50 - \$57.50}{\$62.50} = \frac{\$5}{\$62.50} = 8\%$$

(c) The cost of retained earnings, k_s, is:

$$k_s = \frac{D_1}{P_0} + g = \frac{\$5.42}{\$62.50} + 5\% = 8.67\% + 5\% = 13.67\%$$

(d) The cost of new common stock, k_e, is:

$$k_e = \frac{D_1}{P_0(1-f)} + g = \frac{\$5.42}{\$62.5(1-0.08)} + 5\% = \frac{\$5.42}{\$57.50} + 5\%$$
$$= 9.43\% + 5\% = 14.43\%$$

10.9 Weighted Average Cost of Capital. The Gamma Products Corporation has the following capital structure, which it considers optimal:

Bonds, 7% (now selling at par)	$ 300,000
Preferred stock, $5.00	240,000
Common stock	360,000
Retained earnings	300,000
	$1,200,000

Dividends on common stock are currently $3 per share and are expected to grow at a constant rate of 6 percent. Market price per share of common stock is $40, and the preferred stock is selling at $50. Flotation cost on new issues of common stock is 10 percent. The interest on bonds is paid annually. The company's tax rate is 40 percent.

Calculate (a) the cost of bonds, (b) the cost of preferred stock, (c) the cost of retained earnings (or internal equity), (d) the cost of new common stock (or external equity), and (e) the weighted average cost of capital.

SOLUTION

(a) Since the bonds are selling at par, the before-tax cost of bonds (k_i) is the same as the coupon rate, that is, 7 percent. Therefore, the after-tax cost of bonds is

$$k_d = k_i(1-t)$$
$$= 7\%(1-0.4) = 4.20\%$$

(b) The cost of preferred stock is:

$$k_p = \frac{d_p}{p} = \frac{\$5}{\$50} = 10\%$$

(c) The cost of retained earnings is:

$$D_1 = D_0(1+g) = \$3(1+0.06) = \$3.18$$

$$k_s = \frac{D_1}{P_0} + g = \frac{\$3.18}{\$40} + 6\% = 7.95\% + 6\% = 13.95\%$$

(d) The cost of new common stock is:

$$k_e = \frac{D_1}{P_0(1-f)} + g = \frac{\$3.18}{\$40(1-0.1)} + 6\% = 8.83\% + 6\% = 14.83\%$$

(e) The weighted average cost of capital is computed as follows:

Source of Capital	Capital Structure	Percentage	Cost	Weighted Cost
Bonds	$ 300	25%	4.20%	1.05 %
Preferred stock	240	20	10.00%	2.00
Common stock	360	30	13.95%	4.185
Retained earnings	300	25	14.83%	3.708
Totals	$1,200	100%		10.943%

Weighted average cost of capital = 10.943%

10.10 Weighted Average Cost of Capital. Valie Enterprises, Inc., has compiled the following investments:

Type of Capital	Book Value	Market Value	After-Tax Cost
Long-term debt	$3,000,000	$2,800,000	4.8%
Preferred stock	102,000	150,000	9.0%
Common stock	1,108,000	2,500,000	13.0%
	$4,210,000	$5,450,000	

(a) Calculate the weighted average cost of capital, using (1) book value weights and (2) market value weights. (b) Explain the difference in the results obtained in (a).

SOLUTION

(a) (1) Book value weights are computed as follows:

Type of Capital	Book Value	Weight	Cost	Weighted Cost
Long-term debt	$3,000,000	0.713	4.8%	3.422%
Preferred stock	102,000	0.024	9.0%	0.216
Common stock	1,108,000	0.263	13.0%	3.419
	$4,210,000	1.000		7.057%

(2) Market value weights are computed as follows:

Type of Capital	Market Value	Weight	Cost	Weighted Cost
Long-term debt	$2,800,000	0.514	4.8%	2.467%
Preferred stock	150,000	0.028	9.0%	0.252
Common stock	2,500,000	0.458	13.0%	5.954
	$5,450,000	1.000		8.673%

(b) The book value weights give the firm a much greater leverage (or debt position) than the market value weights. The cost of capital based on market value weights is more realistic, since it is based on the prevailing market values. Since common stock usually sells at a higher value than its book value, the cost of capital is higher when using market value weights.

10.11 Cost of Capital. The Conner Company has the following capital structure:

Mortgage bonds, 6%	$ 20,000,000
Common stock (1 million shares)	25,000,000
Retained earnings	55,000,000
	$100,000,000

Mortgage bonds of similar quality could be sold at a net of 95 to yield $6\frac{1}{2}$ percent. Their common stock has been selling for $100 per share. The company has paid 50 percent of earnings in dividends for several years and intends to continue the policy. The current dividend is $4 per share. Earnings are growing at 5 percent per year. If the company sold a new equity issue, it would expect to net $94 per share after all costs. Their marginal tax rate is 50 percent.

Conner wants to determine a cost of capital to use in capital budgeting. Additional projects would be financed to maintain the same relationship between debt and equity. Additional debt would consist of mortgage bonds, and additional equity would consist of retained earnings. (a) Calculate the firm's weighted average cost of capital, and (b) explain why you used the particular weighting system. (CMA, adapted.)

SOLUTION

(a)

	Amount	Proportion	After-Tax Cost	Weighted Average
Bonds	20	20%	3.25% [a]	0.65%
Common stock	25	25	9.0 [b]	2.25
Retained earnings	55	55	9.0	4.95
	100	100%		7.85%

[a] $3.25\% = 6.5\%(1 - 0.5)$

[b] The cost of equity capital is:

$$k_e = \frac{D_1}{P_0} + g = \frac{4.00}{100.00} + 0.05 = 9.0\%$$

Market value weighting (in millions) produces the following cost of capital:

Bonds	19	16%	3.25%	0.52%
Common and retained earnings	100	84	9.00%	7.56
	119	100%		8.08%

(b) The weighting to be used should reflect the mix of capital the company intends to use (presumably based upon its understanding of the optimal mix). The problem states that the company intends to maintain the same relationship between debt and equity. If that relationship is defined as the book value relationship, then that should be used to calculate the weighted average cost of capital. If the relationship referred to means the market value weighted average cost of capital, then that relationship should be used.

10.12 Cost of Capital Comparison. The treasurer of a new venture, Start-Up Scientific, Inc., is trying to determine how to raise $6 million of long-term capital. Her investment adviser has devised the alternative capital structures shown below:

Alternative A		Alternative B	
$2,000,000	9% debt	$4,000,000	12% debt
$4,000,000	Equity	$2,000,000	Equity

If alternative A is chosen, the firm would sell 200,000 shares of common stock to net $20 per share. Stockholders would expect an initial dividend of $1 per share and a dividend growth rate of 7 percent.

Under alternative B, the firm would sell 100,000 shares of common stock to net $20 per share. The expected initial dividend would be $0.90 per share, and the anticipated dividend growth rate 12 percent.

Assume that the firm earns a profit under either capital structure and that the effective tax rate is 50 percent. (*a*) What is the cost of capital to the firm under each of the suggested capital structures? Explain your result. (*b*) Explain the logic of the anticipated higher interest rate on debt associated with alternative B. (*c*) Is it logical for shareholders to expect a higher dividend growth rate under alternative B? Explain your answer. (CMA, adapted.)

SOLUTION

(*a*) The cost of capital for a firm is computed as a weighted average of the component costs of the sources used to raise capital where the weights relate to the percentage of total capital raised. In this case the two components are debt and equity.

$$\text{Cost of debt } (k_d) = (\text{interest rate})(1 - \text{tax rate})$$

$$\text{Cost of equity } (k_e) = \frac{\text{dividend}}{\text{price}} + \text{growth}$$

$$\text{Overall cost of capital } (k_o) = (\text{weight of debt})(k_d) + (\text{weight of equity})(k_e)$$

For alternative A:

$$k_d = 0.09(1 - 0.5) = 4.5\%$$

$$k_e = \frac{\$1}{\$20} + 0.07 = 12\%$$

$$k_o = \tfrac{2}{6} \times 0.045 + \tfrac{4}{6} \times 0.12 = 9.5\%$$

For alternative B:

$$k_d = 0.12(1 - 0.5) = 6\%$$

$$k_e = \frac{\$0.90}{\$20} + 0.12 = 16.5\%$$

$$k_o = \tfrac{4}{6} \times 0.06 + \tfrac{2}{6} \times 0.165 = 9.5\%$$

The weighted average cost of capital is the same for alternatives A and B because the risk = return trade-offs for A and B balance each other.

(*b*) The interest rate on debt is higher for alternative B because the financial risk is greater due to the increased use of leverage. As a result, the probability of not being able to meet the high fixed payment increases, causing the bond market to have a higher required rate of return to offset this greater risk.

(*c*) It is logical for shareholders to expect a higher dividend growth rate under alternative B because of the additional financial risk and increased fixed interest requirement. Equity holders will demand a higher return to compensate them for the additional financial risk. Dividends per share should grow at a faster rate than alternative A because earnings per share grow faster due to the greater amount of leverage (smaller base). In addition, assuming a given payout rate, it follows that dividends per share would also grow faster than alternative A.

10.13 Cost of Capital. Timel Company is in the process of determining its capital budget for the coming fiscal year. Timel Company's balance sheet reflects five sources of long-term funds. The current outstanding amounts from these five sources are shown below and represent the company's historical sources of funds fairly accurately.

Source of Funds	$ Amount (in Millions)	%
Mortgage bonds ($1,000 par, $7\frac{1}{2}\%$)	135	15.0
Debentures ($1,000 par, 8%, due 19X5)	225	25.0
Preferred stock ($100 par, $7\frac{1}{2}\%$)	90	10.0
Common stock ($10 par)	150	16.7
Retained earnings	300	33.3
	900	100.0

Timel will raise the funds necessary to support the selected capital investment projects so as to maintain its historical distribution among the various sources of long-term funds. Thus, 15 percent will be obtained from additional mortgage bonds on new plant, 25 percent from debentures, 10 percent from preferred stock, and 50 percent from some common equity source. Timel's policy is to reinvest the funds derived from each year's earnings in new projects. Timel issues new common stock only after all funds provided from retained earnings have been exhausted.

Management estimates that its net income after taxes for the coming year will be $4.50 per common share. The dividend payout ratio will be 40 percent of earnings to common shareholders ($1.8 per share), the same ratio as the prior 4 years. The preferred stockholders will receive $6.75 million. The earnings retained will be used as needed to support the capital investment program.

The capital budgeting staff, in conjunction with Timel's investment broker, has developed the following data regarding Timel's sources of funds if it were to raise funds in the current market.

Source of Funds	Par Value ($)	Interest or Dividend Rate (%)	Issue Price ($)
Mortgage bonds	1,000	14	1,000.00
Debentures	1,000	$14\frac{1}{2}$	1,000.00
Preferred stock	100	$13\frac{1}{2}$	99.25
Common stock	10		67.50

The estimated interest rates on the debt instruments and the dividend rate on the preferred stock are based upon the rates being experienced in the market by firms which are of the same size and quality as Timel. The investment banker believes that the price of $67.50 for the common stock is justified, since Timel's price/earnings ratio of 15 is consistent with the 10 percent earnings growth rate that the market is capitalizing.

Timel is subject to a 40 percent income tax rate.

Calculate (a) the after-tax marginal cost of capital for each of the five sources of capital for Timel Company, and (b) Timel Company's after-tax weighted average cost of capital. (c) Timel Company follows a practice that 50 percent of any funds raised will be derived from common equity sources. Determine the point of expansion at which Timel's source of common equity funds would switch from retained earnings to new common stock in the coming year. (d) If the basic business risks are similar for all firms in the industry in which Timel Company participates, would all firms in the industry have approximately the same weighted average cost of capital? Explain your answer. (CMA, adapted.)

SOLUTION

(a) For a mortgage bond:

$$k_d = \text{current yield } (1 - \text{tax rate}) = 14\% (1 - 0.4) = 8.4\%$$

For a debenture:

$$k_d = \text{current yield } (1 - \text{tax rate}) = 14.5\% (1 - 0.4) = 8.7\%$$

For preferred stock:

$$k_p = \frac{\text{dividend}}{\text{issue price}} = \frac{\$13.5}{\$99.25} = 13.6\%$$

For common stock:

$$k_e = \frac{\text{current dividend}}{\text{current price}} + \text{expected growth rate} = \frac{\$1.80}{\$67.50} + 10\% = 12.67\%$$

For retained earnings:

$$k_s = \text{opportunity rate of return on common stock} = k_e = 12.67\%$$

(b) The weighted average cost of capital is calculated as follows:

Source	Current Component Cost (%)	×	Weights	=	Weighted Average Cost
Mortgage bond	8.4		0.15		0.0126
Debenture	8.7		0.25		0.0217
Preferred stock	13.6		0.10		0.0136
Common stock	12.67		0.167		0.0212
Retained earnings	12.67		0.333		0.0422
Total					0.1113

The weighted average cost of capital is 11.13 percent.

(c) The maximum expansion from retained earnings before a new common stock is required is calculated as follows (in millions of dollars):

Net income (\$4.50/common share × 15 million shares)	\$67.5
Less: Dividend payout (\$1.80/common share × 15 million shares)	27.0
Preferred stock dividend	6.75
Retained earnings available for expansion	\$33.75

If common equity is to be 50 percent of total capital, then the \$33.75 million increase in retained earnings would be matched by raising an additional \$33.75 million from debt and preferred stock for a total of \$67.5 million expansion before common shares would be issued.

(d) The weighted average cost of capital may vary among firms in the industry even if the basic business risk is similar for all firms in the industry. This is true because each firm selects the degree of financial leverage it desires. A firm with a high degree of financial leverage would be assigned a high risk premium by investors.

10.14 Cost of Capital and Weighting System. Electro Tool Co., a manufacturer of diamond drilling, cutting, and grinding tools, has \$1 million of its 8 percent debenture issue maturing on September 1, 19X1. The \$1 million that has been accumulated to retire this debt is now going to be used to acquire additional manufacturing machinery. To meet the debt and purchase of machinery, an additional $1 million must be raised. One proposal that has been particularly appealing is the sale and lease-back of the company's general office building. This proposal has a lower interest cost than the financing program proposed by the equipment vendor.

The building would be sold to FHR, Inc., for $1 million and leased back on a 25-year lease. The lease calls for Electro Tool to pay $110,168 annually, which permits FHR, Inc., to recover its investment and earn 10 percent on the investment. Electro Tool will pay for all maintenance costs, property taxes, and insurance during the lease period. At the end of the 25 years Electro Tool will reacquire the building for a very small payment. The sale and lease-back will be treated the same for both financial reporting and income tax purposes.

The current capital structure and cost of the individual components for Electro Tool Co. are shown below.

Capital Component	Amount per Recent Balance Sheet	Before-Tax Component Cost
8% debentures (including the $1,000,000 to be retired)	$ 5,000,000	8%
9% preferred stock	1,000,000	9%
Common stock	2,000,000	13%
Retained earnings	2,000,000	12%
	$10,000,000	

Electro Tool is subject to a 40 percent income tax rate.

(a) Using the data provided, calculate the historical weighted average cost of capital of Electro Tool Co. (1) before the retirement of the debentures and the sale and lease-back action, and (2) after the retirement of the debentures and the sale and lease-back transaction. (b) If the component costs and weightings used to calculate the weighted average cost of capital in (a) (1) are different from those used in (a) (2), explain why. If the amounts used to calculate (a) (1) are the same as those used in (a) (2), explain why. (c) Market values for the capital components were not presented. What arguments are given to support the use of market values in calculating the weighted average cost of capital? (CMA, adapted.)

SOLUTION

(a) (1) The historical weighted average cost of capital before the retirement of the debentures and the sale and lease-back transaction is 8.3 percent, as calculated below.

	(1) Amount per Recent Balance Sheet	(2) % of Total	(3) Before-Tax Cost	(4) After-Tax Cost	(5) Weighted Cost (2) × (4)
8% debentures	$ 5,000,000	50%	0.08	0.048	0.024
9% preferred stock	1,000,000	10	0.09	0.09	0.009
Common stock	2,000,000	20	0.13	0.13	0.026
Retained earnings	2,000,000	20	0.12	0.12	0.024
	$10,000,000	100%			0.083

(2) The historical weighted average cost of capital after the retirement of the debentures and the sale and lease-back transaction is 8.42 percent as calculated below.

	(1) Amount per Recent Balance Sheet	(2) % of Total	(3) Before-Tax Cost	(4) After-Tax Cost	(5) Weighted Cost (2) × (4)
Lease	$ 1,000,000	10%	0.10	0.06	0.006
Debentures	4,000,000	40	0.08	0.048	0.0192
Preferred stock	1,000,000	10	0.09	0.09	0.009
Common stock	2,000,000	20	0.13	0.13	0.026
Retained earnings	2,000,000	20	0.12	0.12	0.024
	$10,100,000	100%			0.0842

(b) The component costs and weightings used to calculate the historical weighted average cost of capital are different in (a) (1) and (a) (2) because lease financing is substituted for a portion of the debentures. Therefore, the debentures now represent only 40 percent of the total capital and the lease 10 percent. The after-tax cost of the lease is $0.10 \times 0.60 = 0.06$, whereas the after-tax cost of the debentures is $0.08 \times 0.60 = 0.048$. The overall cost of capital is increased because a higher cost component replaced a lower cost component.

(c) Market values should be used in calculating the weighted average cost of capital because the cost of capital calculation is used to estimate the current marginal cost of capital for the company. The use of market values (1) recognizes the current investor attitudes regarding the company's risk position and thus will reflect current rates for capital, (2) recognizes better the capital proportions the company must consider in the capital sources decision, and (3) ignores the influence of past values which are not relevant to future decisions.

10.15 Bond Rating and Cost of Capital. Two bond rating agencies, Moody's and Standard and Poor's, lowered the ratings on Appleton Industries' bonds from triple-A to double-A in response to operating trends revealed by the financial reports of recent years. The change in the ratings is of considerable concern to the Appleton management because the company plans to seek a significant amount of external financing within the next 2 years.

(a) Identify several events or circumstances which could have occurred in the operations of Appleton Industries that might have influenced the factors the bond rating agencies use to evaluate the firm and, as a result, caused the bond rating agencies to lower Appleton's bond rating. (b) If Appleton Industries maintains its present capital structure, what effect will the lower bond ratings have on the company's weighted average cost of capital? Explain your answer. (c) If Appleton Industries' capital structure was at an optimal level before the rating of its bonds was changed, explain what effect the lower bond ratings will have on the company's optimal capital structure. (CMA, adapted.)

SOLUTION

(a) Factors or circumstances which may have caused the rating agencies to lower the bond rating of Appleton Industries include:

1. Lowered long-term solvency reflected by a reduction in the times-interest-earned ratio or a reduction in the fixed-charge-coverage ratio

2. Lowered short-term liquidity reflected by a decrease in the current ratio or quick ratio

3. Lowered profitability reflected by a reduced market share, lower return on sales, or decreased profits

4. An increased risk of financial stability due to major pending litigation which would be damaging to the firm or a large increase in earnings variability

5. A major change in management which is perceived negatively by the financial community

(b) The weighted average cost of capital can be expected to rise. The lower bond rating is usually relied upon as an indication of greater risk being assumed by the bond investors. This change will be noted by the investors of other Appleton securities. Thus the investors in each capital component of Appleton Industries can be expected to require a higher return.

(c) Appleton Industries capital structure will shift toward greater equity with less debt. The fact that the bond rating was lowered would indicate to investors that the risk has increased. To reduce the risk and minimize the increase in the cost of capital, the optimal capital structure will have to shift toward one with an increased percentage of equity.

10.16 Earnings Multiple and Cost of Capital. The Jefferson Corporation is contemplating a $50 million expansion project. Over the years, the firm's board of directors has adhered to a policy of rejecting any investment proposal that would jeopardize the market value of the firm's common stock.

A preliminary analysis projected a rate of return on the new project of around 14 percent before taxes. Jefferson has reached tentative agreement with an insurance company to finance the project through a private placement of the $50 million in the form of 10 percent notes.

The firm's common stock has been historically selling at 10 times after-tax earnings. Current earnings per share are $2.70 and the firm faces a 50 percent corporate income tax rate.

Long-term debt (8%)	$ 10,000,000
Common stock ($2 par, 10,000,000 shares outstanding)	20,000,000
Paid-in capital, in excess of par	70,000,000
Retained earnings	100,000,000
Total capitalization	$200,000,000

(a) One of the members of Jefferson Corporation's board of directors argued that the firm should immediately place the notes, since the before-tax marginal cost of capital for the project is only 10 percent (the interest on the notes), and indications are that the project's before-tax rate of return would be greater than 10 percent. Discuss.

(b) Assuming Jefferson's earnings multiple declines to 9, what level of annual earnings must the new project generate in order to meet the director's objective? (CMA, adapted.)

SOLUTION

(a) The board members' conclusion is not valid because the facts seem to indicate the Jefferson Corporation's capitalization is not in equilibrium. The issuance of the notes will move debt from 5 percent of total capitalization (10/200) to 24 percent (60/250). This increases the financial risk that common equity must bear through increased fixed interest payments, and the increased risk can be expected to be manifested by a decline in the earnings multiple. While the marginal cost of capital appears to be 10 percent (the cost of the private placement), the marginal cost of capital is a combination of explicit interest cost on the notes and the additional costs of earnings that must occur to compensate the common stockholders for the decline in the earnings multiple.

Jefferson Corporation should have calculated the weighted average cost of capital according to the following formula:

$$\left(\begin{array}{c}\text{Percent of new funds}\\\text{raised from debt}\end{array}\right) \times (\text{cost of debt}) + \left(\begin{array}{c}\text{percent of funds}\\\text{raised from equity}\end{array}\right) \times (\text{additional cost of equity})$$

The 14 percent rate of return on this project should be compared to the firm's average cost of capital. If the project's return is at least as great as the weighted average cost of capital, then the value of the firm's stock will not decrease.

(b) The stock is now selling at 10 times earnings:

$$P_0 = 10(\$2.70) = \$27.00$$

This is the price that must be maintained upon taking on the new project. If the new project causes the P/E ratio to fall to 9 and offers no additional earnings, the price of stock would fall by $2.70 to $24.30.

In order to get the price of stock back up to $27, the earnings provided by the new asset must equal X:

$$(\text{New P/E})(\text{new EPS}) = \$27$$
$$9(\$2.70 + X) = \$27$$
$$\$2.70 + X = \$3$$
$$X = \$0.30$$

This assumes that currently held assets are capable of continuing to provide $2.70 in earnings per share.

The annual earnings the new project must generate to meet Jefferson Corporation's objective is determined as follows:

(1) Required EPS to maintain $27 price with a multiple of 9:

$$\frac{\$27.00}{9} = \$3.00$$

(2) Required earnings after taxes:

$$\$3.00 \times 10,000,000 \text{ shares} = \$30,000,000$$

(3) Required earnings before taxes:

$$\frac{\$30,000,000}{0.5} = \$60,000,000$$

(4) Interest expense:

$$(\$10,000,000)(0.08) + (\$50,000,000)(0.10) = \$800,000 + \$5,000,000 = \$5,800,000$$

(5) Required earnings before interest and taxes:

$$\$60,000,000 + \$5,800,000 = \$65,800,000$$

(6) Old earnings before interest and taxes:

$$\frac{(\$2.70 \times 10,000,000 \text{ shares})}{0.5} + \$800,000 = \$54,800,000$$

(7) Additional before interest and taxes earnings required:

Projected earnings	$65,800,000
Old earnings	54,800,000
	$11,000,000

10.17 The MCC and IOS Schedules. Rhonda Pollak Company is considering three investments whose initial costs and internal rates of return are given below:

Project	Initial Cost ($)	Internal Rate of Return (%)
A	100,000	19
B	125,000	15
C	225,000	12

The company finances all expansion with 40 percent debt and 60 percent equity capital. The after-tax cost is 8 percent for the first $100,000, after which the cost will be 10 percent. Retained earnings in the amount of $150,000 is available, and the common stockholders' required rate of return is 18 percent. If the new stock is issued, the cost will be 22 percent.

Calculate (*a*) the dollar amounts at which breaks occur, and (*b*) calculate the weighted cost of capital in each of the intervals between the breaks. (*c*) Graph the firm's weighted marginal cost of capital (MCC) schedule and investment opportunities schedule (IOS). (*d*) Decide which projects should be selected and calculate the total amount of the optimal capital budget.

SOLUTION

(*a*)   Breaks (increases) in the weighted marginal cost of capital will occur as follows:
      For debt:

$$\frac{\text{Debt}}{\text{Debt/assets}} = \frac{\$100,000}{0.4} = \$250,000$$

      For common stock:

$$\frac{\text{Retained earnings}}{\text{Equity/assets}} = \frac{\$150,000}{0.6} = \$250,000$$

The debt break is caused by exhausting the lower cost of debt, while the common stock break is caused by using up retained earnings.

(*b*)   The weighted cost of capital in each of the intervals between the breaks is computed as follows:
      With $0–$250,000 total financing:

Source of Capital	Weight	Cost	Weighted Cost
Debt	0.4	8%	3.2%
Common stock	0.6	18%	10.8
			$k_o = \underline{\underline{14.0\%}}$

      With over $250,000 total financing:

Source of Capital	Weight	Cost	Weighted Cost
Debt	0.4	10%	4.0%
Common stock	0.6	22%	13.2
			$k = \underline{\underline{17.2\%}}$

(*c*)   See Fig. 10-2.

(*d*)   Accept projects A and B for a total of $225,000; which is the optimal budget.

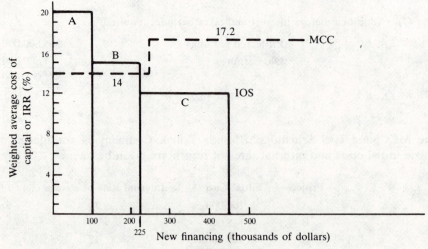

Fig. 10-2

10.18 The MCC and IOS Schedules. John Constas & Company has to decide which of the following
four projects should be selected:

Project	Initial Investment ($)	Internal Rate of Return (%)
A	250,000	16
B	300,000	10
C	100,000	12
D	150,000	13

The company has the following capital structure:

Debt (long-term only)	30%
Equity	70%

The company's last earning per share was $400.

It pays out 50 percent of its earnings as dividends. The company has $210,000 of retained
earnings available for investment purposes. The cost of debt (before taxes) is 10 percent for
the first $180,000. The cost of any additional debt (before taxes) is 14 percent. The company's
tax rate is 40 percent; the current market price of its stock is $43; the flotation cost is
15 percent of the selling price; the expected growth rate in earnings and dividends is 8 percent.

(*a*) How many breaks are there in the MCC schedule, and at what dollar amounts do the
breaks occur? (*b*) What is the weighted cost of capital in each of the intervals between the
breaks? (*c*) Graph the MCC and IOS schedules. (*d*) Which projects should the company
accept and what is the total amount of the optimal capital budget?

SOLUTION

(*a*) There are two breaks in the MCC schedule:

For common stock: $\dfrac{\text{Retained earnings}}{\text{Equity/assets}} = \dfrac{\$210,000}{0.7} = \$300,000$

For debt: $\dfrac{\text{Debt}}{\text{Debt/assets}} = \dfrac{\$180,000}{0.3} = \$600,000$

(*b*) The weighted cost of capital in each of the intervals between the breaks is calculated as follows:
With 0$ − $300,000:

Source of Capital	Weight	After-Tax Cost	Weighted Cost
Debt	0.3	6% [a]	1.8%
Retained earnings	0.7	13% [b]	9.1
			$k_o = \underline{10.9\%}$

[a] $k_d = k_i(1 - t) = 10\%(1 - 0.4) = 6\%$

[b] $k_s = \dfrac{D_1}{P_0} + g = \dfrac{(\$2.00)(1 + 0.08)}{\$43} + 8\% = \dfrac{\$2.16}{\$43} + 8\% = 13.0\%$

With $300,000 − $600,000:

Source of Capital	Weight	After-Tax Cost	Weighted Cost
Debt	0.3	6%	1.80%
External equity	0.7	13.9% [a]	9.73
			$k_o = \underline{11.53\%}$

[a] $k_e = \dfrac{D_1}{P_0(1-f)} + g = \dfrac{(\$2.00)(1 + 0.08)}{\$43(1 - 0.15)} + 8\% = \dfrac{\$2.16}{\$36.55} + 8\% = 13.9\%$

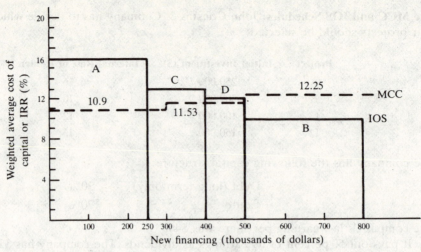

Fig. 10-3

Above $600,000:

Source of Capital	Weight	After-Tax Cost	Weighted Cost
Debt	0.3	8.4% [a]	2.52%
External equity	0.7	13.9	9.73
			$k_o = \underline{\underline{12.25\%}}$

---

[a] $k_d = k_i(1 - t) = 14\%(1 - 0.4) = 8.4\%$

(c) The MCC and IOS schedules are shown in Fig. 10-3.

(d) The company should select projects A, D, and C for a total optimal capital budget of $500,000.

Chapter 11

Leverage and Capital Structure

11.1 LEVERAGE DEFINED

Leverage is that portion of the fixed costs which represents a risk to the firm. *Operating leverage*, a measure of operating risk, refers to the fixed operating costs found in the firm's income statement. *Financial leverage*, a measure of financial risk, refers to financing a portion of the firm's assets, bearing fixed financing charges in hopes of increasing the return to the common stockholders. The higher the financial leverage, the higher the financial risk, and the higher the cost of capital. Cost of capital rises because it costs more to raise funds for a risky business.

11.2 BREAK-EVEN POINT, OPERATING LEVERAGE, AND FINANCIAL LEVERAGE

A discussion of *break-even analysis*, broadly known as *cost/volume/profit analysis*, is necessary for understanding the nature and importance of operating leverage.

Break-Even Analysis

The *break-even point* is the level of sales at which no profit or loss results. To determine the break-even point, the costs must be divided into (1) *variable costs* which are costs that vary in direct proportion to a change in volume, and (2) *fixed costs*, which are costs that are constant regardless of volume.

The break-even point can be found easily by setting sales just equal to the total of the variable costs plus the fixed costs:

Let S = Sales ($)
       X = Sales volume in units
       P = Selling price per unit
      V = Unit variable cost
    VC = Variable operating costs
    FC = Fixed operating costs

Then

$$S = VC + FC$$

$$PX = VX + FC$$

$$(P - V)X = FC$$

$$X = \frac{FC}{P - V}$$

or

$$\frac{\text{Break-even sales}}{\text{in units}} = \frac{\text{fixed operating costs}}{\text{unit selling price} - \text{unit variable cost}}$$

EXAMPLE 11.1 The Wayne Company manufactures and sells doors to home builders. The doors are sold for $25 each. Variable costs are $15 per door, and fixed operating costs total $50,000. The company's break-even point is:

$$X = \frac{FC}{P - V} = \frac{\$50,000}{\$25 - \$15} = 5,000 \text{ doors}$$

Therefore, the company must sell 5,000 doors to break even.

Cash Break-Even Point

If a firm has a minimum of available cash or the opportunity cost of holding excess cash is high, management may want to know the volume of sales that will cover all cash expenses during a period. This is known as the *cash break-even point*.

Not all fixed operating costs involve cash payments. For example, depreciation expenses are noncash charges. To find the cash break-even point, the noncash charges must be subtracted from total fixed operating costs. Therefore, the cash break-even point is lower than the usual break-even point. The formula is:

$$X = \frac{FC - d}{P - V}$$

where d is depreciation expenses.

EXAMPLE 11.2   Assume from Example 11.1 that the total fixed operating costs of $50,000 include depreciation in the amount of $2,000. Then the Wayne Company cash break-even point is:

$$X = \frac{FC - d}{P - V} = \frac{\$50,000 - \$2,000}{\$25 - \$15} = \frac{\$48,000}{\$10} = 4,800 \text{ doors}$$

The company has to sell 4,800 doors to cover only the fixed costs involving cash payments of $48,000 and to break even.

Operating Leverage

Operating leverage is a measure of operating risk and arises from fixed operating costs. A simple indication of operating leverage is the effect that a change in sales has on earnings. The formula is:

$$\text{Operating leverage at a given level of sales } (X) = \frac{\% \text{ change in EBIT}}{\% \text{ change in sales}} = \frac{(P - V)X}{(P - V)X - FC}$$

where

$$\text{EBIT} = \text{earnings before interest and taxes}$$
$$= (P - V)X - FC$$

EXAMPLE 11.3   From Example 11.1, assume that the Wayne Company is currently selling 6,000 doors per year. Its operating leverage is:

$$\frac{(P - V)X}{(P - V)X - FC} = \frac{(\$25 - \$15)(6,000)}{(\$25 - \$15)(6,000) - \$50,000} = \frac{\$60,000}{10,000} = 6$$

which means if sales increase by 10 percent, the company can expect its net income to increase by six times that amount, or 60 percent.

Financial Leverage

Financial leverage is a measure of financial risk and arises from fixed financial costs. One way to measure financial leverage is to determine how earnings per share are affected by a change in EBIT (or operating income).

$$\text{Financial leverage at a given level of sales } (X) = \frac{\% \text{ change in EPS}}{\% \text{ change in EBIT}} = \frac{(P - V)X - FC}{(P - V)X - FC - IC}$$

where EPS is earnings per share, and IC is fixed finance charges, i.e., interest expense or preferred stock dividends. [Preferred stock dividend must be adjusted for taxes i.e., preferred stock dividend/$(1 - t)$.]

EXAMPLE 11.4 Using the data in Example 11.3, the Wayne Company has total financial charges of $2,000, half in interest expense and half in preferred stock dividend. The corporate tax rate is 40 percent. What is their financial leverage? First,

$$IC = \$1,000 + \frac{\$1,000}{(1-0.4)} = \$1,000 + \$1,667 = \$2,667$$

Therefore, Wayne's financial leverage is computed as follows:

$$\frac{(P-V)X - FC}{(P-V)X - FC - IC} = \frac{(\$25 - \$15)(6,000) - \$50,000}{(\$25 - \$15)(6,000) - \$50,000 - \$2,667} = \frac{\$10,000}{\$7,333} = 1.36$$

which means that if EBIT increases by 10 percent, Wayne can expect its EPS to increase by 1.36 times, or by 13.6 percent.

Total Leverage

Total leverage is a measure of total risk. The way to measure total leverage is to determine how EPS is affected by a change in sales.

$$\text{Total leverage at a given level of sales }(X) = \frac{\%\text{ change in EPS}}{\%\text{ change in sales}}$$

$$= \text{operating leverage} \times \text{financial leverage}$$

$$= \frac{(P-V)X}{(P-V)X - FC} \times \frac{(P-V)X - FC}{(P-V)X - FC - IC}$$

$$= \frac{(P-V)X}{(P-V)X - FC - IC}$$

EXAMPLE 11.5 From Examples 11.3 and 11.4, the total leverage for Wayne Company is:

$$\text{Operating leverage} \times \text{financial leverage} = 6 \times 1.36 = 8.16$$

or

$$\frac{(P-V)X}{(P-V)X - FC - IC} = \frac{(\$25 - \$15)(6,000)}{(\$25 - \$15)(6,000) - \$50,000 - \$2,667}$$

$$= \frac{\$60,000}{\$7,333} = 8.18 \text{ (due to rounding error)}$$

11.3 THE THEORY OF CAPITAL STRUCTURE

The theory of capital structure is closely related to the firm's cost of capital. Capital structure is the mix of the long-term sources of funds used by the firm. The primary objective of capital structure decisions is to maximize the market value of the firm through an appropriate mix of long-term sources of funds. This mix, called the *optimal capital structure*, will minimize the firm's overall cost of capital. However, there are arguments about whether an optimal capital structure actually exists. The arguments center on whether a firm can, in reality, affect its valuation and its cost of capital by varying the mixture of the funds used. There are four different approaches to the theory of capital structure:

1. Net operating income (NOI) approach
2. Net income (NI) approach
3. Traditional approach
4. Modigliani-Miller (MM) approach

All four use the following simplifying assumptions:

1. No income taxes are included; they will be removed later.
2. The company makes a 100 percent dividend payout.
3. No transaction costs are incurred.
4. The company has constant earnings before interest and taxes (EBIT).
5. The company has a constant operating risk.

Given these assumptions, the company is concerned with the following three rates:

1.
$$k_i = \frac{I}{B}$$

where k_i = yield on the firm's debt (assuming a perpetuity)
       I = annual interest charges
       B = market value of debt outstanding

2.
$$k_e = \frac{EAC}{S}$$

where k_e = the firm's required rate of return on equity or cost of common equity (assuming
       no earnings growth and a 100 percent dividend payout ratio)
EAC = earnings available to common stockholders
       S = market value of stock outstanding

3.
$$k_o = \frac{EBIT}{V}$$

where k_o = the firm's overall cost of capital (or capitalization rate)
EBIT = earnings before interest and taxes (or operating earnings)
       V = B + S and is the market value of the firm

In each of the four approaches to determining capital structure, the concern is with what happens to k_i, k_e, and k_o when the degree of leverage, as denoted by the debt/equity (B/S) ratio, increases.

The Net Operating Income (NOI) Approach

The net operating income approach suggests that the firm's overall cost of capital, k_o, and the value of the firm's market value of debt and stock outstanding, V, are both independent of the degree to which the company uses leverage. The key assumption with this approach is that k_o is constant regardless of the degree of leverage.

EXAMPLE 11.6   Assume that a firm has $6,000 in debt at 5 percent interest, that the expected level of EBIT is $2,000, and that the firm's cost of capital, k_o, is constant at 10 percent. The market value (V) of the firm is computed as follows:

$$V = \frac{EBIT}{k_o} = \frac{\$2,000}{0.10} = \$20,000$$

The cost of external equity (k_e) is computed as follows:

$$EAC = EBIT - I = \$2,000 - (\$6,000 \times 5\%)$$
$$= \$2,000 - \$300 = \$1,700$$

$$S = V - B = \$20,000 - \$6,000 = \$14,000$$

$$k_e = \frac{EAC}{S} = \frac{\$1,700}{\$14,000} = 12.14\%$$

The debt/equity ratio is

$$\frac{B}{S} = \frac{\$6,000}{\$14,000} = 42.86\%$$

Assume now that the firm increases its debt from $6,000 to $10,000 and uses the proceeds to retire $10,000 worth of stock and also that the interest rate on debt remains 5 percent.

The value of the firm now is:

$$V = \frac{EBIT}{k_o} = \frac{\$2,000}{0.10} = \$20,000$$

The cost of external equity is

$$EAC = EBIT - I = \$2,000 - (\$10,000 \times 5\%)$$
$$= \$2,000 - \$500 = \$1,500$$

$$S = V - B = \$20,000 - \$10,000 = \$10,000$$

$$k_e = \frac{EAC}{S} = \frac{\$1,500}{\$10,000} = 15\%$$

The debt/equity ratio is now:

$$\frac{B}{S} = \frac{\$10,000}{\$10,000} = 100\%$$

Since the NOI approach assumes that k_o remains constant regardless of changes in leverage, the cost of capital cannot be altered through leverage. Hence this approach suggests that there is no one optimal capital structure, as evidenced in Fig. 11-1.

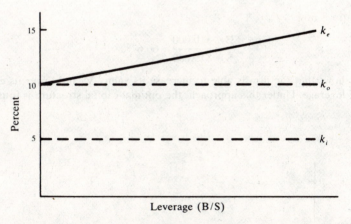

Fig. 11-1 Costs of capital: Net operating income approach

The Net Income (NI) Approach

Unlike the net operating income approach, the net income approach suggests that both the overall cost of capital, k_o and the market value of the firm, V, are affected by the firm's use of leverage. The critical assumption with this approach is that k_i and k_e remain unchanged as the debt/equity ratio increases.

EXAMPLE 11.7 Assume the same data given in Example 11.6 except that k_e equals 10 percent. The value of the firm, V, is computed as follows:

$$EAC = EBIT - I = \$2,000 - (\$6,000 \times 5\%) = \$1,700$$

$$V = S + B = \frac{EAC}{k_e} + B$$

$$= \frac{\$1,700}{0.10} + \$6,000 = \$17,000 + \$6,000 = \$23,000$$

The firm's overall cost of capital is:

$$k_o = \frac{EBIT}{V} = \frac{\$2,000}{\$23,000} = 8.7\%$$

The debt/equity ratio in this case is:

$$\frac{B}{S} = \frac{\$6,000}{\$17,000} = 35.29\%$$

Now assume, as before, that the firm increases its debt from $6,000 to $10,000, uses the proceeds to retire that amount of stock, and that the interest rate on debt remains at 5 percent. Then the value of the firm is:

$$EAC = EBIT - I = \$2,000 - (\$10,000 \times 5\%) = \$1,500$$

$$V = S + B = \frac{EAC}{k_e} + B$$

$$= \frac{\$1,500}{0.10} + \$10,000 = \$15,000 + \$10,000 = \$25,000$$

The overall cost of capital is

$$k_o = \frac{EBIT}{V} = \frac{\$2,000}{\$25,000} = 8\%$$

The debt/equity ratio is now

$$\frac{B}{S} = \frac{\$10,000}{\$15,000} = 66.67\%$$

The NI approach shows that the firm is able to increase its value, V, and lower its cost of capital, k_o, as it increases the degree of leverage. Under this approach, the optimal capital structure is found farthest to the right in Fig. 11-2.

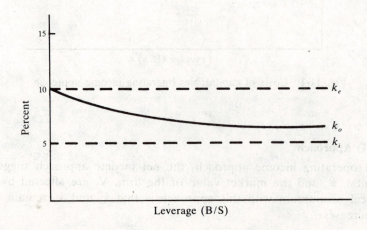

Fig. 11-2 Cost of capital: Net income approach

Traditional Approach

The traditional approach to valuation and leverage assumes that there is an optimal capital structure and that the firm can increase its value through leverage. This is a moderate view of the relationship between leverage and valuation that encompasses all the ground between the NOI approach and the NI approach.

EXAMPLE 11.8 Assume the same data given in Example 11.6. Assume, however, that k_e is 12 percent, rather that the 12.14 percent or 10 percent with the NOI or NI approaches illustrated previously. The value of the firm is:

$$EAC = EBIT - I = \$2,000 - (\$6,000 \times 5\%) = \$1,700$$

$$V = S + B = \frac{EAC}{k_e} + B$$

$$= \frac{\$1,700}{0.12} + \$6,000 = \$14,167 + \$6,000 = \$20,167$$

The overall cost of capital is:

$$k_o = \frac{EBIT}{V} = \frac{\$2,000}{\$20,167} = 9.9\%$$

The debt/equity ratio is:

$$\frac{B}{S} = \frac{\$6,000}{\$14,167} = 42.35\%$$

Assume, as before, that the firm increases its debt from \$6,000 to \$10,000. Assume further that k_i rises to 6 percent and k_e at that degree of leverage is 14 percent. The value of the firm, then, is:

$$EAC = EBIT - I$$
$$= \$2,000 - (\$10,000 \times 6\%) = \$2,000 - \$600 = \$1,400$$

$$V = S + B = \frac{EAC}{k_e} + B$$

$$= \frac{\$1,400}{0.14} + \$10,000 = \$10,000 + \$10,000 = \$20,000$$

The overall cost of capital is:

$$k_o = \frac{EBIT}{V} = \frac{\$2,000}{\$20,000} = 10.0\%$$

The debt/equity ratio is:

$$\frac{B}{S} = \frac{\$10,000}{\$10,000} = 100\%$$

Thus the value of the firm is lower and its cost of capital slightly higher than when the debt is \$6,000. This result is due to the increase in k_e and, to a lesser extent, the increase in k_i. These two observations indicate that the optimal capital structure occurs before the debt/equity ratio equals 100 percent as shown in Fig. 11-3.

Miller-Modigliani (MM) Position

Miller-Modigliani (MM) advocates that the relationship between leverage and valuation is explained by the NOI approach. More specifically, MM's propositions are summarized below.

1. The market value of the firm and its cost of capital are independent of its capital structure.
2. k_e increases so as to exactly offset the use of cheaper debt money.
3. The cutoff rate for capital budgeting decisions is completely independent of the way in which an investment is financed.

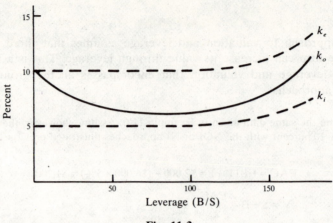

Fig. 11-3

Factors Affecting Capital Structure

Many financial managers believe, in practice, that the following factors influence financial structure:

1. Growth rate of future sales
2. Stability of future sales
3. Competitive structures in the industry
4. Asset makeup of the individual firm
5. Attitude of owners and management toward risk
6. Control position of owners and management
7. Lenders' attitude toward the industry and a particular firm

11.4 EBIT-EPS ANALYSIS

The use of financial leverage has two effects on the earnings that go to the firm's common stockholders: (1) an increased risk in earnings per share (EPS) due to the use of fixed financial obligations, and (2) a change in the level of EPS at a given EBIT associated with a specific capital structure.

The first effect is measured by the degree of financial leverage previously discussed. The second effect is analyzed by means of *EBIT-EPS* analysis. This analysis is a practical tool that enables the financial manager to evaluate alternative financing plans by investigating their effect on EPS over a range of EBIT levels. Its primary objective is to determine the EBIT break-even, or indifference, points among the various alternative financing plans. The indifference points between any two methods of financing can be determined by solving for EBIT in the following equality:

$$\frac{(EBIT - I)(1 - t) - PD}{S_1} = \frac{(EBIT - I)(1 - t) - PD}{S_2}$$

where t = tax rate
          PD = preferred stock dividends
   S_1 and S_2 = number of shares of common stock outstanding after financing for plan 1 and plan 2, respectively.

EXAMPLE 11.9 Assume that ADI Company, with long-term capitalization consisting entirely of $5 million in stock, wants to raise $2 million for the acquisition of special equipment by (1) selling 40,000 shares of common stock at $50 each, (2) selling bonds, at 10 percent interest, or (3) issuing preferred stock with an 8 percent dividend. The present EBIT is $8 million, the income tax rate is 50 percent, and 100,000 shares of common stock are now outstanding. In order to compute the indifference points, we begin by calculating EPS at a projected level of $1 million.

	All Common	All Debt	All Preferred
EBIT	$1,000,000	$1,000,000	$1,000,000
Interest		200,000	
Earnings before taxes (EBT)	$1,000,000	$ 800,000	$1,000,000
Taxes	500,000	400,000	500,000
Earning after taxes (EAT)	$ 500,000	$ 400,000	$ 500,000
Preferred stock dividend			160,000
EAC	$ 500,000	$ 400,000	$ 340,000
Number of shares	140,000	100,000	100,000
EPS	$3.57	$4.00	$3.40

Now connect the EPSs at the level of EBIT of $1 million with the EBITs for each financing alternative on the horizontal axis to obtain the EPS-EBIT graphs. We plot the EBIT necessary to cover all fixed financial costs for each financing alternative on the horizontal axis. For the common stock plan, there are no fixed costs, so the intercept on the horizontal axis is zero. For the debt plan, there must be an EBIT of $200,000 to cover interest charges. For the preferred stock plan, there must be an EBIT of $320,000 [$160,000/(1 − 0.5)] to cover $160,000 in preferred stock dividends at a 50 percent income tax rate; so $320,000 becomes the horizontal axis intercept. See Fig. 11-4.

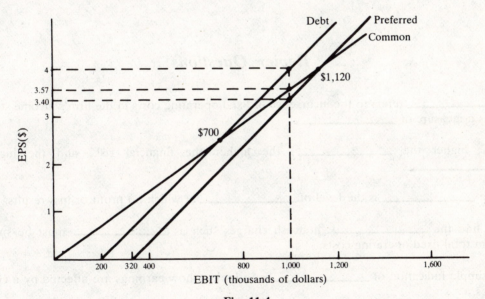

Fig. 11-4

In this example, the indifference point between all common and all debt is:

$$\frac{(\text{EBIT} - \text{I})(1 - t) - \text{PD}}{S_1} = \frac{(\text{EBIT} - \text{I})(1 - t) - \text{PD}}{S_2}$$

$$\frac{(\text{EBIT} - 0)(1 - 0.5) - 0}{140,000} = \frac{(\text{EBIT} - 200,000)(1 - 0.5) - 0}{100,000}$$

Rearranging yields:

$$0.5(\text{EBIT})(100,000) = 0.5(\text{EBIT})(140,000) - 0.5(200,000)(140,000)$$
$$20,000 \; \text{EBIT} = 14,000,000,000$$
$$\text{EBIT} = \$700,000$$

Similarly, the indifference point between all common and all preferred would be:

$$\frac{(EBIT - I)(1 - t) - PD}{S_1} = \frac{(EBIT - I)(1 - t) - PD}{S_2}$$

$$\frac{(EBIT - 0)(1 - 0.5) - 0}{140,000} = \frac{(EBIT - 0)(1 - 0.5) - 160,000}{100,000}$$

Rearranging yields:

$$0.5(EBIT)(100,000) = 0.5(EBIT)(140,000) - 160,000(140,000)$$
$$20,000 \ EBIT = 22,400,000,000$$
$$EBIT = \$1,120,000$$

Based on the above computations, we can draw the following conclusions:

1. At any level of EBIT, debt is better than preferred stock.

2. At a level of EBIT above $700,000, debt is better than common stock. If EBIT is below $700,000, the reverse is true.

3. At a level of EBIT above $1,120,000, preferred stock is better than common. At or below that point, the reverse is true.

Review Questions

1. _____ refers to the incurrence of fixed operating costs in the firm's income statement. It is a measure of _____.

2. The higher the _____, the higher the financial risk, and the higher the _____.

3. The _____ is the level of _____ at which no profit or loss results.

4. To find the _____, noncash charges such as _____ must be subtracted from total fixed operating costs.

5. A simple indication of _____ is to look at how earnings are affected by a change in sales.

6. Total leverage is a measure of _____. It measures how _____ is affected by a change in sales.

7. Total leverage is the _____ of _____ and _____.

8. There are four positions regarding the relationship between valuation and leverage. They are the _____, the _____, the _____ and the _____.

9. Under the _____, there is no such thing as optimal capital structure.

10. The key assumption underlying the net income approach is that the cost of _____ and the cost of _____ remain unchanged as the _____ increases.

11. The _____ to valuation and leverage assumes that there is a(n) _____ capital structure and that the firm can increase _____ through _____ .

12. The primary objective of the _____ is to determine the _____ break-even, or _____ , points between the various alternative financing plans.

13. _____ refers to the mix of long-term financing sources used.

14. Debt has a(n) _____ advantage over preferred stock in that _____ is a tax-deductible expense while _____ are not.

15. The theory of capital structure assumes no _____ and no _____ .

Answers: 1. Operating leverage, operating risk; 2. financial leverage, cost of capital; 3. break-even point, sales; 4. cash break-even point, depreciation; 5. operating leverage; 6. total risk, EPS; 7. product, operating leverage, financial leverage; 8. net income (NI) approach, net operating income (NOI) approach, traditional approach, Miller-Modigliani (MM) approach; 9. net operating income (NOI) approach; 10. common equity, debt, debt/equity ratio; 11. traditional approach, optimal, its value, leverage; 12. EBIT-EPS analysis, EBIT, indifference; 13. Capital structure; 14. tax, interest, preferred stock dividends; 15. income taxes, transaction costs.

Solved Problems

11.1 **Break-Even and Cash Break-Even Points.** The following price and cost data are given for firms A, B, and C:

	A	B	C
Selling price per unit	$25	$12	$15
Variable cost per unit	$10	$6	$5
Fixed operating costs	$30,000	$24,000	$100,000

Calculate (*a*) the break-even point for each firm, and (*b*) the cash break-even point for each firm, assuming $5,000 of each firm's fixed costs are depreciation. (*c*) Rank these firms in terms of their risk.

SOLUTION

(*a*)

$$X = \frac{FC}{P - V}$$

$$\text{Firm A:} \quad \frac{\$30,000}{\$15} = 2,000 \text{ units}$$

$$\text{Firm B:} \quad \frac{\$24,000}{\$6} = 4,000 \text{ units}$$

$$\text{Firm C:} \quad \frac{\$100,000}{\$10} = 10,000 \text{ units}$$

(b)
$$X = \frac{FC - d}{P - V}$$

Firm A: $\dfrac{\$30{,}000 - \$5{,}000}{\$15} = 1{,}667$ units

Firm B: $\dfrac{\$24{,}000 - \$5{,}000}{\$6} = 3{,}167$ units

Firm C: $\dfrac{\$100{,}000 - \$5{,}000}{\$10} = 9{,}500$ units

(c) Firm A seems least risky, followed by B and then C, based on increasing break-even points. It is important to recognize, however, that operating leverage is only one measure of risk.

11.2 Operating and Financial Leverages. John Tripper Soft Drinks, Inc., sells 500,000 bottles of soft drinks a year. Each bottle produced has a variable cost of $0.25 and sells for $0.45. Fixed operating costs are $50,000. The company has current interest charges of $6,000 and preferred dividends of $2,400. The corporate tax rate is 40 percent.

(a) Calculate the degree of operating leverage, the degree of financial leverage, and the degree of total leverage. (b) Do part (a) at the 750,000 bottle sales level. (c) What generalizations can you make comparing (a) to (b) after first finding the break-even point?

SOLUTION

(a)
$$\text{Operating leverage} = \frac{(P - V)X}{(P - V)X - FC}$$

$$= \frac{(\$0.45 - \$0.25)(500{,}000)}{(\$0.45 - \$0.25)(500{,}000) - \$50{,}000} = \frac{\$100{,}000}{\$50{,}000} = 2$$

$$\text{Financial leverage} = \frac{(P - V)X - FC}{(P - V)X - FC - IC^a}$$

$$= \frac{(\$0.45 - \$0.25)(500{,}000) - \$50{,}000}{(\$0.45 - \$0.25)(500{,}000) - \$50{,}000 - \$10{,}000} = \frac{\$50{,}000}{\$50{,}000 - \$10{,}000} = 1.25$$

^{a} $IC = \$6{,}000 + \dfrac{\$2{,}400}{1 - 0.4} = \$6{,}000 + \$4{,}000 = \$10{,}000$

$$\text{Total leverage} = \frac{(P - V)X}{(P - V)X - FC - IC} = \frac{\$100{,}000}{\$40{,}000} = 2.5$$

(b)
$$\text{Operating leverage} = \frac{(0.45 - \$0.25)(750{,}000)}{(\$0.45 - \$0.25)(750{,}000) - \$50{,}000} = \frac{\$150{,}000}{\$100{,}000} = 1.5$$

$$\text{Financial leverage} = \frac{\$100{,}000}{\$100{,}000 - \$10{,}000} = 1.11$$

$$\text{Total leverage} = \frac{\$150{,}000}{\$90{,}000} = 1.667$$

or

$$\text{Total leverage} = 1.5 \times 1.11 = 1.667$$

(c)
$$\text{Break-even point} = \frac{FC}{P - V} = \frac{\$50{,}000}{\$0.45 - \$0.25} = 250{,}000 \text{ units}$$

The degree of operating leverage decreases the further the company moves from break-even operations. The addition of financial leverage to operating leverage magnifies the effect of a change in sales on earnings per share. With financial leverage the break-even point moves to 300,000 units.

$$\frac{\$50,000 + \$10,000}{\$0.45 - \$0.25} = 300,000 \text{ units}$$

11.3 Financial Leverage. Herken Company is a closely held corporation with a capital structure composed entirely of common stock and retained earnings. The stockholders have an agreement with the company that states the company will purchase the stock of a shareholder should a shareholder want to sell his or her holdings in the company. The agreement states that the stock will be purchased at a price equal to the stock's previous year-end book value per share.

Early in October 19X1 Mrs. John Vader, a widow of one of Herken's major stockholders, expressed an interest in selling her stock in accordance with the buy-back pricing arrangement. Mrs. Vader owns 600,000 shares of the 3 million shares of Herken Company common stock.

The board of directors has concluded that the company must replace the capital used to repurchase the shares. The board has assurances that it would be able to finance the acquisition of stock by borrowing the necessary funds on 10-year notes through private placement at an annual interest rate of 10 percent. Thus the company would have capital provided by debt and perhaps be able to take advantage of financial leverage.

The board and Mrs. Vader agreed that the exchange will take place on January 1, 19X2. The book value per share of common stock is projected to be $50 on December 31, 19X1.

The controller of Herken Company had prepared a forecast and pro forma statements for the 19X2 year.

An excerpt of the forecasted earnings statement for the year ended December 31, 19X2, is presented below (in thousands of dollars). Herken used a 40 percent income tax rate in the forecasted statement. The pro forma statements do not reflect the repurchase of Mrs. Vader's shares or the new issue of debt required to pay for the shares.

Income before income taxes	$50,000
Less income taxes (40%)	20,000
Net income	$30,000

(*a*) Revise the excerpt from Herken Company's forecasted earnings statement for the year ended December 31, 19X2, to reflect the long-term debt financing to be used to purchase Mrs. Vader's common stock. Assume the 40 percent tax rate will still be applicable. (*b*) Explain the impact the long-term debt financing would have on Herken Company's earnings per share and return on stockholders' equity using the forecasted data for 19X2. (*c*) Identify and discuss the advantages and disadvantages of financial leverage for a company that has a capital structure similar to that of Herken Company before and after this long-term debt has been added. (CMA, adapted.)

SOLUTION

(*a*)

Herken Company
Revised Profit Forecast
(In Thousands of Dollars)
For the Year Ended Dec. 31, 19X2

Earnings before interest & taxes	$50,000
Interest—new debt ($30,000 × 10%)	3,000
Earnings before tax	$47,000
Income tax (40%)	18,800
Net income	$28,200

With 2,400 shares outstanding, earnings per share is $11.75 and dividends per share (assumed no change) is $0.

(b) The effects of the financial leverage is to increase the earnings per share because the reduction in after-tax earnings caused by the after-tax impact of the interest expense is more than offset by the impact of having fewer shares outstanding. Return on equity would also increase because the book value decreases 20 percent while the earnings are only decreasing by 6 percent (from $30,000 to $28,200).

(c) The basic advantages of financial leverage where the earnings on assets exceed the after-tax cost of the debt are increased earnings per share (EPS) and increased return on equity (ROE). The disadvantages of financial leverage include: (1) the risk that earnings will drop below the cost of debt, which would result in negative financial leverage that would lower both EPS and ROE, (2) increased financial risk to the owners through variability in net income due to the fixed cost associated with debt, and (3) the prospect of increased cost of capital due to creditors' assessment of increased financial risk.

11.4   **The NI Approach.** Equipment Company has earnings before interest and taxes (EBIT) of $10 million. The company currently has outstanding debt of $20 million at a cost of 7 percent. Ignore taxes.

(a) Using the net income (NI) approach and a cost of equity of 12.5 percent, (1) compute the total value of the firm and the firm's overall weighted average cost of capital (k_o), and (2) determine the firm's market debt/equity ratio. (b) Assume that the firm issues an additional $10 million in debt and uses the proceeds to retire stock; the interest rate and the cost of equity remain the same. (1) Compute the new total value of the firm and the firm's overall cost of capital, and (2) determine the firm's market debt/equity ratio.

SOLUTION

(a)
$$\text{EBIT} = \$10,000,000$$
$$I = \$20,000,000 \times 7\% = \$1,400,000$$
$$k_e = 12.5\%$$

(1) The total value of the firm, V, can be found as follows:

$$\text{EAC} = \text{EBIT} - I = \$10,000,000 - \$1,400,000 = \$8,600,000$$
$$S = \frac{\text{EAC}}{k_e} = \frac{\$8,600,000}{0.125} = \$68,800,000$$
$$V = S + B = \$68,800,000 + \$20,000,000 = \$88,800,000$$

Therefore,

$$k_o = \frac{\text{EBIT}}{V} = \frac{\$10,000,000}{\$88,800,000} = 11.26\%$$

(2) The firm's market debt/equity ratio is:

$$\frac{B}{S} = \frac{\$20,000,000}{\$68,800,000} = 29\%$$

(b) (1)
$$I = \$30,000,000 \times 7\% = \$2,100,000$$
$$\text{EAC} = \text{EBIT} - I = \$10,000,000 - \$2,100,000 = \$7,900,000$$
$$S = \frac{\text{EAC}}{k_e} = \frac{\$7,900,000}{0.125} = \$63,200,000$$
$$V = S + B = \$63,200,000 + \$30,000,000 = \$93,200,000$$

Therefore,

$$k_o = \frac{\text{EBIT}}{\text{V}} = \frac{\$10,000,000}{\$93,200,000} = 10.73\%$$

(2)   The debt/equity ratio is:

$$\frac{\text{B}}{\text{S}} = \frac{\$30,000,000}{\$63,200,000} = 47\%$$

11.5   The NOI Approach. Assume the same data as given in Problem 11.4. (*a*) Using the net operating income (NOI) approach and an overall cost of capital of 12 percent, (1) compute the total value, the stock market value of the firm, and the cost of equity; and (2) determine the firm's market debt/equity ratio. (*b*) Determine the answer to (*a*) if the company were to sell the additional $10 million in debt, as in Problem 11.4(*b*).

SOLUTION

(*a*)

$$\text{EBIT} = \$10,000,000$$
$$k_o = 12\%$$
$$\text{EAC} = \$8,600,000$$

(1)

$$\text{V} = \frac{\text{EBIT}}{k_o} = \frac{\$10,000,000}{12\%} = \$83,330,000$$

$$\text{S} = \text{V} - \text{B} = \$83,330,000 - \$20,000,000 = \$63,330,000$$

Therefore,

$$k_e = \frac{\text{EAC}}{\text{S}} = \frac{\$8,600,000}{\$63,330,000} = 13.6\%$$

(2)   The debt/equity ratio is:

$$\frac{\text{B}}{\text{S}} = \frac{\$20,000,000}{\$63,330,000} = 31.58\%$$

(*b*)   (1)

$$\text{S} = \text{V} - \text{B} = \$83,330,000 - \$30,000,000 = \$53,330,000$$

Therefore,

$$k_e = \frac{\text{EAC}}{\text{S}} = \frac{\$8,600,000}{\$53,330,000} = 16.1\%$$

(2)   The debt-equity ratio is:

$$\frac{\text{B}}{\text{S}} = \frac{\$30,000,000}{\$53,330,000} = 56.3\%$$

11.6   The NI Approach. Happy-Day Industries, Inc., is financed entirely with 100,000 shares of common stock selling at $50 per share. The firm's EBIT is expected to be $400,000. The firm pays 100 percent of its earnings as dividends. Ignore taxes.

(*a*) Using the NI approach, compute the total value of the firm and the cost of equity. (*b*) The company has decided to retire $1 million of common stock, replacing it with 9 percent long-term debt. Compute the total value of the firm and the overall cost of capital after refinancing.

SOLUTION

(a) Since there is no debt, B = 0 and I = 0.

$$S = V - B = (100{,}000 \text{ shares} \times \$50) - 0 = \$5{,}000{,}000$$

$$EAC = EBIT - I = \$400{,}000 - 0 = \$400{,}000$$

Therefore,

$$k_e = \frac{EAC}{S} = \frac{\$400{,}000}{\$5{,}000{,}000} = 8\%$$

which is also k_o.

(b)

$$I = \$1{,}000{,}000 \times 9\% = \$90{,}000$$

$$EAC = EBIT - I = \$400{,}000 - \$90{,}000 = \$310{,}000$$

$$S = \frac{EAC}{k_e} = \frac{\$310{,}000}{0.08} = \$3{,}875{,}000$$

$$V = S + B = \$3{,}875{,}000 + \$1{,}000{,}000 = \$4{,}875{,}000$$

Therefore,

$$k_o = \frac{EBIT}{V} = \frac{\$400{,}000}{\$4{,}875{,}000} = 8.2\%$$

11.7 The NOI Approach. Assume the same data as given in Problem 11.6. (a) Using the NOI approach and an overall cost of capital of 10 percent, compute the total value, the stock market value of the firm, and the cost of equity. (b) Determine the answers to (a) if the company decided to retire $1 million of common stock, replacing it with 9 percent long-term debt.

SOLUTION

(a)

$$V = \frac{EBIT}{k_o} = \frac{\$400{,}000}{0.10} = \$4{,}000{,}000$$

$$S = V - B = \$4{,}000{,}000 - \$0 = \$4{,}000{,}000$$

Therefore,

$$k_e = \frac{EAC}{S} = \frac{\$400{,}000}{\$4{,}000{,}000} = 10\%$$

(b)

$$S = V - B = \$4{,}000{,}000 - \$1{,}000{,}000 = \$3{,}000{,}000$$

Therefore,

$$k_e = \frac{EAC}{S} = \frac{\$400{,}000}{\$3{,}000{,}000} = 13.3\%$$

11.8 EPS Calculation. The balance sheet of the Delta Corporation shows a capital structure as follows:

Current liabilities	$ 0
Bonds (6% interest)	100,000
Common stock	900,000
Total claims	$1,000,000

Its rate of return before interest and taxes on its assets of $1 million is 20 percent. The value of each share (whether market or book value) is $30. The firm is in the 50 percent tax bracket. Calculate its earnings per share.

SOLUTION

EBIT (20% × $1,000,000)	$200,000
Less: Interest (6% × $100,000)	6,000
Earnings before tax (EBIT)	$194,000
Less: Income tax (50%)	97,000
Earnings after tax (EAT)	$ 97,000

Number of common shares outstanding is:

$$\frac{\$900,000}{\$30} = 30,000 \text{ shares}$$

$$\text{EPS} = \frac{\$97,000}{30,000 \text{ shares}} = \$3.23$$

11.9 **The EBIT-EPS Analysis.** DMC Corporation currently has 100,000 shares of common stock outstanding with a market price of $50 per share. It also has $2 million in 7 percent bonds (currently selling at par). The company is considering a $4 million expansion program that it can finance with either (I) all common stock at $50 per share, or (II) all bonds at 9 percent. The company estimates that if the expansion program is undertaken, it can attain, in the near future, $1 million in EBIT.

(*a*) The company's tax rate is 40 percent. Calculate the EPS for each plan. (*b*) Draw the EBIT-EPS graph. (*c*) What is the indifference point between the alternatives? (*d*) If the expected EBIT for the near future is greater than your answer in (*c*), what form of financing would you recommend?

SOLUTION

(*a*) The EPS is computed as follows:

	(I) All Stock	(II) All Bonds
EBIT	$1,000,000	$1,000,000
Interest	140,000 [a]	500,000 [b]
EBT	$ 860,000	$ 500,000
Tax (40%)	344,000	200,000
EAT	$ 516,000	$ 300,000
Number of shares	180,000 [c]	100,000
EPS	$2.87	$3.00

[a] $2,000,000 × 7% = $140,000

[b] $4,000,000 × 9% = $360,000

 $360,000 + $140,000 = $500,000

[c] $4,000,000 ÷ $50 per share = 80,000 shares. Therefore,

 100,000 + 80,000 = 180,000 shares

(*b*) The EBIT-EPS graph is shown in Fig. 11-5.

(*c*)
$$\text{EPS} = \frac{(\text{EBIT} - \text{I})(1 - t) - \text{PD}}{\text{Number of shares outstanding}}$$

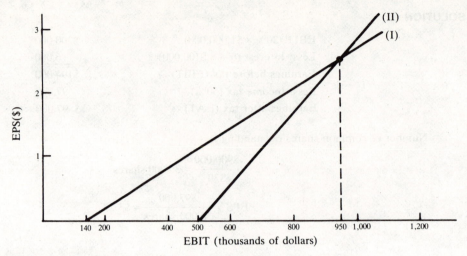

Fig. 11-5

The EBIT-EPS indifference points between plans (I) and (II) are calculated as follows:

$$\text{EPS under plan (I)} = \text{EPS under plan (II)}$$

$$\frac{(\text{EBIT} - 140,000)(1 - 0.4) - 0}{180,000} = \frac{(\text{EBIT} - 500,000)(1 - 0.4) - 0}{100,000}$$

$$(0.6\,\text{EBIT} - 84,000)(100,000) = (0.6\,\text{EBIT} - 300,000)(180,000)$$

$$48,000\,\text{EBIT} = 45,600,000,000$$

$$\text{EBIT} = \$950,000$$

(d) Plan (II), all bonds, is preferred.

11.10 The EBIT-EPS Analysis. Amsterdam Products, Inc., is evaluating two financing plans. Key data are given below. Assume a 50 percent tax rate and an expected EBIT of $400,000.

	Plan A	**Plan B**
Bonds	$80,000 at 9%	$150,000 at 10%
Preferred stock	8,000 shares of $3	4,000 shares of $3.50
Common stock	20,000 shares	23,000 shares

Determine (a) the EPS for each plan, and (b) the financial break-even points for each plan. (c) Draw the EBIT-EPS graph. (d) At what level of EBIT would the company be indifferent as to which of these two plans is selected?

SOLUTION

(a) The earnings per share (EPS) for each plan is given below.

	Plan A	**Plan B**
EBIT	$400,000	$400,000
Interest	7,200	15,000
EBT	$392,800	$385,000
Tax (0.5)	196,400	192,500
EAT	$196,400	$192,500
Preferred stock dividend	24,000	14,000
EAC	$172,400	$178,500
Number of shares outstanding	20,000 shares	23,000 shares
EPS	$8.62	$7.76

(*b*) In order to draw the EBIT-EPS graph for the two plans, two coordinates are needed and are given by the financial break-even points:

For plan A:

$$\$7,200 + \frac{\$24,000}{0.5} = \$55,200$$

For plan B:

$$\$15,000 + \frac{\$14,000}{0.5} = \$43,000$$

In other words, the company must have $55,200 in EBIT under plan A to cover interest charges and preferred stock dividends. It must have $43,000 in EBIT under plan B to cover its interest charges and preferred stock dividends.

(*c*) The EBIT-EPS chart is shown in Fig. 11-6.

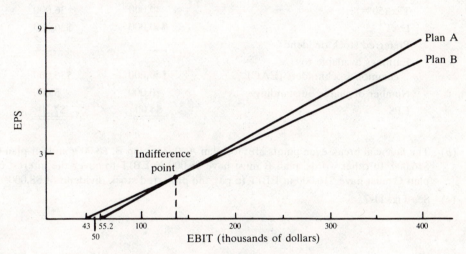

Fig. 11-6

(*d*) The indifference point is calculated as follows:

$$\text{EPS} = \frac{(\text{EBIT} - \text{I})(1 - t) - \text{PD}}{\text{number of shares outstanding}}$$

EPS under plan A = EPS under plan B

$$\frac{(\text{EBIT} - 7,200)(1 - 0.5) - 24,000}{20,000} = \frac{(\text{EBIT} - 15,000)(1 - 0.5) - 14,000}{23,000}$$

$$\frac{0.5\,\text{EBIT} - 3,600 - 24,000}{20,000} = \frac{0.5\,\text{EBIT} - 7,500 - 14,000}{23,000}$$

$$(0.5\,\text{EBIT} - 27,600)(23,000) = (0.5\,\text{EBIT} - 21,500)(20,000)$$
$$1,500\,\text{EBIT} = 204,800,000$$
$$\text{EBIT} = \$136,533$$

Therefore, below the level of $136,533, plan B is preferred; above the level of $136,533, plan A is preferred.

11.11 The EBIT-EPS Analysis. Parker Brothers, Inc., is considering three financing plans. The key information follows. Assume a 50 percent tax rate.

Plan A	Plan B	Plan C
Common stock: $200,000	Bonds at 8%: $100,000	Preferred stock at 8%: $100,000
	Common stock: $100,000	Common stock: $100,000

In each case the common stock will be sold at $20 per share. The expected EBIT is $80,000. Determine (*a*) the EPS for each plan, and (*b*) the financial break-even point for each plan. (*c*) Draw the EBIT-EPS graph. (*d*) Indicate over what EBIT range each plan is preferred.

SOLUTION

(*a*)   The EPS calculation is shown below:

	Plan A	Plan B	Plan C
EBIT	$80,000	$80,000	$80,000
Interest		8,000	
EBT	$80,000	$72,000	$80,000
Tax (50%)	40,000	36,000	40,000
EAT	$40,000	$36,000	$40,000
Preferred stock dividend			8,000
Earnings available to common stockholders (EAC)	$40,000	$36,000	$32,000
Number of shares outstanding	10,000	5,000	5,000
EPS	$4.00	$7.20	$6.40

(*b*)   The financial break-even points are: for plan A, 0; for plan B, $8,000; and for plan C, $8,000 ÷ 0.5 = $16,000. In other words, plan B must have $8,000 in EBIT to cover the interest charge of $8,000; plan C must have $16,000 in EBIT to pay the preferred stock dividend of $8,000.

(*c*)   See Fig. 11-7.

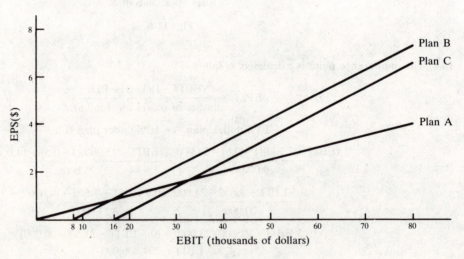

Fig. 11-7

(*d*)   From Fig. 11-7, the EBIT-EPS graph in (*c*), we see that plan B will always dominate plan C at any level of EBIT. Thus, only alternatives A versus B and A versus C need be evaluated. The indifference points are computed as follows:

For plan A versus plan B:

$$\frac{(\text{EBIT} - 0)(1 - 0.5) - 0}{10,000} = \frac{(\text{EBIT} - 8,000)(1 - 0.5) - 0}{5,000}$$

$$0.5 \text{ EBIT}(5,000) = (0.5 \text{ EBIT} - 4,000)(10,000)$$
$$2,500 \text{ EBIT} = 40,000,000$$
$$\text{EBIT} = \$16,000$$

For plan A versus plan C:

$$\frac{(\text{EBIT} - 0)(1 - 0.5) - 0}{10,000} = \frac{(\text{EBIT} - 0)(1 - 0.5) - 8,000}{5,000}$$

$$\frac{0.5 \text{ EBIT}}{10,000} = \frac{0.5 \text{ EBIT} - 8,000}{5,000}$$

$$0.5 \text{ EBIT}(5,000) = (0.5 \text{ EBIT} - 8,000)(10,000)$$
$$2,500 \text{ EBIT} = 5,000 \text{ EBIT} - 80,000,000$$
$$2,500 \text{ EBIT} = 80,000,000$$
$$\text{EBIT} = \$32,000$$

If EBIT is expected to exceed $16,000, plan B is preferred over plan A. If EBIT is expected to exceed $32,000, plan C is preferred over plan A.

11.12 EBIT-EPS Analysis. The Morton Company is planning to invest $10 million in an expansion program which is expected to increase earnings before interest and taxes by $2.5 million. The company currently is earning $5 per share on 1 million shares of common outstanding. The capital structure prior to the investment is:

Debt	$10,000,000
Equity	30,000,000
	$40,000,000

The expansion can be financed by sale of 200,000 shares at $50 net each, or by issuing long-term debt at a 6 percent interest cost. The firm's recent profit and loss statement was as follows:

Sales	$101,000,000
Variable cost	$ 60,000,000
Fixed cost	30,500,000
	$ 90,500,000
Earnings before interest and taxes	$ 10,500,000
Interest	500,000
Earnings before taxes	$ 10,000,000
Taxes (50%)	5,000,000
Earnings after taxes	$ 5,000,000

(a) Assuming the firm maintains its current earnings and achieves the anticipated earnings from the expansion, what will be the earnings per share (1) if the expansion is financed by debt? (2) if the expansion is financed by equity? (b) At what level of earnings before interest and taxes will the earnings per share under either alternative be the same amount? (c) The choice of financing alternatives influences the earnings per share. The choice might also influence the earnings multiple used by the market. Discuss the factors inherent in the choice between the debt and equity alternatives that might influence the earnings multiple. Be sure to indicate the direction in which these factors might influence the earnings multiple. (CMA, adapted.)

SOLUTION

(a)

		(1) Debt-Financed	(2) Equity-Financed
Earnings before interest and taxes—present		$10,500,000	$10,500,000
Added earnings—expansion		2,500,000	2,500,000
		$13,000,000	$13,000,000
Interest		1,100,000	500,000
		$11,900,000	$12,500,000
Taxes		5,950,000	6,250,000
Net income		$ 5,950,000	$ 6,250,000
Common shares outstanding		1,000,000	1,200,000
Earnings per share		$5.95	$5.21

(b)

$$EPS = \frac{(EBIT - I)(1 - t)}{no.\ of\ shares}$$

$$\frac{(EBIT - 1,100,000)(1 - 0.50)}{1,000,000} = \frac{(EBIT - 500,000)(1 - 0.50)}{1,200,000}$$

$$EBIT = \$4,100,000$$

(c) A major factor that is inherent in the choice between debt and equity financing is the change in the risk for the equity holders. If the expansion is financed by debt, the increase in risk appears in two forms. (1) There is increased risk of insolvency because the debt requires regular fixed cash outlay for interest and principal. Equity financing does not incur the legal obligations of the regular cash outlay. (2) The other effect is on the variability of earnings to common stockholders. The fixed charges against income reduces the amount of income available to stockholders. The relative variability of earnings available to common stockholders increases. Both these risks would tend to reduce the earnings multiple. (Note, the market value of a share does not necessarily decrease with the debt expansion.)

11.13 Rate of Return and Optimal Capital Structure. Central Furniture Company recently announced plans to expand its production capacity by building and equipping two new factories to operate in parallel with existing production facilities. The expansion will double the assets of the firm. The proposed expansion has received a lot of attention from industry observers due to the cyclical nature of the furniture industry and the size of the project. The new plants will require fewer workers than current plants of similar capacity because the new facilities will be highly automated.

Central Furniture must now decide how the plant expansion will be financed. The project will require $5 million in new funds and the expected return on the new assets is estimated at 12 percent before taxes, the same return that is currently earned on the existing assets. The two alternatives proposed to raise the needed funds are (1) private placement of long-term debt at an interest rate of 10 percent, and (2) issuance of new common stock at $25 per share. Currently the company is financed equally by debt and equity as follows:

Long-term debt (8%)	$2,500,000
Common stock ($1 par)	$100,000
Paid-in capital on common stock	$400,000
Retained earnings	$2,000,000

Central Furniture's common stock is currently traded on a stock exchange at a market price of $27 per share. Central Furniture is subject to a tax rate of 40 percent.

(a) Compute Central Furniture Company's anticipated rate of return on stockholders' equity if the expansion project is financed by (1) private placement of long-term debt, and (2) issuance of common stock. (b) One of the two alternatives—long-term debt or common stock—will move Central Furniture Company to a more optimum capital structure. (1) What criteria are used to judge optimum capital structure? (2) Explain what factors influence the determination of an optimum capital structure (CMA, adapted.)

SOLUTION

(a) (1)

Earnings before interest and taxes ($10,000,000 × 0.12)		$1,200,000
Less: Interest expense		
Present debt (0.08 × $2,500,000)	$200,000	
New debt (0.10 × $5,000,000)	500,000	700,000
Earnings before taxes		$ 500,000
Taxes (40%)		200,000
Net income		$ 300,000

$$\text{Return on stockholders' equity} = \frac{\$300,000}{\$2,500,000} = 12\%$$

(2)

Earnings before interest and taxes ($10,000,000 × 0.12)		$1,200,000
Less: Interest expense (0.08 × $2,500,000)		200,000
Earnings before taxes		$1,000,000
Taxes (40%)		400,000
Net income		$ 600,000

$$\text{Return on stockholders' equity} = \frac{\$600,000}{\$7,500,000} = 8\%$$

(b) (1) Optimum capital structure is the lowest weighted average cost of capital that a given firm is able to obtain given its risk constraints. (2) The optimum capital structure for a firm is influenced by the relationship of its return to the risks of earning the return. Specific factors influencing these two items would include:

1. The growth rate of income
2. Cash flow available to service debt
3. The amount of operating risk
4. Lender and investor interpretation of the financial risk of the firm and industry

11.14 Alternative Sources of Financing. The Drew Furniture Company is considering the introduction of a new product line. Plant and inventory expansion equal to 50 percent of present asset levels will be necessary to handle the anticipated volume of the new product line. New capital will have to be obtained to finance the asset expansion. Two proposals have been developed to provide the added capital.

1. Raise the $100,000 by issuing 10-year 12 percent bonds. This will change the capital structure from one with about 20 percent debt to one with almost 50 percent debt. The investment banking house estimates the price/earnings ratio, now 12 to 1, will be reduced to 10 to 1 if this method of financing is chosen.

2. Raise the $100,000 by issuing new common stock. The investment banker believes that the stock can be issued to yield $33⅓. The price/earnings ratio would remain at 12 to 1 if the stock were issued. The present market price is $36.

The company's most recent financial statements are as follows:

Drew Furniture Company
Balance Sheet
As of December 31, 19X1

ASSETS		EQUITIES	
Current	$ 65,000	Debt 5%	$ 40,000
Plant and equipment	135,000	Common stock	100,000
		Retained earnings	60,000
	$200,000		$200,000

Income Statement
For the Year Ended December, 31, 19X1

Sales	$600,000
Operating costs	538,000
Operating income	$ 62,000
Interest charges	2,000
Net income before taxes	$ 60,000
Federal income taxes	30,000
Net income	$ 30,000

(*a*) The vice president of finance asks you to calculate the earnings per share and the market value of the stock (assuming the price/earnings ratios given are valid estimates) for the two proposals assuming total sales (including the new product line) of: (1) $400,000, (2) $600,000, and (3) $800,000. Costs exclusive of interest and taxes are about 90 percent of sales. (*b*) Which proposal would you recommend? Your answer should indicate: (1) the criteria used to judge the alternatives, (2) a brief defense of the criteria used, and (3) the proposal chosen in accordance with the criteria. (*c*) Would your answer change if a sales level of $1,200,000 or more could be achieved? Explain. (*d*) What reason(s) would the investment broker give to support the estimate of a lower price/earnings ratio if debt is issued? (CMA, adapted.)

SOLUTION

(*a*)   Proposal 1, for 10-year 12 percent bonds:

Drew Furniture Company
Income Statement
For the Year Ended December 31, 19X1

	Estimated Sales Levels		
	$400,000	$600,000	$800,000
Sales	$400,000	$600,000	$800,000
Operating costs	360,000	540,000	720,000
Operating income	$ 40,000	$ 60,000	$ 80,000
Interest charges	14,000	14,000	14,000
Net income before taxes	$ 26,000	$ 46,000	$ 66,000
Federal income taxes	13,000	23,000	33,000
Net income	$ 13,000	$ 23,000	$ 33,000

$$\text{Outstanding shares} = \frac{30,000}{3} = 10,000$$

Earnings per share	$1.30	$2.30	$3.30
Price/earnings ratio	10 times	10 times	10 times
Estimated market value	$31	$23	$33

Proposal 2, for common stock issue to yield $33\frac{1}{3}$:

Drew Furniture Company
Income Statement
For the Year Ended December 31, 19X1

	Estimated Sales Levels		
Sales	$400,000	$600,000	$800,000
Operating costs	360,000	540,000	720,000
Operating income	$ 40,000	$ 60,000	$ 80,000
Interest charges	2,000	2,000	2,000
Net income before taxes	$ 38,000	$ 58,000	$ 78,000
Federal income taxes	19,000	29,000	39,000
Net income	$ 19,000	$ 29,000	$ 39,000

$$\text{Outstanding shares} = \frac{100,000}{33\frac{1}{3}} + 10,000 = 13,000 \text{ shares}$$

Earnings per share	$1.46	$2.23	$3.00
Price/earnings ratio	12 times	12 times	12 times
Estimated market value	$17.52	$26.76	$36.00

(b) Within the constraints of this problem, two possible objectives emerge: profit maximization as measured by earnings per share, and wealth maximization as measured by the price of the common stock. If profit maximization is used, the firm should choose to finance the new product by selling bonds, since earnings per share is higher for each of the three levels of sales. On the other hand, wealth maximization would require the sale of new common stock because stock price is higher at each sales level.

Wealth maximization is the preferred criterion for financial decision making. Unlike profit maximization, wealth maximization represents a measure of the total benefits to be enjoyed by the shareholders, adjusted for both the timing of benefits and the risk associated with their receipt. A criterion which ignores these two important determinants of value cannot be expected to provide a proper guide to decision making.

Because wealth maximization is the preferred objective, the sale of common stock is the recommended financing technique.

(c) Proposal 2 would still be the choice because the market value remains above that of proposal 1. The difference is smaller than is shown with the lower sales estimates, which means that proposal 1 would become attractive if sales reached a higher level (approximately $1.6 million).

(d) The investment banker would suggest that the lower price/earnings ratio with debt financing is a reflection of the greater returns demanded by stockholders in compensation for the greater variability in earnings and higher risk of bankruptcy created by the fixed commitment to pay debt interest and principal.

Examination II

Chapters 6–11

I. Put a T (true) or F (false) in the space provided below:

_____ **1.** Finding present values is simply the inverse of compounding.

_____ **2.** A perpetuity is an annuity that continues for 20 years.

_____ **3.** Risk is defined as the variation in returns about a standard deviation.

_____ **4.** Through diversification, an investor can reduce the systematic risk, or beta.

_____ **5.** A proxy for the risk-free rate is the Treasury bills yield.

_____ **6.** The cost of capital is the weighted average of the various capital costs.

_____ **7.** Total leverage is the product of operating leverage and financial leverage.

_____ **8.** The optimal capital structure can be defined as the mix of financing sources that minimize the company's debt cost.

_____ **9.** Projects that are negatively correlated tend to be less risky than those that move together in the same direction.

_____ **10.** The NPV method and the IRR approach assume the same rate for reinvestment.

II. Select the best answer:

1. Which of the following takes into account the time value of money?

    (*a*) Average rate of return

    (*b*) Payback period

    (*c*) Internal rate of return

    (*d*) None of the above

2. The NPV method and the IRR method may produce conflicting ranking when

    (*a*) projects are mutually exclusive

    (*b*) projects are independent and not competing for limited funds

    (*c*) both of the above

    (*d*) none of the above

3. Which of the following is concerned with the relationship between the firm's EBIT and EPS?

    (*a*) Beta

    (*b*) Operating leverage

    (*c*) Sales revenue

    (*d*) Financial leverage

4. Through diversification a firm can stabilize its earnings and most effectively reduce its risk when projects are

    (*a*) perfectly positively correlated

    (*b*) independent of each other

    (*c*) perfectly negatively correlated

    (*d*) none of the above

5. Under the CAPM, the required rate of return on a security is the sum of a risk premium and

   (*a*) financial risk
   (*b*) operating risk
   (*c*) diversifiable risk
   (*d*) risk-free rate

6. All the following elements are necessary for the computation of the cost of common stock under the Gordon's growth model, except

   (*a*) tax rate
   (*b*) growth rate in dividends or earnings
   (*c*) market price
   (*d*) dividend

7. Which one of the following must be adjusted for taxes?

   (*a*) Cost of retained earnings
   (*b*) Cost of common stock
   (*c*) Cost of preferred stock
   (*d*) Cost of debt

8. Which of the following is not a method for adjusting for risk in capital budgeting?

   (*a*) Risk-adjusted rate
   (*b*) Simulation
   (*c*) Certainty equivalent approach
   (*d*) Break-even analysis

9. The traditional approach to capital structure implies

   (*a*) there is a minimum cost of capital that is determined by an optimal capital structure
   (*b*) there is no such thing as optimal capital structure
   (*c*) all the above
   (*d*) none of the above

10. The simple expression for the total value of the firm is

   (*a*) stocks/bonds
   (*b*) stocks × bonds
   (*c*) stocks + bonds
   (*d*) none of the above

III.

1. If a firm's earnings and dividends grow from $2.15 per share to $4 per share over an 8-year period, what is the rate of growth?

2. How much would you be willing to pay today for an investment that would return $1,250 each year for the next 10 years, assuming a discount rate of 12 percent?

3. The risk-free rate is 5 percent, the market return is 12 percent and the stock's beta coefficient is 1.25. If the dividend expected during the coming year is $3 and grows at an 8 percent rate, at what price should the stock sell?

4. The Sawyer Company has just issued $10 million of $1,000, 8 percent, 10-year bonds. Due to the current market rates the firm had to sell the bonds at a discount of $40 from their face value. (*a*) Calculate the before-tax cost, or yield to maturity, of the bond, using the shortcut formula, and (*b*) calculate the after-tax cost of the bond, assuming the firm's tax rate is 40 percent.

5. The Desert Products Company is considering six investment proposals of similar risk, for which the funds available are limited. The projects are independent and have the following initial investment and present values of cash inflows associated with them:

Project	Initial Cost (I) ($)	PV ($)
A	15,000	21,000
B	8,000	12,000
C	5,000	7,500
D	4,000	6,400
E	2,000	3,500
F	1,000	1,900

(*A*) Compute the profitability index and NPV for each project. (*b*) Under capital rationing, which projects should be selected, assuming a total budget of $25,000? (*c*) Which projects should be selected if the total budget is reduced to $24,000?

6. A firm is considering two alternative plans to finance a proposed $7 million investment. Plan A: Issue debt (9 percent interest rate). Plan B: Issue common stock (at $20 per share, 1 million shares currently outstanding). The company's income tax rate is 40 percent. (*a*) Calculate the indifference level of EBIT, or the break-even point for each plan, and (*b*) plot these two plans on the EBIT-EPS chart.

7. ABC System, Inc., plans to sell new shares of common stock at $35. The flotation cost is 10 percent. What is the cost of external equity? Both earnings and dividends are expected to grow at a constant rate of 6 percent and the annual dividend per share is $2.

8. Alta-Data, Inc., is considering an investment proposal. The company's board of directors indicated that the firm's present 70 percent owners' equity and 30 percent long-term debt structure should be maintained. The company's projected earnings accompanied by periodic common stock sales will permit it to maintain the present 70 percent owners' equity structure of 40 percentage points from retained earnings and 30 percentage points from common stock.

   After consultation with the firm's investment banker, the company has determined that the debt could be sold to yield 9 percent and new common stock could be sold to provide proceeds of $40 per share to the firm. The company is currently paying a dividend of $2 per share, and the dividends are expected to grow at a constant rate of 6 percent. The firm's income tax rate is 40 percent.

   Calculate the after-tax cost of capital that the company can use for its capital budgeting decision.

Answers to Examination II

I. **1.** T; **2.** F; **3.** F; **4.** F; **5.** T; **6.** T; **7.** T; **8.** F; **9.** T; **10.** F

II. **1.** (*c*); **2.** (*a*); **3.** (*d*); **4.** (*c*); **5.** (*d*); **6.** (*a*); **7.** (*d*); **8.** (*d*); **9.** (*a*); **10.** (*c*)

III.

1.
$$F_n = P \cdot FVIF_{i,n}$$
$$\$4.00 = \$2.15(FVIF_{i,8})$$
$$FVIF_{i,8} = \frac{\$4.00}{\$2.15} = 1.8605$$

From Appendix A, $FVIF_{8\%,8} = 1.8509$. Therefore, the firm's approximate rate of growth is 8 percent.

2.
$$PV = \$1,250(PVIFA_{12\%,10}) = \$1,250(5.6502) = \$7,062.75$$

3.
$$r = r_f + b(r_m - r_f)$$
$$= 5\% + 1.25(12\% - 5\%) = 5\% + 8.75\% = 13.75\%$$

$$P_0 = \frac{D_1}{r - g} = \frac{\$3}{13.75\% - 8\%} = \frac{\$3}{0.0575} = \$52.17$$

4. (*a*)
$$\text{Yield to maturity} = \frac{I + \dfrac{(M - V)}{n}}{\dfrac{(M + V)}{2}} = \frac{\$80 + (\$1,000 - \$960)/10}{(\$1,000 + \$960)/2}$$

$$= \frac{\$80 + \$4}{\$980} = 8.57\%$$

(*b*)
$$\text{After-tax cost of debt} = 8.57\%(1 - 0.4) = 5.14\%$$

5. (*a*) NPV = PV − I and the profitability index is PV/I.

Project	Initial Cost (I) ($)	NPV ($)	Profitability Index (PI)
A	15,000	6,000	1.40
B	8,000	4,000	1.50
C	5,000	2,500	1.50
D	4,000	2,400	1.60
E	2,000	1,500	1.75
F	1,000	900	1.90

(*b*)

Project	I	PV	NPV	PI
A	$ 5,100	$21,000	$ 6,000	1.40
C	5,000	7,500	2,500	1.50
D	4,000	6,400	2,400	1.60
F	1,000	1,900	900	1.90
Totals	$25,000	$36,800	$11,800	

No combination within the $25,000 total budget constraint would show as much NPV as the one listed above. Note that project E is not included even though its 1.75 PI is higher than three of the included projects.

(c)

Project	I	PV	NPV	PI
B	$ 8,000	$12,000	$ 4,000	1.50
C	5,000	7,500	2,500	1.50
D	4,000	6,400	2,400	1.60
E	2,000	3,500	1,500	1.75
F	1,000	1,900	900	1.90
Totals	$20,000	$31,300	$11,300	

It is not necessary to use all the available $24,000 budget in order to maximize NPV. For example, two combinations that do use the entire $24,000 but which have lower NPV are shown below.

Project	I	PV	NPV	PI
A	$15,000	$21,000	$ 6,000	1.40
B	8,000	12,000	4,000	1.50
F	1,000	1,900	900	1.90
Totals	$24,000	$34,900	$10,900	

Project	I	PV	NPV	PI
A	$15,000	$21,000	$ 6,000	1.40
C	5,000	7,500	2,500	1.50
D	4,000	6,400	2,400	1.60
Totals	$24,000	$34,900	$10,900	

6. (a)

$$\frac{(\text{EBIT})(1-0.4)}{1,500,000} = \frac{(\text{EBIT} - \$900,000)(1-0.4)}{1,000,000}$$

$$\text{Break-even EBIT} = \$2,700,000$$

(b) See Fig. E-1.

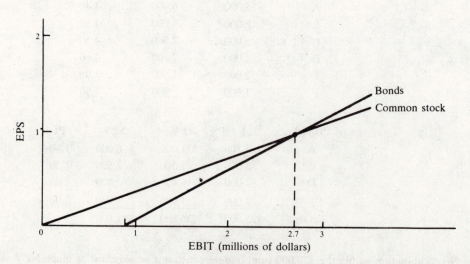

Fig. E-1

7.

$$k_e = \frac{D_1}{P_0(1-f)} + g$$

$$= \frac{\$2.00(1+0.06)}{\$35(1-0.1)} + 6\% = \frac{\$2.12}{\$31.5} + 6\% = 6.7\% + 6\% = 12.7\%$$

8.

$$\text{After-tax cost of debt} = 9\%(1-0.4) = 5.4\%$$

$$\text{Cost of new common stock} = \frac{D_1}{P_0} + g = \frac{\$2.00}{\$40} + 6\% = 11\%$$

$$\text{Cost of retained earnings} = \frac{\$2.00}{\$42} + 6\% = 10.76\%$$

Therefore, the after-tax cost of capital, or weighted average of individual capital component costs, is computed as follows:

	Weights	Weighted Average
Debt, 5.4%	0.3	1.62%
New common stock, 11%	0.4	4.4
Retained earnings, 10.76%	0.3	3.23
After-tax cost of capital		9.25%

Chapter 12

Dividend Policy

12.1 INTRODUCTION

Corporate earnings distributed to stockholders are called dividends. Dividends are paid in either cash or stock and are typically issued quarterly. They may be paid only out of retained earnings and not from invested capital such as capital stock or the excess received over stock par value. In general, the more stable a company's earnings, the more regular its issue of dividends.

A company's dividend policy is important for the following reasons:

1. It bears upon investor attitudes. For example, stockholders look unfavorably upon the corporation when dividends are cut, since they associate the cutback with corporate financial problems. Further, in setting a dividend policy, management must ascertain and fulfill the objectives of its owners. Otherwise, the stockholders may sell their shares, which in turn may bring down the market price of the stock. Stockholder dissatisfaction raises the possibility that control of the company may be seized by an outside group.

2. It impacts the financing program and capital budget of the firm.

3. It affects the firm's cash flow position. A company with a poor liquidity position may be forced to restrict its dividend payments.

4. It lowers stockholders' equity, since dividends are paid from retained earnings, and so results in a higher debt to equity ratio.

If a company's cash flows and investment requirements are volatile, the company should not establish a high regular dividend. It would be better to establish a low regular dividend that can be met even in years of poor earnings.

Relevant dates associated with dividends are as follows:

1. *Declaration date.* This is the date on which the board of directors declares the dividend. On this date, the payment of the dividend becomes a legal liability of the firm.

2. *Date of record.* This is the date upon which the stockholder is entitled to receive the dividend.

3. *Ex-dividend date.* The ex-dividend date is the date when the right to the dividend leaves the shares. The right to a dividend stays with the stock until 4 days before the date of record. That is, on the fourth day prior to the record date, the right to the dividend is no longer with the shares, and the seller, not the buyer of that stock, is the one who will receive the dividend. The market price of the stock reflects the fact that it has gone ex-dividend and will decrease by approximately the amount of the dividend.

EXAMPLE 12.1 The date of record for the dividend declared by the Acme Company is October 20. Harris sells Jones her 100 shares of Acme Company on October 18. Harris, not Jones, will receive the dividend on the shares.

4. *Date of payment.* This is the date when the company distributes its dividend checks to its stockholders.

Dividends are usually paid in cash. A cash dividend is typically expressed in dollars and cents per share. However, the dividend on preferred stock is sometimes expressed as a percentage of par value.

EXAMPLE 12.2 On November 15, 19X1, a cash dividend of $1.50 per share was declared on 10,000 shares of $10 par value common stock. The amount of the dividend paid by the company is $15,000 (10,000 × $1.50).

EXAMPLE 12.3   Jones Corporation has 20,000 shares of $10 par value, 12 percent preferred stock outstanding. On October 15, 19X1, a cash dividend was declared to holders of record as of December 15, 19X1. The amount of dividend to be paid by Jones Corporation is equal to:

$$20,000 \text{ shares} \times \$10 \text{ par value} = \$200,000 \times 12\% = \$24,000$$

Some companies allow stockholders to automatically reinvest their dividend in corporate shares instead of receiving cash. The advantage to the stockholder is that he or she avoids the brokerage fees associated with buying new shares. However, there is no tax advantage since the stockholder must still pay ordinary income taxes on the dividend received.

12.2   DIVIDEND POLICY

A finance manager's objectives for the company's dividend policy is to maximize owner wealth while providing adequate financing for the company. When a company's earnings increase, management does not automatically raise the dividend. Generally, there is a time lag between increased earnings and the payment of a higher dividend. Only when management is confident that the increased earnings will be sustained will they increase the dividend. Once dividends are increased, they should continue to be paid at the higher rate. The various types of dividend policies are:

1. *Stable dividend-per-share policy.* Many companies use a stable dividend-per-share policy since it is looked upon favorably by investors. Dividend stability implies a low-risk company. Even in a year that the company shows a loss rather than profit the dividend should be maintained to avoid negative connotations to current and prospective investors. By continuing to pay the dividend, the shareholders are more apt to view the loss as temporary. Some stockholders rely on the receipt of stable dividends for income. A stable dividend policy is also necessary for a company to be placed on a list of securities in which financial institutions (pension funds, insurance companies) invest. Being on such a list provides greater marketability for corporate shares.

2. *Constant dividend-payout-ratio (dividend per share/earnings per share) policy.* With this policy a constant percentage of earnings is paid out in dividends. Because net income varies, dividends paid will also vary using this approach. The problem this policy causes is that if a company's earnings drop drastically or there is a loss, the dividends paid will be sharply curtailed or nonexistent. This policy will not maximize market price per share since most stockholders do not want variability in their dividend receipts.

3. *A compromise policy.* A compromise between the policies of a stable dollar amount and a percentage amount of dividends is for a company to pay a low dollar amount per share plus a percentage increment in good years. While this policy affords flexibility, it also creates uncertainty in the minds of investors as to the amount of dividends they are likely to receive. Stockholders generally do not like such uncertainty. However, the policy may be appropriate when earnings vary considerably over the years. The percentage, or extra, portion of the dividend should not be paid regularly; otherwise it becomes meaningless.

4. *Residual-dividend policy.* When a company's investment opportunities are not stable, management may want to consider a fluctuating dividend policy. With this kind of policy the amount of earnings retained depends upon the availability of investment opportunities in a particular year. Dividends paid represent the *residual* amount from earnings after the company's investment needs are fulfilled.

Theoretical Position

Theoretically, a company should retain earnings rather than distribute them when the corporate return exceeds the return investors can obtain on their money elsewhere. Further, if the company obtains a return on its profits that exceeds the cost of capital, the market price of its stock will be maximized. Capital gains arising from the appreciation of the market price of stock has a tax advantage over dividends. On the other hand, a company should not, theoretically, keep funds for investment if it earns less of a return than what the investors can earn elsewhere. If the owners have better investment opportunities outside the firm, the company should pay a high dividend.

Although theoretical considerations from a financial point of view should be considered when setting dividend policy, the practicality of the situation is that investors expect to be paid dividends. Psychological factors come into play which may adversely affect the market price of the stock of a company that does not pay dividends.

12.3   FACTORS THAT INFLUENCE DIVIDEND POLICY

A firm's dividend policy is a function of many factors, some of which have been described. Other factors that influence dividend policy are as follows:

1.   *Company growth rate.* A company that is rapidly growing, even if profitable, may have to restrict its dividend payments in order to keep needed funds within the company for growth opportunities.

2.   *Restrictive covenants.* Sometimes there is a restriction in a credit agreement that will limit the amount of cash dividends that may be paid.

3.   *Profitability.* Dividend distribution is keyed to the profitability of the company.

4.   *Earnings stability.* A company with stable earnings is more likely to distribute a higher percentage of its earnings than one with unstable earnings.

5.   *Maintenance of control.* Management that is reluctant to issue additional common stock because it does not wish to dilute its control of the firm will retain a greater percentage of its earnings. Internal financing enables control to be kept within.

6.   *Degree of financial leverage.* A company with a high debt-to-equity ratio is more likely to retain earnings so that it will have the needed funds to meet interest payments and debts at maturity.

7.   *Ability to finance externally.* A company that is capable of entering the capital markets easily can afford to have a higher dividend payout ratio. When there is a limitation to external sources of funds, more earnings will be retained for planned financial needs.

8.   *Uncertainty.* Payment of dividends reduces the chance of uncertainty in stockholders' minds about the company's financial health.

9.   *Age and size.* The age and size of the company bear upon its ease of access to capital markets.

10.   *Tax penalties.* Possible tax penalties for excess accumulation of retained earnings may result in high dividend payouts.

Stockholder Tax Considerations

The answer to the question of which is preferred by stockholders—income from dividends or from capital gains (sale of stock)—depends on the individual stockholder's tax bracket. Capital gains arising from appreciation in market price is subject to a long-term capital gain deduction. Only 40 percent of the gain on the sale of stock that has been held more than 6 months is subject to taxation. Of course, a broker's commission will have to be paid on the sale. Dividends are considered ordinary income and are taxed at the full rate (less a $100 dividend exclusion). Taxpayers in low tax brackets or those who rely on a fixed income favor greater dividend distribution. The theoretical dispute regarding dividend policy relates to investor psychology in terms of whether earnings should be taken as capital gains or as dividends.

EXAMPLE 12.4 Ms. Smith is in the 45 percent tax bracket. She sells stock that she has held for more than 6 months at a gain of $50,000. Her tax computation on the sale follows:

Gain	$50,000
Capital gain deduction	×40%
Gain subject to tax	$20,000
Tax rate	×45%
Tax	$ 9,000

Controversy

The dividend policy controversy can best be described by presenting the approaches put forth by various authors:

1. Gordon et al. believe that cash flows of a company having a low dividend payout will be capitalized at a higher rate because investors will perceive capital gains resulting from earnings retention to be more risky than dividends.

2. Miller and Modigliani argue that a change in dividends impacts the price of the stock since investors will perceive such a change as being a statement about expected future earnings. They believe that investors are generally indifferent to a choice between dividends or capital gains.

3. Weston and Brigham et al. believe that the best dividend policy varies with the particular characteristics of the firm and its owners, depending on such factors as the tax bracket and income needs of stockholders, and corporate investment opportunities.

12.4 STOCK DIVIDENDS

A stock dividend is the issuance of additional shares of stock to stockholders. A stock dividend may be declared when the cash position of the firm is inadequate and/or when the firm wishes to prompt more trading of its stock by reducing its market price. With a stock dividend, retained earnings decrease but common stock and paid-in capital on common stock increase by the same total amount. A stock dividend, therefore, provides *no change* in stockholders' wealth. Stock dividends increase the shares held, but the proportion of the company each stockholder owns remains the same. In other words, if a stockholder has a 2 percent interest in the company before a stock dividend, he or she will continue to have a 2 percent interest after the stock dividend.

EXAMPLE 12.5 Mr. James owns 200 shares of Newland Corporation. There are 10,000 shares outstanding; therefore, Mr. James holds a 2 percent interest in the company. The company issues a stock dividend of 10 percent. Mr. James will then have 220 shares out of 11,000 shares issued. His proportionate interest remains at 2 percent (220/11,000).

12.5 STOCK SPLIT

A stock split involves issuing a substantial amount of additional shares and reducing the par value of the stock on a proportional basis. A stock split is often prompted by a desire to reduce the market price per share, which will make it easier for small investors to purchase shares.

EXAMPLE 12.6 Smith Corporation has 1,000 shares of $20 par value common stock outstanding. The total par value is $20,000. A 4-for-1 stock split is issued. After the split 4,000 shares at $5 par value will be outstanding. The total par value thus remains at $20,000. Theoretically, the market price per share of the stock should also drop to one-fourth of what it was before the split.

The differences between a stock dividend and a stock split are as follows:

(1) With a stock dividend, retained earnings are reduced and there is a pro rata distribution of shares to stockholders. A stock split increases the shares outstanding but does not lower retained earnings.

(2) The par value of stock remains the same with a stock dividend but is proportionally reduced in a stock split.

The similarities between a stock dividend and a stock split are:

(1) Cash is not paid.

(2) Shares outstanding increase.

(3) Stockholders' equity remains the same.

12.6 STOCK REPURCHASES

Treasury stock is the name given to previously issued stock that has been purchased by the company. Buying treasury stock is an alternative to paying dividends. Since outstanding shares will be fewer after stock has been repurchased, earnings per share will rise (assuming net income is held constant). The increase in earnings per share may result in a higher market price per share.

EXAMPLE 12.7 Travis Company earned $2.5 million in 19X1. Of this amount, it decided that 20 percent would be used to purchase treasury stock. At present there are 400,000 shares outstanding. Market price per share is $18. The company can use $500,000 (20% × $2.5 million) to buy back 25,000 shares through a tender offer of $20 per share.

Current earnings per share is:

$$\text{EPS} = \frac{\text{net income}}{\text{outstanding shares}} = \frac{\$2,500,000}{400,000} = \$6.25$$

The current P/E multiple is:

$$\frac{\text{Market price per share}}{\text{Earnings per share}} = \frac{\$18}{\$6.25} = 2.88 \text{ times}$$

Earnings per share after treasury stock is acquired becomes:

$$\frac{\$2,500,000}{375,000} = \$6.67$$

The expected market price, assuming the P/E ratio remains the same, is:

$$\text{P/E multiple} \times \text{new earnings per share} = \text{expected market price}$$
$$2.88 \times \$6.67 = \$19.21$$

To stockholders, the advantages arising from a stock repurchase include the following: (1) If market price per share goes up as a result of the repurchase, stockholders can take advantage of the capital gain deduction. This assumes the stock is held more than 6 months and is sold at a gain. (2) Stockholders have the option of selling or not selling the stock, while if a dividend is paid, stockholders must accept it and pay tax.

To the company, the advantages from a stock repurchase include the following:

(1) If there is excess cash flow that is deemed temporary, management may prefer to repurchase stock than to pay a higher dividend that they feel cannot be maintained.

(2) Treasury stock can be used for future acquisitions or used as a basis for stock options.

(3) If management is holding stock, they would favor a stock repurchase rather than a dividend because of the favorable tax treatment.

(4) Treasury stock can be resold in the market if additional funds are needed.

To stockholders, the disadvantages of treasury stock acquisitions include the following:

(1) The market price of stock may benefit more from a dividend than a stock repurchase.

(2) Treasury stock may be bought at an excessively high price to the detriment of the remaining stockholders. A higher price may occur when share activity is limited or when a significant amount of shares are reacquired.

To management, the disadvantages of treasury stock acquisition include the following:

(1) If investors feel that the company is engaging in a repurchase plan because its management does not have alternative good investment opportunities, a drop in the market price of stock may ensue.

(2) If the reacquisition of stock makes it appear that the company is manipulating the price of its stock on the market, the company will have problems with the Securities and Exchange Commission (SEC). Further, if the Internal Revenue Service (IRS) concludes that the repurchase is designed to avoid the payment of tax on dividends, tax penalties may be imposed because of the improper accumulation of earnings as specified in the tax code.

Review Questions

1. The basic types of dividends are _____ and _____ .

2. Dividends are usually issued _____ .

3. The date that a dividend becomes a legal liability of the corporation is called the _____ .

4. The right to a dividend stays with the stock until _____ days before the date of record.

5. The receipt of dividends is favored by stockholders in _____ tax brackets.

6. The dividend payout ratio is equal to _____ divided by _____ .

7. Under a residual-dividend policy, dividends are paid _____ the firm's investment needs have been satisfied.

8. A stock dividend provides _____ real income for investors.

9. Mr. X owned 100 shares of $10 par value stock. He then received in exchange 200 shares of $5 par value stock. This is referred to as a(n) _____ .

10. _____ refers to shares reacquired by the company.

Answers: (1) cash, stock; (2) quarterly; (3) declaration date; (4) 4; (5) lower; (6) dividends per share, earnings per share; (7) after; (8) no; (9) stock split; (10) Treasury stock.

Solved Problems

12.1 **Dividends per Share.** Lakeside Corporation's net income for 19X1 was $300,000. It retained 40 percent. The outstanding shares are 100,000. Determine the dividends per share.

SOLUTION

$$\frac{\text{Dividends}}{\text{Shares}} = \frac{\$300,000 \times 60\%}{100,000 \text{ shares}} = \frac{\$180,000}{100,000} = \$1.80$$

12.2 **Cash Dividend.** The Dover Corporation has 10,000 shares of common stock outstanding. On March 5, the company declared a cash dividend of $5 per share payable to stockholders of record on April 5. What is the amount of the dividend?

SOLUTION

$$10,000 \times \$5 = \$50,000$$

12.3 **Tax.** Ms. Jones is in the 35 percent tax bracket. How much tax will she have to pay in each of the following cases?

(*a*)   Dividend income = $10,000

(*b*)   Long-term capital gain = $10,000

SOLUTION

(*a*) $10,000 − $100 (dividend exclusion) = $9,900 × 35% = $3,465

(*b*) $10,000 × 40% (capital gain rate) = $4,000 taxable × 35% = $1,400

12.4 **Dividend Policy.** Robert Corporation pays out 70 percent of its earnings in the form of dividends.

(*a*) Evaluate this policy assuming most stockholders are senior citizens in low tax brackets.

(*b*) Evaluate this policy assuming most stockholders are in high tax brackets.

SOLUTION

(*a*) A high dividend payout is appropriate in the case of senior citizens since they rely on the fixed income. Because they are in a low tax bracket, capital gains will not help them that much.

(*b*) A low dividend payout is called for with high-tax-bracket stockholders. Dividends serve as ordinary income. Capital gains is most beneficial for them since only 40 percent of the gain is taxable for securities held more than 6 months.

12.5 **Market Price per Share.** Company A and company B are identical in every respect except for their dividend policies. Company A pays out a constant percentage of its net income (60 percent dividends), while company B pays out a constant dollar dividend. Company B's market price per share is higher than that of company A. The financial manager of company A does not understand why her market price per share is lower even though in some good years company A's dividends exceed those of company B. Explain.

SOLUTION

The reason why company B has a higher market price per share than company A is because the stock market looks favorably upon stable dollar dividends. They reflect less uncertainty about the firm.

12.6   External Equity to Be Issued. Travis Company's net income for the year was $3 million. It pays out 30 percent of its earnings in dividends. The company will acquire $5 million in new assets of which 35 percent will be financed by debt. What is the amount of external equity that must be issued?

SOLUTION

Net income	$3,000,000
Percent of net income retained	×0.7
Retained earnings	$2,100,000
New assets	$5,000,000
Percent financed by equity	×0.65
Equity financing required	$3,250,000
Retained earnings	2,100,000
External equity to be issued	$1,150,000

12.7   Dividend Payout. Most Corporation had a net income of $800,000 in 19X1. Earnings have grown at an 8 percent annual rate. Dividends in 19X1 were $300,000. In 19X2, the net income was $1,100,000. This, of course, was much higher than the typical 8 percent annual growth rate. It is anticipated that earnings will go back to the 8 percent rate in future years. The investment in 19X2 was $700,000.

How much dividends should be paid in 19X2 assuming: (*a*) a stable dividend payout ratio of 25 percent? (*b*) a stable dollar dividend policy is maintained? (*c*) a residual-dividend policy is maintained and 40 percent of the 19X2 investment is financed with debt? (*d*) the investment for 19X2 is to be financed with 80 percent debt and 20 percent retained earnings? Any net income not invested is paid out in dividends

SOLUTION

(*a*) $1,100,000 × 25\% = $275,000

(*b*)   Dividend in 19X2 is:

$$\$300,000 \times 1.08 = \$324,000$$

(*c*)   The equity needed is:

$$\$700,000 \times 60\% = \$420,000$$

Because net income is greater than the equity needed, all the $420,000 of equity investment will be derived from net income.

$$\text{Dividend} = \$1,100,000 - \$420,000 = \$680,000$$

(*d*)   Earnings retained = $700,000 × 20\% = $140,000

$$\text{Dividend} = \text{net income} - \text{earnings retained}$$
$$\$960,000 = \$1,100,000 - \$140,000$$

12.8   Trend in Dividends. Many corporations attempt to maintain a sustained rather than a fluctuating cash dividend per share payment. The payment is gradually adjusted to changes in earnings over time. As a consequence, corporations apparently establish a target payout ratio range. Explain why corporation managements desire sustained cash dividends per share with an increasing trend and attempt to avoid fluctuating cash dividend payments. (CMA, adapted.)

SOLUTION

Corporations tend to follow a policy of sustained cash dividends per share with an increasing and stable trend over time because they believe that such a dividend policy helps maintain or increase the firm's common stock price over time. Corporations following this policy feel that investors will pay a higher price for the stock of a firm with a stable dividend policy because stability provides investors with a reduced level of uncertainty regarding the cash returns provided by the firm.

Another argument for a stable dividend policy leading to higher stock price is that many investors look at cash dividends as a source of funds for their living expenses. Such investors cannot easily plan their income when dividends are fluctuating. Thus, to assist their planning, investors will pay a premium for stock with stable dividend policies.

12.9   Dividend Payout. The Xylon Company has experienced rapid growth in the past 5 years. In order to finance the growth, the board of directors has followed a policy of controlled borrowing, a low dividend payout ratio, and regular stock dividends.

The percent of debt in the capital structure has remained constant since 19X0. The funds generated from operations have been reinvested in productive assets. Each January, for the past 4 years, Xylon's board of directors has declared and paid a 10 percent dividend. A $0.20 per share cash dividend on the stock outstanding on June 15 has been paid each July for the past 5 years. Management estimates that the earnings for 19X7 will be $250,000. The closing price of Xylon Company's stock at November 30, 19X7 was $25.50 per share.

The board anticipates a challenge to its intention to continue this dividend policy by two stockholders who are survivors of two of the founders. Selected data related to the company's earnings and dividends are presented below:

Year	Earnings ($)	Shares Outstanding as of Dec. 31	Cash Dividends		Market Price per Share as of Dec. 31 ($)
			Per Share ($)	Total Payout ($)	
19X2	100,000	100,000	0.20	20,000	10.00
19X3	120,000	110,000	0.20	22,000	12.00
19X4	144,000	121,000	0.20	24,200	14.30
19X5	172,800	133,100	0.20	26,620	17.00
19X6	207,360	146.410	0.20	29,282	22.00

Prepare a response from the perspective of Xylon Company's board of directors which (*a*) justifies the low cash dividend payout, and (*b*) rationalizes the use of stock dividends. (CMA, adapted.)

SOLUTION

(*a*)   The low cash dividend payout is required to finance from internal sources investment opportunities which exceed the cost of capital in order to continue the income and market value growth pattern established. Financing growth through retained earnings has been good for the company and the stockholders, as demonstrated by the increased earnings per share, the increased market price per share, and the increase in total cash dividends paid because of the annual stock dividends.

(*b*)   The continued use of stock dividends allows stockholders who need cash to sell a few shares without reducing the original number of shares owned. In addition, those sales can be taxed at the capital gains rate as opposed to ordinary income rates. This may be important to the shareholders of this company because they are wealthy and likely to be in high tax brackets. The use of stock dividends increases the payout in future years even though the dividend rate per share does not increase.

12.10   Stock Dividend. The Benson Corporation has 9,000 shares of common stock having a par value of $120 outstanding. A 10 percent stock dividend is declared. The fair market value of the stock is $124 per share.

(a) By how much will retained earnings be reduced? (b) What is the par value of the common stock to be issued? (c) What is the paid-in capital on common stock?

SOLUTION

(a) $$9,000 \text{ shares} \times 10\% = 900 \text{ shares} \times \$124 = \$111,600$$

(b) $$900 \text{ shares} \times \$120 = \$108,000$$

(c) $$900 \text{ shares} \times \$4 = \$3,600$$

12.11 Reformulated Capital Structure. Blake Company's capital structure on December 30, 19X1, was:

Common stock ($1 par, 100,000 shares)	$100,000
Paid-in capital on common stock	20,000
Retained earnings	680,000
Total stockholders' equity	$800,000

The company's net income for 19X1 was $150,000. It paid out 40 percent of earnings in dividends. The stock was selling at $6 per share on December 30.

Assuming the company declared a 5 percent stock dividend on December 31, what is the reformulated capital structure on December 31?

SOLUTION

The stock dividend is 5,000 shares (5% × 100,000 shares). Retained earnings is reduced by the fair market value of the stock dividend of $30,000 ($6 × 5,000 shares), paid-in capital on common stock is increased by $25,000 ($5 × 5,000 shares), and common stock is increased at the par value of the shares issued of $5,000 ($1 × 5,000 shares).

The reformulated capital structure on December 31 is:

Common stock ($100,000 + $5,000)	$105,000
Paid-in capital on common stock ($20,000 + $25,000)	45,000
Retained earnings ($680,000 − $30,000)	650,000
	$800,000

Notice that after the stock dividend, total stockholders' equity remains the same.

12.12 Stock Split. The Simpson Company has 50,000 shares of common stock having a par value of $12 per share. The board of directors decided on a 2-for-1 stock split. The market price of the stock was $20 before the split.

(a) Record the stock split. (b) What will the market price per share be immediately after the split?

SOLUTION

(a) No entry is needed since the company's account balances remain the same. However, there should be a memorandum to the effect that there are now 100,000 shares having a par value of $6 per share.

(b) $10 ($20/2)

12.13 Dividend Last Year. Subsequent to a 3-for-1 stock split, Ace Corporation paid a dividend of $5 per share. This was a 10 percent increase over the prior year's dividend (before the split). Determine the dividend for last year.

SOLUTION

Dividend subsequent to split is: $5 × 3 = $15. Last year's dividend is:

$$\frac{\$15}{1.10} = \$13.64$$

12.14 Earnings per Share. Blake Company's net income for 19X2 was $3 million. Of this amount, 40 percent will be used to purchase treasury stock. Currently, there are 1 million shares outstanding and the market price per share is $9.

(*a*) How many shares can the company buy back through a tender offer of $12 a share? (*b*) What is the current earnings per share? (*c*) What is the current P/E ratio? (*d*) What will earnings per share be after the treasury stock acquisition? (*e*) What is the expected market price per share assuming the present P/E ratio remains the same?

SOLUTION

(*a*) Funds available for repurchase of stock are computed as follows:

$$\$3 \text{ million} \times 40\% = \$1,200,000$$

Shares to be repurchased are computed as follows:

$$\frac{\$1,200,000}{\$12} = 100,000 \text{ shares}$$

(*b*)
$$\text{EPS} = \frac{\text{net income}}{\text{shares outstanding}} = \frac{\$3,000,000}{1,000,000} = \$3$$

(*c*)
$$\text{P/E ratio} = \frac{\text{market price per share}}{\text{earnings per share}} = \frac{\$9}{\$3} = 3 \text{ times}$$

(*d*)
$$\text{EPS} = \frac{\$3,000,000}{900,000} = \$3.333$$

(*e*)
$$\text{Market price per share} = \text{P/E ratio} \times \text{new EPS}$$
$$3 \quad \times \quad \$3.333 = \$10$$

Chapter 13

Term Loans and Leasing

13.1 INTERMEDIATE-TERM BANK LOANS

Intermediate-term loans are loans with a maturity of more than 1 year. Intermediate-term loans are appropriate when short-term unsecured loans are not, such as when a business is acquired. The interest rate on an intermediate-term loan is generally higher than on a short-term loan because of the longer maturity date. The interest rate may be either fixed or variable (according to, for example, changes in the prime interest rate). The cost of an intermediate-term loan varies with the amount of the loan and the financial strength of the borrower.

Ordinary intermediate-term loans are payable in periodic equal installments except for the last payment, which may be higher (referred to as a balloon payment). The schedule of loan payments should be based on the borrower's cash flow position to satisfy the debt.

The amortization payment in a term loan equals:

$$\text{Amortization payment} = \frac{\text{amount of loan}}{\text{present value factor}}$$

EXAMPLE 13.1 XYZ Company contracts to repay a term loan in five equal year-end installments. The amount of the loan is $150,000 and the interest rate is 10 percent. The amortization payment each year is:

$$\text{Amortization payment} = \frac{\text{amount of loan}}{\text{present value factor}} = \frac{\$150,000}{3.7908^a} = \$39,569.48$$

----

[a] Present value of annuity for 5 years at 10 percent.

EXAMPLE 13.2 Charles Company takes out a term loan in 20 year-end annual installments of $2,000 each. The interest rate is 12 percent. The amount of the loan is:

$$\text{Amortization payment} = \frac{\text{amount of loan}}{\text{present value factor}}$$

$$\$2,000 = \frac{\text{amount of loan}}{7.4694^a}$$

$$\text{Amount of loan} = \$2,000 \times 7.4694 = \$14,938.80$$

----

[a] Present value of annuity for 20 years at 12 percent.

The amortization schedule for the first 2 years is:

Year	Payment	Interest[a]	Principal	Balance
0				$14,938.80
1	$2,000	$1,792.66	$207.34	$14,731.46
2	$2,000	$1,767.78	$232.22	$14,499.24

----

[a] 12 percent times the balance of the loan at the beginning of the year.

Revolving credit, typically used for seasonal financing, may have a 3-year maturity, but the notes evidencing the revolving credit are short-term, typically 90 days. The advantages of revolving credit are flexibility and readily available credit. Within the time period of the revolving credit agreement, the company may renew a loan or engage in additional financing up to a specified maximum amount.

Compared to a line of credit arrangement, there are generally fewer restrictions on revolving credit but at the cost of a slightly higher interest rate.

Restrictive provisions to protect the lender in an intermediate-term loan agreement may be in the form of:

1. General provisions used in most agreements which vary depending upon the borrower's situation. Examples are working capital and cash dividend requirements.

2. Routine (uniform) provisions that are used universally in most agreements. Examples are the payment of taxes and the maintenance of proper insurance to assure maximum lender protection.

3. Specific provisions that are tailored to a given situation. Examples are the placing of limits on future loans and the carrying of adequate life insurance for executives.

The advantages of intermediate-term loans are:

1. Flexibility in that the terms may be altered as the financing requirements of the company change.

2. Financial information of the company is kept confidential, since no public issuance is involved.

3. The loan may be arranged quickly, compared to a public offering.

4. It avoids the possible nonrenewal of a short-term loan.

5. Public flotation costs are not involved.

The disadvantages of intermediate-term loans are:

1. Collateral and possible restrictive covenants are required, as opposed to none for commercial paper and unsecured short-term bank loans.

2. Budgets and financial statements may have to be submitted periodically to the lender.

3. "Kickers," or "sweeteners," such as stock warrants or a share of the profits are sometimes requested by the bank.

13.2 INSURANCE COMPANY TERM LOANS

Insurance companies and other institutional lenders may extend intermediate-term loans to companies. Insurance companies generally accept loan maturity dates exceeding 10 years, but their rate of interest is often higher than that of bank loans. Insurance companies do not require compensating balances, but usually there is a prepayment penalty involved, which is typically not the case with a bank loan. A company may take out an insurance company loan when it desires a longer maturity range.

13.3 EQUIPMENT FINANCING

Equipment may serve as collateral for a loan. An advance is made against the market value of the equipment. The more marketable the equipment is, the higher the advance will be. Also considered is the cost of selling the equipment. The repayment schedule is designed so that the market value of the equipment at any given time exceeds the unpaid principal balance of the loan.

Equipment financing may be obtained from banks, finance companies, and manufacturers of equipment. Equipment loans may be secured by a chattel mortgage or a conditional sales contract. A chattel mortgage serves as a lien on property except for real estate. In a conditional sales contract, the seller of the equipment keeps title to it until the buyer has satisfied all the agreed terms; otherwise the seller will repossess the equipment. The buyer makes periodic payments to the seller over a specified time period. A conditional sales contract is generally used by small companies with low credit ratings.

13.4 LEASING

The parties involved in a lease are the *lessor*, who legally owns the property, and the *lessee*, who uses it in exchange for making rental payments.

The following types of leases exist:

1. *Operating (service) lease.* This type of lease includes both financing and maintenance services. The lessee leases property that is owned by the lessor. The lessor may be the manufacturer of the asset or it may be a leasing company that buys assets from the manufacturer to lease to others. The lease payments required under the contract are generally not sufficient to recover the full cost of the property. There usually exists a cancelation clause that provides the lessee with the right to cancel the contract and return the property prior to the expiration date of the agreement.

2. *Financial lease.* This type of lease does not typically provide for maintenance services, is noncancelable, and the rental payments equal the full price of the leased property.

3. *Sale and lease-back.* With this lease arrangement, a company sells an asset it owns to another company (usually a financial institution) and then leases it back. This allows the firm to obtain needed cash from the sale and still have the property for its use.

4. *Leveraged lease.* In a leveraged lease, there is a third party who serves as the lender. Here, the lessor borrows money from the lender in order to buy the asset. The property is then leased to the lessee.

Leasing has several advantages, including the following:

1. Immediate cash outlay is not required.

2. Typically, a purchase option exists, permitting the lessee to obtain the property at a bargain price at the expiration of the lease. This provides the lessee with the flexibility to make the purchase decision based on the value of the property at the termination date.

3. The lessor's expert service is made available.

4. There are generally fewer financing restrictions (e.g., limitations on dividends) placed on the lessee by the lessor than are imposed when obtaining a loan to buy the asset.

5. The obligation for future rental payment may not have to be reported on the balance sheet.

6. Leasing allows the lessee, in effect, to depreciate land, which is not allowed if land is purchased.

7. In bankruptcy or reorganization, the maximum claim of lessors against the company is 3 years of lease payments. In the case of debt, creditors have a claim for the total amount of the unpaid financing.

8. The lessee may avoid having the obsolescence risk of the property if the lessor, in determining the lease payments, fails to accurately estimate the obsolescence of the asset.

There are several drawbacks to leasing, including the following:

1. A higher cost in the long run than if the asset is purchased.

2. The interest cost associated with leasing is typically higher than the interest cost on debt.

3. If the property reverts to the lessor at termination of the lease, the lessee must either sign a new lease or buy the property at higher current prices. Also, the salvage value of the property is realized by the lessor.

4. The lessee may have to retain property no longer needed (i.e., obsolete equipment).

5. The lessee cannot make improvements to the leased property without the permission of the lessor.

An operating lease is cancelable by the lessee or lessor. The lessee's accounting entry each year is to debit rental expense and credit cash. In a capital lease, the lessee acquires the property in *substance* but not in legal form. According to the Financial Accounting Standards Board (FASB) Statement No. 13, a capital lease exists when any *one* of the following four criteria are met:

1. The lessee obtains title to the property at the end of the lease.
2. There is a bargain purchase option.
3. The lease term equals 75 percent or more of the life of the property.
4. The present value of future minimum rental payments equals or exceeds 90 percent of the fair market value of the property at the inception of the lease.

With a capital lease, the lessee records the leased asset and related obligation on the books at the present value of the future minimum rental payments. In determining the present value of future rental payments, the discount factor to be used is the lower of the lessor's implicit rate or the lessee's incremental borrowing rate. As each rental payment is made, the liability is debited for the principal amount of the payment and interest expense is charged for the interest portion. Since, in theory, the lessee has acquired the property, he or she will depreciate the asset. The recognition of an asset and long-term liability provides a balance sheet that more appropriately reflects the company's financial position and hence allows for more meaningful ratio analysis.

EXAMPLE 13.3 Smith Corporation leased property under a 6-year lease requiring equal year-end annual payments of $20,000. The lessee's incremental borrowing rate is 12 percent.

At the date of lease, the lessee would report an asset and liability at:

$$\$20,000 \times 4.41114^a = \$82,228$$

^{a} Present value of annuity for 6
years at 12 percent.

An amortization schedule for the first 2 years follows:

Year	Payment	Interest^a	Principal	Balance
0				$82,228
1	$20,000	$9,867	$10,133	$72,095
2	$20,000	$8,651	$11,349	$60,746

^{a} 12 percent times present value of the liability at the beginning
of the year.

The lessee should be aware that the lessor can pass along the investment tax credit to him or her if there is a written document to that effect. The investment tax credit can be as much as 10 percent of the cost of the asset.

EXAMPLE 13.4 The cost of an asset having an ACRS 5-year life is $80,000. The investment tax credit is therefore $8,000. The lessee can reduce his or her taxes by $8,000.

The lessee can determine the periodic rental payments to be made under the lease by dividing the value of the leased property by the present value factor associated with the future rental payments.

EXAMPLE 13.5 Wilder Corporation enters into a lease for a $100,000 machine. It is to make 10 equal annual payments at year-end. The interest rate on the lease is 14 percent.

The periodic payment equals:

$$\frac{\$100,000}{5.2161^a} = \$19,171.41$$

^{a} The present value of an
ordinary annuity factor for
$n = 10$, $i = 14\%$ is 5.2161.

EXAMPLE 13.6 Assume the same facts as in Example 13.5, except that now the annual payments are to be made at the beginning of each year.

The periodic payment equals:

Year	Factor
0	1.0
1–9	4.9464
	5.9464

$$\frac{\$100,000}{5.9464} = \$16,816.90$$

The interest rate associated with a lease agreement can also be computed. Divide the value of the leased property by the annual payment to obtain the factor, which is then used to find the interest rate with the help of an annuity table.

EXAMPLE 13.7 Harris Corporation leased $300,000 of property and is to make equal annual payments at year-end of $40,000 for 11 years. The interest rate associated with the lease agreement is:

$$\frac{\$300,000}{\$40,000} = 7.5$$

Going to the present value of annuity table in Appendix D and looking across 11 years to a factor closest to 7.5, we find 7.4987 at a 7 percent interest rate. Therefore, the interest rate in the lease agreement is 7 percent.

The capitalized value of a lease can be found by dividing the annual lease payment by an appropriate present value of annuity factor.

EXAMPLE 13.8 Property is to be leased for 8 years at an annual rental payment of $140,000 payable at the beginning of each year. The capitalization rate is 12 percent. The capitalized value of the lease is:

$$\frac{\text{Annual lease payment}}{\text{Present value factor}} = \frac{\$140,000}{1 + 4.5638} = \$25,162.66$$

Lease-Purchase Decision

Often a decision must be made as to whether it is better to purchase an asset or lease it. Present value analysis may be used to determine the cheapest alternative. This topic was treated in Chapter 8, "Capital Budgeting Including Leasing."

Review Questions

1. Intermediate-term financing applies to a period greater than _____.

2. The interest rate on an intermediate-term loan is typically _____ than on a short-term loan.

3. The interest rate may be either _____ or _____.

4. When the last payment on a loan is higher than the prior periodic installments it is referred to as a(n) _____ payment.

5. In a revolving credit arrangement, the notes evidencing the debt are _____.

6. Restrictive provisions in a loan agreement that vary, based on the borrower's situation, are referred to as _____ provisions.

7. A restriction in a loan agreement that puts a limitation on the borrower's future loans is referred to as a(n) _____ provision.

8. A chattel mortgage has a lien against property except for _____.

9. In a(n) _____ , the seller of equipment retains title until the purchaser has met the terms of the contract.

10. In a(n) _____ lease, there is a third party who acts as the lender.

11. When a company sells an asset it owns and then leases it back, this is referred to as a(n) _____ arrangement.

12. In an operating lease, the entry each year is to debit _____ and credit _____ .

13. In a(n) _____ lease, the lessee records the leased property on his or her books as an asset at the _____ of future minimum rental payments.

14. One of the criteria for a capital lease is that the lease term equals or exceeds _____ of the life of the property.

15. The lessor can pass the _____ on to the lessee.

Answers: (1) 1 year; (2) higher; (3) fixed, variable; (4) balloon; (5) short-term; (6) general; (7) specific; (8) real estate; (9) conditional sales contract; (10) leveraged; (11) sale and lease-back; (12) rent expense, cash; (13) capital, present value; (14) 75 percent; (15) investment tax credit.

Solved Problems

13.1 Intermediate-Term Loans. What are the advantages and disadvantages to intermediate-term loans?

SOLUTION

The advantages of intermediate-term loans are as follows:

1. Flexibility exists regarding terms, since they may be modified based on the changing financial condition of the entity.
2. No public disclosure of the company's financial data is required.
3. The loan may be obtained quickly relative to a public issuance.

The disadvantages of intermediate-term loans are as follows:

1. The company may have to put up collateral.
2. Budgets and financial statements may have to be periodically submitted to the lender.
3. There is a specified maturity date for repayment.
4. The company may have to give the bank "sweeteners" for the loan, such as a share of its net income.

13.2   Amortization Payment. ABC Company agrees to pay a $50,000 loan in eight equal year-end payments. The interest rate is 12 percent.

(a) What is the annual payment? (b) What is the total interest on the loan?

SOLUTION

(a)
$$\text{Amortization payment} = \frac{\text{amount of loan}}{\text{present value factor}} = \frac{\$50,000}{4.9676} = \$10,065.22$$

(b)
Total payments ($8 \times \$10,065.22$)	$80,521.76
Principal	50,000.00
Interest	$30,521.76

13.3   Amount of Loan. Bank Corporation takes out a term loan payable in five year-end annual installments of $3,000 each. The interest rate is 10 percent. What is the amount of the loan?

SOLUTION

$$\$3,000 \times 3.7908 = \$11,372.40$$

13.4   Amortization Schedule. Using the data in Problem 13.3, (a) prepare an amortization schedule for the loan repayment, and (b) explain why the interest is declining over the loan period.

SOLUTION

(a)

Year	Payment ($)	Interest ($)	Principal ($)	Balance ($)
0				11,372.40
1	3,000	1,137.24	1,862.76	9,509.64
2	3,000	950.96	2,049.04	7,460.60
3	3,000	746.06	2,253.94	5,206.66
4	3,000	520.67	2,479.33	2,727.33
5	3,000	272.73	2,727.33 [a]	

[a] Adjusted for slight rounding difference.

(b) Interest is declining because the balance of the loan decreases over time.

13.5   Leasing. What are the advantages and disadvantages of leasing?

SOLUTION

The advantages of leasing include the following:

1. It is not necessary to pay out cash immediately.
2. The lease contract often provides a bargain purchase option that permits the lessee to buy the property for a nominal sum at the lease termination date.
3. Typically, the service technology of the lessor is made available.

4. There are generally fewer financing restrictions set out by the lessor relative to those imposed under other modes of financing.

5. In an operating lease, the lessee does not have to report a liability on his or her books.

The disadvantages of leasing include the following:

1. In the long run, the cost of leasing is higher than the cost of buying.

2. If the lessor receives the property at the end of the lease, the lessee must either enter into a new lease agreement or purchase the property at high current prices.

3. The lessee may have to keep obsolete property.

13.6 Investment Tax Credit. Tristar Corporation leases a $30,000 tangible asset having an ACRS life of 5 years. The lessor agrees in writing to pass the investment tax credit on to the lessee. By what amount can the lessee reduce her taxes for the year?

SOLUTION

$$\$30,000 \times 0.10 = \$3,000$$

13.7 Periodic Payment. Bard Corporation leases a $75,000 machine. It is required to make 15 equal annual payments at year-end. The interest rate on the lease is 16 percent. What is the periodic payment?

SOLUTION

$$\frac{\$75,000}{5.575} = \$13,452.91$$

13.8 Periodic Payment. Assume the same information as in Problem 13.7, except that now the annual payments are to be made at the beginning of the year. What is the periodic payment?

SOLUTION

$$\frac{\$75,000}{1 + 5.468} = \frac{\$75,000}{6.468} = \$11,595.55$$

13.9 Interest Rate. Tint Corporation leased $150,000 of equipment and is to make equal year-end annual payments of $22,000 for 15 years. What is the interest rate on the lease?

SOLUTION

$$\frac{\$150,000}{\$22,000} = 6.818$$

Going to the present value of annuity table in Appendix D and looking across 15 years to a factor closest to 6.818, we find 6.811 at a 12 percent interest rate.

13.10 Capitalized Value of Lease. Property is to be leased for 15 years at an annual rental payment of $40,000 payable at the beginning of each year. The capitalization rate is 10 percent. What is the capitalized value of the lease?

SOLUTION

$$\frac{\text{Annual lease payment}}{\text{Present value factor}} = \frac{\$40,000}{1 + 7.3667} = \$4,780.86$$

Chapter 14

Long-Term Debt

14.1 INTRODUCTION

This chapter discusses the characteristics, advantages, and disadvantages of long-term debt financing. In addition to the various types of debt instruments, the circumstances in which a particular form of debt is most appropriate are mentioned. Bond refunding is also highlighted.

In formulating a financing strategy in terms of source and amount, consider the following:

1. The cost and risk associated with alternative financing strategies.
2. The future trend in capital market conditions and how they will affect future fund availability and interest rates.
3. The existing ratio of debt to equity.
4. The maturity dates of present debt instruments.
5. The existing restrictions in loan agreements.
6. The type and amount of collateral required by long-term creditors.
7. The ability to alter financing strategy to adjust to changing economic conditions.
8. The amount, nature, and stability of internally generated funds.
9. The adequacy of present lines of credit for current and future needs.
10. The inflation rate, since with debt the repayment is made in cheaper dollars.
11. The earning power and liquidity position of the firm.
12. The tax rate.

Sources of long-term debt include mortgages and bonds.

14.2 MORTGAGES

Mortgages represent notes payable that have as collateral real assets and require periodic payments. Mortgages can be issued to finance the acquisition of assets, construction of plant, and modernization of facilities. The bank will require that the value of the property exceed the mortgage on that property. Most mortgage loans are for between 70 percent and 90 percent of the value of the collateral. Mortgages may be obtained from a bank, life insurance company, or other financial institution. It is easier to obtain mortgage loans for multiple-use real assets than for single-use real assets.

There are two kinds of mortgages: a *senior* mortgage, which has first claim on assets and earnings, and a *junior* mortgage, which has a subordinate lien.

A mortgage may have a closed-end provision that prevents the firm from issuing additional debt of the same priority against the same property. If the mortgage is open-ended, the company can issue additional first-mortgage bonds against the property.

Mortgages have a number of advantages, including favorable interest rates, less financing restrictions, and extended maturity date for loan repayment.

14.3 BONDS PAYABLE

Long-term debt principally takes the form of bonds payable and loans payable. A bond is a certificate indicating that the company has borrowed a given sum of money that it agrees to repay at a future date. A written agreement, called an *indenture*, describes the features of the particular bond issue. The indenture is a contract between the company, the bondholder, and the trustee. The trustee makes sure that the company is meeting the terms of the bond contract. In many cases, the trustee is the trust department of a commercial bank. Although the trustee is an agent for the bondholder, it is selected by the company prior to the issuance of the bonds. The indenture provides for certain restrictions on the company such as a limitation on dividends and minimum working capital requirements. If a provision of the indenture is violated, the bonds are in default. The indenture may also have a negative pledge clause, which precludes the issuance of new debt that would take priority over existing debt in the event the company is liquidated. The clause can apply to assets currently held as well as to assets that may be purchased in the future.

Interest

Bonds are issued in $1,000 denominations. Many bonds have maturities of 10 to 30 years. The interest payment to the bondholder is called *nominal interest*, which is the interest on the face of the bond. It is equal to the coupon (nominal) interest rate times the face value of the bond. Although the interest rate is stated on an annual basis, interest on a bond is usually paid semiannually. Interest expense is tax-deductible.

EXAMPLE 14.1   A company issues a 20 percent, 20-year bond. The tax rate is 46 percent. The annual after-tax cost of the debt is:

$$20\% \times 54\% = 10.8\%$$

EXAMPLE 14.2   A company issues a $100,000, 12 percent, 10-year bond. The semiannual interest payment is:

$$\$100,000 \times 12\% \times \tfrac{6}{12} = \$6,000$$

Assuming a tax rate of 30 percent, the after-tax semiannual interest dollar amount is:

$$\$6,000 \times 70\% = \$4,200$$

A bond sold at face value is said to be sold at 100. If a bond is sold below its face value, it is being sold at less than 100 and is issued at a discount. If a bond is sold above face value, it is being sold at more than 100, that is, sold at a premium. A bond may be sold at a discount when the interest rate on the bond is below the prevailing market interest rate for that type of security. A bond is sold at a premium when the opposite market conditions exist. The discount or premium is amortized over the life of the bond. The amortized discount is a tax-deductible expense, while the amortized premium is income subject to tax.

Bond issue costs, also a tax-deductible expense, must also be amortized over the life of the bond.

EXAMPLE 14.3   Travis Corporation issues a $100,000, 14 percent, 20-year bond at 94. The maturity value of the bond is $100,000. Annual cash interest payment is:

$$14\% \times \$100,000 = \$14,000$$

The proceeds received for the issuance of the bond is:

$$94\% \times \$100,000 = \$94,000$$

The amount of the discount is:

$$\$100,000 - \$94,000 = \$6,000$$

The annual discount amortization is:

$$\frac{\$6,000}{20} = \$300$$

EXAMPLE 14.4 A bond having a face value of $100,000 with a 25-year life was sold at 102. The tax rate is 40 percent. The bond was sold at a premium since it was issued above face value. The total premium is $2,000 ($100,000 × 0.02). The annual premium amortization is $80 ($2,000/25). The after-tax effect of the premium amortization is $48 ($80 × 60%).

The yield on a bond is the effective interest rate the company is incurring on that bond. The two methods of computing yield are the simple yield and the yield to maturity. These were fully discussed in Chapter 7.

The price of a bond depends on several factors such as its maturity date, interest rate, and collateral.

EXAMPLE 14.5 Harris Corporation's 6 percent income bonds are due in 19X5 and are selling at $855. The company's $5\frac{1}{2}$% first-mortgage bonds are due in 19X0 and are selling at $950. The first-mortgage bonds which have a lower interest rate compared to the income bonds are selling at a higher price because (1) the bonds are closer to maturity, and (2) the bonds are backed by collateral.

Also, interest is not paid on the income bonds unless there are corporate earnings. This makes them unattractive and hence they will be selling at a lower price.

Types of Bonds

The various types of bonds that may be issued are:

1. *Debentures.* Because debentures represent unsecured debt, they can be issued only by large, financially strong companies with excellent credit ratings.

2. *Subordinated debentures.* The claims of the holders of these bonds are subordinated to those of senior creditors. Debt having a prior claim over the subordinated debentures is set forth in the bond indenture. Typically, in the event of liquidation, subordinated debentures come after short-term debt.

3. *Mortgage bonds.* These are bonds secured by real assets.

4. *Collateral trust bonds.* The collateral for these bonds is the issuer's security investments (bonds or stocks), which are given to a trustee for safekeeping.

5. *Convertible bonds.* These may be converted to stock at a later date based on a specified conversion ratio. Convertible bonds are typically issued in the form of subordinated debentures. Convertible bonds are more marketable and are typically issued at a lower interest rate than are regular bonds. Of course, if bonds are converted to stock, debt repayment is not involved. Convertible bonds are discussed in detail in Chapter 16, "Warrants and Convertibles."

6. *Income bonds.* These bonds require the payment of interest only if the issuer has earnings. However, since interest accumulates regardless of earnings, the interest, if bypassed, must be paid in a later year when sufficient earnings exist.

7. *Guaranteed bonds.* These are debt issued by one party with payment guaranteed by another party.

8. *Serial bonds.* A specified portion of these bonds comes due each year. At the time serial bonds are issued, a schedule is given showing the yields, interest rates, and prices applicable with each maturity. The interest rate on the shorter maturities is lower than the interest rate on the longer maturities. Serial bonds are primarily issued by government agencies.

Bond Ratings

Financial advisory services (e.g., Standard and Poor's, and Moody's) rate publicly traded bonds according to risk in terms of the receipt of principal and interest. An inverse relationship exists between the quality of a bond issue and its yield. That is, low-quality bonds will have a higher yield than high-quality bonds. Thus, a risk-return trade-off exists for the bondholder. Bond ratings are important to financial management because they influence marketability and the cost associated with the bond issue.

EXAMPLE 14.6   The following bond ratings are used by Moody's and Standard & Poor's:

	Moody's			Standard & Poor's
Aaa	Prime quality		AAA	Bank investment quality
Aa	High quality		AA	
A	Upper medium grade		A	
Baa	Medium grade		BBB	
Ba	Lower medium grade		BB	Speculative
B	Speculative		B	
Caa, Ca	Very speculative to near or in default		CCC	
C	Lowest grade		CC	
			C	Income bond
			DDD	Bond is in default
			DD	
			D	

14.4   DEBT FINANCING

The advantages of issuing long-term debt include:

1. Interest is tax-deductible, while dividends are not.
2. Bondholders do not participate in superior earnings of the firm.
3. The repayment of debt is in cheaper dollars during inflation.
4. There is no dilution of company control.
5. Financing flexibility can be achieved by including a call provision in the bond indenture. A call provision allows the company to pay the debt before the expiration date of the bond.
6. It may safeguard the company's future financial stability, for example, in times of tight money markets when short-term loans are not available.

The disadvantages of issuing long-term debt include:

1. Interest charges must be met regardless of corporate earnings.
2. Debt must be repaid at maturity.
3. Higher debt infers greater risk in the capital structure, which may increase the cost of capital.
4. Indenture provisions may place stringent restrictions on the company.
5. Overcommitments may arise due to forecasting errors.

To investors, bonds have the following advantages:

1. There is a fixed interest payment each year.
2. Bonds are safer than equity securities.

To investors, bonds have the following disadvantages:

1. They do not participate in incremental profitability.
2. There is no voting right.

The proper mixture of long-term debt to equity in a company depends on the type of organization, credit availability, and after-tax cost of financing. Where a high degree of financial leverage exists, the firm may wish to take steps to minimize other corporate risks.

Debt financing is more appropriate when:

1. Stability in revenue and earnings exists.
2. There is a satisfactory profit margin.
3. There is a good liquidity and cash flow position.
4. The debt/equity ratio is low.
5. Stock prices are currently depressed.
6. Control considerations are a primary factor.
7. Inflation is expected.
8. Bond indenture restrictions are not burdensome.

An entity experiencing financial difficulties may wish to refinance short-term debt on a long-term basis such as by extending the maturity dates of existing loans. This may alleviate current liquidity and cash flow problems.

As the default risk of the firm becomes higher, so the interest rate will become high on the debt to compensate for the greater risk.

EXAMPLE 14.7 Arl Corporation has $10 million of 12 percent mortgage bonds outstanding. The indenture permits additional bonds to be issued provided all the following conditions are satisfied:

1. The pretax times-interest-earned ratio exceeds 5.
2. Book value of the mortgaged assets are at least 1.5 times the amount of debt.
3. The debt/equity ratio is below 0.6.

The following additional information is provided:

1. Income before tax is $9 million.
2. Equity is $30 million.
3. Book value of assets is $34 million.
4. There are no sinking fund payments for the current year. (A sinking fund is money set aside to be used to retire a bond issue.)
5. Half the proceeds of a new issue would be added to the base of mortgaged assets.

Only $7 million more of 12 percent debt can be issued based on the following calculations:

1. The before-tax times-interest-earned ratio is:

$$\frac{\text{Income before tax and interest}}{\text{Interest}} = \frac{\$9,000,000 + \$1,200,000^{a}}{\$1,200,000 + 0.12X} = 5$$

$$\frac{\$10,200,000}{\$1,200,000 + 0.12X} = 5$$

$$\$10,200,000 = \$6,000,000 + 0.60X$$

$$X = \$7,000,000$$

---

[a] Interest is:

$$\$10,000,000 \times 0.12 = \$1,200,000$$

2.
$$\frac{\text{Book value of mortgaged assets}}{\text{Debt}} = \frac{\$34,000,000 + 0.5X}{\$10,000,000 + X} = 1.5$$

$$\$34,000,000 + 0.5X = \$15,000,000 + 1.5X$$

$$X = \$19,000,000$$

3.
$$\frac{\text{Debt}}{\text{Equity}} = \frac{\$10,000,000 + X}{\$30,000,000} = 0.6$$

$$\$10,000,000 + X = \$18,000,000$$

$$X = \$8,000,000$$

The first condition is controlling and hence limits the amount of new debt to $7 million.

14.5 BOND REFUNDING

Bonds may be refunded by the company prior to maturity through either the issuance of a serial bond or exercising a call privilege on a straight bond. The issuance of serial bonds allows the company to refund the debt over the life of the issue. A call feature in a bond enables the issuer to retire it before the expiration date. The call feature is included in many corporate bond issues.

When future interest rates are anticipated to decline, a call provision in the bond issue is recommended. Such a provision enables the firm to buy back the higher-interest bond and issue a lower-interest one. The timing for the refunding depends on expected future interest rates. A call price is usually established in excess of the face value of the bond. The resulting call *premium* equals the difference between the call price and the maturity value. The issuer pays the premium to the bondholder in order to acquire the outstanding bonds before the maturity date. The call premium is generally equal to 1 year's interest if the bond is called in the first year, and it declines at a constant rate each year thereafter. Also involved in selling a new issue are flotation costs. Both the call premium and flotation costs are tax-deductible expenses.

A bond with a call provision typically will be issued at an interest rate higher than one without the call provision. The investor prefers not to have a situation where the company can buy back the bond at its option prior to maturity. This is because the company will tend to buy back high-interest bonds early and issue lower-interest bonds when interest rates decline. The investor would obviously want to hold onto a high-interest bond when prevailing interest rates are low.

EXAMPLE 14.8 A $100,000, 10 percent, 20-year bond is issued at 95. The call price is 102. Four years after issue the bond is called. The call premium is equal to:

Call price	$102,000
Face value of bond	100,000
Call premium	$ 2,000

EXAMPLE 14.9 A $40,000 callable bond was issued. The call price is 104. The tax rate is 35 percent. The after-tax cost of calling the issue is:

$$\$40,000 \times 0.04 \times 0.65 = \$1,040$$

The desirability of refunding a bond requires present value analysis. The present value technique was discussed in Chapter 8, "Capital Budgeting."

EXAMPLE 14.10 Tracy Corporation has a $20 million, 10 percent bond issue outstanding that has 10 years to maturity. The call premium is 7 percent of face value. New 10-year bonds in the amount of $20 million can be issued at an 8 percent interest rate. Flotation costs associated with the new issue are $600,000.

Refunding of the original bond issue should take place as shown below.

Old interest payments ($20,000,000 × 0.10)	$2,000,000
New interest payments ($20,000,000 × 0.08)	1,600,000
Annual savings	$ 400,000

Call premium ($20,000,000 × 0.07)	$1,400,000
Flotation cost	600,000
Total cost	$2,000,000

Year	Calculation	Present Value
Year 0	−$2,000,000 × 1	−$2,000,000
Years 1–10	$400,000 × 6.71 [a]	+2,684,000
Net present value		$ 684,000

[a] Present value of annuity factor for $i = 8\%$, $n = 10$.

EXAMPLE 14.11 Ace Corporation is considering calling a $10 million, 20-year bond that was issued 5 years ago at a nominal interest rate of 10 percent. The call price on the bonds is 105. The bonds were initially sold at 90. The discount on bonds payable at the time of sale was, therefore, $1 million and the net proceeds received were $9 million. The initial flotation cost was $100,000. The firm is considering issuing $10 million, 8 percent, 15-year bonds and using the net proceeds to retire the old bonds. The new bonds will be issued at face value. The flotation cost for the new issue is $150,000. The company's tax rate is 46 percent. The after-tax cost of new debt ignoring flotation costs, is 4.32 percent ($8\% × 54\%$). With the flotation cost, the after-tax cost of new debt is estimated at 5 percent. There is an overlap period of 3 months in which interest must be paid on the old and new bonds.

The initial cash outlay is:

Cost to call old bonds ($10,000,000 × 105%)	$10,500,000
Cost to issue new bond	150,000
Interest on old bonds for overlap period ($10,000,000 × 10% × 3/12)	250,000
Initial cash outlay	$10,900,000

The initial cash inflow is:

Proceeds from selling new bond		$10,000,000
Tax-deductible items		
Call premium	$ 500,000	
Unamortized discount ($1,000,000 × 15/20)	750,000	
Overlap in interest ($10,000,000 × 10% × 3/12)	250,000	
Unamortized issue cost of old bond ($100,000 × 15/20)	75,000	
Total tax-deductible items	$1,575,000	
Tax rate	×0.46	
Tax savings		724,500
Initial cash inflow		$10,724,500

The *net* initial cash outlay is therefore:

Initial cash outlay	$10,900,000
Initial cash inflow	10,724,500
Net initial cash outlay	$ 175,500

The annual cash flow for the old bond is:

Interest (10% × $10,000,000)		$1,000,000
Less: Tax-deductible items		
Interest	$1,000,000	
Amortization of discount ($1,000,000/20 years)	50,000	
Amortization of issue cost ($100,000/20 years)	5,000	
Total tax-deductible items	$1,055,000	
Tax rate	×0.46	
Tax savings		485,300
Annual cash outflow with old bond		$ 514,700

The annual cash flow for the new bond is:

Interest		$800,000
Less: Tax-deductible items		
Interest	$800,000	
Amortization of issue cost ($150,000/15 years)	10,000	
Total tax-deductible items	$810,000	
Tax rate	×0.46	
Tax savings		372,600
Annual cash outflow with new bond		$427,400

The net annual cash savings with the new bond compared to the old bond is:

Annual cash outflow with old bond	$514,700
Annual cash outflow with new bond	427,400
Net annual cash savings	$ 87,300

The net present value associated with the refunding is:

	Calculation	Present Value
Year 0	−$175,500 × 1	−$175,500
Years 1–15	$87,300 × 10.38[a]	+906,174
Net present value		$730,674

---

[a] Present value of annuity factor for $i = 5\%$, $n = 15$.

Since a positive net present value exists, the refunding of the old bond should be made.

Sinking fund requirements may exist with regard to a bond issue. With a sinking fund, the company is required to set aside money to purchase and retire a portion of the bond issue each year. Usually, there is a mandatory fixed amount that must be retired, but occasionally the retirement may relate to the company's sales or profit for the current year. If a sinking fund payment is not made, the bond issue may be in default.

In many cases, the company can handle the sinking fund in one of the following two ways:

1. It can call a given percentage of the bonds at a stipulated price each year, for example, 5 percent of the original amount at a price of $1,080.
2. It can buy its own bonds on the open market.

The least expensive alternative should be selected. If interest rates have increased, the price of the bonds will have decreased, and the open market option should be used. If interest rates have decreased, the bond prices will have increased, and so calling the bonds is the preferred choice.

EXAMPLE 14.12 XYZ Company has to reduce bonds payable by $300,000. The call price is 104. The market price of the bonds is 103. The company will elect to buy back the bonds on the open market because it is less expensive, as indicated below.

Call price ($300,000 × 104%)	$312,000
Purchase on open market ($300,000 × 103%)	309,000
Advantage of purchasing bonds on the open market	$ 3,000

Review Questions

1. A(n) _____ mortgage prohibits the company from issuing further debt of the same priority against the property.

2. A(n) _____ is the written agreement specifying the terms of a bond issue.

3. A(n) _____ clause in a bond agreement prevents the issuance of new debt having priority over existing debt.

4. Bonds are stated in $ _____ denominations.

5. The interest payment based on the face value of a bond is called _____ interest.

6. As the maturity date of a bond lengthens, the interest rate _____.

7. When a bond is sold at an amount in excess of its face value, it is sold at a(n) _____.

8. A(n) _____ is an unsecured bond.

9. A(n) _____ bond pays interest only if the issuer has earnings.

10. Bond issues that mature periodically are called _____ bonds.

11. The issuance of bonds has an advantage in _____ times in that the company will be paying back the debt in _____ dollars.

12. A(n)_____ provision enables the firm to buy back bonds at a date prior to maturity.

13. _____ is tax-deductible, whereas dividends are not.

Answers: (1) closed-end; (2) indenture; (3) negative pledge; (4) 1,000; (5) nominal; (6) increases; (7) premium; (8) debenture; (9) income; (10) serial; (11) inflationary, cheaper; (12) call; (13) Interest.

Solved Problems

14.1   Interest. A company issues a $300,000, 10 percent, 20-year bond. The tax rate is 40 percent. What is the after-tax semiannual interest dollar amount?

SOLUTION

$$\$300,000 \times 10\% \times \tfrac{6}{12} = \$15,000 \text{ (before taxes)}$$

$$\$15,000 \times 60\% = \$9,000 \text{ (after taxes)}$$

14.2   Bond Issuance. Boxer Corporation issues a $300,000, 16 percent, 10-year bond at 108.

(*a*) What is the maturity value? (*b*) What is the annual cash interest payment? (*c*) What are the proceeds the company receives upon issuance of the bond? (*d*) What is the amount of the premium? (*e*) What is the annual premium amortization?

SOLUTION

(*a*) $300,000

(*b*) $16\% \times \$300,000 = \$48,000$

(*c*) $108\% \times \$300,000 = \$324,000$

(*d*) $\$324,000 - \$300,000 = \$24,000$

(*e*) $\dfrac{\$24,000}{10} = \$2,400$

14.3   Amortization. A bond with a face value of $200,000 with a 20-year life was sold at 105. The tax rate is 35 percent. What is the after-tax effect of the premium amortization?

SOLUTION

Total premium is:

$$\$200,000 \times 0.05 = \$10,000$$

Annual premium amortization is:

$$\frac{\$10,000}{20} = \$500$$

After-tax effect of premium amortization is:

$$\$500 \times 0.65 = \$325$$

14.4 Bond Ratings. Match the description in column A with Moody's bond rating in column B.

	Column A		Column B
(a)	Speculative	(1)	C
(b)	Prime quality	(2)	Aaa
(c)	Lowest grade	(3)	Ba
(d)	Lower medium grade	(4)	B
(e)	Near or in default	(5)	Ca

SOLUTION

(a) (4); (b) (2); (c) (1); (d) (3); (e) (5).

14.5 Bond Rating. The two bond rating agencies, Moody's and Standard & Poor's, lowered the ratings on Appleton Industries' bonds from triple-A to double-A in response to operating trends revealed by the financial reports of recent years. The change in the ratings is of considerable concern to the Appleton management because the company plans to seek a significant amount of external financing within the next 2 years.

(a) Identify several events or circumstances which could have occurred in the operations of Appleton Industries which could have influenced the factors the bond rating agencies use to evaluate the firm and, as a result, caused the bond rating agencies to lower Appleton's bond rating. (b) If Appleton Industries maintains its present capital structure, what effect will the lower bond ratings have on the company's weighted average cost of capital? Explain your answer. (c) If Appleton Industries' capital structure was at an optimal level before the rating of its bonds was changed, explain what effect the lower bond ratings will have on the company's optimal capital structure. (CMA, adapted.)

SOLUTION

(a) Factors or circumstances which could have caused the rating agencies to lower the bond rating of Appleton Industries include:

1. Lowered long-term solvency reflected by a reduction in the times-interest-earned ratio or a reduction in the fixed-charge-coverage ratio

2. Lowered short-term liquidity reflected by a decrease in the current or quick ratios

3. Lowered profitability reflected by a reduced market share, lower return on sales, or decreased profits

4. An increased risk of financial stability due to major pending litigation which would be damaging to the firm or a large increase in earnings variability

5. A major change in management which is perceived negatively by the financial community

(b) The weighted average cost of capital can be expected to rise. The lower bond rating is usually relied upon as an indication of greater risk being assumed by the bond investors. This change will be noted by the investors of other Appleton securities. Thus the investors in each capital component of Appleton Industries can be expected to require a higher return.

(c) Appleton Industries' capital structure will shift toward greater equity with less debt. The fact that the bond rating was lowered would indicate to investors that the risk has increased. To reduce the risk and minimize the increase in the cost of capital, the optimal capital structure will have to shift toward one with an increased percentage of equity.

14.6 Amount of Debt. Boston Corporation has $30 million of 10 percent mortgage bonds outstanding. The indenture allows the issuance of additional bonds provided the following conditions are met: (1) The before-tax times-interest-earned ratio exceeds 4, (2) book value of the mortgaged assets is at least two times the amount of debt, and (3) the debt/equity ratio is less than 0.5.

The following additional data are provided: (1) Income before tax is $11 million, (2) equity is $90 million, (3) book value of mortgaged assets is $80 million, and (4) forty percent of the proceeds of a new issue would be added to the base of mortgaged assets.

How much additional debt can be issued?

SOLUTION

The before-tax times-interest-earned ratio is:

$$\frac{\text{Income before tax and interest}}{\text{Interest}} = \frac{\$11,000,000 + \$3,000,000^a}{\$3,000,000 + 0.10X} = 4$$

$$\frac{\$14,000,000}{\$3,000,000 + 0.10X} = 4$$

$$\$14,000,000 = \$12,000,000 + 0.40X$$

$$X = \$5,000,000$$

---

^{a} Interest $30,000,000 \times 0.10 = \$3,000,000$

The book value of the mortgaged assets is:

$$\frac{\text{Book value of mortgaged assets}}{\text{Debt}} = \frac{\$80,000,000 + 0.4X}{\$30,000,000 + X} = 2$$

$$\$80,000,000 + 0.4X = \$60,000,000 + 2X$$

$$X = \$12,500,000$$

The debt/equity ratio is:

$$\frac{\text{Debt}}{\text{Equity}} = \frac{\$30,000,000 + X}{\$90,000,000} = 0.5$$

$$\$30,000,000 + X = \$45,000,000$$

$$X = \$15,000,000$$

The first condition is controlling and thus limits the amount of new debt to $5 million.

14.7   Call Premium. Mider Corporation issued a $100,000, 14 percent, 15-year bond at 98. The call price is 104. Seven years after issue the bond is called. What is the call premium?

SOLUTION

Call price	$104,000
Face value of bond	100,000
Call premium	$ 4,000

14.8   After-Tax Cost of Call. A $30,000 callable bond was issued. The call price is 105. The tax rate is 46 percent. What is the after-tax cost of calling the issue?

SOLUTION

$$\$30,000 \times 0.05 \times 0.54 = \$810$$

14.9　Bond Refunding. Smith Corporation has a $40 million, 14 percent bond issue outstanding, with 15 years remaining. The call premium is 8 percent of face value. A new 15-year bond issue for $40 million can be issued at a 10 percent interest rate. Flotation costs applicable to the new issue are $350,000. Should Smith Corporation call the original bond issue?

SOLUTION

Old interest payments		
($40,000,000 × 0.14)		$5,600,000
New interest payments		
($40,000,000 × 0.10)		4,000,000
Annual savings		$1,600,000
Call premium ($40,000,000 × 0.08)		$3,200,000
Flotation cost		350,000
Total cost		$3,550,000

	Calculations	Present Value
Year 0	−$3,550,000 × 1	−$ 3,550,000
Year 1–15	1,600,000 × 7.6061 [a]	+12,169,760
Net present value		$ 8,619,760

[a] Present value of annuity factor for $i = 10\%$, $n = 15$.

The company should retire the original bond issue because doing so results in a positive net present value.

14.10　Bond Refunding. Jones Corporation is considering calling a $20 million, 30-year bond that was issued 10 years ago at a face interest rate of 14 percent. The call price on the bonds is 104. The bonds were initially sold at 97. The initial flotation cost was $200,000. The company is considering issuing $20 million, 12 percent, 20-year bonds in order to net proceeds and retire the old bonds. The new bonds will be issued at face value. The flotation costs for the new issue are $225,000. The tax rate is 46 percent. The after-tax cost of new debt ignoring flotation costs is 6.48 percent (12% × 54%). With flotation costs, the after-tax cost of new debt is anticipated to be 7 percent. There is a 2-month overlap in which interest must be paid on the old bonds and new bonds. Should refunding take place?

SOLUTION

The initial cash outlay is:

Cost to call old bonds	
($20,000,000 × 104%)	$20,800,000
Cost to issue new bond	225,000
Interest on old bonds for overlap	
period ($20,000,000 × 14% × 2/12)	466,667
Initial cash outlay	$21,491,667

The initial cash inflow is:

Proceeds from selling new bond		$20,000,000
Tax-deductible items		
Call premium	$ 800,000	
Unamortized discount		
($600,000 × 20/30)	400,000	
Unamortized issue cost of old bond		
($200,000 × 20/30)	133,333	
Overlap in interest		
($20,000,000 × 14% × 2/12)	466,667	
Total tax-deductible items	$1,800,000	
Tax rate	×0.46	
Tax savings		828,000
Initial cash inflow		$20,828,000

The *net* initial cash outlay is therefore:

Initial cash outlay	$21,491,667
Initial cash inflow	20,828,000
Net initial cash outlay	$ 663,667

The annual cash flow for the old bond is:

Interest (14% × $20,000,000)		$2,800,000
Less: Tax-deductible items		
Interest	$2,800,000	
Amortization of discount		
($600,000/30 years)	20,000	
Amortization of issue cost		
($200,000/30 years)	6,667	
Total tax-deductible items	$2,826,667	
Tax rate	×0.46	
Tax savings		1,300,267
Annual cash outflow with old bond		$1,499,733

The annual cash flow for the new bond is:

Interest (12% × $20,000,000)		$2,400,000
Less: Tax-deductible items		
Interest	$2,400,000	
Amortization of issue cost		
($225,000/20 years)	11,250	
Total tax-deductible items	$2,411,250	
Tax rate	×0.46	
Tax savings		1,109,175
Annual cash outflow with new bond		$1,290,825

The net annual cash savings with the new bond compared to the old bond is:

Annual cash outflow with old bond	$1,499,733
Annual cash outflow with new bond	1,290,825
Net annual cash savings	$ 208,908

The net present value associated with the refunding is:

	Calculations	Present Value
Year 0	−$663,667 × 1	− $ 663,667
Years 1–20	$208,908 × 10.59 [a]	+2,212,336
Net present value		$1,548,669

[a] Present value of annuity factor for $i = 7\%$, $n = 20$.

Since a positive net present value exists, the refunding should take place.

14.11 Purchase of Bonds on the Open Market. Drifter Company has to reduce bonds payable by $500,000. The call price of its bonds is 103. The market price of the bonds is 101. Should the bonds be called or bought back on the open market?

SOLUTION

Call price ($500,000 × 103%)	$515,000
Purchase on open market ($500,000 × 101%)	505,000
Advantage of purchasing bonds on the open market	$ 10,000

The bonds should be bought back.

Chapter 15

Preferred and Common Stock

15.1 INTRODUCTION

This chapter discusses equity financing. The advantages and disadvantages of issuing preferred and common stock are addressed, along with the various circumstances in which either financing source is most suited. Stock rights are also described. Consideration is given to the advantages and disadvantages of public versus private placement, or sale. Also discussed is the role of the investment banker.

15.2 INVESTMENT BANKING

Investment banking involves public flotation, or sale, of a security issue. Investment bankers perform the following functions:

1. *Underwriting.* The investment banker buys a new security issue, pays the issuer, and markets the securities. The underwriter's compensation is the difference between the price at which the securities are sold to the public, and the price paid to the company for the securities.

2. *Distributing.* The investment banker markets the security issue.

3. *Giving advice.* The investment banker provides valuable advice to the company concerning the best way to raise funds. The investment banker is familiar with the various sources of long-term funds, debt and equity markets, and Securities and Exchange Commission (SEC) regulations.

4. *Providing funds.* The investment banker furnishes funds to the issuing company during the distribution period.

When a number of investment bankers get together as a group because a particular issue is large and/or risky, they are referred to as a *syndicate*. A syndicate is a temporary association of investment bankers brought together for the purpose of selling new securities. One investment banker among the group will be selected to manage the syndicate. The investment banker so selected is called the *originating house*, which underwrites the major amount of the issue. One bid price for the issue is made on behalf of the group, but the terms and features of the issue are established by the company.

There are two types of underwriting syndicates, divided and undivided. In a *divided* account, the liability of each member investment banker is limited in terms of participation. Once a member sells the securities assigned, that investment banker has no additional liability regardless of whether the other members are able to sell their portion of the security or not. In an *undivided* account, each member is liable for unsold securities up to the amount of its percentage participation irrespective of the number of securities that investment banker has sold. Most syndicates are based on the undivided account arrangement.

In another approach to investment banking, the investment banker agrees to sell the securities on a best-efforts basis, or as an agent for the company. Here, the investment banker does not serve as underwriter but rather sells the stock and receives a commission on the sale. An investment banker may insist on this type of arrangement when he or she has reservations about the success of the security offering in the market.

Besides investment bankers, there are firms that specialize in more specific financial functions with regard to stock. A *dealer* buys securities and holds them in inventory for later resale, expecting to make a profit on the spread. The *spread* is the price appreciation of the securities. A *broker* receives and forwards purchase orders for securities to the applicable stock exchange or over-the-counter market. The broker is compensated with a commission on each sale.

15.3 PUBLIC VERSUS PRIVATE PLACEMENT OF SECURITIES

Equity and debt securities may be issued either publicly or privately. A consideration in determining whether to issue securities publicly or privately is the type and amount of the needed financing.

In a public issuance, the shares are bought by the general public. In a private placement, the company issues the securities directly to either one or a few large investors. The large investors involved are financial institutions such as insurance companies, pension funds, and commercial banks.

Private placement has the following advantages, when compared to a public issuance:

1. The flotation cost is less. Flotation cost is the expense of registering and selling the stock issue. Examples are brokerage commissions and underwriting fees. The flotation cost for common stock exceeds that for preferred stock. Flotation cost expressed as a percentage of gross proceeds is higher for smaller issues than for larger ones.

2. It avoids SEC filing requirements.

3. It avoids the disclosure of information to the public at large.

4. There is less time involved in obtaining funds.

5. It may not be practical to issue securities in the public market when a company is so small that an investment banker would not find it profitable.

6. The company's credit rating may be low, and as a consequence investors may not be interested in buying securities when the money supply is limited.

Private placement has the following disadvantages, when compared to a public issuance:

1. It is more difficult to obtain significant amounts of money privately compared to publicly.

2. Large investors usually employ stringent credit standards requiring the company to be in a strong financial position.

3. Large institutional investors may watch more closely the company's activities than smaller investors in a public issue.

4. Large institutional investors are more capable of obtaining voting control of the company.

15.4 PREFERRED STOCK

Preferred stock may be issued when the cost of common stock is high. The best time to issue preferred stock is when the company has excessive financial leverage and an issue of common stock might create control problems for the owners. Many utilities offer preferred stock. Preferred stock is a more expensive way to raise capital than a bond issue because the dividend payment is not tax-deductible.

Preferred stock may be cumulative or noncumulative. *Cumulative* preferred stock means that if any previous year's dividend payments have been missed, they must be paid before dividends can be paid to common stockholders. If preferred dividends are in arrears for a long period of time, a company may find it difficult to resume its dividend payments to common stockholders. With *noncumulative* preferred stock, the company need not pay missed preferred dividends. Preferred stock dividends are limited to the rate specified, which is based on the total par value of the outstanding shares.

EXAMPLE 15.1 As of December 31, 19X6, Ace Company has 6,000 shares of $15 par value, 14 percent, cumulative preferred stock outstanding. Dividends have not been paid in 19X4 and 19X5. Assuming the company has been profitable in 19X6, the amount of the dividend to be distributed is:

$$\text{Par value of stock} = 6,000 \text{ shares} \times \$15 = \$90,000$$

Dividends in arrears	
($90,000 × 14% × 2 years)	$25,200
Current year dividend ($90,000 × 14%)	12,600
Total dividend	$37,800

Participating preferred stock means that if declared dividends exceed the amount normally given to preferred stockholders and common stockholders, the preferred and common stockholders will participate in the excess dividends. Unless stated otherwise, the distribution of the excess dividends will be based on the relative total par values.

EXAMPLE 15.2 Boston Corporation has the following equity securities outstanding:

Preferred stock, participating—10,000 shares, $10 par value, 12% dividend rate	$100,000
Common stock—4,000 shares, $20 par value	$80,000

The dividend rate declared on the common stock is 10 percent. If the dividends declared for the year are $25,000, the amounts assigned to preferred stock and to common stock are:

	Preferred Stock	Common Stock
Regular dividend		
Preferred (12% × $100,000)	$12,000	
Common (10% × $80,000)		$ 8,000
Excess dividend—allocation based on relative par value		
Preferred [($100,000/$180,000) × $5,000]	2,778	
Common [($80,000/$180,000) × $5,000]		2,222
Total dividend	$14,778	$10,222

Preferred stock may be callable, which means that the company can buy it back at a later date at a specified call price. The call provision is advantageous when interest rates decline, since the company has the option of discontinuing payment of dividends at a rate that has become excessive by buying back preferred stock that was issued when bond interest rates were high. Unlike bonds, preferred stock rarely has a maturity date associated with it. However, if preferred stock has a sinking fund associated with it, this, in effect, establishes a maturity date for repayment.

In the event of corporate bankruptcy, preferred stockholders are paid after creditors and before common stockholders. In such a case, preferred stockholders receive the par value of their shares, dividends in arrears, and the current year's dividend. Any asset balance then goes to the common stockholders.

The cost of preferred stock can be determined by dividing the dividend payment by the net proceeds received.

EXAMPLE 15.3 Blick Corporation sells preferred stock amounting to $2 million. The flotation cost is 11 percent of gross proceeds. The dividend rate is 14 percent. The effective cost of the preferred stock is:

$$\frac{\text{Dividend}}{\text{Net proceeds}} = \frac{0.14 \times \$2,000,000}{\$2,000,000 - (0.11 \times \$2,000,000)} = \frac{\$280,000}{\$1,780,000} = 15.7\%$$

The company should estimate the amount it will receive per share and the number of shares it must sell in order to finance the business.

EXAMPLE 15.4 Brady Corporation is considering expanding its operations. It anticipates a need for $5 million to finance the expansion through the issuance of preferred stock. The preferred stock has a par value of $100 and a dividend rate of 10 percent. Similar issues of preferred stock are currently providing a yield of 12 percent.

For each share, the company will receive:

$$\frac{\text{Dividend}}{\text{Market yield}} = \frac{0.10 \times \$100}{0.12} = \frac{\$10}{0.12} = \$83.33$$

The amount of shares that must be issued is:

$$\frac{\text{Funds required}}{\text{Price per share}} = \frac{\$5,000,000}{\$83.33} = 60,002 \text{ shares (rounded)}$$

To a company, a preferred stock issue has the following advantages:

1. Preferred dividends do not have to be paid, whereas interest on debt must be paid.

2. Preferred stockholders cannot force the company into bankruptcy.

3. Preferred shareholders do not share in unusually high profits of the company.

4. A growth company can generate better earnings for its original owners by issuing preferred stock having a fixed dividend rate than by issuing common stock.

5. Preferred stock issuance does not dilute the ownership interest of common stockholders in terms of earnings participation and voting rights.

6. The company does not have to collateralize its assets as it may have to do if bonds are issued.

To a company, a preferred stock has the following disadvantages:

1. Preferred stock requires a higher yield than bonds.

2. Preferred dividends are not tax-deductible.

To an investor, a preferred stock offers the following advantages:

1. Preferred stock usually provides a constant return in the form of a fixed dividend payment.

2. Preferred stockholders come before common stockholders in the event of corporate bankruptcy.

3. Preferred dividends are subject to an 85 percent dividend exclusion for *corporate* investors. For example, if a company holds preferred stock in another company and receives dividends of $10,000, only 15 percent (or $1,500) is taxable. On the other hand, interest income received on bonds is fully taxable. The *individual* investor does not quality for the 85 percent dividend exclusion.

To an investor, the disadvantages of a preferred stock are:

1. The return is limited because of the fixed dividend rate.

2. There is greater price fluctuation with preferred stock than with bonds because of the nonexistence of a maturity date.

3. Preferred stockholders cannot require the company to pay dividends if the firm has inadequate earnings.

15.5 COMMON STOCK

The owners of a corporation are called stockholders. They elect the board of directors, who in turn select the officers of the firm. When the election occurs, management sends proxy statements, which ask stockholders to give management the right to vote their stock. Effective control of the corporation can exist with less than 50 percent common stock ownership since many stockholders do not bother to vote. Stockholders have limited liability in that they are not personally liable for the debts of the company.

Authorized shares represent the maximum amount of stock the company can issue according to the corporate charter. *Issued shares* represent the number of authorized shares which have been sold by the firm. *Outstanding shares* are the issued shares actually being held by the investing public. *Treasury stock* is stock that has been reacquired by the firm. It is not retired but, rather, held for possible future resale, a stock option plan, to use in purchasing another company, or to prevent a takeover by an outside group. Outstanding shares are therefore equal to the issued shares less the treasury shares. Dividends are based on the outstanding shares.

The *par value* of a stock is a stated amount of value per share specified in the corporate charter. The firm typically cannot sell stock at a price below par value since stockholders would be liable to creditors for the difference between par value and the amount received.

A closely held corporation is one having only a few stockholders. They keep full control and are not required to publicly disclose financial information about the company. However, a company having 500 or more stockholders must file an annual financial statement with the Securities and Exchange Commission.

A company may issue different classes of common stock. Class A is stock issued to the public and usually has no dividends specified. However, it does have voting rights. Class B stock is usually kept by the company's organizers. Dividends are typically not paid on it until the company has generated sufficient earnings.

Common stockholders enjoy the following rights:

1. The right to receive dividends.
2. The right to receive assets upon the dissolution of the business.
3. The right to vote.
4. The preemptive right to buy new shares of common stock prior to their sale to the general public. In this way, current stockholders can maintain their proportionate percentage ownership in the company.
5. The receipt of a stock certificate which evidences ownership in the firm. The stock certificate may then be sold by the holder to another in the secondary security matket.
6. The right to inspect the company's books.

In some states there also exists *cumulative voting*, which allows for multiple votes for a particular director. Cumulative voting is designed to allow a minority group to be able to elect one director.

A number of options exist for equity financing in the case of small businesses, including:

1. Venture capital (investor) groups
2. Issuances directly to institutional investors
3. Issuances to relatives or friends
4. Issuances to major customers and suppliers

A determination of the number of shares that must be issued to raise sufficient funds to meet the capital budget may be required.

EXAMPLE 15.5 Brady Corporation presently has 650,000 shares of common stock outstanding. The capital budget for the upcoming year is $1.8 million.

Assuming new stock may be issued for $16 a share, the number of shares that must be issued to provide the necessary funds to meet the capital budget is:

$$\frac{\text{Funds needed}}{\text{Market price per share}} = \frac{\$1,800,000}{\$16} = 112,500 \text{ shares}$$

The new shareholders will now own 14.8 percent of the total shares outstanding as computed below.

$$\frac{\text{Newly issued shares}}{\text{Total shares}} = \frac{112{,}500}{650{,}000 + 112{,}500} = \frac{112{,}500}{762{,}500} = 14.8\%$$

EXAMPLE 15.6 Smith Corporation wishes to raise $3 million in its first public issue of common stock. After its issuance, the total market value of stock is anticipated to be $7 million. Currently, there are 140,000 outstanding shares that are closely held.

Determine the number of new shares that must be issued to raise the $3 million.

The new shares will have $\frac{3}{7}$ ($3 million/$7 million) of the outstanding shares after the stock issuance. Therefore, current stockholders will be holding $\frac{4}{7}$ of the shares.

$$140{,}000 \text{ shares} = \tfrac{4}{7} \text{ of the total shares}$$
$$\text{Total shares} = 245{,}000$$
$$\text{New shares} = \tfrac{3}{7} \times 245{,}000 = 105{,}000 \text{ shares}$$

Subsequent to the stock issuance, the anticipated price per share is:

$$\text{Price per share} = \frac{\text{market value}}{\text{shares outstanding}} = \frac{\$7{,}000{,}000}{245{,}000 \text{ shares}} = \$28.57$$

A company that first issues its common stock publicly is referred to as "going public." The estimated price per share to sell the securities is equal to:

$$\frac{\text{Anticipated market value of the company}}{\text{Total outstanding shares}}$$

For an established company, the market price per share can be computed as follows:

$$\frac{\text{Expected dividend}}{\text{Cost of capital} - \text{growth rate in dividends}}$$

EXAMPLE 15.7 Golden Corporation expects the dividend for the year to be $10 a share. The cost of capital is 13 percent. The growth rate in dividends is expected to be constant at 8 percent. The price per share is:

$$\text{Price per share} = \frac{\text{expected dividend}}{\text{cost of capital} - \text{growth rate in dividends}} = \frac{\$10}{0.13 - 0.08} = \frac{\$10}{0.05} = \$200$$

Another approach to pricing the share of stock for an existing company is through the use of the price/earnings (P/E) ratio, which is equal to:

$$\frac{\text{Market price per share}}{\text{Earnings per share}}$$

EXAMPLE 15.8 Grace Corporation's earnings per share is $7. It is expected that the company's stock should sell at eight times its earnings. The market price per share is therefore

$$\text{P/E} = \frac{\text{market price per share}}{\text{earnings per share}}$$

$$\text{Market price per share} = \text{P/E multiple} \times \text{earnings per share} = 8 \times \$7 = \$56$$

The financial manager may wish to determine the market value of a company's stock. There are a number of different ways to do this.

EXAMPLE 15.9 Assuming an indefinite stream of future dividends of $300,000 and a required rate of return of 14 percent, the market value of the stock equals:

$$\text{Market value} = \frac{\text{expected dividends}}{\text{rate of return}} = \frac{\$300,000}{0.14} = \$2,142,857$$

If there are 200,000 shares, the market price per share is:

$$\frac{\text{Market value}}{\text{Number of shares}} = \frac{\$2,142,857}{200,000} = \$10.71$$

EXAMPLE 15.10 Technical Corporation is considering a public issue of its securities. The average price/earnings multiple in the industry is 15. The company's net income is $400,000. There will be 100,000 shares outstanding subsequent to the issuance of the stock. The expected price per share is:

$$\text{Total market value} = \text{net income} \times \text{price/earnings multiple}$$
$$= \$400,000 \times 15 = \$6,000,000$$

$$\text{Price per share} = \frac{\text{market value}}{\text{number of shares}} = \frac{\$6,000,000}{100,000} = \$60$$

EXAMPLE 15.11 Pinston Corporation issues 400,000 new shares of common stock to present stockholders at a $25 price per share. The price per share prior to the issue is $29. Currently, there are 500,000 outstanding shares. The expected price per share after the new issue is:

Value of outstanding shares	
(500,000 × $29)	$14,500,000
Value of newly issued shares	
(400,000 × $25)	10,000,000
Value of entire issue	$24,500,000

$$\text{Value per share} = \frac{\text{value of entire shares}}{\text{total number of shares}} = \frac{\$24,500,000}{900,000} = \$27.22$$

EXAMPLE 15.12 Prider Corporation is considering building a new plant. The firm has typically distributed all its earnings in the form of dividends. Capital expansion has been financed through common stock issuance. In the capital structure, there is no outstanding preferred stock or debt.

The following expectations exist:

Net income	$23,000,000
Shares outstanding	5,000,000
Construction cost of new plant	$16,000,000

Incremental annual earnings expected because of the new plant is $2 million. The rate of return anticipated by stockholders is 12 percent per annum. The total market value of the firm if the plant is financed through the issuance of common stock is:

$$\frac{\text{Total net income}}{\text{Rate of return}} = \frac{\$25,000,000}{0.12} = \$208,330,000$$

The financial manager may wish to compute the company's price/earnings ratio and required rate of return.

EXAMPLE 15.13 Davis Corporation has experienced an 8 percent growth rate in earnings and dividends. Next year, it anticipates earnings per share of $4 and dividends per share of $2.50. The company will be having its first public issue of common stock. The stock will be issued at $50 per share.

The price/earnings ratio is:

$$\frac{\text{Market price per share}}{\text{Earnings per share}} = \frac{\$50}{\$4} = 12.5 \text{ times}$$

The required rate of return on the stock is:

$$\frac{\text{Dividends per share}}{\text{Market price per share}} + \text{growth rate in dividends}$$

$$\frac{\$2.50}{\$50} + 0.08 = 0.13$$

When the degree of financial leverage is excessive, the company would be better off financing with an equity issue.

Financing with common stock has the following advantages:

1. There is no requirement to pay dividends.

2. There is no repayment date.

3. A common stock issue improves the company's credit rating relative to the issuance of debt.

Financing with common stock has the following disadvantages:

1. Dividends are not tax-deductible.

2. Ownership interest is diluted. The additional voting rights could vote to take control away from the current ownership group.

3. Earnings and dividends are spread over more shares outstanding.

4. The flotation costs associated with a common stock issue are higher than with preferred stock and debt financing.

It is always cheaper to finance operations from internally generated funds. Financing out of retained earnings involves no flotation costs.

Stockholders are generally better off when a firm cuts back on its dividends rather than issuing common stock as a source of needed additional funds. First, when earnings are retained rather than new stock issued, the market price per share of existing stock will rise, as indicated by higher earnings per share. Second, if stock is held for more than 6 months and then sold at a gain, the investor will get a tax advantage with a capital gain deduction. The capital gain deduction is 40 percent, which means that only 40 percent of the gain is taxable. However, cash dividends are fully taxable. Thus, there is a tax benefit to investors, with a reduction in dividends. One caution, however: Lower dividend payments may be viewed negatively in the market and may result in a reduction in the market price of stock due to psychological factors.

15.6 STOCK RIGHTS

Stock rights represent the option to purchase securities at a specified price at a future date. The preemptive right provides that existing stockholders have the first option to buy additional shares in the company. Exercising this right permits them to maintain voting control and protects against dilution in ownership and earnings.

EXAMPLE 15.14 Charles Corporation has 500,000 shares of common stock outstanding and is planning to issue another 100,000 shares through stock rights. Each current stockholder will receive one right per share. Each right enables the stockholder to buy $\frac{1}{5}$ of a share of new common stock (100,000 shares/500,000 shares). Hence, 5 rights are needed to acquire one share of stock. Hence, a shareholder holding 10,000 shares would be able to purchase 2,000 new shares ($10,000 \times \frac{1}{5}$). By exercising his or her right, the stockholder would now have a total of 12,000 shares, constituting a 2 percent interest (12,000/600,000) in the total shares outstanding. This is the same 2 percent ownership (10,000/500,000) the stockholder held before the rights offering.

In a rights offering, there is a date of record, which states the last day that the receiver of the right must be the legal owner as reflected in the firm's stock ledger. Because of a lag in bookkeeping, stocks are often sold *ex rights* (without rights) 4 business days before the record date. Before this point, the stock is sold *rights on*, which means that purchasers receive the rights.

The recipient of the rights can exercise them, sell them, or let them expire. Since stock rights are transferable, many are traded on the stock exchange and over-the-counter markets. They may be exercised for a given period of time at a *subscription price*, which is set somewhat below the prevailing market price.

After the subscription price has been determined, management must ascertain the number of rights necessary to purchase a share of stock. The total number of shares that must be sold equals:

$$\text{Shares to be sold} = \frac{\text{amount of funds to be obtained}}{\text{subscription price}}$$

The number of rights needed to acquire one share equals:

$$\text{Rights per share} = \frac{\text{total shares outstanding}}{\text{shares to be sold}}$$

EXAMPLE 15.15 Star Corporation wishes to obtain $800,000 by a rights offering. There are currently 100,000 shares outstanding. The subscription price is $40 a share. The shares to be sold equal:

$$\text{Shares to be sold} = \frac{\text{amount of funds to be obtained}}{\text{subscription price}} = \frac{\$800,000}{\$40} = 20,000 \text{ shares}$$

The number of rights needed to acquire one share equals:

$$\text{Rights per share} = \frac{\text{total shares outstanding}}{\text{shares to be sold}} = \frac{100,000}{20,000} = 5$$

Thus, 5 rights will be required to purchase each new share at $40. Each right enables the holder to buy $\frac{1}{5}$ of a share of stock.

Value of a Right

The value of a right should, theoretically, be the same whether the stock is selling with rights on or with ex rights.

When stock is selling with rights on, the value of a right equals:

$$\text{Value of right} = \frac{\text{market value of stock with rights on} - \text{subscription price}}{\text{number of rights needed to buy one share} + 1}$$

EXAMPLE 15.16 Charles Company's common stock sells for $55 a share with rights on. Each stockholder is given the right to buy one new share at $35 for every four shares held. The value of each right is:

$$\text{Value of right} = \frac{\text{market value with rights on} - \text{subscription price}}{\text{number of rights needed to buy one share} + 1}$$
$$= \frac{\$55 - \$35}{4 + 1} = \frac{\$20}{5} = \$4$$

When stock is traded ex rights, the market price is anticipated to decline by the value of the right. The market value of stock trading ex rights should theoretically equal:

$$\text{Market value of stock with rights on} - \text{value of a right when stock is selling rights on}$$

The value of a right when stock is selling ex rights equals:

$$\text{Value of right} = \frac{\text{market value of stock trading ex rights} - \text{subscription price}}{\text{number of rights needed to buy one new share}}$$

EXAMPLE 15.17   Assuming the same facts as those in Example 15.16, the value of the right of Charles Company stock trading ex rights should equal:

Market value of stock with rights on − value of a right when stock is selling rights on

$$\$55 - \$4 = \$51$$

The value of a right when stock is selling ex rights is therefore:

$$\text{Value of right} = \frac{\text{market value of stock trading ex rights} - \text{subscription price}}{\text{number of rights needed to buy one new share}}$$

$$= \frac{\$51 - \$35}{4} = \frac{\$16}{4} = \$4$$

Notice that the theoretical value of the right is identical when the stock is selling rights on or ex rights.

15.7 STOCKHOLDERS' EQUITY SECTION OF THE BALANCE SHEET

The stockholders' equity section of a company's balance sheet consists of:

1. *Capital stock*, which includes the stock issued by the corporation and stated at par value. The two types of capital stock are preferred and common. Also included in the capital stock section are stock rights.

2. *Paid-in capital*, which represents the excess over par value received by a corporation for the issuance of stock.

3. *Retained earnings*, which refers to the accumulated earnings of the company less any dividends paid out.

The company records the issuance of stock only when it *initially* sells it to the stockholder.

When one stockholder sells his or her shares, the transaction is not entered on the corporation's books. The company need only change the name on its records to that of the new stockholder so that dividends may be properly paid.

Treasury stock is shown in the stockholders' equity section as a deduction when computing total stockholders' equity.

15.8 GOVERNMENTAL REGULATION

When securities are issued publicly, they must conform to federal and state regulations. State rules are referred to as *blue sky laws*. The major federal laws are the Securities Act of 1933 and the Securities Exchange Act of 1934. The 1934 act applies to existing security transactions, while the 1933 act deals with regulation of new security issues. The acts require full disclosure to investors concerning the company's affairs. Prior to the issuance of a new security, the company must prepare a prospectus for investors which contains a condensed version of the registration statement filed with the SEC.

15.9 FINANCING STRATEGY

The corporation financial manager is concerned with selecting the best possible source of financing based on the facts of the situation. This section describes various circumstances in which a particular financing source is most suited.

EXAMPLE 15.18   Tart Corporation is considering issuing either debt or preferred stock to finance the acquisition of a plant costing $1.3 million. The interest rate on the debt is 15 percent. The dividend rate on the preferred stock is 10 percent. The tax rate is 46 percent.

The annual interest payment on the debt is:

$$15\% \times \$1,300,000 = \$195,000$$

The annual dividend on the preferred stock is:

$$10\% \times \$1,300,000 = \$130,000$$

The required earnings before interest and taxes to meet the dividend payment is:

$$\frac{\$130,000}{(1 - 0.46)} = \$240,741$$

If the company anticipates earning $240,741 without difficulty, it should issue the preferred stock.

EXAMPLE 15.19   Charles Corporation has previously used short-term financing. It is now considering refinancing its short-term debt with equity or long-term debt securities. The financial manager decided to list the factors that should be taken into account when selecting an appropriate means of financing. These factors are:

1. The costs of the instruments
2. The company's earnings compared to the cost of debt and preferred stock
3. The recurrence in sales and earnings
4. The degree of financial leverage
5. The maturity and degree of success of the firm
6. The degree of dilution in voting control to be tolerated
7. The firm's solvency status

EXAMPLE 15.20   Pride Corporation has sales of $30 million a year. It needs $6 million in financing for capital expansion. The debt/equity ratio is 68 percent. The company is in a risky industry, and net income is not stable year to year. The common stock is selling at a high P/E ratio relative to the competition. Under consideration is either the issuance of common stock or a convertible bond.

Because the company is in a high-risk industry and has a high debt/equity ratio and fluctuating earnings, the issuance of common stock is preferred.

EXAMPLE 15.21   Wilson Corporation is a mature company in its industry. It has a limited ownership. The company has a fluctuating sales and earnings stream. The firm's debt/equity ratio is 70 percent relative to the industry standard of 55 percent. The after-tax rate of return is 16 percent. Since Wilson's is a seasonal business, there are given times during the year when its liquidity position is deficient. The company is undecided on the best means of financing.

Preferred stock is one possible means of financing. Debt financing is not recommended because of the already high debt/equity ratio, the variability in earnings, and the poor liquidity position. Because of the limited ownership, common stock financing may not be appropriate since this would dilute the ownership.

EXAMPLE 15.22   A new company is established and it plans to raise $15 million in funds. The company anticipates that it will obtain contracts that will provide $1,200,000 a year in before-tax profits. The firm is considering whether to issue bonds only or an equal amount of bonds and preferred stock. The interest rate on AA corporate bonds is 12 percent. The tax rate is 50 percent.

The firm will probably have difficulty issuing $15 million of AA bonds because the interest cost of $1,800,000 (12% × $15,000,000) associated with these bonds is greater than the estimated earnings before interest and taxes. The issuance of debt by a new company is a risky alternative.

Financing with $7.5 million in debt and $7.5 million in preferred stock is also not recommended. While some debt may be issued, it is not feasible to finance the balance with preferred stock. In the event that $7.5 million of AA bonds were issued at the 12 percent rate, the company would be obligated to pay $900,000 in interest. In this event, a forecasted income statement would look as follows:

Earnings before interest and taxes	$1,200,000
Interest	900,000
Taxable income	$ 300,000
Taxes	150,000
Net income	$ 150,000

The amount available for the payment of preferred dividends is only $150,000. Hence, the maximum rate of return that could be paid on $7.5 million of preferred stock is:

$$\frac{\$150,000}{\$7,500,000} = 0.02$$

Stockholders would not invest in preferred stock that offers only a 2 percent rate of return.

The company should consider financing with common stock.

EXAMPLE 15.23 Boyser Corporation wishes to construct a plant that will take about $1\frac{1}{2}$ years to build. The plant will be used to manufacture a new product line, for which Boyser anticipates a high demand. The new plant will significantly increase the company's size. The following costs are expected to occur:

1. The cost to build the plant, $800,000
2. Funds required for contingencies, $100,000
3. Annual operating costs, $175,000

The asset, debt, and equity positions of the firm are similar to industry standards. The market price of the firm's stock is less than it should be, considering the future earning power of the new product line. What would be an appropriate way to finance the construction?

Because the market price of stock is less than it should be and considering the potential of the product line, convertible bonds and installment bank loans might be appropriate means of financing, since interest expense is tax-deductible. Further, the issuance of convertible bonds might not require repayment, since the bonds are likely to be converted to common stock because of the firm's profitability. Installment bank loans can be gradually paid off as the new product generates cash inflow. Funds required for contingencies can be in the form of open bank lines of credit.

If the market price of the stock was not at a depressed level, financing through equity would be an alternative financing strategy.

EXAMPLE 15.24 Davis Company wishes to acquire Gortman Corporation but has not decided on an optimum means to finance the purchase. The current debt/equity position is within the industry guideline. In previous years, financing has been accomplished through the issuance of short-term debt.

Earnings have shown instability over the years and consequently the market price of the stock has fluctuated. At present, however, the market price of stock is strong.

The company's tax bracket is low.

The acquisition should be financed through the issuance of equity securities for the following reasons:

1. The market price of stock is presently at a high level.
2. The issuance of long-term debt will result in more instability in earnings due to high fixed interest charges. As a result, there will be greater instability in the company's stock price.
3. The issuance of more debt will cause the firm's debt/equity ratio to rise above the industry norm. This will adversely affect the company's cost of capital and availability of financing.
4. Because it will take a long time to derive the funds necessary for the acquisition cost, short-term debt should not be issued. If short-term debt is issued, the debt would have to be met prior to the receipt of the return from the acquired business.

EXAMPLE 15.25 Breakstone Corporation wishes to undertake a capital expansion program and must, therefore, obtain $7 million in financing. The company has a good credit rating. The current market price of its common stock is $60. The interest rate for long-term debt is 18 percent. The dividend rate associated with preferred stock is 16 percent, and Breakstone's tax rate is 46 percent.

Relevant ratios for the industry and the company are:

	Industry	Breakstone
Net income to total assets	13%	22%
Long-term debt to total assets	31%	29%
Total liabilities to total assets	47%	45%
Preferred stock to total assets	3%	0
Current ratio	2.6	3.2
Net income plus interest to interest	8	17

Dividends per share is $8, the dividend growth rate is 7 percent, no sinking fund provisions exist, the trend in earnings shows stability, and the present ownership group wishes to retain control. The cost of common stock is:

$$\frac{\text{Dividends per share}}{\text{Market price per share}} + \text{dividend growth rate}$$

$$\frac{\$8}{\$60} + 0.07 = 20.3\%$$

The after-tax cost of long-term debt is 9.7 percent (18% × 54%). The cost of preferred stock is 16 percent. How should Breakstone finance its expansion?

The issuance of long-term debt is more appropriate for the following reasons:

1. Its after-tax cost is the lowest.

2. The company's ratios of long-term debt to total assets and total liabilities to total assets are less than the industry average, pointing to the company's ability to issue additional debt.

3. Corporate liquidity is satisfactory based on the favorable current ratio relative to the industry standard.

4. Fixed interest charges can be met, taking into account the stability in earnings, the earning power of the firm, and the very favorable times-interest-earned ratio. Additional interest charges should be met without difficulty.

5. The firm's credit rating is satisfactory.

6. There are no required sinking fund provisions.

7. The leveraging effect can take place to further improve earnings.

In the case that the firm does not want to finance through further debt, preferred stock would be the next best financing alternative, since its cost is lower than that associated with common stock and no dilution in the ownership interest will take place.

EXAMPLE 15.26 Harris Corporation has experienced growth in revenue and net income but is in a weak liquidity position. The inflation rate is high. At the end of 19X5, the firm needs $600,000 for the following reasons:

New equipment	$175,000
Research and development	95,000
Paying overdue accounts payable	215,000
Paying accrued liabilities	60,000
Desired increase in cash balance	55,000
	$600,000

Presented below are the financial statements for 19X5.

Harris Corporation
Balance Sheet
Dec. 31, 19X5

ASSETS

Current assets

Cash	$ 12,000	
Accounts receivable	140,000	
Notes receivable	25,000	
Inventory	165,000	
Office supplies	20,000	
Total current assets		$362,000
Fixed assets		468,000
Total assets		$830,000

LIABILITIES AND STOCKHOLDERS' EQUITY

Current liabilities

Loans payable	$ 74,000	
Accounts payable	360,000	
Accrued liabilities	55,000	
Total current liabilities		$489,000
Long-term debt		61,000
Total liabilities		$550,000
Stockholders' equity		
Common stock	$200,000	
Retained earnings	80,000	
Total stockholders' equity		280,000
Total liabilities and stockholders' equity		$830,000

Harris Corporation
Income Statement
For the Year Ended Dec. 31, 19X5

Sales	$1,400,000
Cost of sales	750,000
Gross margin	$ 650,000
Operating expenses	480,000
Income before tax	$ 170,000
Tax	68,000
Net income	$ 102,000

It is anticipated that sales will increase on a yearly basis by 22 percent and that net income will increase by 17 percent. What type of financing is best suited for Harris Corporation?

The most suitable source of financing is long-term. A company in a growth stage needs a large investment in equipment, and research and development expenditure. With regard to 19X5, $270,000 of the $600,000 is required for this purpose. A growth company also needs funds to satisfy working capital requirements. Here,

45.8 percent of financing is necessary to pay overdue accounts payable and accrued liabilities. The firm also needs sufficient cash to capitalize on lucrative opportunities. The present cash balance to total assets is at a low 1.4 percent.

Long-term debt financing is recommended for the following reasons:

1. The ratio of long-term debt to stockholders' equity is a low 21.8 percent. The additional issuance of long-term debt will not impair the overall capital structure.

2. The company has been profitable and there is an expectation of future growth in earnings. Internally generated funds should therefore ensue, enabling the payment of fixed interest charges.

3. During inflation, the issuance of long-term debt generates purchasing power gains because the firm will be repaying creditors in cheaper dollars.

4. Interest expense is tax-deductible.

Review Questions

1. The two sources of equity financing are _____ and _____.

2. A(n) _____ enables the future purchase of stock.

3. A(n) _____ purchases and distributes new securities of a company.

4. When a group of investment bankers handle a large issue, the group is referred to as a(n) _____.

5. The investment banker who manages the group is called the _____.

6. The two types of underwriting syndicates are _____ and _____.

7. A(n) _____ purchases securities and holds them in inventory for later resale.

8. A(n) _____ handles transactions for securities on the stock exchanges.

9. When securities are _____ they are sold to a few institutional investors.

10. The expense related to registering and selling a security is called _____ cost.

11. One advantage of a private placement is that it avoids _____ filing requirements.

12. _____ preferred stock means that if dividends are not paid in a particular year, they must be paid in a later year before any distributions are given to common stockholders.

13. Preferred dividends are based on the total _____ of the outstanding shares.

14. _____ preferred stock means that preferred shareholders will participate with common shareholders in any excess dividends.

15. For corporate investors, dividends received are subject to a(n) _____ dividend exclusion.

16. A(n) _____ statement gives management the right to vote a common stockholders' shares.

17. The maximum amount of shares the company can issue as per the corporate charter are the _____ shares.

18. Shares that have been sold to the public are called _____ shares.

19. _____ is stock which has been bought back by the company.

20. _____ equal issued shares less treasury shares.

21. Each stock has a(n) _____ that is specified in the corporate charter.

22. The _____ right allows a stockholder to purchase new shares of stock before they are sold to the general public.

23. The stockholders' equity section of a company's balance sheet consists of the _____, _____, and _____ sections.

Answers: (1) common stock, preferred stock; (2) stock right; (3) investment banker; (4) syndicate; (5) originating house; (6) divided, undivided; (7) dealer; (8) broker; (9) privately placed; (10) flotation; (11) SEC; (12) Cumulative; (13) par value; (14) Participating; (15) 85%; (16) proxy; (17) authorized; (18) issued; (19) Treasury stock; (20) Outstanding shares; (21) par value; (22) preemptive; (23) capital stock, paid-in capital, retained earnings.

Solved Problems

15.1 Dividends Payable to Preferred. On December 31, 19X4, Arco Company had 5,000 shares of $10 par value, 15 percent, cumulative preferred stock outstanding. Dividends are in arrears for 3 years. Since 19X4 was a profitable year, the company paid its dividend in full. What is the total dividend payable to preferred stockholders?

SOLUTION

Total par value (5,000 shares × $10)	$50,000
Dividends in arrears	
($50,000 × 15% × 3 years)	$22,500
Current year dividend ($50,000 × 15%)	7,500
Total dividend	$30,000

15.2 Dividends. Harris Corporation has the following equity securities outstanding:

Preferred stock, participating, 20,000 shares,	
$15 par value, 14% dividend rate	$300,000
Common stock, 5,000 shares, $20 par value	$100,000

The dividend rate declared on the common stock is 12 percent, and dividends declared for the year are $60,000. Determine the amount of the dividend to be paid to preferred stockholders and common stockholders.

SOLUTION

	Preferred Stock	Common Stock
Regular preferred dividend (14% × $300,000)	$42,000	
Regular common dividend (12% × $100,000)		$12,000
Excess dividend allocated based on relative par value:		
Preferred $\left(\dfrac{\$300,000}{\$400,000} \times \$6,000\right)$	4,500	
Common $\left(\dfrac{\$100,000}{\$400,000} \times \$6,000\right)$		1,500
Total dividend	$46,500	$13,500

15.3   Effective Cost of Preferred Stock. Star Corporation issued $5 million of preferred stock. The flotation cost was 10 percent of gross proceeds. The dividend rate is 16 percent. What is the effective cost of the preferred stock?

SOLUTION

$$\frac{\text{Dividend}}{\text{Net proceeds}} = \frac{0.16(\$5,000,000)}{\$5,000,000 - 0.10(\$5,000,000)} = \frac{\$800,000}{\$4,500,000} = 17.8\%$$

15.4   Receipt per Share. Appel Corporation is considering expanding. It plans to finance the expansion by issuing $4 million in preferred stock. The preferred stock has a par value of $50 and a dividend rate of 12 percent. Similar issues of preferred stock are presently yielding 14 percent.

(a) How much will the company receive for each share? (b) How many shares must be issued?

SOLUTION

(a) $\dfrac{\text{Dividend}}{\text{Market yield}} = \dfrac{0.12 \times \$50}{0.14} = \dfrac{\$6}{0.14} = \$42.86$

(b) $\dfrac{\text{Funds required}}{\text{Price per share}} = \dfrac{\$4,000,000}{\$42.86} = 93,327 \text{ shares (rounded)}$

15.5   Shares to Be Sold. Simon Corporation has 800,000 common shares outstanding. The capital budget for the upcoming year is $2 million. New stock may be sold for $20 a share.

(a) What is the number of shares that must be sold to obtain the needed funds? (b) What percent of the total shares outstanding will the new stockholders own?

SOLUTION

(a) $\dfrac{\text{Funds needed}}{\text{Market price per share}} = \dfrac{\$2,000,000}{\$20} = 100,000 \text{ shares}$

(b) $\dfrac{\text{Newly issued shares}}{\text{Total shares}} = \dfrac{100,000}{800,000 + 100,000} = \dfrac{100,000}{900,000} = 11.1\%$

15.6   Expected Price. Saft Corporation wants to obtain $4 million in its first public issue of common stock. After the issuance, the total market value of stock is estimated at $10 million. At present, there are 120,000 closely held shares.

(a) What is the amount of new shares that must be issued to obtain the $4 million? (b) After the stock issuance, what will be the expected price per share?

SOLUTION

(a)   The new shares will be 40 percent ($4 million/$10 million) of the outstanding shares subsequent to the stock issuance. Thus, current stockholders will be holding 60 percent of the shares.

$$120,000 \text{ shares} = 60\% \text{ of the total shares}$$
$$\text{Total shares} = 200,000$$
$$\text{New shares} = 40\% \times 200,000 = 80,000 \text{ shares}$$

(b) $$\text{Price per share} = \frac{\text{market value}}{\text{outstanding shares}} = \frac{\$10,000,000}{200,000} = \$50$$

15.7   Price per Share. Gallagher Corporation anticipates a $6 dividend per share for the year. Its minimum rate of return is 12 percent. The dividend growth rate is 6 percent. What is the price per share?

SOLUTION

$$\frac{\text{Expected dividend}}{\text{Minimum return} - \text{dividend growth rate}} = \frac{\$6}{0.12 - 0.06} = \frac{\$6}{0.06} = \$100$$

15.8   Market Value. A company expects an indefinite stream of future dividends of $200,000 and a required rate of return of 16 percent. There are 100,000 shares.

(a) What is the market value of the stock? (b) What is the market price per share?

SOLUTION

(a) $$\text{Market value} = \frac{\text{expected dividends}}{\text{rate of return}} = \frac{\$200,000}{0.16} = \$1,250,000$$

(b) $$\text{Market price per share} = \frac{\text{market value}}{\text{number of shares}} = \frac{\$1,250,000}{100,000} = \$12.50$$

15.9   Expected Price. Wolinsky Corporation is considering a public issuance of its securities. The average P/E ratio in the industry is 12. The firm's reported earnings are $300,000. After the issuance of the stock, there will be 200,000 shares outstanding. What is the expected price per share?

SOLUTION

$$\text{Total market value} = \text{earnings} \times \text{P/E} = \$300,000 \times 12 = \$3,600,000$$

$$\text{Price per share} = \frac{\text{market value}}{\text{shares outstanding}} = \frac{\$3,600,000}{200,000} = \$18$$

15.10   Expected Price. Nelson Corporation issues 200,000 new shares of common stock to current stockholders at a $15 price per share. The price per share before the issue was $18. At present, there are 300,000 shares outstanding. What is the expected price per share after the new issue?

SOLUTION

Value of outstanding shares	
($300,000 \times \$18$)	\$5,400,000
Value of newly issued shares	
($200,000 \times \$15$)	3,000,000
Value of entire issue	\$8,400,000

$$\text{Value per share} = \frac{\text{value of entire shares}}{\text{total shares}} = \frac{\$8,400,000}{500,000} = \$16.80$$

15.11 Total Market Value. Stephens Corporation is thinking about constructing a new facility. The company has usually distributed its earnings in the form of dividends. Common stock has typically been issued to finance capital expansion. Preferred stock and debt are not in the capital structure.

The company's expectations follow:

Net income	\$18,000,000
Outstanding shares	2,000,000
Construction cost of new facility	\$10,000,000

The expected additional earnings due to the new facility is \$2 million. The expected stockholder rate of return is 16 percent per annum. What is the total market value of the company, assuming the facility is financed with common stock?

SOLUTION

$$\frac{\text{Total net income}}{\text{Rate of return}} = \frac{\$20,000,000}{0.16} = \$125,000,000$$

15.12 P/E Ratio. Wilson Corporation anticipates a 10 percent growth in net income and dividends. Next year, the company expects earnings per share of \$5 and dividends per share of \$3. Wilson will be having its first public issuance of common stock. The stock will be issued at \$40 per share.

(*a*) What is the P/E ratio? (*b*) What is the required rate of return on the stock?

SOLUTION

(*a*)
$$\frac{\text{Market price per share}}{\text{Earnings per share}} = \frac{\$40}{\$5} = 8 \text{ times}$$

(*b*)
$$\frac{\text{Dividends per share}}{\text{Market price per share}} + \text{dividend growth rate} = \frac{\$3}{\$40} + 0.10 = 17.5\%$$

15.13 Preemptive Right. Barker Company has 400,000 shares of common stock outstanding and is considering issuing another 100,000 shares through stock rights. Each current stockholder will obtain one right per share. Mr. A owns 40,000 shares of common stock.

(*a*) What amount of each new share of common stock can a stockholder acquire by each right? (*b*) How many rights are required to purchase one new share of common stock? (*c*) How many new shares will Mr. A be able to obtain? (*d*) What will Mr. A's percentage interest in the company be after exercising all his rights? (*e*) Did his percentage ownership change after exercising his rights relative to what it was before the rights offering?

SOLUTION

(a)
$$\text{Rights per share} = \frac{\text{shares to be sold}}{\text{shares outstanding}} = \frac{100,000}{400,000} = \frac{1}{4}$$

(b)
$$\text{Rights required for 1 share} = \frac{\text{shares outstanding}}{\text{shares to be sold}} = \frac{400,000}{100,000} = 4$$

(c)
$$\text{Share available to a stockholder} = \text{shares held} \times \text{right per share} = \frac{40,000 \times 1}{4} = 10,000 \text{ shares}$$

(d)
$$\% \text{ Ownership} = \frac{\text{shares held} + \text{shares bought on rights}}{\text{total shares outstanding}} = \frac{50,000}{500,000} = 10\%$$

(e) No. The percentage ownership is the same. Before the rights offering Mr. A also held a 10 percent interest (40,000/400,000).

15.14 Rights per Share. Mason Corporation intends to raise $1.5 million in a rights offering. At present, there are 240,000 shares outstanding. A subscription price of $25 a share is assigned.

(a) How many shares must be sold? (b) How many rights are needed to purchase one share of stock?

SOLUTION

(a)
$$\text{Shares to be sold} = \frac{\text{amount of funds to be obtained}}{\text{subscription price}} = \frac{\$1,500,000}{\$25} = 60,000 \text{ shares}$$

(b) The number of rights needed to acquire one share equals:

$$\text{Rights per share} = \frac{\text{total shares outstanding}}{\text{shares to be sold}} = \frac{240,000}{60,000} = 4$$

15.15 Value per Right. Charles Corporation stock sells at $78 a share with rights on. The subscription price is $60, and five rights are needed to purchase a new share of stock. What is the value of each right?

SOLUTION

$$\text{Value of right} = \frac{\text{market value with rights on} - \text{subscription price}}{\text{number of rights to buy 1 share} + 1} = \frac{\$78 - \$60}{5 + 1} = \frac{\$18}{6} = \$3$$

15.16 Value per Right. Assume the same facts as in Problem 15.15. (a) What will be the market value of the stock trading ex rights? (b) What is the value of a right when the stock is selling ex rights?

SOLUTION

(a) Value of stock, ex rights = market value of stock with rights on − value of right = $78 − $3 = $75

(b) Value of right (when stock sells ex rights) = $\dfrac{\text{market value of stock, ex rights} - \text{subscription price}}{\text{number of rights to buy 1 share}}$

$$= \frac{\$75 - \$60}{5} = \frac{\$15}{5} = \$3$$

15.17 Cost of Financing. Mason Corporation is considering the issuance of either debt or preferred stock to finance the purchase of a facility costing $1.5 million. The interest rate on the debt is 16 percent. Preferred stock has a dividend rate of 12 percent. The tax rate is 46 percent.

(*a*) What is the annual interest payment? (*b*) What is the annual dividend payment? (*c*) What is the required income before interest and taxes to satisfy the dividend requirement?

SOLUTION

(*a*)
$$\text{Annual interest} = 16\% \times \$1,500,000 = \$240,000$$

(*b*)
$$\text{Annual dividend} = 12\% \times \$1,500,000 = \$180,000$$

(*c*)
$$\text{Before-tax income required for dividend} = \frac{\text{dividend}}{1-t} = \frac{\$180,000}{(1-0.46)} = \$333,333$$

15.18 Common Stock versus Debt. Blake Corporation has $20 million in sales a year. It requires $3.5 million in financing for capital expansion. The debt/equity ratio is 70 percent. The industry has inherent risk, and earnings show variability. The common stock is selling at a high P/E ratio. The company is considering issuing either common stock or debt. Which type of financing is recommended?

SOLUTION

Since Blake is in a high-risk industry, has a high debt/equity ratio, and shows variability in earnings, issuing more debt would be expensive, restrictive, and potentially dangerous to Blake's future financial health. Common stock should therefore be issued, although this will dilute ownership.

15.19 Type of Financing. Krul Corporation is an established company in its industry. It has a limited ownership. The trend in revenue and earnings has shown variability. The company's debt/equity ratio is considerably higher than the industry norm. The after-tax rate of return is 18 percent. The company's business is seasonal. What method of financing is most suitable?

SOLUTION

Debt financing is inadvisable due to the high debt/equity ratio, the earnings variability, and the seasonal nature of the business. Issuance of common stock is not suggested because of the limited ownership. Preferred stock appears to be the best means of financing.

15.20 Financing Strategy. A new company plans to obtain $18 million in financing. The company expects to obtain a yearly income of $2 million before interest and taxes. The firm is considering issuing bonds or an equal amount of bonds and preferred stock. The interest rate on bonds is 14 percent. The tax rate is 46 percent. What financing strategy would you recommend?

SOLUTION

It would be difficult to issue $18 million in bonds because the interest cost of $2,520,000 (14% × $18,000,000) exceeds the anticipated before-tax profit. Also, there is always risk when a new company issues debt.

Financing equally with debt and preferred stock is not advisable. With the issuance of $9 million in debt at 14 percent, the company incurs $1,260,000 in interest charges. The following forecasted income statement applies to this plan:

Income before interest and taxes	$2,000,000
Interest	1,260,000
Taxable income	$ 740,000
Taxes	340,400
Net income	$ 399,600

The amount available to pay preferred dividends is only $399,600. Thus, the maximum return that can be derived on the $9 million of preferred stock is:

$$\frac{\$399,600}{\$9,000,000} = 4.4\%$$

Investors would not be interested in buying preferred stock having a rate of return of only 4.4 percent.

15.21 Means of Financing. Midas Corporation wants to build a new facility that will produce a new product line. The company expects the following costs to arise:

Cost to construct facility	$1,100,000
Funds needed to meet contingencies	$200,000
Annual operating costs	$225,000

The new facility will materially increase the corporate size. The asset and debt ratios of the firm are in conformity with industry norms. Taking into account the future earning potential of the new product line, the company's market price per share is less than what it should be. What is an appropriate means of financing the new facility?

SOLUTION

Since the market price of stock is temporarily depressed and considering the potential success of the product line, convertible bonds appear to be a wise financing strategy. With convertible bonds interest expense is tax-deductible. Also, the issuance of convertible bonds will not mandate repayment because the bonds will probably be converted to common stock as the company becomes more profitable due to the new product line. Another possible financing source is installment bank loans, which may be paid off gradually as cash flow is derived from the new product. Open bank lines of credit may be used to meet possible contingencies.

15.22 Means of Financing. Sunder Corporation wants to acquire another company but is unsure of the best basis to finance the purchase. The company's financial leverage is about the same as the industry average. In prior years, short-term debt has been used for financing. Net income and price per share have shown variability over the years. However, the market price of stock is now strong. The firm is in a low tax bracket.

What means of financing is recommended?

SOLUTION

Equity securities appear to be a good financing source for the following reasons:

1. The price per share is currently high.
2. If long-term debt is issued, there will be higher fixed charges resulting in greater variability in earnings. This in turn will cause instability in the price per share. Also, debt issuance will make the company's degree of financial leverage higher than the industry norm. This may impair the firm's cost of financing and availability of funds.
3. Short-term debt should not be employed, since the debt will have to be met before the receipt of the return from the acquired business.

15.23 Cost of Financing. Morgan Corporation must obtain $8 million in financing for its expansion plans. The firm's credit rating is good. Common stock is now selling at $50 per share. Preferred stock has a dividend rate of 15 percent. Long-term debt has an interest rate of 19 percent. The tax rate is 46 percent.

Applicable ratios for Morgan and the industry are:

	Industry	Morgan
Net income to total assets	15%	24%
Long-term debt to total assets	29%	26%
Total liabilities to total assets	48%	44%
Preferred stock to total assets	4%	0
Current ratio	3.1	3.8
Net income plus interest to interest	9	15

Dividends per share are $6. The growth rate in dividends is 5 percent, there is no sinking fund provision, net income and sales show stability, and the current ownership group wants to maintain its control.

(a) What is the cost of common stock? (b) What is the cost of preferred stock? (c) What is the cost of long-term debt? (d) What source of financing is recommended?

SOLUTION

(a)
$$\frac{\text{Dividends per share}}{\text{Market price per share}} + \text{growth rate in dividends}$$

$$\frac{\$6}{\$50} + 0.05 = 17\%$$

(b) 15%

(c) 19% × 54% = 10.3%

(d) Long-term debt should be issued for the following reasons:

1. It has the lowest after-tax cost.

2. The firm's debt ratios are below the industry norms, indicating that Morgan can take on additional debt.

3. The company's liquidity is satisfactory, as indicated by the favorable current ratio.

4. Additional interest charges can be satisfied based on the stability in revenue and earnings as well as the favorable interest coverage ratio.

5. The firm has a good credit rating.

6. No sinking fund provisions exist.

7. Assuming the return earned on debt funds exceeds the after-tax interest cost, increased profitability will occur due to the leveraging effect.

8. No dilution in ownership will occur.

15.24 Recommended Financing. Frost Corporation has shown growth in sales and earnings but has a liquidity problem. The rate of inflation is high. At year-end 19X8, the company requires $500,000 for the following reasons:

New machinery	$200,000
Research and development	80,000
Paying overdue obligations	130,000
Paying accrued expenses	25,000
Desired increase in cash balance	65,000
	$500,000

Partial financial statements for 19X8 are shown below.

Frost Corporation
Balance Sheet
Dec. 31, 19X8

ASSETS

Current assets		
Cash	$ 10,000	
Other current assets	320,000	
Total current assets		$330,000
Noncurrent assets		570,000
Total assets		$900,000

LIABILITIES AND
STOCKHOLDERS' EQUITY

Current liabilities		$500,000
Long-term debt		100,000
Total liabilities		$600,000
Stockholders' equity		
Common stock	$250,000	
Retained earnings	50,000	
Total stockholders' equity		300,000
Total liabilities and stockholders' equity		$900,000

Frost Corporation
Income Statement
For the Year Ended Dec. 31, 19X8

Sales	$1,300,000
Cost of sales	600,000
Gross margin	$ 700,000
Operating expenses	500,000
Income before tax	$ 200,000
Tax	86,000
Net income	$ 114,000

The company expects that sales and earnings will increase by 25 percent and 20 percent, respectively

What type of financing is recommended?

SOLUTION

The best type of financing is on a long-term basis. A growing company requires a significant investment in machinery and in research and development. In 19X8, 56 percent of the financing is required for this purpose. A growing company also requires financing to meet working capital needs. Here, 31 percent of the financing is required to pay overdue obligations and accrued expenses. Money is also needed to take advantage of favorable business opportunities. At the current time, the ratio of cash to total assets is a low 1.1 percent.

Financing with long-term debt is recommended for the following reasons:

1. The ratio of long-term debt to stockholders' equity is a low 33.3 percent. Further debt issuance will not hurt the overall capital structure.

2. There is growth in revenue and earnings. As a result, internally generated funds will be able to be used to satisfy the fixed interest charges.

3. In inflationary times, the company will be paying back debt in cheaper dollars.

4. Interest is tax-deductible.

15.25 Financing Options. On average over the past 10 years, Tektronix's return on equity has not been sufficient to finance growth of the business, thus an infusion of new capital from outside sources has been required. Most of the additional capital has been in the form of long-term debt, which represented 13 percent of total capital in fiscal 1977 and 21 percent of total capital in fiscal 1981.

With expansion of the business expected to accelerate in the next few years after the current lull, but, with return on equity likely to remain somewhat depressed because of competitive factors and costs associated with "preparing for the 1980s," a need for additional capital is developing. Also, of the $146 million of long-term debt outstanding at the fiscal 1981 year-end, nearly $65 million matures in the fiscal 1982 to fiscal 1984 period. Thus, it is possible that as much as $100 million of capital may have to be raised to meet all requirements.

In anticipation of capital needs, Tektronix in fiscal 1981 borrowed funds in the commercial paper market, and the company intends to replace these commercial paper borrowings at some future time with long-term financing.

Given the foregoing circumstances, and also given that Tektronix common stock currently is quoted on the New York Stock Exchange at 160 percent of book value and that the current interest rate on newly issued triple-A industrial bonds of long maturity is 14 percent, evaluate on an immediate and longer term basis each of the following options. Include in your answers economic and capital market assumptions. (a) Tektronix is selling 2 million shares of common stock at $50 per share, (b) Tektronix is selling a $100 million straight debenture issue maturing in 20 years, and (c) Tektronix is selling a $100 million bond issue convertible into common stock and maturing in 20 years. (CFA, adapted.)

SOLUTION

(a) From the timing viewpoint, selling equity is attractive considering price-to-book rates (160 percent) and comparatively modest dilution (2 million shares represents 11 percent of currently outstanding shares, less impact of after-tax cost of borrowing to be retired). However, price soon could move higher given a better economic environment, earnings recovery, and resultant stronger general stock market. Long-term, selling equity is expensive, as continuing dividend service is with after-tax dollars. Also, immediate return on equity capital will diminish with reduced leverage as debt matures.

(b) Increasing debt, net of maturities, to a larger part of total capital is tolerable by most standards. According to the data provided, debt of about $146 million would increase to around $181 million ($146 + $100 − $65), and by 1984 this sum presumably would not represent much more than the current 21 percent subject to earnings retention during the interim. However, this would be an appealing option only if interest rate assumptions indicate other than a rather meaningful decline over the next year or two, and if pro forma interest charge coverage and/or the current lull in the business do not seriously impact the rating and issue price of the bonds. The after-tax cost of debt service will be comparatively low, and so would be the net cost of capital. Another consideration will be sinking fund requirements and call restrictions and price.

(c) A convertible bond issue has certain disadvantages but it also has advantages; (1) it can be sold at a lower interest cost than a straight debt, and (2) the potential dilution is less than an issue of common reflecting the premium over the common market.

Examination III

Chapters 12–15

1. Travis Company has 10,000 shares of common stock with a par value of $10 per share. A 4-for-1 stock split is made. The market price of the stock was $16 prior to the split. (*a*) Record the stock split. (*b*) What will the market price per share be immediately subsequent to the stock split?

2. Bravo Corporation's net income for the year was $2.5 million. It pays out 40 percent of its profit in dividends. The company will buy $4 million in new assets, and 55 percent of the assets will be financed by debt. What is the amount of external equity that must be issued?

3. Blake Company had net income of $600,000 in 19X1. Net income has grown at a 5 percent annual rate. Dividends in 19X1 were $200,000. In 19X2, the net income was $700,000. This of course exceeded the 5 percent annual growth rate. It is expected that earnings will return to a 5 percent growth rate in later years.

    What should the dividends paid out in 19X2 be, assuming (*a*) a stable dividend payout ratio of 20 percent, and (*b*) a stable dollar dividend policy is maintained?

4. Whitestone Corporation leases a $60,000 machine. It must make 10 equal year-end annual payments. There is a 14 percent interest rate. What is the annual payment?

5. Mall Corporation leased $120,000 of equipment and is to make year-end annual payments of $19,000 for 16 years. What is the interest rate on the lease?

6. Drake Corporation takes out a term loan payable in 12 year-end annual installments of $5,000 each. The interest rate is 14 percent. (*a*) What is the amount of the loan? (*b*) Prepare an amortization schedule for the loan repayment for the first 2 years.

7. Shillinglaw Corporation has $5 million of 16 percent mortgage bonds outstanding. The indenture permits additional bonds to be issued as long as the following conditions are satisfied: (*a*) The before-tax times-interest-earned ratio is greater than 3. (*b*) Book value of the mortgaged assets are at least four times the amount of debt. (*c*) The debt/equity ratio is less than 0.8.

    The following additional data are given: Income before tax is $12 million, equity is $30 million, book value of mortgaged assets is $60 million, and 20 percent of the proceeds of a new issue would be added to the base of mortgaged assets.

    What amount of additional debt can be issued for each of the conditions (*a*), (*b*), and (*c*)?

8. Blake Company has a $30 million, 12 percent bond issue outstanding with 20 years remaining. The call premium is 7 percent of face value. A new 20-year bond issue for $30 million can be issued at a 10 percent interest rate. Flotation costs related to the new issue are $800,000. Should a refunding of the bond issue take place?

9. Ajax Corporation issued a $400,000, 15 percent, 20-year bond at 96. The call price is 102. Six years after issue the bond is called. What is the call premium?

10. Sharav Corporation has the following equity securities outstanding:

Preferred stock, participating, 15,000 shares,
$10 par value, 12% dividend rate $150,000
Common stock, 10,000 shares, $20 par value ... $200,000

The dividend rate declared on the common stock is 10 percent, and dividends declared for the year are $50,000.

Determine the amount of the dividend to be paid to preferred stockholders and common stockholders.

11. Smith Corporation issued $6 million of preferred stock. The flotation cost was 15 percent of gross proceeds. The dividend rate is 18 percent. What is the effective cost of the preferred stock?

12. Knab Corporation expects to raise $2 million in a rights offering. Currently, there are 250,000 shares outstanding. A subscription price of $40 a share is assigned. (*a*) How many shares must be sold? (*b*) How many rights are required to purchase one share of stock?

13. Barnum Company stock sells at $70 a share with rights on. The subscription price is $55. Four rights are needed to purchase a new share of stock. What is the value of each right?

14. Assume the same facts as in Problem 13. (*a*) What will be the market value of the stock trading ex rights? (*b*) What is the value of a right when the stock is selling ex rights?

Answers to Examination III

1. (*a*) No entry is required, because the company's account balances remain the same. However, a memorandum is required to the effect that there are now 40,000 shares having a par value of $2.50 per share.

(*b*)
$$\frac{\$16}{4} = \$4$$

2.

Net income	$2,500,000
Percent of net income retained	×0.6
Retained	$1,500,000
New assets	$4,000,000
Percent financed by equity	×0.45
Equity financing required	$1,800,000
Retained earnings	1,500,000
External equity to be issued	$ 300,000

3. (*a*)
$$\$700,000 \times 20\% = \$140,000$$

(*b*)
$$\text{Dividend in 19X1} = \$200,000 \times 1.05 = \$210,000$$

4.
$$\frac{\$60,000}{5.216} = \$11,503.07$$

5.
$$\frac{\$120,000}{\$19,000} = 6.316$$

Looking at the present value of annuity table in Appendix D and going across 16 years to a factor nearest to 6.316 find 6.2651 at a 14 percent interest rate.

6. (a)
$$\$5,000 \times 5.6603 = \$28,301.50$$

(b)

Year	Payment	Interest	Principal	Balance
0				$28,301.50
1	$5,000	$3,962.21	$1,037.79	$27,263.71
2	$5,000	$3,816.92	$1,183.08	$26,080.63

7. (a) The before-tax times-interest-earned ratio is:

$$\frac{\text{Income before tax and interest}}{\text{Interest}} = \frac{\$12,000,000 + \$800,000^a}{\$800,000 + 0.16X} = 3$$

$$\frac{\$12,800,000}{\$800,000 + 0.16X} = 3$$

$$\$12,800,000 = \$2,400,000 + 0.48X$$

$$X = \$21,666,667$$

––––––––––––––––

[a] Interest $5,000,000 \times 0.16 = \$800,000$

(b)
$$\frac{\text{Book value of mortgaged assets}}{\text{Debt}} = \frac{\$60,000,000 + 0.2X}{\$5,000,000 + X} = 4$$

$$\$60,000,000 + 0.2X = \$20,000,000 + 4X$$

$$X = \$10,526,315$$

(c)
$$\frac{\text{Debt}}{\text{Equity}} = \frac{\$5,000,000 + X}{\$30,000,000} = 0.8$$

$$\$5,000,000 + X = \$24,000,000$$

$$X = \$19,000,000$$

The second condition is controlling and thus restricts the amount of new debt to $10,526,315.

8.

Old interest payments ($30,000,000 × 0.12)	$3,600,000
New interest payments ($30,000,000 × 0.10)	3,000,000
Annual savings	$ 600,000
Call premium ($30,000,000 × 0.07)	$2,100,000
Flotation cost	800,000
Total cost	$2,900,000

	Calculations	Present Value
Year 0	− $2,900,000 × 1	− $2,900,000
Years 1–20	+ $600,000 × 8.5136 [a]	+ 5,108,160
Net present value		+ $2,208,160

––––––––––––––

[a] Present value of annuity factor for $i = 10\%$, $n = 20$.

A refunding of the bond issue should occur, since it results in a positive net present value.

9.

Call price	$408,000
Face value of bond	400,000
Call premium	$ 8,000

10.

	Preferred Stock	Common Stock
Regular dividend		
Preferred (12% × $150,000)	$18,000	
Common (10% × $200,000)		$20,000
Excess dividend		
Preferred [($150,000/$350,000) × $12,000]	5,143	
Common [($200,000/$350,000) × $12,000]		6,857
Total dividend	$23,143	$26,857

11.
$$\frac{\text{Dividend}}{\text{Net proceeds}} = \frac{18\% \times \$6,000,000}{\$6,000,000 - 0.15(\$6,000,000)} = \frac{\$1,080,000}{\$5,100,000} = 21.18\%$$

12. (a)
$$\text{Shares to be sold} = \frac{\text{amount of funds to be obtained}}{\text{subscription price}} = \frac{\$2,000,000}{\$40} = 50,000 \text{ shares}$$

(b)
$$\text{Rights per share} = \frac{\text{total shares outstanding}}{\text{shares to be sold}} = \frac{250,000}{50,000} = 5$$

13.
$$\frac{\$70 - \$55}{4 + 1} = \frac{\$15}{5} = \$3$$

14. (a)
$$\$70 - \$3 = \$67$$

(b)
$$\frac{\$67 - \$55}{4} = \frac{\$12}{4} = \$3$$

Chapter 16

Warrants and Convertibles

16.1 INTRODUCTION

Warrants and convertibles are unique relative to other types of securities in the sense that they may be converted into common stock at will by the holder. This chapter defines warrants and convertibles, discusses their valuation, presents their advantages and disadvantages, and discusses when their issuance is most appropriate.

16.2 WARRANTS

A *warrant* refers to the option to purchase a given number of shares of stock at a given price. Warrants can be either detachable or nondetachable. A detachable warrant may be sold separately from the bond with which it is associated. Thus, the holder may exercise the warrant but not redeem the bond if he or she wishes. A *nondetachable* warrant is sold with its bond to be exercised by the bond owner simultaneously with the convertible bond.

To obtain common stock the warrant must be given up along with the payment of cash called the *exercise price*. Although warrants typically expire on a given date, some are perpetual, that is, never expire. A holder of a warrant may exercise it by purchasing the stock, sell it on the market to other investors, or continue to hold it. The company cannot force the exercise of a warrant. An investor may wish to hold a warrant rather than exercise or sell it because there exists a possibility of achieving a high rate of return. But there are several drawbacks to warrants, including a high risk of losing money, no voting rights, and no receipt of dividends.

If desired, a company may have the exercise price associated with a warrant vary over time (e.g., increase each year).

If there is a stock split or stock dividend before the warrant is exercised, the option price of the warrant is typically adjusted for it.

Through warrants additional funds are received by the issuer. When a bond is issued with a warrant, the warrant price is typically set between 10 percent and 20 percent above the stock's market price. If the company's stock price goes above the option price, the warrants will, of course, be exercised at the option price. The closer the warrants are to their expiration date, the greater the chance is that they will be exercised.

Valuation of a Warrant

The theoretical value of a warrant may be computed by a formula. The formula value is typically less than the market price of the warrant. This is because the speculative appeal of a warrant permits the investor to obtain a good degree of personal leverage.

Value of a warrant = (market price per share − exercise price)
        × number of shares that may be purchased through exercise of the warrant

EXAMPLE 16.1 A warrant for XYZ stock gives the owner the right to buy one share of common stock at $25 a share. The market price of the common stock is $53. The formula price of the warrant is:

Value of warrant = (market price per share − exercise price)
        × number of shares which may be purchased through exercise
        = ($53 − $25) × 1 = $28

If the owner had the right to buy three shares of common stock with one warrant, the theoretical value of the warrant would be

$$(\$53 - \$25) \times 3 = \$84$$

In the event the stock is selling for an amount below the option price, there will be a negative value. Because this is illogical, we use a formula value of zero.

EXAMPLE 16.2   Assume the same facts as in Example 16.1, except that the stock is selling at $21 a share. The formula amount is

$$(\$21 - \$25) \times 1 = -\$4$$

However, zero will be assigned.

Warrants do not have an investment value because there is no interest or dividends paid on them. Hence, the market value of a warrant is solely attributable to its convertibility value into common stock. But the market price of a warrant is typically more than its theoretical value, which is referred to as the *premium* on the warrant. The lowest amount that a warrant will sell for is its theoretical value.

The value of a warrant depends on the remaining life of the option, dividend payments on the common stock, the fluctuation in the price of the common stock, whether the warrant is listed on the exchange, and the opportunity cost of funds for the investor. A high value is associated with a warrant when its life is long, the dividend payment on common stock is small, the stock price is volatile, it is listed on the exchange, and the value of funds to the investor is great (because the warrant requires a lesser investment).

EXAMPLE 16.3   ABC stock currently has a market value of $50. The exercise price of the warrant is also $50. Therefore, the theoretical value of the warrant is $0. However, the warrant will sell at a premium (positive price) as long as there is a possibility that the market price of the common stock will surpass $50 before the expiration date of the warrant. The further into the future the expiration date is, the greater will be the premium, since there is a longer period for possible price appreciation.

Of course, the lower the market price is relative to the exercise price, the less the premium is.

EXAMPLE 16.4   Assume the same facts as in Example 16.3, except that the current market price of the stock is $35. The warrant's premium in this case will be much lower, since it would take a long time for the stock's price to increase above $50 a share. If investors expected that the stock price would not rise above $50 at a later date, the value of the warrant would be $0.

If the market price of ABC stock rises above $50, the market price of the warrant will increase and the premium will decrease. In other words, when the stock price is in excess of the exercise price, the market price of the warrant approximately equals the theoretical value causing the premium to disappear. The reduction in the premium arises because of the lessening of the advantage of owning the warrant compared to exercising it.

Advantages and Disadvantages of Warrants

The advantages of issuing warrants include the following:

1.   They allow for balanced financing between debt and equity.
2.   They permit the issuance of debt at a low interest rate.
3.   They serve as a "sweetener" for an issue of debt or preferred stock.

The disadvantages of issuing warrants include the following:

1.   When exercised they will result in a dilution of common stock.
2.   They may be exercised at a time when the business has no need for additional capital.

Warrant versus Stock Right

There is a difference between a warrant and a *stock right*. A stock right is given *free* to current stockholders, who may either exercise them by purchasing new shares or sell them in the market. Also, a stock right has a shorter duration than a warrant.

16.3 CONVERTIBLE SECURITIES

A *convertible security* is one that may be exchanged for common stock by the holder according to agreed upon terms. Examples are convertible bonds and convertible preferred stock. A specified number of shares of stock are received by the holder of the convertible security when he or she makes the exchange. This is referred to as the *conversion ratio*, which equals:

$$\text{Conversion ratio} = \frac{\text{par value of convertible security}}{\text{conversion price}}$$

The *conversion price* applies to the effective price the holder pays for the common stock when the conversion is effected. The conversion price and the conversion ratio are set at the time the convertible security is issued. The conversion price should be tied to the growth potential of the company. The greater the potential, the greater the conversion price should be.

A convertible bond is a quasi-equity security because its market value is tied to its value if converted rather than as a bond.

EXAMPLE 16.5 If the conversion price of common stock is $25 per share, a $1,000 convertible bond is convertible into 40 shares ($1,000/$25).

EXAMPLE 16.6 A $1,000 bond is convertible into 30 shares of stock. The conversion price is $33.33 ($1,000/30 shares).

EXAMPLE 16.7 A share of convertible preferred stock with a par value of $50 is convertible into four shares of common stock. The conversion price is $12.50 ($50/4).

EXAMPLE 16.8 A $1,000 convertible bond is issued that entitles the holder to convert the bond into 10 shares of common stock. Hence, the conversion ratio is 10 shares for 1 bond. Since the face value of the bond is $1,000 the holder is tendering this amount upon conversion. The conversion price equals $100 per share ($1,000/10 shares).

EXAMPLE 16.9 An investor holds a $1,000 convertible bond that is convertible into 40 shares of common stock. Assuming the common stock is selling for $35 a share, the bondholder can convert the bond into 40 shares worth $1,400.

EXAMPLE 16.10 Y Company issued a $1,000 convertible bond at par. The conversion price is $40. The conversion ratio is:

$$\text{Conversion ratio} = \frac{\text{par value of convertible security}}{\text{conversion price}} = \frac{\$1,000}{\$40} = 25$$

The conversion value of a security is computed as follows:

$$\text{Conversion value} = \text{common stock price} \times \text{conversion ratio}$$

When a convertible security is issued, it is priced higher than its conversion value. The difference is referred to as the *conversion premium*. The percentage conversion premium is computed in the following manner:

$$\text{Percentage conversion premium} = \frac{\text{market value} - \text{conversion value}}{\text{conversion value}}$$

EXAMPLE 16.11 LA Corporation issued a $1,000 convertible bond at par. The market price of the common stock at the date of issue was $48. The conversion price is $55.

$$\text{Conversion ratio} = \frac{\text{par value of convertible security}}{\text{conversion price}} = \frac{\$1,000}{\$55} = 18.18$$

$$\text{Conversion value of the bond} = \text{common stock price} \times \text{conversion ratio} = \$48 \times 18.18 = \$872$$

The difference between the conversion value of $872 and the issue price of $1,000 represents the conversion premium of $128. The conversion premium may also be expressed as a percentage of the conversion value. The percent in this case is:

$$\text{Percentage conversion premium} = \frac{\text{market value} - \text{conversion value}}{\text{conversion value}} = \frac{\$1,000 - \$872}{\$872} = \frac{\$128}{\$872} = 14.7\%$$

The conversion terms may not be static but may increase in steps over specified time periods. Thus, as time goes on fewer common shares are exchanged for the bond. In some cases, after a specified period of time the conversion option may expire.

Usually the convertible security contains a clause that protects it from dilution caused by stock dividends, stock splits, and stock rights. The clause typically prevents the issuance of common stock at a price lower than the conversion price. Also, the conversion price is reduced by the percentage amount of any stock split or stock dividend. This enables the shareholder of common stock to maintain his or her proportionate interest.

EXAMPLE 16.12 A 3-for-1 stock split takes place, which requires a tripling of the conversion ratio. A 20 percent stock dividend necessitates a 20 percent increase in the conversion ratio.

EXAMPLE 16.13 Assume the same facts as in Example 16.8 coupled with a 4-for-1 split. The conversion ratio now becomes 40, and the conversion price now becomes $25.

The voluntary conversion of a security by the holder depends on the relationship of the interest on the bond compared to the dividend on the stock, the risk preference of the holder (stock has a greater risk than a bond), and the current and expected market price of the stock.

Valuation of Convertibles

In a sense, a convertible security is a hybrid security, since it has attributes that are similar to common stock and bonds. The expectation is that the holder will eventually receive both interest yield and a capital gain. Interest yield relates to the coupon interest relative to the market price of the bond when purchased. The capital gain yield applies to the difference between the conversion price and the stock price at the issuance date and the anticipated growth rate in stock price.

EXAMPLE 16.14 A $10,000, 12 percent, 5-year bond is purchased at 95. The simple interest yield is:

$$\frac{\text{Coupon interest}}{\text{Market price of bond}} = \frac{0.12 \times \$10,000}{\$9,500} = \frac{\$1,200}{\$9,500} = 12.6\%$$

The interest yield of 12.6 percent is above the coupon interest rate of 12 percent because the bond was purchased at a discount of 95 percent from its face value ($9,500). At maturity, the holder will get back the face value of $10,000. By purchasing the bond at a discount, the holder has improved his or her rate of return.

The investment value of a convertible security is the value of the security, assuming it was not convertible but had all other attributes. For a convertible bond, its investment value equals the present value of future interest payments plus the present value of the maturity amount. For preferred stock, the investment value equals the present value of future dividend payments plus the present value of expected selling price.

Conversion value refers to the value of stock received upon converting the bond. As the price of the stock goes up so will its conversion value.

EXAMPLE 16.15   A $1,000 bond is convertible into 18 shares of common stock with a market value of $52 per share. The conversion value of the bond equals:

$$\$52 \times 18 \text{ shares} = \$936$$

EXAMPLE 16.16   At the date a $100,000 convertible bond is issued, the market price of the stock is $18 a share. Each $1,000 bond is convertible into 50 shares of stock. The conversion ratio is thus 50. The number of shares the bond is convertible into is:

$$100 \text{ bonds } (\$100,000/\$1,000) \times 50 \text{ shares} = 5,000 \text{ shares}$$

The conversion value is:

$$\$18 \times 5,000 \text{ shares} = \$90,000$$

If the stock price is expected to grow at 6 percent per year, the conversion value at the end of year 1 is:

Shares	5,000
Stock price ($18 × 1.06)	$ 19.08
Conversion value	$95,400

The conversion value at the end of year 2 is:

Shares	5,000
Stock price ($19.08 × 1.06)	$ 20.22
Conversion value	$101,100

A convertible security will not sell at less than its value as straight debt (nonconvertible security). This is because the conversion privilege has to have some value in terms of its potential convertibility to common stock and in terms of reducing the holder's risk exposure to a declining price in the bond (convertible bonds fall off less in price than straight debt issues). Market value will equal investment value only when the conversion privilege is worthless due to a low market price of the common stock relative to the conversion price.

When convertible bonds are issued, the business expects that the value of common stock will appreciate and that the bonds will eventually be converted. If conversion does take place, the company could then issue another convertible bond. Such a financial policy is referred to as *leapfrog financing*.

Of course, if the market price of common stock declines rather than rises, there will be no conversion of debt into equity. In this case, the convertible security remains as debt and is termed a *hung* convertible.

A convertible security holder may prefer to hold the security rather than convert it even though the conversion value exceeds the price paid for it. First, as the price of the common stock goes up so will the price of the convertible security. Second, the holder receives regular interest payments or preferred dividends. To force conversion, companies issuing convertibles often have a call price. The call price is above the face value of the bond (approximately 10 percent to 20 percent higher). This forces the conversion of stock as long as the price of the stock is greater than the conversion price. Everyone would rather have a higher-value common stock than a lower call price for the bond.

EXAMPLE 16.17   The conversion price on a $1,000 debenture is $40 and the call price is $1,100. In order for the conversion value of the bond to equal the call price, the market price of the stock would have to be $44 ($1,100/25). If the conversion value of the bond is 15 percent higher than the call price, the approximate market price of common stock would be $51 (1.15 × $44). At a $51 price, conversion is virtually guaranteed, since if the investor did not convert he or she would incur a material opportunity loss.

EXAMPLE 16.18 Max Company's convertible bond has a conversion price of $80. The conversion ratio is 10. The market price of the stock is $140. The call price is $1,100. The bondholder would rather convert to common stock with a market value of $1,400 ($140 × 10) than have his or her convertible bond redeemed at $1,100. In this case, the call provision forces the conversion when the bondholder might be tempted to wait longer.

Advantages and Disadvantages of Convertibles

To the company, the advantages of convertible security issuance are:

1. It serves as a "sweetener" in a debt offering by giving the investor an opportunity to take part in the price appreciation of common stock. By selling common stock at a gain if held for more than 6 months the stockholder will receive a favorable tax treatment in the form of a capital gain deduction. Here, only 40 percent of the gain is subject to tax.

2. The issuance of convertible debt allows for a lower interest rate on the financing relative to issuing straight debt.

3. A convertible security may be issued in a tight money market, when it is difficult for a creditworthy firm to issue a straight bond or preferred stock.

4. There are fewer financing restrictions involved with a convertible security issuance.

5. Convertibles provide a means of issuing equity at prices higher than present market prices.

6. The call provision enables the firm to force conversion whenever the market price of the stock is greater than the conversion price.

7. In the event the company issued straight debt now and common stock later to meet the debt, they would incur flotation costs twice, whereas with convertible debt, flotation costs would occur only once, with the initial issuance of the convertible bonds.

To the holder, the advantages of convertible securities are:

1. They offer the potential of a significant capital gain due to price appreciation of the common stock.

2. They offer the holder protection if corporate performance falls off.

3. The margin requirement associated with buying convertible bonds is lower than that associated with buying common stock. Therefore, more money could be borrowed from the broker to invest in convertibles.

To the company, the disadvantages of convertible security issuance are:

1. If the company's stock price appreciably increases in value, it would have been better off financing through a regular issuance of common stock by waiting to issue it at the higher price instead of allowing conversion at the lower price.

2. The company is obligated to pay the convertible debt if the stock price does not increase.

To the holder, the disadvantages of convertible securities are:

1. The yield on a convertible security is lower than that on a comparable security not having the conversion option.

2. A convertible bond is usually subordinated to other debt obligations. Thus, it typically has a lower bond rating.

Corporate Financing Strategy

When a company's stock price is currently depressed, convertible debt rather than common stock issuance may be called for if the price of stock is expected to rise. Establishing a conversion price above the current market price of stock will involve the issuance of fewer shares when the bonds are converted relative to selling the shares at a current lower price. Also, less share dilution will be involved. Of course, the conversion will take place only if the price of the stock goes above the conversion price. The drawback here, however, is that if the stock price does not rise and conversion does not occur, an additional debt burden is placed upon the firm.

The issuance of convertible debt is recommended when the company wishes to leverage itself in the short run but wishes not to incur interest cost and pay principal on the convertible debt in the long run (due to its conversion).

A convertible issue is often a good financing vehicle for a growth company. The quicker the growth rate, the earlier the conversion. For example, a convertible bond may act as a temporary source of funds in a construction period. It is a relatively inexpensive source for financing growth. A convertible issuance is not recommended for a company with a modest growth rate, since it would take a long time to force conversion. During such a time the company will not be able to easily issue additional financing. A long conversion interval may imply to the investing public that the stock has not done as well as expected. The growth rate of the firm is a prime consideration in determining whether convertibles are the best method of financing.

Financial Statement Analysis

When engaging in financial statement analysis, the creditor should consider a convertible bond having an attractive conversion feature as equity rather than debt since in all probability it will be converted into common stock. The future payment of interest and principal on the debt, then, will not be required.

Convertibles versus Warrants

The differences between convertibles and warrants are as follows:

1. Exercising convertibles does not generally provide additional funds to the firm, while the exercise of warrants does.

2. When conversion takes place the debt ratio is reduced. However, the exercise of warrants adds to the equity position with debt still remaining.

3. Due to the call feature, the company has greater control over the timing of the capital structure with convertibles than with warrants.

Review Questions

1. The _____ is the cash paid when a warrant is given up to acquire common stock.

2. Dividends are not received on holding _____.

3. A(n) _____ warrant is sold separately from the bond.

4. The option price must be adjusted for a(n) _____ dividend.

5. Warrants may be issued as _____ for a risky debt or preferred stock issue.

6. If stock has a market price below the option price, the value of the warrant is _____.

7. The _____ of a warrant relates to its convertibility value into common stock.

8. The longer the remaining life of a warrant, the _____ its value.

9. A(n) _____ dividend payment on common stock means a lower value associated with the warrant.

10. The difference between a warrant and stock right is that the latter is _____ to existing stockholders.

11. The _____ applies to the number of shares received by a holder of a convertible security when he or she makes the exchange.

12. The effective price when a holder pays for common stock to effect conversion is termed the _____ .

13. The market value of a convertible bond relates to its value _____ rather than its bond value.

14. A(n) _____ is a good financing tool for a growth company.

15. Convertible debt involves a(n) _____ interest rate than straight debt.

16. The margin requirement on purchasing convertible bonds is _____ than on purchasing common stock.

17. Interest yield equals _____ divided by the market price of the bond.

18. The investment value of a convertible bond equals the present value of _____ plus the present value of the _____ .

19. _____ is the term used when a new convertible security is issued after an old one has been converted.

20. The term _____ convertible is used when a convertible security continues as debt.

21. For financial statement analysis purposes, a convertible bond with an attractive conversion feature is considered _____ rather than _____ .

Answers: (1) exercise price; (2) warrants; (3) detachable; (4) stock; (5) "sweeteners"; (6) zero; (7) market value; (8) higher; (9) high; (10) free; (11) conversion ratio; (12) conversion price; (13) if converted; (14) convertible security; (15) lower; (16) lower; (17) coupon interest; (18) future interest payments, maturity amount; (19) Leapfrog financing; (20) hung; (21) equity, debt.

Solved Problems

16.1 Warrant Value. A warrant for Ace Corporation stock enables the holder to purchase one share of common stock at $30 a share. The stock has a market price of $47 a share. What is the value of the warrant?

SOLUTION

Warrant value = (market price per share − exercise price) × number of shares that may be purchased
$$= (\$47 - \$30) \times 1 = \$17$$

16.2 Warrant Value. Assume the same facts as in Problem 16.1, except that the holder can purchase four shares of common stock for each warrant. What is the value of the warrant?

SOLUTION

$$(\$47 - \$30) \times 4 = \$68$$

16.3 Warrant Value. Assume the same facts as Problem 16.1, except that the stock has a market price of $28 a share. What is the value of the warrant?

SOLUTION

$$(\$28 - \$30) \times 1 = -\$2$$

Since there can never be a negative value for a warrant, zero is the amount assigned to the warrant.

16.4 Premium. The market price of Harris Corporation stock is $45. Its exercise price is similarly $45. Will the stock warrant sell at a premium?

SOLUTION

Yes. The warrant will sell at a premium, since there exists the possibility that the market price of the common stock will exceed $45 prior to the expiration date of the warrant.

16.5 Bond to Common Shares. The conversion price of common stock is $20 a share. Into how many shares will a $1,000 convertible bond be converted?

SOLUTION

$$\frac{\$1,000}{\$20} = 50 \text{ shares}$$

16.6 Conversion Price. A $1,000 bond is convertible into 60 shares of stock. What is the conversion price?

SOLUTION

$$\frac{\$1,000}{60 \text{ shares}} = \$16.67$$

16.7 Conversion Ratio. A $1,000 convertible bond permits the holder to convert the bond into five shares of common stock. (*a*) What is the conversion ratio? (*b*) What is the conversion price?

SOLUTION

(*a*)   Five shares for each bond

(*b*)
$$\frac{\$1,000}{5 \text{ shares}} = \$200 \text{ per share}$$

16.8   Conversion Ratio. T Corporation issued a $1,000 bond at par. The conversion price is $20. What is the conversion ratio?

SOLUTION

$$\text{Conversion ratio} = \frac{\text{par value of convertible security}}{\text{conversion price}} = \frac{\$1,000}{\$20} = 50$$

16.9   Convertibility. Tristar Corporation issued a $1,000 bond at par. The common stock has a market price of $45. The conversion price is $58. (*a*) Into how many shares can the bond be converted? (*b*) What is the conversion value of the bond? (*c*) What is the conversion premium?

SOLUTION

(*a*)
$$\frac{\$1,000}{\$58} = 17.24 \text{ shares}$$

(*b*) $\text{Conversion value} = (\text{common stock price}) \times (\text{conversion ratio}) = \$45 \times 17.24 = \$776$

(*c*) $\$1,000 - \$776 = \$224$

16.10   Percentage Conversion Premium. A $1,000 bond is issued at par. The market price of the common stock at the issue date was $20. The conversion price is $25. (*a*) What is the conversion ratio? (*b*) What is the conversion value? (*c*) What is the percentage conversion premium?

SOLUTION

(*a*)
$$\frac{\$1,000}{\$25} = 40$$

(*b*) $\$20 \times 40 = \$800$

(*c*) $\text{Percentage conversion premium} = \dfrac{\text{market value} - \text{conversion value}}{\text{conversion value}} = \dfrac{\$1,000 - \$800}{\$800} = \dfrac{\$200}{\$800} = 25\%$

16.11   Conversion Ratio. What effect will a 2-for-1 stock split have on a conversion ratio?

SOLUTION

The conversion ratio will double.

16.12   Conversion Value. A $1,000 bond is convertible into 25 shares of common stock having a market value of $47 per share. What is the conversion value?

SOLUTION

$$\$47 \times 25 \text{ shares} = \$1,175$$

16.13 Conversion Ratio. When a $50,000 convertible bond is issued, the market price of the stock is $25 a share. Each $1,000 bond is convertible into 40 shares of stock. (a) What is the conversion ratio? (b) What is the conversion value? (c) Assuming the stock price is anticipated to grow at 8 percent annually, what is the conversion value at the end of the first year?

SOLUTION

(a)
$$\frac{\$50,000}{\$1,000} = 50 \text{ bonds} \times 40 \text{ shares} = 2,000 \text{ shares}$$

(b)
$$\$25 \times 2,000 \text{ shares} = \$50,000$$

(c)

Shares	2,000
Stock price ($25 × 1.08)	×$27
	$54,000

16.14 Simple Interest Yield. A $30,000, 15 percent, 10-year bond is bought at 102. What is the simple interest yield?

SOLUTION

$$\frac{\text{Coupon interest}}{\text{Market price of bond}} = \frac{0.15 \times \$30,000}{\$30,600} = \frac{\$4,500}{\$30,600} = 14.7\%$$

16.15 Market Price of Stock. For a $1,000 convertible bond, the conversion price is $50. The call price is $1,200. (a) If the conversion value of the bond equals the call price, what should the market price of the stock be? (b) What is the approximate market price of common stock if the conversion value of the bond is 20 percent higher than the call price?

SOLUTION

(a)
$$\frac{\$1,200}{20} = \$60$$

(b)
$$\$60 \times 1.20 = \$72$$

16.16 Call Price. Drake Corporation's convertible bond has a conversion price of $90. The conversion ratio is 15. The market price of the stock is $130. The call price is $1,800. Would the bondholder rather convert to common stock or receive the call price?

SOLUTION

Market value of common stock received upon conversion is:

$$\$130 \times 15 = \$1,950$$

$$\text{Call price} = \$1,800$$

The bondholder would rather convert, since he or she receives a benefit of $150.

16.17 Attractiveness of Convertible Debenture. Great Northern Oil Shale Company is a company actively engaged in the oil services industry. The company provides replacement parts for drilling rigs and has just begun to test a device that measures shale oil content in certain rock formations.

The company has an 8 percent convertible subordinated debenture outstanding due in the year 2001. The convertible is callable at 106 and has a conversion price of $50. The common stock is currently paying a dividend of $1.40 on earnings per share of $3. Consensus among analysts is that long-term interest rates will be stable to lower over the next year. The common stock is currently selling for $30 and the convertible bond at 66. Nonconvertible bonds of companies in this industry having similar quality ratings (triple-B) are yielding 14 percent to maturity.

(*a*) Discuss four characteristics of the convertible debenture, and (*b*) explain whether you consider the convertible debenture or the common stock more attractive for purchase. (CFA, adapted.)

SOLUTION

(*a*)   Characteristics of this convertible industrial debenture include the following:

   (1)   The quality of the bond is not high but average for most convertible bonds.

   (2)   The outlook for interest rates is stable to lower. This is a plus, as bond prices should be stable to rising.

   (3)   Minimum value as straight debt is around 60, or about 9 percent under current market of 66. This is well within reasonable limits of, say, 15 percent or below.

   (4)   The current price of the common is 10 percent below the bonds' conversion value. Conversion value is [(1,000/50) × $30]. This is within reasonable limits of, say, maximum of 20 percent or so.

   (5)   The current yield on the bond of 12.0 percent seems favorable at more than twice 4.7 percent on the common.

   (6)   The call risk is remote (call price of 106 versus market price of 66).

(*b*)   The convertible looks more attractive because of the modest premiums involved—upside leverage and downside cushion, compared to the common. The convertible also looks more attractive because of the higher income relative to the common, assuming that the common stock price has the potential to rise by a sizable amount from the current price of 33 to the 40-plus level.

Chapter 17

Mergers and Acquisitions

17.1 INTRODUCTION

Internal growth comes about when a company invests in products it has developed, while external growth occurs when a company buys the existing assets of another company through a merger. Financial managers are sometimes required to evaluate the attractiveness of a potential merger as well as participate in merger negotiations. In addition to growth, mergers may allow an organization to diversify.

There are three common ways of joining two or more companies. The following definitions will distinguish the difference between a merger, consolidation, and a holding company:

Merger. A merger is the combination of two or more companies into one, where only the acquiring company retains its identity. Typically, the larger of the two companies is the acquiring company whose identity is maintained.

Consolidation. In a consolidation, two or more companies are combined to form a new company. None of the consolidation firms legally survive. In effect, the consolidating firms are dissolved and a new company is formed.

EXAMPLE 17.1 Companies X and Y give all their assets, liabilities, and stock to the new company, Z, in return for Z's stock, bonds, or cash. The combining of companies X and Y with new company Z emerging is a consolidation.

Holding Company. A holding company holds, or owns, enough shares of common stock to have voting control of one or more other companies. The holding company comprises a group of businesses, each operating as a separate corporate entity. By holding more than 50 percent of the voting rights through common stock, the holding company ensures control of the other companies. In reality, a holding company can have effective control of another company with a smaller percent of ownership, such as 20 percent. The holding company is called the *parent*, and each company controlled is called a *subsidiary.*

Depending on the intent of the combination, there are three common ways businesses get together to gain advantage in their market. The three types of business combinations are:

1. *Vertical.* A vertical merger takes place when a company combines with a customer or supplier. For example, when a furniture manufacturer combines with a chain of furniture stores, the combination is vertical.

2. *Horizontal.* A horizontal combination is when two companies in a similar business combine, for example, when one oil company buys another oil company.

3. *Conglomerate.* A conglomerate is when two companies in unrelated industries combine. For example, when an appliance manufacturer combines with a book publisher, a conglomerate is formed.

17.2 MERGERS

The merger of two companies can be accomplished in one of two ways. The acquiring company can negotiate with management of the other company, which is the preferred approach, or it can make a tender offer directly to the stockholders of the company it wants to take over. A *tender offer* is an offer of cash for shares of stock held by stockholders.

In negotiating with management, often the acquiring company makes a stock offer based on a specified exchange ratio. The merger may take place if the acquired company receives an offer at an acceptable premium over the present market price of its stock. Sometimes to satisfy the management of the acquired business, certain contingent payments, such as stock purchase warrants, are made part of the merger contract. If the negotiations break down, a tender offer may be made directly to the company's stockholders. The tender offer is made at a premium above the market price of the stock and is offered to all stockholders of the company. Tender offers are fully discussed later in this chapter.

There are various financing packages that buyers may use for mergers such as common stock, preferred stock, convertible securities, cash, debt, and warrants. A prime consideration in selecting the final package is its impact on current earnings per share.

When common stock is exchanged, the seller's stock is given in exchange for the buyer's stock. The advantage of a stock trade is that it represents a tax-free exchange. A disadvantage is that issuing the stock increases the buyer's outstanding shares, thus diluting earnings per share. When there is an exchange of cash for common stock, the selling firm's stockholders receive cash for their common stock, resulting in a taxable transaction. Such an exchange may improve earnings per share because the buying company is getting new earnings without increasing outstanding shares.

Reasons for Mergers

There are several reasons why a company would prefer external growth through merger rather than internal growth:

1. The company may want diversification to reduce the risks involved with a seasonal business.

2. A company may expect a synergistic effect by merging with another. Through synergism the results are greater than the sum of the parts. That is, greater earnings may be obtained from the combined company than would be possible from each individual company because of efficiency and cost savings. There is a greater chance of synergistic gains from a horizontal merger, since duplicate facilities may be eliminated.

3. A merger may permit one firm to obtain something it lacks, such as superior management talent or a research capability.

4. A company may improve its ability to raise funds when it combines with another having highly liquid assets and low debt.

5. The net income of the new large company may be capitalized at a low rate, resulting in a high market value for its stock. The stock of a large company is usually more marketable than that of a small one. These attributes may result in a high P/E ratio for the stock.

6. In some cases, it is possible to finance an acquisition when it would not be possible to finance internal expansion. For instance, acquiring another company by exchanging stock may be less costly than constructing a new plant, which requires a substantial cash payment.

7. An acquisition can result in a good return on the investment when the market value of the acquired company is significantly below its replacement cost.

8. By acquiring a company that has been operating at a net loss, the acquiring company may not only get the acquired company at a good price, but will also obtain a tax-loss-carryforward benefit. The acquiring company can use the tax-loss-carryforward benefit to offset its own profitability and thus lower its tax payment. The tax loss may be carried forward for 15 years to reduce the acquiring company's future earnings. In effect, the government is financing part of the acquisition.

EXAMPLE 17.2 Ace Company is considering buying Jones Company. Jones Company has a tax loss of $700,000. Ace expects before-tax profits of $300,000 a year for the next 3 years. The tax rate is 46 percent.

The taxes to be paid for each of the next 3 years after the acquisition follow:

For year 1:

Ace Company's earnings	$300,000
Jones Company's tax loss carryforward	300,000
Taxable income	$ 0
Tax	$ 0

For year 2:

Ace Company's earnings	$300,000
Jones Company's tax loss carryforward	300,000
Taxable income	$ 0
Tax	$ 0

For year 3:

Ace Company's earnings	$300,000
Unused tax loss carryforward ($700,000 − $600,000)	100,000
Taxable income	$200,000
Tax (46% rate)	$ 92,000

Disadvantages of Mergers

The disadvantages that may result from mergers are:

1. A merger may not work out financially because the anticipated benefits (e.g., cost reductions) do not occur.
2. Friction may arise between the management of the two companies.
3. Dissenting minority stockholders may cause problems.
4. Government antitrust action may block or delay the proposed merger.

Evaluating a Potential Merger

In evaluating a possible merger, the financial manager must consider the effect the merger may have on the performance of the company, such as:

1. *Earnings per share.* The merger should improve earnings per share or enhance its stability.
2. *Dividends per share.* The dividends paid prior to the merger should be maintained to stabilize the market price of stock.
3. *Market price per share.* The essential variable to consider is the effect of the merger on the market price of the company's stock.
4. *Risk.* The merger should reduce the business and financial risk of the resulting enterprise.

17.3 ACQUISITION TERMS

When determining the terms of the acquisition, consideration should be given to the following factors:

1. The absolute amount of earnings as well as the earnings growth rate

2. Dividends

3. Market price of the stock

4. Book value per share

5. Net working capital per share

The weight each factor bears on a merger varies, based on the particular circumstances involved.

Earnings.   In ascertaining the value of earnings in a merger, consideration should be given to anticipated future profit and the projected P/E multiple. A company in a rapid growth stage is expected to have a high P/E multiple.

EXAMPLE 17.3   Company S and company T are planning a merger. Company S has the higher P/E ratio. The earnings of company S are expected to show a greater growth rate than that of company T. If the merger occurs, the acquiring company T will be obtaining a company with superior growth potential. Therefore, company T's profitability subsequent to the merger should increase faster than before. The new growth rate will approximate the weighted average growth rates on the individual companies with the weight based on the relative total earnings prior to the merger. The key considerations involved in this analysis are the past and projected growth rates of the business, their size, the P/E multipliers, and the exchange ratio. The combination of these factors influences the EPS of the surviving company.

Dividends.   Dividends impact the acquisition terms, since they constitute income to stock-holders. However, the greater a company's growth rate and profitability, the lesser the impact dividends will have on the per share market price of the companies. Conversely, when profits are declining, dividends will have a more significant effect on the market price of the stock.

Market Price of the Stock.   Since the price per share takes into account potential earnings and dividends, current market value must be considered in the merger. The value given to the firm in the acquisition will probably be greater than the current market price per share under the following circumstances:

1. The company is in an industry with financial problems and thus will have a currently depressed market price.

2. The acquired company may have more of a value to the acquirer (e.g., assist in diversification) than to the stock market in general.

3. To encourage stockholders to give up their shares, an amount greater than the current market price may be given.

Book Value per Share.   Generally speaking, book value is not an important ingredient in the merger process because it is based on historical cost rather than current values. But book value may be relevant when it exceeds market price. In such a case, there may be an expectation that the market price of the stock will increase because of new and better management.

Net Working Capital per Share.   Net working capital per share may impact the merger terms due to the liquidity of one of the combining companies. For example, if the acquired company has a very low debt position, the acquiring company may borrow the funds needed for the acquisition by using the acquired company's good liquidity position to meet the loan following the merger. Or the liquid assets of the acquired company can provide needed collateral for the issuance of debt.

17.4   ACQUISITIONS

Acquisition of a Company

The acquisition of a going concern is evaluated through capital budgeting techniques. When a company buys another having a financial structure materially different from its own, the impact of the new capital structure on the company's overall cost of capital must be projected.

EXAMPLE 17.4 Sharav Company is considering purchasing Shillinglaw Corporation for $80,000 in cash. Sharav's current cost of capital is 15 percent. Shillinglaw's estimated overall cost of capital is expected to become 12 percent after the acquisition. The estimated cash inflows from years 1 to 12 are $10,000.

The net present value is:

	Calculations	Present Value
Year 0	$-$80,000 \times 1$	$-$80,000
Years 1–12	$+$10,000 \times 6.194$	$+61,940$ [a]
Net present value		$-$18,060

[a] Using 12 percent as the discount rate.

Since the net present value is negative, the acquisition should not take place.

EXAMPLE 17.5 Boston Corporation is considering acquiring Masters Corporation for $200,000 in cash. Boston's cost of capital is 16 percent primarily due to its high debt position. If the acquisition is made, Boston expects that its overall cost of capital will be 14 percent because Masters Corporation is financed mostly with equity. The acquisition is anticipated to generate yearly cash inflows of $28,000 for the next 10 years.

The net present value is:

	Calculations	Present Value
Year 0	$-$200,000 \times 1$	$-$200,000
Years 1–10	$+$28,000 \times 5.216$	$+146,048$
Net present value		$-$ 53,952

Since the net present value is negative, the acquisition should not take place.

Acquisition of Assets for Cash

When one company acquires another for cash, capital budgeting may be used to examine the financial feasibility of the acquisition. To ascertain whether the purchase of assets is financially justifiable, the company must predict the costs and benefits of the assets.

EXAMPLE 17.6 The Davis Company wants to buy certain fixed assets of Boris Company. However, Boris wants to sell out its entire business. The balance sheet for Boris Company follows:

ASSETS	
Cash	$ 3,000
Accounts receivable	7,000
Inventories	12,000
Equipment 1	15,000
Equipment 2	25,000
Equipment 3	40,000
Building	100,000
Total assets	$202,000

LIABILITIES AND STOCKHOLDERS' EQUITY	
Total liabilities	$ 90,000
Total stockholders' equity	112,000
Total liabilities and stockholders' equity	$202,000

Davis needs only equipment 2 and 3 and the building. The other assets excluding cash can be sold for $30,000. The total cash received is therefore $33,000 ($30,000 + $3,000 initial cash balance). Boris wants $45,000 for the entire business. Davis will thus have to pay a total of $135,000, which is $90,000 in total liabilities and $45,000 for its owners. The actual net cash outlay is therefore $102,000 ($135,000 − $33,000). It is expected that the after-tax cash inflows from the new equipment will be $25,000 per year for the next 6 years. The cost of capital is 10 percent.

The net present value associated with this acquisition follows:

	Calculations	Present Value
Year 0	−$102,000 × 1	−$102,000
Years 1–6	+$25,000 × 4.355	+108,875
Net present value		+$ 6,875

Since the net present value is positive, the acquisition is recommended.

EXAMPLE 17.7 Miles Corporation is thinking of acquiring Piston Corporation for $50,000. Piston has liabilities of $75,000. Piston has equipment that Miles desires. The remaining assets would be sold for $58,000. By acquiring the equipment, Miles will have an increase in cash flow of $17,000 each year for the next 12 years. The cost of capital is 10 percent.

The net cost of the equipment is:

$$\$50,000 + \$75,000 - \$58,000 = \$67,000$$

Miles should make the acquisition since, as indicated below, the net present value is positive.

	Calculations	Present Value
Year 0	−$67,000 × 1	−$ 67,000
Years 1–12	+$17,000 × 6.814	+115,838
Net present value		+$ 48,838

Acquisition by Exchanging Stock

A company is often acquired by exchanging common stock. The exchange will be in accordance with a predetermined ratio. The amount the acquiring firm offers for each share of the acquired business is usually more than the current market price of the traded shares. The *ratio of exchange* is equal to:

$$\frac{\text{Amount paid per share of the acquired company}}{\text{Market price of the acquiring company's shares}}$$

EXAMPLE 17.8 Company A wants to acquire company B. Company A's stock sells for $80 per share. Company B's stock sells for $55 per share. Because of the merger negotiations, company A offers $60 per share. The acquisition is made through an exchange of securities.

$$\text{Ratio of exchange} = \frac{\text{amount paid per share of the acquired company}}{\text{market price of the acquiring company's shares}} = \frac{\$60}{\$80} = 0.75$$

Company A must exchange 0.75 share of its stock for one share of company B's stock.

17.5 THE EFFECT OF A MERGER ON EARNINGS PER SHARE AND MARKET PRICE PER SHARE OF STOCK

When a merger takes place, there may be a favorable or unfavorable effect on net income and market price per share of stock. The effect on earnings per share can easily be seen in Example 17.9.

EXAMPLE 17.9   The following data are presented:

	Company X	Company Y
Net income	$30,000	$54,000
Shares outstanding	4,000	9,000
Earnings per share	$7.50	$6.00
P/E ratio	10	12.5
Market price	$75	$75

Company Y is the acquiring company and will exchange its shares for company X's shares on a one-for-one basis. The exchange ratio is based on the market prices of X and Y. The impact on EPS follows:

	Y Shares Owned after Merger	EPS Prior to Merger	EPS Subsequent to Merger
X stockholders	4,000	$7.50	$6.46[a]
Y stockholders	9,000	$6.00	$6.46[a]
Total	13,000		

[a] Total net income is calculated as follows:

4,000 shares × $7.50	$30,000
9,000 shares × $6.00	54,000
New EPS	$84,000

$$\text{EPS} = \frac{\text{total net income}}{\text{total shares}} = \frac{\$84,000}{13,000} = \$6.46$$

EPS decreases by $1.04 for X stockholders but increases by $0.46 for Y stockholders.

The impact on market price is not clear. Assuming the combined company has the same P/E ratio as that of company Y, the market price per share will be $80.75 (12.5 × $6.46). In this example, the stockholders of each firm enjoy a higher market value per share. The increased market value comes about because the net income of the combined company is valued at a 12.5 P/E ratio, the same as company Y, while before the merger, company X had a lower P/E multiple of 10. But if the combined company is valued at company X's multiplier of 10, the market value would be $64.60 (10 × $6.46). In this instance, the stockholders in each firm will have experienced a decline in market value of $10.40 ($75.00 − $64.60).

Since the effect of a merger on market value per share is not clear, EPS is given the prime consideration.

EXAMPLE 17.10   The following data are given:

Case	Market Price per Share of Acquiring Company	Market Price per Share of Acquired Company	Price per Share Offered
1	$60	$20	$25
2	$100	$130	$140

In each of the following cases, the exchange ratio in (1) shares and (2) market price are:

Case	Exchange Ratio Shares	Exchange Ratio Market Price
1	$25/$60 = 0.42	$25/$20 = 1.25
2	$140/$100 = 1.4	$140/$130 = 1.08

EXAMPLE 17.11   Joy Corporation wishes to acquire Davis Corporation. Data for the companies follow:

	Joy	Davis
Net income	$30,000	$14,000
Shares outstanding	22,000	7,000

Joy Corporation issues its shares to make the acquisition. The ratio of exchange is 2.2 to 1. The EPS based on the original shares of each company follows:

$$\text{EPS of the merged entity} = \frac{\text{combined net income}}{\text{total shares}} = \frac{\$30,000 + \$14,000}{22,000 + (7,000 \times 2.2)}$$

$$= \frac{\$44,000}{22,000 + 15,400} = \frac{\$44,000}{37,400 \text{ shares}} = \$1.18$$

$$\text{EPS of Joy} = \$1.18$$

$$\text{EPS of Davis} = \$1.18 \times 2.2 = \$2.60$$

EXAMPLE 17.12   Andrew Company wants to acquire Stella Company by exchanging 0.6 share of its stock for each share of Stella. Financial data follow:

	Andrew	Stella
Net income	$180,000	$36,000
Shares outstanding	60,000	18,000
EPS	$3	$2
Market price	$30	$14
P/E ratio	10	7

Andrew issues its shares to make the acquisition. The shares Andrew has to issue in the acquisition are:

$$18,000 \text{ shares} \times 0.6 = 10,800 \text{ shares}$$

Assuming the earnings of each company remain the same, the EPS after the acquisition is:

$$\frac{\$180,000 + \$36,000}{60,000 + 10,800} = \frac{\$216,000}{70,800 \text{ shares}} = \$3.05$$

The amount earned per share on the original shares of Stella stock is:

$$\$3.05 \times 0.6 = \$1.83$$

The amount earned per share on the original shares of Andrew stock is $3.05.

EXAMPLE 17.13   Arnold Corporation wishes to acquire Jack Corporation by exchanging 1.5 shares of its stock for each share of Jack. Arnold Corporation expects to have the same P/E ratio after the merger as before. The following financial data are presented:

	Arnold	Jack
Net income	$400,000	$100,000
Shares	200,000	25,000
Market price per share	$40	$48

The exchange ratio of market price is:

$$\frac{\text{Price per share offered}}{\text{Market price of Jack}} = \frac{\$40 \times 1.5}{\$48} = \frac{\$60}{\$48} = 1.25$$

EPS and P/E multiples for each firm are:

	Arnold	**Jack**
EPS	$400,000/200,000 shares = $2	$100,000/25,000 shares = $4
P/E ratio	$40/$2 = 20 times	$48/$4 = 12 times

The P/E ratio used in obtaining Jack is:

$$1.5 \times \$40 = \$60$$

$$\frac{\$60}{\$4} = 15 \text{ times}$$

The EPS of Arnold after the acquisition is:

$$\frac{\$500,000}{200,000 + (25,000 \times 1.5)} = \frac{\$500,000}{237,500 \text{ shares}} = \$2.11$$

The anticipated market price per share of the merged company is:

$$\$2.11 \times 20 \text{ times} = \$42.20$$

17.6 HOLDING COMPANY

A holding company is one that has the sole purpose of owning the stock of other businesses. A holding company can acquire a small percent of another company (e.g., 10 percent), which may be sufficient to obtain a significant influence over the other, especially when stock ownership is widely disbursed. A holding company that wants to obtain voting control of a business may make a direct market purchase or a tender offer to get the additional shares. What would prompt the officers of a company to turn it into a holding company? A company in a declining industry, for example, may decide to move out of its basic operations by liquidating assets and use the funds obtained to invest in other companies having good growth potential.

Since the operating companies held by the holding company are distinct legal entities, the obligations of any one are isolated from the others. If one of them goes under, there is no claim on the assets of another. However, a loan officer that lends to one company may require a guarantee by the other companies. This will in effect join the assets of the companies. In any case, a major financial setback involving one company is not the responsibility of the others.

The advantages of a holding company arrangement include the following:

1. The ability of the holding company to acquire a large amount of assets with a small investment. In effect, the holding company can control more assets than it could acquire through a merger.

2. There is risk protection because the failure of one of the companies does not cause the failure of the other companies or the holding company. The failure of one invested company would not cost the holding company more than its investment in that firm.

3. It is easy to gain control of another company because all that is involved is buying enough stock in the market place. Unlike a merger in which stockholder or management approval is needed, no approval is needed for a holding company.

The disadvantages of a holding company arrangement are as follows:

1. There is multiple taxation since the income the holding company receives from its subsidiaries is in the form of cash. Before paying dividends, the subsidiary must pay taxes on its earnings. When the earnings are distributed to the holding company as dividends, it must pay tax on the dividends received less the 85 percent dividend exclusion. However, if the holding

company owns 80 percent or more of the subsidiary's stock, there will be a 100 percent dividend exemption. There is no multiple taxation for a subsidiary that is part of a merged company.

EXAMPLE 17.14   A holding company owns 60 percent of another business. Dividends received by the holding company are $15,000. The tax rate is 46 percent. The tax paid on the dividends follow:

Dividend	$15,000
Dividend exclusion (85%)	12,750
Dividend subject to tax	$ 2,250
Tax rate	×46%
Tax	$ 1,035

The effective tax is 6.9% ($1,035/$15,000 or 15% × 46%).

2. A holding company is typically more costly to administer than a single company emanating from a merger. The increased costs arise from not achieving the economies that would normally occur in a merger.

3. The U.S. Department of Justice may consider the holding company a near monopoly and force dissolution of some of the companies by disposal of stock.

4. By acquiring stock ownership in other companies there may occur a financial leverage effect through increased debt which will magnify either earnings or losses. The more the financial leverage involved, the higher the risk of variability in earnings.

A holding company can get a large amount of control for a small investment by obtaining voting control in a company for a minimal amount and then using that firm to gain voting control in another, and so on.

EXAMPLE 17.15   Matz Company holds stock in company X and company Y and has voting control over both. Balance sheet information follows:

Matz Company

Investment		Long-term liabilities	$ 40,000
Company X	$ 30,000	Preferred stock	20,000
Company Y	70,000	Common stock equity	40,000
Total	$100,000	Total	$100,000

Company X

Current assets	$120,000	Current liabilities	$100,000
Noncurrent assets	480,000	Long-term liabilities	350,000
		Common stock equity	150,000
Total	$600,000	Total	$600,000

Company Y

Current assets	$200,000	Current liabilities	$150,000
Noncurrent assets	600,000	Long-term liabilities	400,000
		Common stock equity	250,000
Total	$800,000	Total	$800,000

The percent of total assets controlled by Matz Corporation emanating from its common stock equity is:

$$\frac{\text{Common stock equity of Matz}}{\text{Total assets of company X and company Y}} = \frac{\$40,000}{\$1,400,000} = 2.9\%$$

Assuming another company owns 18 percent of the common stock of Matz and has voting control, the percent of the total assets controlled by the other company's equity is:

$$2.9\% \times 18\% = 0.52\%$$

17.7 TENDER OFFER

The takeover of another company is often accomplished through negotiation. In the event the management of the target company does not want to be merged, the company can be acquired against its will by the buyer making a tender offer. A *tender offer* is made when the buyer goes directly to the stockholders of the target business to *tender* (sell) their shares, typically for cash. The tender in some cases may be shares in the acquiring company rather than cash. If the buyer obtains enough stock, it can gain control of the target company and force the merger. Stockholders are induced to sell when the tender price substantially exceeds the current market price of the target company stock. Typically, there is an expiration date to the tender. Good takeover candidates are cash-rich businesses and those with low debt/equity ratios.

The management of a targeted company can fight the takeover attempt, if it wishes, in the following ways:

1. Furnish publicity against the raider.
2. Purchase treasury stock to make fewer shares available for tendering.
3. Initiate legal action to prevent the takeover, such as by applying antitrust laws.
4. Postpone the tender offer. Many states have laws that can delay the tender offer.
5. Seek out a merger with a different, friendlier, company.
6. Declare an attractive dividend to keep stockholders happy.

With regard to tender offers, the following disclosure requirements exist:

1. The acquiring business must furnish to the management of the potential acquired company and to the SEC, 30 days' notice of its intent to acquire.
2. The name of the group furnishing the money for the acquisition must be disclosed when significant amounts of stock are purchased on the stock exchange. Typically, the acquired stock is in the *street name* of the broker who is acting for the true owner.

Due to the disclosure requirements, competition may arise in the takeover attempt. The competing acquiring companies may increase the acquisition price significantly by bidding higher than the pretakeover market price of stock.

Review Questions

1. A combination of two or more companies into one where only the acquiring company retains its identity is referred to as a(n) _____ .

2. A consolidation is when two or more companies combine to form a(n) _____ company.

3. A(n) _____ company owns common stock of other companies.

4. A(n) _____ business combination is when two companies in a similar business combine.

5. A(n) _____ is when two companies in unrelated industries combine.

6. A good combination may result in a(n) _____ effect.

7. A tax loss may be carried forward _____ years.

8. If a holding company owns 80 percent or more of the subsidiary's stock, there will be a(n) _____ percent dividend exemption.

9. A(n) _____ is made when an acquiring company goes directly to the stockholders of the target business to buy their shares.

Answers: (1) merger; (2) new; (3) holding; (4) horizontal; (5) conglomerate; (6) synergistic; (7) 15; (8) 100; (9) tender offer.

Solved Problems

17.1 Tax-Loss-Carryforward Benefit. In 19X1, Burton Corporation acquires Weiss Corporation, which has a tax-loss-carryforward benefit of $600,000. Burton Corporation has earnings of $500,000 in 19X1 and $800,000 in 19X2. The tax rate is 46 percent. Determine the tax to be paid by Burton in 19X1 and 19X2.

SOLUTION

In 19X1:		
	Burton Corporation earnings	$500,000
	Weiss tax loss carryforward	500,000
	Taxable income	$ 0
	Tax	$ 0

In 19X2:		
	Burton Corporation earnings	$800,000
	Unused Weiss Corporation's tax loss carryforward ($600,000 − $500,000)	100,000
	Taxable income	$700,000
	Tax (46% rate)	$322,000

17.2 Acquisition of a Company. Yohai Corporation is thinking of purchasing Klein Corporation for $70,000 in cash. Yohai's current cost of capital is 16 percent. Klein's estimated overall cost of capital is anticipated to be 14 percent after the acquisition. Forecasted cash inflows from years 1 to 15 are $8,000. Should the acquisition be made?

SOLUTION

	Calculations	Present Value
Year 0	−$70,000 × 1	−$70,000
Years 1–15	+$8,000 × 6.142	+49,136 [a]
Net present value		−$20,864

[a] Using 14 percent as the discount rate.

Since the net present value is negative, the acquisition should not be made.

17.3 Acquisition of Assets for Cash. Master Corporation wants to buy certain fixed assets of Smith Corporation. However, Smith Corporation wants to dispose of its entire business. The balance sheet of Smith follows:

ASSETS

Cash	$ 2,000
Accounts receivable	8,000
Inventories	20,000
Equipment 1	10,000
Equipment 2	20,000
Equipment 3	35,000
Building	90,000
Total assets	$185,000

LIABILITIES AND STOCKHOLDERS' EQUITY

Total liabilities	$ 80,000
Total stockholders' equity	105,000
Total liabilities and stockholders' equity	$185,000

Master needs only equipment 1 and 2 and the building. The other assets excluding cash can be sold for $35,000. Smith wants $48,000 for the entire business. It is anticipated that the after-tax cash inflows from the new equipment will be $30,000 a year for the next 8 years. The cost of capital is 12 percent.

(a) What is the initial net cash outlay? (b) Should the acquisition be made?

SOLUTION

(a)

Total payment:		
Liabilities	$80,000	
Owners	48,000	$128,000
Cash available ($2,000 + $35,000)		37,000
Initial net cash outlay		$ 91,000

(b)

	Calculations	Present Value
Year 0	$-\$91,000 \times 1$	$-\$ 91,000$
Years 1–8	$+\$30,000 \times 4.968$	$+149,040$
Net present value		$+\$ 58,040$

Since the net present value is positive, the acquisition should be made.

17.4 Acquisition of Assets for Cash. Knab Corporation is considering acquiring Deerson Corporation for $40,000. Deerson has liabilities of $62,000. Deerson has machinery that Knab wants, and the remaining assets would be sold for $55,000. The machinery will furnish Knab with an increase in annual cash flow of $7,000 for the next 10 years. The cost of capital is 12 percent.

(a) What is the net cost of the machinery? (b) Should the acquisition be made?

SOLUTION

(a)
$$\$40,000 + \$62,000 - \$55,000 = \$47,000$$

(b)

	Calculations	Present Value
Year 0	$-\$47,000 \times 1$	$-\$47,000$
Years 1–10	$\$7,000 \times 5.650$	$+39,550$
Net present value		$-\$\ 7,450$

Since the net present value is negative, the acquisition should not be made.

17.5   Acquisition by Exchanging Stock. Company R wishes to acquire company S. Company R's stock sells for $100 per share. Company S's stock sells for $40 a share. Due to merger negotiations, company R offers $50 a share. The acquisition is done through an exchange of securities. What is the ratio of exchange?

SOLUTION

$$\frac{\text{Amount paid per share of the acquired company}}{\text{Market price of the acquiring company's shares}} = \frac{\$50}{\$100} = 0.5$$

17.6   Earnings per Share. The following data concerning companies A and B are presented:

	Company A	Company B
Net income	$35,000	$50,000
Shares outstanding	5,000	10,000
Earnings per share	$7.00	$5.00
P/E ratio	10	14
Market price	$70	$70

Company B is the acquiring company, exchanging its shares on a one-for-one basis for company A's shares. The exchange ratio is based on the market prices of company A and company B stock.

(a) What will earnings per share be subsequent to the merger? (b) What is the change in earnings per share for the stockholders of companies A and B?

SOLUTION

(a)

	B Shares Owned after Merger	EPS before Merger	EPS after Merger
A stockholders	5,000	$7.00	$5.67[a]
B stockholders	10,000	$5.00	$5.67[a]
Total	15,000		

---

[a] Total net income is calculated as follows:

5,000 shares × $7	$35,000
10,000 shares × $5	50,000
New EPS	$85,000

$$\text{EPS} = \frac{\text{total net income}}{\text{total shares}} = \frac{\$85,000}{15,000} = \$5.67$$

(b) EPS decreases by $1.33 for company A stockholders but increases by $0.67 for company B stockholders.

17.7   Exchange Ratio. The following information is provided:

Case	Market Price per Share of Acquiring Company	Market Price per Share of Acquired Company	Price per Share Offered
1	$80	$40	$50
2	$120	$160	$180

For each case, determine (*a*) the exchange ratio in shares, and (*b*) the exchange ratio in market price.

SOLUTION

Case	(*a*) Shares	(*b*) Market Price
1	$50/$80 = 0.625	$50/$40 = 1.25
2	$180/$120 = 1.5	$180/$160 = 1.125

17.8   Earnings per Share of Merged Company. Paula Company wants to acquire David Company. Relevant data follows:

	Paula	David
Net income	$40,000	$25,000
Shares outstanding	20,000	5,000

Paula issues its shares to make the acquisition. The ratio of exchange is 2.5. (*a*) What is the earnings per share of the merged company based on the original shares of each company? (*b*) What is the earnings per share of Paula? (*c*) What is the earnings per share of David?

SOLUTION

(*a*)   The merged company's earnings per share is:

$$\frac{\text{Combined net income}}{\text{Total shares}} = \frac{\$65,000}{20,000 + (5,000 \times 2.5)} = \frac{\$65,000}{20,000 + 12,500} = \frac{\$65,000}{32,500 \text{ shares}} = \$2$$

(*b*)   Paula's earnings per share is $2.

(*c*)   David's earnings per share is:

$$\$2 \times 2.5 = \$5$$

17.9   Earnings per Share. Shim Company wishes to acquire Siegel Company by exchanging 0.8 share of its stock for each share of Siegel. Financial data follow:

	Shim	Siegel
Net income	$200,000	$40,000
Shares outstanding	50,000	20,000
Earnings per share	$4	$2
Market price	$40	$16
P/E ratio	10	8

Shim issues its shares to make the acquisition. (*a*) How many shares must Shim issue in the acquisition? (*b*) Assuming the net income of each firm remains the same, what is the earnings per share after the acquisition? (*c*) What is the amount earned per share on the original shares of Siegel stock? (*d*) What is the amount earned per share on the original shares of Shim stock?

SOLUTION

(a)
$$20{,}000 \text{ shares} \times 0.8 = 16{,}000 \text{ shares}$$

(b)
$$\frac{\$200{,}000 + \$40{,}000}{50{,}000 + 16{,}000} = \frac{\$240{,}000}{66{,}000} = \$3.64$$

(c)
$$\$3.64 \times 0.8 = \$2.91$$

(d) $3.64

17.10 EPS, P/E Ratio, and Market Price. Harris Corporation wants to acquire Logo Corporation by exchanging 1.6 shares of its stock for each share of Logo. Harris anticipates having the same P/E ratio subsequent to the merger as prior to it. The following financial data are given:

	Harris	Logo
Net income	$500,000	$150,000
Shares	100,000	25,000
Market price per share	$35	$40

(a) What is the exchange ratio of market prices? (b) What is the EPS and the P/E ratio for each company? (c) What was the P/E ratio used in obtaining Logo? (d) What is the EPS of Harris after the acquisition? (e) What is the expected market price per share of the merged company?

SOLUTION

(a)
$$\frac{\text{Price per share offered}}{\text{Market price of Logo}} = \frac{\$35 \times 1.6}{\$40} = \frac{\$56}{\$40} = 1.4$$

(b)

	Harris	Logo
EPS	$500,000/100,000 shares = $5	$150,000/25,000 shares = $6
P/E ratio	$35/$5 = 7 times	$40/$6 = 6.67 times

(c)
$$1.6 \times \$35 = \$56$$

$$\frac{\$56}{\$6} = 9.33 \text{ times}$$

(d)
$$\frac{\$650{,}000}{\$100{,}000 + (25{,}000 \times 1.6)} = \frac{\$650{,}000}{140{,}000 \text{ shares}} = \$4.64$$

(e)
$$\$4.64 \times 7 \text{ times} = \$32.48$$

17.11 Dividend Exclusion. A holding company owns 40 percent of another business. It received dividends of $20,000. The tax rate is 40 percent. What is the tax to be paid on the dividends?

SOLUTION

Dividend	$20,000
Dividend exclusion (85%)	17,000
Dividend subject to tax	$ 3,000
Tax rate	×40%
Tax	$ 1,200

17.12 Holding Company. Usry Company holds stock in company A and company B and possesses voting control over both. Balance sheet data follow:

Usry Corporation

Investment		Long-term liabilities	$ 30,000
Company A	$ 20,000	Preferred stock	10,000
Company B	80,000	Common stock equity	60,000
Total	$100,000	Total	$100,000

Company A

Current assets	$200,000	Current liabilities	$100,000
Noncurrent assets	300,000	Long-term liabilities	200,000
		Common stock equity	200,000
Total	$500,000	Total	$500,000

Company B

Current assets	$300,000	Current liabilities	$200,000
Noncurrent assets	400,000	Long-term liabilities	350,000
		Common stock equity	150,000
Total	$700,000	Total	$700,000

(*a*) What is the percent of total assets controlled by Usry Corporation resulting from its common stock equity? (*b*) Assuming another company owns 25 percent of the common stock of Usry and has voting control, what is the percent of the total assets controlled by the other firm's equity?

SOLUTION

(*a*)
$$\frac{\text{Common stock equity of Usry}}{\text{Total assets of company A and company B}} = \frac{\$60,000}{\$1,200,000} = 5.0\%$$

(*b*)
$$5.0\% \times 25\% = 1.25\%$$

Chapter 18

Failure and Reorganization

18.1 INTRODUCTION

When a business fails it can be either reorganized or dissolved depending on the circumstances. A number of ways exist for business failure to occur, including a poor rate of return, technical insolvency, and bankruptcy.

Deficient Rate of Return. A company may fail if its rate of return is negative or poor. If operating losses exist, the company may not be able to meet its obligations. A negative rate of return will cause a decline in the market price of its stock. When a company does not earn a return greater than its cost of capital, it may fail. If corrective action is not forthcoming, perhaps the firm should liquidate. A poor return, however, does not constitute legal evidence of failure.

Technical Insolvency. Technical insolvency means that the business cannot satisfy current debt when due even if total assets are greater than total liabilities.

Bankruptcy. In bankruptcy, liabilities are greater than the fair market value of assets. There exists a negative real net worth.

According to law, failure of a company can be either technical insolvency or bankruptcy. When creditor claims against a business are in question, the law permits creditors recourse against the company.

Some causes of business failure include:

1. Poor management
2. An economic downturn affecting the company and/or industry
3. The end of the life cycle of the firm
4. Overexpansion
5. Catastrophe

18.2 VOLUNTARY SETTLEMENT

A voluntary settlement with creditors permits the company to save many of the costs that would be present in bankruptcy. Such a settlement is done out of court. The voluntary settlement enables the company to either continue or be liquidated and is initiated to enable the debtor firm to recover some of its investment.

A creditor committee may decide to allow the firm to continue to operate if it is expected that the company will recover. Creditors may also continue to do business with the company. In sustaining the firm's existence, there may be:

1. An extension
2. A composition
3. Creditor control
4. Integration of each of the above

Extension

In an *extension*, creditors will receive the balances due but over an extended period of time. Current purchases are made with cash. It is also possible that the creditors may agree not only to lengthen the maturity date for payment but also to subordinate their claims to current debt for suppliers furnishing credit in the extension period. The creditors expect the debtor will be able to work out his or her problems.

The creditor committee may require certain controls, including legal control over the company's assets or common stock, obtaining a security interest in assets, and approval of all cash payments.

If there are creditors dissenting to the extension agreement, they may be paid immediately to prevent them from having the company declared bankrupt.

Composition

In a *composition*, there is a voluntary reduction of the amount the debtor owes the creditor. The creditor obtains from the debtor a stated percent of the obligation in *full* settlement of the debt regardless of how low the percent is. The agreement is designed to allow the debtor to continue to operate. The creditor may try to work with the debtor in handling the firm's financial problems, since a stable customer may ensue. The advantages of a composition are that court costs are eliminated as well as the stigma of a bankrupt company.

If there are dissenting stockholders, they may be paid in full or they may be permitted to recover a higher percentage so that they do not force the business to close.

For an extension or composition to be practical, the following should exist:

1. An ethical debtor who will not use the company's assets for personal use.

2. An expectation that the debtor will recover.

3. Present business conditions must be such as to promote the debtor's recovery.

Creditor Committee Takes Control

A committee of creditors may decide to take control of the business if they are not happy with present management. They will operate the business in order to satisfy their claims. Once paid, the creditors may recommend that new management replace the old before further credit is given. The drawback with such an agreement is the possibility of mismanagement lawsuits brought by stockholders against the creditors.

Integration

The creditors and the company negotiate a plan that involves a combination of extension, composition, and creditor control. For instance, the agreement may allow for a 20 percent cash payment of the balance owed plus five future payments of 12 percent, typically in the form of notes. The total payment is thus 80 percent.

The advantages of negotiated settlements are that:

1. They are less formal than bankruptcy proceedings.

2. They cost less (e.g., they avoid or reduce legal expenses).

3. They are easier to implement than bankruptcy proceedings.

4. They usually provide creditors with the greatest return.

The following disadvantages may arise:

1. If the troubled debtor still has control over its business affairs, there may occur further decline in asset values. Creditor controls can, however, be implemented to provide some degree of protection.

2. Unrealistic small creditors may make the negotiating process a drain by demanding full payment.

18.3 BANKRUPTCY REORGANIZATION

If no voluntary settlement is agreed upon, the company may be put into bankruptcy by its creditors. The bankruptcy proceeding may either reorganize or liquidate the firm.

Bankruptcy takes place when a company cannot pay its bills or when liabilities are greater than the fair market value of the assets. Here, legal bankruptcy may be declared. A company may file for reorganization under which it will formulate a plan for continued life.

Chapter 7 of the Bankruptcy Reform Act of 1978 outlines the procedures to be followed for liquidation. This chapter applies when reorganization is not feasible. Chapter 11 goes into the steps of reorganizing a failed business. If a reorganization is not possible under Chapter 11, the company will be liquidated in accordance with Chapter 7.

The two types of reorganization petitions are:

1. *Voluntary.* The firm petitions for its own reorganization. The company does not have to be insolvent to file for voluntary reorganization.

2. *Involuntary.* Creditors file for an involuntary reorganization of the company. An involuntary petition must establish either that the debtor firm is not meeting its debts when due or that a creditor or another party has taken control over the debtor's assets. In general, most of the creditors or claims must support the petition.

The five steps involved in a reorganization are:

1. A reorganization petition is filed under Chapter 11 in court.

2. A judge approves the petition and either appoints a trustee or lets the creditors elect one to handle the disposition of the assets.

3. The trustee presents a fair plan of reorganization to the court.

4. The plan is given to the creditors and stockholders of the firm for approval.

5. The debtor pays the expenses of the parties rendering services in the reorganization proceedings.

The trustee in a reorganization plan is required to:

1. Value the company

2. Recapitalize the company

3. Exchange outstanding debts for new securities

Valuation

In valuing the firm, the trustee must estimate its liquidation value versus its value as a going concern. Liquidation is called for when the liquidation value exceeds the continuity value. If the firm is more valuable when operating, reorganization is the answer. Future earnings must be predicted when arriving at the value of the reorganized company. The going concern value represents the present value of future earnings.

EXAMPLE 18.1 A petition for reorganization of X Company was filed under Chapter 11. The trustee determined that the company's liquidation value after subtracting expenses was $4.3 million. The trustee estimates that the reorganized business will generate $540,000 in annual earnings. The cost of capital rate is 12 percent. Assuming the earnings would continue indefinitely, the value of X Company as a going concern is:

$$\$540,000 \times \frac{1}{0.12} = \$4,500,000$$

Since the company's value as a going concern ($4.5 million) exceeds the value in liquidation ($4.3 million), reorganization is called for.

Recapitalization

Assuming the trustee recommends reorganization, a plan must be developed to carry it out. The obligations may be extended or equity securities may be issued in substitution of the debt. *Income bonds* may be given for the debentures. With an income bond, interest is paid only when there are earnings. This process of exchanging liabilities for other types of liabilities or equity securities is referred to as *recapitalization*. In recapitalizing the firm, the purpose is to have a mixture of debt and equity that will permit the company to meet its debts and provide reasonable profits for the owners.

EXAMPLE 18.2 The current capital structure of Y Corporation is presented below.

Debentures	$1,500,000
Collateral bonds	3,000,000
Preferred stock	800,000
Common stock	2,500,000
Total	$7,800,000

There exists high financial leverage:

$$\frac{\text{Debt}}{\text{Equity}} = \frac{\$4,500,000}{\$3,300,000} = 1.36$$

Assuming the company is deemed to be worth $5 million as a going concern, the trustee can develop a less leveraged capital structure having a total capital of $5 million as follows:

Debentures	$1,000,000
Collateral bonds	1,000,000
Income bonds	1,500,000
Preferred stock	500,000
Common stock	1,000,000
Total	$5,000,000

The income bond of $1.5 million is similar to equity in appraising financial leverage, since interest is not paid unless there is income. The new debt/equity ratio is safer:

$$\frac{\text{Debt} + \text{collateral bonds}}{\text{Income bonds} + \text{preferred stock} + \text{common stock}} = \frac{\$2,000,000}{\$3,000,000} = 0.67$$

Exchange of Obligations

In exchanging obligations to achieve the best capital structure, priorities must be followed. Senior claims are taken care of before junior claims. Senior debt holders must receive a claim on new capital equal to their prior claims. The last priority goes to common stockholders in receiving new securities. A debt holder usually receives a combination of different securities. Preferred and common stockholders may receive nothing. Usually, however, they retain some small ownership. After the exchange, the debt holders may become the firm's new owners.

EXAMPLE 18.3 A $1 million mortgage bondholder may receive in exchange $500,000 in income bonds, $300,000 in preferred stock, and $200,000 in common stock.

Common stockholders receive nothing in exchange.

18.4 LIQUIDATION DUE TO BANKRUPTCY

When a company becomes bankrupt it may be liquidated under Chapter 7 of the Bankruptcy Reform Act of 1978. The key elements of liquidation are *legal considerations*, *claim priority*, and *dissolution*.

Legal Considerations

When a company is declared bankrupt, creditors must meet between 10 and 30 days subsequent to that declaration. A judge or referee takes charge of the meeting in which the creditors provide their claims. A trustee is appointed by the creditors. The trustee handles the property of the defaulted company, liquidates the business, maintains appropriate records, evaluates the claims of creditors, makes payments, and provides relevant information regarding the liquidation process. Many times three trustees are appointed and/or an advisory committee of at least three creditors is formed.

Claim Priority

Some claims against the company take precedence over others in bankruptcy. The following rank order exists in meeting claims:

1. *Secured claims.* Secured creditors receive the value of the secured assets in support of their claims. If the value of the secured assets is insufficient to satisfy their claims in full, the balance reverts to general creditor status.

2. *Bankruptcy administrative costs.* These costs include any expenses related to handling the bankruptcy such as legal and trustee expenses.

3. *Unsecured salaries and commissions.* These claims are limited to $2,000 per individual and must have been incurred within 90 days of the bankruptcy petition.

4. *Unsecured customer deposit claims.* These claims are limited to $900 each.

5. *Taxes.* Tax claims apply to unpaid taxes due the government.

6. *General creditor claims.* General creditors are those who have loaned money to the company without specific collateral. Included are debentures and accounts payable.

7. *Preferred stockholders.*

8. *Common stockholders.*

In most cases, once creditor obligations have been settled with the remaining assets there is nothing left for stockholders.

Bankruptcy distribution in principle should be based on *absolute priority*, in which creditor claims are satisfied strictly following the priority listing. Junior claims are supposed to be met after senior claims are fully satisfied. However, in practice, courts sometimes use *relative priority* in distributing assets in which junior claims receive a partial distribution even though all senior claims have not been fully met.

Dissolution

After claims have been met in priority order and an accounting made of the proceedings, there may then be instituted an application to *discharge* the bankrupt business. A *discharge* occurs when the court releases the company from legitimate debts in bankruptcy, with the exception of debts that are immune to discharge. As long as a debtor has not been discharged within the prior 6 years and was not bankrupt due to fraud, the debtor may then start a new business.

EXAMPLE 18.4 The balance sheet of Ace Corporation for the year ended December 31, 19X4, follows:

Balance Sheet

Current assets	$400,000	Current liabilities	$475,000
Fixed assets	410,000	Long-term liabilities	250,000
		Common stock	175,000
		Retained earnings	(90,000)
Total assets	$810,000	Total liabilities and stockholders' equity	$810,000

The company's liquidation value is $625,000. Rather than liquidate, there could be a reorganization with an investment of an additional $320,000. The reorganization is expected to generate earnings of $115,000 per year. A multiplier of 7.5 is appropriate. If the $320,000 is obtained, long-term debt holders will receive 40 percent of the common stock in the reorganized business in substitution for their current claims.

If $320,000 of further investment is made, the firm's going-concern value is $862,500 (7.5 × $115,000). The liquidation value is given at $625,000. Since the reorganization value exceeds the liquidation value, reorganization is called for.

EXAMPLE 18.5 Plant and equipment having a book value of $1.5 million was sold for $1.3 million. There are mortgage bonds on the plant and equipment in the amount of $1.8 million. The proceeds from the collateral sale are insufficient to satisfy the secured claim. The unsatisfied portion of $500,000 ($1,800,000 − $1,300,000) of the claim becomes a general creditor claim.

EXAMPLE 18.6 Land having a book value of $1.2 million was sold for $800,000. Mortgage bonds on the land are $600,000. The surplus of $200,000 will be returned to the trustee to pay other creditors.

EXAMPLE 18.7 Charles Corporation is bankrupt. The book and liquidation values follow:

	Book Value	Liquidation Value
Cash	$ 600,000	$ 600,000
Accounts receivable	1,900,000	1,500,000
Inventory	3.700,000	2,100,000
Land	5,000,000	3,200,000
Building	7,800,000	5,300,000
Equipment	6,700,000	2,800,000
Total assets	$25,700,000	$15,500,000

The liabilities and stockholders' equity at the date of liquidation are:

Current liabilities		
Accounts payable	$1,800,000	
Notes payable	900,000	
Accrued taxes	650,000	
Accrued salaries	450,000 [a]	
Total current liabilities		$ 3,800,000
Long-term liabilities		
Mortgage on land	$3,200,000	
First mortgage—building	2,800,000	
Second mortgage—building	2,500,000	
Subordinated debentures	4,800,000	
Total long-term liabilities		13,300,000
Total liabilities		$17,100,000
Stockholders' equity		
Preferred stock	$4,700,000	
Common stock	6,800,000	
Retained earnings	(2,900,000)	
Total stockholders' equity		8,600,000
Total liabilities and stockholders' equity		$25,700,000

---

[a] The salary owed to each worker is below $2,000 and was incurred within 90 days of the bankruptcy petition.

Expenses of the liquidation including legal costs were 15 percent of the proceeds. The debentures are subordinated only with regard to the two first-mortgage bonds.

The distribution of the proceeds follows:

Proceeds		$15,500,000
Mortgage on land	$3,200,000	
First mortgage—building	2,800,000	
Second mortgage—building	2,500,000	
Liquidation expenses (15% × $15,500,000)	2,325,000	
Accrued salaries	450,000	
Accrued taxes	650,000	
Total		11,925,000
Balance		$ 3,575,000

The percent to be paid to general creditors is:

$$\frac{\text{Proceeds balance}}{\text{Total owed}} = \frac{\$3,575,000}{\$7,500,000} = 47.66667\%$$

The balance due general creditors follows:

General Creditors	Owed	Paid
Accounts payable	$1,800,000	$ 858,000
Notes payable	900,000	429,000
Subordinated debentures	4,800,000	2,288,000
Total	$7,500,000	$3,575,000

EXAMPLE 18.8 The balance sheet of the Oakhurst Company is presented below.

ASSETS

Current assets		
Cash	$ 9,000	
Marketable securities	6,000	
Receivables	1,100,000	
Inventory	3,000,000	
Prepaid expenses	4,000	
Total current assets		$4,119,000
Noncurrent assets		
Land	$1,800,000	
Fixed assets	2,000,000	
Total noncurrent assets		3,800,000
Total assets		$7,919,000

LIABILITIES AND STOCKHOLDERS' EQUITY

Current liabilities

Accounts payable	$ 180,000	
Bank loan payable	900,000	
Accrued salaries	300,000 [a]	
Employee benefits payable	70,000 [b]	
Customer claims—unsecured	80,000 [c]	
Taxes payable	350,000	
Total current liabilities		$1,880,000

Noncurrent liabilities

First mortgage payable	$1,600,000	
Second mortgage payable	1,100,000	
Subordinated debentures	700,000	
Total noncurrent liabilities		3,400,000
Total liabilities		$5,280,000

Stockholders' equity

Preferred stock (3,500 shares)	$ 350,000	
Common stock (8,000 shares)	480,000	
Paid-in capital	1,600,000	
Retained earnings	209,000	
Total stockholders' equity		2,639,000
Total liabilities and stockholders' equity		$7,919,000

[a] The salary owed to each worker is below $2,000 and was incurred within 90 days of the bankruptcy petition.

[b] Employee benefits payable have the same limitations as unsecured wages and satisfy for eligibility in bankruptcy distribution.

[c] No customer claim is greater than $900.

Additional data are as follows:

1. The mortgages apply to the company's total noncurrent assets.

2. The subordinated debentures are subordinated to the bank loan payable. Therefore, they come after the bank loan payable in liquidation.

3. The trustee has sold the company's current assets for $2.1 million and the noncurrent assets for $1.9 million. Therefore, a total of $4 million was received.

4. The business is bankrupt, since the total liabilities of $5.28 million are greater than the $4 million of the fair value of the assets.

Assume that the administration expense for handling the bankrupt company is $900,000. This liability is not reflected in the above balance sheet.

The allocation of the $4 million to the creditors is shown on the following page.

Proceeds		$4,000,000
Available to secured creditors		
First mortgage—payable from $1,900,000 proceeds of noncurrent assets	$1,600,000	
Second mortgage—payable from balance of proceeds of noncurrent assets	300,000	1,900,000
Balance after secured creditors		$2,100,000
Next priority		
Administrative expenses	$ 900,000	
Accrued salaries	300,000	
Employee benefits payable	70,000	
Customer claims—unsecured	80,000	
Taxes payable	350,000	1,700,000
Proceeds available to general creditors		$ 400,000

Now that the claims on the proceeds from liquidation have been met, general creditors receive the balance on a pro rata basis. The distribution of the $400,000 follows:

General Creditor	Amount	Pro Rata Allocation for Balance to Be Paid
Second-mortgage balance ($1,100,000 − $300,000)	$ 800,000	$124,031
Accounts payable	180,000	27,907
Bank loan payable	900,000	248,062 [a]
Subordinated debentures	700,000	0
Total	$2,580,000	$400,000

[a] Since the debentures are subordinated, the bank loan payable must be satisfied in full before any amount can go to the subordinated debentures. The subordinated debenture holders therefore receive nothing.

EXAMPLE 18.9 Nolan Company is having severe financial problems. Jefferson Bank holds a first mortgage on the plant and has an $800,000 unsecured loan that is already delinquent. The Alto Insurance Company holds $4.7 million of the company's subordinated debentures to the notes payable. Nolan is deciding whether to reorganize the business or declare bankruptcy.

Another company is considering acquiring Nolan Company by offering to take over the mortgage of $7.5 million, pay the past due taxes, and pay $4.38 million for the firm.

Nolan's balance sheet follows:

ASSETS	
Current assets	$ 2,800,000
Plant assets	11,700,000
Other assets	3,000,000
Total assets	$17,500,000

**LIABILITIES AND
STOCKHOLDERS' EQUITY**

Current liabilities		
Accounts payable	$ 1,800,000	
Taxes payable	170,000	
Bank note payable	260,000	
Other current liabilities	1,400,000	
Total current liabilities		$ 3,630,000
Noncurrent liabilities		
Mortgage payable	$ 7,500,000	
Subordinated debentures	5,300,000	
Total noncurrent liabilities		12,800,000
Total liabilities		$16,430,000
Stockholders' equity		
Common stock	$ 1,000,000	
Premium on common stock	2,300,000	
Retained earnings	(2,230,000)	
Total stockholders' equity		1,070,000
Total liabilities and stockholders' equity		$17,500,000

The impact of the proposed reorganization on creditor claims is indicated below.

Outstanding obligations		$16,430,000
Claims met through the reorganization		
Mortgage payable	$7,500,000	
Taxes payable	170,000	
Total		7,670,000
Balance of claims		$ 8,760,000

The cash arising from reorganization is given as $4.38 million, which is 50 percent ($4,380,000/$8,760,000) of the unsatisfied claims.

The distribution to general creditors follows:

General Creditor	Liability Due	50%	Adjusted for Subordination
Bank note payable	$ 260,000	$ 130,000	$ 260,000 [a]
Subordinated debenture	5,300,000	2,650,000	2,520,000
Other creditors (accounts payable + other current liabilities)	3,200,000	1,600,000	1,600,000
Total	$8,760,000	$4,380,000	$4,380,000

[a] The bank note payable is paid in full before the subordinated debenture.

Review Questions

1. _____ means that the company is unable to meet current debt when due.

2. If a company's liabilities exceed the fair market value of its assets, it is _____.

3. In the case of a(n) _____, creditors receive the balances owed them over an extended time period.

4. A voluntary reduction of the amount the debtor owes the creditor is referred to as a(n) _____.

5. A bankruptcy proceeding may either _____ or _____ the business.

6. _____ of the Bankruptcy Reform Act of 1978 outlines the procedures to be followed in liquidation.

7. Liquidation is called for when the _____ value is greater than the _____ value of the business.

8. _____ is the process of exchanging liabilities for other types of liabilities or equity securities.

9. _____ creditors have a higher priority in bankruptcy than unsecured creditors.

10. In bankruptcy, unsecured salaries are limited to $ _____ per individual.

11. In bankruptcy, _____ are paid last.

12. A(n) _____ means that the court releases the business from legitimate debts in bankruptcy.

Answers: (1) Technical insolvency; (2) bankrupt; (3) extension; (4) composition; (5) reorganize, liquidate; (6) Chapter 7; (7) liquidation, continuity; (8) Recapitalization; (9) Secured; (10) 2,000; (11) common stockholders; (12) discharge.

Solved Problems

18.1   Going-Concern Value. There was a petition for reorganization of Hazel Corporation filed under Chapter 11. It was determined by the trustee that the firm's liquidation value, after considering expenses, was $5.3 million. The trustee predicts that the reorganized business will derive $500,000 in annual profit. The cost of capital rate is 10 percent. Assume profits will continue indefinitely. Is reorganization or liquidation recommended?

SOLUTION

The value of the business as a going concern equals:

$$\$500,000 \times \frac{1}{0.10} = \$5,000,000$$

Since the value of the company as a going concern ($5 million) is less than its value in liquidation ($5.3 million), the business should be liquidated.

18.2   Debt/Equity Ratio. The present capital structure of Jones Corporation is shown below.

Debentures	$1,200,000
Collateral bonds	2,800,000
Preferred stock	700,000
Common stock	2,600,000
Total	$7,300,000

There is a high financial leverage position:

$$\frac{\text{Debt}}{\text{Equity}} = \frac{\$4,000,000}{\$3,300,000} = 1.21$$

The business is worth $4.7 million as a going concern. The trustee has formulated a less leveraged capital structure having a total capital of $4.7 million as follows:

Debentures	$ 800,000
Collateral bonds	1,500,000
Income bonds	1,300,000
Preferred stock	400,000
Common stock	700,000
Total	$4,700,000

What is the new debt/equity ratio?

SOLUTION

The income bond of $1.3 million is similar to equity in evaluating financial leverage because interest is not paid unless income exists. The new debt/equity ratio is lower at:

$$\frac{\text{Debt} + \text{collateral bonds}}{\text{Income bonds} + \text{preferred stock} + \text{common stock}} = \frac{\$2,300,000}{\$2,400,000} = 0.96$$

18.3   Reorganization or Liquidation. The balance sheet of Morris Corporation for the year ended December 31, 19X3, follows:

Balance Sheet

Current assets	$ 500,000	Current liabilities	$ 550,000
Fixed assets	520,000	Long-term liabilities	300,000
		Common stock	250,000
		Retained earnings	(80,000)
		Total liabilities and	
Total assets	$1,020,000	stockholders' equity	$1,020,000

The firm's liquidation value is $700,000. Instead of liquidating, there could be a reorganization with an investment of an additional $400,000. The reorganization is anticipated to provide earnings of $150,000 a year. A multiplier of 8 is appropriate. If the $400,000 is obtained, long-term debt holders will receive 35 percent of the common stock in the reorganized firm in substitution for their current claims. Is reorganization or liquidation recommended?

SOLUTION

Assuming the $400,000 of further investment is made, the company's going-concern value is $1.2 million ($8 \times $150,000$). The liquidation value is stated at $700,000. Because the reorganized value is greater than the liquidation value, reorganization is recommended.

18.4   Secured Creditors. Plant and equipment with a book value of $2.3 million was sold for $2 million. The mortgage bonds on the plant and equipment are $2.6 million. How will the mortgage bondholders be treated in liquidation?

SOLUTION

The proceeds from the collateral sale are not enough to meet the secured claim. The unsatisfied portion of $600,000 of the claim becomes a general creditor claim.

18.5   Secured Creditors. Plant and equipment having a book value of $800,000 was sold for $600,000. Mortgage bonds on the plant and equipment are $500,000. How will the mortgage bondholders be treated in liquidation?

SOLUTION

The mortgage bondholders will be fully satisfied in liquidation. The surplus of $100,000 will be returned to the trustee to pay other creditors.

18.6   Distribution in Bankruptcy. Blake Corporation is bankrupt. The book and liquidation values of its assets follow.

	Book Value	Liquidation Value
Cash	$ 500,000	$ 500,000
Accounts receivable	1,700,000	1,400,000
Inventory	3,400,000	2,200,000
Land	4,700,000	3,500,000
Building	8,000,000	5,600,000
Equipment	7,000,000	3,000,000
Total assets	$25,300,000	$16,200,000

The liabilities and stockholders' equity at the liquidation date follow.

Current liabilities		
Accounts payable	$2,000,000	
Notes payable	1,000,000	
Accrued taxes	700,000	
Accrued salaries	400,000 [a]	
Total current liabilities		$ 4,100,000
Long-term liabilities		
Mortgage on land	$3,500,000	
First mortgage—building	4,000,000	
Second mortgage—building	1,600,000	
Subordinated debentures	4,500,000	
Total long-term liabilities		13,600,000
Total liabilities		$17,700,000
Stockholders' equity		
Preferred stock	$4,500,000	
Common stock	6,500,000	
Retained earnings	(3,400,000)	
Total stockholders' equity		7,600,000
Total liabilities and stockholders' equity		$25,300,000

[a] The salary owed to each worker is below $2,000 and was incurred within 90 days of the bankruptcy petition.

Expenses associated with the bankruptcy administration were 12 percent of the proceeds. The debentures are subordinated only to the two first-mortgage bonds.

Determine the distribution of the proceeds.

SOLUTION

The distribution of the proceeds follow.

Proceeds		$16,200,000
Mortgage on land	$3,500,000	
First mortgage—building	4,000,000	
Second mortgage—building	1,600,000	
Liquidation expenses (12% × $16,200,000)	1,944,000	
Accrued salaries	400,000	
Accrued taxes	700,000	
Total		12,144,000
Balance		$ 4,056,000

The percent to be paid to general creditors is:

$$\frac{\text{Proceeds balance}}{\text{Total owed}} = \frac{\$4,056,000}{\$7,500,000} = 0.5408$$

General Creditor	Owed	Paid
Accounts payable	$2,000,000	$1,081,600
Notes payable	1,000,000	540,800
Subordinated debentures	4,500,000	2,433,600
Total	$7,500,000	$4,056,000

18.7   Distribution in Bankruptcy. The balance sheet of Larkin Corporation is shown below.

ASSETS

Current assets

Cash	$ 7,000	
Marketable securities	5,000	
Receivables	1,000,000	
Inventory	2,800,000	
Prepaid expenses	3,500	
Total current assets		$3,815,500

Noncurrent assets

Land	$1,700,000	
Fixed assets	2,200,000	
Total noncurrent assets		3,900,000
Total assets		$7,715,500

LIABILITIES AND STOCKHOLDERS' EQUITY

Current liabilities

Accounts payable	$ 200,000	
Bank loan payable	950,000	
Accrued salaries	250,000[a]	
Employee benefits payable	80,000[b]	
Customer claims—unsecured	70,000[c]	
Taxes payable	300,000	
Total current liabilities		$1,850,000

Noncurrent liabilities

First-mortgage payable	$1,700,000	
Second-mortgage payable	1,200,000	
Subordinated debentures	600,000	
Total noncurrent liabilities		3,500,000
Total liabilities		$5,350,000

Stockholders' equity

Preferred stock	$ 400,000	
Common stock	490,000	
Paid-in capital	1,400,000	
Retained earnings	75,500	
Total stockholders' equity		2,365,500
Total liabilities and stockholders' equity		$7,715,500

---

[a] The salary owed to each worker is below $2,000 and was incurred within 90 days of the bankruptcy petition.

[b] Employee benefits payable have the same limitations as unsecured wages and satisfy for eligibility in bankruptcy distribution.

[c] No customer claim is greater than $900.

Additional data are as follows:

1. The mortgages relate to the firm's total noncurrent assets.
2. The subordinated debentures are subordinated to the bank loan payable.
3. The trustee has sold the current assets for $2 million and the noncurrent assets for $1.8 million.
4. The administration expense related to bankruptcy proceedings was $700,000.

Determine the distribution of the proceeds.

SOLUTION

Proceeds		$3,800,000
First mortgage—payable from $1,800,000 proceeds of noncurrent assets	$1,700,000	
Second mortgage—payable from $1,800,000 proceeds of noncurrent assets	100,000	1,800,000
Balance after secured creditors		$2,000,000
Next priority		
Administration expenses	$ 700,000	
Accrued salaries	250,000	
Employee benefits payable	80,000	
Customer claims—unsecured	70,000	
Taxes payable	300,000	1,400,000
Proceeds available to general creditors		$ 600,000

The distribution of the $600,000 to general creditors follows:

General Creditor	Amount	Pro Rata Allocation for Balance to Be Paid
Second-mortgage balance ($1,200,000 − $100,000)	$1,100,000	$231,579
Accounts payable	200,000	42,105
Bank loan payable	950,000	326,316[a]
Subordinated debentures	600,000	0
Total	$2,850,000	$600,000

[a] Since the debentures are subordinated, the bank loan payable must be met in full before any amount can go to the subordinated debentures. Thus, subordinated debenture holders receive nothing.

The holders of preferred and common stock receive nothing, since the unsecured creditors themselves have not been fully paid.

18.8   Distribution in Bankruptcy. Hover Company's balance sheet follows:

ASSETS	
Current assets	$1,200,000
Land	3,000,000
Plant and equipment	2,400,000
Total assets	$6,600,000

LIABILITIES AND STOCKHOLDERS' EQUITY

Current liabilities

Accounts payable	$ 500,000	
Notes payable	1,200,000	
Accrued taxes	300,000	
Total current liabilities		$2,000,000
Noncurrent liabilities		
Mortgage bonds	$1,800,000 [a]	
Debentures	1,000,000	
Total noncurrent liabilities		2,800,000
Total liabilities		$4,800,000
Stockholders' equity		
Preferred stock	$ 500,000	
Common stock	1,300,000	
Total stockholders' equity		1,800,000
Total liabilities and stockholders' equity		$6,600,000

[a] Mortgage bonds are secured against plant and equipment.

The liquidation value for the total assets is $4 million, $1.2 million of which was received for plant and equipment. Bankruptcy costs were $150,000. Determine the distribution of the proceeds.

SOLUTION

Proceeds		$4,000,000
Mortgage bonds—secured against plant and equipment	$1,200,000	
Bankruptcy costs	150,000	
Accrued taxes	300,000	1,650,000
Balance available to general creditors		$2,350,000

The distribution to general creditors follows:

General Creditor	Owed	Pro Rata Distribution
Mortgage bonds ($1,800,000 − $1,200,000)	$ 600,000	$ 427,273
Accounts payable	500,000	356,060
Notes payable	1,200,000	854,545
Debentures	1,000,000	712,122
Total	$3,300,000	$2,350,000

Holders of preferred and common stock will receive nothing.

Examination IV

1. A warrant for Jack Corporation permits the holder to buy five shares of common stock at $25 a share. The market price of the stock is $37. What is the value of the warrant?

2. Smith Corporation issued a $1,000 bond at par. The common stock has a market price of $34. The conversion price is $40. (*a*) Into how many shares may the bond be converted? (*b*) What is the conversion value of the bond? (*c*) What is the conversion premium?

3. Tunick Corporation's convertible bond has a conversion price of $80. The conversion ratio is 12. The market price of the stock is $115. The call price is $1,200. Would the bondholder rather convert to common stock or receive the call price?

4. The following data are provided:

	Company A	Company B
Net income	$40,000	$60,000
Shares outstanding	8,000	20,000
Earnings per share	$5.00	$3.00
P/E ratio	9	15
Market price	$45	$45

Company B is the acquiring company, exchanging on a one-for-one basis its shares for the shares of company A. The exchange ratio is based on the market prices of A and B. (*a*) What will the EPS be after the merger? (*b*) What is the change in EPS for the stockholders of companies A and B?

5. The following data are provided:

Market Price per Share of Acquiring Company	Market Price per Share of Acquired Company	Price per Share Offered
$75	$25	$35

What is the exchange ratio in: (*a*) shares? (*b*) market price?

6. Jones Company wishes to acquire Masters Company. Relevant data follow:

	Jones	Masters
Net income	$60,000	$45,000
Shares outstanding	30,000	5,000

Jones Company issues its shares to make the acquisition. The ratio of exchange is 3.0 (*a*) What is the EPS of the merged company based on the original shares of each firm? (*b*) What is the EPS of Jones? (*c*) What is the EPS of Masters?

7. Glory Corporation wishes to acquire Jerry Corporation by exchanging 1.5 shares of its stock for each share of Jerry. Glory expects to have the same P/E ratio after the merger as before it. The following data are given:

	Glory	Jerry
Net income	$600,000	$200,000
Shares	200,000	25,000
Market price per share	$50	$40

(*a*) What is the exchange ratio of market prices? (*b*) What are the EPS and P/E ratios for each firm? (*c*) What was the P/E ratio used to obtain Jerry? (*d*) What is the EPS of Glory after the acquisition? (*e*) What is the anticipated market price per share of the merged company?

8. Brother Corporation is considering acquiring Davis Company for $190,000 in cash. Brother's current cost of capital is 12 percent. Davis has an estimated cost of capital of 10 percent after the acquisition. Anticipated cash inflows from years 1 to 12 are $20,000. Should the acquisition be made?

9. Company T wants to acquire company Z. Company T's stock sells for $90 per share. Company Z's stock sells for $35 per share. Because of merger negotiations, company T offers $45 a share. The acquisition is accomplished by an exchange of securities. What is the exchange ratio?

10. The balance sheet of Jason Corporation for the year-ended December 31, 19X4, follows:

Balance Sheet

Current assets	$ 800,000	Current liabilities	$ 600,000
Noncurrent assets	300,000	Long-term liabilities	250,000
		Common stock	300,000
		Retained earnings	(50,000)
		Total liabilities and	
Total assets	$1,100,000	stockholders' equity	$1,100,000

The company's liquidation value is $800,000. Rather than liquidating, a reorganization could occur with an investment of another $350,000. The reorganization is expected to generate earnings of $120,000 a year. A multiplier of 6 is appropriate. If the $350,000 is obtained, long-term debt holders will receive 40 percent of the common stock in the reorganized business in substitution for their current claims. Is reorganization or liquidation recommended?

11. Calcot Corporation is bankrupt. The book and liquidation values of its assets follow.

	Book Value	Liquidation Value
Cash	$ 400,000	$ 400,000
Accounts receivable	1,600,000	1,300,000
Inventory	3,200,000	2,000,000
Land	5,000,000	3,800,000
Building	10,000,000	6,000,000
Equipment	8,000,000	4,000,000
Total assets	$28,200,000	$17,500,000

The liabilities and stockholders' equity at the liquidation date follow.

Current liabilities

Accounts payable	$3,000,000	
Notes payable	1,500,000	
Accrued taxes	800,000	
Accrued salaries	300,000 [a]	
Total current liabilities		$ 5,600,000

Long-term liabilities

Mortgage on land	$3,800,000	
First mortgage—building	4,000,000	
Second mortgage—building	2,000,000	
Subordinated debentures	4,200,000	
Total long-term liabilities		14,000,000
Total liabilities		$19,600,000

Stockholders' equity

Preferred stock	$3,500,000	
Common stock	7,000,000	
Retained earnings	(1,900,000)	
Total stockholders' equity		8,600,000
Total liabilities and stockholders' equity		$28,200,000

[a] The salary owed to each worker is less than $2,000 and was incurred within 90 days of the bankruptcy petition.

Expenses applicable to the bankruptcy administration were 15 percent of the proceeds. The debentures are subordinated only with regard to the two first-mortgage bonds. What is the distribution of the proceeds?

12. Michael Corporation's balance sheet is presented below.

ASSETS

Current assets	$1,400,000	
Land	3,500,000	
Plant and equipment	2,500,000	
Total assets		$7,400,000

LIABILITIES AND STOCKHOLDERS' EQUITY

Current liabilities

Accounts payable	$ 400,000	
Notes payable	1,000,000	
Accrued taxes	200,000	
Total current liabilities		$1,600,000

Noncurrent liabilities

Mortgage bonds	$2,000,000 [a]	
Debentures	1,200,000	
Total noncurrent liabilities		3,200,000
Total liabilities		$4,800,000

Stockholders' equity

Preferred stock	$ 800,000	
Common stock	1,800,000	
Total stockholders' equity		2,600,000
Total liabilities and stockholders' equity		$7,400,000

[a] Mortgage bonds are secured against plant and equipment.

The liquidation value of the total assets was $4.6 million, $1.4 million of which was received for plant and equipment. Bankruptcy costs were $120,000.

What is the distribution of the proceeds?

Answers to Examination IV

1.
$$(\$37 - \$25) \times 5 = \$60$$

2. (a)
$$\frac{\$1,000}{40} = 25 \text{ shares}$$

(b)
$$\text{Conversion value} = \text{common stock price} \times \text{conversion ratio} = \$34 \times 25 = \$850$$

(c)
$$\$1,000 - \$850 = \$150$$

3. The market value of common stock received upon conversion is:
$$\$115 \times 12 = \$1,380$$

The call price is $1,200. The bondholder would rather convert, since he or she receives a benefit of $180.

4. (a)

	B Shares Owned after Merger	EPS before Merger	EPS after Merger
A stockholders	8,000	$5.00	$3.57[a]
B stockholders	20,000	$3.00	$3.57[a]
Total	28,000		

[a] The new EPS is calculated as follows:

8,000 shares × $5	$ 40,000
20,000 shares × $3	60,000
Total net income	$100,000

$$\text{EPS} = \frac{\text{total net income}}{\text{total shares}} = \frac{\$100,000}{28,000} = \$3.57$$

(b) EPS is lower by $1.43 for A stockholders but rises by $0.57 for B stockholders.

5. (a)
$$\frac{\$35}{\$75} = 0.467$$

(b)
$$\frac{\$35}{\$25} = 1.4$$

6. (a)
$$\frac{\text{Combined net income}}{\text{Total shares}} = \frac{\$105,000}{30,000 + (5,000 \times 3)} = \frac{\$105,000}{45,000} = \$2.33$$

(b) $2.33

(c) $2.33 \times 3 = \$6.99$

7. (a)
$$\frac{\text{Price per share offered}}{\text{Market price of Jerry}} = \frac{\$50 \times 1.5}{\$40} = \frac{\$75}{\$40} = 1.875$$

(b)

	Glory	Jerry
EPS (net income/number of shares)	3.0	8.0
P/E	16.67	5

(c)

$$1.5 \times \$50 = \$75$$

$$\frac{\$75}{\$8} = 9.4 \text{ times}$$

(d) Total net income is:

200,000 shares × \$3	\$600,000
25,000 shares × \$8	200,000
Total net income	\$800,000

Net EPS is:

$$\frac{\text{Total net income}}{\text{Total shares}} = \frac{\$800,000}{237,500} = \$3.37$$

(e)   Anticipated market price = P/E × new EPS 16.67 × \$3.37 = \$56.18 (rounded)

8.

Year	Calculations	Present Value
0	−\$190,000 × 1	−\$190,000
1–12	+\$20,000 × 6.814	+136,280 [a]
		−\$ 53,720

[a] Using 10 percent as the discount rate.

The net present value is −\$53,720. Since it is negative the acquisition should not be made.

9. $$\frac{\text{Amount paid per share of the acquired company}}{\text{Market price of the acquiring company's shares}} = \frac{\$45}{\$90} = 0.5$$

10. Assuming the \$350,000 of further investment is made, the company's going concern value is \$720,000 (6 × \$120,000). The liquidation value is given as \$800,000. Since the liquidation value exceeds the going concern value, liquidation is called for.

11. The distribution of the proceeds follow:

Proceeds		\$17,500,000
Mortgage on land	\$3,800,000	
First mortgage—building	4,000,000	
Second mortgage—building	2,000,000	
Liquidation expenses (15% × \$17,500,000)	2,625,000	
Accrued taxes	800,000	
Accrued salaries	300,000	
Total		13,525,000
Balance		\$ 3,975,000

Percent to be paid to general creditors:

$$\frac{\text{Proceeds balance}}{\text{Total owed}} = \frac{\$3,975,000}{\$8,700,000} = 0.4568965$$

General Creditor	Owed	Paid
Accounts payable	$3,000,000	$1,370,690
Notes payable	1,500,000	685,345
Subordinated debentures	4,200,000	1,918,965
Total	$8,700,000	$3,975,000

12.

Proceeds		$4,600,000
Mortgage bonds—secured against plant and equipment	$1,400,000	
Bankruptcy costs	120,000	
Accrued taxes	200,000	1,720,000
Balance available to general creditors		$2,880,000

The distribution to general creditors follows:

General Creditor	Owed	Pro Rata Distribution
Mortgage bonds ($2,000,000 − $1,400,000)	$ 600,000	$ 540,000
Accounts payable	400,000	360,000
Notes payable	1,000,000	900,000
Debentures	1,200,000	1,080,000
Total	$3,200,000	$2,880,000

Preferred stock and common stockholders will receive nothing.

Future Value of $1: FVIF$_{i,n}$

Period	1%	2%	3%	4%	5%	6%	7%	8%	9%	10%	12%	14%	15%	16%	18%	20%	24%	28%	32%	36%
1	1.0100	1.0200	1.0300	1.0400	1.0500	1.0600	1.0700	1.0800	1.0900	1.1000	1.1200	1.1400	1.1500	1.1600	1.1800	1.2000	1.2400	1.2800	1.3200	1.3600
2	1.0201	1.0404	1.0609	1.0816	1.1025	1.1236	1.1449	1.1664	1.1881	1.2100	1.2544	1.2996	1.3225	1.3456	1.3924	1.4400	1.5376	1.6384	1.7424	1.8496
3	1.0303	1.0612	1.0927	1.1249	1.1576	1.1910	1.2250	1.2597	1.2950	1.3310	1.4049	1.4815	1.5209	1.5609	1.6430	1.7280	1.9066	2.0972	2.3000	2.5155
4	1.0406	1.0824	1.1255	1.1699	1.2155	1.2625	1.3108	1.3605	1.4116	1.4641	1.5735	1.6890	1.7490	1.8106	1.9388	2.0736	2.3642	2.6844	3.0360	3.4210
5	1.0510	1.1041	1.1593	1.2167	1.2763	1.3382	1.4026	1.4693	1.5386	1.6105	1.7623	1.9254	2.0114	2.1003	2.2878	2.4883	2.9316	3.4360	4.0075	4.6526
6	1.0615	1.1262	1.1941	1.2653	1.3401	1.4185	1.5007	1.5869	1.6771	1.7716	1.9738	2.1950	2.3131	2.4364	2.6996	2.9860	3.6352	4.3980	5.2899	6.3275
7	1.0721	1.1487	1.2299	1.3159	1.4071	1.5036	1.6058	1.7138	1.8280	1.9487	2.2107	2.5023	2.6600	2.8262	3.1855	3.5832	4.5077	5.6295	6.9826	8.6054
8	1.0829	1.1717	1.2668	1.3686	1.4775	1.5938	1.7182	1.8509	1.9926	2.1436	2.4760	2.8526	3.0590	3.2784	3.7589	4.2998	5.5895	7.2058	9.2170	11.703
9	1.0937	1.1951	1.3048	1.4233	1.5513	1.6895	1.8385	1.9990	2.1719	2.3579	2.7731	3.2519	3.5179	3.8030	4.4355	5.1598	6.9310	9.2234	12.166	15.916
10	1.1046	1.2190	1.3439	1.4802	1.6289	1.7908	1.9672	2.1589	2.3674	2.5937	3.1058	3.7072	4.0456	4.4114	5.2338	6.1917	8.5944	11.805	16.059	21.646
11	1.1157	1.2434	1.3842	1.5395	1.7103	1.8983	2.1049	2.3316	2.5804	2.8531	3.4785	4.2262	4.6524	5.1173	6.1759	7.4301	10.657	15.111	21.198	29.439
12	1.1268	1.2682	1.4258	1.6010	1.7959	2.0122	2.2522	2.5182	2.8127	3.1384	3.8960	4.8179	5.3502	5.9360	7.2876	8.9161	13.214	19.342	27.982	40.037
13	1.1381	1.2936	1.4685	1.6651	1.8856	2.1329	2.4098	2.7196	3.0658	3.4523	4.3635	5.4924	6.1528	6.8858	8.5994	10.699	16.386	24.748	36.937	54.451
14	1.1495	1.3195	1.5126	1.7317	1.9799	2.2609	2.5785	2.9372	3.3417	3.7975	4.8871	6.2613	7.0757	7.9875	10.147	12.839	20.319	31.691	48.756	74.053
15	1.1610	1.3459	1.5580	1.8009	2.0789	2.3966	2.7590	3.1722	3.6425	4.1772	5.4736	7.1379	8.1371	9.2655	11.973	15.407	25.195	40.564	64.358	100.71
16	1.1726	1.3728	1.6047	1.8730	2.1829	2.5404	2.9522	3.4259	3.9703	4.5950	6.1304	8.1372	9.3576	10.748	14.129	18.488	31.242	51.923	84.953	136.96
17	1.1843	1.4002	1.6528	1.9479	2.2920	2.6928	3.1588	3.7000	4.3276	5.0545	6.8660	9.2765	10.761	12.467	16.672	22.186	38.740	66.461	112.13	186.27
18	1.1961	1.4282	1.7024	2.0258	2.4066	2.8543	3.3799	3.9960	4.7171	5.5599	7.6900	10.575	12.375	14.462	19.673	26.623	48.038	85.070	148.02	253.33
19	1.2081	1.4568	1.7535	2.1068	2.5270	3.0256	3.6165	4.3157	5.1417	6.1159	8.6129	12.055	14.231	16.776	23.214	31.948	59.567	108.89	195.39	344.53
20	1.2202	1.4859	1.8061	2.1911	2.6533	3.2071	3.8697	4.6610	5.6044	6.7275	9.6463	13.743	16.366	19.460	27.393	38.337	73.864	139.37	257.91	468.57
21	1.2324	1.5157	1.8603	2.2788	2.7860	3.3996	4.1406	5.0338	6.1088	7.4002	10.803	15.667	18.821	22.574	32.323	46.005	91.591	178.40	340.44	637.26
22	1.2447	1.5460	1.9161	2.3699	2.9253	3.6035	4.4304	5.4365	6.6586	8.1403	12.100	17.861	21.644	26.186	38.142	55.206	113.57	228.35	449.39	866.67
23	1.2572	1.5769	1.9736	2.4647	3.0715	3.8197	4.7405	5.8715	7.2579	8.9543	13.552	20.361	24.891	30.376	45.007	66.247	140.83	292.30	593.19	1178.6
24	1.2697	1.6084	2.0328	2.5633	3.2251	4.0489	5.0724	6.3412	7.9111	9.8497	15.178	23.212	28.625	35.236	53.108	79.496	174.63	374.14	783.02	1602.9
25	1.2824	1.6406	2.0938	2.6658	3.3864	4.2919	5.4274	6.8485	8.6231	10.834	17.000	26.461	32.918	40.874	62.668	95.396	216.54	478.90	1033.5	2180.0
26	1.2953	1.6734	2.1566	2.7725	3.5557	4.5494	5.8074	7.3964	9.3992	11.918	19.040	30.166	37.856	47.414	73.948	114.47	268.51	612.99	1364.3	2964.9
27	1.3082	1.7069	2.2213	2.8834	3.7335	4.8223	6.2139	7.9881	10.245	13.110	21.324	34.389	43.535	55.000	87.259	137.37	332.95	784.63	1800.9	4032.2
28	1.3213	1.7410	2.2879	2.9987	3.9201	5.1117	6.6488	8.6271	11.167	14.421	23.883	39.204	50.065	63.800	102.96	164.84	412.86	1004.3	2377.2	5483.8
29	1.3345	1.7758	2.3566	3.1187	4.1161	5.4184	7.1143	9.3173	12.172	15.863	26.749	44.693	57.575	74.008	121.50	197.81	511.95	1285.5	3137.9	7458.0
30	1.3478	1.8114	2.4273	3.2434	4.3219	5.7435	7.6123	10.062	13.267	17.449	29.959	50.950	66.211	85.849	143.37	237.37	634.81	1645.5	4142.0	10143.
40	1.4889	2.2080	3.2620	4.8010	7.0400	10.285	14.974	21.724	31.409	45.259	93.050	188.88	267.86	378.72	750.37	1469.7	5455.9	19426	66520	*
50	1.6446	2.6916	4.3839	7.1067	11.467	18.420	29.457	46.901	74.357	117.39	289.00	700.23	1083.6	1670.7	3927.3	9100.4	46890	*	*	*
60	1.8167	3.2810	5.8916	10.519	18.679	32.987	57.946	101.25	176.03	304.48	897.59	2595.9	4383.9	7370.1	20555	56347	*	*	*	*

* FVIF > 99,999

439

Sum of an Annuity of $1: FVIFA$_{i,n}$

Number of Periods	1%	2%	3%	4%	5%	6%	7%	8%	9%	10%	12%	14%	15%	16%	18%	20%	24%	28%	32%	36%
1	1.0000	1.0000	1.0000	1.0000	1.0000	1.0000	1.0000	1.0000	1.0000	1.0000	1.0000	1.0000	1.0000	1.0000	1.0000	1.0000	1.0000	1.0000	1.0000	1.0000
2	2.0100	2.0200	2.0300	2.0400	2.0500	2.0600	2.0700	2.0800	2.0900	2.1000	2.1200	2.1400	2.1500	2.1600	2.1800	2.2000	2.2400	2.2800	2.3200	2.3600
3	3.0301	3.0604	3.0909	3.1216	3.1525	3.1836	3.2149	3.2464	3.2781	3.3100	3.3744	3.4396	3.4725	3.5056	3.5724	3.6400	3.7776	3.9184	4.0624	4.2096
4	4.0604	4.1216	4.1836	4.2465	4.3101	4.3746	4.4399	4.5061	4.5731	4.6410	4.7793	4.9211	4.9934	5.0665	5.2154	5.3680	5.6842	6.0156	6.3624	6.7251
5	5.1010	5.2040	5.3091	5.4163	5.5256	5.6371	5.7507	5.8666	5.9847	6.1051	6.3528	6.6101	6.7424	6.8771	7.1542	7.4416	8.0484	8.6999	9.3983	10.146
6	6.1520	6.3081	6.4684	6.6330	6.8019	6.9753	7.1533	7.3359	7.5233	7.7156	8.1152	8.5355	8.7537	8.9775	9.4420	9.9299	10.980	12.135	13.405	14.798
7	7.2135	7.4343	7.6625	7.8983	8.1420	8.3938	8.6540	8.9228	9.2004	9.4872	10.089	10.730	11.066	11.413	12.141	12.915	14.615	16.533	18.695	21.126
8	8.2857	8.5830	8.8923	9.2142	9.5491	9.8975	10.259	10.636	11.028	11.435	12.299	13.232	13.726	14.240	15.327	16.499	19.122	22.163	25.678	29.731
9	9.3685	9.7546	10.159	10.582	11.026	11.491	11.978	12.487	13.021	13.579	14.775	16.085	16.785	17.518	19.085	20.798	24.712	29.369	34.895	41.435
10	10.462	10.949	11.463	12.006	12.577	13.180	13.816	14.486	15.192	15.937	17.548	19.337	20.303	21.321	23.521	25.958	31.643	38.592	47.061	57.351
11	11.566	12.168	12.807	13.486	14.206	14.971	15.783	16.645	17.560	18.531	20.654	23.044	24.349	25.732	28.755	32.150	40.237	50.398	63.121	78.998
12	12.682	13.412	14.192	15.025	15.917	16.869	17.888	18.977	20.140	21.384	24.133	27.270	29.001	30.850	34.931	39.580	50.894	65.510	84.320	108.43
13	13.809	14.680	15.617	16.626	17.713	18.882	20.140	21.495	22.953	24.522	28.029	32.088	34.351	36.786	42.218	48.496	64.109	84.852	112.30	148.47
14	14.947	15.973	17.086	18.291	19.598	21.015	22.550	24.214	26.019	27.975	32.392	37.581	40.504	43.672	50.818	59.195	80.496	109.61	149.23	202.92
15	16.096	17.293	18.598	20.023	21.578	23.276	25.129	27.152	29.360	31.772	37.279	43.842	47.580	51.659	60.965	72.035	100.81	141.30	197.99	276.97
16	17.257	18.639	20.156	21.824	23.657	25.672	27.888	30.324	33.003	35.949	42.753	50.980	55.717	60.925	72.939	87.442	126.01	181.86	262.35	377.69
17	18.430	20.012	21.761	23.697	25.840	28.212	30.840	33.750	36.973	40.544	48.883	59.117	65.075	71.673	87.068	105.93	157.25	233.79	347.30	514.66
18	19.614	21.412	23.414	25.645	28.132	30.905	33.999	37.450	41.301	45.599	55.749	68.394	75.836	84.140	103.74	128.11	195.99	300.25	459.44	700.93
19	20.810	22.840	25.116	27.671	30.539	33.760	37.379	41.446	46.018	51.159	63.439	78.969	88.211	98.603	123.41	154.74	244.03	385.32	607.47	954.27
20	22.019	24.297	26.870	29.778	33.066	36.785	40.995	45.762	51.160	57.275	72.052	91.024	102.44	115.37	146.62	186.68	303.60	494.21	802.86	1298.8
21	23.239	25.783	28.676	31.969	35.719	39.992	44.865	50.442	56.764	64.002	81.698	104.76	118.81	134.84	174.02	225.02	377.46	633.59	1060.7	1767.3
22	24.471	27.299	30.536	34.248	38.505	43.392	49.005	55.456	62.873	71.402	92.502	120.43	137.63	157.41	206.34	271.03	469.05	811.99	1401.2	2404.6
23	25.716	28.845	32.452	36.617	41.430	46.995	53.436	60.893	69.531	79.543	104.60	138.29	159.27	183.60	244.48	326.23	582.62	1040.3	1850.6	3271.3
24	26.973	30.421	34.426	39.082	44.502	50.815	58.176	66.764	76.789	88.497	118.15	158.65	184.16	213.97	289.49	392.48	723.46	1332.6	2443.8	4449.9
25	28.243	32.030	36.459	41.645	47.727	54.864	63.249	73.105	84.700	98.347	133.33	181.87	212.79	249.21	342.60	471.98	898.09	1706.8	3226.8	6052.9
26	29.525	33.670	38.553	44.311	51.113	59.156	68.676	79.954	93.323	109.18	150.33	208.33	245.71	290.08	405.27	567.37	1114.6	2185.7	4260.4	8233.0
27	30.820	35.344	40.709	47.084	54.669	63.705	74.483	87.350	102.72	121.09	169.37	238.49	283.56	337.50	479.22	681.85	1383.1	2798.7	5624.7	11197.9
28	32.129	37.051	42.930	49.967	58.402	68.528	80.697	95.338	112.96	134.20	190.69	272.88	327.10	392.50	566.48	819.22	1716.0	3583.3	7425.6	15230.2
29	32.450	38.792	45.218	52.966	62.322	73.689	87.346	103.96	124.13	148.63	214.58	312.09	377.16	456.30	669.44	984.06	2128.9	4587.6	9802.9	20714.1
30	34.784	40.568	47.576	56.084	66.438	79.058	94.460	113.28	136.30	164.49	241.33	356.78	434.74	530.31	790.94	1181.8	2640.9	5873.2	12940	28172.2
40	48.886	60.402	75.401	95.025	120.79	154.76	199.63	259.05	337.88	442.59	767.09	1342.0	1779.0	2360.7	4163.2	7343.8	22728	63977	*	*
50	64.463	84.579	112.79	152.66	209.34	290.33	406.52	573.76	815.08	1163.9	2400.0	4994.5	7217.7	10435	21813	45497	*	*	*	*
60	81.669	114.05	163.05	237.90	353.58	533.12	813.52	1253.2	1944.7	3034.8	7471.6	18535	29219	46057	*	*	*	*	*	*

* FVIFA > 99.999

Appendix C

Appendix D

Present Value of $1: PVIF$_{i,n}$

Period	1%	2%	3%	4%	5%	6%	7%	8%	9%	10%	12%	14%	15%	16%	18%	20%	24%	28%	32%	36%
1	.9901	.9804	.9709	.9615	.9524	.9434	.9346	.9259	.9174	.9091	.8929	.8772	.8696	.8621	.8475	.8333	.8065	.7813	.7576	.7353
2	.9803	.9612	.9426	.9246	.9070	.8900	.8734	.8573	.8417	.8264	.7972	.7695	.7561	.7432	.7182	.6944	.6504	.6104	.5739	.5407
3	.9706	.9423	.9151	.8890	.8638	.8396	.8163	.7938	.7722	.7513	.7118	.6750	.6575	.6407	.6086	.5787	.5245	.4768	.4348	.3975
4	.9610	.9238	.8885	.8548	.8227	.7921	.7629	.7350	.7084	.6830	.6355	.5921	.5718	.5523	.5158	.4823	.4230	.3725	.3294	.2923
5	.9515	.9057	.8626	.8219	.7835	.7473	.7130	.6806	.6499	.6209	.5674	.5194	.4972	.4761	.4371	.4019	.3411	.2910	.2495	.2149
6	.9420	.8880	.8375	.7903	.7462	.7050	.6663	.6302	.5963	.5645	.5066	.4556	.4323	.4104	.3704	.3349	.2751	.2274	.1890	.1580
7	.9327	.8706	.8131	.7599	.7107	.6651	.6227	.5835	.5470	.5132	.4523	.3996	.3759	.3538	.3139	.2791	.2218	.1776	.1432	.1162
8	.9235	.8535	.7894	.7307	.6768	.6274	.5820	.5403	.5019	.4665	.4039	.3506	.3269	.3050	.2660	.2326	.1789	.1388	.1085	.0854
9	.9143	.8368	.7664	.7026	.6446	.5919	.5439	.5002	.4604	.4241	.3606	.3075	.2843	.2630	.2255	.1938	.1443	.1084	.0822	.0628
10	.9053	.8203	.7441	.6756	.6139	.5584	.5083	.4632	.4224	.3855	.3220	.2697	.2472	.2267	.1911	.1615	.1164	.0847	.0623	.0462
11	.8963	.8043	.7224	.6496	.5847	.5268	.4751	.4289	.3875	.3505	.2875	.2366	.2149	.1954	.1619	.1346	.0938	.0662	.0472	.0340
12	.8874	.7885	.7014	.6246	.5568	.4970	.4440	.3971	.3555	.3186	.2567	.2076	.1869	.1685	.1372	.1122	.0757	.0517	.0357	.0250
13	.8787	.7730	.6810	.6006	.5303	.4688	.4150	.3677	.3262	.2897	.2292	.1821	.1625	.1452	.1163	.0935	.0610	.0404	.0271	.0184
14	.8700	.7579	.6611	.5775	.5051	.4423	.3878	.3405	.2992	.2633	.2046	.1597	.1413	.1252	.0985	.0779	.0492	.0316	.0205	.0135
15	.8613	.7430	.6419	.5553	.4810	.4173	.3624	.3152	.2745	.2394	.1827	.1401	.1229	.1079	.0835	.0649	.0397	.0247	.0155	.0099
16	.8528	.7284	.6232	.5339	.4581	.3936	.3387	.2919	.2519	.2176	.1631	.1229	.1069	.0930	.0708	.0541	.0320	.0193	.0118	.0073
17	.8444	.7142	.6050	.5134	.4363	.3714	.3166	.2703	.2311	.1978	.1456	.1078	.0929	.0802	.0600	.0451	.0258	.0150	.0089	.0054
18	.8360	.7002	.5874	.4936	.4155	.3503	.2959	.2502	.2120	.1799	.1300	.0946	.0808	.0691	.0508	.0376	.0208	.0118	.0068	.0038
19	.8277	.6864	.5703	.4746	.3957	.3305	.2765	.2317	.1945	.1635	.1161	.0829	.0703	.0596	.0431	.0313	.0168	.0092	.0051	.0029
20	.8195	.6730	.5537	.4564	.3769	.3118	.2584	.2145	.1784	.1486	.1037	.0728	.0611	.0514	.0365	.0261	.0135	.0072	.0039	.0021
25	.7798	.6095	.4776	.3751	.2953	.2330	.1842	.1460	.1160	.0923	.0588	.0378	.0304	.0245	.0160	.0105	.0046	.0021	.0010	.0005
30	.7419	.5521	.4120	.3083	.2314	.1741	.1314	.0994	.0754	.0573	.0334	.0196	.0151	.0116	.0070	.0042	.0016	.0006	.0002	.0001
40	.6717	.4529	.3066	.2083	.1420	.0972	.0668	.0460	.0318	.0221	.0107	.0053	.0037	.0026	.0013	.0007	.0002	.0001	*	*
50	.6080	.3715	.2281	.1407	.0872	.0543	.0339	.0213	.0132	.0085	.0035	.0014	.0009	.0006	.0003	.0001	*	*	*	*
60	.5504	.3048	.1697	.0951	.0535	.0303	.0173	.0099	.0057	.0033	.0011	.0004	.0002	.0001	*	*	*	*	*	*

*The factor is zero to four decimal places.

441

Present Value of an Annuity of \$1: $PVIFA_{i,n}$

Number of payments	1%	2%	3%	4%	5%	6%	7%	8%	9%	10%	12%	14%	15%	16%	18%	20%	24%	28%	32%
1	0.9901	0.9804	0.9709	0.9615	0.9524	0.9434	0.9346	0.9259	0.9174	0.9091	0.8929	0.8772	0.8696	0.8621	0.8475	0.8333	0.8065	0.7813	0.7576
2	1.9704	1.9415	1.9135	1.8861	1.8594	1.8334	1.8080	1.7833	1.7591	1.7355	1.6901	1.6467	1.6257	1.6052	1.5656	1.5278	1.4568	1.3916	1.3315
3	2.9410	2.8839	2.8286	2.7751	2.7232	2.6730	2.6243	2.5771	2.5313	2.4869	2.4018	2.3216	2.2832	2.2459	2.1743	2.1065	1.9813	1.8684	1.7663
4	3.9020	3.8077	3.7171	3.6299	3.5460	3.4651	3.3872	3.3121	3.2397	3.1699	3.0373	2.9137	2.8550	2.7982	2.6901	2.5887	2.4043	2.2410	2.0957
5	4.8534	4.7135	4.5797	4.4518	4.3295	4.2124	4.1002	3.9927	3.8897	3.7908	3.6048	3.4331	3.3522	3.2743	3.1272	2.9906	2.7454	2.5320	2.3452
6	5.7955	5.6014	5.4172	5.2421	5.0757	4.9173	4.7665	4.6229	4.4859	4.3553	4.1114	3.8887	3.7845	3.6847	3.4976	3.3255	3.0205	2.7594	2.5342
7	6.7282	6.4720	6.2303	6.0021	5.7864	5.5824	5.3893	5.2064	5.0330	4.8684	4.5638	4.2883	4.1604	4.0386	3.8115	3.6046	3.2423	2.9370	2.6775
8	7.6517	7.3255	7.0197	6.7327	6.4632	6.2098	5.9713	5.7466	5.5348	5.3349	4.9676	4.6389	4.4873	4.3436	4.0776	3.8372	3.4212	3.0758	2.7860
9	8.5660	8.1622	7.7861	7.4353	7.1078	6.8017	6.5152	6.2469	5.9952	5.7590	5.3282	4.9464	4.7716	4.6065	4.3030	4.0310	3.5655	3.1842	2.8681
10	9.4713	8.9826	8.5302	8.1109	7.7217	7.3601	7.0236	6.7101	6.4177	6.1446	5.6502	5.2161	5.0188	4.8332	4.4941	4.1925	3.6819	3.2689	2.9304
11	10.3676	9.7858	9.2526	8.7605	8.3064	7.8869	7.4987	7.1390	6.8052	6.4951	5.9377	5.4527	5.2337	5.0286	4.6560	4.3271	3.7757	3.3351	2.9776
12	11.2551	10.5753	9.9540	9.3851	8.8633	8.3838	7.9427	7.5361	7.1607	6.8137	6.1944	5.6603	5.4206	5.1971	4.7932	4.4392	3.8514	3.3868	3.0133
13	12.1337	11.3484	10.6350	9.9856	9.3936	8.8527	8.3577	7.9038	7.4889	7.1034	6.4235	5.8424	5.5831	5.3423	4.9095	4.5327	3.9124	3.4272	3.0404
14	13.0037	12.1062	11.2961	10.5631	9.8986	9.2950	8.7455	8.2442	7.7862	7.3667	6.6282	6.0021	5.7245	5.4675	5.0081	4.6106	3.9616	3.4587	3.0609
15	13.8651	12.8493	11.9379	11.1184	10.3797	9.7122	9.1079	8.5595	8.0607	7.6061	6.8109	6.1422	5.8474	5.5755	5.0916	4.6755	4.0013	3.4834	3.0764
16	14.7179	13.5777	12.5611	11.6523	10.8378	10.1059	9.4466	8.8514	8.3126	7.8237	6.9740	6.2651	5.9542	5.6685	5.1724	4.7296	4.0333	3.5026	3.0882
17	15.5623	14.2919	13.1661	12.1657	11.2741	10.4773	9.7632	9.1216	8.5436	8.0216	7.1196	6.3729	6.0472	5.7487	5.2223	4.7746	4.0591	3.5177	3.0971
18	16.3983	14.9920	13.7535	12.6593	11.6896	10.8276	10.0591	9.3719	8.7556	8.2014	7.2497	6.4674	6.1280	5.8178	5.2732	4.8122	4.0799	3.5294	3.1039
19	17.2260	15.6785	14.3238	13.1339	12.0853	11.1581	10.3356	9.6036	8.9501	8.3649	7.3658	6.5504	6.1982	5.8775	5.3162	4.8435	4.0967	3.5386	3.1090
20	18.0456	16.3514	14.8775	13.5903	12.4622	11.4699	10.5940	9.8181	9.1285	8.5436	7.4694	6.6231	6.2593	5.9288	5.3527	4.8696	4.1103	3.5458	3.1129
25	22.0232	19.5235	17.4131	15.6221	14.0939	12.7834	11.6536	10.6748	9.8226	9.0770	7.8431	6.8729	6.4641	6.0971	5.4669	4.9476	4.1474	3.5640	3.1220
30	25.8077	22.3965	19.6004	17.2920	15.3725	13.7648	12.4090	11.2578	10.2737	9.4269	8.0552	7.0072	6.5660	6.1772	5.5168	4.9789	4.1601	3.5693	3.1242
40	32.8347	27.3555	23.1148	19.7928	17.1591	15.0463	13.3317	11.9246	10.7574	9.7791	8.2438	7.1050	6.6418	6.2335	5.5482	4.9966	4.1659	3.5712	3.1250
50	39.1961	31.4236	25.7298	21.4822	18.2559	15.7619	13.8007	12.2335	10.9617	9.9148	8.3045	7.1327	6.6605	6.2463	5.5541	4.9995	4.1666	3.5714	3.1250
60	44.9550	34.7609	27.8756	22.6235	18.9293	16.1614	14.0392	12.3766	11.0480	9.9672	8.3240	7.1401	6.6651	6.2492	5.5553	4.9999	4.1667	3.5714	3.1250

Appendix E

Normal Probability Distribution Table

Area of normal distribution that is z standard deviations
to the left or right of the mean

Number of Standard Deviations from Mean (z)	Area to the Left or Right (One tail)	Number of Standard Deviations from Mean (z)	Area to the Left or Right (One tail)
0.00	.5000	1.55	.0606
0.05	.4801	1.60	.0548
0.10	.4602	1.65	.0495
0.15	.4404	1.70	.0446
0.20	.4207	1.75	.0401
0.25	.4013	1.80	.0359
0.30	.3821	1.85	.0322
0.35	.3632	1.90	.0287
0.40	.3446	1.95	.0256
0.45	.3264	2.00	.0228
0.50	.3085	2.05	.0202
0.55	.2912	2.10	.0179
0.60	.2743	2.15	.0158
0.65	.2578	2.20	.0139
0.70	.2420	2.25	.0122
0.75	.2264	2.30	.0107
0.80	.2119	2.35	.0094
0.85	.1977	2.40	.0082
0.90	.1841	2.45	.0071
0.95	.1711	2.50	.0062
1.00	.1577	2.55	.0054
1.05	.1469	2.60	.0047
1.10	.1357	2.65	.0040
1.15	.1251	2.70	.0035
1.20	.1151	2.75	.0030
1.25	.1056	2.80	.0026
1.30	.0968	2.85	.0022
1.35	.0885	2.90	.0019
1.40	.0808	2.95	.0016
1.45	.0735	3.00	.0013
1.50	.0668		

Index